Praise

"I work with teenagers from all over the world, and what they need most is someone who understands them and helps them to believe in themselves. Jodi is [the] perfect example of this. She inspires me through how she helps teenagers increase confidence that they have the power to heal and create their own life, especially when they don't see it. She helps us all see how the future can be better than the past. With warmth and compassion, Jodi's workbook activates this empowerment with practical and timeless principles that are easily accessible to anyone."
—Clint G Rogers PhD, author of *Ancient Secrets Of A Master Healer*

"Jodi Aman does a fantastic job speaking directly to teens in an engaging and entertaining way. Teenagers will soak up the knowledge and skills she offers and will be empowered to go head to head with anxiety."
—Natasha Daniels LCSW, author of *Anxiety Sucks! A Teen Survival Guide*

"Aman's *Anxiety . . . I'm So Done with You* is an incredibly helpful tool for any teen—or parent—to have in their survival toolbox. As the mother of someone who has suffered terribly with anxiety, I can honestly say that I wish this book had been available years ago. If your teen in anxious, you need this book."
—Jennifer Browne, author of *Understanding Teenage Anxiety* and the *Anti-Anxiety Cookbook*

"Ever wanted to not only understand fear—but get rid of it? Do you need help choosing relationships that are mutually beneficial rather than toxic? I recommend Jodi Aman's workbook because it has what young people need to harness their personal power and thrive in what we often perceive as a cold, cruel world."
—Gabe Howard, author of *Mental Illness is an A**hole* and founder of The Psych Central Podcast

"Adolescence with all its remarkable changes is also more likely to trigger stress and anxiety as young people navigate the many challenges they face. *Anxiety . . . I'm So Done with You* combines Jodi's experiences of anxiety together with her many years of experience as a therapist to provide an informative workbook on how to manage anxiety-related emotional distress. Emoji's, engaging graphics, and a warm, personal style of writing provides young people with an understanding of what anxiety is, how it impacts on you, and outlines key steps to making change. The book includes a helpful chapter on managing self-harm behavior and a detachable guide for parents. This unique book is well worth a read."

—Dr. Nihara Krause, founder of the Calm Harm app

"This book helps young people, even if they've experienced very hard things, learn how to take control of their lives."

—Matthew Pappas, Director of Operations at CPTSD Foundation

"Jodi Aman has done an amazing job showing teens how to eliminate anxiety from their lives and find their personal power. *Anxiety . . . I'm So Done with You* shows a practical and effective approach any teen can use to gracefully navigate the challenges of modern day life. It's a must read!"

—Jaya Jaya Myra, author of *Vibrational Healing and The Soul of Purpose*

"In the chaotic world we live in, teens are inundated with high-stress situations and experience a roller coaster of emotions. It is so important to have resources such as this workbook that will actually help teens to eliminate anxiety and rewire their developing brains away from the sympathetic nervous system (fight/flight) and back into their parasympathetic system (calm). Not only will that help them to show up to their teenage lives in an easier manner, but will create skills and neuropathways that can last a lifetime. Jodi Aman has done a fantastic job with this wonderful resource. This workbook has everything young people need to trust their personal power to thrive in this modern world."

—Teralyn Sell, PhD, brain health

Anxiety . . . I'm So Done with You

Dedication

For Generation Z, who trust me with their inner thoughts, showing me that they are abundantly adaptable and skilled. Especially for the three kiddos who share my heart, Calin, Leo, and Lily. #ibowtoyou

Anxiety . . . I'm So Done with You

A Teen's Guide to Ditching Toxic Stress and Hardwiring Your Brain for Happiness

Jodi Aman, LCSW

Skyhorse Publishing

Skyhorse Publishing books may be purchased in bulk at special discounts for sales promotion, corporate gifts, fund-raising, or educational purposes. Special editions can also be created to specifications. For details, contact the Special Sales Department, Skyhorse Publishing, 307 West 36th Street, 11th Floor, New York, NY 10018 or info@skyhorsepublishing.com.

Skyhorse® and Skyhorse Publishing® are registered trademarks of Skyhorse Publishing, Inc.®, a Delaware corporation.

Visit our website at www.skyhorsepublishing.com.

10 9 8 7 6 5 4 3 2 1

Library of Congress Cataloging-in-Publication Data is available on file.

Cover design by Erin Seaward-Hiatt
Cover illustrations: © kentarcajuan/Getty Images (background);
 © Hulinska_Yevheniia/Getty Images (clouds)
Interior artwork by Leo Aman

Print ISBN: 978-1-5107-5134-7
Ebook ISBN: 978-1-5107-5135-4

Printed in the United States of America

Table of Contents

INTRODUCTION:
Spoiler Alert!

"We delight in the beauty of the butterfly, but rarely admit the changes it has gone through to achieve that beauty."

–Maya Angelou

Dear Reader,

 Adolescence is a time of great turbulence, but unlike the caterpillar who goes into a safe cocoon while it's transforming, we, humans, have to be exposed to a chaotic world while we are doing one of the hardest things in our life—becoming ourselves. 🦋

If you feel like the adults in your life don't understand, I've got you covered. I have added a parent resource section at the back of this book (page 203). Cut those pages out and staple them together. Let your adult read them while you go through this book yourself.

Before we start, let me ask you: Are you ready to get your life back?

♥

Jodi

Will I be ok?

Yes! You will be okay. You can definitely feel better than this. Let that sink all the way into your heart.

It. Is. Possible. To. Feel. Better. Period.

That's how much confidence I have that you won't feel like this forever.

In your hands is everything you need to crush doubt, lack of confidence, anxiety, and depression in order to feel good and create lasting peace in your life. When you get rid of feeling powerless, worthless, and out of control, you will . . .

👍 Feel comfortable in your body
👍 Wake up confident and hopeful in the morning
👍 Have a clear life purpose
👍 Enjoy soul-fulfilling adventures
👍 Understand how the world works
👍 Share close, loving relationships

Me, please! 🐨

Getting there is not hard, and it is not dangerous. But it will take some of the know-how in this book and a bit of practice. Not only do I trust that you can get there, but more important, I know you deserve to get there. You deserve it because this is not your fault.

Nope. It's really not.

Once you ditch this toxic stress called anxiety, then happiness is available to you. I'll show you how to get it. But first, let me tell you why I know exactly how you feel.

"They're dead," my father said.

"What's *dead* mean?" I asked. I was five years old.

Dad's neck grew long, and his face went pale. The lightheartedness of our evening evaporated as he became serious.

"It means when someone is not alive anymore."

I read the panic in his eyes. *This must be bad.*

"It's like sleeping without waking up," he continued.

What?

"We all die."

My stomach dropped, and alarms went off in my head.

People. Die.

I. Am. In. Danger.

Bad. Things. Happen.

Earlier, we were at an activity night learning about the US presidents George Washington and Abraham Lincoln. As we arrived home, it dawned on me that I never saw those guys around. So I asked, "Where are the presidents now, Daddy?"

His two-word answer "They're dead" changed my life.

Jodi, meet Anxiety. Anxiety, meet Jodi. *It is horrible to meet you.*

Now that I knew "bad things could happen," new thoughts took hold in my brain. Feelings of anxiety, worry, and hopelessness moved in and showed me a world where "the worst" could happen. I panicked over this daily:

☻ *I might see a dead body.*
☺ *I would lose the people I loved.*
☻ *What would they look like dead?*
☺ *I will die someday.*
☻ *It might be painful.*
☻ *What would I look like dead?*

These ideas haunted me. I virtually experienced the terror of death, over and over, even though I was physically healthy. For a long time, I didn't tolerate the dark, couldn't be alone, experienced stomachaches, and had trouble eating. For the next twenty years, anxiety was an unwanted companion. Sometimes the panicking subsided for a while when I was distracted, but any reminders of my vulnerability, such as a horrific headline or a scary movie, brought it flooding back. I lived as if trapped in a prison. When anxiety came, I ran like that powerless five-year-old to the corner of my cell, with the monster of anxiety guarding the locked door.

Anxiety sucks. Ⓦ I know because I experienced much of what you can experience with this problem during those two decades: the weight loss, the weight gain, the sleeplessness, the oversleeping, the social isolation, the relationship issues, the low self-worth, the obsessions, every physical symptom in the book, the despair, the desire to hurt myself, the depression, the loneliness, and the feeling of being misunderstood, different, and like an alien from outer space. AND, the I-give-up-on-everything-because-I-am-too-beaten-down-and-exhausted-to-go-on-fighting feeling.

Hi. I'm Jodi (white, she/her, cis, straight). I was your age once. (Does that mean squat when adults say "I was your age once"?) Maybe you don't find the adults in your life to be understanding. Let's get real. If you are anything like I was, you don't find *people* to be understanding. For me, my inner critic told me that I was so different, weird, and unusual that no one could possibly get me. This. Was. Devastating.

But it is not true. People actually do understand. I promise you that in the twenty-plus years of being a counselor and hearing the inner dialogues of my clients, there is one thing I've learned: People have very similar personal thoughts and feelings. Because they are not commonly shared and because we use different words to describe them, your inner critic can convince you that your thoughts and feelings are unique and strange. On top of everything, this makes you feel very alone in the world.

[Insert your anxiety story here.]

You probably have times when you feel hopeless and when you think that your anxiety is not curable. Maybe you've tried many medicines and combinations of medicines. Perhaps you've done groups, seen doctors, distracted yourself, tried to motivate yourself, attempted to let go of it, read books, heeded advice, sampled meditation, and watched videos. Maybe you get somewhat better temporarily, but you haven't felt *cured*.

So, you try harder. 💪

You've heard these things work for many people, but for some reason, they just don't work for you. It's not fair. It hurts. And since you don't know the reason it's not working for you, you're powerless to do anything about it. It's totally deflating.

I was in this place for many years with anxiety holding power over me. I was convinced that my anxiety was strange and unusual. And since nothing worked, I concluded I was incurable. And so, anxiety stuck around . . . for what seemed like forever. #scaredofmyownshadow

When I was in my twenties, I experienced a particularly long and horrible anxiety episode. I was a social worker in an outpatient psychiatric center, and one day we participated in a clinical case meeting where we took turns sharing our hardest cases.

"He cries most of the day and can't go to work," said my colleague Beth. The familiar dread brewed in my belly. "His wife can't talk to him about anything. He's having trouble making plans or decisions. He habitually picks the skin on his nose. He's lost forty pounds, and the medicine isn't helping him."

It was the third presentation that day, and sweat tingled under my arms. I peered at the other faces around the table, searching for something to keep me in the here and now before my mind tumbled into a confusion of rapid thoughts. But it didn't help.

I'm worse, I thought. *My anxiety is worse than the client's. I'm supposed to be the person who helps them, but I'm helpless to stop what's going on in my own mind.*

I became hyper-aware of the room—the smell of the coffee, the pen tapping on the table, the back of my coworker's head as he nodded at the doctor's advice—these were like beacons for my attention.

Then, suddenly, the room blurred out of focus. Blinking, I looked down at the table. *Hold yourself together!* Tears threatened. *You're falling apart.* My heart rate increased, and the walls of the room started to close in.

How am I going to handle life like this?

Unable to sit in that conference room another minute, I awkwardly got up and walked out. Shame reddened my face. I was certain all eyes were on my back, judging what a mess I was.

I slipped out the door and made for the stairwell. On the first floor, I bolted for the exit. *I'm running again.*

I practically dove into my car and shoved the key into the ignition. Holding my hands at ten and two, I held my breath and looked in my rearview mirror before backing out. What I saw in my reflection stopped me in my tracks.

My neck was long, and my face was pale—that same haunted face of my father telling me about death for the first time when I was five years old.

I exhaled. And all of my attention was on that breath slowly flowing out. My mind focused. Inhale. Exhale. I looked into my eyes—twenty years of this. Enough was enough. I wondered, with a glimmer of hope, *If I learned this thing called anxiety, is it possible that I could unlearn it?*

Seeing anxiety as "something that was constructed on the outside of me," something I had learned, rather than as "a mental illness inside me," gave me hope for the first time in years. I finally glimpsed healing as a POSSIBILITY for me, but I realized I needed more information. I was determined to get better and committed to finding out what caused anxiety and what I had to do to ditch it, and then to practice what I discovered with my whole heart and soul.

That day, the power dynamic between anxiety and me shifted. If anxiety attempted to imprison me, I was no longer going to cower in the corner and let it. I decided to take back my life.

Searching for answers, I chewed through articles, books, and trainings like a very hungry caterpillar. I used trial and error and experienced bad days and so-so days in the learning cocoon I had created. Gradually, I started to recover. I became calmer, much more comfortable with myself, and more confident in my relationships.

When I emerged fully transformed, I felt . . . happy . . . prepared . . . relieved.

I was so cured of my anxiety that, a few years later, it didn't even flare up when the worst happened: my fourteen-year-old stepson, Calin, was hospitalized with spinal meningitis.

My six-year-old son, Leo, was standing with me in the hallway, watching his father quickly pack a few things before making the drive to Cal's bedside.

In his precious little-boy voice, Leo asked, "Mommy, is Calin going to die?"

Time stopped, and I felt the significance of the moment.

I relaxed my face.

Squatting down to meet his eyes, I responded, "Whatever happens, we will handle it together." I nodded with confidence to emphasize my faith in that. Leo moved on to the next moment, satisfied.

I could feel my adrenaline pumping and the intensity of what was happening, but I knew *what* it was, so I wasn't scared. I understood that anxiety wouldn't and couldn't help the situation so I used that adrenaline to swing into action: educating myself on meningitis, praying, communicating, making food, and opening my heart to caring for everyone involved.

Calin miraculously recovered. ⚡

I had broken the anxiety legacy. Leo grew up without my anxieties or preoccupation with death. And now, this new anxiety-free Jodi is so much happier because instead of getting lost down the **rabbit hole**, I am able to stay in service to others.

After many, many late nights of pacing, missed events, lost relationships, and years of suffering and hopelessness, something changed when I saw possibility. Hope. It was only when I believed that I *could* feel better—which sparked a determined desire to do whatever possible—that I figured out how to get rid of it. For good.

Rabbit hole?

The rabbit hole is a reference to *Alice's Adventures in Wonderland* by Lewis Carroll. It means to enter a thought process or activity that is strange, troubling, and chaotic and that becomes increasingly complex the deeper you travel through it.

Rabbits live in warrens, an underground network of interconnecting burrows and tunnels. It's dark in there. One can get lost in the maze of cycling negative thoughts and images with no light to find the way out.

You can lose a lot of time and energy in a "rabbit hole." ☺

Reflecting on my journey, it became clear that I had walked through five distinct steps to get to this new way of being. Since they worked for me, I started teaching them to my clients. Over twenty years, I have shown thousands of kids, teens, and adults how to do them, too.

These are the steps to getting rid of anxiety:

- 🦋 Understand what anxiety is
- 🦋 Reveal the lies of anxiety
- 🦋 Activate your personal **agency**
- 🦋 Make peace with yourself
- 🦋 Practice happiness-sustaining habits

What's *agency*?

Think of yourself as an agent in your life. You know how a music agent gets the band jobs and contracts to propel its career? You are an agent of yourself and the band is your life. For example, you decide who you spend time with, what opportunities to go after, and how hard you try for them. Even when something bad happens, you choose how to respond to it. Your response can make you thrive despite it, or it can make it worse. This is called personal agency. You have it. I have it. Everyone has this inner power source that influences how good a life we have. 💪

This means your happiness level is not determined by what happens to you. It's built on how you respond to what happens.

Anxiety wants you to think that you have no agency (no skills or abilities to handle and create a life that you want). Too bad for anxiety ☺ because you do have it. Once you see your personal agency and activate it, life gets so much easier. More on this soon!

And now, it's your turn.

Remember what I learned in my anxiety recovery cocoon and what has been confirmed over and over in my work as a counselor: the people who feel better faster are the people who believed that they could. Belief is everything, here. Anxiety wants you to believe you are powerless, worthless, and out of control, so you stay subservient. Once you realize you are empowered, worthy, and in control, the game changes.

Repeat this to yourself over and over: "I can and will feel better."

YOU. CAN. DO. THIS. I'll be right beside you, cheering you on!

So, bring your worries, the perceived deficits, and your wary hearts and minds. Lay down those heavy burdens so your hands are free to receive the beauty and uniqueness that is you.

I'm ready. You're ready. Let's get you better! #imyourbiggestfan

> One more thing: it may seem like you have no one to go to for help, but that is often the anxiety wanting you to be isolated, so you stay vulnerable. Hear me: it is a lie. You are not alone. People do care. Use your skills in observation to find an adult whom you can trust. Don't go to an adult or peer who is not trustworthy and say, "See, everyone hurts me." Pick a good person. They are out there, I promise.

Okay, two more things . . . At the end of each section of the book, you'll find an activity to practice under the heading "What's in Your Hand?" This is about what is at your disposal right now: the actions you can take with the skills and abilities you have in your hands. Anxiety preys on you by shoving into your face what you can't control. In this section, you will practice what is in your control. It will help you notice the gumption, the skills, the unique abilities, and the ideas and agency you have right at this present moment to shift the energy of a situation, a mood, a relationship, or a thought pattern. None of these actions are dangerous. They are easy (and sometimes even fun)! You may find that some work better than others at shifting your relationship with anxiety, but you'll never know which will bring your biggest "aha" moments until you try.

💪 They will get you to act (which you are already doing anyway, so you might as well choose to take the specific actions that make you happier rather than the ones that make you exhausted).

💪 They will connect you to your inner wisdom, and help you build trust in yourself so anxiety can no longer keep you down.

What's in Your Hand?

Watch my YouTube video "Why You Think Anxiety Is Not Curable" by searching my name and the title in the search bar. (Or, find it at jodiaman.com/ditchanxiety.) In the space below, reflect on these four reasons that cause people to stay anxious by answering the questions below.

- 🐾 You are still scared of it.
- 🐾 You don't like yourself.
- 🐾 You are staying still.
- 🐾 You don't believe that you can.

Can you relate to any of these reasons from the video?
How are you participating in staying stuck?
Equipped with this knowledge, what would you like to do about it?

....

....

....

....

....

....

....

....

For the first two decades of this journey, I had the urge to run whenever I felt anxious. I wanted to escape! However, I started to notice that instead of freeing myself, I ran toward a story that anxiety told me about safety: *You'll be safe in your room, alone.* Though I was trying to escape the anxiety, this action did the opposite. It was a trap. I was "safe" (e.g., curled up in bed), but I was left to my negative thinking and I missed everything life had to offer. It sucked. I had done exactly what anxiety wanted me to do—live in its prison. It stood guard, saying, "I'm protecting you!" when it was really keeping me away from happiness.

Reflect below. What story does anxiety tell you? That you should stay in bed? That it would be safer there? That you can't handle this or that? That you are not good enough? Do you feel like running when you feel anxious? Which way do you run: Are you running into anxiety's prison? Or toward healing and freedom?

Here is what I know: Healing from physical, emotional, and spiritual problems generally consists of three steps. I call them the "Formula for Happiness." They are:

1. Get rid of what makes you suffer.
2. Bring into your life what brings you joy.
3. Practice 1 and 2 daily.

We, humans, tend to complicate the first step, feel undeserving of the second, and feel too defeated to do the third. Or, we do the first and second once, but don't do the third because we didn't know it was a thing. ☺

1. Get rid of what makes you suffer.

The past and your cynical inner critic can weigh you down. You know that you want to get rid of what is making you feel bad, and in this book, I will show you exactly how.

2. Bring into your life what brings you joy.

You may not know all the things in this life that you want to do. But I am sure you have some interests already. We'll start there and pair that with what the research says makes people happy.

3. Practice 1 and 2 daily.

Healing is not a singular event. We must commit to our emotional well-being daily in order to sustain it. That's why the third step is a BIGGIE. It is the trick to transforming the power*less*ness to power*ful*ness. In fact, getting you accustomed to practicing is why this book is an activity book. You stay out of your negative thinking through activity. You activate your agency (your ability to respond to your situation) through activity. You build confidence through activity. You get to know yourself, and your values, through activity. Therefore, you create your new happy, fulfilled, successful identity through activity.

I like the word *practice*, because when you have to *DO* something, you can fail at it. I don't know about you, but I am high-key against failing things. Unfortunately, fear of failing sometimes makes me unwilling to try *doing* something in the first place. That sucks, because then I stay stuck in place. But when I'm just *practicing* it, the stumbles are allowed and expected as part of the practice. I mean, you can't ever fail at practicing, since you are *just practicing*.

This anxiety-provoking world with its viral pandemics, global warming, social pressure, and violence in schools, can make you feel powerless, worthless and out of control. These do cause anxiety. But you don't have to keep the anxiety. Anxiety is curable. Most people who are struggling with anxiety wait a long time to get help. I am glad you are reading my book. Why suffer if you don't have to? Work through this book, watch videos, see a counselor, connect to your inner wisdom, start a creative project, talk to a friend, and find something to do that you enjoy. The worst thing you can do is pull back from everything in life and give all your attention to worries. That will just spin your mind into more chaos. Though anxiety would love you to stay in this abusive relationship, it will make you feel worse.

What's in Your Hand?

Name some things in your life that don't serve your happiness. (Don't include things that will benefit you in the end, even if you don't like doing them, such as "School," "Chores," or "Paying for things." ☺ Please list things from which nothing good comes, like specific worries, insecurity, self-harm.)

....

....

....

Name some things that you enjoy or that make you happy:

....

....

....

Circle the things you can actively increase in your life if you choose to.

CHAPTER 1:
"It's Not Me, It's You."

Anxiety thrives on being mysterious. The mystery gives it a lot of power because you can't control what you don't understand. In Chapter 1, we'll expose anxiety mentally, biologically, and culturally. When you understand what anxiety is and what it isn't, you have the upper hand.

Time to take anxiety down a notch! ☻

1.

THE HYPER MONKEY MIND

In the millions of years of evolution, human minds had to develop a vast capacity for thinking about how to survive the dangerous world. In 2005, the National Science Foundation published an article showing that the average person has between 12,000 and 60,000 thoughts per day. This is the thing: our current living conditions are so much easier than they were during the hunter-gatherer times that we don't have enough important things to think about. When that happens, we simply MAKE UP MORE IDEAS to fill the space! Unfortunately, that same study says that these made-up thoughts are 80 percent negative. That's ten thousand negative ideas a day! #nowonderifeeloutofcontrol #feelskindahopeless

Humans have daily experiences that set off both emotional responses (a.k.a. feelings) and cognitive responses (a.k.a. thoughts). Feelings come on their own, and thoughts are us figuring out what happened and what it means. And what those thoughts decide has happened then triggers a new set of emotions.

For example, if you arrive at class and realize you forgot your homework, you might immediately feel embarrassed or angry or nervous. (If you care about that. ☺) The thoughts that follow those negative emotions might express blame, such as "My brother moved it!" or self-blame, like, "I'm so stupid!" or worry, like, "I'll get a zero!" which evoke more anger, self-depreciation, or anxiety, compounding the emotional turmoil.

In today's world? There are way too many things that can make you feel bad! Like the example above, these feelings get your inner critic online pronto, which adds self-doubt, worries, and blame into the situation. Because it is easier to tame something that has a name, I'm going to go ahead and call this inner critic the **monkey mind** 🐵.

Why the monkey mind?

The founder of Buddhism, Gautama Buddha, coined the term *monkey mind* to describe mind chatter. He likened the monkey, who swings through the trees grabbing one branch and letting it go only to seize another, to mind chatter where we swing rapidly from one negative thought to the next, increasing emotional chaos.

The monkey mind is not the initial feelings of being sad, scared, and angry; instead, it is your subsequent thoughts that analyze, judge, and worry about those feelings. "Why do I still feel so bad?" "What is wrong with me?" "Why can't I get myself together?"

At its worse, it keeps you stuck, worried, down on yourself, preoccupied, distracted, and resentful. It makes up, exaggerates, and twists what's wrong with you. When you feel so horrible about yourself, you feel raw, vulnerable, and exhausted.

Let me give you an example of spiraling anxiety. When people experience a breakup, they might feel heartbroken:

So that we can track what happens, let's pretend there are units that measure emotional pain. Heartbreak is one of the most painful feelings, so let's say that the size of this heartbroken circle represents many, many units of pain.

Almost immediately . . .

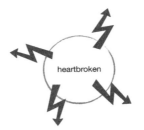

The monkey mind sends stories about what happened. This often starts with negative self-judgments: *Am I overreacting? I'm not good enough. I messed this up! Why does everyone leave me?* (Usually more!) Each of these thoughts has units of emotional pain represented by larger-sized circles. The stories add some chaos to the pain, so now it is better described as "turmoil."

Nope. It doesn't stop there. The monkey worries, especially since it just concluded that you are useless. Worries might sound like: *How am I going to do this? How long is this going to last? I can't handle this! OMG! OMG! I'm losing my mind!* (There might be many more.)

The amount of emotional turmoil is growing. At this size, it is almost unbearable. The original heartbroken circle looks tiny now. You're losing your 💩, and it's not done. The monkey tosses new negative self-judgments on top: *I can't believe I can't do this. Other people would be over it by now. I am so weak to have this bother me so much. This is all my fault.* (And yeah, plus more.)

The circles get bigger as the chaos ensues.

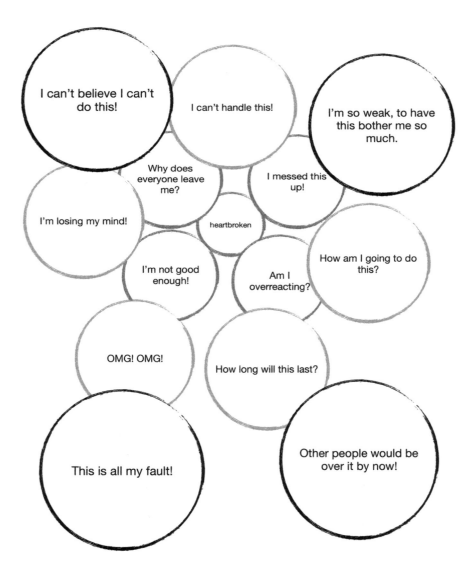

The judgments and worries take you from 0 to 100 within moments. Look at the size differences of the original emotional hurt and the resulting massive amounts of emotional turmoil. What would you rather have?

NOW YOU SEE WHAT THE MONKEY MIND CAN DO.

1. It makes you think that you can't trust yourself to handle anything.
2. Intensifies anxiety and depression.
3. Keeps you stuck in shame and guilt, lengthening the healing process.
4. Has you thinking that the whole emotional turmoil comes from the original hurt—which, I hate to say it, increases your worry and judgment that you are overreacting.
5. Distracts you from attending to and healing the original hurt by having you focus on your deficits.
6. Delays recovery. Healing often occurs naturally over time, but the judgments and worries prevent this.

You are not "crazy" for adding these circles, and you are not going "insane." ☺ You are not weird or strange or different. This is a human reaction to living. And it is not just you. The problem is that many elements of our current Western culture (which we'll touch on in the next section) encourage our inner critic, causing an influx of feelings of powerlessness and worthlessness and feeling out of control, which instigates anxiety, panic, depression, and low self-worth, especially and devastatingly among young people. That means your experience is both common in humans and absolutely understandable in today's world. So, you can stop blaming yourself for your emotional turmoil right now.

(Get rid of that "It's all my fault!" circle!)

> If it is human to have a monkey mind, am I just destined to live like this?

> No, thank goodness. Actually, some individuals and communities have been able to gain mastery over the mind for millennia. And it is learnable!

You can tame the mind. Awareness is the first step. You used to think the whole thing was your reaction to the initial hurt. But once you know these are all separate circles, you can begin to peel them off, one by one, and let them go. I find that the outer judgments hold in the inner judgments and worries, so if you peel off the outer ones, the inner ones fall off much easier.

What's in Your Hand?

Label the diagram on the next page based on a recent experience in your life.

1. Label the original hurt in the small central circle.
2. Write down, using exact wording, the negative self-judgments as you thought them.
3. Write down some worries that have arisen.
4. Add the second layer of negative self-judgments on top of them all.
5. Add circles if you have more. Notice that you are not only creating more circles, but that the outer circles are also bigger and thus more impactful on your feelings.

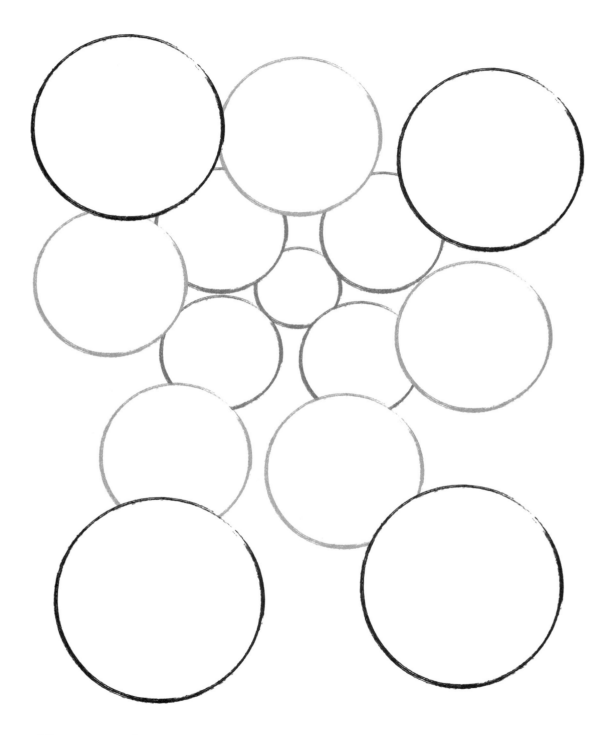

2.

THE CONSTANT DIGITAL CHATTER

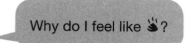

Thought so.

#theworldatyourfingertips #FOMOisreal #theveryhungrymonkey

You're not going to like this part, but I think you already know what I am about to say. That phone in your hand increases emotional turmoil. Big time.

When you're on your phone, you are bombarded with thousands of messages a day. Add up posts, videos, ads, stories, headlines, content, direct messages, and texts!

Okay. Not all of them cause anxiety. We can agree that there is a lot of inspiration and entertainment out there. However, there are many, many things that *do cause anxiety*. I've singled out three main beliefs that have caused our personal stress to skyrocket in the last decade with the rise of smart phones. They are:

☺ **Other people are better than you.**
😱 **The world is a dangerous place.**
😎 **You deserve cool stuff "just because."**

These ideas leave you feeling powerless, helpless, and out of control. We often think of these as symptoms of anxiety, but as a psychotherapist for over twenty years, and as a former sufferer myself, I know them *as causes of it*. Let me explain.

☺ Other people are better than you.

Social media and the like encourage us to compare ourselves to the ideal pictures that we see. We don't see the messy parts of celebrities' or our peers' lives, and this tricks us into thinking that they don't have any. (Meanwhile, you're up close and personal with your own messy parts.) On social media, everyone seems happy, confident, loved, and successful. It appears that these smiling people are just born lucky rather than putting in any effort to get there. (Then, they get so many ♥s and comments, making it worse!)

By now, you've probably heard the research: the more time teens spend on social media, the more depressed and anxious they report feeling. Because. They. Are. Comparing. Themselves.

Hear me: when you compare yourself to a thin slice at the end of someone's success story, you don't take into account the failure, hard work, and mistakes that got them there. And, so, you will always find yourself inadequate in comparison because things seem "harder for you."

😱 The world is a dangerous place.

The second belief is that traumatic events in your feeds make life on earth appear more and more dangerous. During the Spring of 2020, at the time of this writing, we are stuck at home (out of our routine and isolated) with 24-7 coverage of the novel coronavirus. Media outlets share the scary bits—reminding us what we don't know yet. The headlines are written to evoke fear so you are compelled to click through to find out if you'll be okay or not.

We can watch shocking and traumatic scenes in the palm of our hands. Before the dawn of video, when you experienced a threat, you were present and could use up your adrenaline to respond to the situation. Now, we witness danger from very far away, and there's nothing to do but feel out of control and helpless from our couch.

😎 You deserve cool stuff "just because."

This last one is a big contributor to today's mental health pandemic. It is marketing that touts, "You need this cool thing because you deserve it." It manipulates viewers into dropping the ideals of work ethic, making them think they don't have to put effort into creating and receiving their desires. Companies know that if you believe you have to work for something to get it, sales drastically decrease. Common Sense Media reported that children under the age of eighteen see an average of 1.5 million of these[1] entitled ads a year. This saturation of marketing messages that say "You're supposed to have this!" becomes a paradigm through which you see yourself and the world. #toomanyhoursofyoutube

Of course, that's not how it works. You don't get everything you want. Not having integrated cause and effect, this disappointment is nuanced with confusion. I mean, your mind totally gets it, but your sense of worth feels a bit slighted. Your heart doesn't understand why you can't have it, and so it comes up with its own false conclusion: *I guess I don't deserve it.*

---

1   "Advertising to Children and Teens: Current Practices," *A Common Sense Media Research Brief,* January 28, 2014: 16. https://www.commonsensemedia.org/research/advertising-to-children-and-teens-current-practices.

While this mainly happens below awareness, you can probably relate to feeling a pang of unworthiness when you can't afford something everyone else has. You try to figure out why you are unworthy, which is an invitation for the monkey to look for a problem. (This is the thing: when you let the monkey look for a problem, it will oblige you.) Then, since you're already feeling bad, the monkey's problem sounds smart and logical: *You've made lots of mistakes. You annoy people. You are ugly.*

You also wonder: *What did I do wrong?* If you can't answer that—and you can't because you didn't do anything wrong—then you can't fix it, and it increases your distress. ☕ #negativityspiral

You feel increasingly worthless, powerless, and out of control. #nosedivedowntherabbithole 🐇 #thegenzfrenzy

If we don't do something, the mental health crisis will get worse.

👫 US teenagers spend on average over 4.5 hours a day on their phone. [2]US teenagers spend on average 9 hours a day on digital technology, not including schoolwork. US tweens, aged eight to twelve, spend 6 hours on average.

👫 Teens who spend more than 3 hours a day on electronic devices are 35 percent more likely to have a risk factor for suicide than those who spend less than an hour.

👫 Teens who spend more than 5 hours a day on their phones are 71 percent more likely to have a risk factor for suicide.

👫 Teenagers report greater contentment within hours of a break from their devices.[3]

When you think of yourself as powerless, you feel like you can't handle challenges, changes, or the unknown. And in an uncertain world, this is terrifying.

---

2   This data is from 2019. Due to stay-at-home orders this will likely increase dramatically for 2020. "The Common Sense Census: Media Use By Tweens and Teens in 2019," A Common Sense Media Research Brief, October 28, 2019: 3. https://www.commonsensemedia.org /research/advertising-to-chil-dren-and-teens-current-practices.

3   Jean M. Twenge, Thomas E. Joiner, Megan L. Rogers, Gabrielle N. Martin, "Increases in Depressive Symptoms, Suicide-Related Outcomes, and Suicide Rates Among U.S. Adolescents After 2010 and Links to Increased New Media Screen Time," *Clinical Psychological Science* 6, no. 1 (November 2017): 3–17, https://doi.org/10.1177/2167702617723376.

With this constant message bombardment, even adults are freaking out! How can young people not be completely, totally, and utterly overwhelmed?

What's worse is what people do when they feel out of control. They try to get *in control*. Unfortunately, too many go down paths of what I call "pseudo-power." Because it feels like power, but it is fleeting and not ultimately satisfying, so you have to keep seeking and demanding it. Yet, you still feel anxious.

Teens try to either control themselves through resistance, rebellion, food over-indulgence or restriction, demanding self-perfection, overusing video games, or obsession with social media, to name a few. These are bad enough, but in the extremes, this feeling of being out of control leads some kids to use drugs; be sexually promiscuous; practice self-harm; or, most tragically, think about, attempt, or complete suicide.

Though less frequent, some teens even try to get control over others through bullying, sex, or violence.

When we are anxious, we are desperate for relief, and we step back from activities to try to decrease our stress. (That is another attempt to have control.) Unfortunately, that reinforces helplessness, keeping anxiety in power. What is worse, the isolation and lack of mental engagement leave your mind idle and more vulnerable to spiraling negative thoughts. ☺

If the consequences of the world chatter make you feel hopeless, don't fear! I share this to lay the framework for understanding how you can feel better. These messages may have been unconsciously affecting you before I explained them, but now that you're in the know, you're equipped to dismiss the distorted beliefs that they encourage.

You don't have to give up your phone. I love my phone and understand if you adore yours, too. (I even get it if you have a love-hate relationship with it.) Phones are not going away. But knowing the dangers will help you make smarter choices going forward—for example, spending some designated time away from your phone each day, and hopefully engaging in some physical movement. Or, making sure you are involved in creative activities and conducting in-person relationships with good, uplifting people for a significant part of your day.

What's in Your Hand?

Let's practice stimulating the mind from outside these digital influences, through real-life experiences. This activity involves taking a short break from screens. You are going to take a walk outside. Yes. You. Are.

And you are going to leave your phone at home.

You can walk as long as you want to, but challenge yourself to be out for at least ten minutes to start. (If you don't wear a watch, simply guess the time.)

While you are strolling, look around you. The practice here is *to notice*. See? It's easy. You've got this! I want to hone your skills in reading the world, so we are going to start right now using basic skills in observation. I am purposefully taking you away from the bombardment of messages telling you what to think, so you can remember YOUR ability to think for yourself. (You still have it, I promise!) Building these skills will help you feel safer in the future.

When you are out there, notice the shapes of the trees and other plants that you see. What different colors and textures are there in nature that you hadn't noticed before? Look at the buildings, houses, or other structures. Notice the architecture and those colors and shapes. What material was used to build them? Do you see any critters? Squirrels? Birds? Insects? A cat in a window? Do any of your neighbors have decorations that spark your curiosity? Notice the different ways your neighbors care for their yards.

You may see beautiful, cool or funny things; you wish you can snap a pic to post! But this is not a reason to bring your phone.

When you return, write down something that you noticed that you never noticed before. Say a bit about what it's making you think.

....

....

....

....

Um . . . it's freezing outside . . .

I don't know what the weather is wherever and whenever you are reading this. If it is too hot, go outside in the evening or morning when it is cooler. If it is cold, dress warmly.

In the past, frigid temperatures felt like an attack on my senses. Mentally, it made me annoyed, tense, feeling vulnerable, and HATING it. My grandparents used to say, "You'll catch a cold," and I believed them.

Then, while watching the Olympics, I saw professional athletes use icy tubs to build strength and muscle. I learned that cold doesn't make you sick—germs do—and that being outside actually improves the immune system. Once I knew it was "good for me," my attitude for colder weather did a 180. Now with a PMA, I walk twelve months a year, feeling empowered and strong. ☺

3.

THE HELLISH SYMPTOMS

I know what anxiety feels like. It feels like hell. Sometimes the symptoms of anxiety make you feel like something else is wrong, which tends to freak you out more. If you knew that it was just anxiety and not a heart attack or a brain tumor, it would help. Understanding it physically will take away more of the mystery. So, let's get into what this "just anxiety" is.

All anxiety, embarrassment, stress, confusion, panic, fear, nervousness, and worry triggers (and is the result of) a hormone called adrenaline. ALL of the symptoms of distress are body responses of having adrenaline released in your system. Including the negative thoughts! You can have a little adrenaline or a lot of it, and that affects how intensely you feel it.

Here are just a few symptoms of anxiety/panic from the adrenaline:

☺ Shortness of breath. Or feeling like you cannot get enough air in. Sometimes feeling like you can't breathe.

☺ Racing mind. Negative thoughts abound, especially about the worst-case scenario and how ill-equipped you are to handle it. Negative self-judgments fly, too.

☺ Temperature change. Too hot or so chilled you can't stop shaking. Redness in the face or turning pale.

☺ Shaking. Feeling like you want to jump out of your skin or run a marathon.

☺ Being frozen. Not being able to do anything.

☺ Excessive worry.

☺ Physical pain, headaches, backaches, foot and hand pain, and chest pain.

☺ Numbness anywhere in the face, body, or limbs.

☺ Nervous stomach, nausea, constipation, and diarrhea.

☺ Obsessions and compulsions.

☺ Difficulty sleeping and eating (too much or too little).

☺ Tension in the body: face, jaw, shoulders, stomach, etc. Inability to relax. Numbness and tingling. Dizziness.

☺ Weak or restless legs.

☺ Mistrust of yourself and others.

☺ Judgmental, irritable, depressed.

☺ Empty mind. Feeling like you have lost touch with reality. Feeling like you're going crazy.

☺ Intense fear of relatively safe things: driving over bridges, flying, heights, spiders, social situations.

☺ Focused vision. Blurred vision.

☺ Pulling back from friends and family.

☺ Fear of the feelings you are feeling.

Do any of those sound familiar? Gulp!
I feel sweaty just thinking of them!

This is how I understand it: anxiety is the leftover fear response (adrenaline's effects on the body and mind) when you are not in physical danger. This definition separates anxiety from the fear response, making it clear so there is no debate: anxiety is wholly unnecessary. The fear response, on the other hand, is an amazing thing your body does even though you don't need it most of the time.

I know. I know. There are so many messages (even from mental health professionals and advocates!) saying that there is "normal anxiety," and then there is an "anxiety disorder." Or that there is "rational fear" and "irrational fear." It's not helpful to think of it in this duality. In fact, I've found these ideas delay people's recovery *by years!*

Because . . .

1. they validate that some anxiety is logical and correct,
2. which supports anxiety's claim that "it is protecting you,"
3. and hides the fact that it is your skills and abilities that protect you.

Why would you get rid of something that you think protects you? You don't. You keep it. Also, trying to figure out good anxiety from bad anxiety will get you over-thinking about which type you have, giving anxiety your undivided attention. This means you will have no energy or attention for healing! Anxiety wants you to believe it is real, rational, good, helpful, and protecting. When you believe that, you are sunk, and anxiety reigns.

Example 1: If a new, lovely person wants to get to know you, anxiety might say, "They seem too good to be true. They could hurt you, and you can't handle that. It's better to keep them at a distance." You can convince yourself that this decision is "healthy" and "safe." But this is what anxiety actually means: "Stay in horrible suffering alone with me indefinitely so I can protect you from some slight possibility of future suffering that may or may not happen."

Example 2: "Stay vigilant; something bad might happen" sounds smart and prepared. But, TBH daily panic attacks weaken your energy and keep your anxiety powerful. Building confidence and honing skills are what protect and prepare you for future challenges.

Anxiety doesn't make you wear a seatbelt or a helmet, or stay with friends at a party rather than go off with a stranger. Common sense does that. When we call it common sense, there is no question if it is good or bad. You can fully embrace it and call it a survival skill. You are empowered and in control.

If anxiety is the leftover fear response when you're not in physical danger AND you learn what releases and decreases adrenaline in your body, then you have the power and ability to control it. When your adrenaline decreases, the anxiety symptoms will fade away. You will learn how adrenaline is controlled in the next section when we go deep into the sympathetic nervous system. #goodbyeanxietygoodriddance #omgineverthoughtitwouldleave

What's in Your Hand?

List the things that cause your anxiety:

....

....

....

....

List some things a friend is anxious about that you are not:

....

....

....

....

Why aren't you afraid of these things? Why would your friend be afraid?

....

....

....

....

4.

THE STRAIGHTFORWARD BIOLOGY

Anxiety holds a certain power because it is mysterious. It keeps us wondering why we have it, so we are too distracted to get rid of it! Let's break down the biology of fear and anxiety so that you can see what anxiety really is—and that it *isn't* what you thought it was.

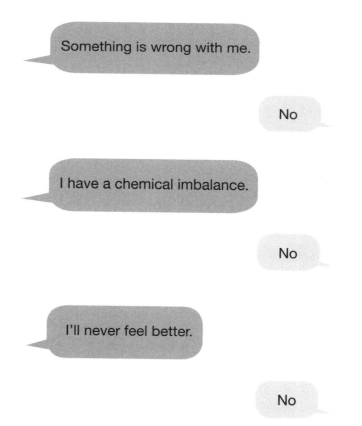

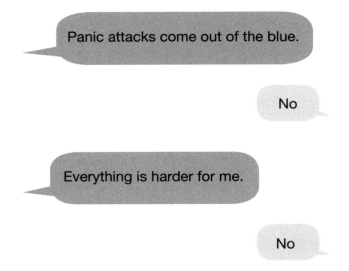

Those ideas about anxiety and depression make you feel out of control, heavy, alone, and hopeless. They increase your struggle. ☹

Fear, however, is different. It has a purpose. It calls our awareness to suspected danger in order to increase our capabilities and skills to make decisions and take actions. You may know the sympathetic nervous system as the fear response, a.k.a. the "fight or flight" response.

Here are the nuts and bolts of it:

A **fear stimulus** is present (or felt, or thought of). Then, the amygdala, a tiny almond-shaped cluster in the middle of the brain, triggers the release of adrenaline into your bloodstream. That fills you with energy, preparing your body to perform beyond your usual limits in order to fight off or run away from the danger.

This preparation includes:

1. Sending your blood away from your belly to your limbs. This interrupts digestion in favor of getting the oxygenated blood to your large muscles. (Yes, this is where the butterflies, nausea, cramps, and unfortunately diarrhea come in! 😲)
2. Increasing heart and respiratory rates to get oxygen to the large muscles.
3. Warming your body to maximize the performance of those muscles (just like during a fever, a warm body can make you feel hot or cold).

4. Focusing your eyes (tunnel vision) so you are not distracted by anything but surviving.
5. Hyper-arousal in the prefrontal cortex—the cognitive "thinking" part of the brain.

Merely nanoseconds later, but AFTER the above is underway, the amygdala sends the message to the (already energized) prefrontal cortex: "All hands on deck! Something is wrong! Find out what is happening! What should we dooooooooo?????"

When the fear stimulus is a literal danger, like a hungry bear in the woods, these preparations come in handy! You use each one when taking action to survive. Running away, outwitting the bear, or climbing a tree to avoid being a bear's lunch relieves the amygdala of its job because your body and mind take over. This is the thing: the fear is only there to get the adrenaline party started. It's unnecessary once you engage in the action, because the action takes over. (Remember this! 🏃)

People have been known to do outrageous, superhuman acts under this kind of duress, such as lifting cars off people! The way our sympathetic nervous system evolved to do this is practically a miracle!

On November 28, 2015, Eric Heffelmire was fixing something under his truck when his jack slipped and the truck fell on his chest, knocking over some gasoline cans, which caught fire. Ten minutes later, his nineteen-year-old daughter, Charlotte, acting on a hunch that "something seemed weird," went to the garage.[4] Barefoot and blinded by smoke, she miraculously lifted the 7000-pound (3175 kg) truck, rested it on her hip, and pulled her father out from under it. She then had the wherewithal to pull the truck out of the garage so the engine wouldn't blow up and risk injury to her family inside the house. The only explanation for this superhuman feat is mad adrenaline. #yourockamygdala #makehaywiththefearresponse

Let's review the sequence: a fear stimulus triggers the amygdala, and the amygdala sets off the adrenaline. The body gets hot, heart rate and breathing increase,

---

4 Peggy Fox, "Teen girl uses 'crazy strength' to lift burning car off dad," *USA Today*, January 12, 2016. https://www.usatoday.com/story/news/humankind/2016/01/12/teen-girl-uses-crazy-strength-lift-burning-car-off-dad/78675898/

blood goes to large muscles, etc. The amygdala sends the message to the prefrontal cortex (already doused by the adrenaline) to assess the situation and decide a course of action. The "clear and present" danger is identified, survival tactics engaged, and hopefully you make it—destined to live another day.

(Big, giant *however* coming . . .)

HOWEVER, there is only a clear and present danger about 2 percent of the time. The other 98 percent of the time, the system is triggered by a stimulus that is NOT a current and physical threat to your body. Biologically and evolutionarily, you can see why the system was designed to trigger *before the danger is confirmed.* (It is better to have it when you don't need it than to not have it when you do!) And, just think: in the first two million years of the human brain's evolution, if a situation was weird and confusing, or if someone looked at you funny, it could have very well meant you'd be clubbed to death. ⚠

#notsureifcavepeoplehadmanners #genzhavemanners

What's a fear stimulus?

It's something in your mind or environment that evokes fear, stress, confusion, discomfort, embarrassment, frustration, and pain.

Why does my anxiety come out of the blue?

Emotions trigger the amygdala to ensure the body is flushed with adrenaline as quickly as possible. Thoughts would be too slow to be useful here. Emotions are immediately connected to your nervous system. An emotional trigger can be a feeling, a smell, an image, a sound, and more.

Even though negative and scary thoughts can make you anxious, it is the emotions that come with the thought that trigger the amygdala. This is why anxiety seems to come out of the blue at times. Your body is often flooded with adrenaline before your thinking mind knows what has happened. Watch my YouTube video "Why Anxiety Comes Out of the Blue."

If the cortex discovers that there is no physical threat, it reports to the amygdala that all is well, and the parasympathetic nervous system (the opposite of the sympathetic nervous system) returns us to calm. Most notable is the GABA hormone, which puts the brakes on adrenaline. GABA is released if you know everything is fine, *and* when you take action and survive. I like imagining GABA as pushing the brakes in a car. (Yeah, I know. I wish it were that easy.)

In modern times, these systems have become wonky for a couple of reasons, which have exponentially increased anxiety and stress in humans.

☹ If you have chronic high stress or something physiological (e.g., thyroid disease) that causes an increase in adrenaline, your hormones are consistently so high that it takes very little trigger to push you higher.

☺ The message pathway from the amygdala to the prefrontal cortex is highly developed, since the evolution of our brain, as it is essential to get that message through quickly, according to neuroscientist Michael Fanselow from the University of California, Los Angeles. The faster your cortex is online, the quicker it makes a survival plan, increasing the chance of success. However, his research found that the message system from the cortex back to the amygdala, which tells the amygdala that "everything is okay," is not as well-developed, since calming down quickly isn't necessary for survival.

🙂 When the amygdala sends the message to the prefrontal cortex to see what is going on, the cortex takes a look around and says, "I don't see the danger, but I feel it; keep pumping those hormones! I will find out what is wrong!" Thoughts fly, and the mind diligently finds the first awful thing that comes into it and then ruminates, increasing the perception of the threat. As I said, when looking, the monkey will always "discover" a problem. And it has the skill to make it sound horrible, too. The amygdala, in service to survival, continues to trigger increasing the adrenaline level in the blood. Panic ensues. #youareabsolutelyphysicallysafebutemotionallyfreakingout

😣 After the first time you feel the terror of anxiety, the very thought of it or the threat of it coming can become its own amygdala trigger.

This review of the biology of the sympathetic nervous system reveals two main things that will help you most in getting your power back.

1. When you are **bothered**, anxiety perpetuates.
2. GABA is released when you take action, and this calms you down.

Bothered?

I used to say that anxiety needs you to be "scared" for it to stay in power. More recently, I have understood that anxiety can get you with:

fear,

frustration,

anger,

self-doubt,

bitterness,

grief,

being upset,

annoyance,

self-blame,

confusion,

disgust,

and more, because they all trigger adrenaline.

Now I realize that anxiety spirals ℮ if you are bothered in any way, shape, or form.

What's in Your Hand?

Anxiety can be very distracting, so it's helpful to plan ahead and determine what actions you can take in different circumstances to take your attention away from the anxiety, and thus release the GABA.

Write down three situations where you might experience anxiety. Under each one, make a list of five actions you can take the next time you feel the adrenaline starting. If you need additional ideas, you can download my list of twenty things you can do when you have anxiety here: jodiaman.com/20ways.

Example:

When I have anxiety during _the moments before bedtime_ ,

I can:

1. *Get organized for tomorrow*
2. *Plan for or think of something I'm looking forward to*
3. *Read or listen to music*
4. *Pet my dog*
5. *Take a shower*

Your turn:

When I have anxiety during ....

I can:

1. ....

2. ....

3. ....

4. ....

5. ....

When I have anxiety during ....

I can:

1. ....

2. ....

3. ....

4. ....

5. ....

When I have anxiety during ....

I can:

1. ....

2. ....

3. ....

4. ....

5. ....

5.

THE 💔 TRIGGERS

The amygdala knows/learns what is and what isn't a fear stimulus from 1) instinct stored in the DNA from dangers your ancestors experienced, and 2) from your own scary experiences in this life. The good news is that you have the power to affect and change both of these! Before we go into that, let me describe how scary experiences affect us.

Intensely threatening experiences are called traumas. Trauma reaction is the consequences of having lived through a traumatic experience—a deeply distressing or disturbing event when the mind, body and/or soul felt grave risk.

Traumatic experiences include but are not limited to:

- sexual, physical, or emotional abuse
- living through a violent event
- a life-threatening accident
- public humiliation, bullying
- a shocking loss
- a panic attack
- your parent's divorce
- a breakup
- abandonment
- a sudden illness of yourself or someone you love
- war experience
- a natural disaster
- poverty
- racism
- discrimination

During a traumatic event, our fear response is triggered and for good reason: we need that superpower to survive.

Unfortunately, a person may feel consequences a long time after the trauma experience. Here are three major consequences of trauma.

1. Body tension. People who experience acute or chronic stress have higher levels of the stress hormone cortisol, which causes perpetual tension that gets stored in the body and affects the DNA, causing acute or long-term physical pain. #yourissuesareinyourtissues

2. Emotional turmoil. Trauma is often devastating to a person's sense of worth, which increases the susceptibility of insecurity, depression, and anxiety.

3. A new trigger, or multiple triggers, are born as the event and circumstances are logged into your amygdala. This is so that if anything similar happens, it can, quick-as-lightning, trigger the superhuman hormone adrenaline to help you survive.

As pervasive and often all-consuming these consequences are on a person who has experienced trauma, they don't have to be a life sentence.

1. The body can be taught to relax, and cortisol levels can decrease.

2. You can learn or relearn to trust yourself.

3. The amygdala can be taught that a trigger that was previously a threat or thought of as a threat is no longer dangerous.

So, you don't have to feel bad forever even if you have experienced the worst of humanity. ☺

Two important reminders to keep at the top of your mind!

🛑 A panic attack can be experienced as a traumatic event (whether the person has a traumatic history or not). Since the sufferer feels physically and emotionally threatened, the amygdala registers the anxiety itself as dangerous.

🛑 To stop the adrenaline, you need to 1) not be bothered, and 2) take some action.

To illustrate what I mean by not being bothered and how an amygdala trigger can be unlearned, let me share with you an example from my life.

Note: I have purposely picked a relatively benign vignette so that you are not upset by something horrible while you try to understand the process of untriggering the amygdala.

A few years ago, I assisted my colleague Jon at a weeklong meditation workshop at a prominent retreat center. Afterward, our liaison from the venue told Jon that three of the forty attendees listed complaints about the workshop on their feedback forms. Though only one of the three expressed an issue with a guided meditation on forgiveness that I had facilitated, Jon called me and left me an indignant and accusatory voicemail, saying that I had ruined his reputation. My stomach dropped as I listened, shocked and humiliated by his anger at my "unprofessionalism." He clearly threw me under the bus to the liaison, as I later learned I was no longer welcome to teach at this venue. Though he had been a trusted colleague for years, Jon stopped speaking to me. I felt confused, betrayed, powerless, and alone.

For a long while after this, an incoming call or voicemail notification would trigger my amygdala, and I'd spiral into anxiety and panic. My amygdala logged both "phone calls" and the "emotional reaction of anxiety" as threats. When a voicemail came in, it would take me days to check it. (I know I am aging myself here, but this was before texting became as popular as it is now. And before transcribed voicemails.)

The first thing you do once you identify an amygdala trigger is to see if it would be safe for you to get rid of it.

In the prehistoric age, emotional rejection and abandonment meant certain death because humans and pre-humans needed a community to survive. In modern times, rejection from *one* person, or *one* group, doesn't mean a rejection from humanity (even if it feels like it). In the midst of my voicemail anxiety, I *felt* like I was dying, but I also knew cognitively that my life was not physically threatened. Because of this, I determined it was safe and beneficial for me to retrain my amygdala to realize that neither phone calls, nor anxiety about them, is dangerous.

(Let me explain why I am distinguishing if a situation is safe: if a person is abusive to you, and being around that person triggers you, you wouldn't want to untrigger your amygdala about them. Instead, you'd want to keep your distance from them! Same as when you wouldn't want to teach yourself to calmly walk across a busy street without looking out for traffic.)

Retraining my brain not to be bothered by these triggers began with my imagination, where it is safe to practice these things. First, I visualized my phone ringing, while at the same time imagining that I felt calm and relaxed in my body. I did this guided imagery a few times a day for a few days.

This preparation built my confidence for the next time it happened IRL. My mind was learning the association of phone calls and calm. And then, when the phone did ring, I would step into a mode of observing myself. This is like taking a mental step back in the mind, out of the chaos of anxiety, into seeing a bigger picture view.

Then, I said: *I feel the adrenaline flowing through my arms. Yep, there it is! Wow! I feel my heart beating faster. That's the adrenaline.*

I observed the adrenaline symptoms with no negative judgment. (I pretended I wasn't afraid as best I could. This was slightly easier since I had practiced first in my imagination.) Next, I'd say:

Thanks, amygdala, if I needed you, this would be amazing! But I don't need you right now. I am physically safe.

Because that message system from the cortex to the amygdala is not as developed, I had to tell the amygdala myself.

Immediately, I would engage myself in some action at hand so that the GABA could push on the brakes and my body could calm down. I repeated this process during any subsequent calls I received, until, many calls later, the anxiety around phone calls stopped.

(The gratitude part of this untriggering process is essential here. Saying "Thanks, amygdala. If I needed you, this would be great . . ." transforms the negative, powerless dread to a positive, empowering sensation.)

Have you ever been concentrating on something, or had earphones on, and then someone startled you when you didn't hear them approaching you in advance, causing you to scream like a chicken and jump ten feet out of your chair? Once you realized it was just your mom or a friend, you both laughed. You've felt the adrenaline at those times, haven't you?

You knew the reason why you felt that adrenaline buzz, and so you were not freaked out by it. Plus, you knew you were okay. How long did the adrenaline take to go away? When I ask people this, they say one minute or a few minutes. Pretty darn quick, right? That's how long GABA works when you are not afraid, or otherwise emotionally bothered, by adrenaline symptoms! *It takes only minutes to go away!!*

That seems easier to handle than however long your anxiety was last time! I know anxiety is scary, but what you can do is briefly act as if you are not afraid.

I am not flippantly saying, "Just get your mind off it." (I know how hurtful that can be.)

Instead, I'm saying, "I totally understand how bad the anxiety is and how hard it is to live with it. I see how much effort you are making each day. I also understand why you have it, and that it is not your fault. But you are suffering. I want to help you feel better. Anxiety needs you to be scared to continue having power over you. You take all its power away and give it ALL back to yourself if you *act as if* you are not bothered by it in the moment. You have already decided it is not dangerous. Yes, I know it *feels scary*, and so it is hard not to be afraid. Anyone would be afraid of the feeling. But you can *practice pretending to not be afraid.* This will result in having less frequent, smaller intensity, and shorter anxiety episodes—even if it is a little at first. It won't make you feel invisible to pretend. It'll make you feel better."

You may think **pretending** is hard. But the loneliness is also hard, the fact that you have anxiety is hard, and the actual anxiety experience is hard. The brief acting as if you are not afraid is not so hard compared to those. You can do it.

> I pretend I don't have anxiety all the time, but this doesn't help.

> Sometimes we pretend to other people for fear that they'll judge us. This makes anxiety worse, since we are so afraid they'll notice anyway. That makes you feel more alone, so I don't recommend it.
>
> When I'm saying "act as if" here, I mean temporarily overriding your feelings of fear (from your own brain) when you've already established that you're safe.
>
> Drastically different.

You can do this with any trigger you have that you don't need, like car rides, your boss being upset that you were late, classrooms, sports practice, swimming, restaurants, storms, and more.

What's in Your Hand?

Discern: There have been times in your life when your fear response was needed and helpful to get you out of, or to get you through, a dangerous situation or problem. And there are also many examples when your fear response was not needed.

Fill out the prompt below.

The fear response helped me when ....

....

....

Isn't that amazing that your body does this? Tell it that you think so.

Dear amygdala,

Thank you for ....

....

....

The fear response was not needed when ....

....

....

....

....

....

....

....

6.

THE BASIC FEARS

Recently, on my Facebook page (@jodiamanlove), I asked, "What are you all dealing with today?" and immediately a comment popped up: "Feeling alone, invisible and wishing I felt more important."

As a therapist, I have worked with thousands of people. One day I did the math. Twenty years, thirty-five people a week, and about three problems an hour. It came out to 105,000 problems that I have helped men, women, and children unpack.

When you uncover 105,000 problems, you learn a lot about people and more than you'd ever want to know about problems. And do you know what I discovered? When I peeled off the judgment-circles of blame and low self-esteem. When I blasted through worry-circles to peek into what is keeping the heaviness in their hearts—I found something that gave me goosebumps.

There was the same thing below ALL 105,000 problems 😊.

Know what it was? Fear.

These basic fears are pure unadulterated monkey food. When my kids were little, we took them to a candy museum where they got to eat some chocolate samples. They were so off-the-wall silly from that sugar high that we took videos. You can see their minds going a million miles a minute. This is what I picture the monkey is like on fear.

Fear's purpose is to propel you into action, but instead we are getting saturated and stalled in fear, and immobilized by it when it turns into anxiety. Scientists say there are three basic fears: fear of being trapped, fear of rejection, and fear of failure. #holymolythosearetheworst

Can you relate to the fear of being trapped?
Living through stay-at-home orders? Yes! Anxiety likes this one—it makes you feel trapped in the anxiety when you feel powerless to stop it, or trapped in a situation you can't handle. Anxiety is recognizable by the sensation of being trapped.

How about rejection?

Believe it or not, you are not the only person who thinks nobody likes them. Feeling alone increases anxiety because you don't have anyone to help you counter the negative thoughts in your head.

And what about the fear of failure?

When your standards are too high, you feel inadequate. If you see yourself as having no skills, you expect that you can't handle anything, and life is terrifying.

Yep. Yep. Yep. 😈

In my conversations with people, I unpacked each of these fears one more layer. Can you guess what is behind them?

Yep. More fear.

Underneath each of the three basic fears is the ultimate fear . . . of being unworthy and/or unloved. Let me explain.

The *fear of rejection* is the fear that you are not lovable or worthy enough to be kept, or that you do not belong because you're different from (or less than) other people. (This is why exclusion and discrimination are so hurtful.)

The *fear of failure* is that you are not good enough, a.k.a. not worthy enough, to have success.

The *fear of being trapped* is the loss of autonomy—a doozy for so many teens: you are afraid of being trapped in your situation (having to do something you don't want to do), in your deficits, and in your isolation. You fear being trapped in "being out of control" because you are not skilled enough (or good enough, worthy enough, loved enough) to figure out how to *be in control*. #lifesuckswhenyoudontfeelgoodenough

What does this ultimate fear have to do with anxiety and depression? The expectations and pressures we place on ourselves—to be perfect, good-looking, talented, bright, smart, young, thin, healthy, and happy—are increasing in this fast-paced, competitive society. Not being able to meet these high standards convinces us that we're a failure at life. If we feel inadequate, then we believe we have no skills to handle life, and this breeds anxiety and depression.

This kind of worry feeds itself, building momentum like a repeating, self-sustaining cycle. We think we are inadequate and we feel bad about ourselves, which makes us feel more inadequate and even worse about ourselves. We feel unable to do anything about it and feel so out of control that we are terrified. Fear sucks the life out of us.

Michel Foucault, a French historian who studied the pitfalls of modern culture, explains that we control ourselves by perceived assessment by our peers—we think we are in a fishbowl, and we measure our actions so that we behave in ways that we hope will prevent the people around us from excluding or judging us as inadequate.

Like on social media, where many kids only leave their story live if there are enough likes. If not, they take it down.

Humans are social beings—we need each other for physical and emotional survival. We are DESPERATE NOT TO BE left out. But in our worry about this, we set our standards for fitting in so high that we can't meet them and so constantly judge ourselves as inadequate.

You may recognize this in your real life or your social life online, feeling like you're in a fishbowl, like everyone is watching you to make sure you are ACCEPTABLE, and afraid that they are (probably) judging you for being an ugly, awkward odd-ball.

Young people—in fact, people of all ages—frequently ask me if what they feel is normal. Even if they are not asking, they are simply assuming they are not normal. "Normal" is undefinable, so you can never achieve it. And trying to will just make you feel bad.

The basic fears are deeply felt, but none of them are totally true.

1. You are never 100 percent *trapped* in your mind, body, and soul. Usually, being trapped in the mind affects us the most, which is, fortunately, the easiest to control once you know how!
2. Even if you are *rejected* by one person, several people, or a group, you are NEVER rejected by EVERYONE on earth. There are always nice people out there that you can trust. The biggest risk of this fear is avoiding asking for help. Thinking we're supposed to do everything on our own is a huge self-worth issue that has become increasingly problematic in the last fifty years. Hear me out: no one is supposed to do everything alone.
3. *Failure* assumes the absolute end of possibility, and as long as you are breathing and there is a chance for change, you can never truly fail. Plus, failure is relative. It changes when the standards and expectations for success change. (We'll go over that in Chapter 4!)

What's in Your Hand?

Think of a story that has upset you. Describe it below in one or two sentences.

....

....

....

....

....

Unpack it by asking yourself: Why does that bother me?

....

....

....

....

....

....

And again, by asking: What bothers me about that (what you just wrote)? Keep asking what bothers you about each answer until you strip it down to a basic fear.

....

....

....

....

....

....

....

....

....

....

What did you uncover was your most prominent basic fear?

....

....

....

....

....

Why is it important to you that this doesn't happen?

....

....

....

....

....

....

....

....

7.

THE DANG STIGMA

Most people with anxiety wait three to ten years before getting help, mainly because they think, *I got myself into this; I need to get myself out of it.* ☺ This is especially true in communities of color, where there is little access to treatment, and mental illness is considered a sign of weakness.

Even though many teens today are more open about their anxiety and depression than ever before, and many celebrities share stories of their own emotional challenges, the Western societal value of being independent and a preexisting mental illness stigma are still in effect. Teens still feel "different" and embarrassed about what they are going through. On the one hand, they are parroting that it is not their fault, because it is a **"chemical imbalance,"** and on the other, they DO blame themselves and feel responsible, because people are supposed to be strong and take care of themselves, right?

Does this happen to you? Is there a war inside of you, debating which one is right, leaving no place for you to just be *you*?

According to the National Center for Health Statistics, 12.7 percent of the US population over the age of twelve currently takes antidepressant medication prescribed for treating depression and anxiety.[5] They are often told that their brain is an "anxious brain" or a "depressed brain" and that **they need antidepressants like people with diabetes need insulin**. This explanation is meant to decrease one's negative self-judgment about taking medicine by attempting to eliminate the shame, since it implies, "It's not your fault; you were born this way."

The now debunked diabetes-depression analogy was created by pharmaceutical companies that want people to think that it's simply black and white—*you have an illness, and antidepressants are the only way to help it*—in order to promote their medicines.[6] Even though pharmaceuticals no longer use this comparison in

---

5   L.A. Pratt, D.J. Brody and Q. Gu, "Antidepressant use among persons aged 12 and over: United States, 2011–14," *National Center for Health Statistics Data Brief*, no. 283 (2017).

6   L.M. McMullen, and K.J. Sigurdson, "Depression is to diabetes as antidepressants are to insulin: the unraveling of an analogy?" *Health Communication* 29, no. 3 (2014): 309–317.

their written marketing, it has gained truth status in society. Many doctors, as well as mental health practitioners, continue to use this analogy in educating their patients.

Unfortunately, while their intentions are to help patients, in reality, I've noticed that, overall, it has the opposite effect of decreasing shame. At first this analogy feels like a relief, but soon the truth of what it means sets in. And it is so insidious that the effects are not even linked to its falsehood.

It HAS YOU BELIEVING that you have no control over an illness that is and will always be in your brain, emphasizing that you're "different," and stripping you of your agency. This hijacks the healing process by bringing forth the circles of negative self-judgment and worry that transforms your sadness from its originally small-sized circle into a massive chaotic mess of horrible depression.

I am not against medicine. It is a powerful tool available to you on your wellness journey. However, how you relate to the medication is important! It is hurtful to your treatment to think taking medicine is something you need to do because you are sick in the head. On the flip side, it is helpful to your treatment to think about the decision to take medicine as an empowered choice you consciously make. The latter will keep intact your self-trust and self-esteem, which will magnify the results. You are using the tool, instead of the tool using you.

When making the conscious choice, you weigh the benefits against the risks. Ask yourself:

1. Can this medicine assist me in getting out of bed, staying alive, having more energy, holding enough hope, or caring about recovery so that I can more easily use the emotional tools to feel better?
2. Are those benefits worth the risk of any possible **side effects**?
3. How urgent is my current state?
4. Is there something additional I can do to help myself?
5. If I do take it, will I have (and will I allow) supports around me?

If you decide the benefits outweigh the risks, be empowered and claim, "I'm choosing to take these medications because of the benefits. Thank goodness they are available!" Say "yes" while you swallow it. (As opposed to being disempowered by the notion "I need this because something is wrong with me" and ingesting guilt with every dose.)

But isn't it a chemical imbalance?

Not really. There is no quantifiable mix of mysterious pathological chemicals that sit on a scale which can tip to one side. ⚖ The word chemical sounds foreign and abnormal, but it just refers to regular hormones and neurotransmitters found in everyone. These hormones shift and change constantly with every physical context, ingestion, feeling, and emotion. While they affect our mood, and are affected by our mood, we can manipulate them with our thoughts, actions, and surroundings. Also, serotonin is not measurable. We don't know how much there is in the brain, so we can't know if you have a deficit. You need a definable balance for something to be imbalanced. This false analogy has been so hurtful to getting rid of the mental health stigma.

Isn't depression like diabetes?

Not even a little. Type 1 diabetes is physically definable: the cells in the pancreas lose their ability to produce insulin. There is a test for diagnosing it. However, depression is NOT definable. Different hypotheses are available to explain depression, and many of these have been discredited. There is no objective test to diagnose it. Type 1 diabetes does not improve without some form of intervention. Depression recovery varies, with or without pharmaceutical intervention. The way insulin works to relieve the symptoms of diabetes is known, but the way SSRIs (the main type of antidepressant) work for depression is unknown.[7]

PLUS: You can increase the hormones and neurotransmitters that make you feel good—serotonin, GABA, tryptophan, and endorphins—with many different practices, and by continuing those practices, you can keep them nourished and abundant. Likewise, you can decrease your adrenaline, cortisol, and inflammation with similar practices. You can do this even if you have other reasons like genetics or environment impacting these hormones, for example, low vitamin D, low magnesium, or thyroid or kidney issues.

---

7   McMullen et al., "Depression is to diabetes," 309.

What are the side effects of antidepressants?

Possible side effects of antidepressants:

- Increases in suicidal ideation among children and young adults
- Long-term weight gain
- Tiredness
- Insomnia
- Nausea and diarrhea
- Sexual dysfunction, which affects 70 to 80 percent of people on SSRIs
- Increased risk of stroke and death among older adults
- Greater risk of relapse after recovery
- Disconnects you with your personal agency

Most young people assume that antidepressants are effective for all people. Opinions on the effectiveness vary, but a quick online search reveals studies that find between 33 and 66 percent effectiveness.[8] When you think of medicine as something you *need,* and you realize it doesn't work? It. Is. Devastating. For. Realsies.

I applaud denouncing the stigma of mental illness, and I appreciate the intention to ease self-blame. This is so needed! However, these myths don't do that. They increase stigma by confirming for people that they are different. Unfortunately, many mental health "advocates" spend a lot of time and energy trying to convince everyone that they *are different*, hoping this will take stigma down. But what they

---

8   A. Qaseem, et al. "Using Second-Generation Antidepressants to Treat Depressive Disorders: A Clinical Practice Guideline from the American College of Physicians," *Annals of Internal Medicine* 149, no. 10 (November 2008): 725–33.

haven't realized is that a patient seeing themselves as "different" has a long-lasting, horrible impact that sustains anxiety and depression.

- 💔 First, it attaches you more firmly to the problem. To quote the author Richard Bach, "Argue your limitation, and you get to keep them." The more you convince people that they have big problems, the more they'll believe (and experience) those big problems.
- 💔 Second, it dismisses the fact that the problems are changeable and treatable, which is necessary to believe for recovery.
- 💔 Third, "different" means that you don't belong, which is crushing to the soul.

Here is a better way to decrease stigma: start a campaign to acknowledge their efforts!

The real reason the person dealing with anxiety or depression tries to convince others that they are different because of their mental illness is not just a desire for others to understand how bad they are suffering. The person actually craves other people to notice their efforts: the considerable energy needed to get through a regular day, and the Herculean effort it takes to get through a difficult day. Other people are so focused on trying to help them feel better that nobody, neither the person suffering nor their family or friends, is acknowledging this effort. Instead, the family and friends are all worried and focused on what the person is unable to do, which feels very judgmental.

For now, do me a favor: try not to make changing the minds of people who don't understand you your responsibility right now. Send them my way. I will train them on how to be better humans. Instead, you focus on healing.

I will explain how easy and common it is for anyone to get caught up by anxiety in our cultural climate. I will tell these people who don't understand that depression is a human reaction to traumatic histories, challenging contexts, disempowerment, and tumultuous relationships. I'll share how emotional struggles are awful and how they make life so hard and lonely that they suck the very spirit out of the person suffering, so they need lots of hugs and love to feel better. And, I will tell these people to let the person suffering know that we see them by recognizing their efforts. When this compassion validates their work, then stigma and shame dissipate. Then, they'll land on solid ground and can step back, see the situation from a broader perspective, and feel secure and supported enough to find a way out.

❤

Don't let perceived worthlessness from emotional turmoil convince you not to ask for help. Remember that we are social creatures, and we are not meant to do anything alone. People experience shame when asking for assistance because they think they ought to be able to do it alone. The societal value placed on independence is a farce, and it hurts and isolates people. When you have shame about asking for assistance, it makes you feel needier, and your shame increases, making you even more needy . . . ℮.

Without shame, you'll feel good about reaching out for support. It's win-win, because other people will also feel accepted, needed, and worthy when they are allowed to help you. Your loved ones want to help. If they seemed frustrated with you, it is often because they are feeling helpless. Let them know exactly what they can do to help, and thank them when they do it—and you'll both feel better.

What's in Your Hand?

Despite how bad a situation is, people are survivors. They use their agency even if they are not aware of it. What are some of the things you have done to get through your worst times? Make a list.

Example:

1. played music
2. called a friend
3. got out of bed when I didn't feel like it.

1. ....

2. ....

3. ....

4. ....

5. ....

People engage in actions for a conscious purpose. When you are not conscious of it, you are not empowered by it. Let's change that. Below, I want you to share why you took an action, and in the parentheses, write down what that says about what is important to you. This seems simple, but it is powerful to open that awareness of what you hold precious. This awareness will activate your potential and keep you integrated with your higher self.

Example:

1. I was hoping the music would make me feel better (feeling better)
2. I promised my friend I would _____ (my friend's feelings)
3. I wanted to do well on the test (good grades)

1. ....

2. ....

3. ....

4. ....

5. ....

Consider doing this exercise daily! Get a journal. Each night, write down three things that you managed to do that day despite how intense the anxiety and depression are. Anxiety and depression don't want you to see the skills that lead to your daily successes because this takes away their power. Luckily, once your skills are familiar to you, you will have better access to them. This is how you'll build the trust in yourself that you'll need for a full recovery.

If you share these successes with loved ones, their acknowledgment will significantly contribute to lowering the effects of anxiety and depression beating you down.

Watch the following videos on YouTube: "I'm a Mess," "Anxiety and Trust Issues," and "The Five Things People with Anxiety Want You to Know." (Find them at jodiaman.com/ditchinganxiety. You can also find my channel "Jodi Aman" and search those titles.)

CHAPTER 2:
"I'm Done with Your Lies."

In Chapter 1, you learned what anxiety is. In Chapter 2, I will show you how anxiety entraps you in its snare. Once you know the ways anxiety exerts its power (by lying to your face), you can see it coming from a mile away and not be bothered, not believe it, not be available to it, and, yes, not even care what it has to say!

We are not just going to help you ditch anxiety when it arrives; we are going to take down anxiety's power *before* it comes. All. The. Way. To. Zilch.

Lie #1:

"YOU HAVE TO KNOW WHAT'S WRONG."

Whether it's meeting with folks one-on-one, speaking, or being interviewed on television and podcasts, I get asked the same question over and over:
How do you know if you have anxiety?
Here are the worries implied in that query:

Do I have a diagnosable mental illness?
Am I normal?
Is something wrong with me?
Would you consider me sick?
Am I irrational, or rational?
Am I crazy?
What do I have?
Do I need, or even, deserve help?
I need to figure it out.

This is what I know: people spend a lot of time and energy trying to understand exactly what they are up against, thinking that they will feel more in control once they know it. They assume the name of the problem will reveal how to handle it, and what to do to get rid of it.

On the one hand, they assume right. Something powerful happens when we know the name of our problem. We feel validated that we are not making it up! But more important, with a name, it becomes an entity outside of ourselves that we can take a stand against, and change our relationship with, so it becomes tangible. If this is your attitude, great! This will support your belief that you can heal and be on the path to healing quickly.

On the other hand, it becomes hazardous if and when the label becomes part of your identity (e.g., "I am mentally ill."). Negative labels don't feel good since they increase your shabby view of yourself. And, let's face it: sometimes, even with a name, the monkey doubts it and takes your attention and energy on a wild goose chase because, *What if you are wrong?* It'll keep you wondering as long as you give it attention. That's exactly what the anxiety wants. You're stuck looking behind, spinning your wheels, and beating yourself up instead of going forward. From this place, it is hard to see how you will ever feel better.

One sneaky way anxiety holds power is by hiding behind other problems and issues, so you stay distracted figuring out what you are up against. To do this, anxiety goes by many different names. Time to call it out.

Here are some of the names **anxiety** hides behind: (Don't just scan the list! Read each name and think about how you relate to these. Circle the ones that resonate!)

Fear
Worry
Worrier
Worrywart
Nervousness
Anxiety
Panic
Shyness
Mental illness
Mental health
Emotional
Attention seeking
Embarrassment
Discomfort
Desperation
Out of control
Control freak (controlling)
Stress
Distress
PTSD
Confusion
Overwhelmed

Stress
Distress
OCD
Resistance
Emotional block
Terror (terrified)
Shook
Stuck
Weak
Immobilized
Irritable
Impatient
Frustration
Dissociation
Depression
Grief
Eating disorder
Disinterested
Breakdown (nervous breakdown)
Losing it (your mind)
Weird feeling
Dread

Manic

Obsessed

Preoccupied

Rumination

Monkey mind

Selfish

Sensitive

Needy

Doubt

Disinterest

Hopeless

Worthless

No point

A mess

Phobia(s) (acrophobia, agoraphobia, claustrophobia, emetophobia, arachnophobia)

All of these are anxiety?

You may think "some of these aren't anxiety" because "real anxiety is worse" than these. Please note: people feel suffering in different intensities and use different words. This doesn't mean they are not feeling it as badly as you. It is entirely possible that they feel it worse than you, but call it something you'd consider less of a big deal.

Happens all the time.

A girl, who suffered panic attacks, was quite offended every time her friend said, "That gives me such bad anxiety!" when the class was assigned an English essay. She thought her friend was making light of anxiety. Listen, anxiety is invisible. How many people have no idea you have it? Most people? Yep. So many more people have it even though they may look like they don't have it. In fact, rarely does someone look like they have it. It is more probable that her friend suffers from real and horrible anxiety rather than making light of it.

It doesn't matter if you have *enough anxiety* or are *truly mentally ill* to warrant help. These terms are relative. "Relative" means you cannot define them exactly. Though each has become a term that we recognize, there is no universal definition for anxiety or mental illness. They mean what they mean to the person who is uttering them. While the *Diagnostic and Statistical Manual of Mental Disorders* outlines a list of symptoms for each diagnosis, a great deal of the practitioner's subjectivity (opinion) comes into play when they make a diagnosis. This is why I prefer to use words as *descriptions* rather than labels, because then the subjectivity is implied, for example, feeling anxious, feeling suffering, and feeling emotional turmoil.

You might be able to handle having a bad day once in a while, but if it turns into weeks, or even months, why stay there just because you don't know if the situation is bad enough to warrant help? All that matters is that you want a change. You deserve support anytime your emotions are bothering your life.

What's in Your Hand?

Let's call the anxiety out so it doesn't get to hide behind anything you think you "just have to live with." List all of the names you use to describe what you experience.

....

....

....

....

....

....

....

....

Lie #2:

"YOU NEED TO LOOK AT ME."

Anxiety is such a bully. It knew just what to say to get my full attention. *"This is bad!! Look at what might happen to you! Violence! The apocalypse! Painful death!"* #youhadmeathello #itcouldhappen

Anxiety wants your undivided attention, so it will use what works *on you*. It'll use your past, your basic fears, your loved ones, your body, your intelligence, or anything that has meaning for you, to get to you to listen. It has no ethical qualms against worrying you about random remote risks by acting like they are big and current. However slight these risks are, the fact that there is a *possibility* enables your anxiety to appear justified, and it seems risky to let it go. *I better be ready, or . . . or . . . I won't be ready!*

"Someone *could* bring a knife on a school bus."
"It *could* be brain cancer."
"Someone *could* break in."

The thought of imminent and tragically painful death used to snap me into full alert, though as a healthy, white, cis teen living in suburban America, the small risk was not worth the hours of panic attacks I had every day.

Before I learned how to get rid of it, I used to temporarily escape anxiety by reading fiction. When I was in one of my worse episodes, I was reading a novel about a woman who fell off a horse and subsequently had panic attacks whenever she got near horses. I remember thinking, *I wish I had that anxiety; that seems so much easier to get over than what I have . . .*

Mine felt more "real." The dangers (violence, the apocalypse, and painful death) felt riskier, more horrible, and more possible. *I mean, it's death. (DEATH!)*

BTW I ♥ 🐎 and I've never fallen off one, so horse-riding anxiety didn't work on me. But, my "death anxiety" got me hook, line, and sinker.

A few years ago, I met with Tina[1] (Asian, "she," cis, straight) for a therapy session. She was anxious about getting sick because she worried about missing class and assignments. In the evenings, as well as in the mornings before school, she was preoccupied with and anxious about the possibility of coming into contact with someone with germs the following day. Tina's mother, an immigrant who had left her home country during wartime, could not relate. She worried she was raising her daughter with such little hardship that Tina was anxious about things that "weren't something to worry about."

Tina turned the tables and told me her mom was afraid of driving, especially in wintery conditions, so much so that she rarely drove. Her mom defended herself by saying, "But *driving* is dangerous!" I am sure you guessed that Tina had no problem with driving in any conditions and could not relate to her mom's anxiety, either.

It's hard to see how anxiety is lying when what you fear is "possible"—even if it is only remotely possible. Here is how you know it's lying: the probability of it happening doesn't warrant the emotional time and effort that anxiety wants you to give it right now. Anxiety tells you it is worth worrying about, but honestly, it is not worth the suffering you are devoting to it.

Anxiety uses the scariness and threat within words (the *content* of anxious thoughts)—"You might crash," "You can't finish it," "It will be hard," "You might get hurt," "You're not good enough for her," "The world is going to end," etc.— to convince you that you need to feel vulnerable and out of control about this RIGHT NOW. The content catches your attention, and you are down that rabbit hole trying to solve, resolve, defend, deny, or otherwise contend with what it says the problem is.

Anxiety will say anything to get and keep your attention on it. You believe the content is the issue because if the content came true, it would be horrible.

BUT, the content is 💩.

It is a red herring—something that is meant to be misleading or distracting. This is it: anxiety needs you to ENGAGE in the content for it to have power. Enough of this charade!

---

1   My client names have been changed to protect identity.

What if you pulled back from the content and thought of it as just "anxiety"? You can call it "anxiety chatter" or "negative thoughts" instead of paying attention to *the meaning* of what it says. You remind yourself that it's nonsense, not currently happening, not probable, and not something terrible that you must figure out. It will be much easier to disengage.

Think about it this way: if you have a brush burn on your knee, and you kept touching it and picking at it, it wouldn't heal. Same with anxiety. *You have to stop touching it.* Here is how:

What's in Your Hand?

Let's reveal "the man behind the curtain." #wizardofoz

The anxious thought content is that scary, loud holographic head that everyone thinks is the "great and powerful Wizard of Oz." The anxiety is the powerless wimp in the control booth, manipulating the sound and smoke and saying, "Pay no attention to the man behind the curtain." The ominous head tricks you into thinking it is powerful. The lights, dry ice, and angry voice grab your attention! *Look at me! This is bad!*

It appears extremely threatening, but it is actually caused by a powerless bully in the corner pushing levers. (If you don't know *The Wizard of Oz*, you can find a video of this scene on YouTube by searching: "Pay no attention to the man behind the curtain.")

Part A: Write down the lies that anxiety uses with you in Column A. (See example.)

Part B: In Column B, explain how you know each of these lies is ridiculous by adding the counterpoint to anxiety's threat. In other words, say why it is wrong. (See example.)

NOTE: If an anxious thought comes from a significant loss or trauma, you may need outside help to challenge it. Please know that it is possible to heal, and you don't have to do it alone. Peers may not be equipped to help you process a traumatic experience, so please find a trusted adult.

Examples:

A	B
This will be horrible	I've done it before and it wasn't bad
You can't handle that	I've dealt with worse
You are not good	Sometimes I manage
No one likes you	Some people like me
I might die	No evidence that it will happen soon

A	B

Share your chart with a friend you trust to get validation for why the anxiety is lying!

Part C: Practice.

Now that you've proved that the holographic head is saying nonsense, it is time to disengage. It is time to quit being mad at, worrying about, or arguing with it. *Yes, even the act of arguing with anxiety means you've engaged with it!* This is the mistake that many people in recovery make: they do the exercise that we just did, and every time the anxiety comes, they desperately repeat their counterpoint in Column B to themselves, thinking they are using the skill of positive self-talk. This sometimes helps calm anxiety, but as you probably know, it doesn't entirely dismiss anxiety and keep it from returning. As long as you engage with it, the monkey will keep playing with your emotions. It's like you are knitting a scarf as fast as you can, but the monkey keeps unraveling it. You will not finish the scarf until you get the monkey out of there.

Once you expose anxiety lies (A) and prove them wrong (B), you should have completed the healing around each fearful thought. (This may take longer if you have some history of trauma or marginalization since those lies have been deeply embedded and ingrained.)

This processing of the problem doesn't mean the anxious thoughts don't come back. They come back because they are familiar, not because you are unhealed. Next time it terrorizes you with its horrible content (that you've already proven wrong), skip Part B—you've already done it—and go right to Part C: it's time to stop engaging with the content that anxiety is pushing toward you. You don't want to worry about it or argue with it. Instead, lump all of the *what-ifs* and *oh-nos* into a general term that describes what it really is (e.g., "anxiety chatter," "negative thoughts," "intrusive thoughts," or "self-doubt"). Acknowledge its presence, and then dismiss it.

"Oh hey, anxiety chatter, I knew that you would come back. Have a seat. I am busy right now."

And then, AND THIS IS CRUCIAL, pull your attention away from it and onto some physical or mental task immediately. Anxiety will keep trying to get your attention. Keep briefly acknowledging that it is lying—don't acknowledge its content—and reengage your mind elsewhere. It may come back very soon at first.

Expect that. Don't get surprised, upset, or judge-y. That attaches your mind back to it, handing the power back to anxiety. (This is why we say, "I knew you'd come back," to remind ourselves not to be bothered.)

Anxiety has been telling you for a long time that you have to figure out *[fill in the blank]*. That's a dirty trick to keep it on your mind. Let that falsehood go.

Healing from anxiety is gradual, and the timeline is different for everyone. This practice is the key to shortening the timeframe and getting you to freedom. The less you engage, the quicker you'll get your life back.

Lie #3:

"YOU MUST HANDLE IT RIGHT."

Social media is loaded with people acting as if being spiritually evolved means that you maintain positive vibes at all costs, never let negativity bother you—be bold, be brave, never complain, never break a sweat, have healthy boundaries, prioritize your self-care, respect yourself, be kind above all, have great people around you, love everyone, stand up for the little guy, don't antagonize, breathe, think positive, be VERY happy, and be chill. You. Must. Get. OVER. It. Immediately. And get "inner peace."

That is not spiritually evolved. That is *fake positivity,* and it contributes to the stigmatization of emotional problems. Rather than lifting you up, this fake positivity often leads you to negatively judge your appropriate human reactions to painful situations. It makes you feel shame about feeling any sadness, frustration, or anxiety even when you are going through a horribly hard time. This is not good. When you avoid, deny, ignore, or self-medicate to not deal with your feelings, they stay pushed down inside you where, TBH, they affect you anyway (in much worse ways than if you process them).

"There is no greater agony than bearing an untold story inside of you."
—Maya Angelou

There is no one "right" way to deal with negative feelings. And complete positivity is impossible anyway, so expecting that will just make you feel like you have failed at handling whatever it is you are going through. #sososomuchworse

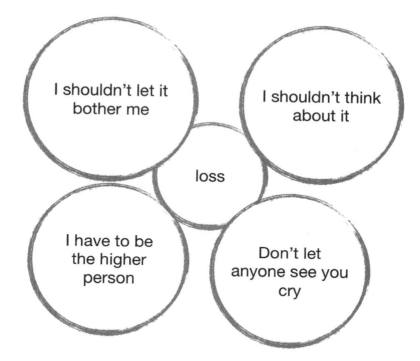

Look how the negative self-judgment circles are surrounding the "loss" feeling as if they are guards, not letting it go. It has to stay put. If you slam your human feelings because you judge them as not "woke," you are unwittingly bringing the energy of them more fully into your consciousness, where you don't want them. #Iwouldnotlikethemhereorthere #iwouldnotlikethemanywhere

In other words, you have to *allow yourself to feel and process feelings* in order to let them go. If you get angry over a friend who betrayed your trust, getting mad at feeling the anger will increase it. However, having (1) compassion for yourself and understanding what made you angry—it's human to hurt when someone lets you down—will help you feel validated. The validation will allow you to (2) take that mental step back and see the situation from a big-picture view. Here, you will have a great perspective to learn about yourself and how and why people act the way they do. This helps you not take things personally and allows you to feel calm and in control of the situation. Then, (3) your next actions will come from this grounded place and will always be for your highest good. (More about these three steps in "Chapter 3: 1. Activate Your Power.")

Compassion and validation are the opposite of self-judgment. Allowing yourself to feel emotions like anger means you won't burden yourself with extra circles. And when you're not imprisoned, the anger can and will dissipate.

That said, we can also cross a line where we pay too much attention to the negative feelings and end up feeding them, instead of feeling and releasing them. Sometimes my kids vent their problems to me, and for a while they seem to be relieving their burdens to their mother. It feels amazing to get things OUT, and when they feel validated and heard, this helps to dissolve feelings.

But occasionally the 😈 gets that sugar-high from the negativity, and the conversation turns a corner. This is when their inner critic and past regrets join the party, and pretty soon, their whole life feels doomed and hopeless. 😵 OOPS! We left the land of resolving and processing and started feeding a frenzy of negativity that is making things infinitely worse! I call this opposite extreme *spiraling negativity,* and it is just as harmful as **fake positivity**.

People sometimes get caught in spiraling negativity when they feel invalidated by other people, by themselves, or by both. For example, if someone hurts you, and when you tell this to your friend, they may reply, "You can't take it personally!" So you say to yourself, *I shouldn't let it bother me*. It's a double whammy: You're hurt, AND you are handling it wrong. This drives you to make defenses for why it hurt so bad, and to build this defense, your mind remembers all of the old hurts and painful past situations that were similar. This ups the ante on analyzing the issue, and worrying about it. 😱

If there are two extremes, fake positivity and spiraling negativity, that are not helpful, then what is helpful?

You can balance the shuffle between 1) facing your problems so you can learn, resolve, and evolve from them, and then, at some point, 2) taking your attention away from the problem and putting it toward creating happiness, oftentimes earlier than you think.

Happy people are not just focused on the positive all the time. They allow themselves to feel sadness but don't stay stuck there. They feel it, have compassion for it, take a step back, and then let go of it. (More on how to let go soon!) Then, they focus on bringing good stuff back into their lives. Remember the Formula for Happiness from page xix? Here's a reminder:

1. Get rid of the stuff that makes you suffer (by processing, not denying).
2. Bring into your life what makes you joyful.
3. Practice 1 and 2 every day.

There is no perfect way to handle anything. Life is hard. A lot of things can happen to a person. You are going to be hurt, angry, sad, and anxious sometimes. There is nothing wrong with you for feeling those emotions. It means you are human. Anxiety will always try to make you feel bad for anything so it can stay in power. Enough is enough. Embrace your humanity so that you are with yourself, instead of against yourself.

There is a risk of spiraling negativity when teens commiserate. Often there are pockets of kids in school who connect around problems. This could happen in a moment of a group venting about something. Or, a small friend group can construct a culture in sharing experiences of anxiety, depression, and self-harm. At first, this feels so good to belong. Humans long for belonging, and when they are struggling, they crave it even more.

When you find one or more peers who get you, it feels like chapstick on dry lips. Don't get mad at me for saying this, but if you are in a group like this, it is sometimes hard to get happy because that would mean you no longer belong. Also, the negativity grows as most kids in these groups are sensitive and empathetic. They feel each other's pain. Worrying about your friends adds to your stress. Unfortunately, in this mini-culture of negativity, the struggle becomes something equated with worth. Even if it is negative, you are part of something, and that can become addicting. I am not saying to leave your friends behind. Your recovery can inspire the whole group to change. Or, better yet, you can all consciously decide that you want to lift each other up and out of it together!

What's in Your Hand?

Write a goodbye letter to "Anxiety." Here's an example from a former client who has allowed me to share it.

Dear Anxiety,

At points in my life, I thought I needed you and that you were a part of me. A huge and dark part of me. With time, support, and practice, I have learned you are not a part of me at all, but a lingering menace holding me back from my full potential. Through years of isolation, regret, despair, and pain, I have learned that you were not protecting me, but instead vilifying a world full of beauty, love, and potential.

Instead of living with you, I live despite you, and our battles continue, but I know I am so much stronger, braver, and wiser since I have acknowledged your face and tactics. I can feel the sunshine and see the flowers bloom without the fear that you may overcome me again, because I know I am stronger than you think I am.

Although my peers struggle with you, as a team we are so much bolder together that your combined attacks are nothing we cannot handle together. I see you . . .

In fact, I want to thank you for making me understand pain in the darkest places of my mind, so that I can appreciate my journey in the light, the sunshine, and the shield of my community. I am always learning new ways to challenge you. You can continue to try, but remember: I am stronger, and no matter what new tricks you pull, I will overcome. I am prepared like warrior to battle, and you no longer dictate my life, because I say so.

Standing in the sun,
Sam

Your turn.

Dear Anxiety . . .

....

....

....

....

....

....

....

....

....

....

....

....

....

....

Lie #4:

"YOU MUST BE IN CONTROL!"

Feeling in control is one of our main desires, because being out of control feels dangerous. *If I am not in control, and something bad happens, I can't DO anything!* This idea can paralyze even the strongest person.

People crave control because it makes them feel safe. Unfortunately, trying to control everything will end up making us feel more out of control since we'll realize rather quickly that . . . We. Can't. Control. ANYTHING!!! 😤

To manage the panic that ensues, we grasp more desperately to control something—*anything*: other people, chance, institutions, the weather. However, each of those have their own agenda, and they won't cooperate with our need to have everything the way we want it. We spiral into heightened helplessness. Anxiety increases. When you view *possible risk* as a real and valid threat, you won't feel peace anywhere. #likeacontrolfreakonamonsterenergydrink

Remember: Anxiety is LYING to you. Lack of control may have you feeling vulnerable, but it is hardly ever actually dangerous. This is crucial to distinguish! Vulnerability isn't dangerous by itself. Vulnerability, when you are safe, is SAFE.

Cate (white, "she," cis, straight) is a young woman who meets with me. "Someone treating her as unworthy" is a fear stimulus for her, ever since she was bullied by her aunts and an ex-boyfriend. This means her brain registers any interaction with someone who is being passive aggressive, who treats her as invisible, who acts selfishly, or who is inconsiderate as a *physical threat*. Her anxiety is UNDERSTANDABLE from both an emotional, and biological, standpoint. However, the problem is that many regular, relatively harmless people act in these ways all the time. Therefore, she is frequently panicking, even though she is literally physically safe.

So, Cate doubles down and attempts to avoid people that she can't control. But this is no way to live. Her anxiety and isolation are worse risks to her emotional well-being, IMO. She can continue shutting down when she feels unworthy, lamenting that she cannot control other people, hide away, and avoid all social situations, while she continues to feel anxious thinking about the dangers "out there." But that's not a life. In our work together, she realized that instead of putting herself through all of this suffering, she could separate the notion of worth and safety.

To do this, we focused on her skills in assessing the safety of a situation, specifically in being able to distinguish between the dangerous people, who are trying to get power over her, from harmless people, who may act self-centered because of insecurity or out of ignorance. (As it turns out, she, like many of you, is already quite skilled at assessing who is in which category. #yourshouldbeamarvelhero)

> Our social identifiers (race, preferred pronoun, gender, sexuality) affect our experience. For people with marginalizing identifiers, we would take into account a higher risk of danger during and after these microaggressions.

Once she decides who is who, she can choose her course of action, from an eye roll dismissal to a *Get away from this person right now,* and everything in between. This discussion helped her become aware of what is in her control: namely, how she has the power to discard insensitive comments or get safe if the situation is legitimately dangerous. Even though the real danger may be a minimal risk, she learned that planning for it helps her to let go of the worry of how she would respond in the future. She began to relax in public, feeling empowered rather than out of control. She learned that these things just happen in life. Many things are benign (not harmful) and don't matter too much. Most things that do matter are manageable and not even scary. Some are different degrees of annoying but bring many lessons with them. Very, very few things that happen are horrible. Even at those times, you can adapt, survive, and thrive.

Being stuck because you are feeling out-of-control-while-you-are-trying-to-control-everything-due-to-some-remote-possibility-of-something-horrible-happening is not only wasting your life; it is pure suffering. News flash: if we live in fear, we don't truly live.

Anxiety picks out the ways you don't have control and tries to put all your attention on them. Meanwhile, there are so many other parts of life that you absolutely have control over. You can keep your attention on one, or the other. And you know which one anxiety wants you to pay attention to. Which will you choose? #covidtaughtushowtoletgowhatwecantcontrol

What's in Your Hand?

Here are five things you can do to regain a sense of control:

🤚 Make to-do lists.

Writing things down helps you be accountable to yourself. It enables you to divide a big overwhelming job into smaller steps, propelling you to start tackling the tasks instead of being frozen and overwhelmed by the whole of them. And when you cross the finished tasks off, you are reminded of your agency and ability to do what you put your mind and intentions to. Also, results of your accomplishments will reinforce your power, since you made this happen.

🤚 Meditate.

Meditation is a practice of taking your attention from one thing to another. Anxiety needs your attention, and meditation trains you to gently guide your mind away from what feels out of control to what feels in control. We will talk about this more in Chapter 5. For now, know that there are many ways to meditate. Even coloring! Color the next page. (Find my "21 Guided Meditations" on my book resource page online: jodiaman.com/ditchinganxiety.)

🤚 Learn new things.

Learning new things will help you feel in control. It reminds you that new skills affect positive change in our lives.

🤚 Do something hard.

This builds confidence and problem-solving skills. The more challenging things you do, the more you'll know that you have the skills to figure things out when there is a problem. The story Will Smith tells about the wall he built when he was young illustrates this perfectly. To watch, search YouTube for "Will Smith Wall."

🤚 Be around like-minded people.

There is no substitute for having a family or community where there are people who see you, listen to you, care about you, and have your back. We are social beings; there's more power and safety in a group. Post the colored page on your Facebook or Instagram story to inspire others. Tag @jodiamanlove and use #ditchinganxiety.

Lie #5:

"YOU SHOULDN'T HAVE TO DO IT."

Obligation, or pressure, to do something feels restrictive for teens who are busy attempting to individuate (become your own self-governing person). It triggers resistance, then often resentment toward the person who ordered the task.

A significant pressure to do something
+ A strong urge to resist that pressure
───────────────────────────────
Feeling out of control

Unfortunately, this combo brings teens into conflict with people and opportunities. Young people feel a stronger and stronger pull to avoid doing what they don't want to do.

However, the conflict increases your misery, lowers self-worth, and affects your performance. Let me explain what's happening so you can get your control back.

Your brain has two main jobs:

1. To survive/thrive.
2. To conserve calories.

Sounds funny doesn't it?

For the first two-million-plus years of human evolution, conserving calories was a purposeful and necessary survival mechanism. One burned a ton of calories hunting and gathering food, which wasn't always available. However, in the last hundred years, grocery stores have rendered this tool useless. Unfortunately, qualities that evolved because we needed them in the past stay with us even though they are no longer needed. #seethelittletoe 🦶

This means your brain quickly assesses anything you come across to see if it is necessary for your *surviving, or thriving,* in life. If yes, you (obvs!) deem it as worth your caloric expense. On the other hand, if you don't think you need it to survive or thrive, you will experience biological, mental, and emotional RESISTANCE to use calories to do, read, engage, or otherwise give any attention to it. This is human and biological. Keep in mind: it doesn't just happen when there is a food shortage; it happens *in case there is one.*

Your brain is continually making this assessment all day, every day. Activities will be considered worth the caloric expenditure if they are necessary, impact survival, satisfy a basic need, affect something important, are pleasurable, or generate preferred results. The anticipated physical and mental effort and the expectation of positive outcome also play into the decision to engage. The least amount of energy for the highest results is valued, since efficiency meant survival during those first two million years.

If the activity is considered unnecessary, you feel resistance to it. This is a big reason you feel tired all the time. Your brain is on repeat, "Rest! Rest!" Just in case.

Then, there are those times when you assess something to be *against* surviving or thriving, and resistance shoots up even higher. This is why you feel like rejecting all tasks and events that feel challenging, tedious, out of control, emotionally dangerous, or anything that could potentially evoke discomfort or anxiety. It feels like more than a lack of desire, though—it feels *unsafe*. (Because biologically starving is unsafe.)

Teens have a reputation for being unmotivated. But I don't think you are unmotivated at all. I see you as highly motivated *to resist!* 🖑 ⚠️

The resistance is annoying enough, but what is worse is that we attach meaning to this resistance, and that usually builds more resistance. For example, the combination of obligation and resistance gives you a feeling of oppression (the state of being subject to unjust treatment or control) where you feel like a victim and trapped. Have you ever felt resentful of having to follow some authority's rules or of not being able to make your own decisions? Homework? Chores? Going somewhere you didn't want to go?

All the time? Did anyone accuse you of being rebellious, insubordinate, or lazy for feeling this way? 😑

When you have to do something you don't want to do, you might defend yourself, causing conflicts with folks, thus feeding the spiral of negativity. You might even spend more calories digging your heels in than you would on the actual task, LOL. Yet, it feels like you're defending your honor, so you keep going. Then (unless you wear down the authority figure enough that they give up), you still have to DO THE TASK on top of all that!

What feels like "oppression" from the combination of pressure and resistance is not always oppression. Oppression is the act of unjustly controlling a person or community. The demands of the oppressor are intended to maintain power and control and to disempower the oppressed. The demands benefit only the person/people in power and serve to maintain that power differential. If the request, recommendation, or limit is from someone who cares about you and your future, and the task is for your highest good, your classmates' highest good, your family's highest good, etc., then it is not oppression.

Real oppression is a soul trauma because it is dehumanizing. Some of you have had real experiences of oppression, from an abuser or a corrupt government or institution, and they might have come in the forms of racism, sexism, classism, ableism, xenophobia, ageism, or heterosexism. But we risk rendering those things invisible when we confuse it with your teacher scheduling a test tomorrow that you don't want to do, or your parents giving you a curfew.

Resistance also affects how you see yourself. When you feel tired all the time, it's a quick jump to worrying that something is wrong with you: "I'm so tired all the time. Why am I so tired?" The teens I know frequently say this aloud, so I can only assume they say it in their heads even more.

The repetition is like laying heavy blankets on you, making you feel more and more tired, but also disconnected and apart from the group. And it makes you worry that you are a victim/lazy/mentally ill/physically ill/weak/incapable/stuck/stupid/self-sabotaging, etc., which, again, will make you feel more out of control. This spiral of thoughts is distracting, self-deprecating, and conflict-producing, which then becomes the priority to deal with, and the original task gets lost in the shuffle. This is unfortunate when the task is for your highest good.

What is worse is that, if it's not understood, this resistance leads to long-lasting negative identity conclusions, where you take on as your identity what the worries just accused you of (e.g., you are a victim/lazy/mentally ill, etc.). Those labels stick, even though you were just a regular human having biologically appropriate resistance. Over months and years of seeing yourself this way, things spiral, and the ensuing isolation of this negative self-judgment brings ongoing depression, anxiety, addiction, OCD, and more. You assumed you had a mental illness, and it becomes a self-fulfilling prophecy.

However, if you understand this as a *biological resistance to conserve calories,* you can decide what to do from outside the influence of this negative self-judgment. You'll have the mental space to assess whether:

1. there are benefits to the task (it DOES contribute to thriving in life),
2. you are safe doing it, and
3. you have enough food to support the physical and mental efforts of doing it. 🍨

With one or more yeses, you'll decide to override the resistance.

Also, doing tedious chores regularly makes them familiar and more comfortable, and therefore will take less effort, decreasing resistance. The less resistance, the less negative energy around those chores and so the quicker they are done with less energy expended.

If you hate everything that you have to do, your energy is sucked right out of you. You become depleted and exhausted. When my to-do list is a mile long and I want to hide under my covers and lose myself in some fan fiction, what helps me most is to remember: *everything I do, I am choosing to do.* I chose it because I want the benefits of doing it, and don't want the consequences of not doing it. This helps me feel empowered instead of disempowered, allowing me to have my energy for the task.

What's in Your Hand?

Write a list of some tasks/chores that you resist doing, especially those that give you anxiety. Next to each, write if there would be any benefit to you, or to something/someone important to you, in doing it.

If you can't find a benefit, please ask someone else if they can help you think of a benefit. There may or may not be a benefit, but it's very helpful to double check with a trusted friend.

Using this information, decide if the tasks are worth doing or not. Circle those that are worth it and cross out those that aren't.

Read this blog post: "Benefits of Chores" (find the link on jodiaman.com/ditchinganxiety).

....

....

....

....

....

....

....

....

....

....

....

....

Lie #6:

"YOU CAN'T TRUST ANYONE."

I have been around my share of difficult people. People who are so miserable that negativity oozes out of their pores. They are passive-aggressive, mean-spirited, grumpy, judgmental, and often humorless (unless it's at someone else's expense). They are not easy to be around. Energy is contagious. Excitement and happiness spread, and so does negativity. One difficult person can take down a whole room, especially when they are mean.

Miserable people have so many negative feelings that they overflow onto everyone around them. Mean people may seem confident because they act self-important, but this is just overcompensation as they have little belief in themselves.

This is the thing: people are not mean because they don't like you; they are mean because they don't like themselves. If the "mean girls" are judging you, it's because they are **judging** themselves 10x more.

What do you mean that people who judge, judge themselves more?

The higher standards people have for themselves, the less they can live up to them, so the more inadequate they feel. To compensate for this, they tend to put other people down to make themselves feel better, like the stereotypical bully from the movies.

However, sometimes the judging person has good intent. They do care and love you, but they point out your flaws to "help you." The imperfection is making them worry about you, because, in their eyes, it means you could be vulnerable. Or, it feels out of control to them. Their intentions may be honorable, but they are still responsible for hurting you with their negative judgment.

I wish they didn't do this! If I had their ear, I'd tell them to stop; but for now, I can only let you know how to protect yourself!

Are there many people who are mean to you, and your monkey mind has on repeat: "It must be me, because a lot of people are mean to me; I'm the most common denominator"? #nopeitsnotyou

Many people are mean to you because *many people* don't like themselves. It is not fair or okay that they treat you this way, but unfortunately, you can't control them. However, if you think you are helpless in the midst of difficult people, you will exude that helplessness, leaving your mind and heart open to their negativity. I have been there a million times. It's especially hard when you've come into the situation already feeling fragile. But it doesn't have to be this way.

You may feel helpless, but you are not! You have 100 percent of your personal agency to respond to a situation in any way you like. You can empower yourself to protect yourself and set firm boundaries on what you are available for. You can even shift the energy of the room by spreading positivity. (Watch my videos "Dealing with Difficult People" and "Setting Awesome Personal Boundaries" on YouTube.)

You may have heard that no one can make you feel bad unless you let them. That's overly simplistic, and so not always helpful. It makes you judge yourself. Of course, encountering mean and negative people will bother you. You feel devalued, unimportant, and unworthy. It's not because you are weak, or sensitive, or overreacting—it just doesn't feel good because you are HUMAN.

Have lots of loving compassion for yourself about feeling hurt. You can understand why you would be hurt, so tell yourself so! Mean people make you feel devalued. Compassion returns your value. It is only then that you can take a step back and see that This. Is. About. THEM. Not you. Once you stop judging yourself and your feelings, the hurt gradually dissolves, and you can figure out how to respond.

You will have to deal with people like this your whole life. It is awful to experience, but with practice, it becomes easier to recover. Here are two options to respond to difficult people: 1) get physical space, and 2) get emotional space.

1. The best way to be unavailable to negative people is to get physically where they can't reach you. This includes blocking people on your cell or social media. Do it.

2. Getting emotional space is when you intentionally block their words, actions, and attitude from coming into your heart. This means you reject the energy they are conveying BEFORE you take it in. (Once it is in your heart, it is harder to get rid of!) Think of this as an energetic force field around yourself that won't let anything negative through. You can do this in two ways.

   a. One is by guided meditation where you imagine a light shield around yourself before going into situations when you know you might or will be interacting with someone negative.

   b. The other way is the energetic eye roll. The eye roll is a rejection, rendering unworthy what a person says/does to you. The energetic eye roll is an attitude that says what they are sending you has no value, so your mind, body, and soul won't take it in. It gives you the power to control the situation, without risking causing the other person to become more negative. (You don't do the eye roll physically!)

Imagine if the insult or negativity were in physical form, coming toward you. These impenetrable barriers would stop it, and it would drop to the ground, powerless and harmless in front of you.

Believing you can protect yourself from difficult people makes a huge difference. When you don't believe this, you'll feel powerless and vulnerable. When you do, this confidence shields you, making anything they say and do roll off like water off a duck's back.

Once you know you are safe, and only when you are safe, you can try to spread positivity. You might even change a negative person into a positive person! #lukesavesanakinskywalker

Remind yourself that people are mean because they don't like themselves. When you understand this, you will realize that people attack because they are lacking, and so needing, love. Giving LOVE (acknowledgment) heals a person because it gives them worth when they feel worthless.

While it is not your responsibility to heal mean or negative people, you can try it as an experiment. The "experiment" will protect you from taking things personally and positions you as an observer/researcher—a much more powerful, and less attached, stance than "victim." This is what you do: pick a person that is a bit crabby, and give them genuine compliments every day or so. After a few weeks of acknowledgment, notice if anything changes.

Abort the experiment at any time for any reason. Some people's pain goes deeper than a little acknowledgment can heal, and getting physical space for your own safety is necessary. Don't open yourself to being hurt because you think you can save someone. Being able to hurt you will never help them to change.

If you care about someone who is hurting you and really don't want to abandon them, don't worry, you can send them healing energy from a distance when you are out of harm's way.

Don't try this experiment if you are in a manipulative relationship. Continuing to take a person's abuse is not the same as giving them the love they need to stop abusing. Pleasing an abuser reinforces their control and they will continue their pattern.

They need you to feel bad about yourself for you to stay with them, so they are always saying no one else would love you. They may say they love you, but they are confusing love with possession. They are miserable people, and they try to stabilize themselves by getting control over others. (This is an example of that pseudo power I told you about.) It is not sustainable, so they constantly feel out of control again, and they have to continue to exercise control over you.

If you are dating someone who is insulting, controlling, mean, or abusive, the best thing you can do is tell someone (especially if you are not sure, either because they are nice some of the time or if you have feelings for them). You may be too close to the situation to see clearly. Get an outside opinion from someone you trust. They might tell you that you are not crazy, and that it is as bad as you think, and that you don't deserve it. (You need to hear this because the abuser probably has fed you with lies that their behavior is not that bad, or that it is all your fault.)

Isolation makes it harder for you to get out of the relationship. That's why abusers control who you spend time with, hiding this behavior behind being jealous, needing you, or having distrust of other people. Connect (stay connected) with people outside the relationship at all costs!

Plus, a community will help you heal after you finally leave the person. Often, we carry the voice of the abuser in our own self-critic even long after the abuser is no longer around, and we'll need those friends to help us let go of that.

I plan to write a whole book for you about how to get away from a person like this. Since I haven't written it yet, watch my videos on Navigating Teen Relationships at jodiaman.com/ditchinganxiety. Also here's a short book that I suggest, *The Narcissist: A Guide Book* by Lori Hoeck and Betsy Wuebker.

What's in Your Hand?

Inspired by the meme "Dear 13-year-old me," I wrote a letter to my younger self, explaining why I ought not worry about what everyone else thinks.

Read my letter to my thirteen-year-old self. After, write your reflections answering my prompts.

Dear thirteen-year-old Jodi,

You made it! I almost don't know how you did it given what you were feeling at your age. (That's not true. I believed in you the whole time!) It's inspiring how you kept trusting and searching for answers for how to feel better. Even though you rarely found something that worked, you didn't give up.

This is what I want you to know: you are so much more amazing than you feel like you are. You are kind and observant. You always saw what people needed and were willing to help them. You tried so hard, even though you were tired of being teased and treated like you were strange and unwelcome. Even though some days you felt like you couldn't stand it another minute, you kept going.

It doesn't matter that your body seems behind the rest of the class. You'll catch up later. Don't get so down on yourself that you can't write well. You care, and that's what's important. This will give you the tenacity to practice and hone your skills. It doesn't matter that you dress like a dork; you'll figure that out, too. Don't listen to what the boys say.

I know our mom told you that boys are mean when they like you. Please know that you don't have to tolerate this. It is never okay for them to be mean. They may have a crush on you and be confused and embarrassed and tease you, but this doesn't mean it's okay. It means you don't have to take it personally. Please don't pay those boys any mind until they learn to get over themselves and treat you with kindness. If they continue to express affection by putting you down, NEVER give them the time of day. And know this has NOTHING to do with you and does not mean you don't deserve to be treated well.

You are lovely and worthy, and you will find the love of your life when you get older. You don't have to worry about it too much. Even though you will feel quite passed over for many more years, trust me, it works out great.

There are many things you don't have to worry too much about. You don't have to worry about doing things the right way all the time. There are many ways to do things, and you have good, creative ideas. In fact, you are awesome at problem-solving, being motivated, and planning. You will be a leader through high school, college, and graduate school. And you will help a lot of people during that time.

You don't have to worry about being different. Eventually, you will be happy that you are unique. Being silly won't always be embarrassing, but joyful. You don't have to worry about being invisible. You are not invisible. Many people see you and think you are great; you just don't see it right now. Sometimes it is hard in the moment. I understand. But you are loved.

I know friendships are hard sometimes. People are hard. They say things that hurt you and don't seem to care. It's mostly because they don't know they've hurt you. They are dealing with their own insecurities, and what they say has nothing to do with you. All of your friends are trying hard to figure out their own lives. When they say something mean, it is because they need a bit more love.

This doesn't mean you should be a doormat. You can love them without taking their mean words into your heart. You'll feel better, and you might help them, too. That may seem strange to you right now, but you'll understand when you are older. Please practice giving yourself some compassion. Whatever you are feeling, tell yourself, "It's okay, I understand." Allow yourself to feel that because this will keep your sense of self intact. You will feel validated and worthy instead of alone.

Little Jodi, you are a cutie-pie! I know you are worried you won't make it, but you can do this. In fact, you will do great things in your life. Subtle, small things, but they will mean the world to a few people. You will save lives by seeing the good in people. You'll learn to celebrate yourself, and this will give you energy to do more.

You can trust yourself. Just try it a little for now.

Much love,
Older-wiser-happier Jodi

Did you read anything in the letter that you need to hear right now? What was it?

....

....

....

....

....

If you could imagine yourself as an older, wiser person, what would you most need to hear right now?

....

....

....

....

....

....

....

....

....

....

....

Lie #7:

"YOU CAN'T."

That dang inner critic! We would never put up with someone saying this to us, but we have no problem saying these horrible things to ourselves. Our own inner critic is often worse to us than an enemy might be.

You can't do this.
You can't do that.
They're not going to like you.
You'll mess up.
You're stupid.
Nobody likes it when you do . . .
You're annoying.
You don't know how to.
It's too hard.
It's going to be overwhelming.
You can't handle it.

Lies. All lies.
You are not what your mind says you are. Not by a long shot. And, you DON'T deserve to be berated like that.
You are not ugly.
Not stupid.
Not unlovable.
You don't mess everything up.
You can feed your inner critic with your precious attention and energy, or you can give that attention and energy to your wise voice that reminds you:
You belong.
You are kind . . . a survivor . . . and so much more skilled than you think you are!!

When your inner critic whispers how terrible you are, it is often with an emotionally charged delivery, as if it is NEWS. You feel renewed devastation, even though your critic has said the same thing for months, or years. What if you expected the critic and responded with, "Yep, that's what you always say," removing the emotional charge? You'll take it less seriously, with no attachment, and you'll find it easier to let go.

Silencing your inner critic is doable. It takes a bit of discipline and practice. When you start to doubt and judge yourself negatively, say, "I knew you'd come back. I get it. Just have a seat; I am busy right now." Self-compassion is again the key to letting go of what you no longer want in your life. #makelikeatreeandleave 🌳

What's in Your Hand?

Write down some of the typical complaints your self-critic says. Next to them, write down how long you have been saying this to yourself.

....

....

....

....

....

Do you deserve what it says? Why, or why not?

....

....

....

....

If you answered "yes," or even if you hesitated rather than answer "no," do this: imagine you are one of your dear friends (a trusted one who loves you). Ask yourself, *as your friend*, "Does your friend, *[your name]* , deserve what her inner critic is saying? Why not?"

....

....

....

....

....

....

....

....

....

....

....

....

....

....

CHAPTER 3:
"I'm a Single-Pringle!"

In this chapter, you'll learn how to claim your personal power and take control of your life. Every action you take is an extension of your values and beliefs. When you are conscious of your actions, values and beliefs, you control them. Each section will outline an ability that will help you activate your agency and transform how you approach life.

Shhhh! Anxiety doesn't want you to know these strategies.

1.

ACTIVATE YOUR POWER

When I was struggling with anxiety, I wasn't willing to "accept my powerlessness" or "surrender needing to be in control," like people were suggesting. Not a chance. 💔 Even the thought of surrender made me want to cringe and grab on to "control" tighter—though it was painful. It showed up in decisions like these:

If I don't spend much time with my peers, then they won't know how stupid I am and they won't hate me.

If I don't put the papers in my bag in the right order, I might forget one. (Sift through folder) I have to do it so I don't mess up. Wait, let me check one more time . . . (Sift through folder) . . . Did I see them all? (Sift through folder . . .)

If I didn't control situations, I thought they would control me.

I was wrong.

Okay, yes, there are things outside your control, like other people's choices and behaviors, natural disasters, and accidents. And, of course, they affect you. However, there is something that is 100 percent in your control: your responses and reactions to what has happened. You can:

1. blow up those effects, increasing your suffering 🛑, or
2. process and release the feelings 👍

What actually happened only affects a very small percentage of your mood, emotional turmoil/wellness, comfort/discomfort in the world, and view of yourself. You are actually MOSTLY affected by how you think about what happened, how you make sense of it, and what you do next. (You have absolute power over those.)

The initial pain from what happened to you is that first "heartbroken" circle from "Chapter 1: 1. The Monkey Mind." Instead of the monkey piling up circles of negative self-judgments, blame, and worries, it is infinitely better to create uplifting rays around that heartbroken circle of growth, compassion, understanding, empowered actions, and deep connections, and watch that circle fade away.

More important:

You.
Do.
Not.
Need.
To.
Give.
Up.
Control.

You can claim 100 percent of control over what matters most to your life: your happiness, sense of peace, relationships, identity, and your view of the world.

Despite what happens, you decide what you can do next to create the best result for you, and you CAN hone your skills to improve on that action's impact. Your personal agency is your most precious asset because it has the potential to make, or break, your life. You go from powerless → to having much more power than you thought possible.

It is real and lasting power that makes you feel secure and worthy. And there are bonuses! This power both highlights what is important to you and also reflects what you think you deserve, strongly informing your future decisions. These things become more conscious and aligned, which means safer, controlled, and better results for you.

When you have no sense of agency, you end up defaulting to pseudo-power tactics (bullying, blaming, and controlling yourself and others) to try to stabilize. These tactics will hurt you and your relationships, increasing suffering. You'll end up with negative identity conclusions, like, "I am a loser," and you'll feel terrified as life feels ever more anxiety-provoking.

There will always be things you can control, and things you can't. You have a choice about what you give attention to. **Anxiety** throws what you can't control in your face to keep your focus on that line of thinking. If you want anxiety to lose its power, give your time and energy over to what you can control.

Activating your power will allow you to live happier and create lasting peace in yourself, so you can bring joy, opportunity, and positive change to your families and communities, now and in the future. The world needs you right now. And you need joy, peace, happiness, and opportunities, too! #lifeisshort #dontwasteanotherminutesuffering.

Anxiety makes me feel out of control.

To keep you feeling vulnerable, it wants you to think you might "go off some insanity cliff." I promise the insanity cliff is nonexistent, and I have never heard of anybody, in thousands of clients in my over two decades as a psychotherapist, lose their personal agency. You always have your wits about you. You are still making decisions. In fact, the adrenaline makes you hyper-aware 😫 and in the mode of action-taking.

What's in Your Hand?

If you were in physical danger, you'd take action to survive first. If (or once) you are SAFE, these are the steps to activating your agency when something goes wrong.

1. Have self-compassion.
2. Take a mental step back.
3. Decide what to do.

💬 Have self-compassion.

Compassion is the first step before, during, and after any event, especially when that event is negative or difficult. Self-compassion is not feeling sorry for yourself. Nor is it okaying a negative feeling so it can stay. It is an acknowledgment of the feeling by saying, "I get it," or, *"I understand why I feel sad about that."*

This acknowledgment is the thing that prevents the monkey mind from piling on the spirals of negative self-judgment and worry that immediately compound the original feeling. Compassion eliminates these thoughts:

- 🐵 *Why do I feel that way?*
- 🐵 *What is wrong with me?*
- 🐵 *Am I overreacting?*
- 🐵 *Why am I overreacting?*
- 🐵 *When will this stop?*
- 🐵 *Why did I do that?*
- 🐵 *Why didn't I stop myself?*
- 🐵 *What should I feel?*
- 🐵 *Why don't I feel that?*

You will feel so much better without those questions.

You are upset because you, or something important to you, has been devalued. So, validating you, or it, with your compassion, will heal you.

Can we try it? Is there a current situation that you are processing? Whatever you feel about the situation—sad, frustrated, hurt, annoyed, angry—put your hand over your heart and say, "I totally get why I feel that." Send yourself a little love at the feeling and your experience.

When I do this, I kiss my pointer finger on the inside third knuckle (put your hand in a loose fist and bring it to your mouth with your pointer facing your lips). Then I bring my hand to my heart and place it in a flat palm. I pull my shoulders in a shrug as if I am cuddling that hand. And I smile and imagine my compassion embracing my hurt feelings.

How did that feel?

....

....

....

....

....

....

It is only after you are validated that you can move on to this next step.

🗨🗨 Take a mental step back.

In your mind, imagine you are floating above a replay of the event. From this position, you are outside the chaos, blame, and fear. You have the advantage to see behind the scenes, have insight into each player, and know why they took that action, considering perspectives from all sides. Close your eyes and imagine yourself above your scenario. Knowing you are safe because you are above the fray, you can take your time here and gain a deep understanding. What do you notice that you didn't before?

....

....

....

....

🗨🗨🗨 Decide what to do.

Close your eyes again and go back above the situation. Think of different responses you can make and imagine what might happen next. You can imagine a few responses. When you find a response that is realistic, safe, encourages good results, and has you acting like how you want to be in the world, decide to do that response. Write down your next action steps regarding this situation. #whentheygolowwegohigh #myreligioniskindness

....

....

....

....

....

2.

ACTIVATE TRUST

Do you wonder who to trust and not to trust? These are not easy determinations, and the monkey mind loves slinging evidence from the past at you "to prove" that you are terrible at knowing who might betray you. It says, *You have made mistakes and gotten burned, so you are not good at knowing who you can trust.* You may feel paralyzed and conclude "it is safer" not to trust anyone, which means you and the monkey are in solitary confinement, without connections or love to bail you out. Psst! Being alone with the monkey. Is. Not. Safe.

"Trust issues" are a big thing nowadays. Everybody's got them. It's easy to see why we have trust issues because it means that TRUST is important to you. Why wouldn't it be? Trust is needed to waylay our basic fears. We'd love to *trust* that someone will not reject or abandon us. Unfortunately, trusting someone doesn't guarantee they won't hurt you one day. Even the nicest people in the world make mistakes and inflict pain without intending it. This is it: you cannot control other people. Period. (Thus, "trust issues.")

But what if I told you that this doesn't matter as much as you think it does? The truth is: the essential person to trust is yourself. You have to trust that you can:

👀 Read people.
👟 Keep on your ruby slippers.
💪 Handle it.

Let me explain . . .

👀 Read people.
Anyone who has been through a hard time (a.k.a., everyone in the world) gets good at watching and noticing how other people act in certain situations. Trust in this skill, and it will continue to develop because it is your best protector!

For example, when meeting new people, you can look at their face and catch their vibe. Some people show their negative true colors right away, and you can sidestep them and keep walking. Otherwise, you should be able to tell if they are initially approachable, cheerful, and good-natured. It is worth the first step of small talk with those folks to get to know them better.

Take your time assessing people. You can get to know people, laugh, make memories, get out of your head, learn, and feel inspired without opening yourself fully to someone whom you don't know very well. Experience them in different circumstances and see them interacting with a variety of people to make sure there are no **red flags**. Kindness can only be faked for a short time.

> What are red flags?

Red flags are behaviors that signal that a relationship with a person is potentially dangerous. Here are some common red flags to look for, but this is not an exclusive list:

They keep saying how perfect you are.
They text or call you annoyingly often.
They tell you they would die without you.
They don't respect your boundaries.
They want to get close way too quickly.
They act jealous or angry about you being with other friends.
They roll their eyes or try to act like you're overreacting.
They are mean when arguing (name-calling, blaming).
They use drugs or alcohol.
They are not kind to people (their parents, adults, your friends).
They have rapid, cycling, unexplained mood changes.
They are secretive.
They make lots of excuses.
They make you feel stupid or guilty.
They let you pay for everything.
They need lots of assurances.
They don't apologize.

Watch my Red Flags video on the resource page, jodiaman.com/ditchinganxiety!

Remember: you will attract the people you think you deserve. So, if you deeply respect yourself, you will reject anyone who doesn't treat you well. PLEASE involve your friends and families in your relationships. They know you and love you and can help you assess who you can trust with your time and energy. Hiding the way someone treats you, or hiding the whole relationship, is a sign that something is not right. #toomanyteenskilledbypeopletheymeetonline #friendswillhaveyourback #nottoday

🍂 Keep on your ruby slippers.

(Sorry, not sorry, about another *The Wizard of Oz* reference, because it tracks!) Dorothy is given the Wicked Witch of the East's "ruby slippers" when she first arrives in the strange land of Oz. Through the story, she is on a quest to find the wizard to get back home to Kansas. In the end, the @#$* wizard tells her that she had the power to get herself home all along in the magical ruby slippers!

Imagine you had such ruby slippers imbued with magic! They symbolize your personal agency—the power to act, respond, and create a life that you want.

Would you ever walk into a party and hand another person your magical shoes, and ask them to like you (not any old ruby slippers, but YOUR ruby slippers—the ones that control *your* life, *your* opinion of yourself, how *you* act, what *you* do and think, and *your* total worth)?

No?

I see teens (and adults) do this all the time. Take them back. You're going to want to keep those puppies on.

💪 Handle it.

People are limited. No one is perfect. Humans make mistakes. People have their own insecurities that affect their choices. They change their mind, or more often they don't know their mind, or *they pull back to protect or isolate themselves.* And you get brushed. Even if you take your time reading people, and keep your ruby slippers on, occasionally, you will still get hurt. (Much less often, though!)

Most of us are worried because we feel like we will not be able to handle even a little bit of heartbreak. But you can handle it! You've gotten through difficult situations before, and you will again. When you remember this, life is a lot less scary. Things happen, and you can trust yourself to minimize the consequences because you know you can have compassion for yourself and take a step back, and from that position you can work out what happened, make sense of it, and decide what to do next.

Why do people pull away?

Even though pulling away from others is the worse thing an upset person can do, it is often their first inclination. Alone feels safer. But it is not! Inside the mind, negative thoughts fester and exponentially grow in power.

Sad and alone, they may deeply desire connection but, feeling undeserving of it, they may feel guilty about this desire and continue to pull away. Much of the time when a friend is pulling back, this is what is going on in their heads. It is not you!

What's in Your Hand?

People survive so many things, yet they come away with the negative effects of the hardship instead of the confidence that, given what they had been up against, they had kicked butt at getting through it.

If you gave your survival skills more attention, would the view of yourself change? Instead of "broken," you might see "empowered." Instead of "victim," you'd see "strength against the odds." Instead of a "mess," you'd think of an "amazing problem-solver." This viewpoint will develop trust in yourself. Anxiety will wane. And you will feel more comfortable in the world. You'll be confident that your unique abilities can prevent and protect you from future problems.

In the following space, describe a recent problem and how you solved it or otherwise recovered from it.

....

....

....

....

....

....

....

....

One way to build trust is to connect with your own inner guidance system. You use it all the time, but becoming aware of it helps you have greater access to more trust in your future. This is why I teach teens how to connect with their intuition. Look up "Develop Your Intuition for Teens" at jodiaman.com/ditchinganxiety.

3.

ACTIVATE MOTIVATION

Being a student is a lot. It feels like you're being pulled in a million different directions: schoolwork, social pressure, job, extracurricular schedules, and home responsibilities. So much to do—completing homework, securing supplies for a project, finding something clean to wear that looks good on you, filling out that form, asking your parents for permission to do something, showering, walking the dog, babysitting your little sibling, doing chores, memorizing your lines for a play, visiting your grandparents—and starting each new task is overwhelming. All too often, this steals your energy, and you hesitate. Quickly, you're pulled into your head and out of the present moment. Hesitation signals to your brain that there might be something wrong, 1) releasing adrenaline and 2) setting your mind to look for a problem.

Oh crap! We know what that means. 🐵

It will find your inadequacy, your past failures, your exhaustion, and the difficulty of the job, and it will tell you it's hopeless and provide so many more reasons or excuses to postpone or never start the task. Then, the conserving-calorie resistance kicks in, and there is even less motivation (or rather, *lots of motivation to resist*).

With no belief in yourself, and a mountain of resistance, goals seem unreachable, and your failure is concluded before you've begun. You think, *If I don't want to be disappointed, it is better to just not have any goals, dreams, desires, or hopes.* #ihopethisisanexaggeration #itsprobablynot

But that's not true. You want goals (and dreams, and desire and hopes!). You have things you crave to do in this life—projects you are interested in creating, money you want to make, a world of adventures to have, and communities you are eager to serve.

If you think you are unmotivated, don't get worried that there is something wrong with you. Remember that conserve-calorie brain goal. You are not alone here. I know that other people might seem productive from the outside, but they have to override their brain's resistance, too. The good news is that you can make a habit of motivating yourself to do what you want to do (and to do the things that benefit you even if you don't like the task), making it easier and more natural going forward.

Here are four ways to get and stay motivated.

♔ Decide to do it.

Get clear that you want the results of your actions, and commit to taking the actions to get those results. When you approach something as an option, it is open for debate. It is easy to delay and make excuses. However, when you stay focused on the benefits of the actions, you commit. Then, there is nothing left to do *but do*. Commitment gives your actions a purpose and connects the results to thriving, valuing the task, and minimizing your resistance.

♔ Write it down.

This not only helps you remember; it also makes you a witness to yourself whenever you read what you previously wrote, which increases your follow-through.

♔ Start immediately.

It is easier to do something, especially something tedious or challenging, when you don't allow yourself to think about it. Many people say that the hardest part is starting. I agree! I trick my brain into at least starting by saying, "Do it for at least ten minutes!" Once I begin, continuing it is a cinch, especially because my attention is on the task and off the resistance of it.

♔ Celebrate your wins.

Most teens in our deficit-minded culture finish a task and immediately lament the dozens of things they haven't gotten to yet. This zaps your energy and makes you want to hide under the covers. Resistance shoots through the roof! Instead, celebrate every page of homework, every pile of laundry, and every sports practice as you complete them. This means taking a moment to look at what you've finished and smile, knowing that you have done that. You'll feel happy, empowered, and energized by this celebration and be invigorated for the next task. You will feel more connected with your abilities and really believe in yourself.

(This is the biggest secret to success and happiness.)

Anxiety may say, "It's not worth it!" But that. Is. Not. True.

Goals are worth it. They give you a purpose. Without them, you'll feel untethered and depressed. Even the smallest step propels you forward. Keep in mind: the less you do, the less you want to do. If you haven't felt motivation for a long time, it will be hard to get into the swing of it. You have to push yourself to do small things, such as help a family member with something, clean out a drawer, do one piece of homework, or accompany someone on an errand. They might be hard at first, but eventually they will feed you with energy to try bigger things.

Have goals. Write them down. Commit to them. Start and celebrate them. You matter. You have gifts that are uniquely designed to benefit the world. It's your life's purpose to deliver these. Not only is it good for your mental, emotional, physical, and spiritual health to live out your purpose, but everyone around you, and the community at large, will benefit.

What's in Your Hand?

Successful people have this in common: they write down their goals. You can practice doing it here, but I encourage you to also take this exercise out of this book and into a notebook dedicated just to this purpose. Among young people, *Bullet Journaling* is all the rage because it is an efficient system of organizing tasks.

You can get a to-do list app or use the notes app on your phone. Try this for a few months and see if it doesn't bring more motivation and self-trust.

Benefits of list-making:

1. Work becomes efficient.
2. Priorities and benefits are clear.
3. Progress and accomplishments get tracked.
4. The anxiety of forgetting something is eliminated.
5. The pressure in your head is relieved.
6. The likeliness of completion is increased ninefold.
7. Your confidence is raised.
8. Your adrenaline and attention are channeled into something productive.
9. There is less hesitation and resistance.

Try to list tasks for the day, tasks for the week, and one big goal for the month below. Write down everything you've remembered you must do, and also what you want to do. Keep the book handy with you today, add more as you think of them, and cross off what you accomplish. Reflect on how that feels. Making lists may take a bit of practice to get into, like anything else you are not used to. If you try this for a month or so, you may find that it settles your mind and you start to enjoy it.

To-do today:

....

....

....

....

....

....

To-do this week:

....

....

....

....

....

....

To-do this month:

....

....

....

....

....

....

Sharing your goals with friends helps keep you accountable. Pick a goal that is not too private and fill out the square below. Snap a picture and post it to IG. Tag me @jodiamanlove with the hashtag #ditchinganxiety.

MY GOAL

@jodiamanlove
#ditchinganxiety

4.
ACTIVATE RESPONSIBILITY

In Chris Pratt's acceptance speech for MTV's 2018 Movie & TV Award Generation Award, he shared his "Nine Rules to Life."[1] (You can find his funny speech, which includes some friendly advice, on YouTube.) His rule #5 is: "Doesn't matter what it is: earn it."

Earning means getting something that you've worked for. Not only do you get what you want, but you also feel empowered, in control, and skilled on account of having earned it. And once you've done it, you'll know how to access that power again in the future. Earning is firsthand evidence that there is *cause and effect*. You realize that anxiety was wrong; the world is not random and out of control. You have the power to react and respond to change situations. Embracing your agency is being responsible.

Without understanding the influence you have, "responsibility" can be something that teens dread. It feels like someone in authority is trying to control you. But, hear me out . . . what if you associated responsibility with freedom, opportunity, and getting what you desire? That doesn't sound so bad, does it?

Charlie's (white, "he," cis, undefined) family was seeing me in therapy. His mom was worried about him because he played video games all evening. She wanted him to be active, spend time outside, and hang out with kids his age or with the family. Charlie would game nonstop if she didn't intervene, and when she did, he protested, loudly. The power struggle between Charlie and his mom became so frustrating that she finally hid his gaming console so he couldn't play at all.

During our session, I explained to Charlie the secret of how to earn something (or earn it back) from your parents: *be responsible.*

The system of cause and effect exists between parents and kids. When you do things like stick up for someone, act with kindness, get to school on time, study hard for a math test, walk the dog, or help a sibling, most parents will feel so proud

---

1   Chris Pratt, "Chris Pratt's 9 Rules Acceptance Speech | 2018 MTV Movie & TV Awards," filmed June 16, 2018 in Santa Monica, CA, video, 4:15, https://www.youtube.com/watch?v=EihqXHqxri0.

of you that they want to reward you. They wish to feed you, help you with something, take you somewhere, or give you a privilege, such as staying out later.

Charlie quickly came up with some ways he could show his mom his responsibility in balancing his life. He decided that if he finished his chores and homework, took a bike ride around the neighborhood, and ate dinner with the family, he could then relax with video games. Mom was satisfied.

Before our meeting, Charlie was feeling out of control, trapped in a punishment that he couldn't see his way out of, and his mom was the enemy. He was trying to wield pseudo-power by being angry and passive-aggressive with his mom for taking away his gaming system. Some parents capitulate under this treatment, especially when they don't feel good about themselves, but it was lucky for Charlie that his mom did not.

This reasoning may sound strange and seem like it is against Charlie. However, when we are not taught that responsibility brings us freedom, we risk learning that angry outbursts get us what we want. Then we go forth with that corrupt belief. Pseudo-power is not real. It's confusing because it does seem to work occasionally; however, it damages relationships, it's not sustainable, and it's emotionally fraught with lifelong problems of depression, unworthiness, exclusion, and anxiety.

After our conversation, Charlie was equipped to wield real power, and he no longer felt trapped. He understood that he had 100 percent of the ability to change his situation. While riding his bike was not something he desired, he knew that he could do it and that it would please his mom, therefore giving him a bargaining chip to ask for what he wanted. Good negotiation skills are a must! You'll want to know what the other person wants so you can offer that in exchange for what you want. People are more willing to negotiate with people they can trust, so deliver what you offer first!

When you are irresponsible, you lose freedom by being punished. Although freedom, opportunity, and abundance are not equally distributed in our world, in general, the effort you put forth contributes to achieving your desired outcome.

Besides, the effort feels good to the soul. Pushing yourself builds confidence and skills. For Charlie, the physical exertion will connect him to his body. Being outside will connect him to nature, his neighborhood, and even some peers. He will notice things and learn to read the world a little differently. He will have new experiences, and maybe a few adventures.

I'll just put this right here.

The World Health Organization has added video game addiction to the International Classification of Diseases database, recognizing how detrimental it is for video games to take time away from other life interests, especially during essential brain development for people younger than twenty-five.

So . . . gaming is fun, but have some limits!

P.S. Chris Pratt's Rule #3 is also fly: "Don't be a turd. If you are strong, be a protector; and if you're smart, be a humble influencer. Strength and intelligence can be weapons. Do not wield them against the weak. That makes you a bully. Be bigger than that."

What's in Your Hand?

To feel good about yourself, you need a sense of purpose. Goals give you purpose. When you set goals, you'll practice and hone skills in negotiating real power in your life. Let's try it.

List some things that you desire and then list the ways you can get it, writing out the first step.

Something material that I want is:

....

Ways to get that:

....

The first step is:

....

An achievement goal is:

....

Ways to get that:

....

The first step is:

....

A privilege that I want is:

....

Ways to get that:

....

The first step is:

....

5.

ACTIVATE CONFIDENCE

Social anxiety is legit. It is one of the most common forms of anxiety that people experience. Hidden behind labels such as introvert, sensitive, and shy, it affects how you see yourself. It tries to convince you that you are different and limited, *and so maybe it is better to hide . . .*

Social anxiety is rampant. You know those cultural expectations that dictate that we must measure up to being cool enough, smart enough, eloquent enough, interesting enough, fashionable enough, and having the best body, all while being kind, tough, assertive, spontaneous, organized, loyal (the best friend anyone could ever have), and otherwise PERFECT in every way? ☺ Yeah, those. They make you want to hide in a cave for the rest of your life to protect your vulnerable heart.

You might be afraid of being left out when you don't measure up. But you might not even care to join the group because it takes too much energy anyway. You may not be sure what you want—belong or be alone?

Confidence is the key. If we build your confidence and your belief in yourself, then the social situation will feel easier. You can work on this by doing the following:

1. Hone your skills in noticing.

When you are socially anxious, you think of social situations as moments when everyone is watching you. Reverse this in your mind and begin thinking of it as your opportunity to watch everyone else. It's more tolerable, and you're in control that way! (Besides, you probably have excellent skills in noticing.)

Have you ever sat in a mall or on a park bench just to people watch? You can tell by their mannerisms that they rarely even register that you are there! From this vantage point, you can notice things. Notice their faces. And then, practice the next three points.

2. Understand that people are just as afraid as you, or worse.

Remember the time when you were young and afraid of bugs? Your parents told you, "They are more afraid of you than you are of them."

This same sentiment stands in social situations. You think of yourself as one person afraid of the crowd. But in every crowd, there is a large percentage of other folks fearful of the social situation, too. Social anxiety is that common. Imagine that, at any time, there are collectively more people afraid of you than the one of you who is scared of them. Anxiety may make you feel intimidated by others, where everyone seems confident and secure! (Nope. Anxiety is invisible, and most of them are hiding it!) If you knew that many people feel the same way you do, they wouldn't be as intimidating, right? And you would know you are not so different.

3. Realize that people are in their own heads.
When you look at the faces of other people, you'll see that preoccupied look, as if their monkey is swinging from thought to thought. THEY are worrying about who's looking at them, their future, if there is time for what's next on their to-do list, who is ghosting them, a past mistake, if their parents will find out such-and-such, and more. Not many people are focused on you. They are busy dealing with their own stuff 🙃.

4. Don't expect perfection.
No one is perfect, because perfection doesn't exist. Trying to measure up to unreasonable expectations makes you feel inadequate and out of control. Perfectionism separates you from people, strips you of confidence. It takes unnecessary time and gets you nowhere. It is like a hamster on a wheel. You exhaust yourself, yet you remain in the same place as when you first started. Look around. Nobody else is perfect. So, you can drop those expectations of yourself.

5. Find an anchor.
A great skill to have when you're nervous in social situations is to have an anchor. This is a touchstone for when your nervousness starts to rise. When my forty-year-old friend is in a social situation and she needs a break, she finds the younger kids and hangs out with them for a while. (They are less intimidating than the adults.) I make sure I have a friend on-call to text when I need low-key fortification in social situations. Most places have a bathroom or a space to step outside in the open air for a moment when you need some room to breathe. You can also keep a worry stone in your pocket to hold when you need support. Or, you can use #6 as an anchor.

6. Focus on others.

A helpful way to keep your mind busy and not thinking about your anxiety in the social situation is to focus on doing things for others. There's someone in any context who could use a compliment or some encouragement. If you have a goal to deliver random acts of kindness to three people, then you have a purpose to focus on throughout the event. In addition, those connections will make you feel uplifted and spread some joy around.

7. Have an exit strategy.

"You'll be stuck there, freaking out" is one of the manipulations that anxiety uses to discourage you from going out in public. To avoid having this worry, prepare an **exit strategy** or a plan of how to leave the event if you choose to, so you don't feel trapped. Knowing you have the power to go at any time can get you to the event. Most people feel better once they arrive at a place and realize they don't even need the exit strategy; they are glad anxiety didn't talk them into missing one more thing. However, if you don't feel okay while you're at the event, you can employ the exit strategy!

But what if I use my exit strategy? Then anxiety wins . . . 🕊️ 🏚️

Oh Love, if you believe it is a failure to use your exit strategy, then you don't really have an exit strategy. This pressure will make you feel more trapped, spiking your anxiety and, with it, your desire to leave. You will feel devastated by your weakness and feel worse than before.

Don't think of yourself as using the exit strategy because you have to—you use it because you consciously choose it by weighing the risks and benefits. This helps you feel empowered instead of powerless. Whether you use it or not, YOU WENT, so you get a gold star! ⭐ Now, do #8.

8. Celebrate wins.

Take time to celebrate any steps you've taken outside your comfort zone no matter what the result. If the results are good, add those into the celebration! This will increase your confidence and give you energy for the next step you take outside your comfort zone.

9. Don't forget #8 . . . Seriously!

10. Get some downtime.

Always make sure you take some breaks to relax. It requires a lot of energy to be around groups of people and to steady your nerves. Please recognize that rests are a part of the self-care practice, rather than a sign of weakness. You can embrace and enjoy your rest more when you are proud of what you accomplish!

11. Hone your intuition.

Many people identify as highly sensitive or as an empath. This often comes with the burden of taking on the negativity of others and situations. If you find that you are a sensitive person, it is a great idea to hone your intuition. This will have you deeply trusting yourself, so you are ready to play in the joy life has to offer and to stay fully protected from negativity. For videos on how to get started, visit jodiaman.com/ditchinganxiety.

What's in Your Hand?

Go to a park or someplace where you can sit on a bench in the corner, and observe people. See what you can read from the things you notice.

Do some people look tired? Are some of them dressed nicely, and others sloppily? What might that say about how they view themselves? Is anyone touching their hair or adjusting their clothes like they feel uncomfortable with their bodies? What might they be thinking?

When you see the people who look impeccable, how do you think about them? How do people interact with the people they are walking next to (whether strangers or people they are with)? Can you guess how they are related?

How many people look approachable? How many look happy? How many look sad?

Write down some observations:

....

....

....

....

....

....

....

....

....

....

What would be a supportive anchor for you when you do something challenging (See #5)?

....

....

....

Think of an upcoming event that makes you nervous:

....

....

What are some ideas of "random acts of kindness" that you can have in your pocket for that event? (For example, compliment three people, help someone who's lost something, get someone food, accompany someone to the parking lot so they don't have to walk alone.)

....

....

....

....

....

....

....

6.
ACTIVATE COURAGE

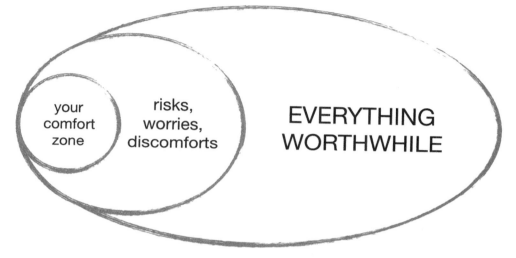

"We have to stop preparing the path for our kids and start preparing kids for the uncertain path. Teach them to sit in uncertainty and discomfort. Comfort is so overrated. It's okay to be uncomfortable; that's what it feels like to be brave."
—Brene Brown
(Watch Brene's TEDx talk on jodiaman.com/ditchinganxiety)

We are bombarded daily with consumeristic messages touting that we deserve to be comfortable at every moment in every part of our body, just because we exist. "Don't live with discomfort; buy this thing and feel better!" ads say.

When you hear this proclaimed four thousand times a day, it stops being just an idea and graduates to a *belief*. It makes us think we are entitled to comfort, much like we feel entitled to happiness. But comfort and happiness are vastly different things. Discomfort and risk-taking often lead to fantastic results that bring joy and happiness into our lives. And comfort? Comfort sometimes feels wonderful, especially at the end of an adventure, or a long day of hard work, but consistent comfort is a recipe for boredom, unworthiness, loneliness, emptiness, and anxiety.

I've noticed a trend in teens who feel increasingly weary when they do things they don't want to do, or that make them uncomfortable. They unconsciously feel controlled by HAVING to do these things. The undesired, uncomfortable activity is an attack on their happiness and freedom, bringing on anxiety. Then, they mistakenly think that if they avoid what makes them uncomfortable, they'll control their anxiety. But it is the opposite: being stuck inside your comfort zone is GIVING the anxiety power.

Here it is: discomfort and undesirable tasks are daily occurrences. When you feel attacked by them, life is pretty frustrating. However, the more practice you have at handling them, the less fear, the less discomfort, the less resistance, and the less displeasure you'll feel—resulting in an easier life.

My son, Leo (white, "he," cis, straight), rowed crew in high school. In addition to intense daily practices, the team participated in weekly regattas. On those race days, the team spent thirteen hours carrying shells, rigging and unrigging, and rowing long distances in sweltering heat or freezing cold. Basically, they were uncomfortable 100 percent of the time. To get through it, he'd focus on the present moment—the oar in his hands—using a mantra, "One more stroke."

After twelve grueling seasons, he built endurance through this discomfort and confidence that he could get through just about anything. In his freshman fall semester of college, when he felt overwhelmed by a new life and culture away from home, he repeated, "one more stroke" to himself. He KNEW he could withstand the discomfort, and that gave him the hope he needed to get through the tough part until he got used to life on campus.

Discomfort challenges us and charges up our minds and bodies to do something. When we withstand it, our confidence grows to be more robust. The human brain is designed to solve problems, not to be idle. You don't want devastating problems (some of you have already had them), but you do need discomfort, challenges, and adventures daily to stimulate the brain and connect with your survival and life skills. They make you brave and more equipped when new challenges come. When you are consistently comfortable and unchallenged, your mind must make up its own problems. And, since they are made up, you can't solve them, and you can get stuck in the helplessness and anxiety that brings. #idlemindisthedevilsworkshop #youcantphoneitin

What's in Your Hand?

Complete this graph. A) List the things that are inside your comfort zone. B) List the risks, worries, and discomforts that keep you wanting to stay there. C) List the joys and adventures you can have if you pushed through B. Try to list as many things as you can. Now circle a couple of items in C that you're willing to do in the next month.

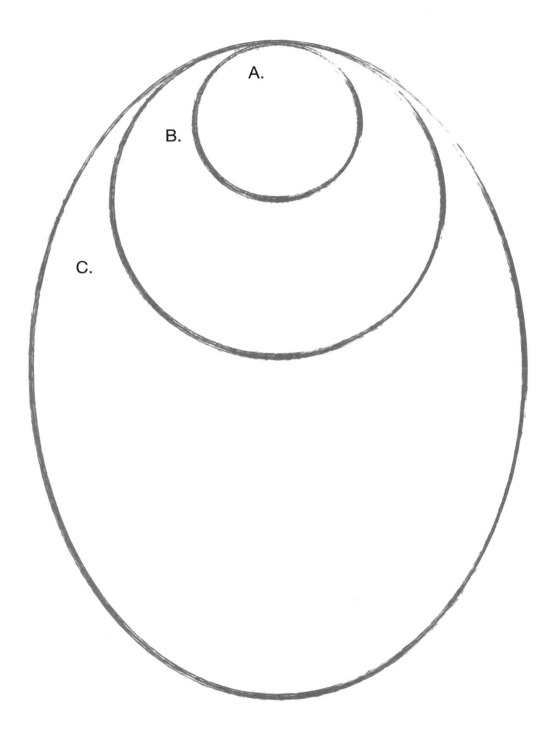

7.

ACTIVATE YOUR UNIQUE SKILLS

"Whether you think you can, or think you can't—you're right."
—Henry Ford

Parents bring their teens to see me in counseling and say, "Please teach them 'coping skills' so they can feel better."

In my experience, teens already have coping skills. In fact, you have mad coping skills! How could you have survived this long in life without them? The problem is that you don't see your awesome skills.

And, really, if I tried to teach you coping skills, you'd check right out. First of all, giving advice ends a conversation, and I want to really hear what you have to say. Second, you would feel invisible since all the effort you have been putting in up to this point would go completely unnoticed. Third, you would just see me as an old authority figure and not someone who understands what you are going through or is aligned with your dream of feeling better. None of these would be okay.

I'd rather listen to how you've been managing what you are dealing with and get glimpses into your personal agency. It is my job to point out the skills that you already have, so you have more access to them when you need them. When problems are big, you don't see all the Herculean things you are doing despite how bad you feel. #youwentthedistance 👟

After a while, you'll start to notice your abilities, skills, know-how, and unique qualities that you can use to affect situations in favor of yourself, as well as what and who is important to you. You look down and realize you've had your ruby slippers on all along.

Hopefully, by now you are starting to believe in yourself as a skilled person. Once you are in touch with your personal agency, life is less scary. With a "can-do" attitude, meeting any goals will be invigorating and reinforcing of your abilities rather than a prison of obligation. You are someone with skills who trusts themselves. You are in control.

From here, you can do anything. You can grow, evolve, expand, have deeper friendships, have greater adventures, take bigger opportunities, earn abundantly, and experience MORE LOVE.

Plus, a person who heals themselves heals everyone around them. #withgreat powercomesgreatresponsibility

What's in Your Hand?

Photocopy and cut out each positive action on the next page. Put them in a jar. Each morning, challenge yourself to pick one out and do it.

Today, I will help someone.

Today, I will try something new.

Today, I will make or create something.

Today, I will set a new goal.

Today, I choose to have a great day.

Today, I will tell someone how much they mean to me.

Today, I will list three things I love about myself.

Today, I will smile at three strangers.

Today, I will find out an answer to a question I have.

Today, I will spend time in nature.

Today, I will be patient with _____.

Today, I will say "thank you" and "I love you."

Today, I will list three things I love about my family.

Today, I will focus on what is working instead of what's not.

Today, I will cheer on a friend.

Today, I will look for opportunities to help someone.

Today, I will write a letter to a friend.

Today, I will offer to help with dinner or clean-up.

Today, I will give my full attention to someone talking.

Today, I will take on a new challenge.

CHAPTER 4:
My Time to Shine

When you don't like yourself, your mistakes, problems, and deficits become your identity. They blind you or at least cloud the view of your abilities, unique gifts, survival skills, and values. Existing in this uncertain world is terrifying when you think you don't have these gifts. It makes you vulnerable to believing the monkey's manipulation and lies: *You can't do anything right! You make mistakes! You can't make decisions! You can't handle it!*

The road to getting rid of fear and anxiety is paved with self-acceptance. That might be easy if there weren't so many barriers in your way! In Chapter 4, we will reveal, disempower, and release obstacles from your life and help you embrace what brings you self-confidence and self-love. You need this more than ever right now.

Trigger warning: in Chapter 4, "6. Embrace Hope," we will talk about strategies to prevent self-harm and suicide. My intentions here are to help you heal, but if you think it will be counterproductive because the very topic triggers you, kindly listen to that inner wisdom and skip that section. But if you do so, please find an adult whom you trust and tell them what you're going through right away.

1.

EMBRACE MAKING MEANING

Humans are meaning-makers. After each experience we have, we go through a mental process, deciding what it means to us. This meaning is highly influenced by our previous experiences and preconceived understandings about ourselves and the world, so it represents our perception rather than the truth. For example, let's say you text a friend and they don't text back . . .

. . . there are many different ways to interpret this. Based on your history with friendships, which would you guess?

They don't like you anymore — They are angry — They lost their phone — They did write a message, but forgot to hit send — They are on vacation — They changed their number — Someone told them bad gossip about you — They are in a coma.

Until we know for sure, the mind keeps questioning and guessing. This feels chaotic and very stressful, and we don't like that. We desire an exact and complex, yet clear, definitive, and objective meaning to any situation tied up neatly in a bow so that we can restore order and feel in control of the world. 📔

We want to know exactly what it is . . .

what to do with it . . .

. . . and what to expect, ASAP!

#justwritebackandtellmewhatiswrongsoicansleep #orderorderinthecourt

Imagine a forest. It's messy. The trees don't grow in lines, the trunks are different diameters and heights, and branches shoot off in every which way. Logs, leaves, and seed pods litter the ground without rhyme or reason. Total chaos. Nature is chaotic.

If we bring a person into the woods and tell them to stay in one place under a specific tree for several hours, something interesting will happen. Upon returning to get them, we will see that they have begun to organize their small patch of wilderness. Rather than sit still among the disorder, they might have designed a game of batting an acorn with a stick. They might balance rocks in a cairn, or make a little moss cushion to sit on. You can try this with many people, and there's no question that they'll all do *something*. Human minds crave order over disorder.

Horrible experiences like abuse, betrayal, rejection, and loss are nonsensical. In these highly chaotic times, humans are desperate for order to stabilize themselves. It is common to have the sense that you will lose all control (lose your very self) if you don't make sense of what happened immediately. In this urgency, people usually pick the meaning that comes to mind first. Unfortunately, this is blame.

This means that many people, desperate to understand what happened, will conclude that it is their fault, especially if they are young and alone, or if the trauma is particularly out of the ordinary. "I must have done something to cause this; no one else would do this." Or, "I allowed it to happen to me." Even though this conclusion doesn't answer all the questions, it is the only thing that seems to make some sense in the chaotic moment. In a clear moment, this doesn't make sense at all, but because the choice to blame oneself happens below awareness, it usually comes off as a fact, instead of a guess. As you can imagine, believing that it was your fault compounds and sustains the self-deprecating consequences of trauma and is why most people undeservedly and overwhelmingly feel guilt, shame, and blame after a traumatic event. It actually causes more chaos.

To compound the suffering further, there is an additional layer of negative self-judgment: If one believes they had done something wrong, but don't know what it was, they will further blame themselves for "not knowing what." This incites a fear that they will not be able to prevent it from happening again in the future. Also, because they "allowed" it, they sometimes feel like they deserve to feel bad, and so they don't try to feel better. Or, they decide they need to work hard to deserve to feel better, and so they might:

- try to please everyone,
- try to figure out the problem,
- overwork to prove their worth,
- accept blame from others,
- over-apologize, or
- attempt to protect themselves by isolating.

Like running on a hamster wheel, these take huge effort with no results, conjuring even more blame because they "can't get better." #agneswantsherwheelback #thesedonthelpyouanyway ℮

People blame themselves even through mild chaos. That combined with our sense of inadequacy from unrealistic standards is why guilt and shame are so overwhelmingly present in modern culture. These ultra-damaging emotions are the hallmark of self-contempt. I've seen them cause self-hatred, self-abuse, intrusive thoughts, intense panic, devastating depression, overworking, addiction, isolation, and more.

On the other hand, you might also blame others. This may lead to more questioning: "How could they do something like this?" "Why would someone . . . ?" "I don't understand."

Much of the time, actually, I have noticed that too many people go back and forth, blaming both.

← *I made a mistake.*
→ *That was horrible.*
← *Did I do it?*
→ *It was their fault.*
← *I allowed it.*
→ *Why did they do it?*
← *It was me.*
→ *It was them.*
← *Was it me?*

This creates a war inside of us where we are pitted for and against ourselves—both blaming ourselves and defending ourselves. It's exhausting, distracting, and anxiety-provoking, and people can get stuck here for years.

And as you may have surmised, in spite of the effort of trying to gain order, these all create more chaos. And then you have to lift your beaten-up psyche off the ground and diligently try to figure it all out again. The 🐵 can be such a 🐴.

Many people don't know blame is something that affects you on top of the effects of the painful event (again, think of the circles from page 6); instead, they believe ALL of these overwhelming emotions come from the original incident. But now that you know blame is an additional and multiplying factor, hopefully it will be easier to let go.

What's in Your Hand?

To release blame, you may need to make meaning of what happened. Fortunately, you are not in a rush this time, so you can take the time to decide the meaning of the situation in a way that will help you heal. Let's do it together.

Think of a stressful event.

Read this list of why things happen:

🐟 Accidents happen when you are at the wrong place at the wrong time. Or because someone was neglectful or made an unintentional mistake.

🐟 Natural disasters happen.

🐟 People are limited. Some make bad choices, some are selfish, and some are mean, and we know why. Bad decisions, selfish actions, mean-spiritedness, and violence happen for the following reasons: when people don't know better; when they are taught that it is okay to be violent; when they are distracted, psychotic, or under the influence of substances; if they want something; or if they feel miserable, powerless, or worthless.

🐟 Because *people are limited*, institutions, government, and communities can be corrupt and can treat people unequally.

🐟 Also, humans contradict themselves. They can love someone and then break up with them. They can be kind sometimes and selfish other times. They can act confidently but be very insecure. They can seem like really cool people and yet be silent amid injustice.

Stop asking why someone did something. People make bad choices all the time. The monkey will try to tell you it isn't that simple. This is an excuse for it to continue to wreak havoc. It IS that simple.

Circle the reasons above that resonate with a situation that happened to you.

Here is how to understand your stressful event:

It happened.
It wasn't okay.
You did not deserve it.
It doesn't have to define you.

Fill in the blanks.

_____ happened.

_____ wasn't okay.

I did not deserve _____.

It doesn't have to define me.

"It happened" validates you and your memory. You need this because, let's face it, your mind might still be questioning if it happened the way you remember it. The truth is, the intensity of a situation usually improves memory. You have remembered it correctly. Firmly decide that it happened. Period. And stop questioning it.

"It was not okay" validates that you are not overreacting and also that you are worthy of being respected and treated well. It is definitive. The decision is now made, and there is no more speculation. It was not okay that it happened.

"I did not deserve it" tells the truth—because you didn't. It was not your fault. I know your mind questions this from every angle, so let's settle it. You. Didn't. Deserve. To. Be. Treated. Poorly.

But? No, you didn't.

But? No. You didn't.

But? No. No. No. Say "I didn't do anything to deserve it" over and over until you take it into your heart, please. (Watch the *Good Will Hunting* "It's Not Your Fault Scene" on my book resource page: jodiaman.com/ditchinganxiety. #justwatchthewholemovieitssogood)

Lastly: "It doesn't have to define me." Most of the time, we take on the identity of the experience, using labels like "broken," "loser," and "worthless" that create a whole host of additional meanings as you step into those negative perceptions of yourself. These self-imposed labels can hurt you for years after the bully is gone or the event has passed. Remember: you are so much more, and you are not what happened to you.

Don't try to do this alone. Get some help! Some issues are so big—even huge—that you need help understanding them. This doesn't mean that you are weak. The bravest, smartest, luckiest, most insightful, and confident people get help.

Who do you trust who can help you with this?

....

....

....

When will you tell them?

....

....

....

Once you decide on this clear new meaning—*it happened, it wasn't okay, I did not deserve it, it doesn't have to define me*—you can put this whole figuring-it-out business to bed. Night, night.

Now, you can step out, without that anvil of blame around your ankle, knowing you deserve to let go of the energy, identities, fears, and emotional turmoil around this event. Onward!

2.

EMBRACE LETTING GO

Do you want to move on from the pain of your past? Do you wish it would stay where it belongs, *in the past,* so you can create a present and a future without the pain and fear that it caused?

Yes, please!

I know because I have been there, trying to let go of my past, too.

After one particularly painful situation, I was beside myself. I'd ruminate, sifting through the timeline of the scenario, fantasizing about confronting the person who had hurt me, and searching for the answer to the age-old question: *Why did they do that?* I longed for validation and understanding but thought I needed it from the person who hurt me. I vented about it, wrote about it . . . obsessed about it. Part of me felt that if I let it go, it would mean it didn't matter that she had hurt me.

When I spoke to my friends, they would say, "Don't take it personally." And while they meant well, to me it was a double-whammy: *I was betrayed, AND I'm not handling it right!*

A few times, I gathered my courage and proclaimed, "I'm going to let go of this!"

I was so proud. *Great! I'm free and ready to take on the world!* ✸

But, mere minutes later, the darn monkey lobbed the pain story back into my consciousness, and blame started to spiral . . .

I can't believe it happened . . . if she would only listen . . . am I overreacting? . . . What is she thinking? . . . How did I let that happen? . . . I should have known better . . . Arghh! I'm thinking about it again. Stop thinking about it!

I tried to return to the task at hand. But before I could focus entirely on what I was supposed to be doing, the rascal had another go at me: "But, THIS!" he said.

I was so frustrated with myself.

I'm so stupid! I have no idea how to let this go. What's THE PROBLEM? Why am I doing this to myself?

This went on for months, until one day, I hiked a trail to a waterfall, hoping to clear my mind. However, instead of enjoying the beauty all around me, I found myself ruminating over this old situation. Even though I had set the intention to let go a million times, I was consumed with it again! I was so PO-ed with myself.

It's been months, Jodi! What is wrong with you?

Once I arrived at the waterfall, I sat on the riverbank to meditate. I looked up and saw countless small, yellow leaves falling down from the trees high above on the cliff. Because of the upward air pressure near the waterfall, the leaves were floating as if suspended in mid-air. Curious, I stared at them for a few moments.

I thought, *Those leaves are coming down as fast as they possibly can.*

And it hit me.

Humans = the leaves. When your feelings are hurt, it takes as long as it takes to heal. Sometimes the process is slow. Other times, it is very slow. ☺ I decided to stop beating myself up for feeling pain, and instead made an intention to accept and love myself through my gentle recovery.

I also realized that there is so much more to letting go than just deciding to do it. (The declaration "I'm going to let this go!" is just the easiest part!) That day under the waterfall, I formulated a three-step process to help myself—and others— to let go of the past.

Here is the nitty-gritty I came up with that day: clear, doable, practical steps:

Step 1: Decide that you deserve to let it go.
Step 2: Set the intention.
Step 3: Practice.

If you are like me, you've tried the second step and only the second step. And then, you berate yourself for being inadequate, unskilled, or too dumb to get the job done. What's worse is that because holding on to things is invisible, you assume everyone else IS free and clear of their past EXCEPT for you.

Nope. Because we are not taught these steps in middle school (wouldn't that have been useful!), nobody knows them. Luckily, we have done a lot of the prep work in this book, so you won't be starting from scratch. It is time to feel better.

Step 1: Decide that you deserve to let it go.

You did this process in the "What's in Your Hand?" exercise of the previous section.

Step 2: Set the intention.

This is the easy one. Just decide to let go, and say it out loud. Have some fun by doing a ceremony around your intention. This serves to deepen the meaning of the commitment, which helps you sustain it. It can be simple, like blowing the energy of it into a rock and throwing it into a lake, writing it on paper and burying it in the ground, or making an offering like putting a vase of flowers in your room. It is not only a physical act to symbolize your mental commitment but also a talisman for the intentional energy to amplify.

Step 3: Practice.

Don't take this step for granted, because it is THE step. Even if you have done what you needed to do to process and integrate the past, the rumination often continues. When your mind was hooked on something, it created a habit. Even when you don't believe it anymore, the former thoughts can continue to barrage you with their negativity. (See the "What's in Your Hand?" from Chapter 2, "Lie #2: 'You need to look at me.'")

We mistakenly assume this means that we didn't fix the problem and 1) continue blaming and questioning, and 2) try to figure it out again. As you can imagine, this will keep it attached to you.

After working through Step 1 and Step 2, now you can begin the process to unhook it. It takes practice and patience. (This is what the floating yellow leaves taught me.) When you get frustrated with the lack of progress, you'll feel powerless, and it will hook you harder. Conversely, the kinder you are to yourself, the faster it will release its hold.

So, this is what you do: expect the rumination to come back. Be waiting and ready for it, so you have the power. Then, when it comes, gently and lovingly (with no judgment) remind yourself that you have already decided to let it go. Here is the script:

"Hi, hurt feelings! I knew that you'd come back. I already decided to let go, so I'm all set. Just sit down here [pat the seat next to you]*; I am busy right now."*

Then, get your mind and body engaged in some other task at hand.

You are acknowledging without judgment (showing yourself compassion), reminding yourself of your commitment, and then taking your attention off the negative emotion and putting it onto what you'd prefer to have your attention on.

You may have to do this a hundred times a day at first. The less bothered you are by that frequency, the quicker the feeling will dissipate. (As you can imagine, being bothered feeds the rumination.) Gradually, it will come less often, with less intensity, and for a shorter duration until it is gone.

Compassion is an integral component of each step to letting go. When the mind brings up feelings about the past that you want to let go of, you will be ready for it. Whatever you feel, whether it is sadness, frustration, or hurt, say, "I get it." "I understand why I feel that way." This kindness is essential.

When I am practicing letting go, I find it helpful to make a physical gesture to signify this compassion. As I shared in Chapter 3, "1. Activate Your Power," I kiss my hand and touch my heart, expressing to my mind, body, and soul that I understand why that would have hurt me. I don't try to avoid it, move it out of my mind, or fight it. I lovingly acknowledge it. And then, just as immediately, I stop giving it attention by focusing on some present activity.

Without feeding the rumination, it has less and less energy and soon fades away.

This is easy, doable, and relatively risk-free. It is neither fake positivity nor spiraling negativity. It has helped me heal hurt feelings from many painful situations, saving my mind tons of unnecessary suffering. I have taught it to my friends, family, and clients, and I have seen it save them, too. I know it can save you.

What's in Your Hand?

A ceremony might seem like a novel idea to you, but humans around the world have always used ceremony to give meaning and witness, and thus sustenance, to their commitments toward a new way of being: think weddings, graduations, receiving awards. Have fun, but add reverence, so it feels important to you. Dress up and clean up the place you are holding your ceremony. The energy you put toward planning is part of the meaning-making, and it will help your heart get behind this commitment.

Use this planning template to create a Letting Go Ceremony that fits your personality. (I provided some examples to get your juices flowing, but as long as it is safe, you can be creative in your answers.)

What are your hopes and intentions for this ceremony?

....

....

....

....

....

....

....

When will you have it?

....

....

Where? (e.g., in your room, at a special tree, in a park)

....

....

What will represent the feelings or event that you want to let go? (e.g., piece of paper with words written on it, rock, photograph, memento)

....

....

What will you do with it to symbolize the release? (e.g., throw it in a lake, bury it, rip it up into little pieces, step over it)

....

....

Who are you asking for support? (e.g., friends, family, your inner wisdom, or a higher power)

....

....

How will you symbolically or physically invite their presence?

....

....

How will you integrate (start to get a sense of) the new, lighter you? (e.g., listen to a poignant song expressing your conviction to be free, dance, bathe, run, meditate, laugh with friends, eat)

....

....

How will you express gratitude for your new freedom? (e.g., water a tree, make a small donation, clean up some litter, plant a seed, wear a meaningful necklace or color)

....

....

Now do it! After you hold the ceremony, write a reflection about how it was and what you are thinking and feeling here.

....

....

....

....

....

....

....

3.

EMBRACE REALISTIC EXPECTATIONS

In modern Western society, we have the sovereign personal agency to be any way we want to be.

Yay! ☺

Except, also, boo! ☹

This freedom is tempered by the fact that we also really, really, really, really want to be included. The modern message is: *You are free to express yourself however you like, BUT it must be exactly like it "should" be, or else people might not like you.*

To avoid exclusion, we constantly, and harshly, judge how we measure up to the societal expectations as we perceive them to be: *Am I pretty, thin, straight, cool, popular, smart, rich, perfect, fun,* (fill in the blank) *enough?*

Unfortunately, because "enough" is not clear, the expectations are impossible to reach, and failure is inevitable. Negative self-judgment feeds and attaches us to our problems. Remember these SOBs? (Spirals of 🐂 💩.)

Even being "healthy" is an unreasonable standard that we try to measure ourselves against. Because it is undefinable, it's impossible to know if you reach it, so you can't *not* fail. Unfortunately, the shame felt over being "unhealthy" is for realsies. This makes some people overwork toward a perfect standard, or it makes them shrink away from putting any effort into it because "they will probably fail anyway."

Does this sound familiar? *I'd rather not try, because if I try my hardest and fail, there will be no hope and I won't be able to bear the disappointment.* 💔 Let me get this straight: to *protect* yourself, you avoid putting effort into feeling better and allow yourself to *stay in suffering.* On purpose. (If you knew this is what you were doing, would you keep doing it?)

Failure is devastating because it appears to be conclusive, definite, and inflexible. *You are not enough. Period. End of story.* But it is relative to your interpretation of the standard you measure success against: What is the pinnacle of thin? How do you know you reached "thin" enough?

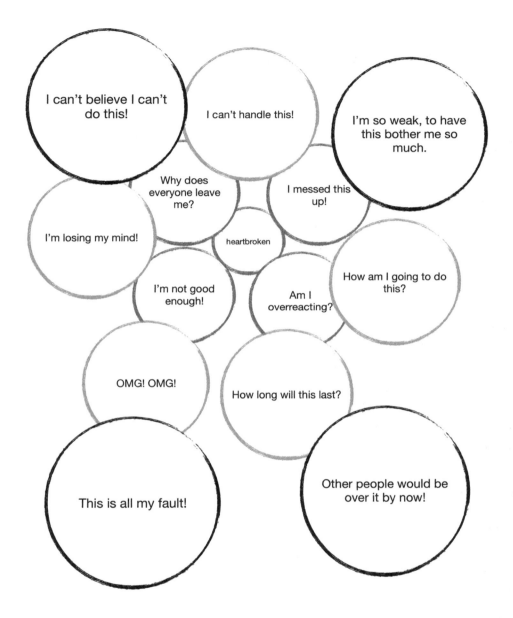

Unreasonable, undefinable standards and expectations suck up precious time and energy and starve us of self-appreciation, self-acceptance, and self-love. To let go of negative self-judgment, you have to make the expectation R-E-A-L-I-S-T-I-C. Let's try it.

What's in Your Hand?

Time to call out your unreasonable, unrealistic standards and expectations! Once they are exposed, you can consciously decide to take them down a notch. Invisible, they reign. Visible, you reign. 💪 Here are some examples:

I have to lose twenty pounds in three weeks.
I'm supposed to eat under 1300 calories a day.
I need to get straight As.
I need to act cool at all times.
I need to hide my femininity.
I need to know what the teacher means.
I need to have perfect makeup on every day.
I can't make waves.
I need to ace this test.
People can't know _____ about me.
I have to be the perfect girlfriend/boyfriend/friend.
I have to be strong.
I have to not care what people think.
I can't go out if I have pimples.
My clothes need to be from_____.
I have to text back immediately.
I need to do it alone.
I am supposed to know what I want to do with my life.
I need to understand_____.
I need to act like it doesn't bother me.
I need to pass my driver's test the first time.
I need to book that audition.
They cannot see me cry.
I need to let this go.
I shouldn't be angry.
I should be positive.

Do you see the "supposed-tos," the "need-tos," the "can'ts," and the "have-tos"? They imply that it's either that or failure. There is no in-between. Plus, these expectations are undefinable, so you have to overshoot even to consider yourself half-way there. There is no space to be human. And no chance of fully accepting yourself.

Your turn. List four expectations you have of yourself. (Once you get started you may notice more and more. Use additional paper to write all of them down! To gain the full power of your choice to accept yourself as you are, you'll want to become aware of them ALL.)

1. ....

2. ....

3. ....

4. ....

Next, take a look at each one. How can you redefine them so you can be successful and still grow and evolve? Here are three examples.

Expectation: *"I need to understand . . . "*
Redefined: *I am interested in understanding, and I can take some action to research, or ask questions, but I can also be patient because some things take a while to be understood.*

Expectation: *"I need to be fun to be around."*
Redefined: *I love having fun and being an inspiration for my friends to have fun. Some days this works out better than others, and that is life. I can enjoy the good days. If I love myself through the lesser days, I will have more good days.*

Expectation: *"I need to pass my driver's test the first time."*
Redefined: *Loads of people have to take the test more than once, but everyone eventually passes, and once I get my driver's license, it won't matter.*

Expectation 1: " .... "
Redefined:

....

....

....

....

Expectation 2: " .... "
Redefined:

....

....

....

....

Expectation 3: " .... "
Redefined:

....

....

....

....

4.

EMBRACE CONNECTION

Over the time we worked together, Melanie (black, "she," cis, bi) had some periods where her anxiety was so bad she stopped attending school, slept all day, and stayed up all night. After a few days/weeks of this extreme isolation, her lack of motivation to feel better worsened. Her lack of interest in anything—change, relief, happiness, joy—went beyond the usual hopelessness and "protecting herself from disappointment." Melanie's negative thoughts had nowhere to go and no one to counter them (between her sessions with me), so they just grew to epidemic proportions inside her head.

Not to be contrite, but isolation is also boring. It numbs your mind—stops the **dopamine** releasing—and you stop remembering what it was like to feel joy. Melanie was almost completely shut down emotionally, and she stopped caring whether she'd ever feel good again.

What the heck is dopamine?

The neurotransmitter dopamine releases in the nervous system (brain) when you experience something pleasurable. The dopamine feels so amazing that it makes you want more of it, so you repeat the activity.

This wasn't the first or last time I've seen the extreme negative consequences of isolation. It is one of the things I worry affects our mental health the most in modern society. Especially with Gen Z. 💔

Capitalism values the individual over community, and it has contributed to smaller and smaller living communities, sometimes consisting of just one or two people in a household. And it is affecting us. A study out of the University of

Oxford[1] reported that, generally, kids who had a high level of grandparent involvement had fewer emotional and behavioral problems. In homes where there are more bodies, there's more communication, storytelling, emotional support, tradition, helping, touching, sharing, and problem-solving.

But even if there are people available, some teens isolate themselves anyway. It is developmentally appropriate for teens to spend more time in their rooms, and to hug and cuddle their parents with less and less frequency. In this digital age, where teens can be entertained by a device in their hand, some of them are hardly physically around anyone. You might feel like you are connected to friends because you are keeping up a text messaging streak, but it is not the same. You are not touching them, reading their body language, sharing food, or having stimulating conversations face to face.

Most people have countless negative thoughts swirling up in their heads. When you experience that negativity in isolation, you think you are the only crazy person who feels like that. Without anyone else to tell you that they feel those things, too, and that they are not true, the thoughts will stay there, bullying you. The shame about them grows, and you feel so horrible you can end up hating yourself. You may crave belonging, but hate that you are "needy," and so you suppress it! It feels like everyone's inside a warm house having a party, and you are out in the cold rain looking through the windows, not allowed in because you are such a loser.

I wish this made you get out and be with people! But all too often, it makes people isolate themselves more, because they think, *Who would want to be with a loser?* At the extreme (and it is too easy to cross into extremes), your brain may lose interest in anything fun, in any people, and even in getting better. I see this too often. And I am heartbroken thinking about the thousands of kids that I don't know who are going through this as well. The statistics for suicide and self-harm are going up and up.

Unfortunately, when someone feels anxiety or depression, isolation is one of the first tendencies. They might be embarrassed to reach out, or they were betrayed once when they shared their feelings in the past, or they don't want to

---

1   Ann Buchanan, ed., and Anna Rotkirch, ed., *The Role of Grandparents in the 21st Century: Global Perspectives on Changing Roles and Consequences* (New York: Routledge, 2018).

bother anyone, or they don't feel worthy of help. Or, they may simply not care. But that self-isolation can cause many, many more days of increasingly more intense anxiety and depression. Over time, you may have pulled back so much, feel so unworthy about what you have become, and feel like there is no one out there who cares about you. (Isolation will tell you no one cares even when there are people who care.)

This section is important, but it has been depressing! I hope you now agree that isolation is one of your worst enemies. When you are in its lair, it can be a fight for your life to get out. I want you to get all the help you can to feel better, and the first thing we have to do is get you out and about.

What if you are with someone who is mean to you?

Sometimes when teens feel bad, they surround themselves with people they think they deserve: people who don't treat them well. Bullies make sure you are isolated because it makes you an easier target. And isolation is the right environment for you to continue the bully's torment even when they are no longer present.

If you are in this situation, the first step you can take is talking to someone you trust about it!

What's in Your Hand?

If you can relate to anything in this section, imagine me sending a hug through the pages right now. I see you. You do not have to stay like this. Please, tell an adult you can trust, immediately.

If you feel like you don't have many friends at school, the first thing to do is observe. Take two weeks, and decide to use the time to watch people. Keep track of the kids who you notice are consistently kind and undramatic. People like that are present everywhere. Once you identify them, start to smile when you catch their eye and look for opportunities for small talk. Look at the clubs and extracurricular activities that these kinds of kids are drawn to, and if the group interests you, join, too.

Then pick one of these ten activities below and try it today.

1. Go to a coffee shop, order something, and compliment the cashier (e.g., "Nice earrings!" "This frappuccino is delicious!").
2. Find an opportunity to be around younger children (children are easier to be around because they bridge a gap between self-isolation and you being around peers or adults who feel intimidating when you're vulnerable).
3. Find someone to video chat.
4. Invite someone to meet you somewhere.
5. Offer to help someone with a task.
6. Go to a library or store and set a goal to exchange small talk with at least three people.
7. Walk down a busy street.
8. Watch TV with someone in your family.
9. Listen to familiar music.
10. Hang out with your pet.

Reflect on this experience:

....

....

....

....

....

....

....

....

....

....

....

....

....

....

....

....

I love being alone.

Isolation that comes from self-shame worries me, and it is not the same as "me time." Some people relish time after a social situation to relax on their own. They intend to calm and center themselves. Taking a walk, dancing in your room to some good music, or taking some quiet time to read a good book can feed the soul.

It is when someone is stuck in their head in a negative spiral that I DO NOT RECOMMEND being alone.

You mention touching a few times . . .

Teens have increasingly fewer opportunities for touching unless they are dating someone. Humans are the only primates who don't do social grooming (where apes, monkeys, and chimps sit and pick bugs off of each other). Being socially groomed has many benefits besides decreasing bug infestations (ick!). The touching calms the nervous system. It is how primates regulate their adrenaline and ease the stress that has built up that day. With this pandemic of anxiety, humans need touching badly! Have you ever cuddled with someone for a while? It can be so healing emotionally, mentally, and physically! Contact sports, tickling, and ice-breaker games—since there are lots of touching—can be stress-reducing (and fun!).

Don't confuse this with "bad touching." Inappropriate sexual touching is abusive. It has the opposite effect. If this is happening to you, or if you are unsure, tell an adult whom you trust.

5.

EMBRACE A POSITIVE MENTAL ATTITUDE

Anxiety has us so focused on *what is wrong*, so much so that examples of our mistakes, deficits, and inadequacies are like beacons for our attention. Noticing and lamenting what we don't have, didn't win, haven't gotten done, and aren't is ingrained in us from a young age. Complaints fall easily from our tongue, and we sometimes forget to see what we *do have*.

It can be beneficial to vent about disappointments and negative experiences with a loyal friend or trusted adult. Your thoughts, memories, and emotions come up and out of your ruminating mind. You feel validated, and so process and resolve your feelings. However, if you continue to complain *without effort toward resolution,* there are unfortunate effects on your brain.

⚠ It can engage spiraling negativity, where even small disappointments grow into desperation and hopelessness.

⚠ It creates neuron bridges. Repeated behavior kicks the brain into creating efficiently to conserve energy. It will link the neurons for that action and emotion so that it is easier to repeat it in the future. Eek! Over time, it becomes easier to think negative than it is to think positive. (I'm sure you can think of someone in your life for whom negativity is their default way of seeing things.)

⚠ It releases the stress hormone cortisol. Besides making you feel overwhelmed, over time, cortisol compromises your immune system.

⚠ It is contagious. Those around us mirror our feelings and energy. I've said this before: one negative person can take down a whole room. You never know who is around and what they are going through, so you may not know the consequences of your negativity on others.

Disappointments happen all the time. Most of the time they are little, but they can be annoying anyway. When you're in the rabbit hole, it can feel like tracking the negative will protect us from disappointment, making it hard to let go of it. But it is the opposite: focusing too much on what is wrong, which conjures negative memories, will bring us more disappointment. Imagine having an armful of balloons representing all the negative things you are contemplating, and then something good comes along. You won't have a free hand to grab it.

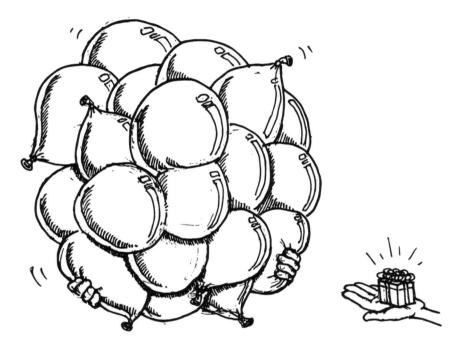

Having a positive mental attitude (PMA) is not about "ignoring the negative" like fake positivity does. It is knowing that despite frustrations, there are positive things you can do to shift a bad experience and get through it faster. Disappointment is easier to handle once you know how to do it.

Here is how to make lemonade out of lemons:

🫘 Allow yourself to feel: feeling bad about a disappointing situation is appropriate! No need to judge yourself here. (Remember: judging causes problems to stick to you!) Instead, be compassionate. It is only once compassion honors your feelings that you can see clearly what you should do next to recover.

🫘 Let go of self-blame: when we get disappointed, it often triggers all our past disappointments. This can send us into a spiral of analysis—thinking we have to figure out the pattern and about how it is our fault. No. This is how minds work—a new occurrence triggers an old occurrence—unless you intercede. If you halt the process, self-blame won't add to your anxiety and overwhelm, and you'll have the focus to move forward.

● Pacify yourself with a substitute. Be open about what else could make you happy in this moment. Being rigid—only being satisfied with ONE outcome—leaves you at risk for increased disappointment. Be willing to soften and be flexible. There are always other choices, and some will end up being better than what you had wanted in the first place.

● Know that there will be a next time. There is always a next time. Honor that it might not feel good right now, but be open to the possibility that something different (and possibly even better) is on its way.

One of my biggest secrets to maintaining a positive attitude amidst so much pull to look at my deficits and inadequacies is to celebrate my wins (See Chapter 3: 6. Activate Courage). I rejoice at even the smallest actions, like getting the dishes washed! Celebrating reminds me to feel good about myself because I have abilities despite my human imperfections. When I finish one job, or get through one hardship, I pause and acknowledge that I did it by literally saying, "I did it!" to myself out loud. This keeps me focused on my agency and abundance instead of feeling like a victim of what I've lost or haven't got. This invigorates and empowers me for the next step, big or small. It keeps me happy because I trust in myself to make my life what I want. I see how I affect it and don't feel powerless or unconnected.

Psychologist Steven Sussman, cofounder of the Child & Teen Success Centers, says that young people need eight to fifteen praising comments to balance each criticism received.[2] OMG! We need to do a lot of celebrating to counter all the negative self-talk that rattles around in our mind!

---

2   Steven Sussman, "Parenting Success - 8:1 ratio of positive to negative interactions," filmed October 2013 in New Jersey, video 2:17, https://youtu.be/AIR3KJORHE4

What's in Your Hand?

Check out Will Bowen's book *A Complaint Free World: How to Stop Complaining and Start Enjoying the Life You Always Wanted*. Or check out his videos at jodiaman.com/ditchinganxiety. While you are there, watch my YouTube video "I'm such a mess!"

Read this story.

There is a Chinese story of an old farmer who owned a bony plow horse. One spring afternoon, the horse ran away. The old man's friends, trying to console him, said, "We're so sorry about your horse, old man. What a misfortune you've had."

But the old farmer said, "Bad news, good news—who knows?"

A few days later the horse returned home leading a herd of wild horses. Again, the friends came running. Filled with jubilation, they cried, "How wonderful! You have more horses."

But the old man whispered, "Good news, bad news—who knows?"

Then the next day, when the farmer's son was trying to ride one of the new horses, he was thrown to the ground and broke both legs. The friends gasped and lamented this catastrophe.

Again, the old man stood still and said, "Bad news, good news—who knows?"

And a short time later when the village went to war and all the young men were drafted to fight, the farmer's son was excused because of his two broken legs.

Write down one thing that seemed like bad luck at the time but that turned out better than what you had wanted in the first place.

....

....

....

....

....

Write down three things you have accomplished in the last three days.

....

....

....

....

....

Why is it so amazing that you accomplished these? What stresses and feelings were you up against, yet you made this happen anyway?

....

....

....

....

....

....

....

....

....

....

6.

EMBRACE HOPE

Deep breath. This is a biggie. It's about *hope*. (And what to do if it seems like there is no light at the end of the tunnel.)

When you have been in pain for a while, you get used to it. Yeah, it's a suffering, but it's a suffering that *you know*. There is some notion of "safety" because it is familiar. EVEN. IF. IT. IS. AWFUL.

"Healing" actually feels out of control because it's unknown. We worry: *What if it's worse?*

No.

Just. No.

Can't happen. Healing, by definition, is better. You CANNOT feel worse when you feel better. If you don't feel better, you are not better; you are worse, and that's NOT better.

It is a ridiculous tactic of doubt to dissolve your hope.

Despair can have you too weighed down to take another step. When the intensity of feelings is too much to bear, people have been known to hurt themselves physically. The most common **self-harm** behavior among teens is cutting or scratching the skin. Teens do this to turn emotional pressure into something physical, thus releasing the pressure. They often report feeling "instant relief." Ostensibly, this makes it appear to be "beneficial," and so they continue using it. I totally get the motivation to relieve oneself of intense emotions, and I have total compassion for that.

However, people who engage in self-harm may not notice the risks: mere minutes after they felt the emotional relief of (1) harming themselves, they (2) feel crazy about it, thinking, *Normal people don't do this. But I need to do it. I'm losing it. My parents would be so upset.* This brings on (3) shame and guilt, reemphasizing that they're out of control, and the (4) negative feelings intensify again, necessitating (5) another release, and then (6) more shame.

And on and on.

These risks often go unnoticed because the sequence of the whole process (1 to 6) is not separated into individual steps; it's viewed as one big lump of chaos that needs releasing.

In conversations with young people about self-harm, I discovered that they engaged in self-harm when they believed it was *necessary* to handle their emotions. Even though this plummeted their overall mental health, they decided that they simply needed it. They were making a choice, and since they felt it was necessary, they didn't experience it as a choice.

I also tracked when teens decided to stop using self-harm. Once they realized that the risks outweighed the benefits, they stopped thinking of themselves as needing it, and so they decided to stop doing it. They simply stopped. Not even a bad day would tempt them, because they knew it made them worse.

What are the risks of self-harm?

Scars, infections, nerve damage, pain, reckless behavior, loved ones feeling hurt or worried, friends being triggered, shame, feeling more out of control, addiction to it, worsening of mental health overall, preoccupation with it, embarrassment if people see it, fear of people judging or misunderstanding you, your parents not allowing you to be alone, and more.

What are the benefits?

A sense that you have control that lasts only a few moments.

> What if you replaced self-harm with something else physical you could do to give you the emotional release, with NO risks? Like do twenty squats, practice deep breathing, take a shower, or sing a song at the top of your lungs? Download the Calm Harm phone app, which gives you a list of alternatives at the touch of your hands!

Thinking about dying is another thing people do when their emotions are intense and they feel little hope. If you have thought or are thinking about suicide, please know that you are not alone. Most people think about it at one time or another. It means you don't like how you feel and want to get out of that feeling. I want you to get out of that feeling, too, just not by dying.

There's hope! When you are feeling at your lowest, please remember that there is one guarantee in life—THINGS CHANGE.

You.
Will.
Not.
Feel.
Like.
This.
Forever.

I know so many people my age and older who survived a suicide attempt or two when they were younger, and they are all leading very rich lives now—they are in love, have kids, have traveled the world, love their jobs, have helped people, and have lots of friends. They still experience trials and tribulations, but they are so glad they survived their attempt because, if not, they would have missed out on so much happiness.

I've seen clients in the most intense pain that you can imagine, and I've watched them recover. 🦋 Witnessing this transformation over and over, I can predict that I don't have to worry about the next person walking into my office being lost forever. They might feel broken and hopeless, but I've seen butterflies emerge enough times to believe in my bones that this new soul won't stay a caterpillar either. People. Get. Better.

Do you believe that there is "no light at the end of the tunnel?" Listen, I promise you that it is there. It's just that something is blocking your view of it. Maybe the obstacle is this very belief that no light exists. When you believe that things can get better, you'll take actions that will take you out of the suffering faster.

While you are waiting to feel better, GET OUT OF ISOLATION IMMEDIATELY.

And then, find something to live for: a person/people who would be devastated if you are gone. A bucket list item that you're unwilling to give up. A challenge to learn something or help someone. You need to have a purpose to make the suffering worth getting through. This will carry you until you feel better and want to live again.

If you are thinking about killing yourself, you have to tell an adult that you can trust today. This is not optional. Isolation is your worst enemy right now. If you don't know who to tell first, call the national suicide hotline, and they will help you decide: 1-800-273-8255 (If you are in a country outside the US, look online for your national number.) Check out my videos on suicide prevention on the book resource page, jodiaman.com/ditchinganxiety.

Teenagers often experience their peers talking about suicide. If you have a friend who does this, it can be overwhelming. You may not know what to do or what to say, even if you want to do something! Here are four ways to respond.

✍ Be calm and understanding.

"Suicide" has a way of freaking people out. But when we freak out, it becomes about us and not the person who is suffering. They feel lost, invisible, and shamed when we freak out. People who think of suicide are usually scared by their thoughts because they worry they are "messed up." Tell them that there is nothing to be ashamed of; tell them you understand that they don't want to feel so bad anymore.

✍ Always tell someone.

This is too heavy to deal with alone. Never promise your friend that you will not tell anyone. If they say, "I have something to tell you, but you can't tell anyone." Let them know you can't agree to promise that until you know what it is. Say you can't keep a secret if someone is in danger. Tell a trusted adult—a teacher or counselor if you are at school, or your parents if you are at home.

♪ Touch them.

People who are this sad feel very lonely, unloved, and disconnected. A kind word and a hug can do wonders. Being close to another person makes people feel worthy. Many who are overwhelmed by their emotions can use a good cry in loving arms. Occasionally, people are uncomfortable about being touched, so always ask and respect touching boundaries.

♪ Be present.

Once your friend is in a safe place with trusted adults around them, your visits can become a fun distraction to help them get through. You aren't the therapist! Your job is to bring lightness into their day. Try to get them to laugh. Laughing with a friend is the most effective, cheapest, risk-free way to release built-up tension, get out of your head, and pass the time until you feel better.

💔

Many people feel hopeless about a future where things are better. They have no energy to put effort into healing. EVERYTHING SEEMS HARD. As long as you're going to keep living, even if it is for only one more day, you might as well try doing something on my "Easy Things" list. Why not?

I am not sure how much better you'll feel by doing any of these, because it depends. Sometimes it is 3 percent improvement, or 9 percent or 18 percent. But it doesn't matter because these activities are so easy that any little relief makes them worth the small effort. And they are free!

As one thing uplifts you, you may have a bit of energy for the next small step in healing! Each improvement in percentage will make you feel better and better, and soon you'll have greater and greater hope knowing you are not staying in this space forever.

This list is not just for folks who feel like their life is hopeless. ANYONE can use these activities to improve their emotional wellness and re-instill hope.

Do the Easy Things

1. Stretch your body, squeezing and releasing tension.
2. Drink more water.
3. Go to sleep and wake up at the same time each day.
4. Listen to music.
5. Light a candle and set an intention.
6. Have self-compassion.
7. Eat more fruits and vegetables.
8. Spend time outside.
9. Breathe deeply.
10. Pet a pet.
11. Compliment someone.
12. Watch funny videos.
13. Listen to an uplifting podcast.
14. Send a thank-you note.
15. Take pictures of beautiful things.
16. Color or draw.

What's in Your Hand?

We are going to try an easy thing! First, rate the intensity of your feelings before doing the easy thing: _____
(From 1 to 10, with 10 being the worst feeling ever)

Pick one thing on the above list and do it. Come back and write a reflection on how easy/hard it was. Ask yourself: How did you feel doing it? What happened next?

The easy thing I did:

....

....

How I feel now: _____
(From 1 to 10, 10 being the worst feeling ever)

How was it?

....

....

....

....

....

....

....

7.

EMBRACE COMPASSION

People get so mad at their anger. They hate it. I tell them that they have to allow themselves to feel the anger, and they argue, "No, I don't want it! It feels awful. I don't want to feel this way!" See—their annoyance just intensifies the anger.

The first step to letting go is to understand that negative feelings, like frustration, annoyance, pain, worry, and anger, are felt when something precious to you is threatened or lost.

Examples:

~A friend betrays you—you feel frustration because having a loyal friend is something you value; having your feelings respected is important to you.

~Someone calls your friend a racial slur—you get angry because you care about equality, your friend being respected is important to you, your friend feeling good about themselves is what you want.

~Someone steals your book bag—you get angry because the bag and its contents have significant worth, there may have been things in there that are not replaceable.

~A friend changes plans—you feel annoyed because you liked the original plan and were looking forward to it.

When you have things that are important to you (check) AND you live in this uncertain world (check), you are going to be frustrated sometimes. You cannot avoid anger altogether. Unfortunately, "anger" has a bad reputation and people don't like to feel it. Like most negative feelings, it brings those negative self-judging circles to surround the smaller original feeling that was appropriate to the situation. This is distracting. Assuming that the whole chaos of feelings is the actual anger, people often worry that they are overreacting. This encourages another layer of circles.

In that process of spiraling negativity, there is no longer focus on the importance of your feelings, your friend's feelings, the value of your book bag and its contents, or your appreciation for the original plan. Your feelings stay unresolved, while anger, resentment, and rage keep building up. Unfortunately, when the next injustice happens, your frustration explodes bigger.

Instead of hating anger, you can let it go by having compassion for it. Anytime you feel anger, frustration, annoyance, and pain, take a breath. Ask yourself what it is that is being lost or threatened. Get clear on what is important to you that has been devalued by the person or event. First of all, when you recognize this, then your anger is not only *understandable*, but it is *honorable*. You can feel compassion for yourself instead of negative self-judgment. "I get why I feel this way."

Now, step back to see the big picture. When you focus on what is important to you, then you can decide on a course of action to lift it back up. If a friend is threatened, you can stick up for them and help them process what happened. If something was lost, you can take steps to find it or start replacing it. If someone passes away, you can give their life meaning by creating a fundraiser for a charity in their name.

There are other reasons people hold on to anger and resentment even though it feels like 👏. One is that they think if they let it go, the person who hurt them gets away with the injustice scot-free. My friend, you staying in pain does not hold a person from your past accountable for what they did to you. Instead, it is like staying in a cage so "they stay in that cage, too." 🏚️ Um, they are long gone. They are not experiencing punishment when you do this. You are.

Step out of your cage, and fly away. 🦋 You have living to do! They've had enough power in your life up until this point. Enough is enough. Don't worry if they don't deserve you letting go. This is not about having compassion for them; it is about having compassion for yourself. #dontwasteanothermomentonthem #youdeservetobefree

People also worry that letting go means you "accept" what was done to you. This feels like it didn't matter that it happened, which translates to you not mattering. Seriously, we hold on to emotional pain because *we want to matter*. This happens way too often. But I assure you, it is not working out well for your sense of worth to sit in that cage.

When self-help gurus say you have to "accept it," they don't mean accept what happened. They mean to have compassion for how you feel about it.

Remember: *It happened. It wasn't okay that it happened. You didn't deserve that it happened. But you don't have to let what happened define you . . . as "unworthy," "destined to be in pain," a "victim," "messed-up," "inadequate," or any negative term that makes you feel less than your best self.* You are worth healing. You didn't deserve this pain in the first place, so you sure as heck deserve to be free of it!

> Some people worry that if they let go, they'd forget and be vulnerable to it happening again. Anger and resentment don't protect you; instead, they break you down further and further. This is the thing: you learn from every experience, especially the bad ones. You are stronger, smarter, and more capable for the next challenges in your life. When you embrace and honor your survival skills, you'll keep them, and this is how you keep yourself safe in the future.

Now that you know how to process and release negative feelings, you will have room and space to embrace self-love. Some people don't know how to love themselves. But you don't have to do anything to love yourself; self-worth is innate. It is the reason you defend yourself, eat, sleep, and do anything. You are protecting what it is you value.

However, if you just don't *feel it*, it just means negative judgments are in your way. With compassion, the fear, resentment, angst, and chaos are cared for, and then they will fade away. What's left is peace and contentment.

What's in Your Hand?

What is something that you have been angry at recently?

....

....

....

What was lost or threatened that made you angry?

....

....

....

Breathe, acknowledging how important that thing is/was to you.

What can you next do to re-honor the thing that is/was important to you?

....

....

....

....

....

....

....

CHAPTER 5:
Self-Care Is the New Health Care

According to Dan Buettner, author of *The Blue Zones,* happiness can be measured by 1) life satisfaction, 2) a fulfilling purpose, and 3) the experience of enjoyment. When studying these measures on different populations around the world, he and his team from *National Geographic* discovered that 40 percent of happiness is dictated by **genes**, 10 to 15 percent is determined by **luck**, and the last 45 to 50 percent depends on **you**. In this chapter, we'll dive into each of these factors.

First is genes. Epigenetics, the study of gene modification, says that frequencies can change your genetic code (adversely and positively). Emotions, words,[1] colors, music, lights, foods, flowers, and pretty much everything has a frequency and can influence that figure of 40 percent. (Check out jodiaman.com/ditchinganxiety for more on epigenetics.)

Then, there's luck. Luck is out of your control, and so it invites anxiety. But think about it. Luck only affects 10 to 15 percent of happiness. That includes good luck, benign, and only mildly bad luck. This leaves a very small percent of your overall happiness for *bad* luck! (IDK, maybe 6 percent, conservatively?) Also, has something bad already happened to you? Yes? Then, some of that percentage is used up already, phew!

We know that anxiety wants you to obsess about the things you have no control over. It puffs them up and makes them out to be a monster in size and intimidation, as it controls 99 percent of your life. *Nope! Less than 6 percent!* It is not

---

1   Fosar Grazyna and Franz Bludorf, *Vernetzte Intelligenz* (Aachen, Germany: Omega Verlag, 2001).

worth stressing over. Just keep honing your skills to handle challenges, and you'll trust yourself to handle future bad luck.

Lastly, there's the **you** percent. Your personal agency is in your hands—45 to 50 percent of your life can be actively orchestrated by releasing what is not serving you and bringing in what improves your satisfaction, purpose, and enjoyment on the daily. Who knew? ✒

Well, YOU know. Because I've told you.

What you can't control is dwarfed by the ability and potential of your response to improve, understand, or save the situation. AND (!) your actions *mean* more to your emotional, spiritual, and physical health than the things you cannot control. Actions rule your relationships, opportunities, and choices, and how you see yourself.

In Chapter 5, we'll harness the You Percent. When you are proactively practicing these habits in your life, so much is possible. Specifically, happiness; happiness is possible. 🎁

1.

PRIORITIZE UPLIFTING RELATIONSHIPS

"Good relationships keep us happier and healthier. Period." concludes an eighty-year-old human development study from Harvard University.[2]

Isolation has a long-term negative impact on emotional wellness. In fact, social and familial conflicts are the number-one reason teens come to counseling. They are also the number-one reason teens participate in self-harm and think about or attempt suicide. For example, nearly 40 percent of transgender people attempt suicide at least one time in their lives.[3] When teens feel like an outlier, feel "different," or feel like they don't belong, for any reason, it affects how they think of themselves, how they feel, how they see relationships, and really how they interpret everything else.

When the relationship issues are resolved and a person feels a sense of social belonging, anxiety and depression decrease. When teens are involved in a community who accepts them as they are, they begin to feel happiness again. Having good, close relationships is a factor that tops every happiness and longevity research study I've found. People need other supportive people to feel worthy, safe, and have a sense of belonging—three essential elements of life satisfaction. Surround yourself with happy people who love you, and this energy will naturally rub off on you.

In the time of social distancing, this is more important than ever. We have to be a bit more creative about connecting, but since humans are highly adaptive, we can manage. Reaching out not only helps you feel like you're not alone in the universe, it helps the friends and family that you are reaching out know that someone is thinking of them. Supporting others fulfills your need for purpose, making life meaningful.

---

2   Liz Mineo, "Harvard study, almost 80 years old, has proved that embracing community helps us live longer, and be happier," *The Harvard Gazette*, April 11, 2017, https://news.harvard.edu/gazette/story/2017/04/over-nearly-80-years-harvard-study-has-been-showing-how-to-live-a-healthy-and-happy-life/

3   S.E. James, et al., *The Report of the 2015 U.S. Transgender Survey*, (Washington, DC: National Center for Transgender Equality, 2016), 5.

A psychology study from Kobe College in Japan divided 175 college students into two groups.[4] One group did nothing different from their usual lifestyles for a week, while the other group were given the task of counting their acts of kindness during the week. (They weren't asked to *try* to do things for others, just write down what they had done.) After a week, the second group reported higher levels of happiness. We need to see that we are making a difference. Having a purpose makes the daily grind, the effort, and the suffering *worth* it!

> "There are three ways to ultimate success. The first is to be kind. The second way is to be kind. The third way is to be kind."
> —Mr. Rogers

What's in Your Hand?

List the people in your life whom you can trust. Circle the long-term relationships.

....

....

....

....

....

....

---

4   Keiko Otake et al., "Happy People Become Happier Through Kindness: A Counting Kindnesses Intervention." *Journal of Happiness Studies* 7, no 3 (September 2006): 361–375, https://doi. org/10.1007/s10902-005-3650-z

Write a thank-you note to someone from the list, letting them know what they mean to you. You can write the draft here and then copy it to send it to them:

....

....

....

....

....

....

....

....

....

....

....

....

....

....

....

....

Ask someone to write you a note about what they love about you. Tape it to this page so you can read it on bad days!

(I keep a "jodi love" folder in my email inbox, and anytime I get kind notes, I file them there so that, if I have a down day, I can look through them to cheer myself up. You can also take screenshots of kind comments on social media. Keep them in an album in your photos app so you can locate them easily when you need encouragement!)

PASTE NOTE HERE

2.
PRIORITIZE ENERGIZING SURROUNDINGS

When you enter a new friend's home for the first time, the appearance of their bedroom is hardly a surprise. It often matches their energy and personality. Eclectic creatives look a certain way, unorganized friends appear as expected, and high-strung friends' rooms fit them, too. When you enter the room of a happy friend, you can often feel the positive energy as you enter, even if you can't put your finger on it. You probably find cool, unique, and meaningful tokens in there that mirror them.

Since our surroundings are so reflective of a person, it is hard to doubt that the things around us—people, pets, plants, light, design, cleanliness, convenience factor, etc., are related to their happiness. Feng Shui, an ancient Chinese ideology that seeks to harmonize individuals with their surrounding environment, explains that every item in your house attaches to your energy. This idea renders clutter, so common in modern homes, worrisome. Studies in California found that all family members in cluttered homes have more of the stress hormone cortisol than those in uncluttered homes.[5] The Kondo phenomenon (from her book *The Life-Changing Magic of Tidying Up* and her Netflix show "Tidying Up with Marie Kondo") has inspired people to clear out their clutter, and this is having a huge impact on emotional wellness. Marie recommends that if the item gives you pleasure or joy, keep it. If not, get rid of it. #nextnetflixbinge

☀

Colors make a huge difference to mood. My office is decorated with the brightest hues I could find, surrounded by four large windows. The vibrancy and vitality you encounter when entering the room instantly connect you with *your* vibrancy and vitality. 🎀 By being invited in, you belong to this beauty, too. This is felt

---

5   D. Saxbe and R. L. Repetti, "For better or worse? Coregulation of couples' cortisol levels and mood states." *Journal of Personality and Social Psychology,* 98 no. 1 (2010), 92–103, https://doi.org/10.1037/a0016959

consciously, as people's dopamine makes them feel good, and unconsciously as it prepares them to feel worthy of the healing that is coming. The aesthetics of the room affect the expectation of what will happen in that space. My clients come to see me because they want to feel better, but upon entering, they shift to expecting something great. With the preferred results in sight, motivation to take action toward those results kicks in.

ㅗㅊ

The beauty and fresh, oxygenated air of nature calms and calibrates the mind and body. Here are some ways that spending time surrounded by nature will improve emotional wellness:

🦋 Connection

When I am stressed, I lie right on the ground. I let all my troubles flow out of my body and into the earth. In that moment, nothing matters, and I feel supported, connected to this vast planet under me. Emotional turmoil makes us feel separate, like we don't belong to, or can't handle, the world. That "me vs. the world" feeling creates vulnerability. But you can go outside, look at a leaf, smell a flower, watch some chipmunks play, and feel an instant connection to them that provides the security of belonging.

🌳 Helps us understand transience

Everything changes. Flowers sprout, grow, bloom, and fade. One of our biggest fears is loss, but nature shows us that even sadness and loss are temporary. When something goes, something else comes.

☀ Gives us a larger perspective

Our problems are little when paired side by side to this massive world. Things that we think matter so much pale in comparison to a giant ocean. There are more stars in the sky than worries in our heads. Outside, we can let go and be part of something bigger than our thoughts and worries.

🍎 Oxygen

Conscious breathwork is the cheapest, safest, and, I dare say, easiest thing to do to harmonize your nervous system. Since plants give off oxygen, there are added benefits of breathing outside. Go sit by a tree or a plant and introduce yourself—thank it for the oxygen and ask it anything else that comes to mind.

♨ Aromatherapy

Smells are frequencies, so they have healing power. For example, the smell of fresh or dried jasmine and lavender is calming. Natural smells will always feel better to the body than processed smells like air fresheners, fragrance, or essential oils. These are usually too strong, and often full of chemicals.

🌳 Earthing

Earthing is touching the soil or rock with your bare feet. It reduces the **free radicals and free radical damage** in the body, decreasing inflammation, easing physical, and emotional pain, improving sleep, and increasing energy. I love walking barefoot outside. But I also keep big rocks under my desk, so I can take my shoes off and touch them, even in the winter.

> Free radicals are molecules with unattached electrons, which can damage cells. They are caused by toxins in food and environment, as well as electromagnetic field (EMF), a.k.a. electric radiation from household electronics and cell phones.

❧ Gardening

Gardening is great for many reasons. Flowers are beautiful, smell good, and make wonderful gifts to cheer up a friend. A vegetable garden helps you know your food is fresh and without chemicals! The pre- and probiotics in your soil support good gut flora. Not only do you ingest them when eating, but they transfer through the skin of your hands when you plant, weed, and harvest. These microbes enhance digestion, and because 90 percent of serotonin[6] (a.k.a. the "happy hormone") is made in your stomach, this has been linked to greater emotional health.[7] Gardening is fun, too! (No? My kids don't like it either.)

A house plant is a suitable alternative if you can't garden. Studies by NASA show that house plants can decrease the electromagnetic field (plus they are pretty).

● Distraction

Once while on a hike, my son and I saw a raccoon, a chipmunk, three frogs, countless birds, a squirrel, tons of wildflowers, and two butterflies. We forgot about the whole world during that time we were in the woods. It is amazing how twenty minutes of walking can ease anxiety and clear your mind. *Shinrin Yoku* is the Japanese therapeutic practice of walking outside where one engages in nature using all the five senses. Research has suggested that the scent of trees, the sound of brooks, and the feel of sunshine have a physiologically calming effect. It can decrease cortisol by up to 16 percent![8]

Find some green space anywhere, even if it is a houseplant, every day. Then, especially if you are upset at all, look at it, smell it, feel it, and do some deep breathing.

---

6   Jessica M. Yano et al., "Indigenous Bacteria from the Gut Microbiota Regulate Host Serotonin Biosynthesis," *Cell* 161 no. 2 (2015): 264.

7   *The Sensitive Gut: A guide to managing common gastrointestinal disorders.* Boston: Harvard Medical School Health Report, 201

8   B. J. Park et al., "The physiological effects of Shinrin-yoku (taking in the forest atmosphere or forest bathing): evidence from field experiments in 24 forests across Japan." *Environmental Health and Preventive Medicine* 15 no. 1 (January 2010): 18–26, https://www.ncbi.nlm.nih.gov/pubmed/19568835.

What's in Your Hand?

Even as a teenager, you can influence the appearance of part of your home. Focus on your room (even if you can only control a small part of a room if you are sharing it with someone else). Ask yourself:

Do I want my bedroom to be a sanctuary?
When I enter my room, does my mind instantly calm?
Do I open the shades during the day, and allow light to enter?
Or open a window to let fresh air circulate?
Are my dirty clothes on the floor, mixed with clean outfits I tried on but didn't end up wearing?
Do I have clothes and stuff that I don't use, taking up energy and space?
Are my decorations pretty? Negative? Positive? Do they make me feel good? Or do they add to the clutter?

What if your house, or your room, had the energy of a sanctuary where you felt deserving? Don't worry, you don't need a redecorating budget! Getting rid of clutter that drains you is much more important. Making a space neat and clean will give you the sanctuary you seek. There is even a whole movement that says making your bed connects you with your personal agency first thing in the morning, inciting empowerment throughout the day. (On YouTube, watch "University of Texas at Austin 2014 Commencement Address - Admiral William H. McRaven.")

Try something on a small scale right now. Take a look at your backpack. Check all the pockets. What do you have in there? Do you need it all?

List everything in your backpack and put a check mark beside the things you want to keep in there. Give the rest of the things another home or discard them as you desire.

How does it feel when you are done?

If you have time, do this with one drawer, your whole dresser, a bookshelf, or a closet. If you don't have time now, schedule each of them for a later date and complete these tasks until your room looks peaceful and you feel calm and content as soon as you enter.

Check out my videos on jodiaman.com/ditchinganxiety: "Clear Your Clutter" and "7 Easy Ways To Declutter Your Home."

ALSO, GO OUTSIDE! Sit comfortably by a tree or plant. Put your nose up close to it and inhale. Look at the color and shape of the leaves. Close your eyes, and take three long, deep breaths. In your mind, introduce yourself to the tree or plant. Continue to breathe slowly, and see if the plant has any secrets to share with you. Stay for about 5 to 10 minutes, listening or asking questions. Before you end the chat, thank the tree or plant, and give it a little bow before going about your day.

What did you hear?

....

....

....

....

....

....

....

....

....

....

....

3.

PRIORITIZE MOVEMENT

A 2019 University of Vermont study concluded that daily exercise results in an improvement in mood, as reported by 95 percent of participants. I don't think that surprises anyone! Whether or not it informs our behavior, we already KNOW that movement is an essential component for overall health, and in particular mental health. Many of my clients stop therapy when their sports season begins, since, they say, the exercise (and focus on something constructive) regulates their anxiety.

Exercise is a win-win-win-win situation. Here is how exercising makes you happy:

🫴 Physical

Exercise builds strength and endurance. Your *body* grows accustomed to pushing through even when you are tired. It improves your heart and respiratory, musculature, skeletal, and nervous systems.

🎇 Mental

Your *mind* grows accustomed to pushing through even when you are tired (mental strength and endurance). You learn to be goal-oriented, becoming familiar with hard work and the results of it. Watching yourself successfully navigate challenges and hone problem-solving skills builds your confidence. If you commit to something, and continuously honor this commitment, you raise your self-esteem. Movement pulls your attention away from your monkey mind and into your body where it can be in the present moment.

🗨 Relational

You meet people and have a sense of belonging. You learn how to deal with difficult people and authority figures and how to navigate rules. You learn how to work as a team and to be a good sport.

👥 Emotional

Endorphins are released, and you experience an emotional high. You feel proud of yourself that you have exercised. Exercise uses up any extra adrenaline, and you feel calmer and more centered as a result. Another bonus is that exercise provides tryptophan with an unimpeded passage to the brain. (You may have heard of tryptophan, the calming hormone that earned its fame from making people want to nap after a turkey dinner.) Throughout the day, larger proteins travel up to the brain, putting tryptophan, a small molecule, at a disadvantage. But when a person exercises, the larger proteins leave the brain to aid the muscles, and tryptophan, without competition, is allowed to flood the brain.

If you are not a regular exerciser and you attempt to exercise, your brain will say, *That seems hardly worth the effort. Better conserve the calories.* You hear, "I don't think I can do that right now." You forge a story about yourself—"I am not an exerciser" or "I hate exercise." And that becomes an excuse not to do it.

In ancient times, pre-humans physically worked all day to hunt, fight, make/repair shelter, and travel long distances. Food was scarce, so every calorie counted. Extraneous tasks would be wasteful, and so resisting them was essential. In today's world, where you might sit on the couch all day long, safe and fed, the opposite is true. Movement, exercise, keeping busy, and being creative are what will help us thrive.

TBH, I don't like exercise, but I *like having done it.* I override the calorie-conserving resistance I feel each and EVERY time—*You can't exercise today; you are too tired!*—by reminding myself that I'll be happy when it is done and that it will be over soon. In addition, understanding the source of my resistance helps me to pay less attention to it. Since I lift weights and walk outside regularly, I am familiar with how good it can feel to maintain these habits, and that gets me moving.

You can do this, too. When starting, don't overdo it, or it'll be harder tomorrow. Think, fun. Put on music, and have a dance party. The German neuroscientist Dr. Kathrin Rehfeld discovered that dancing reverses the signs of aging on the brain.

I know you are not concerned with aging yet, but this means it reverses damage from emotional and environmental toxins.[9] That is good for you at any age.

Dancing is especially good for you for a few reasons besides the other benefits of exercise I listed above. One benefit is that it requires non-linear movement, so it engages lesser-used muscles. Also, good music is healing to your DNA, creativity is good for the soul, and singing releases endorphins, so definitely belt it out while you dance!

When starting to add movement to your life, start small. Get the 7 Minute Workout app. Watch a ten-minute YouTube exercise video. Grab a friend and take a walk through your neighborhood. The positive effects of exercise will grow over time. You can build up your exercise habits to a longer workout duration once it begins to feel good.

Whether you heed my advice on adding movement to your life or not, please do this one thing that takes minimal effort and will deliver great rewards throughout your whole life:

Stand up straight.

Slouching tells your brain that you have to protect your heart, increasing your feelings of vulnerability, while standing with your shoulders back and down both exudes and builds confidence. (It literally releases the GABA hormone, which puts the breaks on adrenaline.) It makes you more attractive and approachable.

Blame phones, blame couches, blame self-consciousness, blame whatever you want, but posture has taken a beating in modern culture. There are no excuses! The detriment to your spinal cord, and potential for lifelong physical and emotion problems, is too great a risk. You have to fix this, and you can fix this. The first step is awareness. When you notice yourself slouching, straighten up. Keep doing this all day, forever.

A great relaxing way to counter the effects of slouching is to lie on your back with a pillow under your middle or upper back and rest there for ten minutes. Or lie on your stomach and rest up on your elbows to counter the effects of sitting a lot. Also, don't sit a lot.

---

9   Kathrin Rehfeld, et al., "Dancing or Fitness Sport? The Effects of Two Training Programs on Hippocampal Plasticity and Balance Abilities in Healthy Seniors," *Frontiers in Human Neuroscience* 11 (June 15, 2017), https://doi.org/10.3389/fnhum.2017.00305.

What's in Your Hand?

Lie on your bed, face up, with your arms above your head in a "v" and your legs also spread in a "v." If your mattress is too full of pillows and junk, clear it off, or find a body-length space on the floor so that you can be flat.

Lift your right arm and left leg straight up toward the center above you until they touch. Slowly bring it back down. Next, bring the left arm and right leg up in the same way. Do twenty sets.

How do you feel?

....

....

....

....

....

....

....

Circle where your posture is on this chart:

4.

PRIORITIZE WHOLE NOURISHMENT

You need fuel to think, feel, and act. If you see your body as a temple, you become empowered to give it the best medicine that you can. I'm using the word *medicine* as something that heals, repairs, and renews, so this can mean anything that you bring into your mind, body, and soul: healthy food, good advice, bodywork, positive energy, happy news, meditation, prayer, vitamins, exercise, actual pharmaceuticals, and the like.

Keep in mind: everything that comes into your body either heals you or ages you. Focusing on whole foods is essential to good health. When you care about yourself and your well-being, you make nourishing food choices, such as eating lots of fruits and vegetables. Processed food, which is anything made in a factory, is full of free radicals, which cause inflammation. Inflammation is the cause of every illness and disease, including anxiety and depression. This is why eating too much junk food digs you deeper into unhappiness.

People who have migrated to a whole foods–based or an anti-inflammatory diet report a total change in mood. I understand it is hard to motivate yourself to eat less junk food when you don't feel well. If there is an opportunity at your house, try adding more greens to your plate.

There are a ton of things besides food that can nourish us. Learn to make conscious decisions about what you watch, listen to, who you are with, and where you go. Your time and energy are precious! Once you take toxins in, you suffer the effects and have to face the challenge of getting rid of them. However, if you can take a beat and *avoid taking them in* in the first place, you'll be so much better off.

Take an extra moment before engaging in anything to put your hand on your heart and say, "What is the most nourishing thing I can do for myself right now?"

What's in Your Hand?

Because people interact with food daily, unfortunately, food is an easy target for anxiety and depression to hook on to. For one, hunger increases your adrenaline. Then, emotional stress causes stomach issues. And satisfying hunger releases dopamine, giving us a sense of comfort. Even when we are not hungry, this trains us to eat when we seek comfort. In addition, the social standards to be thin and perfect bring anxiety and stress into our relationship with food. Each of these factors can cause us to overeat or undereat. They both feel out of control, and the spiral begins.

If you have concerns about your relationship with food, you can change it.

How would you describe your relationship with food?

....

....

....

....

....

....

....

....

....

....

....

Is there an area in your relationship with food that you would like to improve?

....

....

....

....

....

....

....

What is the first step?

....

....

....

....

....

....

Watch the video "Natural Ways to Build Emotional Wellness" on jodiaman. com/ditchinganxiety.

5.

PRIORITIZE REST

"People who sleep six hours a night are 30 percent less happy than people who sleep more," says Dan Buettner from *Blue Zones*.[10] Wowza!

Although health advisers promote the importance of sleep for healing, longevity, and happiness, 75 percent of adults still get less than seven hours a night. Teens, who need more sleep than adults, often get less than that! No wonder sadness and anxiety are issues!

Your body doesn't shut down when you are asleep. Internal organs and processes are hard at work at night to restore any damage during the day. Notably, the brain clears out harmful toxins during sleep. You know those folds you see when you picture a human brain? Between and around them, there is a liquid called cerebrospinal fluid (CSF). In that liquid are neurotransmitters (like dopamine), where thoughts travel around the brain. When you don't get enough sleep, CSF gets thick like honey. Your mind dulls, and you find it harder to concentrate, make decisions, and problem solve. Plus, you lose things, have slower reactions, have more accidents, eat more, and are more irritable.

This means you feel bad. If you are struggling emotionally, getting enough rest should be a top priority because it improves things with minimal effort.

Lack of Sleep =
Decreases the functionality of your immune system
Increases your appetite
Increases irritability/depression/anxiety
Decreases memory/productivity/concentration/performance
Increases risk of accidents and health problems

---

10 As of February, 2020, bluezones.com had a blogpost, "Nine Questions for Dan Buettner: Happiness Lessons From the Happiest Places in the World," https://www.bluezones.com/2017/10/happiness-lessons-from-happiest-countries-and-cities-in-the-world/

Often when people have trouble falling asleep, they worry that the next day will be ruined. Unfortunately, this worry releases adrenaline, which keeps you alert and further prevents sleep. If you can't sleep, try not to worry about it and trust that you will manage. This will calm you, getting you to sleep faster.

Here are some tips on how to sleep better.

Stick to a routine: A relatively consistent bedtime and wake-up time will enhance overall emotional wellness.

Decrease your daytime sleeping: when you sleep during the day, your body needs less sleep at night, which will leave you to be awake during an isolating time.

Nix the screens in and around your bed: The blue light emitted by screens decreases the production of melatonin, the hormone that controls your sleep-wake cycle or circadian rhythm.[11] Take an electronic radiation break during sleeping to decrease your exposure. #nomorephoneatnight #bedisforsleepingnotsearching

Cool down your bedroom. Temperatures between 60 to 68° F (15 to 20°C) stimulate the production of melatonin.

Exercise.

No afternoon caffeine or energy drinks.

Try warm milk with honey or chamomile tea. #notjustanoldwivestale

Have an optimal bed position. Don't align your bed with the door. Your mind feels safer if you have a better view of anyone entering than they have of you.

Close doors to the bathroom or closet as this also calms the mind.

Clear the clutter in your room, and especially clean out under your bed.

Don't look at the clock; it makes you worry about how little sleep you are getting.

Try deep, slow breathing to bring your attention out of the mind and into the body.

Keep a journal by your bed to write down the worries and to-dos to get them out of your head.

---

11   "Cellular Phones," American Cancer Society, accessed February 20, 2020, https://www.cancer. org/cancer/cancer-causes/radiation-exposure/cellular-phones.html

Think about something benign. Design an outfit, plan your next party, take a tour of your best friend's house in your head, try to recall the last TV show you saw in the chronological order of each scene. See my YouTube video "How to Calm Your Mind at Night" for more details on how to do this!

In addition to getting enough sleep, everyone needs some downtime to revive and restore the nervous system. With stress as the number-one health problem in the twenty-first century, we need to incorporate downtime into our every day. If you could enjoy your downtime with a special person, even better! (I wish humans did do social grooming! See Chapter 4: 4. Embrace Connection.) Choose the downtime activities you prefer, for example, coloring, meditation, walking, listening to music, reading, journaling, cuddling, massage, floating, or drinking tea.

What's in Your Hand?

Write down your preferred bedtime routine.

....

....

....

....

....

....

....

Coloring is a relaxing bedtime activity.

6.

PRIORITIZE A HIGHER PURPOSE

Having faith that things will work out gives us the certainty of outcome, which makes us feel less stressed and more at peace. Faith ignites hope and expectation, informing our decisions and actions to increase our potential and make the world a better place. These actions create purpose, which gives a point to everything you do, especially the hard stuff. Without purpose, people feel untethered, lost, and empty.

Jennice Vilhauer starts her TEDxPeachtree talk[12] by asking the audience, "How many of you want to win the lottery?" Loads of hands shoot up. Then she asks, "How many of you bought lottery tickets this week?" Most of the hands dropped. Brains act on anticipation, she explains. When you think and prepare for what you *expect* might happen—for example, that you'd never win—you participate in that very outcome by not purchasing a scratch-off. It becomes a self-fulfilling prophecy because, without a reason to buy a ticket, you don't buy one.

But when you think and prepare for what you *want* to happen, your sense of purpose shifts action and energy toward those desired results. This is the gist: if you don't have faith that your future can be better than the past, there would be no point to create something better.

Faith is not about religion. It is a belief that you are connected to something beyond yourself, for example, your family, justice, the greater good, higher consciousness, your inner wisdom, your community, energy, mother nature, the collective soul, the Tesseract, or whatever you call a higher being. Faith acts as an internal and external guidance system that helps you trust, make sense of, and take steps on your life's journey. Your thoughts have power, and a higher purpose steers them in a more hopeful and positive direction for you to follow. If your actions matter, you matter.

When you don't feel like you matter, depression cuts deep. You feel worthless and unmotivated. If each human had faith that they had a purpose on earth to be an agent of positive change, they would: Make. Better. Choices.

---

12 Jennice Vilhauer, "Why you don't get what you want; it's not what you expect," filmed May 2015 at TEDxPeachtree, Atlanta, GA, video, 13:13, https://youtu.be/FwLeiY5f7sI

There is a purpose to teaching history: be inspired by the ones who were brave in adversity, and prevent repeating atrocities. But young people need to be guided on how to do that. Sarah, an eighth grader (white, "she," cis, straight), and I were speaking about the nightmares she'd been having since starting her social studies unit on the Holocaust during World War II. In her dreams, she and family members, as well as friends, suffered violent deaths by different methods in a variety of settings.

After hearing about how the teacher had presented the content to thirteen-year-olds, I understood why Sarah was expressing vulnerability and helplessness in her dreams. His lessons consisted of showing them grim photos and videos of the atrocities and describing in detail the torture that the victims had endured. And that was it.

To teens who are already feeling out of control of their world, they need guidance to make this information useful. They ought to be taught what it means and what they can do about it. Without guidance, some students will be indifferent, putting the horror in the same category as other fictional movies. And others will feel more vulnerable and anxious in their lives. (Neither of these give the desired effect of learning history with the intention of making the world a better place.)

Good history teachers ought to embrace the opportunity . . .

⊡ to teach kids how to be reverent about past atrocities and to honor the victims.

⊡ to inspire them that, even in unspeakable oppression, people still can find the courage to exercise their agency and protest.

⊡ to share the skills people used to adapt, survive, and take care of loved ones during horrible times.

⊡ to encourage students to volunteer locally to help hurting or marginalized people.

⊡ to encourage practicing daily acts of kindness to make the world a better place.

⊡ to galvanize kids to stand up to bullies and advocate against injustice.

What's in Your Hand?

We are going to fuel the fire of your faith. Think of an example of something you are hoping for in the future. Write the following reflections.

What do I expect to happen? How is what I am expecting making me feel?

What is it that scares me?

....

....

....

....

....

....

What would I like to happen instead?

....

....

....

....

....

....

What would I need to do to allow what I want to happen?

....

....

....

....

....

....

....

How would it affect my larger community?

....

....

....

....

....

....

7.

PRIORITIZE CREATIVITY

Playing is our first activity to help brain development. It activates the front lobe, teaches emotional regulation, enhances imagination, opens pathways to abstract thinking, hones problem-solving, and builds skills in strategy. Though the kind of playing we do changes as we grow, enjoyment, social interaction, and creativity are essential pieces at any age.

Unfortunately, the way we play has changed in the last few decades. For example, take LEGOs. While it's still fun to build the modern LEGO sets, where you follow instructions to build the design on the outside of the box, you lack the stimulation of creative expression that the LEGOs of the 70s, 80s, and 90s had, when all you had was a box of all varying shapes and colors that you could use to build whatever you wanted. And phones: some phones have creative apps and puzzles; however, teens often use phones to consume content, not create it. They scroll through social media instead of hanging out with their friends, or they watch videos on YouTube rather than come up with their own play activity.

This lack of creative play brings along certain risks. Kids grow up with higher standards, yet they are less connected to their agency. They feel (and so expect that they are) less equipped to handle the world. This is terrifying, and it affects their potential. Adults, teachers, and employers are also worried that members of Generation Z do not have what it takes to adult.

I'm not worried about Gen Z, though. My heart breaks because you are suffering, but I have faith that when push comes to shove, you will step up to the plate and do what you have to do to survive. Humans are highly adaptable, so you will be okay.

But why not practice now? Then, you can feel more comfortable taking risks and following opportunities while you still have a safety net beneath you. This is what you do: always be engaged in some kind of creative project; spend time in playful, joyful pursuits to maintain high brain function; and build trust in yourself. Remember, if you are bored, the monkey will look for problems to solve. Give it something fun to plan, organize, or create. It will gain skills, stay satisfied, and leave you in peace (and bliss).

Creative pursuits can also help you fall in love with something, like drawing, photography, building things, playing ball, producing music, helping people, science, animals, or electronics, and may even lead to you finding out what you want to do with your life. Securing an income around a higher purpose and an activity you enjoy makes for a happy life. Financial independence will give you the freedom to afford the home you want in the location you love, the ideal job, the cool car, the toys you enjoy, and worldwide adventures. In this Information Age, when young people don't have to fit themselves into a job, you have the opportunity to create a career of your dreams doing whatever interests you.

What's in Your Hand?

Is it a phone?

Try this: power it down, put it on a shelf, and spend the next twenty minutes doing some creative project. Draw, explore outside, organize your dresser, make some healthy food, write a list, practice a trick, write a poem, or make some music.

Take a moment to reflect on your future.

What are some of the things you want to be able to afford when you are an adult?

....

....

....

....

....

....

....

What would be your dream career?

....

....

....

....

....

....

How do you want it to impact the world?

....

....

....

....

....

....

....

....

....

What hobbies can you do now to gain skills for that?

....

....

....

....

....

....

....

....

Practice. Practice. Practice. Your monkey repeats things incessantly, so you must be diligent in your repetition of practicing all of your unique skills. Needing practice doesn't mean something is wrong; it means you are human. Remind yourself: you are not doing this work because you are different and have problems; you are doing it because nobody is *just happy* without effort.

EVERY. SINGLE. PERSON needs to consistently generate good things that they enjoy on the daily in order to have lasting happiness.

Remember:

You have a purpose.

There is nothing inherently wrong with you.

You want to feel good. You deserve to feel good.

Now, you know how.

You. Have. Full. Control.

#micdrop #imnotcryingyourecrying #ily

Write something in the box that gives you hope that things will get better. Snap a picture and post to IG. Tag me: @jodiamanlove.

IT WILL BE OKAY BECAUSE

@jodiamanlove
#ditchinganxiety

APPENDIX A:

How to Raise Happy Teens—A Resource for Parents and Caregivers

Hopefully you have parents/guardians/adult helpers who are there for you. Maybe they even bought you this book. Now it is time for them to get some help to support you.

Cut these pages out, staple them, and give them to your parents, guardians, or the adult helper of your choosing.

(Yes, it is also okay for you to read them!)

Dear Love Giver,

Being a parent, caregiver, teacher, guardian, grandparent, coun-selor of Gen Z teens is not for the faint of heart. It is HARD. I know you are doing everything you can. I want you to know that IT IS MAKING A DIFFERENCE. If you don't agree, that is probably because you're being too hard on yourself and excus-ing away your amazing-ness. "What? It's no big deal! It's what anyone would do." No, it's a remarkable feat and it shows how skilled you are. You also might not see the progress because most changes your kids make are subtle. Individuating (becoming a human adult) is a one-step-forward-three-steps-back kind of deal. 😵 I wish it weren't so.

I have three kids. My youngest is fifteen as I write this. I get it. You'd love your independent, happy butterfly to emerge from the cocoon and fly around, successful and surrounded by posi-tive friends and family (and . . . you also want them to appreci-ate everything you did to get them there). But it takes a while to eat enough leaves, deal with body changes, figure out what they want, weave a chrysalis, and transform inside it. And, in our mod-ern world, there is a lot to waylay them from the process.

By the time they are in their twenties, when they finally are mature enough to realize what you've done for them, you might have more scars than they do!

Kids need to make mistakes and encounter disappointments so they can learn how to survive in this crazy world. It breaks your heart to see them struggle, but that's part of their journey. It's not your job to fix it or make it perfect for them. But you do have an important job. To be present so they don't feel alone in the world. To reflect to them their implicit worth. To be their guide and cheerleader.

Here are the four things kids need from their parents.

🦋 Basic needs

Having food, clothes, shelter, and safety will give kids the security to learn how to be in the world. There is a gradual weaning off process of providing basic needs to kids as they grow, when they start practicing fulfilling their own needs and making their own decisions. At first, they'll make small decisions with your guidance, then they'll start to make bigger and bigger decisions. Some of these will turn your hair grey, since learning independence comes with risks and rebellion. 👶 I'm sorry.

🦋 Unconditional love

Families are the first place where kids feel a sense of belonging and worth. Everyone needs this for emotional wellness! Having unconditional love is how kids learn self-acceptance and self-forgiveness. When they make mistakes, they need a place to come back to, where loved ones won't define them by that mistake.

🦋 Opportunities to learn

Kids are sponges. They are taking in everything around them. As parents, one of our biggest jobs is surrounding them with opportunities to learn. They will learn what they enjoy, how to be kind to people, how to take care of themselves, how to do what they don't like to do, how to eat well, when to ask for help, how to act justly, how to read the world, and more. They are always watching 😵, so we need to be models of how we want them to be.

🦋 To notice their uniqueness

As kids grow personalities, it is important to point out their unique skills and values. You noticing their abilities teaches them how to see themselves. This is how they'll step into their personal agency. It's how they build trust and confidence in themselves. You are showing them their empowerment in a seemingly powerless world. This is the best thing you can do to help them live up to their potential.

When kids have anxiety and depression, they first and foremost want to feel understood. These are what kids with anxiety want you to know.

How hard they are trying
Acknowledge how hard it is to just get through the day. When they feel misunderstood about this, they will defend their limitations, which increases how bad they feel. But if they are recognized for their efforts, they will have more access to those efforts.

What helps them
Plan out with your teen a list of what helps them in different scenarios, so you have a toolbox to refer to. Anxiety makes people want to fight with each other, and while you probably can't avoid this altogether, you can prevent some of it by working this out ahead.

What triggers them
When no one knows how you are feeling, it's awful. Sometimes kids need to talk out their problems to see them from different angles. If you know the lies that anxiety tells your teen, you can help them realize they are not true. Teaming up on this is invaluable, because anxiety can be pretty persistent, especially when they are alone.

That distraction helps
One of the greatest skills humans have is to distract themselves. It is easiest to do this when you are not alone. Tell stories, run errands, start a project, or watch funny videos together! Distracting them when they need it is a necessary and rewarding role for you to play; if not, they can get stuck in their own powerlessness. Don't underestimate the power of distraction!

To remind them that it is temporary

One of the first things I convey in this book is that people get through anxiety faster when they *believe that they can.* You have a big influence over how they think about anxiety. If you think it is "something they will have to manage their whole life," they will think that, too, and they will keep it. Anxiety is temporary, but it will last if you don't believe that. Even in heightened anxiety, remembering that it will pass makes it less scary and deflates it. Remind your teen, "This will go away," and tell them that you will not leave them here. Assure them that you will figure this out together. There are so many things you can do to feel better, and you will just try one at a time until it is gone.

Raising kids brings up a lot of your own shizzle. Don't delay addressing this. Getting yourself together is the best thing you can do to help them.

It would be great if you can read this book; however, your kid's copy may not be available. (They may be writing their private thoughts in there.) Get yourself a Kindle version and read along so you are equipped to be their biggest guide and cheerleader. It will help you understand what they are going through, and how to think and talk about anxiety so you can lift them out of it *faster.*

When your teen is struggling, it evokes your own feelings of powerlessness. I get it. That's why I have a page of resources just for you. They are shots in the arm to fortify you to keep up the hard work! You'll find videos, audios, and articles here: jodiaman. com/conscious-parenting.

💉 My TEDxWilmington Talk on why we have an anxiety epidemic

💉 Developing your parental intuition to build trust in yourself

💉 How to know when to seek professional help and understanding the options

💉 What goes in deciding to medicate your teens

- Natural ways to improve mental health
- How to keep lines of communication open
- How to address about suicidality and self-harm behaviors
- How to get your kids off their phones
- How to help your kids get rid of anxiety
- Everything you need to know about raising Gen Z
- How to Help Your Kids with Anxiety Masterclass
- How to prevent giving your kids "your baggage"
- Links to my favorite parenting resources

And here is the book resource page for teens: jodiaman.com/ditchinganxiety.

From there, you can search my YouTube videos that expose the major problems that attack our emotional wellness. I will show you how to navigate around them and get through them with your sanity intact, empowered to take charge of your life! You need to maintain your emotional wellness while you raise the future adults of this world.

We parents have to stick together. Sometimes it feels like we are feeling our way through the dark with Gen Z, because this is unprecedented territory. We are more hands-on than our parents were, yet anxiety and depression keep rising steadily, as if our efforts don't make a difference. We worry that our kids are drowning and ill-equipped to handle life.

Humans are highly adjustable, and when given challenges, they will rise to them. It's easier, of course, when they believe that they can. Enter, you.

No matter how hopeless they become, you can maintain the confidence that they CAN do this, and it will rub off on them. Reflect back to them the different skills they have as evidence that they can get through whatever is happening today. This belief in them will be contagious, and they will start to take it on.

You are making a difference. You strongly influence the tools that they have to cope with life. Just hold signs along their route to guide them, be available for hugs when they need you, and cheer from the sidelines when they don't. Always radiate back to them the good they have in them until they see it, too.

However heartbroken you are to see your kid suffering, and however bleak it seems to be because you've tried everything, don't fear. There is hope. Things don't stay the same. They always change. You have the power to change them for the better, together.

Good luck, and let me know what else I can do for you.

Peace,
Jodi

Come hang out with me!
IG @jodiamanlove
FB.com/jodiamanlove

Bibliography

"Advertising to Children and Teens: Current Practices," *A Common Sense Media Research Brief* (January 28, 2014). https://www.commonsensemedia.org/research/advertising-to-children-and-teens-current-practices

American Cancer Society. "Cellular Phones." Accessed February 20, 2020. https://www.cancer.org/cancer/cancer-causes/radiation-exposure/cellular-phones.html

Bluezones.com. "Nine Questions for Dan Buettner: Happiness Lessons From the Happiest Places in the World." Accessed February 20, 2020. https://www.blue-zones.com/2017/10/happiness-lessons-from-happiest-countries-and-cities-in-the-world/

Bowen, Will. *A Complaint Free World: How to Stop Complaining and Start Enjoying the Life You Always Wanted.* New York: Three Rivers Press, 2013.

Buchanan, Ann, ed., and Rotkirch, Ann, ed. *The Role of Grandparents in the 21st Century: Global Perspectives on Changing Roles and Consequences* (New York: Routledge, 2018).

Buettner, Dan. *The Blue Zones: Lessons for Living Longer From the People Who've Lived the Longest.* Washington, D.C.: National Geographic, 2010.

Collishaw, S., B. Maughan, L. Natarajan, and A. Pickles. Trends in adolescent emotional problems in England: A comparison of two national cohorts twenty years apart. *Journal of Child Psychology and Psychiatry*, 51 (2010): 885–894.

"The Common Sense Census: Media Use By Tweens and Teens in 2019," A Common Sense Media Research Brief, October 28, 2019: https://www.commonsensemedia.org/research/advertising-to-chil-dren-and-teens-current-practices.

Diagnostic And Statistical Manual of Mental Disorders: DSM-5. Arlington, VA: American Psychiatric Association, 2013.

Fanselow, Michael S. "From contextual fear to a dynamic view of memory systems," *Trends in cognitive sciences*, 14 no.1 (2010): 7–15.

Foucault, Michel. *Madness and Civilization: A History of Insanity in the Age of Reason,* trans. by R. Howard, (London: Tavistock, 1965).

Fox, Peggy. "Teen girl uses 'crazy strength' to lift burning car off dad," *USA Today,* January 12, 2016. https://www.usatoday.com/story/news/humankind/2016/01/12/teen-girl-uses-crazy-strength-lift-burning-car-off-dad/78675898/

Grazyna, Fosar, and Bludorf, Franz. *Vernetzte Intelligenz.* Aachen, Germany: Omega Verlag, 2001.

Hayslip, Bert, Fruhauf, Christine A., Dolbin-MacNab, Megan L. "Grandparents Raising Grandchildren: What Have We Learned Over the Past Decade?" *The Gerontologist* 59, no. 3 (June 2019): e152–e163, https://doi.org/10.1093/geront/gnx106

Hoeck, Lori, and Wuebker, Betsy. *The Narcissist: A Guide Book.* CreateSpace Independent Publishing Platform (2012).

James, S. E., Herman, J. L., Rankin, S., Keisling, M., Mottet, L., & Anafi, M. *The Report of the 2015 U.S. Transgender Survey.* Washington, DC: National Center for Transgender Equality, 2016.

Kondo, Marie, and Hirano, Cathy, trans. *The Life-Changing Magic of Tidying Up.* Berkeley: Ten Speed Press, 2014.

McMullen, L.M., and K.J. Sigurdson. "Depression is to diabetes as antidepressants are to insulin: the unraveling of an analogy?" *Health Communication* 29, no. 3 (2014): 309–317.

Mineo, Liz. "Harvard study, almost 80 years old, has proved that embracing community helps us live longer, and be happier." *The Harvard Gazette,* April 11, 2017.

Otake, Keiko, Shimai, Satoshi, Tanaka-Matsumi, Junko, Otsui, Kanako, Fredrickson, Barbara L. "Happy People Become Happier Through Kindness: A Counting

Kindnesses Intervention." *Journal of Happiness Studies* 7, no 3 (September 2006): 361–375. https://doi.org/10.1007/s10902-005-3650-z

Park, B.J., Tsunetsugu, Y., Kasetani, T., Kagawa, T., Miyazaki, Y. "The physiological effects of Shinrin-yoku (taking in the forest atmosphere or forest bathing): evidence from field experiments in 24 forests across Japan." *Environmental Health and Preventive Medicine 15 no. 1.* (January 2010): 18–26. https://www.ncbi.nlm.nih.gov/pubmed/19568835

Pratt, Chris. "Chris Pratt's 9 Rules Acceptance Speech | 2018 MTV Movie & TV Awards." Filmed June 16, 2018 in Santa Monica, CA, video, 4:15, https://www.youtube.com/watch?v=EihqXHqxri0.

Pratt, L.A., D.J. Brody, and Q. Gu. "Antidepressant use among persons aged 12 and over: United States, 2011–14." *National Center for Health Statistics Data Brief* no. 283 (2017).

Qaseem, Amir, Snow, Vincenza, Denberg, Thomas D., Forciea, Mary Ann, and Owens, Douglas K. "Using Second-Generation Antidepressants to Treat Depressive Disorders: A Clinical Practice Guideline from the American College of Physicians," *Annals of Internal Medicine* 149, no. 10, (November 2008): 725–33.

Rehfeld, Kathrin, Müller, Patrick, Aye, Norman, Schmicker, Marlen, Dordevic, Milos, Kaufmann, Jörn, Hökelmann, Anita, and Müller, Notger G. "Dancing or Fitness Sport? The Effects of Two Training Programs on Hippocampal Plasticity and Balance Abilities in Healthy Seniors." *Frontiers in Human Neuroscience* 11 (June 15, 2017), https://doi.org/10.3389/fnhum.2017.00305

Saxbe, D. and Repetti, R. L. "For better or worse? Coregulation of couples' cortisol levels and mood states." *Journal of Personality and Social Psychology,* 98 no. 1 (2010), 92–103. https://doi.org/10.1037/a0016959

Sussman, Steven. "Parenting Success - 8:1 ratio of positive to negative interactions." Filmed October 2013 in New Jersey. Video 2:17, https://youtu.be/AIR3KJORHE4

Tomasi, David, Gates, Sheri, and Reyns, Emily. "Positive Patient Response to a Structured Exercise Program Delivered in Inpatient Psychiatry." *Global Advances in Health and Medicine* 8, (2019), https://doi.org/10.1177/2164956119848657

Twenge, Jean M., Thomas E. Joiner, Megan L. Rogers, Gabrielle N. Martin, "Increases in Depressive Symptoms, Suicide-Related Outcomes, and Suicide Rates Among U.S. Adolescents After 2010 and Links to Increased New Media Screen Time," *Clinical Psychological Science* 6, no. 1, (November 2017): 3–17, https://doi.org/10.1177/2167702617723376

Vilhauer, Jennice. "Why you don't get what you want; it's not what you expect." Filmed May 2015 at TEDxPeachtree, Atlanta, GA. Video, 13:13. https://youtu.be/FwLeiY5f7sI

Wolverton, B.C., Johnson, Anne, and Bounds, Keith. *Interior landscape plants for indoor air pollution abatement (Report)*. Stennis Space Center, MS: NASA, 1989.

Yano, Jessica M., Yu, Kristie, Donaldson, Gregory P., Shastri, Gauri G., Liang Ma, Phoebe Ann, Nagler, Cathryn R., Ismagilov, Rustem F., Mazmanian, Sarkis K., and Hsiao, Elaine Y. "Indigenous Bacteria from the Gut Microbiota Regulate Host Serotonin Biosynthesis." *Cell*, 161 no. 2 (2015): 264.

BC Wolverton; WL Douglas; K Bounds (September 1989). Interior landscape plants for indoor air pollution abatement (Report). NASA. NASA-TM-101766.

Acknowledgments

It has been my honor to witness the resilience and skills of my young clients as you grow up navigating this current world. I appreciate every step you take to making it a better place for our future.

This workbook is deeply rooted in the potential and determination that I observe in the people who consult me and in my online audience each and every day. You are incredible and I couldn't have come through my own emotional turmoil without your inspiration. From the bottom of my heart, thank you.

Thank you to Skyhorse Publishing for bringing this message to a larger audience, especially my editor, Kim Lim, who saw I had something to share and invited me to deliver it to the world.

Thank you to my early readers, Ava Byrne, Monique, Nikky El Hares, Trudi Lebrón, Pidge Hood, and Ted Aman, who gave me invaluable feedback. I appreciate that your comments completely up-leveled this book with each draft. Thank you to Joy Evanns, Arriya Kingrey, and John Carlino, who helped me navigate some of the more intense labor pains of birthing this book.

Thank you to my Gen Z focus groups, my parents, friends, siblings, nieces, nephews, my husband and three kids, and Jenny who patiently gave me their opinion about every potential book title in the known Universe. Thank you to Jen Kondziela, Maureen Hood, Christina Solaris, and my Omega Codex family, who sent me encouraging texts to sustain my energy while I was writing.

And finally, thank you to everyone who has stuck by me through thick and thin, holding up a mirror to invite me to be a better version of myself. I am so grateful and deeply love you all. 🐮

About the Author

Natalie Sinisgalli

As a psychotherapist for over 20 years, Jodi shows people how to create practical miracles even in the most difficult times. As an inspirational speaker, she teaches Generation Z, their parents, and helpers how to find their Diamond Confidence so they feel worthy, empowered and in control. In her online videos, she gives audiences all over the world usable tools to get clarity, push past fear, and develop their intuition. Because Jodi clawed her way out of her own emotional turmoil, she totally gets it. As a mom of teens, she double-dog gets it. Through her TEDxWilmington talk, "Calm Anxious Kids," and her bestselling book, *You 1, Anxiety 0*, Jodi is changing the way we understand the current mental health crisis. She generates her own daily happiness through mindfulness, family time, and walking in the woods with her fur-baby, Winston.

Themis
Bar Review

Law School Essentials:
First-Year Review

Civil Procedure
Constitutional Law
Contracts
Criminal Law
Property
Torts

ISBN 978-1-953593-32-0

Themis
Bar Review

Civil Procedure

CIVIL PROCEDURE

Table of Contents

CIVIL PROCEDURE

I. PERSONAL JURISDICTION

A. IN GENERAL

In personam jurisdiction is the power that a court has over an individual party. It is required whenever a judgment is sought that would impose an obligation on a defendant personally. When such personal jurisdiction exists, the court has the authority to issue a judgment against the party, personally, which can be satisfied by seizure of all of the party's assets. Such a judgment is entitled to full faith and credit in other states.

There are three general types of personal jurisdiction: (i) *in personam* jurisdiction, (ii) *in rem* jurisdiction, and (iii) *quasi in rem* jurisdiction.

B. EFFECT OF STATE JURISDICTIONAL STATUTES ON PERSONAL JURISDICTION IN FEDERAL COURT

In general, a federal court does not have nationwide personal jurisdiction. *Omni Capital Int'l, Ltd. v. Rudolph Wolff & Co., Ltd.,* 484 U.S. 97 (1987). Under Rule 4(k)(1)(A) of the Federal Rules of Civil Procedure (which rules are hereinafter cited as Fed. R. Civ. P. xx, or Rule xx), the service of a summons in a federal action establishes personal jurisdiction over a defendant "who is subject to the jurisdiction of a court of general jurisdiction in the state where the district court is located." A federal court must generally determine personal jurisdiction as if it were a court of the state in which it is situated. Thus, a federal court will look to state jurisdictional statutes (*see* § I.C.4., *infra,* regarding long-arm statutes) to determine if it has authority over the parties before it and will be subject to the restrictions imposed on states by the Due Process Clause of the U.S. Constitution.

1. Exceptions

a. Nationwide service of process

A federal court may have national personal jurisdiction for special types of statutorily created actions, such as federal statutory interpleader actions (*see* § VII.B.4., *infra*).

b. "100-mile bulge" rule

Under Rule 4(k)(1)(B), the so-called "100-mile bulge" rule, a federal court has personal jurisdiction over a party who is served within a Unites States judicial district and not more than 100 miles from where the summons is issued, even if state law would otherwise not permit such service. This special rule applies to only two types of parties: a third-party defendant who is joined under Rule 14 (*see* § VII.B.5., *infra*) and a required party who is joined under Rule 19 (*see* § VII.B.2., *infra*).

c. Rule 4(k)(2)

Four conditions must be present for a federal court to have personal jurisdiction under Rule 4(k)(2):

i) The plaintiff's claims must be based on federal law;

ii) No state court could exercise jurisdiction over the defendants;

iii) The exercise of jurisdiction must be consistent with the laws of the United States; and

iv) The exercise of jurisdiction must be consistent with the U.S. Constitution (i.e., there must be "minimum contacts," *see* § I.C.6.a, *infra*).

2. Consent and Waiver

Unlike subject matter jurisdiction, a party may consent to personal jurisdiction. The consent may be express, implied, or by making a voluntary appearance.

An objection to a court's exercise of jurisdiction over persons and things may also be waived by a party. Under Rule 12(b), the defenses of lack of jurisdiction over the person, insufficiency of process, and insufficiency of service of process must be asserted in a responsive pleading, or by motion before a responsive pleading is submitted. A failure to object in accordance with Rule 12 waives the objection. Rule 12(h).

C. BASES FOR IN PERSONAM JURISDICTION

1. Voluntary Presence

If a defendant is voluntarily present in the forum state and is served with process while there, the state will have personal jurisdiction over the defendant. *Burnham v. Superior Court*, 495 U.S. 604 (1990). However, most courts today have two exceptions to this rule. If a plaintiff fraudulently brings a defendant into the state for the purpose of serving process on him, the service will most likely be invalid. A defendant may also be immune if she is merely passing through the state to attend other judicial proceedings.

2. Domicile

If authorized by statute, a state can have jurisdiction over a person who is domiciled within the state, even if the person is temporarily absent from the state. Domicile is established when a person with capacity enters a state with the intent to make that state her home.

3. Consent

Personal jurisdiction can be established by a party's consent. Under Rule 12(b), the defense of lack of personal jurisdiction must be asserted in a responsive pleading or by motion before a responsive pleading is submitted. The failure to timely object to a court's assertion of personal jurisdiction waives the objection. Rule 12(h).

a. Plaintiffs

Plaintiffs are said to have consented to personal jurisdiction by filing the lawsuit.

b. Defendants

1) Express consent

A defendant may agree in advance by contract to submit to the jurisdiction of the court if a lawsuit is brought by the plaintiff. Such contractual consent will not be effective if the court determines that the contract was a contract of adhesion. A defendant may also stipulate to personal jurisdiction once an action is brought. *Petrowski v. Hawkeye-Security Co.*, 350 U.S. 495 (1956). Consent is said to be given when a person authorizes an agent to accept service of process. Usually, a state will require nonresidents doing business in a heavily regulated industry to appoint an agent.

2) Voluntary appearance

Voluntary appearance of the defendant in court automatically subjects the defendant to personal jurisdiction, unless he is present to object to jurisdiction.

The failure to timely and properly challenge personal jurisdiction will be treated as a waiver of that defense and result in a voluntary appearance.

4. Long-Arm Statutes

Most states have enacted statutes that authorize personal jurisdiction over non-residents who engage in some activity in the state or cause some action to occur within the state. In many states, the long-arm statute authorizes jurisdiction to the extent permissible under the Due Process Clause. Thus, a federal court in those states need only determine whether the exercise of personal jurisdiction comports with due process. A few states have enacted statutes of a more limited scope, which confer jurisdiction on the basis of specific activities undertaken in the state (owning property, committing a tort, or entering into a contract to supply goods or services in the state). These statutes, too, must comport with the Due Process Clause.

5. Attachment

Under "Attachment Jurisdiction" (historically a type of quasi in rem jurisdiction), a plaintiff asserting a personal claim against the defendant would use attachment of the property as a device to obtain jurisdiction and satisfy the judgment, if successful. Since *Shaffer v. Heitner,* 433 U.S. 186 (1977), if the claim is not related to the ownership of the property that has been attached, there must be additional minimum contacts between the defendant and the forum state in order to establish jurisdiction.

Shaffer established that when disputes involve the litigants' interests in the property involved in the case, the minimum contacts requirement is apparent and thus satisfied simply because there is a close relationship between the claim and the "attached" property. However, for cases in which the dispute is unrelated to the ownership of the property and no close relationship is formed, in addition to having the property located in the forum state, minimum contacts must be shown to exist between the defendant and the forum state before jurisdiction will apply. Notice and an opportunity to be heard are also constitutionally required.

6. Due Process Requirements

The Due Process Clause also limits a court's exercise of personal jurisdiction over a defendant. In general, due process is satisfied if the non-resident defendant has certain minimum contacts with the forum state such that the maintenance of the action does not offend traditional notions of fair play and substantial justice. *International Shoe Co. v. State of Washington,* 326 U.S. 310 (1945).

> **EXAM NOTE:** When analyzing a personal jurisdiction question, focus on: (i) the contacts the defendant has or had with the forum state and (ii) whether the assertion of jurisdiction by the court would comport with fair play and substantial justice. Whether personal jurisdiction is proper depends on the facts of each case.

a. Minimum contacts

1) Purposeful availment

To warrant the assertion of in personam jurisdiction, a defendant's contacts with the forum state must be purposeful and substantial, such that the defendant should reasonably anticipate (foresee) being taken to court there. Foreseeability depends on whether a defendant recognizes or anticipates that by running his business, he risks being party to a suit in a particular state. *World-Wide Volkswagen Corp. v. Woodson,* 444 U.S. 286 (1980). This is the "purposeful availment" requirement.

There are situations, however, in which it is difficult to discern whether purposeful availment is present. Such is the case when a product is put into the stream of commerce, not necessarily by the manufacturer, but by a party who purchased the product from the manufacturer to use in his product. The manufacturer's product is then put into the stream of commerce. The question remains, did the manufacturer avail himself of the jurisdiction's benefits and laws? The Court has not been able to reach a cohesive answer. In *Asahi*, while four justices found sufficiency with the mere knowledge that the product being sold would end up in the forum state, four other justices believed that the manufacturer needed to take an additional step to have availed itself of the forum. *Asahi Metal Industry Co. v. Superior Court of California*, 480 U.S. 102 (1987).

3) Specific and general jurisdiction

The scope of the contacts necessary for the assertion of personal jurisdiction depends on the relationship that the cause of action has with the forum state.

When a cause of action arises out of or closely relates to a defendant's contact with the forum state, jurisdiction may be warranted over that action even if that contact is the defendant's only contact with the forum state. This type of jurisdiction is often referred to as "specific personal jurisdiction." On the other hand, "general personal jurisdiction" requires that a defendant be domiciled in the state or have continuous and systematic contacts with the forum state. General jurisdiction confers personal jurisdiction even when the cause of action has no relationship with the defendant's contacts with the state. *Helicopteros Nacionales de Colombia, S.A. v. Hall*, 466 U.S. 408 (1984).

3) Suits based on contract

While the fact that one party to a contract is a resident of the forum state will not, by itself, confer personal jurisdiction over the non-resident party to the contract, the existence of the contract can be a significant factor in determining that minimum contacts exist, such that the exercise of personal jurisdiction over the non-resident is appropriate. *Burger King v. Rudzewicz*, 471 U.S. 462 (1985).

a) Choice-of-law provision

If the contract contains a choice-of-law provision indicating that the forum state's law is to be used in any action with regard to the contract, this will be a significant factor in finding jurisdiction, as it establishes that the non-resident purposefully availed itself of the benefits of the forum's laws.

b) Contracts of adhesion or procured by fraud

If the contract is adhesive or was procured through fraud, personal jurisdiction based on the contract would not be appropriate.

4) Intentional torts

Personal jurisdiction may also be proper when a defendant commits an intentional tort in his own state, but the conduct was aimed at the plaintiff in the forum state. When a defendant intentionally harms a forum state resident, a court may apply the "Calder Effects Test," which allows personal jurisdiction over a party whose conduct was expressly aimed at the forum state, knowing that the brunt of the harmful effects would be felt there. *Calder v. Jones*, 465 U.S. 783 (1984).

5) Internet websites

Merely having a website will not subject a defendant to process everywhere that the site can be viewed. Most courts have followed the approach of *Zippo Mfg. Co. v. Zippo Dot Com. Inc.,* 952 F. Supp. 1119 (W.D. Pa. 1997), which bases jurisdiction over a non-resident's website on the degree of interactivity between the website and the forum. The court set forth a sliding-scale approach with regard to the interactivity of websites, ranging from passive sites to those that are integral to the defendant's business.

Merely making a website accessible to the public and posting information is generally considered passive on the sliding scale and should not result in personal jurisdiction. Websites that are integral to a defendant's business, however, are on the other end of the sliding scale. When a website's purpose is to assist in conducting direct business transactions, courts are more likely to find minimum contacts with a state and assert personal jurisdiction.

Courts are struggling with how to draw the lines for sites that are interactive but that do not involve significant commercial activity. The law in this area continues to evolve. Some courts have applied the Calder Effects Test, *supra,* to Internet cases.

6) Imputed contacts

Under some circumstances, the contacts of one defendant with the forum state may be imputed to another defendant for purposes of determining jurisdiction.

a) Employees/independent contractors

Contacts by a non-resident employer's agents or employees are generally imputed to the employer when the agent or employee is acting within the scope of the agency or employment. An out-of-state corporation, though, is generally not subject to personal jurisdiction solely because of contacts in the state by an independent contractor.

b) Partnerships

Each partner is generally an agent of the partnership for the purpose of its business. Accordingly, a partner's activities on behalf of the partnership can confer personal jurisdiction over the partnership entity. Such contacts, though, may not necessarily establish personal jurisdiction over that partner or the other partners of the partnership in their individual capacities.

c) Corporations

An out-of-state corporation's contacts with the forum state will not automatically establish jurisdiction over a wholly owned subsidiary of the corporation, and contacts by a wholly owned subsidiary will not automatically confer jurisdiction over a corporate parent. *Cannon Mfg. Co. v. Cudahy Packing Co.,* 267 U.S. 333 (1925). If, however, the subsidiary is the corporate parent's alter ego or is specifically acting as the corporate parent's agent, its contacts may be imputed to the corporate parent. *Id.*

b. Fair play and substantial justice

Once minimum contacts are established, a court must still examine the facts to determine if maintenance of the action would "offend traditional notions of fair play and substantial justice." *International Shoe, supra.*

Courts consider a variety of factors—sometimes referred to as the "*Asahi* factors"—when making this determination, including:

    i)   The burden on the defendant of appearing in the case;

    ii)   The interest of the forum state in adjudicating the matter;

    iii) The plaintiff's interest in litigating the matter in the forum state;

    iv) The interest of the judicial system in the efficient resolution of controversies; and

    v)   The shared interests of the states in promoting substantive social policies.

Asahi, supra.

7. In Personam Jurisdiction Over Corporations

a. Resident corporations

For in personam jurisdiction purposes, a corporation will be a resident corporation only if it is incorporated in the forum state. Any action may be brought against a corporation that is incorporated in the forum state. If the corporation is not incorporated in the state, then for purposes of in personam jurisdiction it will constitute a foreign corporation.

b. Foreign corporations

The rules of minimum contacts and substantial fairness apply to a foreign corporation. To determine whether the corporation is subject to a state's general jurisdiction, the proper inquiry is whether a corporation's affiliations with the forum state are so "continuous and systematic" as to render the corporation essentially "at home" in the forum state. *Daimler AG v. Bauman*, 571 U.S. 117 (2014). A corporate defendant is always at home in the state of the corporation's place of incorporation and the state of its principal place of business. In exceptional cases, a corporate defendant's operations in another forum may be so substantial and of such a nature as to render the corporation at home in that state as well. *BNSF Ry. v. Tyrrell*, 137 S. Ct. 1549 (2017); *see, e.g., Perkins v. Benguet Consol. Mining Co.*, 342 U.S. 437 (1952) (holding that when a company's president moved to a state where he temporarily kept an office, maintained the company's files, oversaw the company's activities, and conducted directors' meetings, business correspondence, banking stock transfers, and payment of salaries, these continuous and systematic contacts permitted general jurisdiction over the company).

D. JURISDICTION OVER THINGS

Historically, jurisdiction over property has been divided into in rem jurisdiction and quasi in rem jurisdiction.

1. In Rem Jurisdiction

a. Defined

In rem jurisdiction is the authority of a court to determine issues concerning rights in property, either real or personal. It does not include property brought into the state through fraud. Often, no parties are named and the case is known by the name of the property at issue.

b. Due process

While in rem proceedings are commenced against property, they must still satisfy due process requirements for personal jurisdiction because they affect the rights of individuals in the property. In general, for in rem jurisdiction to exist, the property at issue must be present within the forum state. *Shaffer v. Heitner,* 433 U.S. 186 (1977).

Due process is met if the notice is "reasonably calculated, under all the circumstances, to apprise interested parties of the pendency of the action and afford them an opportunity to present their objections." *Mullane v. Central Hanover Bank & Trust Co.,* 339 U.S. 306 (1950). Thus, it is no longer sufficient to simply post the notice on the property or in a newspaper.

2. Quasi In Rem Jurisdiction

a. Defined

While a judgment in rem determines the interests of all persons in particular property, a quasi-in-rem judgment determines only the interests of the parties to the action regarding property located in the forum state. Traditionally, the judgment was not personally binding on the defendant, could not be sued upon in any other court, and could not be enforced by seizing any of the defendant's property other than the property at issue in the quasi-in-rem action.

b. Due process

In a quasi-in-rem action, as with in rem and in personam actions, the defendant whose property is subject to the judgment generally must have sufficient minimum contacts with the forum state to justify the exercise of personal jurisdiction over the matter. *Shaffer v. Heitner,* 433 U.S. 186 (1977). As a consequence, a quasi-in-rem action either can be pursued as an in personam action due to satisfaction of the minimum contacts test or cannot be brought due to lack of personal jurisdiction over the defendant. When the action directly relates to property rights, such as the foreclosure of a mortgage or other lien, the minimum contacts requirement is satisfied because of the relationship between the claim and the property. Provided the owner of the property is given proper notice and an opportunity to be heard, the judgment is personally binding on the defendant. If the defendant chooses not to appear, the judgment of a federal district court is confined to the property that is the subject of the action. 28 U.S.C. § 1655.

When the underlying action does not relate to property rights, but the property instead serves only as the relief sought, such as in a breach of contract action in which the contract does not involve the in-state property, the minimum contacts requirement likely is not satisfied, and the court lacks personal jurisdiction to adjudicate the matter.

c. Limitation

In an action to determine ownership of real or personal property (e.g., removal of a cloud on the title to the property) or to enforce a lien against real or personal property when the property is located within the district, the federal district court has personal jurisdiction over the claimants to the property. 28 U.S.C. § 1655; Rule 4(n)(1). In other in rem or quasi-in-rem actions, jurisdiction can be obtained by a federal district court under the circumstances and in the manner provided by the law of the state in which the federal district court is located, but only if the federal district court, despite the existence of sufficient minimum contacts, cannot acquire personal jurisdiction over the defendant by service of process under the federal rule (Rule 4). As a consequence, quasi-in-rem jurisdiction is generally limited to exigent circumstances, such as when the defendant is a fugitive or the property is in imminent danger of disappearing. Rule 4(n)(2).

II. NOTICE AND SERVICE OF PROCESS

The Due Process Clause of the U.S. Constitution requires that deprivation of property by adjudication be preceded by notice and opportunity for hearing appropriate to the nature of the case. *Mullane v. Central Hanover Bank & Trust Co.,* 339 U.S. 306 (1950).

A. NOTICE

1. Due Process

Due process is met if the notice is "reasonably calculated, under all the circumstances, to apprise interested parties of the pendency of the action and afford them an opportunity to present their objections." *Mullane, supra*.

2. Form

If the identity and address of an interested party are known or obtainable through reasonable efforts, notice through in-person delivery, registered mail, return receipt requested, or some other means likely to notify the particular individual is required. *Mennonite Board of Missions v. Adams,* 462 U.S. 791 (1983). However, if the plaintiff knows that the defendant(s) did not receive notice, the plaintiff cannot proceed unless there are no other reasonable methods to notify the defendant(s). *Jones v. Flowers,* 547 U.S. 220 (2006).

If the identity or address of in interested party is not obtainable through reasonable efforts, other means, such as publication of notice in newspapers, may be satisfactory. The constitutional test is, generally, what is **reasonable under the circumstances.** The standards are less strict for in rem and quasi in rem cases than for in personam cases. When there are multiple defendants, each defendant must be served, but the manner of service will depend on whether their identities and addresses are known or unknown.

In situations when an agent is appointed, either by contract or statute, the defendant will not be subject to personal jurisdiction if the agent did not advise the defendant of service of process. This rule does not apply when the defendant selects his own agent.

3. Court Rules

Satisfying due process is not the only standard for the sufficiency of notice. State and federal courts have procedural rules that dictate the form and service of process. While a particular form of notice may meet due process standards, it must also meet the specific procedural requirements that govern in the court where the action is to be heard. Certified mail, for example, meets due process standards, but not every court system permits it to be used.

4. Opportunity to Be Heard

In addition to requiring notice of the claim being made, due process requires that a defendant be given an opportunity to be heard whenever there is a state-sponsored interference with a defendant's property interest. The state must be an active participant in the interference for due process to apply.

B. SERVICE OF PROCESS

Rule 4 sets forth the procedure for service of process in a federal action, detailing the form, content, method of issuance, methods of service, and time of service of a summons and complaint. In the absence of service of process (or waiver of service by the defendant), a court ordinarily may not exercise power over a party named as a defendant in a complaint. *Murphy Bros., Inc. v. Michetti Pipe Stringing, Inc.,* 526 U.S. 344 (1999).

1. **Who Must Serve**

    Under Rule 4(c), the plaintiff is responsible for serving the summons and complaint upon the defendant. Service may be made by any non-party who is at least 18 years old.

2. **Time Limit for Service**

    Under Rule 4(m), the plaintiff must serve the summons and complaint within 90 days after filing the complaint. If, however, the plaintiff shows "good cause" why service was not timely made, the court must extend the time for service for an appropriate period. When no such showing is made, the court, on motion or on its own after notice to the plaintiff, must dismiss the action without prejudice against the defendant or order that service be made within a specified time. Rule 4(m).

3. **Methods of Service**

    Rule 4 establishes different procedures for service of process depending on whether the defendant is an individual or a corporation, a governmental entity or subdivision, and domestic or foreign.

    a. **Service generally**

        1) **In the United States**

            Pursuant to Rule 4(e)(2), service may be made by:

            i)   Personally serving the summons and complaint on the defendant;

            ii) Leaving the summons and complaint at the defendant's usual place of abode with a person of suitable age and discretion who resides there; or

            iii) Delivering the summons and complaint to an agent appointed by the defendant or otherwise authorized by law to receive service.

        2) **Outside the United States**

            Pursuant to Rule 4(f), service may be effected in any manner, internationally agreed upon, which is reasonably calculated to give notice. If no international agreement exists, or if an international agreement permits service by other means, service on any competent individual outside the United States may be effected by any method permitted by the law of the foreign country.

    b. **Service on minors and incompetents**

        Minors and incompetents in the United States must be served according to the law for serving such a person of the state where service is made. Rule 4(g).

    c. **Service on corporations and associations**

        1) **Inside the United States**

            Pursuant to Rule 4(h), service on a corporation or association in the United States may be effected by delivering the summons and complaint to an officer, managing agent, general agent, or agent appointed or authorized by law to receive process.

If the agent is one authorized by statute and the statute so requires, the plaintiff must also mail a copy of the summons and complaint to the defendant. Rule 4(h)(1)(B).

2) Outside the United States

Service on corporations and associations outside of the United States may be made using any methods available for service on an individual outside the United States, except personal delivery under Rule 4(2)(c)(i).

d. Service on the United States government and its agencies and officers

1) Service on the United States government

Under Rule 4(i)(1), to serve the United States, a party must:

i)   Deliver a copy of the summons and complaint to the U.S. attorney (or a designee) for the district where the action is brought, or send a copy by registered or certified mail to the civil-process clerk at the U.S. attorney's office;

ii) Send a copy by registered or certified mail to the U.S. Attorney General; and

iii) If the action challenges an order of a non-party agency or officer of the United States, send a copy by registered or certified mail to the agency or officer.

2) Service on U.S. agency, officer, or employee sued in an official capacity

Under Rule 4(i)(2), to serve a U.S. agency, officer, or employee only in an official capacity, a party must serve the United States and also send a copy of the summons and complaint by registered or certified mail to the agency, officer, or employee.

3) Service on U.S. officer or employee sued individually

Under Rule 4(i)(3), to serve a U.S. officer or employee in an individual capacity for an act or omission occurring in connection with duties performed on behalf of the United States, a party must serve the United States and also serve the officer or employee under the normal rules for serving an individual.

4. Waiver of Service

Pursuant to Rule 4(d), a competent individual, corporation, or association that is subject to service has a duty to avoid unnecessary expenses of serving the summons by waiving service. The plaintiff may notify such a defendant that an action has been commenced and request that the defendant waive service. The rule does not apply to government entities, infants, or incompetents.

a. Request for waiver

A plaintiff's notice and request for waiver of service must be in writing and be addressed to the individual defendant, or, for a corporation, to an officer, managing or general agent, or any other agent authorized by appointment or by law to receive service of process.

It must be accompanied by a copy of the complaint, two copies of a waiver form, and a prepaid means for returning the form, and it must give the defendant a reasonable time of at least 30 days after the request was sent (or at least 60 days if sent to a foreign defendant) to return the waiver. Rule 4(d)(1).

b. Effect of waiver

Under Rule 4(d)(3), if a defendant timely returns a waiver of service before being served with process, the defendant does not have to serve an answer to the complaint until 60 days after the request was sent, or 90 days after it was sent to a defendant outside a judicial district of the United States. This is an incentive to waive service, because the normal time period in which an answer must be served is 21 days after service of process. Rule 12(a)(1)(A).

Rule 4(d)(5) specifically provides that waiver of service does not waive any objection to personal jurisdiction or to venue.

If the defendant agrees to waive service, the date on which the plaintiff files the waiver form with the court will be deemed the date of service. Rule 4(d)(4). However, the defendant must still answer the complaint within 60 (or 90, if foreign) days from the date on which the notice was sent.

c. Failure to waive service

Under Rule 4(d)(2), if a defendant located within the United States fails, without good cause, to sign and return a waiver requested by a plaintiff located within the United States, the court must impose on the defendant the expenses that are incurred in making service and the reasonable expenses, including attorney's fees, of any motion required to collect such service expenses.

5. Proof of Service

Under Rule 4(l)(1), if formal service is not waived, the process server must submit proof of service to the court. Generally, this will be by an affidavit of the process server. Failure to make proof of service does not affect the validity of the service.

III. SUBJECT MATTER JURISDICTION

A. IN GENERAL

1. Overview

The term "subject matter jurisdiction" refers to a court's competence to hear and determine cases of the general class and subject to which the proceedings in question belong. In order for a federal court to hear and resolve a claim, it must have subject matter jurisdiction over the claim. The four most common congressional grants of subject matter jurisdiction are: (i) diversity jurisdiction; (ii) federal question jurisdiction; (iii) removal jurisdiction; and (iv) supplemental jurisdiction. Each is discussed below.

2. Presumption

A federal court must presume an absence of jurisdiction until it determines that the matter falls within its rightful jurisdiction. The burden is on the party seeking to invoke the court's jurisdiction.

3. Waiver

Subject matter jurisdiction cannot be waived or agreed to by the parties, unlike personal jurisdiction.

4. Objection to Jurisdiction

An objection to subject matter jurisdiction can be presented at any stage of a proceeding, including on appeal. A court may also raise the issue of subject matter jurisdiction *sua sponte*. If the issue of subject matter jurisdiction was not contested, then a judgment may not ordinarily be challenged collaterally on that basis except under special circumstances of egregious abuses of authority or substantial infringements of the authority of another tribunal or government. *See Travelers Indem. Co. v. Bailey,* 129 S. Ct. 2195 (2009) ("The rule is not absolute, and we have recognized rare situations in which subject-matter jurisdiction is subject to collateral attack.").

B. DIVERSITY JURISDICTION

1. Basis

Article III, section 2 of the U.S. Constitution permits Congress to extend federal judicial power to controversies "between citizens of different states … and between a state or the citizens thereof, and foreign states, citizens or subjects." Under § 1332, Congress gave the U.S. district courts jurisdiction over actions when:

i) The parties to an action are:

a) Citizens of different states,

b) Citizens of a state and citizens or subjects of a foreign state,

c) Citizens of different states and citizens or subjects of a foreign state are additional parties, or

d) A foreign state as plaintiff and citizens of a state or different states, and

ii) The amount in controversy in the action exceeds $75,000.

In general, when these requirements are met, a federal court may exercise jurisdiction over the action, regardless of the legal subject of the controversy. This is known as diversity-of-citizenship jurisdiction or, more commonly, diversity jurisdiction.

a. State law exclusions

Two areas of state law are generally excluded from diversity jurisdiction: probate matters (probate of a will or administration of an estate) and domestic relations actions (divorce, alimony, custody disputes).

b. Suit against a foreign state

Under the Foreign Sovereign Immunities Act (FSIA), a suit may not be brought in federal or state court against a foreign state, including a political subdivision or agency or instrumentality of a foreign state, unless an exception applies. Among the exceptions are engaging in a commercial activity, committing a tort in the United States, or seizing property in violation of international law. § 1602-1611.

2. Complete Diversity Requirement

a. Rule of complete diversity

Diversity jurisdiction requires complete diversity between the parties on different sides of the case. There will be no diversity of citizenship if any plaintiff in the case is a citizen of the same state or is a citizen or subject of the same foreign country as any defendant in the case. *Strawbridge v. Curtiss,* 7 U.S. (3 Cranch) 267 (1806). Two plaintiffs in a case may be from the same state without destroying diversity, as long as no plaintiff is from the same state as any defendant in the case.

Note that under § 1332(e), the term "state" includes the District of Columbia, Puerto Rico, and the U.S. territories.

b. Exceptions: minimal diversity

1) Interpleader

The Federal Interpleader Act, 28 U.S.C. § 1335, allows the holder of property that is claimed by two or more persons to deposit the property with a court to determine ownership. Under the act, there need be only two adverse claimants of diverse citizenship to establish federal jurisdiction (i.e., any defendant is diverse from any plaintiff).

2) Class actions greater than $5 million

For certain class actions in which the amount at issue totals more than $5 million, diversity will be met if any member of the plaintiff class is diverse with any defendant. § 1332(d)(2)(A).

3) Multiparty, Multiforum Trial Jurisdiction Act of 2002

Under the Multiparty, Multiforum Trial Jurisdiction Act of 2002, 28 U.S.C. § 1369(a), for a civil action that "arises from a single accident, where at least 75 natural persons have died in the accident at a discrete location," only one plaintiff need be of diverse citizenship from one defendant for a federal court to have diversity jurisdiction, if:

i) A defendant resides in a state and a substantial part of the accident took place in another state or other location, regardless of whether that defendant is also a resident of the state where a substantial part of the accident took place;

ii) Any two defendants reside in different states, regardless of whether such defendants are also residents of the same state or states; or

iii) Substantial parts of the accident took place in different states.

Even if those requirements are met, however, under § 1369(b), the district court must abstain from hearing the case if:

i) The substantial majority of all plaintiffs are citizens of a single state of which the primary defendants are also citizens; and

ii) The claims asserted will be governed primarily by the laws of that state.

The Act also provides:

i) That anyone involved in the accident is permitted to intervene as a plaintiff; and

ii) Nationwide service of process.

c. "Realignment"

In evaluating whether true diversity exists, courts will look beyond the face of the pleadings to determine the "ultimate interests." If necessary, they will "arrange the parties according to their sides in the dispute." *City of Dawson v. Columbia Ave. Sav. Fund. Safe Deposit, Title & Trust Co.*, 197 U.S. 178 (1905). Thus, courts will not allow, for example, a party that is actually aligned with the plaintiff to be named as a defendant in order to present a false diversity. *See id.*

d. Date of determination of diversity

Diversity is determined at the time the case is filed. There is no requirement that diversity exist at the time the cause of action arose. A change in citizenship after the filing of the case will not affect diversity jurisdiction that was in existence at the time of the filing. In addition, a change in the parties as a result of substitution or intervention will not affect diversity jurisdiction.

3. **Determining Party Citizenship**

   a. **Individuals**

   To be a citizen of a state for the purposes of § 1332, an individual must be a citizen of the United States and a domiciliary of the state.

   1) **Domicile**

   In general, an individual is a domiciliary of the state in which she is present and intends to reside for an indefinite period of time.

   a) **Only one domicile**

   An individual can have only one domicile at a time. The presumption is that a place of domicile continues until it is definitively changed, i.e., when a person:

   i)   Establishes presence in the new place; and

   ii) Manifests intent to remain there for an indefinite period. Consequently, a compulsory change of domicile, such as for incarceration or military purposes, will not result in a change in domicile.

   b) **When determined**

   Domicile is determined at the time the action is commenced. Once subject matter jurisdiction has been established, it will not be affected by a party's change of domicile.

   c) **Factors considered**

   Some factors used in determining domicile include whether a party exercises civil and political rights (e.g., registration to vote), pays taxes, owns real and personal property, and is employed in the state.

   2) **Aliens**

   Diversity jurisdiction based on alienage will be found when there are one or more citizens or subjects of a foreign country (aliens) on one side of the lawsuit, and one or more citizens of a state on the other. The foreign parties need not be from different countries from one another to preserve diversity. There is no diversity jurisdiction in an action by one alien against another. Nor is there jurisdiction when an action is between a citizen of a state and an alien admitted into the United States for permanent residence who is domiciled in the same state as the citizen. § 1332(a)(2). The only way aliens may be adversaries in an action without undermining diversity jurisdiction is if there are one or more citizens of a state on both sides of the action as co-parties of the aliens.

   3) **Stateless persons**

   Under the language of § 1332, the presence of a stateless citizen of the United States, an alien who is present in the United States and who is not a citizen of a foreign state, or a U.S. citizen residing abroad would preclude diversity jurisdiction, as these persons are neither citizens of a U.S. state nor citizens or subjects of a foreign country.

4) Minors, incompetents, decedents, and trusts

The legal representative of a minor, an incompetent, or an estate of a decedent will be deemed a citizen of the same state as that minor, incompetent, or decedent. § 1332(c)(2). As to trusts, the old rule was that they were deemed to be a citizen of the same state as the trustee. *See Navarro Savings Assoc. v. Lee,* 446 U.S. 458 (1980). However, this rule has been placed in doubt by *Carden v. Arkoma Associates,* 494 U.S. 185 (1990), which held that the citizenship of unincorporated associations is determined by the citizenship of all of its members. At least one lower federal court has recently applied the *Carden* holding to trusts, holding that *Carden* requires that diversity would be destroyed if, in a suit against a trust, any beneficiary of the trust is a citizen of the same state as a plaintiff. *See Bergeron ex rel. Ridgewood Elec. Power Trust V v. Ridgewood Elec. Power Trust V,* (D. Mass., Jul. 5, 2007).

An unemancipated minor is generally deemed a citizen of the state in which his parents are domiciled. If a minor's parents are not citizens of the same state, then the child will generally be deemed a citizen of the state of the parent who has custody.

5) Class actions

Diversity in a class action brought pursuant to Rule 23 will generally be determined by the citizenship of the named members of the class bringing the lawsuit (referred to as "class representatives"). *See* § VII.B.6, *infra,* for a discussion of class actions under Rule 23.

For certain class actions, however, in which the amount at issue totals more than $5 million, diversity will be met if any member of the plaintiff class is diverse with any defendant. § 1332(d)(2)(A). *See* § III.B.2. *supra.*

b. Business entities

1) Corporations

A corporation may be a party to a diversity action. Under § 1332(c), for purposes of diversity jurisdiction, "a corporation shall be deemed to be a citizen of every State and foreign state by which it has been incorporated and of the State or foreign state where it has its principal place of business." Thus, corporations, unlike individuals, may be citizens of more than one state for diversity purposes, and diversity jurisdiction will be destroyed if any opposing party is a citizen of any of the states in which the corporation has citizenship.

> A pleader does not have the option of alleging that a corporation's citizenship is either its state of incorporation or the state where the principal place of business is located; both states must be listed in the pleading.

a) Incorporation

A corporation's state of incorporation is the state in which the corporate entity is legally established. Every corporation has at least one state of incorporation, and some have multiple states of incorporation. If a corporation is incorporated in more than one state or foreign country, then it is considered a citizen of each state and foreign country in which it is incorporated.

b) Principal place of business

Determining where a corporation maintains its principal place of business is a question of fact more complicated than determining where a corporation is incorporated. A recent Supreme Court decision did away with looking toward where the corporation's actual physical operations were located. Instead, the Court held that principal place of business refers to the "nerve center" or headquarters of the corporation. *Hertz Corp. v. Friend,* 559 U.S. 77 (2010). The nerve center is generally the location from which the high-level officers direct, control, and coordinate the activities of the corporation. Typically, the nerve center is the corporate headquarters.

Unlike with incorporation, which may involve multiple states, a corporation's principal place of business is in only one state or foreign country.

c) Foreign corporations

A foreign corporation will be deemed a citizen of the country in which it is incorporated. In addition, if the foreign corporation also has its principal place of business in the United States, then it will have citizenship in the state where the principal place of business is located.

d) Date of determination

The corporation's citizenship at the time the action is commenced determines jurisdiction.

e) Liability insurers

Under § 1332(c), a special rule applies when a plaintiff allegedly injured by an insured party brings a direct action against the liability insurer. To avoid automatic federal subject matter jurisdiction in cases in which the liability insurer is incorporated or has its principal place of business in a different state from that where the plaintiff is a citizen, § 1332(c) makes the insurer a citizen of the state or foreign country in which its insured is a citizen, in addition to the other states or foreign countries where it has citizenship.

2) Partnerships and other unincorporated associations

a) Generally

In general, unincorporated associations—such as partnerships—are considered citizens of each state in which each of their partners or members is domiciled. Thus, it is possible that a partnership could be a citizen of all 50 states, if it had partners domiciled in every state. This rule holds for both general and limited partnerships; a limited partnership will therefore be a citizen of every state in which its general and limited partners are domiciled. *Carden v. Arkoma Assocs.,* 494 U.S. 185 (1990).

b) Exception

Rule 23.2 provides an exception for actions brought by or against the members of an unincorporated association as a class. If "it appears that the representative parties will fairly and adequately protect the interests of the association and its members," such an action may be maintained. In that case, the citizenship of the representative parties will control for purposes of diversity jurisdiction. Rule 23.2 may not be used merely to create diversity jurisdiction or if the association has the capacity under state law to sue or be sued as an entity.

4. Devices to Create or Destroy Diversity

Under § 1359: "A district court shall not have jurisdiction of a civil action in which any party, by assignment or otherwise, has been improperly or collusively made or joined to invoke jurisdiction of such court."

a. Real party in interest

The real party in interest is the party who has the right to bring a claim and who will benefit from it, even if the plaintiff is someone else.

b. Assignment of claims

When there is a legitimate assignment of a claim, the assignee becomes the real party in interest and its citizenship, as opposed to the assignor's citizenship, will be determinative. For example, when an insurance company pays an insured for damages caused by a third party and sues the third party in a subrogation action, the company's citizenship, and not the insured's citizenship, controls for diversity purposes.

If the assignment is being effected to manufacture or create diversity jurisdiction "collusively," however, under § 1359, diversity jurisdiction will not exist. *See, e.g., Kramer v. Caribbean Mills, Inc.,* 394 U.S. 823 (1969) (assignment to a nominal party having no real interest in the claim is found to be collusive).

c. Failure to name indispensible parties

The parties may not manufacture diversity jurisdiction by failing to join a non-diverse indispensable party. (*See* § VII.B.2., *infra,* regarding the standards for compulsory joinder under Rule 19.)

d. Voluntary change of state citizenship

A party may voluntarily change state citizenship after the accrual of a cause of action, but before the commencement of a lawsuit, and therefore establish or defeat diversity jurisdiction.

A party's motive for changing citizenship is irrelevant. The change of state citizenship must be genuine, however, to be recognized.

e. Substitution versus replacement of parties

Sometimes there is a need to exchange parties to a lawsuit. Two processes are in place to do so depending on the circumstances. Rule 25 allows for the substitution of a party due to death or incompetence. In this case, the substituted party does not have to satisfy the diversity requirement. The original party's citizenship remains intact and controlling.

A similar doctrine exists when a party must be replaced, such as when the wrong party is named in the complaint. Replacement in such instance is possible so long as the replacing party satisfies the diversity requirement.

> Notice the subtle distinction between substitution and replacement. Substitution calls for the substituted party to step into the shoes of the original party, whereas replacement removes one party to the lawsuit to make way for another party.

5. **Amount in Controversy**

   a. **Rule**

   Under § 1332(a), the amount in controversy must exceed the sum or value of $75,000, exclusive of interest, costs, and collateral effects of a judgment. Although interests and costs are excluded from the amount in controversy, attorney's fees may be made part of the amount in controversy if the fees are recoverable by contract or statute. Punitive damages may be permitted to be made part of the amount in controversy. The amount in controversy is determined at the time the action is commenced in federal court, or, if the action has been removed to federal court, at the time of the removal. The party seeking to invoke federal court jurisdiction must allege that the action satisfies the amount-in-controversy requirement.

   In the case of injunctive relief, when it is difficult to assess a dollar amount, the court will examine either the plaintiff's viewpoint to determine the value of the harm or the defendant's viewpoint to assess the cost of complying with the injunction. If the amount under either test exceeds $75,000, then the amount-in-controversy requirement is satisfied.

   > **EXAM NOTE:** Remember that the amount in controversy must **exceed** $75,000; a claim for exactly $75,000 fails.

   b. **Standard of proof**

      1) **Generally**

         In general, a plaintiff's good-faith assertion in the complaint that the action satisfies the amount-in-controversy requirement is sufficient.

         If an alleged amount in controversy is challenged, then the burden is on the party asserting jurisdiction merely to show that it is not a legal certainty that the claim involves less than the statutory amount.

      2) **Reduction of claim after filing**

         If events after the action has been filed reduce the amount in controversy below the statutory minimum, then jurisdiction will not be lost, so long as the original claim was made in good faith. Additionally, if the plaintiff eventually recovers an amount that is less than the statutory jurisdictional amount, then that fact will not render the verdict subject to challenge on appeal for lack of jurisdiction.

   c. **Aggregation of claims**

      1) **By a single plaintiff against a single defendant**

         If the action involves only one plaintiff and one defendant, then the total value of the plaintiff's claims is calculated to determine the amount in controversy.

      2) **By multiple plaintiffs**

         If the action involves multiple plaintiffs, then the value of their claims may be aggregated only if the multiple plaintiffs are enforcing a single title or right in which they have a common or undivided interest.

         If multiple plaintiffs, each having separate and distinct claims, unite for convenience or economy in a single suit, then each plaintiff must separately meet the amount-in-controversy requirement.

3) By a single plaintiff against multiple defendants

The value of a single plaintiff's claims against each defendant may not be aggregated if the claims are separate and distinct. If the defendants are jointly liable to the plaintiff, then aggregation to meet the amount-in-controversy requirement is permissible.

4) Class actions

In general, if any member of the putative class does not have a claim that meets the statutory jurisdictional amount, then the amount-in-controversy requirement will not be met. *Snyder v. Harris*, 394 U.S. 332 (1969); *Zahn v. International Paper*, 414 U.S. 291 (1973).

Note, though, that the Class Action Fairness Act of 2005 amended § 1332(d) to permit aggregation of claims in certain class actions. (See § IV.E.1.e., Class Actions, *infra.*)

Additionally, when at least one representative plaintiff in a putative class action has a claim that meets the statutory jurisdictional amount, other persons with claims that do not meet the jurisdictional amount can be made part of the class under the doctrine of supplemental jurisdiction. *Exxon Mobil Corp. v. Allapattah Servs., Inc.*, 545 U.S. 546 (2005). (*See* § I.D. Supplemental Jurisdiction, *infra.*)

6. Refusal to Exercise Jurisdiction

Even when jurisdiction is otherwise proper under § 1332, a federal court can refuse to exercise its jurisdiction in a particular matter under the abstention doctrine. This may be proper when a case involving the same parties is currently pending in another court, if the case involves issues of state law that the states should rule upon first, if the state court may have a greater understanding in a complex area of state law, or when parallel litigation is pending in another court.

C. FEDERAL QUESTION JURISDICTION

1. Basis

Article III, Section 2 of the U.S. Constitution provides that federal judicial power shall extend to all cases "arising under this Constitution, the Laws of the United States, and Treaties made, or which shall be made, under their Authority." This constitutional provision authorizes Congress to give federal courts such jurisdiction. Today, the congressional grant of federal question jurisdiction is codified at 28 U.S.C. § 1331, which provides: "The district courts shall have original jurisdiction of all civil actions arising under the Constitution, laws, or treaties of the United States."

2. Concurrent versus Exclusive Jurisdiction

State and federal courts have concurrent jurisdiction of federal question claims, except when Congress expressly provides that jurisdiction of the federal courts is exclusive, as it has with cases under the Securities and Exchange Act of 1934, patent cases, and bankruptcy proceedings.

3. Scope: Essential Federal Element

There is no uniform, bright-line standard for determining whether an action arises under the Constitution, laws, or treaties of the United States. In general, if the cause of action in question is expressly created by federal law, and federal law provides the underlying right, then federal question jurisdiction will exist. If a right is created by federal law, and a cause of action may fairly be implied and was intended by Congress, then federal jurisdiction is likely to be found. If the cause of action is neither expressly nor implicitly created by federal law, then the complaint must involve a real and substantial issue of federal law, and its determination must necessarily depend on resolution of the federal issue. A federal corporation (corporate entity incorporated through an act of Congress) does not, simply by being a federal corporation, have federal jurisdiction. However, if the United States owns more than 50 percent of the corporation's capital stock, then the corporate entity will be considered a federal agency and may then be sued in federal court.

Federal law includes the U.S. Constitution, federal statutes, federal administrative regulations, and U.S. treaties. State laws incorporating standards of federal law are not considered laws of the United States for the purposes of § 1331. *See Merrell Dow Pharmaceuticals, Inc. v. Thompson,* 478 U.S. 804 (1986). *Merrell Dow* held that when a substantive federal statute (e.g., the FDCA) does not provide a federal remedy, then an alleged violation of that statute as an element of a state law complaint does not automatically establish § 1331 jurisdiction. Rather, federal courts have discretion to determine whether a federal issue or interest is important enough in a specific case to justify the exercise of jurisdiction. If a state-law claim necessarily raises a federal issue, actually disputed and substantial, that may be entertained without disturbing any congressionally approved balance of federal and state responsibilities, federal question jurisdiction exists, notwithstanding the absence of an express federal remedy. *Grable & Sons Metal Products, Inc. v. Darue Engineering & Manufacturing,* 545 U.S. 308 (2005).

4. Well-Pleaded Complaint

Federal question jurisdiction exists only when the federal law issue is presented in the plaintiff's complaint. This is the "well-pleaded complaint" rule.

a. Consider only elements of the claim, not defenses

Under the rule, the determination of jurisdiction must be made by considering only the necessary elements of the plaintiff's cause of action, and not potential defenses. It is not sufficient to establish jurisdiction that a plaintiff alleges some anticipated federal law defense. *Louisville & Nashville Railroad v. Mottley,* 211 U.S. 149 (1908). The federal question must appear on the face of the complaint. Thus, an action for declaratory relief, which by its nature anticipates future action or infringement of rights, cannot be brought under federal question jurisdiction unless it provides relief that is not available under state law. *See Skelly Oil Co. v. Phillips Petroleum Co.,* 339 U.S. 667 (1950).

b. Do not consider answers and counterclaims

Answers and counterclaims are also not considered in determining the existence of federal question jurisdiction.

c. Original and removal jurisdiction

The well-pleaded complaint rule applies both to the original jurisdiction of the federal court and to removal jurisdiction.

5. No Amount-in-Controversy Requirement

Unlike for federal diversity jurisdiction, federal question jurisdiction has no amount-in-controversy requirement.

D. REMOVAL JURISDICTION

1. Basis

Under 28 U.S.C. § 1441(a), any civil action commenced in a state court that is within the original jurisdiction of a U.S. district court may generally be removed by the defendant to the district court for the district and division in which the state court action is pending.

The right of removal is a right of the defendant only and is not available to a plaintiff defending a counterclaim that could have originally been brought in federal court. Note that removal jurisdiction is not a substitute for either federal question or diversity jurisdiction, but it is simply a mechanism by which defendants in a state action over which a federal court otherwise has subject matter jurisdiction can get the action into federal court.

a. Removal to another district or division within the same state

The removal statute specifically requires the case to be removed to the district court for the **district and division** in which the state court action is pending. Consequently, a case that is removed to a district court that is within the state but outside the district or division of the original state court is subject to a motion to remand. *Addison v. N.C. Dep't of Crime & Pub. Safety*, 851 F. Supp. 214 (M.D.N.C. 1994). However, since this requirement has been characterized as procedural rather than jurisdictional, some courts have transferred the case to the proper federal court instead of remanding it to the state court. *E.g., Butler v. N.C. DOT*, 154 F. Supp. 3d 252 (M.D.N.C. 2016).

2. Determination

In general, the right of removal is determined by the pleadings filed as of the time of the filing of the petition of removal. In diversity cases, however, diversity must exist at the time of filing the original action as well as at the time the notice of removal is filed, unless the plaintiff dismisses a party who would have destroyed diversity jurisdiction. In other words, removal is permitted when a party who prevents diversity jurisdiction is dismissed from an action.

The federal court to which the action is removed is not precluded from hearing and determining any claim in the action because the state court from which the action was removed did not have jurisdiction over that claim. § 1441(f).

3. Other Removal Statutes

While § 1441 sets forth the general rule regarding removal, other statutes authorize removal in specific cases, including:

i) Suits against the United States, any federal agency, or federal officers for acts under color of office (§ 1442);

ii) Suits against federal employees for injuries caused from their operation of a motor vehicle within the scope of their employment (§ 2679(d)); and

iii) Actions involving international banking (12 U.S.C. § 632).

In addition, certain statutes **prohibit** removal for otherwise removable actions, including:

i) Actions arising under the Federal Employers' Liability Act (FELA) and under the Jones Act against a railroad or its receivers or trustees (§ 1445(a));

ii) Actions against carriers for delay, loss, or damage in shipments, when the amount in controversy does not exceed $10,000 (§ 1445(b));

iii) Actions arising under the workers' compensation laws of the state in which the action is brought (§ 1445(c)); and

iv) Actions arising under section 40302 of the Violence Against Women Act of 1994.

4. Limitation on Removal in Diversity Cases

If removal is sought solely based on diversity jurisdiction, then the claim may be removed only if no defendant is a citizen of the state in which the action was filed. § 1441(b). There is no similar requirement for removal based on federal question jurisdiction or for the removal of class actions.

Example: If a Texas corporation sues Illinois defendants in Illinois state court, then the Illinois defendants are not permitted to remove the action to federal court based on diversity jurisdiction.

5. Removal of Separate and Independent Claims in a Federal Question Jurisdiction Case

If removal is sought on the basis of federal question jurisdiction, and the federal question claims in the state action are joined with claims that are not independently removable, then the entire case may be removed. The district court must then sever and remand to the state court any claims in which state law predominates. § 1441(c). This provision is of questionable validity because federal courts lack supplemental jurisdiction over state law claims that are "separate and independent" from claims that are independently removable.

6. Procedure

a. Notice of removal

1) Generally

Under 28 U.S.C. § 1446, a defendant who wants to remove a state court action to federal district court must file a notice of removal with the district court within 30 days after receipt by or service on that defendant of the initial pleading or summons. The notice must be:

i) Signed pursuant to Rule 11 (*see* § VI.H. Rule 11, *infra*) and contain a short and plain statement of the grounds for removal;

ii) Filed in the district court for the district and division in which the state action is pending; and

iii) Accompanied by copies of all process, pleadings, and orders served on the defendants seeking removal.

In general, all defendants who have been properly joined and served are required to join in or consent to the removal. If the defendants are served at different times and a later-served defendant files a notice of removal, then any earlier-served defendant may join in the removal even though that defendant did not previously initiate or consent to removal. § 1446(b). In cases of removal based on federal question jurisdiction, only those defendants against whom the federal claim is asserted must join in or consent to the removal. § 1441(c)(2). In addition, a class action based on the Class Action Fairness Act of 2005 (CAFA) may be removed by any defendant without the consent of all defendants. § 1453(b).

2) Removal based on diversity

A matter cannot be removed based on diversity of citizenship more than one year after the action is commenced. This one-year rule does not apply, however, if the district court finds that the plaintiff has acted in bad faith (such as by deliberately failing to disclose the actual amount in controversy) to prevent a defendant from removing the action. § 1446(c).

If removal is based on diversity and the plaintiff (i) seeks nonmonetary relief, (ii) is not required under state law to demand a specific sum, or (iii) is permitted by state law to recover more than the amount demanded, then the notice of removal may assert that the amount in controversy exceeds $75,000, and the district court will have jurisdiction if it finds, by a preponderance of the evidence, that the amount does exceed $75,000. A defendant's notice of removal need include only a plausible allegation that the amount in controversy exceeds $75,000; it does not need to contain evidentiary submissions. *Dart Cherokee Basin Operating Co. v. Owens*, 574 U.S. ____, 135 S. Ct. 547 (2014).

b. Additional requirements

Promptly after the notice of removal is filed with the district court, the defendants must give written notice of the filing to all adverse parties and file a copy of the notice of removal with the clerk of the state court from which the action is sought to be removed. § 1446(d).

Once a copy of the removal notice is filed with the state court, the removal acts as a stay of the state court proceedings. The state court is not allowed to take any further action with regard to the case and can be enjoined by the federal court if it does take any action.

c. Procedure in district court following removal

Once the action is removed, procedure follows the Federal Rules of Civil Procedure. New pleadings are not required unless the court orders otherwise. Pleadings filed before removal can be amended pursuant to the federal rules.

The district court may issue all necessary orders and processes to bring before it all proper parties, regardless of whether those parties had been served by process issued by the state court. § 1447(a). If the action was removed before each defendant had been served with process, or if service of process was defective, then service of process can be completed or new process issued in the same manner as in cases originally filed in district court. § 1448.

State court orders issued before removal to district court remain in effect but are subject to district court modification when necessary. § 1450.

7. Remand

a. For lack of subject matter jurisdiction

If at any time before final judgment it appears that the district court lacks subject matter jurisdiction, then the case must be remanded to the state court from which it came. § 1447(c).

b. For other reasons

A party must make any motion to remand the case on the basis of any defect other than lack of subject matter jurisdiction within 30 days after the filing of the notice of removal. § 1447(c).

c. Burden of proof

If the propriety of the removal is challenged, then the burden of establishing proper removal is on the party who removed the case.

d. Costs and attorney's fees

The district court's order remanding the case may require payment of costs, including attorney's fees, incurred as a result of the removal. § 1447(c). The Supreme Court has held that, absent unusual circumstances, federal courts may award attorney's fees under § 1447(c) only when the removing party lacked an objectively reasonable basis for seeking removal. *Martin v. Franklin Capital Corp.,* 546 U.S. 132 (2005).

e. Procedure

A certified copy of the remand order must be mailed by the district court clerk to the clerk of the state court. The state court may thereafter proceed with the case. § 1447(c).

f. Not generally appealable

Under § 1447(d), a remand order is generally not reviewable on appeal or otherwise, with the following exceptions:

i) There is statutory exception for an order remanding a civil rights case removed pursuant to § 1443; or

ii) A remand order is also appealable in a class action, if the application for review is made to the court of appeals not more than ten days after the entry of the order.

g. Discretion to remand when proposed joinder would destroy diversity jurisdiction

Under § 1447(e), if, after removal, the plaintiff seeks to join a defendant who would destroy the federal court's diversity jurisdiction, the court has discretion to deny the joinder and proceed with the action in federal court, or to permit the joinder and remand the action to state court.

E. SUPPLEMENTAL JURISDICTION

1. In General

A district court with jurisdiction may exercise "supplemental jurisdiction" over additional claims over which the court would not independently have subject matter jurisdiction (usually state law claims against a non-diverse defendant) but that arise out of a **"common nucleus of operative fact"** such that all claims should be tried together in a single judicial proceeding. *United Mine Workers v. Gibbs,* 383 U.S. 715 (1986).

2. Federal Question Jurisdiction Cases

When the district court's subject matter jurisdiction for a claim is based on the existence of a federal question, additional claims against the same party can be heard by the court through the exercise of supplemental jurisdiction if the "common nucleus of operative fact" test is met.

Example 1: Plaintiff sues Defendant, her corporate employer, in federal court under Title VII for sex discrimination and retaliation, matters over which the court has federal question jurisdiction. Plaintiff then seeks to sue Defendant for assault and battery under state law, a claim that arises under the same operative facts that applied to her

Title VII claim. The federal court has discretion to exercise supplemental jurisdiction over the assault and battery claim.

Similarly, a district court may have supplemental jurisdiction over claims that involve the joinder or intervention of additional parties over which the court would not otherwise have jurisdiction if the claims involving the additional parties satisfy the "common nucleus of operative fact" test. Such jurisdiction in the past was referred to as "pendent party jurisdiction."

Example 2: Plaintiff sues Defendant 1, her corporate employer, in federal court under Title VII for sex discrimination and retaliation, matters over which the court has federal question jurisdiction. Plaintiff then seeks to sue Defendant 2, her direct supervisor, for assault and battery, a claim that arises under the same operative facts that applied to her Title VII claim against the corporate employer. The federal court could exercise supplemental jurisdiction over the assault and battery claim against the supervisor.

Dismissal of a federal claim on the merits does not preclude a federal court from exercising supplemental jurisdiction over the state claim.

3. Diversity Jurisdiction Cases

When a district court has diversity jurisdiction over a claim, the "common nucleus of operative facts" rule also applies to determine whether the court can exercise supplemental jurisdiction over an additional claim.

a. Permissive joinder

Although the additional claim is **not required to satisfy the amount-in-controversy requirement** for purposes of supplemental jurisdiction, when the additional claim is asserted by a plaintiff seeking to join the action under Rule 20 (permissive joinder), the addition of that party cannot result in a violation of the requirement for **complete diversity of citizenship.**

Example 1: Plaintiff 1, a citizen of Pennsylvania, brings a negligence action in federal court for $500,000 against Defendant, a citizen of New York, based on an automobile accident. Plaintiff 2, also a citizen of Pennsylvania and a passenger in Plaintiff 1's car at the time of the accident, seeks to join Plaintiff 1's action, by filing a negligence claim against Defendant for $30,000. While diversity jurisdiction does not exist for Plaintiff 2's claim because it does not satisfy the $75,000 amount-in-controversy requirement, the court can exercise supplemental jurisdiction over that claim because it meets the "common nucleus of operative facts" test.

Example 2: Assume for this example the same facts as those in Example 1 except that Plaintiff 2 is a citizen of New York. The federal court cannot exercise supplement jurisdiction over Plaintiff 2's claim because the presence of Plaintiff 2 would defeat the requirement for complete diversity.

b. Counterclaims

A counterclaim may be asserted by a defendant against a plaintiff without satisfying the jurisdictional amount when the counterclaim is compulsory. A permissive counterclaim does not qualify for supplementary jurisdiction and therefore must satisfy the jurisdictional amount.

c. Cross-claims

A cross-claim may be asserted by a defendant against another defendant or by a plaintiff against another plaintiff if the cross-claim arises out of the same transaction or occurrence as the initial claim, without regard to the amount in controversy or the citizenship of the parties to the cross-claim as long as the court has subject matter jurisdiction.

d. Precluded claims in diversity cases

Under § 1367(b), in actions where the original jurisdiction of the federal court is based solely on diversity jurisdiction, supplemental jurisdiction is precluded for:

i)   Claims by existing plaintiffs (but not defendants) against persons made parties under one of the following Federal Rules of Civil Procedure: 14 (impleader), 19 (compulsory joinder), 20 (permissive joinder), or 24 (intervention); and

ii) Claims by persons to be joined as plaintiffs pursuant to Rule 19 or claims by persons seeking to intervene as plaintiffs pursuant to Rule 24, in which the exercise of supplemental jurisdiction over such claims would be inconsistent with the requirements for diversity jurisdiction under 28 U.S.C. § 1332.

> **Example 1:** Plaintiff, a citizen of Iowa, sues Defendant, a Nebraska corporation, in federal court under diversity jurisdiction for the wrongful death of Plaintiff's husband. Defendant then impleads Contractor, a citizen of Iowa, under Rule 14, alleging that if Defendant is liable to Plaintiff, then Contractor must indemnify Defendant for any liability to Plaintiff. If Plaintiff then asserts a claim directly against Contractor, because they are both citizens of the same state (Iowa), supplemental jurisdiction in federal court will not apply to the claim, as it would be inconsistent with the requirements for diversity jurisdiction pursuant to § 1367(b). Note that if Defendant's claim against Contractor is for more than $75,000, it would fall within the court's diversity jurisdiction. If the amount were $75,000 or less, Defendant's claim against Contractor would fall within the federal court's supplemental jurisdiction, as it is derived from the same operative facts being considered by the court under the claim over which it has original jurisdiction and is not precluded by § 1367(b).

> **Example 2:** Plaintiff, a citizen of Arkansas, sues Defendant 1 and Defendant 2, both citizens of Oklahoma, in federal court on the basis of diversity jurisdiction, alleging negligence. Defendant 1 seeks to assert a cross-claim for negligence, under the same operative facts, pursuant to Rule 13(g), against Defendant 2. Although there would be no original jurisdiction in federal court for the cross-claim, because Defendant 1 and Defendant 2 are citizens of the same state (Oklahoma) (*see* § III.B.2, *supra*), the federal court could exercise supplemental jurisdiction over the cross-claim, as it is derived from the same operative facts being considered by the court under the claim over which it has original jurisdiction, and it is not excluded under § 1367(b).

4. Discretionary Rejection of Supplemental Jurisdiction

Under § 1367(c) a district court has discretion to decline to exercise supplemental jurisdiction over a claim that would otherwise qualify for supplemental jurisdiction in each of the following circumstances:

i)   The supplemental claim raises a novel or complex issue of state law;

ii) The supplemental claim substantially predominates over the claims within original federal jurisdiction;

iii) All of the claims within the court's original jurisdiction have been dismissed; or

iv) In exceptional circumstances, when there are other compelling reasons for declining jurisdiction.

IV. VENUE

A. IN GENERAL

Sometimes a court may have the power to hear a case (subject matter jurisdiction), but it may not be the proper district to adjudicate the matter. Venue concerns which court among the courts having personal and subject matter jurisdiction is the proper forum for hearing the matter. For cases in federal court, the issue is determining the proper federal judicial district in which a trial should occur. Venue requirements are statutory and are intended to ensure the parties a fair and convenient forum for litigating their dispute.

B. LOCAL AND TRANSITORY ACTIONS

The common law created a distinction between local and transitory actions for purposes of venue. In general, local actions involve title to property and must be brought in a court where the property is located. Transitory actions involve a cause of action based on events that could have taken place anywhere. Many state venue statutes continue to apply this distinction; however, in federal court, local actions and transitory actions are now subject to the same venue provisions.

C. VENUE IN STATE COURT

The requirements of venue in state court actions are established by statute. State venue statutes vary as to what factors determine venue. In many statutes, venue will be proper in the county or judicial district where the defendant resides. Other bases for venue include the location where the cause of action arose or the location of real property to which the title is at issue.

D. VENUE IN FEDERAL COURT

Venue in federal court actions is generally governed by § 1391.

1. General Venue Rule

In general, venue is proper in only one of the following judicial districts:

i) A judicial district in which any defendant resides, if all defendants reside in the same state in which the district is located; or

ii) A judicial district in which a "substantial part of the events or omissions" on which the claim is based occurred, or where a "substantial part of the property" that is the subject of the action is located.

If there is otherwise no judicial district in which the action may be brought, venue is proper in a judicial district in which any defendant is subject to personal jurisdiction with respect to such action. § 1391.

2. Residence

a. Natural person

For venue purposes, a natural person, including an alien lawfully admitted for permanent residence into the United States, is deemed to reside in the judicial district where that person is domiciled. § 1391(c)(1).

b. Business entities

Under § 1391(c)(2), an entity with the capacity to sue and be sued, regardless of whether incorporated, is deemed to reside, if a defendant, in any judicial district in which the entity is subject to personal jurisdiction with respect to the civil action in question. If the entity is a plaintiff, it is deemed to reside only in the judicial district in which it maintains its principal place of business. In a state that contains multiple judicial districts and in which a defendant corporation is subject to personal jurisdiction at the time the action is commenced, the corporation "shall be deemed to reside in any district in that State within which its contacts would be sufficient to subject it to personal jurisdiction if that district were a separate State." If there is no such district, then the corporation will be deemed to reside in the district with which it has the most significant contacts.

> **Example:** X Corporation is incorporated in Delaware, has its principal place of business in Colorado, and maintains a regional sales office in Orlando, Florida (U.S. Middle District Court in Florida), but it conducts no activities anywhere else in Florida. If X Corporation is sued, for federal venue purposes it will reside in the District of Delaware, the District of Colorado, and the Middle District of Florida. Note that Corporation X would not be a resident for federal venue purposes of any other judicial district in Florida.

> **EXAM NOTE:** Keep in mind that this "entity" approach is taken only for venue purposes. It does not apply for the purposes of determining diversity jurisdiction, when a partnership or unincorporated association is considered a citizen of each state in which each of its partners or members is domiciled.

c. Nonresident of the United States

A defendant who is not a resident of the United States may be sued in any judicial district, but the joinder of such a defendant is disregarded when determining proper venue with respect to other defendants. § 1391(c)(3).

3. Special Venue Provisions

There are some provisions for special rules for venue in specific types of cases.

a. Federal officials

Under § 1391(e), actions against officers or employees of the United States or its agencies acting in their official capacity or under color of legal authority may be commenced in a judicial district in which:

i) A defendant in the action resides;

ii) A substantial part of the events or omissions giving rise to the claim occurred, or a substantial part of property that is the subject of the action is situated; or

iii) The plaintiff resides, if no real property is involved in the action.

b. Cases removed from state court

Under § 1441(a), in cases that are removed from state court, venue is automatically proper in the federal district court in the district where the state action was pending. It is immaterial that venue would not have been proper if the action had been brought initially in that district.

c. Cases brought under the Federal Tort Claims Act

Under § 1402(b), venue in a case brought under the Federal Tort Claims Act is proper either in the judicial district where the plaintiff resides or in the judicial district where the act or omission occurred.

4. **Objection to Venue**

An objection to venue, unlike an objection regarding subject matter jurisdiction, may be waived by the parties, and it will be automatically waived if not asserted in a timely manner, i.e., raised in a pre-answer motion to dismiss under Rule 12(b)(3) or in the first responsive pleading, if a motion under Rule 12(b)(3) was not filed.

E. CHANGE OF VENUE IN FEDERAL COURT

1. Change of Venue When Original Venue Is Proper

Under § 1404(a), "[f]or the convenience of parties and witnesses, in the interest of justice, a district court may transfer any civil action to any other district or division where it might have been brought or to any district or division to which all parties have consented." This transfer may be ordered upon motion of the parties or by the court on its own initiative, but it is available only when the jurisdiction and venue of the court considering the issue are proper. The burden of proof with regard to the motion rests on the party seeking the transfer.

a. Diversity cases

In diversity cases, if the motion for change of venue is granted or the court transfers the case on its own initiative, the district court to which the case is transferred must apply the law that would have been applied in the district court that transferred the case. *Ferens v. John Deere Co.,* 494 U.S. 516 (1990).

b. Federal question cases

In federal question cases when transfer is to a district court in another appellate circuit, the district court to which the case is transferred will apply the federal law as interpreted by its Court of Appeals and not the interpretation of the Court of Appeals in which the district court that transferred the matter is located.

c. Forum selection clause

When transfer is sought on the basis of a forum selection clause in a contract, the clause is generally a significant, but not determinative, factor; when the contract is international, the clause is determinative, unless the party attacking venue can show that the clause's application would be unreasonable, unfair, or unjust. *M/S Bremen v. Zapata Off-Shore Co.,* 407 U.S. 1 (1972).

d. No personal jurisdiction

Even in situations in which the court lacks personal jurisdiction over the defendant, the court is not barred from transferring a case to a different venue. § 1404(a).

2. Change of Venue When Original Venue Is Improper

Under § 1406(a), if venue in a case is improper, the district court must dismiss the case, or "if it be in the interest of justice," transfer the case to any district or division in which it could have been brought. Under § 1406(b), if no timely objection is made to venue, nothing prevents the district court from maintaining jurisdiction over the case.

a. Diversity cases

In diversity cases transferred for improper venue under § 1406(a), the district court to which the case is transferred will apply the choice-of-law rules of the state in which it is located, as opposed to the state law of the district court that transferred the case.

b. Federal question cases

In federal question cases transferred for improper venue under § 1406(a), the district court to which the case is transferred will apply the interpretation of federal law in its Circuit Court of Appeals.

3. Transfer to Another Division in the Same District

Under § 1404(b), on motion or by stipulation of all parties, a case may be transferred to a different division within a judicial district at the discretion of the court.

F. FORUM NON CONVENIENS

This doctrine allows a court to dismiss an action—even if personal jurisdiction and venue are otherwise proper—if it finds that the forum would be too inconvenient for parties and witnesses and that another, more convenient, venue is available.

1. Federal Court

In the federal courts, the doctrine has had only limited application since the enactment of § 1404(a), which provides for discretionary transfer based on convenience when venue is proper. In general, the doctrine of forum non conveniens is now used in federal court only when the forum that is deemed most appropriate for the action is a state court or a foreign court, to which § 1404(a) would not apply.

2. State Courts

In state courts, the common-law doctrine continues to apply. Some of the factors that are generally considered include the availability of an alternative forum; the law that will apply; and the location of the parties, witnesses, and evidence. When the doctrine of forum non conveniens is invoked, it is generally the defendant whose convenience is being respected, since the plaintiff has usually indicated his own convenience in the original choice of forum.

V. CHOICE OF LAW: THE ERIE DOCTRINE

A. IN GENERAL

When an action is commenced in U.S. district court, the court must determine the substantive law and rules of procedure that will govern the action.

1. Federal Question Claim

If the action is a federal question claim, federal substantive and procedural law will control.

2. Federal Diversity Claim

a. Substantive law

In a diversity action, the district court is required to apply the substantive state law that would be applied by the state in which the district court is located. *Erie Railroad Co. v. Tompkins,* 304 U.S. 64 (1938).

b. Procedure

1) Applicable federal law

With regard to procedure in a diversity action, however, if a procedural issue is addressed by a valid federal law (a statute, Federal Rule of Civil Procedure, Federal Rule of Evidence, etc.), the federal law will be applied, even if a state rule or statute is in conflict. *Hanna v. Plumer,* 380 U.S. 460 (1965).

2) No applicable federal law

If no federal law applies, the general rule is that the district court must follow state law with regard to substance, but it can choose to ignore state law with regard to procedure, under certain circumstances.

The determination of substance versus procedure and the circumstances under which state procedural law must be followed or may be ignored are discussed below.

3) Other claims

The same rules that apply when a federal court hears a federal diversity claim apply when federal courts hear pendent state claims or state-law counterclaims, cross-claims, and third-party claims that arise in federal cases.

B. SUBSTANCE VERSUS PROCEDURE

1. Analytical Approach

It is sometimes difficult to determine if an issue involves substance or procedure for the purposes of applying the *Erie* doctrine. The following general approach is often used:

i) The district court will start by determining whether there is a **conflict between state and federal law** with respect to the issue before the court. If no conflict exists, then the analysis does not need to proceed any further because the court can apply state and federal law harmoniously to the issue.

ii) If, however, the applicable state and federal laws do conflict, the district court must ask whether a **valid federal statute** or Federal Rule covers the disputed issue. *Hanna, supra.*

    a) If there is a **valid federal statute** or rule of procedure on point, the district court must **apply federal law** rather than state law.

    b) If no federal statute or rule is on point, then the court must determine whether federal common law, rather than state law, should be applied. In making this determination with respect to federal common law, the district court will ask whether the **failure to apply state law will lead to forum shopping and an inequitable administration of the laws.** These are the "twin aims" of *Erie*. *Hanna, supra.*

        1) If the answer is no, then the district court will generally apply federal common law, rather than state law.

        2) If the answer is yes, the court will apply the state law, unless affirmative countervailing federal interests are at stake that warrant application of federal law.

    c) The court may also choose to examine the issue by weighing the interests of the state and federal judiciaries and applying the law whose policy is of greater importance. *Byrd v. Blue Ridge Rural Elec. Co-op., Inc.,* 356 U.S. 525 (1958). If there are strong federal policy interests at stake, the court may choose to apply federal law, notwithstanding a finding that one or both of the twin aims of *Erie* might be implicated.

    d) Finally, the court may ask whether the **failure to apply state law will lead to different outcomes** in state and federal court. *Guar. Trust Co. v. York,* 326 U.S. 99 (1945). Again, if the answer is no, the district court will generally apply federal common law, rather than state law, but if the answer is yes, the court may decide to apply state law.

> In *Gasperini v. Center for the Humanities,* 518 U.S. 415 (1996), the Supreme Court interpreted a Federal Rule extremely narrowly in order to protect an important state interest, while purporting to follow the Court's decision in *Hanna.* While the decision seemed to balance state and federal interests rather than simply apply the Federal Rule, it is unclear whether the Court in *Gasperini* altered existing law.

2. Substantive Law

Examples of specific areas of law that have been held to be substantive rather than procedural include the following.

a. Elements of a claim or defense

The elements of a claim or defense in contract or tort, for example, are considered substantive and are generally controlled by state law in a federal diversity action.

b. Statutes of limitations and tolling provisions

The Supreme Court has indicated that state statutes of limitations and the rules for tolling state statutes of limitations are substantive in nature and are thus applicable in diversity. *Guaranty Trust Co., supra.*

c. Burden of proof

The specification of the applicable standards of proof is considered a substantive matter, and the law of the forum state will govern in a diversity case. *Bank of America Nat. Trust & Sav. Ass'n v. Parnell,* 352 U.S. 29 (1956).

3. Procedural Law

Examples of areas of law that have been determined to be procedural, rather than substantive, include the following.

a. Judge-jury allocation

If there is a jury in a diversity case on a state law claim, the jury, rather than a judge, will decide all factual issues in the case, regardless of whether state law would provide otherwise. *Byrd, supra.*

b. Assessment of attorney's fees

In a diversity case on a state law claim, the federal court may properly use its inherent power to assess attorney's fees as a sanction for a defendant's bad-faith conduct during the litigation, even if the law of the forum state provides that attorney's fees may not be awarded to a successful party. *Chambers v. NASCO, Inc.,* 501 U.S. 32 (1991).

c. Equitable versus legal

Federal law usually governs whether an issue is legal or equitable. *Simler v. Conner,* 372 U.S. 221 (1963).

C. DETERMINING APPLICABLE STATE LAW

Under *Erie,* a U.S. district court with diversity jurisdiction must apply the substantive law—including the choice-of-law rules—of the state in which it is located. *Klaxon v. Stentor Elec. Mfg. Co.,* 313 U.S. 487 (1941).

> **Example:** The U.S. District Court of Delaware will generally apply Delaware substantive law to the diversity actions over which its sits.

1. **Highest State Court's Rulings on Substantive Law Control**

In determining a state's substantive law, the U.S. district court will be bound by the rulings of the state's highest court.

2. **Highest State Court Not Yet Ruled**

If the state's highest court has not spoken on an issue, however, the federal court must try to determine how the state's highest court would rule on the issue, if it did consider it. To make this determination, the federal court will generally look to any lower state court decisions that have considered the issue and will follow a lower court's view, unless it believes that the highest state court would not follow it. If no state court has considered the issue, the federal court will have to determine how it believes the highest court in the state would rule if it looked at the issue today. Some states have procedures that allow the federal district court to certify a question of substantive law to the state supreme court for clarification.

3. **Highest Court Rules After Federal Suit Complete**

If, after the U.S. district court action has been completed, the state's highest court rules on an issue in a way that is different from the way the district court predicted, a federal appeals court is bound by the state court's ruling. *Vandenbark v. Owens-Illinois Glass Co.,* 311 U.S. 538 (1941).

4. **Conflict of Laws**

In diversity actions, a U.S. district court is bound by the conflict-of-law rules of the state in which the district court is located, but only to the extent that the state's rules are valid under the Full Faith and Credit and Due Process Clauses of the U.S. Constitution. *See Allstate Ins. Co. v. Hague,* 449 U.S. 302 (1981), *Klaxon v. Stentor Elec. Mfg. Co.,* 313 U.S. 487 (1941).

State conflict-of-law rules frequently determine whether to apply the law of the forum state or the law of a foreign jurisdiction by considering whether the law to be applied is substantive or procedural. States apply their own procedural laws and sometimes apply the substantive law of a foreign jurisdiction. Although the substance-procedure distinction arises in federal-state choice of law under *Erie,* it is not the same substance-procedure distinction in state-state choice of law under the law of conflicts under *Klaxon.*

Questions about the following issues are generally considered procedural and controlled by the law of the forum state:

i) The proper court in which to bring an action;

ii) The form of the action to be brought;

iii) The sufficiency of the pleadings;

iv) The effect of splitting a cause of action;

v) The proper or necessary parties to an action;

vi) Whether a counterclaim may be brought;

vii) Venue;

viii) The rules of discovery;

ix) The right to a jury trial;

x) Service of process;

xi) The burden of proof;

xii) Trial procedure; and

xiii) The methods of enforcing a judgment.

5. When Venue Is Transferred

If the venue of a diversity action is transferred under § 1404, the court to which the action is transferred must apply the law of the state of the transferor court, including that state's rules regarding conflicts of law. If the transfer is made pursuant to § 1406(a), however, the court to which the case is transferred applies the conflict-of-law rules of the state in which it is located.

6. Substance and Procedure in Choice-of-Law Cases

The substance and procedure distinctions in choice-of-law cases are not necessarily the same as those under *Erie*. If a particular state's conflict-of-law rules treat a certain law as procedural or substantive, a federal court applying those conflict-of-law rules will generally follow the state's distinction.

Example: There is an automobile accident in Maine, and one driver sues the other in federal court in Massachusetts, based on diversity jurisdiction. Maine and Massachusetts have different rules regarding the burden of proof of who was at fault. Maine requires that the defendant prove that the plaintiff was contributorily negligent, while Massachusetts requires the plaintiff to disprove contributory negligence. Because the accident occurred in Maine, the Massachusetts court would follow Maine law as to substantive issues (i.e., what is negligence), but it would treat burden of proof as procedural, and so follow its own rule requiring the plaintiff to disprove contributory negligence.

VI. PLEADINGS

A. NOTICE PLEADING

The Federal Rules provide for notice pleading, as opposed to fact pleading. Federal pleadings need not detail the facts or the legal theory of the case; they must only give fair notice of the pleader's contentions. This means that federal complaints generally have to be less specific than complaints in state court. The purpose of notice pleading is to standardize pleading across all causes of action, to simplify the pleading process, and to shift the emphasis from the pleading to the merits of the case. Complaints should be dismissed on the basis of the pleadings only if "it appears beyond a doubt that the plaintiff can prove no set of facts...which would entitle him to relief." *Conley v. Gibson,* 355 U.S. 41 (1957).

1. Recent Changes

Two recent Supreme Court cases have heightened the pleading requirement of federal cases, requiring that the allegations in the complaint state a "plausible"—not simply possible—case for recovery.

a. *Bell Atlantic Corp. v. Twombly*

In an antitrust case, the plaintiff alleged that the defendants had made an agreement in restraint of trade. The Supreme Court said that the complaint should be dismissed because it did not provide facts sufficient to prove that the allegations were plausible, basically stating that the trial court should inquire into whether a complaint was sufficiently convincing to allow the suit to continue. *Bell Atlantic Corp. v. Twombly,* 550 U.S. 544 (2007).

b. *Ashcroft v. Iqbal*

In a constitutional tort action, the Supreme Court again ruled that the complaint should be dismissed because the plaintiff did not state a claim for relief that was plausible on its face. The Supreme Court further held that the decision in *Bell Atlantic Corp.* was not to be limited to antitrust cases. The case expanded the authority of district judges to dismiss cases that they believe are without merit.

B. COMMENCEMENT OF PROCEEDINGS

1. Manner

Under Rule 3, a civil action is commenced by filing a complaint with the court clerk. In a federal diversity action, state law applies to decide when the action commenced for purposes of the statute of limitations. *Walker v. Armco Steel Corp.,* 446 U.S. 740 (1980). Thus, if state law provides that an action is commenced by service of process on a defendant, rather than by filing with the court, the state rule will control for the purposes of diversity jurisdiction.

2. Time Computation

a. General rule

Rule 6 sets out guidelines for computing time limits that apply throughout the Federal Rules of Civil Procedure, unless otherwise provided. Under Rule 6(a)(1), whenever a time period is stated in days (which is the only time period discussed in this outline), the period excludes the day of the event that triggers the period, includes **every day** following, **including intervening Saturdays, Sundays, and legal holidays,** and includes the last day of the period, **except that** if the last day is a Saturday, Sunday, or legal holiday, the period is continued to the next non-weekend or holiday day. Rule 6(a)(1).

b. Motions, hearings, and affidavits

Under Rule 6(c), a written motion and notice of a hearing must be served at least 14 days prior to the hearing, unless: (i) the motion can be heard ex parte, (ii) the Rules provide for it, or (iii) the court orders otherwise. An opposing affidavit must be served at least seven days before the hearing, unless otherwise ordered.

c. Additional time for responses to electronic and non-paper filings

Under Rule 6(d), when the Rules otherwise provide a time period for responding to a service or filing, and the service or filing is made electronically or otherwise non-traditionally under Rule 5(b), **three days are added** to the prescribed period.

C. COMPLAINT

1. Required Elements

a. In general

The complaint is the initial pleading in an action filed by the plaintiff and serves as notice to the opposing party. Under Rule 8(a), a complaint (or any pleading in which a claim is made) must include:

  i) A short and plain statement of the grounds that establish the court's subject matter jurisdiction;

  ii) A short and plain statement of the claim establishing entitlement to relief (*see* § VI.A., *supra,* for details); and

  iii) A demand for judgment for the relief sought by the pleader.

b. Subject matter jurisdiction

A complaint in federal court must contain an allegation of the subject matter jurisdiction of the court, unless the court already has jurisdiction and the claim needs no new jurisdictional support.

c. Demand for relief

The demand for judgment for the relief sought may include relief in the alternative or different types of relief (e.g., monetary damages, equitable relief, or a declaratory judgment). The demand in a contested case does not limit the nature or scope of relief that the trial court may grant. The plaintiff is entitled to whatever relief is appropriate to the claims alleged in the complaint and proved at trial. Rule 54(c).

2. Special Matters

Rule 9 sets forth certain special rules with regard to pleading, which apply not just in the context of a complaint, but to any pleading. In certain circumstances (below), a party is required to plead with greater detail than under the general rules. Federal courts have no power to require more specific pleading beyond the rules set forth in the Federal Rules of Civil Procedure or by statute. *See Swierkiewicz v. Sorema N.A.,* 534 U.S. 506 (2002).

a. Capacity

Under Rule 9(a), except when required to show that the court has jurisdiction, a pleading need not allege a party's capacity to sue or be sued. To challenge a party's capacity, an opposing party must make a specific denial and state any supporting facts that are peculiarly within the party's knowledge.

b. Fraud or mistake

Under Rule 9(b), a party alleging fraud or mistake must state with particularity the circumstances constituting fraud or mistake.

Malice, intent, knowledge, and other conditions of a person's mind, however, may be alleged generally.

c. Conditions precedent

Under Rule 9(c), in pleading conditions precedent in a contract action, a party may allege generally that all conditions precedent have occurred or been performed. When denying that a condition precedent has occurred or been performed, however, the party must do so with particularity.

d. Official document or act

Under Rule 9(d), in pleading an official document or official act, it is sufficient to allege that the document was legally issued or that the act was legally done.

e. Judgment

Under Rule 9(e), in pleading a judgment or decision of a domestic or foreign court, a judicial or quasi-judicial tribunal, or a board or officer, it is sufficient to plead the judgment or decision without showing any jurisdiction to render it.

f. Special damages

Under Rule 9(g), when an item of special damage is claimed, it must be specifically stated. Special damages are damages that do not normally or necessarily flow from an event.

g. Time and place

When relevant and material, facts regarding time and place must be specified in detail.

3. Time for Filing and Service

A complaint will generally be filed before service on the defendant(s), which must then generally occur within 90 days of filing. Rule 4(m). For time limits, *see* § II.B.2, *supra.*

D. MOTIONS AGAINST THE COMPLAINT

Under Rule 12, within 21 days of service of process, a defendant must respond to a complaint either by an answer or by a pre-answer motion, or she must seek additional time to answer. If a defendant does not take one of these steps, she risks a default.

1. Rule 12(b) Motion to Dismiss

a. Basis

Prior to filing an answer, a defendant may file a motion under Rule 12(b), raising any or all of the following defenses:

i)   Lack of subject matter jurisdiction;

ii)   Lack of personal jurisdiction;

iii)   Improper venue;

iv)   Insufficient process;

v)   Insufficient service of process;

vi)   Failure to state a claim upon which relief can be granted; and

vii) Failure to join a necessary or indispensable party under Rule 19.

Such motions generally seek dismissal of the claim. For the defenses of insufficient process and service of process, though, it is common to make a motion to quash the service of process or the process itself.

b. Timing

The defense of lack of subject matter jurisdiction may be raised at any time, even on appeal. Rule 12(h)(3).

Under Rule 12(h)(1), the defenses of lack of personal jurisdiction, improper venue, insufficient process, and insufficient service of process must be raised in a pre-answer motion or, if no pre-answer motion is made, in the answer, or the defenses will be waived.

Under Rule 12(h)(2), the defenses of failure to state a claim upon which relief can be granted and failure to join a necessary or indispensable party under Rule 19 may be raised in any pleading, in a motion for judgment on the pleadings, or at trial.

2. Motion to Dismiss for Failure to State a Claim Upon Which Relief Can Be Granted

a. Rule 12(b)(6)

Under Rule 12(b)(6), a claim for relief can be dismissed if it either fails to assert a legal theory of recovery that is cognizable at law or fails to allege facts sufficient to support a cognizable claim. In deciding a motion under Rule 12(b)(6), courts treat all well-pleaded facts of the complaint as true, resolve all doubts and inferences in the plaintiff's favor, and view the pleading in the light most favorable to the plaintiff.

b. More than speculation

The U.S. Supreme Court has held that the facts alleged in the complaint must "raise a right to relief above the speculative level ... on the assumption that all the allegations in the complaint are true (even if doubtful in fact)." *Bell Atlantic Corp. v. Twombly,* 550 U.S. 544 (2007). The complaint must state enough facts to raise a reasonable expectation that discovery will reveal evidence of the necessary element.

c. What the court may consider

In ruling on a motion to dismiss under Rule 12(b)(6), the court may consider only the allegations in the complaint, any exhibits attached to the complaint, and any matters subject to judicial notice. If a matter outside the pleadings, such as an affidavit, is presented to the court and is not excluded by the court in its review, the motion must be treated as a motion for summary judgment under Rule 56, and all parties must be given an opportunity to present all material information for the court's consideration. Rule 12(d).

d. Outcome

1) Motion granted

If the claim is dismissed, the plaintiff may generally amend the pleading and continue the action. If the plaintiff does not wish to do so, a judgment will be entered, and the plaintiff can appeal.

2) Motion denied

If the defendant's motion to dismiss is denied, the defendant may either answer the claim or allow a default judgment to be entered and then appeal.

3. Motion for Judgment on the Pleadings

a. In general

After the pleadings are closed, a party may move for judgment on the pleadings pursuant to Rule 12(c). A motion for judgment on the pleadings allows a court to dispose of a case when the material facts are not in dispute and a judgment on the merits can be achieved based on the content of the pleadings. Motions under Rule 12(c) are not often used because of the availability of motions under Rule 12(b)(6) and motions for summary judgment under Rule 56.

b. Timing

A motion under Rule 12(c) must be made after an answer is filed.

c. Standard

The standard for a motion under Rule 12(c) is generally the same as that for a motion under Rule 12(b)(6). Likewise, if matters outside the pleadings are presented to the court and the court does not exclude them, the motion is to be treated as a motion for summary judgment under Rule 56.

4. Motion for a More Definite Statement

a. Vague and ambiguous

If a claim for relief is so vague or ambiguous that a party cannot reasonably draft a responsive pleading, the responding party may move for a more definite statement pursuant to Rule 12(e). The motion must specify the defects in the pleading, as well as the details sought by the party making the motion.

b. Standard

Courts are generally reluctant to grant a motion for a more definite statement, because discovery is available to get more information about an issue. The standard for granting such a motion is whether the pleading provides enough information from which the responding party can draft a responsive pleading and commence discovery. A motion for a more definite statement may be appropriate when the pleader fails to allege facts required to be specifically pleaded, such as allegations of fraud or mistake under Rule 9(b).

c. Timing

The party must make a motion for a more definite statement before filing a responsive pleading. The court may strike a failure to respond to such a motion within 14 days of the notice. Rule 12(e).

5. Motion to Strike

a. Rule 12(f)

Under Rule 12(f), if a pleading contains any insufficient defense, or redundant, immaterial, impertinent, or scandalous material, then the court, upon motion or upon its own initiative, may order that such defense or material be stricken. Defenses that tend to complicate litigation significantly or that are insufficient at law may be stricken to avoid unnecessary time and money in litigating invalid and spurious issues. *See Anchor Hocking Corp. v. Jacksonville Elec. Auth.*, 419 F. Supp. 992. (M.D. Fla. 1976); *SEC v. Gulf & Western Indus., Inc.*, 502 F. Supp. 343 (D.D.C. 1980).

b. Timing

When a responsive pleading is permitted, the responding party must move to strike prior to responding to such a pleading. When no responsive pleading is permitted, the party must make a motion to strike within 21 days after service of the pleading.

E. ANSWER

An answer is a pleading by the defendant that responds to a plaintiff's complaint. A plaintiff would also file an answer if responding to a defendant's counterclaim (i.e., an "answer to a counterclaim" under Rule 7).

1. Admissions or Denials

The answer must admit or deny the allegations of the plaintiff's complaint. Rule 8(b). If the defendant is without knowledge or information sufficient to form a belief as to the truth or falsity of an allegation, then the defendant must say so in the answer. This response has the effect of a denial, pursuant to Rule 8(b). Before pleading lack of sufficient knowledge, however, the defendant must make a reasonable investigation into whether the information exists and how difficult it would be to ascertain.

a. Specific denial

A specific denial is a denial of a particular paragraph or allegation in the complaint or other claim for relief (e.g., counterclaim, cross-claim, etc.). A party can respond to each paragraph of the complaint by either denying the allegation in the paragraph, admitting it, pleading insufficient knowledge to either admit or deny it, or admitting part of the allegation and either denying or pleading insufficient knowledge as to the rest.

b. General denial

Alternatively, a party can make a general denial, stating that she denies each and every allegation of the complaint. This may only be done, however, if the party, in good faith, intends to controvert all of the allegations.

A party could also make a qualified general denial, stating that she denies each and every allegation in the complaint, except certain specified allegations.

c. Effect of failure to deny

An allegation, other than one relating to the amount of damages, will be deemed admitted if a responsive pleading is required and the allegation is not denied.

2. Affirmative Defenses

The answer (or an amended answer) must state any avoidance or affirmative defense that the defendant (or responding party) has, or that defense is deemed waived. Rule 8(c) lists some such affirmative defenses:

i) Accord and satisfaction;

ii) Arbitration and award;

iii) Assumption of risk;

iv) Contributory negligence;

v) Duress;

vi) Estoppel;

vii) Failure of consideration;

viii) Fraud;

ix) Illegality;

x) Injury by fellow servant;

xi) Laches;

xii) License;

xiii) Payment;

xiv) Release;

xv) *Res judicata*;

xvi) Statute of frauds;

xvii) Statute of limitations; and

xviii) Waiver.

This list is non-exclusive; thus, if there are other affirmative defenses that the party has in addition to the ones listed above (e.g., novation, qualified immunity), even if they are inconsistent, they must be raised in the answer as well.

3. Counterclaims

If a defendant has a claim against the plaintiff, the plaintiff may state it as a counterclaim in the answer to the complaint. Under certain circumstances, a counterclaim will be compulsory (*see* § VII.A.2., Counterclaims, *infra*) under Rule 13 and must be pleaded or it will be precluded in any future litigation.

4. **Time for Filing an Answer to a Complaint**

   a. **No motion made under Rule 12**

   If no motion is made under Rule 12, then under Rule 12(a)(1)(A)(i), a defendant must serve an answer within 21 days after being served with the summons and complaint.

   If the defendant has timely waived service under Rule 4(d), the defendant must serve the answer within 60 days after the request for a waiver was sent, or within 90 days after it was sent to the defendant outside any judicial district of the United States. Rule 12(a)(1)(A)(ii).

   b. **Motion made under Rule 12**

   When a motion is made under Rule 12, a defendant will not have to file an answer while the motion is pending. If the court denies or postpones disposition of the motion until a trial on the merits, the answer must be served within 14 days after notice of the court's action. Rule 12(a)(4)(A). If the court grants a motion for a more definite statement under Rule 12(e), the answer must be served within 14 days after service of the more definite statement.

F. **REPLY**

   1. **Defined**

   A reply is a response by the plaintiff to a defendant's answer. It can also be a response by a defendant to a plaintiff's counterclaim answer, a third-party answer, or a cross-claim answer.

   2. **Court Order**

   A reply is made only when the court orders it. Rule 7(a)(7).

   3. **Timing**

   In general, a party must serve a reply to an answer within 21 days after being served with an order to reply, unless the order specifies a different time. Rule 12(a)(1)(C).

G. **AMENDMENTS AND SUPPLEMENTAL PLEADINGS**

   Rule 15 provides the rules with regard to when and how pleadings can be amended or supplemented.

   1. **Amendments**

   a. **By right**

   Under Rule 15(a), a party may amend a pleading once as of right within 21 days if no responsive pleading is required, or, if a responsive pleading is required, within 21 days of service of the responsive pleading, or within 21 days of being served with a motion under Rule 12(b), whichever is earlier. Thus, a plaintiff may amend his complaint even after being served with an answer (up to 21 days), but also is limited to 21 days to amend after being served with a 12(b) motion. A party may amend a pleading during and after a trial, if doing so will conform to the evidence and as long as the opposing party had an opportunity to prepare. Due process is required for the amended pleading.

   b. **By leave of the court**

   The court should freely give leave to amend a pleading when justice so requires. Rule 15(a)(2). Generally, a court will first determine if the proposed amendment to the pleading would be futile because it would immediately be subject to dismissal under Rule 12(b)(6). If it would not, the amendment will generally be permitted unless the amendment would result in undue prejudice to the opposing party. However, when the court has issued an order regarding the trial plan after a final pre-trial conference, which may include the issues for trial, the court may modify that order only to prevent manifest injustice. Rule 16(e).

c. Effect

An amended pleading supersedes the prior pleading.

d. Relation back

1) New claim

Under Rule 15(c)(1), an amendment to a pleading will relate back to the date of the original pleading when the amendment asserts a claim or defense that arose out of the conduct, transaction, or occurrence set out, or attempted to be set out, in the original pleading. This may be important for purposes of complying with the applicable statute of limitations. An amendment will also relate back to the date of the original pleading if the law that provides the applicable statute of limitations allows relation back.

2) New party

Under Rule 15(c)(1)(C), if the amendment changes the party or the naming of the party against whom a claim is asserted, it will relate back to the date of the original pleading if:

i) It asserts a claim or defense that arose out of the conduct, transaction, or occurrence set out, or attempted to be set out, in the original pleading; and

ii) Within 90 days after the filing of the original complaint, the party to be brought in by amendment receives notice of the action such that he will not be prejudiced in defending on the merits; and

iii) The party to be brought in by amendment knew or should have known that the action would have been brought against him, but for a mistake concerning the proper party's identity.

e. Time to respond to an amended pleading

Unless the court orders otherwise, a party must respond to an amended pleading within the later of 14 days after service of the amended pleading or the time remaining for response to the original pleading. Rule 15(a)(3).

2. Supplemental Pleadings

A court has discretion under Rule 15(d) to permit supplemental pleadings that describe events occurring after the filing of an earlier pleading. The court may permit supplementation even though the original pleading is defective in stating a claim or defense. The court may also order that the opposing party respond to the supplemental pleading within a specified time. A supplemental pleading does not supersede an original pleading.

H. RULE 11

Rule 11 establishes the standards that attorneys and individual parties must meet when filing pleadings, motions, or other papers. It also provides for sanctions against parties, attorneys, and law firms for violations of the rule.

1. **Signature**

   Under Rule 11(a), every pleading, every written motion, and other paper filed with the court must be signed by at least one attorney of record, or by a party personally, if unrepresented. The court must strike an unsigned paper unless the omission is promptly corrected after being called to the attention of the attorney or party.

2. **Certification to the Court**

   Under Rule 11(b), by presenting to the court a pleading, written motion, or other paper, an attorney or unrepresented party certifies that to the best of his knowledge, information, and belief, formed after an inquiry reasonable under the circumstances:

   i) The paper is not being presented for any improper purpose, such as to harass, cause unnecessary delay, or needlessly increase the cost of litigation;

   ii) The claims, defenses, and other legal contentions are warranted by existing law or by a non-frivolous argument for extending, modifying, or reversing existing law or for establishing new law;

   iii) The factual contentions have evidentiary support or, if specifically so identified, will likely have evidentiary support after a reasonable opportunity for further investigation or discovery; and

   iv) The denials of factual contentions are warranted on the evidence or, if specifically so identified, are reasonably based on belief or a lack of information.

   "Presenting" a pleading under Rule 11 includes "signing, filing, submitting, or later advocating" a position presented in the pleading.

3. **Sanctions**

   a. **In general**

      Under certain circumstances, after notice and a reasonable opportunity to respond, the court may in its discretion impose sanctions on attorneys, law firms, and parties for violations of Rule 11. Absent exceptional circumstances, a law firm must be held jointly responsible for a violation committed by its partner, associate, or employee. Pursuant to Rule 11(c)(4), sanctions "must be limited to what suffices to deter repetition of the conduct or comparable conduct by others similarly situated."

   b. **How initiated**

      Sanctions can be initiated either by motion or by the court on its own.

      1) **Motion**

         A motion for sanctions must be made separately from any other motion and must describe the specific conduct alleged to violate Rule 11. The motion must be served under Rule 5, but it must not be filed or presented to the court if the challenged paper, claim, defense, contention, or denial is withdrawn or appropriately corrected within 21 days after service or within any other time set by the court.

      2) *Sua sponte*

         On its own initiative, the court may order an attorney, law firm, or party to show cause why conduct specifically described in the order has not violated Rule 11.

c. Types of sanctions

Sanctions may include:

i) Nonmonetary directives;

ii) An order to pay a penalty into court; or

iii) If imposed on motion and warranted for effective deterrence, an order directing payment to the movant for part or the entirety of reasonable attorney's fees and other expenses directly resulting from the violation.

d. Procedure

The court cannot impose a monetary sanction on its own, unless it issued an order to show cause with regard to the matter before voluntary dismissal or settlement of the claims made by or against the party who is, or whose attorneys are, to be sanctioned.

The court also is not permitted to impose a monetary sanction against a represented party for violating the requirement that the claims, defenses, and other legal contentions of the paper be warranted by existing law or by a non-frivolous argument for extending, modifying, or reversing existing law or for establishing new law.

An order imposing a sanction under Rule 11 must describe the sanctioned conduct and explain the basis for the sanction. Rule 11(c)(6).

VII. MULTIPLE CLAIMS AND PARTIES

A. JOINDER OF CLAIMS

1. Permissive Joinder

a. In general

Pursuant to Rule 18(a), a party who can assert a claim, counterclaim, cross-claim, or third-party claim (i.e., a qualifying claim that clearly can be brought under the Federal Rules) may join with it as many independent or alternative claims of whatever nature as the party may have against an opposing party.

> Rule 18 permits joinder of claims, but it does not compel it. However, res judicata (claim preclusion) concerns will often require joinder.

b. Joinder of contingent claims

Pursuant to Rule 18(b), a party may join two claims even though one of them is contingent on the disposition of the other.

> **Example:** A plaintiff may assert both a claim for monetary damages and a claim to set aside a conveyance that was fraudulent as a result of the defendant's transfer of assets to try to frustrate enforcement of the claim for monetary damages.

c. Subject matter jurisdiction

To join a claim under Rule 18, the court must have subject matter jurisdiction over it.

If subject matter jurisdiction is based on diversity jurisdiction, the plaintiff may aggregate all claims against the defendant in order to satisfy the statutory jurisdictional amount-in-controversy requirement.

If the original claim is based on federal question jurisdiction, a non-federal claim may be joined only if diversity jurisdiction exists or if the two claims are part of the same case or controversy as the federal claim such that supplemental jurisdiction applies.

d. Venue

The venue requirements for federal court must be satisfied in order to join a claim under Rule 18.

2. Counterclaims

A counterclaim is a claim for relief made against an opposing party after an original claim has been made. A counterclaim may be asserted in the answer to the complaint and the reply to a counterclaim. Rule 13 governs the requirements for bringing a counterclaim.

A party must serve an answer to a counterclaim (or cross-claim) within 21 days of service. Rule 12(a)(1)(B).

a. Compulsory

1) In general

A pleading is required to state as a counterclaim any claim that, at the time of service, the pleader has against an opposing party if the claim arises out of the same transaction or occurrence that is the subject matter of the opposing party's claim and does not require adding another party over whom the court cannot acquire jurisdiction. Rule 13(a)(1).

However, the pleader is not required to make the claim if, at the time the action was commenced, the claim was the subject of another pending action, or if the opposing party's action is in rem or quasi in rem and the party does not assert any other counterclaim in that action. Rule 13(a)(2).

2) Failure to state a compulsory counterclaim

A party that fails to assert a compulsory counterclaim waives the right to sue on the claim and is generally precluded from ever suing on the claim in federal court.

Rule 13(f), which authorized the court to permit a party to amend a pleading in order to add a counterclaim that had been omitted through oversight, inadvertence, or excusable neglect, was abrogated as of December 2009.

3) Subject matter jurisdiction

A federal court must have subject matter jurisdiction over the counterclaim. By definition, though, a compulsory counterclaim arises out of the same transaction or occurrence as does the original claim before the court. Thus, a compulsory counterclaim (unlike a permissive counterclaim) will likely fall under the supplemental jurisdiction of the federal court and not need independent subject matter jurisdiction from the original claim.

b. Permissive

1) In general

Under Rule 13(b), a pleading may state as a counterclaim against an opposing party any claim that is not compulsory. Thus, a party has discretion as to whether to raise the counterclaim in the action before the court or in a separate action.

2) Subject matter jurisdiction

A permissive counterclaim does not necessarily fall within the supplemental jurisdiction of the federal court, as it does not arise out of the same transaction or occurrence as the original claim. Thus, a permissive counterclaim must on its own meet the requirements for federal subject matter jurisdiction (either diversity or federal question).

c. By third parties

A third-party defendant may file a counterclaim against either an original defendant or an original plaintiff. The rules of Rule 13 regarding what is compulsory or permissive apply.

Pursuant to Rule 13(h), new parties to a counterclaim may be joined so long as they meet the requirements for joinder under Rule 20. New parties must be joined if they are indispensable parties under Rule 19.

3. Cross-Claims

a. In general

A cross-claim is a claim made against a co-party, as when one defendant makes a claim against another defendant.

Under Rule 13(g), a pleading may state as a cross-claim any claim by one party against a co-party that arises out of the same transaction or occurrence that is the subject matter of the original action or of a counterclaim, or if the claim relates to any property that is the subject matter of the original action. The cross-claim may include a claim that the co-party is liable to the cross-claimant for all or part of a claim asserted in the action against the cross-claimant.

b. Cross-claim not mandatory

A party is never required to assert a cross-claim against a co-party. Pursuant to Rule 13(h), new parties to a cross-claim may be joined so long as they meet the requirements for joinder under Rule 20. New parties must be joined if they meet the requirements for joinder under Rule 19.

c. Subject matter jurisdiction

A cross-claim must fall within the subject matter jurisdiction of the federal court. This is generally not a problem, since, by definition, a cross-claim must arise out of the same transaction or occurrence as the subject matter of the original action or of a counterclaim, or it must relate to the property at issue, and therefore would fall under the court's supplemental jurisdiction.

d. In personam jurisdiction and venue

Because the parties are already before the court, personal jurisdiction is satisfied. Additionally, if venue was proper over the original claim, a party cannot object to venue with regard to the cross-claim.

B. JOINDER OF PARTIES

The Federal Rules of Civil Procedure provide for joining parties to existing litigation, generally for reasons of efficiency and economy. Joinder may be permissive, pursuant to Rule 20, or compulsory, pursuant to Rule 19.

1. **Permissive Joinder**

Rule 20 sets forth the circumstances in which a plaintiff may join other plaintiffs in an action, or defendants may be joined in the same action.

a. **Plaintiffs**

Pursuant to Rule 20(a)(1), persons may join in one action as plaintiffs if:

i) They assert any right to relief jointly, severally, or in the alternative with respect to or arising out of the same transaction, occurrence, or series of transactions or occurrences; and

ii) Any question of law or fact common to all plaintiffs will arise in the action.

b. **Defendants**

Pursuant to Rule 20(a)(2), persons may be joined in one action as defendants if:

i) Any right to relief is asserted against them jointly, severally, or in the alternative with respect to or arising out of the same transaction, occurrence, or series of transactions or occurrences; and

ii) A question of law or fact common to all defendants will arise in the action.

c. **Extent of relief**

The same relief need not be demanded among the joined plaintiffs or against the joined defendants. Rule 20(a)(3).

d. **Protective measures**

To avoid unfairness or hardship to any party, the court may order separate trials on any claims joined or may make any other order to prevent delay or undue expense to any party. Rule 20(b).

e. **Jurisdiction and venue**

1) **Subject matter jurisdiction**

A plaintiff or defendant joined still must meet the requirements of federal subject matter jurisdiction to be joined.

a) **Supplemental jurisdiction**

i) **Joinder of defendants**

Note that under 28 U.S.C. § 1367(b), supplemental jurisdiction does not apply to defendants sought to be joined under the permissive joinder rule in a case based exclusively on diversity jurisdiction where exercising jurisdiction would destroy diversity. Thus, if the claims are made solely on the basis of diversity jurisdiction, there must be complete diversity between the plaintiffs and the defendants, and each claim must exceed the jurisdictional amount in controversy of $75,000.

Example: While driving his car, Plaintiff, a citizen of Arizona, is hit by a truck operated by Defendant 1, a citizen of New Mexico. Plaintiff is thrown from his car and is further injured by a car driven by Defendant 2, a citizen of Nevada. Plaintiff brings a negligence suit for $100,000 against Defendant 1 in federal court based on diversity jurisdiction. Plaintiff then joins Defendant 2 under Rule 20, suing for $25,000. Under § 1367(b), there is no supplemental jurisdiction against Defendant 2, and no diversity jurisdiction against Defendant 2, because the statutory jurisdictional amount is not met.

ii) Joinder of plaintiffs

If multiple plaintiffs, however, join together under Rule 20, supplemental jurisdiction is permitted for determining the statutory jurisdictional amount, but the parties must still meet the requirement of complete diversity. *Exxon Mobil Corp. v. Allapattah Services, Inc.,* 545 U.S. 546 (2005).

Example: Plaintiff 1 and Plaintiff 2, who are citizens of California, join together under Rule 20 as plaintiffs against Defendant, a citizen of Oregon, in a diversity suit for negligence. The claims arise out of the same occurrence or transaction. Plaintiff 1 claims $200,000 and Plaintiff 2 claims $25,000. There is supplemental jurisdiction, and the plaintiffs may add their claims together for the purposes of determining the statutory jurisdictional amount. If Plaintiff 2 was a citizen of Oregon, however, there would not be complete diversity, and Plaintiff 2 would have to be dropped from the federal case.

2) In personam jurisdiction

If a defendant is joined pursuant to Rule 20, the court must have in personam jurisdiction over the defendant for joinder to be proper.

3) Venue

Joinder under Rule 20 must also meet any applicable venue requirements.

2. Compulsory Joinder

Rule 19 specifies circumstances in which additional parties must be joined. Note that the requirements of jurisdiction (both subject matter and personal) and venue must still be met in order for compulsory joinder to occur. Under certain circumstances, if compulsory joinder cannot occur because of jurisdictional or venue issues, Rule 19(b) may require the action to be dismissed from federal court.

a. Necessary parties

Under Rule 19(a), a person who is subject to service of process and whose joinder will not deprive the court of subject matter jurisdiction or destroy venue must be joined as a party if:

i) Complete relief cannot be provided to existing parties in the absence of that person; or

ii) Disposition in the absence of that person may impair the person's ability to protect his interest; or

iii) The absence of that person would leave existing parties subject to a substantial risk of multiple or inconsistent obligations.

The Supreme Court has specifically held that tortfeasors facing joint and several liability are **not** parties who must be joined under Rule 19. *Temple v. Synthes Corp., Ltd.,* 498 U.S. 5 (1990).

b. Subject matter jurisdiction

A plaintiff or defendant to be joined under Rule 19 must meet the requirements of federal subject matter jurisdiction. Thus, if the exclusive basis for the court's subject matter jurisdiction is diversity jurisdiction and a party sought to be joined would destroy diversity, joinder is not permitted.

Note that under 28 U.S.C. § 1367(b), supplemental jurisdiction does not apply to the claims of a party sought to be joined under Rule 19 in a case based exclusively on diversity jurisdiction if the exercise of jurisdiction would be inconsistent with the diversity requirements.

c. In personam jurisdiction

There must be personal jurisdiction over the necessary party. A necessary party may be served within 100 miles from where the summons was issued, even if the service is outside of the state and beyond its long-arm statute jurisdiction. Rule 4(k)(1)(B).

d. Venue

If a joined party objects to venue and the joinder would make venue improper, the court must dismiss that party.

e. When joinder is not feasible

Under Rule 19(b), if a person who is required to be joined cannot be joined because of jurisdictional or venue concerns, the court must determine whether, in equity and good conscience, the action should proceed among the existing parties or should be dismissed. Among the factors for the court to consider are:

i) The extent to which a judgment rendered in the person's absence might prejudice that person or the existing parties;

ii) The extent to which any prejudice could be reduced or avoided by protective provisions in the judgment, shaping the relief, or other measures;

iii) Whether a judgment rendered in the person's absence would be adequate; and

iv) Whether the plaintiff would have an adequate remedy if the action were dismissed for non-joinder.

3. Intervention

Rule 24 governs the circumstances under which a non-party may join in a lawsuit. In some circumstances, the non-party may intervene as of right. In other circumstances, the non-party must have the permission of the court. Note that in either case, a motion to intervene must be timely.

a. Intervention as of right

Under Rule 24(a)(1), a non-party has the right to intervene in an action in which a federal statute confers the right and the non-party timely moves to intervene. Additionally, under Rule 24(a)(2), upon a timely motion, a non-party has the right to intervene when:

i) The non-party has an interest in the property or transaction that is the subject matter of the action;

ii) The disposition of the action may, as a practical matter, impair the non-party's interest; and

iii) The non-party's interest is not adequately represented by existing parties.

The criteria for intervention as of right under Rule 24(a)(2) are similar to the criteria for compulsory joinder under Rule 19(a).

The burden of proof is on the person seeking to intervene.

b. Permissive intervention

Under Rule 24(b), the court may allow intervention, upon timely motion, when either:

    i)   The movant has a conditional right to intervene under a federal statute; or

    ii) The movant's claim or defense and the original action share a common question of law or fact.

In exercising its discretion, the court must consider whether the intervention will unduly delay or prejudice the adjudication of the rights of the original parties.

c. Timeliness

The decision of whether the non-party timely moved to intervene is in the discretion of the trial court, considering factors such as:

    i)   The length of time the movant knew or reasonably should have known that its interest was threatened before moving to intervene;

    ii) The prejudice to existing parties if intervention is permitted; and

    iii) The prejudice to the movant if intervention is denied.

d. Subject matter jurisdiction

A claim of an intervenor must be supported by its own jurisdictional basis, unless the claim is closely related to a federal-question claim already asserted in the action.

Pursuant to § 1367(b), supplemental jurisdiction does not apply to the claims of a person seeking to be joined under Rule 24 (either as of right or permissively) in a case based exclusively on diversity jurisdiction if the exercise of jurisdiction would be inconsistent with the requirements of diversity jurisdiction.

> **Example:** X, a citizen of Ohio, sues Y, a citizen of Michigan, in federal court under diversity jurisdiction. Z, a citizen of Michigan, seeks to intervene (as of right or permissively) pursuant to Rule 24. Z cannot intervene because she would destroy diversity jurisdiction in the action. If Z were a citizen of any state other than Michigan, she could intervene, provided the requirements for intervention under Rule 24 were established.

4. Interpleader

Interpleader allows a person holding property (traditionally known as the "stakeholder") to force all potential claimants to the property into a single lawsuit to determine who has a right to the property.

a. Federal interpleader rule

1) Basis

Under Rule 22, persons with claims that may expose a plaintiff to double or multiple liability may be joined as defendants and required to interplead. Such joinder is proper even though the claims of the claimants, or the titles on which their claims depend, lack a common origin or are adverse and independent rather than identical; or the plaintiff denies liability in whole or in part to any or all of the claimants. A defendant who is exposed to similar liability may seek interpleader through a cross-claim or counterclaim. Rule 22(a).

The primary standard for determining the propriety of an interpleader action under Rule 22 is whether the party bringing the action legitimately fears multiple claims against the property.

2) Subject matter jurisdiction

Rule 22 does not create subject matter jurisdiction in interpleader actions. Rather, the court must already have jurisdiction over all parties. Thus, a plaintiff will need federal question jurisdiction or, for diversity jurisdiction, the citizenship of the party bringing the action must be completely diverse from that of the claimants, and the statutory amount in controversy must be met. While the stakeholder needs to be diverse from the claimants, the claimants need not be diverse among themselves.

3) In personam jurisdiction

An interpleader action is an action against the claimants, so the general requirements of in personam jurisdiction in federal court must be met.

4) Venue

Federal venue requirements must also be met in interpleader actions under Rule 22.

b. Federal statutory interpleader

There are some key differences in the requirements for federal statutory interpleader pursuant to § 1335.

1) Subject matter jurisdiction

For statutory interpleader, diversity jurisdiction is met if any two adverse claimants are citizens of different states. With regard to the amount in controversy, in a statutory interpleader action the property at issue must merely be $500 or more in value, not meet the $75,000 threshold required for regular diversity matters.

2) In personam jurisdiction

Statutory interpleader provides for nationwide personal jurisdiction and service of process and permits the federal court to enjoin other federal and state proceedings that may affect the property that is subject to dispute.

3) Venue

Venue is proper in any federal judicial district where one of the claimants resides.

4) Deposit

For statutory interpleader, unlike for federal rule interpleader, the stakeholder is required to either deposit with the court the property at issue or post a bond in an appropriate amount.

5. Third-Party Claims (Impleader)

a. In general

Rule 14 sets out the rules governing impleader (third-party claims). These are claims that are made by a defending party against a non-party for all or part of the defending party's liability on an original claim. Note that the impleaded claim must relate to the original claim against the defending party. The court may sever any third-party claim if justice demands it.

> **Example—Contribution:** If two tortfeasors both injure the plaintiff, and the plaintiff sues only one of them, the defendant has a right to seek contribution from the other tortfeasor for that tortfeasor's share of the plaintiff's injuries. Impleader is permitted here because, given the right of contribution, the second tortfeasor may be liable to the original defendant for part of the defendant's liability to the plaintiff.
>
> **Example—Indemnification:** If a general contractor hires a subcontractor, and the subcontractor's faulty work makes the general contractor liable to the plaintiff, the subcontractor must indemnify the general contractor for defects in the subcontractor's work.

b. Procedure

A defending party—including a plaintiff against whom a counterclaim has been asserted—may assert a third-party claim at any time after the complaint is filed. The defending party, referred to for impleader purposes as the third-party plaintiff, must serve a summons and third-party complaint on the non-party (third-party defendant). The third party must obtain the court's permission if it files more than 14 days after service of the original answer. Rule 14(a)(1). There are some states, however, that do not permit a defendant to implead his own insurance company unless the company has denied coverage.

The third-party defendant may (and in some cases must) assert defenses, counterclaims, and cross-claims against any of the parties as appropriate under the rules and may also implead another non-party who is or may be liable to the third-party defendant for the claim on which he was impleaded. Rule 14(a)(2).

c. Subject matter jurisdiction

A third-party claim must fall within the federal court's subject matter jurisdiction. Because by definition a third-party claim will be closely related to the original claim, the court will generally have supplemental jurisdiction over the matter. If the original claims are based exclusively on diversity jurisdiction, however, under § 1367(b), supplemental jurisdiction will not apply to claims by the plaintiff against a third-party defendant brought in under Rule 14. Such claims need to meet diversity or federal question jurisdiction requirements on their own.

d. In personam jurisdiction

There must be personal jurisdiction over the third-party defendant for impleader to apply. Third parties joined by impleader may be served within 100 miles of where the summons was issued, even if the service is outside of the state and beyond its long-arm statute jurisdiction. Rule 4(k)(1)(B).

6. Class Actions

In a class action, the court authorizes a single person or a small group of people to represent the interests of a larger group. Rule 23 and the Class Action Fairness Act of 2005 govern class actions.

a. Prerequisites

1) Basic requirements

Rule 23(a) establishes four requirements for representative members of a class to sue or be sued on behalf of all members of the class:

i) The class must be so numerous that joinder of all members is impracticable (numerosity);

ii) There must be questions of law or fact that are common to the class (commonality);

iii) The claims or defenses of the representatives must be typical of the class (typicality); and

iv) The representatives must fairly and adequately protect the interests of the class (adequacy).

2) Three types

In addition to the requirements of Rule 23(a), before a class action can be certified, it must also fit within one of the three situations specified in Rule 23(b).

a) Risk of prejudice

Under Rule 23(b)(1), the class is maintainable if the prosecution of separate actions would create the risk that the class opponent would become subject to incompatible standards of conduct resulting from inconsistent adjudications (a so-called "incompatible standards class" under Rule 23(b)(1)(A)), or where prosecution of the claims through separate actions would impair the interests of the class members (a so-called "impeding of interests class" under Rule 23(b)(1)(B), a classic example of which is a limited fund situation in which the combined claims of all class members exceed the defendant's assets).

b) Final equitable relief

Under Rule 23(b)(2), a class seeking final injunctive or declaratory relief may be certified if the class shares a general claim against the opposing party. An additional claim for monetary damages may not be sought, at least when the monetary relief is not incidental to the injunctive or declaratory relief. Moreover, a claim for individualized monetary relief is not available because a claim under Rule 23(b)(2) is available only when a single, indivisible remedy would provide relief to each class member. *Wal-Mart Stores, Inc. v. Dukes*, 564 U.S. 338 (2011) (a claim for back pay due to alleged gender discrimination could not be certified in an action seeking injunction and declaratory relief for such discrimination).

c) Common legal or factual questions

Under Rule 23(b)(3), a class can be certified if questions of law or fact that are common to the class members predominate over any questions affecting only individual members, and a class action is the superior method in bringing about a fair and efficient adjudication of the controversy. In making this determination, the court must consider, among other things:

i) The class members' interests in individually controlling the prosecution or defense of separate actions;

ii) The extent and nature of any litigation concerning the controversy already begun by or against class members;

iii) The desirability or undesirability of concentrating the litigation of the claims in the particular forum; and

iv) The likely difficulties in managing a class action.

The class representatives need not establish that success on a common question of law is likely in order for the class to be certified. *Amgen Inc. v. Conn. Ret. Plans & Tr. Funds*, 568 U.S. 455 (2013).

3) Subject matter jurisdiction

A class action must also satisfy federal subject matter jurisdiction requirements. A class action can invoke federal question jurisdiction or diversity jurisdiction.

a) Diversity jurisdiction

If diversity jurisdiction is invoked in a class action, diversity of citizenship will be satisfied if the class representatives are diverse from the party or parties opposing the claim.

When at least one representative plaintiff of a putative class action has a claim that meets the statutory jurisdictional amount (generally it must exceed $75,000), other persons with claims that do not meet the jurisdictional amount can be made part of the class under the doctrine of supplemental jurisdiction. *Exxon Mobil Corp. v. Allapattah Servs., Inc.*, 545 U.S. 546 (2005).

4) Venue

When the class action involves a defendant class, venue is determined on the basis of the residences of the representative parties, not the residences of all the class members.

5) Class actions under the Class Action Fairness Act of 2005

The Class Action Fairness Act of 2005 (CAFA) made it easier to satisfy federal subject matter jurisdiction for certain large class actions. Subject matter jurisdiction will be met if:

i) The class action involves at least 100 members;

ii) The primary defendants are not states, state officials, or other government entities against whom the district court may be foreclosed from ordering relief;

iii) The action does not involve certain securities-related cases, or litigation concerning the internal affairs or governance of a corporation;

iv) The amount in controversy exceeds the sum or value of $5,000,000, exclusive of interest and costs; and

v) Minimum diversity exists. Minimum diversity is satisfied when any member of a class of plaintiffs is a citizen of a state different from any defendant.

a) Removals and exclusions

Under CAFA, any defendant can remove the case to federal court. If the class action claim is based only on federal securities law or corporate governance, there is no federal jurisdiction under CAFA. This exclusion also applies to primary defendants who are government entities.

b) Protections

The benefit to filing under CAFA is the various protections afforded to the class members. The court will generally protect members against loss in consumer class actions, ensure that the settlement is fair to the members, and ensure that the settlement is equally distributed. It will also notify federal and state officials of the proposed settlement. If no notice is given, the class member may choose not to be bound by the agreement.

c) Limitations on jurisdiction

The court is required to repudiate jurisdiction when the primary injuries were incurred in the state in which the action was filed, when more than two-thirds of the proposed plaintiffs are citizens of the state in which the case was filed, and when significant relief is sought from a defendant who is a citizen of the state in which the case was filed.

If between one-third and two-thirds of proposed plaintiffs and the primary defendants are citizens of the state in which the case was filed, the court is given discretion to decline jurisdiction.

6) Shareholder derivative suits

When a shareholder brings a cause of action on behalf of other shareholders against the corporation, he must represent the class fairly and adequately. He is bound to plead with particularity that he made a demand on the directors when state law requires such a demand, and, if not, he is bound to state the reasons for not making the demand. He must also assert his status as a shareholder at the time the transaction occurred. Finally, he must prove to the court that the action is not a cunning enterprise to impart jurisdiction on the court.

If a corporation displays animus to the plaintiffs, it must be named on the complaint. Otherwise, the court will join the corporation as a defendant to indicate the corporation's animus. Further, the settlement or dismissal of a derivative suit must be approved by the court. In the case of a settlement, the amount awarded is measured by the damages the corporation suffered.

b. Approval of the court

Pursuant to Rule 23(c), if the class meets all of the above requirements, the court must certify the class. If a class is certified, the court's order must define the class and the class's claims, issues, or defenses and must appoint counsel for the class. A party may seek an appeal to the certification even though the certification is not a final judgment.

c. Notice of the class action

Notice of the class action is required only for class actions under Rule 23(b)(3). The notice must be the best notice that is practicable under the circumstances, including individual notice to all members who can be identified through reasonable effort. The notice must clearly and concisely state in plain, easily understood language:

i)   The nature of the action;

ii) The definition of the class;

iii) The class claims, issues, or defenses;

iv) That a class member may enter an appearance through an attorney if the member so desires;

v)   That the court will exclude from the class any member who requests exclusion;

vi) The time and manner for requesting exclusion; and

vii) The binding effect of a class judgment on members.

Rule 23(c)(2)(B). Generally, the cost of notifying the class member is borne by the plaintiff, even in cases in which the plaintiff is likely to succeed. *Eisen v. Carlisle & Jacquelin*, 417 U.S. 156 (1974).

For class actions under Rule 23(b)(1) and (b)(2), notice of the action is at the court's discretion. The court may order that appropriate notice be given to the members of the class, which often can take the form of publication notice. Rule 23(c)(2)(A).

d. Settlement or dismissal

Under Rule 23(e), the claims, issues, or defenses of the certified class may be voluntarily settled or dismissed only with the approval of the court.

1) Notice

When a proposal for settlement or dismissal is made to the court, the court must direct notice in a reasonable manner to all class members who would be bound by the proposal.

2) Standard for approval

If the proposal would bind class members, the court may approve it only after a hearing and on finding that it is fair, reasonable, and adequate. The parties seeking approval must file a statement identifying any collateral agreements made in connection with the proposal.

3) Objection by class members

Any class member may object to the proposal if it requires court approval. Rule 23(e)(5). Once the named representative class members reach a settlement that is approved over the objections of a class member who was not a named representative, the objecting class member's interests diverge from those of the class representatives, and the class member who objects may appeal the court's approval of a settlement. *Devlin v. Scardelletti*, 536 U.S. 1 (2002); *Marino v. Ortiz*, 484 U.S. 301 (1988).

4) Second opt-out opportunity

If a class action was certified under Rule 23(b)(3), the court may refuse to approve of the settlement unless class members are given a second opportunity to "opt out" of the litigation and proceed on their own. Rule 23(e)(4). A class member who fails to opt out is bound by the settlement.

e. Judgment

In general, a valid judgment binds all members of the class. In a class action certified under Rule 23(b)(3), a valid judgment does not bind those class members who opted out of the lawsuit; a class member who does not opt out, however, is bound by the judgment, even when that class member did not have minimum contacts with the forum state. *Phillips Petroleum Co. v. Shutts*, 472 U.S. 797 (1985).

VIII. DISCOVERY

A. MANDATORY DISCLOSURES

Rule 26(a) requires the parties, at three different times prior to trial, to make certain disclosures: initial disclosures, disclosures of expert testimony 90 days before trial, and pre-trial disclosures 30 days before trial. These disclosures are mandatory and must be made even if an opposing party does not ask for such information. Unless otherwise ordered by the court, the disclosures must be in writing, signed, and served.

1. Initial Disclosures

a. In general

Under Rule 26(a)(1), unless otherwise agreed by stipulation or ordered by the court, each party must provide to the other parties:

  i) The name, address, and telephone number of each individual likely to have discoverable information, along with the subjects of that information;

  ii) A copy or description of all documents, electronically stored information, and tangible things that the disclosing party has in its possession, custody, or control;

  iii) A computation of each category of damages claimed by the disclosing party, along with the documents or other evidentiary material on which each computation is based; and

  iv) Any insurance agreement under which an insurance business may be liable to satisfy all or part of a possible judgment in the action or to indemnify or reimburse for payments made to satisfy the judgment.

Pursuant to Rule 26(a)(1)(E), a party must make its initial disclosures based on the information that is then reasonably available to it. A party is not excused from making its disclosures because it has not fully investigated the case, because it challenges the sufficiency of another party's disclosures, or because another party has not made its disclosures.

b. Exceptions

Nine categories of proceedings are excluded from the initial disclosure requirements, including actions for review on administrative records, actions to enforce an arbitration award, and petitions for habeas corpus. Rule 26(a)(1)(B).

c. Time for initial disclosure

A party must make the initial disclosures required by Rule 26(a)(1) at or within 14 days after the parties' Rule 26(f) conference (*see* § VIII.D., *infra*), unless a different time is set by stipulation or court order.

2. Disclosure of Expert Testimony

Rule 26(a)(2) requires parties to disclose the identities of persons who may testify as expert witnesses and to produce an expert report for each such witness. The expert report must be prepared and signed by the expert and contain, among other things: a complete statement of and basis for all opinions to be expressed, the facts or data considered by the expert in forming the opinions, the experts' qualifications (including publication and litigation history), and the experts' compensation.

These disclosures must generally be made 90 days before the date set for trial, unless the court orders otherwise. Rule 26(a)(2)(D).

3. Pre-Trial Disclosures

Pursuant to Rule 26(a)(3)(A), in addition to the initial and expert disclosures, the parties must make certain disclosures regarding evidence that they may present at trial other than for impeachment purposes, including:

    i) The name, address, and telephone number of each witness;

    ii) The designation of those witnesses whose testimony the party expects to present by deposition and, if not taken stenographically, a transcript of the pertinent parts of the deposition; and

    iii) An identification of each document or other exhibit, including summaries of other evidence.

These disclosures must be made at least 30 days before trial. An objection must generally be raised within 14 days after the disclosures are made, or it will be waived, unless excused by the court for good cause or unless the objection relates to relevancy, prejudice, or confusion pursuant to Rules 402 and 403 of the Federal Rules of Evidence. Rule 26(a)(3)(B).

B. DISCOVERY SCOPE

In addition to obtaining information under the mandatory disclosure rules, parties may use a variety of discovery methods set forth in Rules 27–36 and discussed below. Rule 26 sets forth rules establishing the scope and limitations of such discovery.

1. In General

Under Rule 26(b)(1), discovery is generally permitted with regard to any non-privileged matter relevant to any party's claim or defense in the action and proportional to the needs of the case, considering the importance of the issues at stake in the action, the amount in controversy, the parties' relative access to relevant information, the parties' resources, the importance of the discovery in resolving the issue, and whether the burden or expense of the proposed discovery outweighs its likely benefit.

2. Relevance

Information within the scope of discovery need not be admissible in evidence to be discoverable. The test is whether the information sought is relevant to any party's claim or defense.

3. Privilege

a. Generally

Privileged information is not discoverable. In federal question cases, privileges are determined under federal common law, pursuant to Rule 501 of the Federal Rules of Evidence. In diversity or supplemental claims in which a state's substantive laws apply, that state's law determines whether a privilege applies. These privileges may include the priest-penitent privilege, the doctor-patient privilege, and spousal privilege.

b. Attorney-client privilege

The attorney-client privilege protects only communications made between a licensed attorney and a client, for the purposes of seeking legal advice. For a communication to qualify for the privilege, the privilege must not have been waived. Waiver can occur if a communication is disclosed to third parties who are not part of the attorney-client relationship. If a privilege is waived as to a communication, the subject matter of the communication is waived even as to other communications.

c. Work product

Material prepared in anticipation of litigation on behalf of a party is considered work product and is ordinarily not discoverable. However, if another party can show a substantial need for the work product and it cannot get the information in any other way without undue hardship, the court may order its disclosure. Under no circumstance will a court order discovery of an attorney's mental impressions, conclusions, opinions, or legal theories.

> **EXAM NOTE:** While an attorney's notes regarding litigation are protected from discovery, the information within those notes may not be. Additionally, documents prepared by a party before the cause of action arose or in the ordinary course of business are not protected by the work-product rule.

d. Accidental disclosure

Rule 502 provides protection to parties who inadvertently disclose privileged material if (i) the party took reasonable care to protect against the disclosure, and (ii) the disclosure was actually inadvertent.

e. Claims of privilege

Under Rule 26(b)(5)(A), whenever a party withholds information on the basis of a privilege or the attorney work-product doctrine, the party must expressly state the claim of privilege and describe the materials or communications not produced in a manner that will enable other parties to assess the applicability of the privilege or protection.

C. LIMITATIONS ON DISCOVERY

1. Required Limitations

On motion or on its own, the court is required to limit the frequency or extent of discovery otherwise allowed by the rules if it determines that:

  i) The discovery sought is unreasonably cumulative, or can be obtained from some other source that is more convenient or less expensive;

  ii) The party seeking discovery has had ample opportunity to obtain the information by discovery in the action; or

  iii) The proposed discovery is outside the scope permitted by Rule 26(b)(1) (not relevant and proportional).

When discovery is challenged, the court must weigh the party's interests in seeking discovery against the privacy interests of the party resisting discovery. *Eckstein Marine Serv., Inc. v. M/V Basin Pride,* 168 F.R.D. 38 (W.D. La. 1996). For example, discovery with respect to personnel records may be limited due to privacy concerns, *Gehring v. Case Corp.,* 43 F.3d 340, 342-43 (7th Cir. 1994).

2. Discretion to Alter Limits

The court may alter the limits in the rules as to the number of depositions, interrogatories, or requests for admission, or on the length of oral depositions.

3. Limitations on Electronically Stored Information

A party is not required to provide discovery of electronically stored information from sources that the party identifies as not reasonably accessible because of undue burden or cost. If challenged, the party will have the burden to show the undue burden and cost. Even if shown, the court may still order such discovery if the requesting party shows good cause. Rule 26(b)(2)(B). Moreover, the requesting party may specify the form in which the documents should be produced.

4. Protective Orders

Under Rule 26(c), the court may, for good cause, enter orders to protect parties and other persons from annoyance, embarrassment, oppression, or undue burden or expense resulting from discovery. For example, a party may seek a court order limiting the time and manner of conducting a physical examination, and a non-party who is served with a subpoena to attend a deposition may, by filing a motion to squash the subpoena, seek a court order to that effect.

5. Experts

Under Rule 26(b)(4)(A), a party is entitled to depose any expert witness of an opposing party whose opinions may be presented at trial.

As of December 1, 2010, Rule 26(b)(3) protects drafts of any expert report or disclosure required under Rule 26(a)(2). Any communications between the party's attorney and an expert witness who is required to provide a report are also protected, except to the extent that the communications (i) relate to the expert's compensation, (ii) identify facts or data that the party's attorney provided and that the expert considered in forming his opinion, or (iii) identify assumptions that the party's attorney provided and the expert relied upon.

If the expert was retained or specially employed by another party in anticipation of litigation or to prepare for trial but is not expected to be called as a witness, discovery is permitted only on showing exceptional circumstances under which it is impracticable for the party to obtain facts or opinions on the same subject by other means. Rule 26(b)(4)(D).

A report of an examining physician who is not expected to testify, however, can be obtained as provided under Rule 35(b).

6. Supplementation

Pursuant to Rule 26(e)(1)(A), if a party who has made a required disclosure or responded to an interrogatory, request for production, or request for admission learns that the disclosure or response is materially incomplete or incorrect, the party is required to supplement or correct the disclosure or response in a timely manner.

There is no duty to supplement or correct if such information has otherwise been made known to the other parties in discovery or in writing.

As to an expert whose report must be disclosed under Rule 26(a)(2)(B), the party's duty to supplement extends both to information included in the expert's report and to information given during the expert's deposition. Rule 26(e)(2).

D. DISCOVERY CONFERENCE

1. Rule 26(f)

Under Rule 26(f), except in a proceeding exempted from the initial disclosure rules or if the court orders otherwise, the parties must confer as soon as practicable, and in any event at least 21 days before a scheduling conference is to be held or a scheduling order is due under Rule 16(b) (*see* § VIII.H., *infra*) to:

    i) Consider the nature and basis of their claims and defenses and the possibilities for promptly settling or resolving of the case;

ii) Make or arrange for the automatic disclosures required by Rule 26(a)(1);

iii) Discuss any issues about preserving discoverable information; and

iv) Develop a proposed discovery plan.

The attorneys of record and all unrepresented parties that have appeared in the case are jointly responsible for arranging the conference, for attempting in good faith to agree on the proposed discovery plan, and for submitting to the court within 14 days after the conference a written report outlining the plan.

The discovery plan must state the parties' views on the discovery that may be needed in the case; the schedule for such discovery; requested modifications and limits to the scope of discovery; issues about electronically stored information or privilege; and any scheduling or protective order that should be entered by the court.

The discovery plan must also indicate when the initial automatic disclosures were or are to be made.

2. Failure to Participate in the Framing of the Discovery Plan

Pursuant to Rule 37(f), if a party or her attorney fails to participate in good faith in the development and submission of a proposed discovery plan, the court may, after providing an opportunity for a hearing, order the party or attorney to pay the reasonable expenses, including attorney's fees, incurred as a result of such failure.

E. DISCOVERY DEVICES

1. Depositions

Depositions are widely used and can take two forms: oral depositions, which are common to almost all litigation in federal court, and written depositions, which are rarely used.

a. Oral depositions

1) When an oral deposition may be taken

Under Rule 30, a party may take the deposition of any party or non-party witness at any time after the party has made its mandatory initial disclosures pursuant to Rule 26(a).

Without leave of the court, the plaintiffs, the defendants, and the third-party defendants, each as a group, are limited to 10 depositions by oral or written examination.

Unless the parties agree to the deposition, leave of the court must be obtained to:

i) Exceed the 10-deposition limitation;

ii) Depose a witness a second time; or

iii) Depose a person before the deposing party has complied with its initial disclosure requirements under Rule 26(a).

2) Notice of deposition

A party who seeks an oral deposition of a person must obtain a court order and give reasonable written notice, at least 21 days prior to the hearing for the order, to every other party, stating the time and place of the deposition and, if known, the deponent's name and address.

Notice of deposition is all that is needed to compel attendance by any party, even a party who is beyond the reach of the court's subpoena power. To compel attendance by a non-party, a subpoena must be served. Rule 30(b).

3) **Deposing a corporation, partnership, association, or government entity**

When deposing a corporation, partnership, association, or government entity, Rule 30(b)(6) states that the notice must describe with reasonable particularity the areas of inquiry, and it must state that the named entity has the duty to designate a representative with respect to the designated areas of inquiry.

The named entity must then designate one or more officers, directors, or managing agents, or other people who consent to testify on the entity's behalf with regard to those areas.

4) **Conducting an oral deposition**

A deposition must be conducted before an officer who is appointed or designated under Rule 28 to administer oaths and take testimony, unless the parties agree otherwise. By stipulation of the parties or by court order, a deposition may be taken by telephonic or other remote electronic means.

   i)   Examination of the deponent may proceed as permitted at trial under the Federal Rules of Evidence except that cross-examination is not limited to matters raised on direct examination. Rule 30(c).

   ii) The deponent is to be placed under oath and the testimony is to be recorded either by stenographic or electronic means. Rule 30(b).

   iii) Any objections are to be made on the record, but the examination still proceeds. The testimony is taken subject to any objection. Rule 30(c)(2).

   iv) A person may instruct the deponent not to answer only when necessary to preserve a privilege, to enforce a limitation ordered by the court, or to present a motion to terminate or limit the examination. Rule 30(c)(2).

Under Rule 30(d)(1), a deposition is limited to one day of seven hours, unless the parties agree otherwise or the court orders otherwise. The court must allow additional time if needed to fairly examine the deponent, or if the deponent, another person, or any other circumstance impedes or delays the deposition.

5) **Motion to terminate or limit an oral deposition**

At any time during an oral deposition, the deponent or a party may move to terminate or limit such deposition on the ground that it is being conducted in bad faith or in a manner that unreasonably annoys, embarrasses, or oppresses the deponent or party. Rule 30(d)(3)(A).

6) **Failure to attend a deposition**

Pursuant to Rule 30(g), if a party given notice to attend a deposition attends expecting such deposition, and the noticing party fails to attend or proceed with the deposition, the noticing party is subject to a court order requiring payment of reasonable expenses to the other party.

b. Written depositions

Pursuant to Rule 31, depositions may be taken by providing written questions to the deponent. The same rules regarding leave of court and deposing an organization that apply to oral depositions apply to written ones. They are as follows:

i) To take a written deposition, the deposing party must serve the questions and a notice, identifying the deponent and the officer before whom the deposition will be taken, to all other parties (Rule 31(a)(3));

ii) The other parties may then serve cross-questions, re-direct questions, and re-cross-questions on all other parties (Rule 31(a)(5));

iii) The deposing party serves the notice and all questions on the officer designated in the notice (Rule 31(b)); and

iv) The officer asks the written questions of the deponent and records the deponent's oral responses stenographically or by electronic means (*id.*).

c. Irregularities in depositions

Certain errors and irregularities in depositions are waived if not objected to in a timely manner.

2. Interrogatories

a. Availability

Pursuant to Rule 33(a), any party may serve no more than 25 written interrogatories on any other party. Interrogatories may not be used on non-party witnesses.

b. Scope

Pursuant to Rule 33(a)(2), interrogatories may relate to any matters permitted to be inquired into under Rule 26(b)(1) (i.e., non-privileged matters relevant to any party's claim or defense and proportional to the needs of the case). An interrogatory is not objectionable merely because it asks for an opinion or contention that relates to fact or the application of law to fact, but the court may order that the interrogatory need not be answered until designated discovery is complete, or until a pre-trial conference or some other time.

c. Answers and objections

Under Rule 33(b)(1), the interrogatories must be answered by the party to whom they are directed, or if that party is a corporation, partnership, association, or government entity, by any officer or agent, who must furnish the information available to the party.

Each interrogatory must be answered fully and separately under oath, unless the responding party objects to the interrogatory. The grounds for objecting to an interrogatory must be stated with specificity. Any ground not stated in a timely objection is deemed waived, unless the court, for good cause, excuses the failure. Rule 33(b)(2), (3).

The responding party must serve its answers and any objections within 30 days after being served with the interrogatories. The court may order or the parties may stipulate to a shorter or longer time. Rule 33(b)(4).

The person who makes the answers must sign them, and the attorney who objects must sign any objections. Rule 33(b)(5).

d. Option to produce business records

Under Rule 33(d), if the answer to an interrogatory may be ascertained from the business records (including electronically stored information) or summation of the business records of the responding party, and the burden of deriving the answers is substantially the same for the party serving the interrogatories as for the responding party, the responding party may answer the interrogatory by specifying the records from which the answer may be derived and providing the party who served the interrogatories with an opportunity to examine and copy such records.

3. Requests to Produce Documents and Inspect Land

a. In general

Under Rule 34(a)(1), a party may serve on any other party a request to produce and permit the requesting party or its representative to inspect, copy, test, or sample any of the following items in the responding party's possession, custody, or control:

    i) Any designated documents or electronically stored information (including writings, drawings, graphs, charts, photographs, sound recordings, images, and other data or data compilations) stored in any medium from which information can be obtained either directly or, if necessary, after translation by the responding party into a reasonably usable form; or

    ii) Any designated tangible things.

A party may also serve a request to enter onto another party's land to inspect, measure, survey, photograph, test, or sample the property or a designated object or operation on the property, if relevant to the action. Rule 34(a)(2).

While these requests may be directed only to other parties, non-parties may be compelled to produce documents and other things or submit to an inspection pursuant to a subpoena served under Rule 45. Rule 34(c).

b. Contents of request

Pursuant to Rule 34(b)(1), the request must describe the items to be inspected, must set forth a reasonable time and place for inspection, and may specify the form in which electronically stored information should be produced.

c. Responses and objections

The party to whom the request is directed must respond in writing within 30 days after being served or within 30 days after the parties' first rule 26(f) conference, if the request was served prior to that conference unless a shorter or longer time is stipulated by the parties or ordered by the court. If a party fails to respond to a document request or to allow inspection, or objects to a request, then the requesting party may move to compel under Rule 37(a). Rule 34(b)(2)(A). The responding party may state that it will produce copies of documents or electronically stored information instead of permitting inspection. The production must be completed no later than the time for inspection specified in the request or another reasonable time specified in the response. Rule 34(b)(2)(B).

With regard to electronically stored information, if a request does not specify a form for its production, a party must produce it in a form or forms in which it is ordinarily maintained or in a reasonably usable form or forms. A party need not produce the same electronically stored information in more than one form. Rule 34(b)(2)(E).

4. Physical and Mental Exams

a. In general

Under Rule 35(a), if the mental or physical condition (including blood type) of a party or a person in the legal custody or control of a party is in controversy, the court may order such person to submit to a physical or mental examination by a "suitably licensed or certified examiner."

b. Procedure

Such an order may be made only upon motion, for good cause shown, and the person to be examined and all parties must be given prior notice specifying the time, place, conditions, and scope of the examination and the identity of the examiner. Rule 35(a)(2).

A "suitably licensed or certified examiner" need not be a physician and can include others licensed to report on physical or mental conditions, including psychologists and dentists.

c. Report of examiner

On request by the party or person examined, the party who requested the examination must provide a copy of the examiner's written report, including results of all tests, diagnoses, and conclusions, as well as any reports of earlier examinations of the same condition. If the examiner refuses to make a report, the examiner's testimony may be excluded at trial. Rule 35(b).

d. Other examinations

After delivery of the examiner's report, a party who was examined must provide the party who moved for the examination, on request, a report of all other previous or subsequent examinations of the same condition in that party's custody or control. Rule 35(b)(3).

If the party who was examined obtains the report of the examination or conducts a deposition of the examiner, the party waives any privilege it may have regarding the testimony of any other person who has examined or thereafter examines the party with respect to the same condition. Rule 35(b)(4).

5. Requests for Admission

a. In general

Under Rule 36, a party may serve upon any other party a written request for the admission of any relevant, non-privileged matters discoverable under Rule 26. The requested matters may relate to statements or opinions of facts or of the application of law to fact, including the genuineness of any documents described in the request. Rule 36(a)(1). Each matter for which an admission is requested must be set forth separately. A request to admit the genuineness of a document must be accompanied by a copy of the document unless it is, or has been, otherwise furnished or made available for inspection and copying. Rule 36(a)(2).

b. Responses and objections

A matter will be admitted unless, within 30 days after being served, the party to whom the request is directed serves on the requesting party a written answer or objection addressed to the matter and signed by the party or her attorney. Rule 36(a)(3).

If a matter is not admitted, the answer must specifically deny it or state in detail why the answering party cannot truthfully admit or deny it. A denial must fairly respond to the substance of the matter, and when good faith requires that a party qualify an answer or deny only a part of a matter, the answer must specify the part admitted and qualify or deny the rest. Rule 36(a)(4).

An answering party may assert lack of knowledge or information as a reason for failing to admit or deny only if the party states that he has made a reasonable inquiry and that the information he knows or can readily obtain is not sufficient to enable him to admit or deny. *Id.*

c. Effect of an admission

A matter admitted under Rule 36 is conclusively established unless the court, on motion, permits the admission to be withdrawn or amended. An admission under Rule 36 is an admission only in the pending action and cannot be used against the party in any other proceeding. *Id.*

F. USE OF DISCOVERY AT TRIAL

Information gathered through the use of discovery devices is not automatically admissible as evidence at trial. In order to be admissible, the information must comply with the evidentiary rules.

1. Use of Depositions

a. At trial

Depositions may be used by a party to impeach the testimony of the deponent as a witness or for any other purpose permitted by the Federal Rules of Evidence. Rule 32(a)(2). Pursuant to Rule 32(a)(3), an adverse party may use for any purpose the deposition of a party or a person who, when deposed, was the party's officer, director, managing agent, or designated deponent.

In addition, a party may use for any purpose the deposition of a witness, whether or not a party, if the court finds that:

 i) The witness is dead;

 ii) The witness is more than 100 miles from the trial or is outside the United States, unless it appears that the witness's absence was procured by the party offering the deposition;

 iii) The witness cannot attend or testify because of age, illness, infirmity, or imprisonment;

 iv) The party offering the deposition could not procure the witness's attendance by subpoena; or

 v) On motion and notice, exceptional circumstances make it desirable in the interest of justice to permit the deposition to be used.

Rule 32(a)(4). If admissible, a deposition may generally be offered against any party who was present or represented at the deposition, or had reasonable notice of it.

b. Objections to the admissibility of depositions

Pursuant to Rule 32(b), an objection to the admission of any deposition testimony that would be inadmissible if the witness were present and testifying may generally be made at the time the deposition is offered at a hearing or trial.

2. Answers to Interrogatories

Under Rule 33(c), an answer to an interrogatory may be used to the extent allowed by Federal Rule of Evidence 801(d)(2), whereby a party's answer will generally constitute a party admission. An interrogatory answer could, however, constitute hearsay if offered against another party.

G. ENFORCEMENT

1. Motion to Compel

a. In general

Under Rule 37, if a party fails to make the automatic disclosures required by Rule 26(a) or fails to respond to discovery that has been properly served, the party seeking the information may move to compel such disclosure or discovery.

An evasive or incomplete disclosure, answer, or response is treated as a failure to disclose, answer, or respond. Generally, making a motion to compel is a prerequisite to obtaining any sanctions under Rule 37 (*see* § VIII.G.2, *infra*).

b. Procedure

A motion to compel must be served on all parties and be accompanied by a certificate that the movant has in good faith conferred or attempted to confer with the opposing party in an effort to obtain the disclosure or secure the information or material without court action. Rule 37(a)(1).

If the subject of the motion to compel is a party, the motion must be filed with the court where the action is pending. If the subject of the motion is a non-party who was subpoenaed under Rule 45, the motion must be filed in the court that issued the subpoena. Rule 37(a)(2).

c. Fees and expenses

1) If motion is granted

A successful movant is entitled to recover her reasonable expenses incurred in connection with the motion, including reasonable attorney's fees. The court may order the opposing party, his attorney who advised the refusal of disclosure or discovery, or both, to pay the expenses. Rule 37(a)(5)(A).

Expenses cannot be awarded if:

i) The movant failed to make a good-faith effort to secure the information before filing the motion;

ii) The opposing party demonstrates that his nondisclosure, response, or objection was substantially justified; or

iii) Other circumstances render unjust an award of expenses.

2) If motion is denied

If the motion to compel is denied and the court determines that the motion was made without substantial justification, the court must, after providing an opportunity to be heard, require the movant, the attorney filing the motion, or both, to pay the party or deponent who opposed the motion her reasonable expenses incurred in opposing the motion, including attorney's fees. Rule 37(a)(5)(B).

3) If motion is granted in part and denied in part

If the motion is granted in part and denied in part, the court may apportion fees in its discretion, after providing an opportunity for the parties to be heard. Rule 37(a)(5)(C).

2. Sanctions

a. Failure to comply with a court order

If a party fails to obey a court order regarding discovery, the court may impose any of the following sanctions pursuant to Rule 37(b)(2):

i) Directing that the matters addressed in the order or other facts be taken as established for purposes of the action;

ii) Prohibiting the disobedient party from supporting or opposing designated claims or defenses, or from introducing designated matters in evidence;

iii) Striking pleadings in whole or in part;

iv) Staying further proceedings until the order is obeyed;

v) Dismissing the action in whole or in part;

vi) Rendering a default judgment against the disobedient party; and

vii) Treating as contempt of court the failure to obey any order, except an order to submit to a physical or mental examination.

Note that the mere failure to respond to discovery or disclosure obligations is not subject to sanctions under Rule 37; there must be a violation of a court order.

The list of sanctions in Rule 37(b)(2) is not exclusive. The court may order any sanction that is "just." Instead of or in addition to such sanctions, the court may also require the disobedient party, his attorney, or both to pay the movant's reasonable expenses, including attorney's fees incurred as a result of the failure to comply, except when the failure was substantially justified or imposition of fees would be unjust. Rule 37(b)(2)(C).

b. Failure to make automatic disclosures

Under Rule 37(c)(1), if a party fails to make or supplement its automatic disclosures as required by Rules 26(a) and (e), the party will not be permitted to use the documents or witnesses that were not disclosed unless the non-disclosure was substantially justified or was harmless.

This rule applies to the use of such evidence at trial and for motions and hearings, but it does not apply to the use of such evidence for impeachment purposes, since Rule 26(a) does not require disclosure of impeachment evidence or witnesses.

c. Failure to admit under Rule 36

Pursuant to Rule 37(c)(2), when a party fails to admit a matter requested under Rule 36 and another party proves the matter to be true at trial, the party proving the matter can move for the award of reasonable expenses, including reasonable attorney's fees, incurred in proving the matter.

d. Failure of party to attend her own deposition, serve answers to interrogatories, or respond to a request for inspection

Under Rule 37(d)(1)(A)(i), if a party fails to appear at her own deposition after being properly notified, the court may impose sanctions. A failure to appear will not be excused on the ground that the discovery sought was objectionable, unless the party failing to act has a pending motion for a protective order.

The court may also impose sanctions if a party fails to answer or object to properly served interrogatories under Rule 33 or fails to serve a written response to a properly served request for the production of documents or other things under Rule 34. Rule 37(d)(1)(A)(ii). A party moving for sanctions under such circumstances must certify that she conferred or attempted to confer in good faith with the opposing party in an effort to obtain a response without court action. Rule 37(d)(1)(B).

e. Electronically stored information

If electronically stored information that should have been preserved in the anticipation or conduct of litigation is lost because a party failed to take reasonable steps to preserve it, and it cannot be restored or replaced through additional discovery, then the court: (i) upon finding prejudice to another party, may order measures no greater than necessary to cure the prejudice, or (ii) upon finding that the party acted with the intent to deprive another party of the information, may presume the lost information was unfavorable to the party, instruct the jury that it may or must presume the information was unfavorable, or dismiss the action or enter a default judgment. Rule 37(e).

f. "Abuse of discretion" review standard

Sanctions are subject to review under the "abuse of discretion" standard. Generally, the harshest sanctions—dismissal of the action and entry of a default judgment—are reserved for misconduct that is serious, repeated, contumacious, extreme, or inexcusable. Usually, a court should impose lesser sanctions before meting out more severe ones. *See Bachier-Ortiz v. Colon-Mendoza,* 331 F.3d 193 (1st Cir. 2003).

H. PRE-TRIAL CONFERENCES

Under Rule 16(a), the court may direct counsel and unrepresented parties to appear for pre-trial conferences for such purposes as expediting disposition of the action, effective case management, and facilitating settlement. If counsel or a party fails to appear, participate in good faith, or obey a pre-trial conference order, the court may generally impose the same sanctions as those permitted for failure of a party to comply with a discovery order. Dismissal of an action is a severe sanction, and generally is appropriate only when a party's conduct is serious, repeated, extreme, and otherwise inexcusable.

IX. ADJUDICATION WITHOUT TRIAL

A. DISMISSAL

Rule 41 sets forth the procedure for obtaining dismissal of a complaint, counterclaim, cross-claim, or third-party claim. Dismissal can be voluntary or involuntary under the rule.

1. Voluntary

a. By filing notice or by stipulation of the parties

Pursuant to Rule 41(a)(1)(A), a plaintiff may dismiss an action without leave of the court by filing a notice of dismissal at any time before the opposing party serves either an answer or a motion for summary judgment or by filing a stipulation of dismissal signed by all parties who have appeared in the action.

Unless otherwise stated in the notice or stipulation, the voluntary dismissal will be without prejudice. However, if a plaintiff voluntarily dismissed a prior state or federal action based on the same claim by filing a notice of dismissal, then a subsequent dismissal of the same claim by notice will be with prejudice. This is referred to as the "two-dismissal" rule. Rule 41(a)(1)(B).

b. By motion and court order

Except as provided previously, an action may be dismissed at the plaintiff's request only by court order, on terms that the court considers proper. Rule 41(a)(2).

A voluntary dismissal by court order is without prejudice unless the order states otherwise. However, when a plaintiff moves for dismissal without prejudice under Rule 41(a)(2), the decision to dismiss with or without prejudice is left to the discretion of the court, and voluntary dismissal without prejudice is not a matter of right. *See Mobil Oil Corp. v. Advanced Envtl. Recycling Techs., Inc.*, 203 F.R.D. 156 (D. Del. 2001); *Jaskot v. Brown*, 167 F.R.D. 372 (S.D.N.Y. 1996).

c. Counterclaim, cross-claim, or third-party claim

A voluntary dismissal of a counterclaim, cross-claim, or third-party claim must be made before a responsive pleading is served, or, if there is no responsive pleading, before evidence is introduced at a hearing or trial.

2. Involuntary

Under Rule 41(b), if the plaintiff fails to prosecute or to comply with the Rules or a court order, a defendant may move to dismiss the action or any claim against him.

Unless the court's dismissal order specifies otherwise, a dismissal under Rule 41(b) is with prejudice and operates as an adjudication on the merits. A dismissal based on a lack of jurisdiction, improper venue, or failure to join an indispensable party under Rule 19, however, will not operate as an adjudication on the merits.

B. DEFAULT AND DEFAULT JUDGMENT

A default results from the defendant's failure to respond within the timeframe set out under Rule 12. A defendant has 21 days from service of process to respond to a complaint either by an answer or by a pre-answer motion, or to seek additional time to answer. If a defendant does not take one of these steps, she risks a default under Rule 55. This default (defendant's failure to respond) is not the same as a default judgment and does not automatically entitle the plaintiff to relief. It simply begins a process whereby the plaintiff can proceed to recovery. More importantly, however, it cuts off the defendant's right to file a response. A default judgment, on the other hand, creates a legal obligation from the defendant to the plaintiff. It is binding and enforceable against the defendant as any other judgment would be.

Under Rule 55(a), in order for the plaintiff to obtain a default judgment, she must first request that an entry of default for the defendant's failure to respond be entered by the clerk of the court. Generally, the plaintiff must show that (i) service of process was effected on the defendant by filing a proof of service, (ii) the requisite time to respond to the complaint has passed, and (iii) the defendant has failed to respond. Once the default is entered, the plaintiff may then obtain a default judgment, either from the clerk directly if the amount is certain, or, when the amount is not certain, by applying to the court for a default judgment. Rule 55(b).

Even if the defendant is in default, the plaintiff has no absolute right to a default judgment. Rule 55(c) states that "[t]he court may set aside an entry of default for good cause, and it may set aside a default judgment under Rule 60(b)." So long as the defendant is acting in good faith, good cause usually equates to reasons beyond the defendant's control or to an honest oversight by the defendant. Rule 60(b) dictates stricter guidelines for the court to set aside a default judgment because a judgment is an official judicial order granting the plaintiff recovery and is not taken lightly.

C. SUMMARY JUDGMENT

1. Standard

Under Rule 56(c), a motion for summary judgment is applicable to all civil actions and should be granted if the pleadings, the discovery and disclosure materials on file, and any affidavits show that there is no genuine issue as to any material fact and that the movant is entitled to judgment as a matter of law. A genuine issue of material fact exists when a reasonable jury could return a verdict in favor of the non-moving party. *Anderson v. Liberty Lobby, Inc.,* 477 U.S. 242 (1986). In ruling on a motion for summary judgment, the court is to construe all evidence in the light most favorable to the non-moving party and resolve all doubts in favor of the non-moving party.

2. Burden of Proof

The movant has the burden of persuasion on a motion for summary judgment. Once the movant makes a prima facie showing that summary judgment is appropriate, the burden of proof shifts to the opposing party to set forth specific evidence showing the existence of a genuine issue of fact for trial. *Celotex Corp. v. Catrett,* 477 U.S. 317 (1986). "When opposing parties tell two different stories, one of which is blatantly contradicted by the record, so that no reasonable jury could believe it, a court should not adopt that version of the facts for purposes of ruling on a motion for summary judgment." *Scott v. Harris,* 550 U.S. 372, 380 (2007).

3. Evidence

In deciding a motion for summary judgment, the court may consider affidavits, pleadings, deposition transcripts, interrogatory answers, admissions, and stipulations filed by the party, even if they are not presented in a form that is admissible at trial, so long as the facts contained in the submissions are admissible at trial. *Stinnett v. Iron Works Gym/Executive Health Spa, Inc.,* 301 F.3d 610, 613 (7th Cir. 2002). Supporting and opposing affidavits must be made on personal knowledge and must establish the affiant's competency to testify on the matters stated. The judge must view any evidence presented "through the prism" of the "substantive evidentiary standard of proof that would apply at the trial on the merits." *Anderson,* 477 U.S. at 252, 254. If a motion for summary judgment is properly made and supported, an opposing party may not rely merely on allegations or denials in its own pleading, but she must set out specific facts showing a genuine issue for trial. If the opposing party does not so respond, summary judgment, if appropriate, will be entered against that party. Rule 56(e)(2).

4. Partial Summary Judgment

Pursuant to Rule 56(d)(1), if summary judgment is not rendered on the entire action, the court should, to the extent practicable, determine what material facts are not genuinely at issue.

Rule 56(d)(2) also permits the court to grant summary judgment on the issue of liability alone, if a genuine issue of fact is present with regard to damages. Such a judgment will be interlocutory and thus not generally appealable until a final judgment with regard to damages is entered.

5. Time for Making Motion

Under Rule 56(b), a party may move for summary judgment on all or part of the claim at any time set by local rule or until 30 days after the close of discovery; a party opposing such a motion must file a response within the later of 21 days after service or a responsive pleading is due. If a party opposing summary judgment has insufficient information to support her opposition, she may request that the court stay its consideration of the motion pending further discovery under Rule 56(d).

6. Appeal

In general, an order denying summary judgment is not subject to immediate appeal. A grant of full summary judgment is a final disposition on the merits and is subject to appeal.

However, if a party fails to properly support an assertion of fact or properly address another party's assertion of fact as required by Rule 56(c), the court may (i) give an opportunity to properly support or address the fact, (ii) consider the fact undisputed for the purposes of the motion, (iii) grant summary judgment if the motion and supporting materials show that the movant is entitled to it, or (iv) issue any other appropriate order. Rule 56(e).

D. DECLARATORY JUDGMENT

A declaratory judgment is a ruling in which the court tells the parties to a dispute what their rights, responsibilities, or obligations are, without awarding damages or ordering the parties to do (or refrain from doing) anything. Parties generally seek a declaratory judgment in order to resolve uncertainty and avoid the possibility of a future lawsuit. Under the federal Declaratory Judgment Act, 28 U.S.C. § 2201, a federal court may award declaratory relief in actions within the court's original jurisdiction, with the exception of certain actions concerning taxes, bankruptcy, free trade, or drug patents. Most states have enacted statutes permitting their courts to issue declaratory judgments.

X. TRIAL PROCEDURE

A. JURY TRIAL

1. Right to Jury Trial

Rule 38 provides that the right of trial by jury as declared by the Seventh Amendment to the U.S. Constitution, or as provided by a federal statute, is preserved to the parties inviolate. In general, an action at law will be tried on demand to a jury, but an action in equity (e.g., an action for injunction) will not. If a new cause of action that was unknown at common law is created, the court must look to the remedy sought and will generally allow a jury if the relief sought is legal rather than equitable. If an action involves both legal and equitable claims, the jury normally determines the legal claims first, and the court then determines the equitable claims, but the court is bound by the jury's findings on the legal claims. *Beacon Theatres, Inc. v. Westover,* 359 U.S. 500 (1959).

2. Jury Demand and Waiver

Under Rule 38(b), any party may make a demand for trial by jury. The demand must be in writing and served within 14 days after service of the last pleading directed to the issue that is sought to be tried by a jury. A party waives a jury trial unless her demand is properly served and filed.

3. Jury Size

Under Rule 48(a), a jury must initially have at least six and no more than 12 members. Having been selected, a juror must participate in the verdict unless dismissed for good cause. There is no provision in the federal rules for the selection of alternate jurors, as is the practice in some states.

4. Jury Deliberations and Verdicts

a. Deliberations

One of the duties of a juror is to listen to the evidence presented in court and weigh that evidence fairly when reaching a verdict. Jurors may take their notes and all papers or exhibits presented during the trial into the deliberation room. Jurors cannot consider other matters not formally admitted into evidence, nor are they permitted to discuss the facts of the case with any non-jurors.

b. Verdicts

A verdict is formal decision issued by a jury on the issues of fact that were presented at trial. Unless the parties stipulate otherwise, the verdict must be unanimous and must be returned by a jury of at least six members. Rule 48(b).

1) Special

A special verdict is a form of a special written finding on each issue of fact. A court will submit written questions to the jury correlating to each ultimate fact of the case and ask the jury to make a finding on each fact. Rule 49(a).

2) General

A general verdict is the usual form of verdict when a jury's decision in a civil case is in favor of one or the other party.

3) General with special interrogatories

This type of verdict is an ordinary general verdict coupled with special findings of fact, similar to a special verdict. This type of verdict is used to ensure that the jury independently considered the material facts of the case.

4) Verdicts in error

If a party believes that the jury has returned an erroneous verdict that can be corrected, he must raise this issue with the court. The verdict may be set aside if the court believes that the jury did not follow its instructions properly.

5. Polling

The jury must be polled on a party's request, and any lack of unanimity or assent will result in continued deliberations or a new trial. Rule 48(c).

6. Selection

Under Rule 47(a), the court may permit the parties or their attorneys to examine prospective jurors or may do so itself.

a. Peremptory challenges

Peremptory challenges may not be made for racial- or gender-based reasons. *Edmonson v. Leesville Concrete Co.,* 500 U.S. 614 (1991); *J.E.B. v. Alabama,* 511 U.S. 127 (1994). In civil cases, each side has three peremptory challenges. Several defendants or several plaintiffs may be considered as a single party for the purposes of making such challenges, or the court may allow additional peremptory challenges and permit them to be exercised separately or jointly.

b. Challenges for cause

Each party is entitled to an unlimited number of challenges for cause, such as bias or a personal relationship with a litigant. The court rules on such challenges. 28 U.S.C. § 1870.

7. Jury Instructions

Under Rule 51, parties may file and serve proposed instructions for the court to give the jury. The court is required to inform the parties of any instructions it proposes to give prior to the parties' closing arguments to the jury. The parties are then entitled to an opportunity to object on the record and out of the jury's presence before the instructions and arguments are delivered. The court may instruct the jury on the applicable law in the case either before or after closing arguments.

8. Jury Misconduct

Misconduct can occur when a juror conceals facts relating to his qualifications or gives false testimony during voir dire. To obtain a new trial, a party must not only demonstrate that the juror failed to answer honestly a material question on voir dire, but also show that a proper response would have provided a valid basis for a challenge for cause. *McDonough Power Equip. v. Greenwood*, 464 U.S. 548 (1984).

If the juror violates the confidentiality of deliberations, is improperly influenced by nonjurors, or takes it upon himself to investigate facts outside of those presented at trial, then the court may dismiss the juror or, if necessary, order a new trial. Note that, while generally a juror may not impeach her own verdict, she may testify on the question of whether extraneous prejudicial information was improperly brought to the jury's attention or whether any outside influence was improperly brought to bear on a juror. Fed. R. Evid. 606(b).

B. TRIAL BY THE COURT

A case will be tried by the court without a jury if no right to a jury trial exists (or if such right has been waived). The court is the finder of fact; it must find the facts specially and state its conclusions of law separately. The findings and conclusions may be stated on the record after the close of evidence or may appear in an opinion or a memorandum of decision filed by the court. The court is not required to state findings or conclusions when ruling on a motion under Rule 12 (motions against the complaint) or Rule 56 (summary judgment) or, unless the rules provide otherwise, on any other motion. Rule 52(a).

C. CONSOLIDATION ACTIONS AND SEPARATE TRIALS

If actions before the court involve a common question of fact or law, the court may join for hearing or trial any or all matters at issue in the actions, consolidate the actions, or issue any other orders to avoid unnecessary cost or delay. Rule 42(a). Conversely, a court may order a separate trial of one or more issues, claims (including cross-claims, counterclaims, and third-party claims) for convenience, to avoid prejudice, or to expedite and economize. When doing so, the court must preserve any federal right to a jury trial. Rule 42(b).

D. PREJUDGMENT ATTACHMENT

At the commencement and through the course of an action, a plaintiff may file a motion for prejudgment attachment as allowed by the state where the court is located. A prejudgment attachment provides for seizing a person or property to secure satisfaction of a potential judgment. Federal statute governs the extent to which the state statute may be applied, and remedies include arrest, attachment, garnishment, replevin, sequestration, and other equivalent remedies.

In addition to filing the motion, the plaintiff must give the defendant notice and an opportunity to be heard by preparing a writ of attachment in addition to a summons and complaint. A court will grant a prejudgment attachment only if the plaintiff shows that there is a likelihood of success of recovering an amount equal to the amount being sought to attach. Rule 64.

E.   JUDGMENT AS A MATTER OF LAW

Rule 50 provides procedural requirements for challenging the sufficiency of the evidence in a civil jury trial. The rule establishes two separate but related stages for such challenges. Prior to submission of the case to the jury, a party may file a motion for judgment as a matter of law under Rule 50(a). This is also called a "motion for a directed verdict." After the verdict and entry of judgment, a party may renew their motion for judgment as a matter of law pursuant to Rule 50(b). This renewed motion may also be referred to as a "motion for judgment notwithstanding the verdict."

1.   Motion for Judgment as a Matter of Law ("Directed Verdict")

Under Rule 50(a), once a party has been fully heard on an issue at a jury trial, the court may grant a motion for judgment as a matter of law resolving the issue against a party if the court finds that there is insufficient evidence for a jury reasonably to find for that party. The court may also grant such a motion against the party on any claim or defense that is dependent on a favorable finding on that issue.

a.   Standard

The court must view the evidence in the light most favorable to the opposing party and draw all reasonable inferences from the evidence in favor of the opposing party. It may not consider the credibility of witnesses or evaluate the weight of the evidence, and it must disregard all evidence favorable to the moving party that the jury is not required to believe. *Reeves v. Sanderson Plumbing Prods., Inc.*, 530 U.S. 133 (2000). If reasonable persons can draw different inferences, then the issue is for the jury to decide, and the motion cannot be granted.

b.   Procedure and timing

A motion for judgment as a matter of law may be made at any time before the case is submitted to the jury. The motion must specify the judgment sought and the law and facts that entitle the movant to the judgment.

If a party moves for judgment as a matter of law after the close of the plaintiff's case and the motion is denied, then the party may be unable to pursue a renewed motion for judgment as a matter of law after entry of judgment unless the party also moves for judgment as a matter of law after the presentation of all evidence. There is a dispute among the circuit courts as to whether the second motion is always mandatory or whether it is unnecessary when the defendant's evidence could not have caused the court to grant the motion. *Compare Mid-America Tablewares, Inc. v. Mogi Trading Co.*, 100 F.3d 1353 (7th Cir. 1996) (second motion required) *with BE & K Constr. Co. v. United Bhd. of Carpenters & Joiners*, 90 F.3d 1318 (8th Cir. 1996) (second motion not required).

c.   Judgment on partial findings

In a nonjury trial, a defendant, instead of making a motion for a judgment as a matter of law, can move for a judgment on partial findings if the plaintiff has failed to prove his case. Rule 52(c).

2.   Renewed Motion for Judgment as a Matter of Law (JNOV)

Under Rule 50(b), if the court does not grant a motion for judgment as a matter of law, then the court is considered to have submitted the action to the jury subject to the court's later deciding the legal questions raised by the motion. The movant may file a renewed motion for judgment as a matter of law no later than 28 days after the entry of judgment. If the motion addresses a jury issue not decided by a verdict, then the renewed motion must be filed no later than 28 days after the jury was discharged.

A post-verdict motion under Rule 50(b) is only a renewal of the earlier motion made at the close of the evidence, and it can be granted only on grounds advanced in the pre-verdict motion. Therefore, filing a motion under Rule 50(a) for a judgment as a matter of law before the case is submitted to the jury is a requirement for consideration of a renewed motion for judgment as a matter of law under Rule 50(b). If a party fails to move for a judgment as a matter of law before the case goes to the jury, then an appellate court will not review whether a district court erred in refusing to grant the party's renewed motion for judgment as a matter of law. *See, e.g., Catlett v. Local 7370 of United Paper Workers Int'l Union*, 69 F.3d 254 (8th Cir. 1995); *Firestone Tire & Rubber Co. v. Pearson*, 769 F.2d 1471 (10th Cir. 1985).

In ruling on the renewed motion, the court may: (i) allow judgment on the verdict if the jury returned a verdict, (ii) order a new trial, or (iii) direct the entry of judgment as a matter of law. The same standards apply to the entry of the renewed motion as applied to the initial motion.

Under Rule 50(c), if the renewed motion for judgment as a matter of law is granted and the party had alternatively moved for a new trial, the court must also determine whether the motion for a new trial should be granted if the judgment is reversed or vacated on appeal.

F.   JUDGMENT

A judgment is a decree or order by a court that resolves the parties' rights and demands for relief in a manner that permits it to be appealed (*see* IX.B. Appeals, *infra*). Rule 54(a).

1.   Agreement With Pleadings

In general, a judgment should grant a party the relief to which the party is entitled, even if the party has not demanded such relief in its pleadings. However, a default judgment must not differ in kind or exceed in amount what is demanded in the pleadings. Rule 54(c).

2.   Costs

Unless a federal statute, rule, or court order provides otherwise, the prevailing party is allowed court costs, other than attorney's fees, without needing to file a motion. The court clerk may tax costs on 14 days' notice. A party may challenge the clerk's action by serving a motion within seven days. Rule 54(d)(1). By serving on an opposing party an offer to allow judgment on specified terms at least 14 days prior to the date set for trial, a defending party may limit such costs to the costs then accrued if the opposing party does not accept the offer and the judgment is less favorable to the opposing party than the offer. A similar offer may be made once a party is determined to be liable but damages have not been determined. Evidence of an unaccepted offer is not admissible except in a proceeding to determine costs. Rule 68.

3.   Attorney's fees

Unless a statute or court order provides otherwise, a claim for attorney's fees that is not required by law to be proved at trial as an element of damages must be made by a motion filed within 14 days after entry of judgment. Unless the court orders otherwise, this motion does not extend the time for filing an appeal. Rule 54(d)(2).

G.   MOTION TO AMEND OR MAKE ADDITIONAL FINDINGS

In a nonjury trial, a party may make a motion for the court to amend its findings or to make additional findings. This motion must be made within 28 days of the entry of judgment and may be combined with a new trial motion. Rule 52(b).

On appeal, a court's finding of facts can be set aside only if clearly erroneous. The reviewing court must give due regard to the trial court's opportunity to judge the witnesses' credibility. Rule 52(a)(6).

H. MOTION TO ALTER OR AMEND A JUDGMENT

A party may make a motion for the court to alter or amend a judgment. This motion must be made within 28 days of the entry of the judgment. Rule 59(e).

I. MOTION FOR A NEW TRIAL

1. Grounds

Under Rule 59(a), the court may, on motion by a party or on its own, grant a new trial on all issues or with respect to only certain issues or parties. Rule 59 does not specifically list the grounds that will justify a new trial, but in practice, the overarching theme is that the court may grant a new trial to prevent a miscarriage of justice. Some of the reasons that have been held to justify a new trial include:

i) Error at trial that renders the judgment unfair;

ii) Newly discovered evidence that existed at the time of the trial was excusably overlooked and would likely have altered the outcome of the trial;

iii) Prejudicial misconduct of counsel, a party, the judge, or a juror;

iv) The verdict is against the clear weight of the evidence;

v) The verdict is based on false evidence; or

vi) The verdict is excessive or inadequate.

In general, whether a new trial is warranted rests within the sound discretion of the trial court. *Montgomery Ward & Co. v. Duncan,* 311 U.S. 243 (1940). Under Rule 61, the court must disregard all errors and defects that do not affect any party's substantial rights. This is the "harmless error" rule.

After giving the parties notice and an opportunity to be heard, the court may grant a timely motion for a new trial for a reason not stated in a party's motion. The court must specify the reasons in its order.

2. Remittitur and Additur

If the court determines that a verdict was excessive, the court may offer a reduction of the verdict, known as a remittitur, and grant a new trial on the condition that the remittitur is not accepted. *See Hetzel v. Prince William Cnty.,* 523 U.S. 208 (1998). If the court determines that the verdict was inadequate, the court only has the option of ordering a new trial. An additur (enhanced judgment) is not permitted.

3. Timing

Pursuant to Rule 59(b) a motion for a new trial must be filed no later than 28 days after the entry of judgment. When the motion is based on affidavits, those affidavits must be filed with the motion. The opposing party then has 14 days after being served to file opposing affidavits. The court may permit reply affidavits. Rule 59(c).

XI. POST-TRIAL PROCEDURES

A. ALTERATION OF OR RELIEF FROM JUDGMENT

1. Rule 60(a): Correction of a Judgment

Rule 60(a) allows a court to correct a clerical or other mistake resulting from oversight or omission whenever one is found in a judgment, order, or other part of the record.

Fed. R. Civ. P. 60(a). An example of such a mistake would be when a court meant to enter a judgment for the plaintiff for $100,000, and it appeared in the written judgment as "$10,000." The court may make such a correction on its own initiative, with or without notice. However, once an appeal from the judgment or order has been docketed in the appellate court, such a correction can only be made with leave of the appellate court. *Id.*

2. Rule 60(b): Relief from a Judgment or Order

Rule 60(b) allows a court to relieve a party from a final judgment or order for a motion filed:

i) Within a reasonable time, and **no later than one year following the entry of the judgment or order** for:

a) Mistake, inadvertence, surprise, or excusable neglect;

b) Newly discovered evidence that could not have been earlier discovered with reasonable diligence; or

c) Fraud (intrinsic or extrinsic), misrepresentation, or misconduct by an opposing party; or

ii) Within a reasonable time, with no definite limiting period, on the grounds that: a judgment is void; a judgment has been satisfied, released, or discharged; a judgment was based on a judgment that was reversed or vacated; applying the judgment prospectively is no longer equitable; or for any other reason that justifies relief.

In sum, Rule 60(b) allows a court to exercise its equitable jurisdiction to relieve a party from a judgment in any case in which enforcing the judgment would work injustice, and the party seeking relief or its counsel was not guilty of misconduct or gross negligence. If a motion for relief is made, but the court lacks the authority to rule because of the pendency of an appeal, then the court may (i) defer, (ii) deny the motion, or (iii) state that it would grant the motion upon remand. Rule 62.1.

The court may provide any relief that it believes to be appropriate based on the evidence, and it is not limited to the relief requested in the pleadings.

3. Other Remedies

Despite the limitations otherwise imposed by Rule 60, a court may nevertheless:

i) Entertain an independent action to relieve a party from an order, judgment, or proceeding;

ii) Grant relief to a defendant who was not personally notified of the action (28 USC § 1655); or

iii) Set aside a judgment for fraud on the court.

Rule 60(d). Fraud on the court is fraud that is "limited to fraud which seriously affects the integrity of the normal process of adjudication." *Kupferman v. Consol. Research & Mfg. Corp.*, 459 F.2d 1072, 1078 (2d Cir. 1972). "[O]nly the most egregious misconduct, such as bribery of a judge or members of a jury, or the fabrication of evidence by a party in which an attorney is implicated, will constitute a fraud on the court." *Rozier v. Ford Motor Co.*, 573 F.2d 1332, 1338 (5th Cir. 1978).

B. **APPEALS**

1. **Final Judgment Rule**

    Under 28 U.S.C. § 1291, the federal courts of appeals have jurisdiction over appeals from the final judgments of the district courts. A final judgment is a decision by the court on the merits of the entire case.

    Pursuant to Rule 54(b), if more than one claim is presented in a case, or if there are multiple parties, the district court may expressly direct entry of a final judgment as to one or more issues or parties. Any order or other decision, however designated, that adjudicates fewer than all of the claims or the rights and liabilities of fewer than all of the parties will not end the action as to any of the claims or parties, and may be revised at any time before the entry of a judgment adjudicating all of the claims and all of the parties' rights and liabilities.

2. **Appeal of Interlocutory Orders**

    While most interlocutory orders, such as the denial of a summary judgment motion or a motion to dismiss, are not immediately appealable, 28 U.S.C. § 1292(a) makes certain equitable orders reviewable immediately as a matter of right, including:

    i)   An order granting, modifying, refusing, or dissolving an injunction;

    ii) An order appointing or refusing to appoint a receiver; and

    iii) A decree determining the rights and liabilities of the parties to admiralty cases in which appeals from final decrees are allowed.

    In addition, under 28 U.S.C. § 1292(b), if a district court certifies (i) that an order involves a controlling question of law as to which there is substantial ground for difference of opinion, and (ii) that an immediate appeal from the order may materially advance the ultimate termination of the litigation, then a court of appeals has discretion to permit an appeal to be taken from such order. In such a case, however, the application must be made within 10 days after the entry of the order, rather than the 30-day period that applies to an appeal of other interlocutory orders that are immediately appealable as of right.

3. **Collateral Order Rule**

    Under the so-called **collateral-order doctrine**, a court of appeals has discretion to hear and rule on a district court order if it: "1) conclusively determines the disputed question, 2) resolves an important issue that is completely separate from the merits of the action, and 3) is effectively unreviewable on appeal from a final judgment." *Mohawk Indus., Inc. v. Carpenter*, 558 U.S. 100, 105 (2009) (holding that a disclosure order whose enforcement would allegedly violate attorney-client privilege did not qualify for review under the collateral-order doctrine). For example, an order imposing on the defendant 90 percent of the cost of notifying members of a class was appealable under this doctrine. *Eisen v. Carlisle & Jacquelin*, 417 U.S. 156 (1974).

4. **Mandamus Review**

    Under a writ of mandamus, an appellate court can immediately review an order of a lower court that is an abuse of judicial authority. In addition to establishing the existence of an error of law, the petitioner must establish that there is no other adequate means of obtaining the desired relief and that the right to such relief is clear and indisputable. *Compare Kerr v. U.S. Dist. Court*, 426 U.S. 394 (1976) (mandamus inappropriate to vacate a lower court's discovery orders) *with Dairy Queen, Inc. v. Wood*, 369 U.S. 469 (1962) (mandamus appropriate when a trial court denied the right to a jury trial on a legal issue).

5. **Class Action Certification**

A court of appeals has the discretion to permit an appeal from a district court order granting or denying class action certification. The petition for permission to appeal must be filed with the circuit clerk within 14 days after the order is entered. If the appeal is permitted, it does not stay proceedings in the district court unless the district court or the court of appeals so orders. Rule 23(f).

6. **Standards of Review**

The standard of review focuses on the degree to which an appellate court defers to a decision by the trial court or jury. It is a procedural matter that is governed by federal law, even in an action based on diversity jurisdiction.

a. **Review of a trial court's factual findings—clearly erroneous**

A trial court's findings of fact, including a master's findings that have been adopted by the court, may not be set aside unless "**clearly erroneous**." The appellate court must give due regard to the trial court's opportunity to judge the witnesses' credibility. Rule 52(a). A finding is clearly erroneous when, although there is evidence to support it, the appellate court, based on the entirety of the evidence, is left with the definite and firm conviction that a mistake has been committed. *United States v. U.S. Gypsum Co.*, 333 U.S. 364 (1948). A party may challenge the sufficiency of the evidence supporting such findings on appeal even though the party took no action in the trial court with regard to them. Rule 52(a)(5).

b. **Review of legal rulings—de novo**

In general, appellate review of legal rulings is **de novo**. While an appellate court relies on the record created in a trial court and does not entertain the admission of additional evidence, the appellate court reviews the evidence and law without deference to the trial court's legal rulings. Thus, the appellate court may reach its own independent conclusions as to the applicable law.

c. **Review of discretionary rulings—abuse of discretion**

A trial court's rulings on discretionary matters, such as the admissibility of evidence, sanctions for violation of discovery rules, or the granting or denial of a motion to transfer venue or to sever actions, are generally subject to review under the **abuse of discretion** standard. *GE v. Joiner*, 522 U.S. 136 (1997).

d. **Review of jury verdict**

In determining whether to set aside a jury verdict, it is not sufficient that the verdict is against the weight of the evidence. *Lavender v. Kurn*, 327 U.S. 645 (1946). Some appellate courts refuse to set aside a jury verdict if there is substantial evidence supporting the verdict. Other courts require only sufficient evidence to sustain a jury verdict. Still others uphold a jury verdict unless there is no evidence to support the verdict. However, to preserve for appeal a challenge to the sufficiency of the evidence supporting a jury verdict, a party must properly renew a motion for directed verdict with a motion for judgment notwithstanding the verdict under Rule 50(b) or must raise a motion for a new trial under Rule 59. If a party fails to do so, there is no basis for review of the challenge to the overall sufficiency of the evidence in a court of appeals, and appellate review will instead be limited to any specific claims of error that were properly preserved. *Unitherm Food Sys. v. Swift-Eckrich, Inc.*, 546 U.S. 394 (2006).

C.   FULL FAITH AND CREDIT

1.   State to State

Article IV, Section 1 of the Constitution provides that "Full Faith and Credit shall be given in each State to the public Acts, Records, and judicial Proceedings of every other State." The clause is invoked primarily to enforce the judgment of one state court in another state.

If a valid judgment is rendered by a court that has jurisdiction over the parties, and the parties receive proper notice of the action and a reasonable opportunity to be heard, the Full Faith and Credit Clause requires that the judgment receive the same effect in other states as in the state where it was rendered. Thus, a party who obtains a judgment in one state may petition the court in another state to enforce the judgment. In general, the issues are not re-litigated, and the court in the state in which enforcement is sought must honor the judgment of the other state's court.

The same principle applies to challenges based on an alleged lack of personal or subject matter jurisdiction; a party against whom enforcement is sought may collaterally challenge the original state judgment based on lack of personal jurisdiction or subject matter jurisdiction **only** if the jurisdictional issues were not litigated or waived in the original action. *Durfee v. Duke,* 375 U.S. 106 (1963).

The requirement of full faith and credit extends to the preclusive effects of the original state-court judgment. Thus, if the original state-court judgment would bar a subsequent action in the original state, then it acts to bar a subsequent action in any other state. This is the case even if the subsequent action would otherwise be permitted in that state. (*See* § IX.D. Claim Preclusion (Res Judicata), and § IX.E. Issue Preclusion (Collateral Estoppel) *infra,* for a discussion of preclusion generally.)

2.   Federal to State

Under 28 U.S.C. § 1738, federal courts must also give full faith and credit to state court judgments. The same rules as discussed above for states apply with respect to a federal court.

3.   State to Federal in Diversity Cases

Federal law determines the effects under the rules of res judicata of a judgment of a federal court. Restatement (Second) of Judgments, § 87. However, federal common law requires that the claim-preclusive effect of a judgment by a federal court sitting in diversity must be governed by the law of claim preclusion of the federal court's forum state. *Semtek Int'l Inc. v. Lockheed Martin Corp.,* 531 U.S. 497 (2001).

XII.   PRECLUSION DOCTRINE

A.   CLAIM PRECLUSION (*RES JUDICATA*)

1.   In General

The doctrine of claim preclusion (*res judicata*) provides that a final judgment on the merits of an action precludes the parties from successive litigation of an identical **claim** in a subsequent action. *New Hampshire v. Maine,* 532 U.S. 742, 748 (2001).

2. **Requirements**

   a. **Valid final judgment on the merits**

      1) **Valid**

         The judgment must be valid, meaning that the court had both personal and subject matter jurisdiction, and the defendant had proper notice and an opportunity to be heard.

      2) **Final**

         The judgment must also be final, meaning that there is nothing further for the court to do but to order entry of judgment.

      3) **On the merits**

         The decision must have been made in consideration of the merits of the claim or defense, rather than on technical grounds. A claim or defense does not actually have to have been raised in the earlier action to be barred in the later action. If the claim or defense could have been raised in the earlier action, it will be precluded in the later action. A judgment on the merits includes judgment entered after a full trial, summary judgment, judgment as a matter of law, and default judgment where the court has jurisdiction over the subject matter and personal jurisdiction over the parties.

      4) **Voluntary dismissal without prejudice**

         A voluntary dismissal "without prejudice" expressly reserves the right to sue again on the same claim in the same court so long as the statute of limitations has not expired. Unless the notice of dismissal states otherwise, a voluntary dismissal will be "without prejudice." Rule 41(a)(1)(B).

      5) **Voluntary dismissal with prejudice**

         A voluntary dismissal "with prejudice" is treated as a judgment on the merits and will have a preclusive effect in the court that issued the order of dismissal. A dismissal on the merits under Rule 41(b) will bar a plaintiff from re-filing the claim only in the same federal court, not in state court. *Semtek, supra.*

      6) **Involuntary dismissal**

         Unless otherwise provided by the order of dismissal, an involuntary dismissal on non-jurisdictional grounds will constitute an adjudication on the merits. Rule 41(b). While such an involuntary dismissal will bar re-filing of the claim in the same federal court, it does not preclude re-filing of the claim in state court. *Semtek, supra.*

      7) **Dismissal for lack of jurisdiction**

         Under Rule 41(b), a dismissal on jurisdictional grounds, or for lack of venue or failure to join a party under Rule 19, is without prejudice, because a court that has no jurisdiction cannot adjudicate a matter on the merits.

      8) **Diversity jurisdiction**

         If a federal court with diversity jurisdiction over an action issues a judgment, a state court must give such judgment the same claim preclusion effect that the judgment would have been given by the courts of the state where the federal court was located. *Semtek, supra.*

9) Family law decisions

A divorce decree must generally be given a preclusive effect so long as the court had jurisdiction, which usually requires only a long-term connection of plaintiff-spouse with the forum state rather than personal jurisdiction over the defendant-spouse. However, a decision involving property rights, including alimony or child custody, is not entitled to a preclusive effect unless the court had personal jurisdiction over the defendant-spouse. *Estin v. Estin*, 334 U.S. 541 (1948).

b. Sufficiently identical claims

The original and later-filed claims must be sufficiently identical to be barred under claim preclusion. Federal courts apply a transactional approach under which they bar a subsequent claim with respect to all or any part of the transaction, or series of connected transactions, out of which the action arose. If a plaintiff sues on only a portion of a claim arising from a transaction, the unaddressed portions of his claim merge with the judgment if the plaintiff wins, and are barred if the plaintiff loses.

Factors that are considered in determining what constitutes a transaction or series of transactions include:

i)   Whether the facts are related in time, space, origin, or motivation;

ii) Whether the facts form a convenient trial unit; and

iii) Whether treating the facts as a unit conforms to the parties' expectations.

c. Sufficiently identical parties (mutuality)

For claim preclusion to apply, the claimant and defendant must be the same (and in the same roles) in both the original action and the subsequently filed action. Note that claim preclusion is limited to the parties (or their privies, such as agents, proxies, or successors-in-interest). Thus, a similar action by a different party would not be precluded.

B.   ISSUE PRECLUSION (COLLATERAL ESTOPPEL)

1.   In General

The doctrine of issue preclusion, often called "collateral estoppel," precludes the re-litigation of issues of fact or law that have already been necessarily determined by a judge or jury as part of an earlier claim.

2.   Nonparty Preclusion

Unlike claim preclusion, issue preclusion does not require strict mutuality of parties; it requires only that the party against whom the issue is to be precluded (or one in privity with that party) was a party to the original action. Thus, "offensive" use of collateral estoppel is permitted.

Trial courts have "broad discretion" to determine whether offensive collateral estoppel should be applied. If a plaintiff could easily have joined in the earlier action or if offensive estoppel is found to be unfair to a defendant, then a trial judge should not allow it. *Parklane Hosiery Co. v. Shore*, 439 U.S. 322 (1979).

There are six exceptions to the general rule against nonparty preclusion:

i)   A party who agreed to be bound by a judgment;

ii) Certain types of "substantial legal relationships" between the party and the nonparty, such as a bailor-bailee relationship;

iii) A nonparty who was "adequately represented by someone with the same interests," as is found in class action suits or suits by trustees;

iv) A nonparty who "assumes control" over the case;

v) A party who attempts to re-litigate by using a proxy; or

vi) Special statutory schemes that prohibit successive litigation and are consistent with due process.

Taylor v. Sturgell, 553 U.S. 880 (2008). The court has also recognized that there is a narrow exception known as "virtual representation," which requires either special procedures to ensure that nonparty interests are protected or notice and an understanding that "the first suit was brought in a representative capacity." *Richards v. Jefferson County*, 517 U.S. 793 (1996).

3. Requirements

a. Same issue

The issue sought to be precluded must be the same as that involved in the prior action. The facts relevant to the particular issue and the applicable law must be identical in order for issue preclusion to apply. *Commissioner of Internal Revenue v. Sunnen*, 333 U.S. 591 (1948).

b. Actually litigated

The issue must have been actually litigated in the prior action in order for issue preclusion to apply. *Stoll v. Gottlieb*, 305 U.S. 165 (1938) (Issue preclusion applies to findings of jurisdiction that are fully litigated.)

c. Final, valid judgment

The issue must have been determined by a valid and binding final judgment. Generally, this requires that the first determination of the issue was within the authority of the court that decided it, and that the determination was made in a final decision on the merits.

d. Essential to the judgment

The determination of the issue must have been essential to the prior judgment. Generally, an issue that constitutes a necessary component of the decision reached will be considered essential to the judgment.

4. Equitable Issues

Issues decided under a court's equitable power, such as a bankruptcy court's avoidance of preferential transfers, can be precluded from re-litigation just as can be legal issues, if all the requirements for collateral estoppel are met. *See Katchen v. Landy,* 382 U.S. 323 (1966).

5. Criminal Prosecution

Issues determined in a criminal prosecution in favor of the prosecution are generally preclusive in a civil action against the defendant based on the same conduct as in the criminal prosecution. Restatement (Second) of Judgments § 85. Issues determined in a criminal prosecution in favor of the defendant are not preclusive in a civil action against the defendant based on the same conduct as in the criminal prosecution because the plaintiff in the civil action was not a party to the criminal prosecution.

Themis
Bar Review

LSE Key Concepts: Civil Procedure
To be used with online lecture

PERSONAL JURISDICTION (PJ)
Court's jurisdiction over the parties
- *Sovereignty*: Sovereigns (states) cannot reach outside the scope of their geographical limits
- *Fairness*: Required by Due Process Clause; no random justice; most important principle
- Scope of judicial authority determined by state legislature

---

GENERAL JURISDICTION (GEN JX)
Court's power to adjudicate regardless of the nature of the suit
Bases for GEN JX by state and fed. courts:
- *Domicile*—person domiciled in state where court is located
  - Humans—where you reside/intend to remain indefinitely
  - Corporations—principal place of business <u>and</u> incorporation
  - Other entities—Usually principal place of business location

- *Consent*—person who consents to the court's authority
  - Need not be explicit
  - Going to court and failing to object to PJ is enough
  - Plaintiff consents by filing the suit with that court
  - Lack of PJ must be asserted or the objection is forfeited
  - Consent by contract in a choice-of-forum clause

- *Service of Process*—person who is voluntarily present in the state and is served with process while there, unless plaintiff ("P") brings defendant ("D") into state fraudulently or D is merely passing through to attend other judicial proceedings

- *Substantial Business Activity*—State and fed. courts have Gen JX over business whose continuous and systematic activities render it essentially "at home" in the state

❖ Pennoyer v. Neff, 95 U.S. 714 (1878) *(Court did not have general PJ over Neff, a non-resident not properly served)*

❖ Carnival Cruise Lines v. Shute, 499 U.S. 585 (1991) *(Forum selection clause enforceable; choice not unreasonable or unjust)*

❖ Burnham v. Superior Court, 495 U.S. 604 (1990) *(Voluntary presence in CA & service of process while there was sufficient to exercise general PJ over husband in divorce proceeding)*

❖ Daimler AG v. Bauman, 571 U.S. 117 (2014) *(Daimler, a foreign defendant, did not have sufficient business contacts with CA to justify the exercise of general PJ)*

❖ Perkins v. Benguet Consol. Mining Co., 342 U.S. 437 (1952) *(Temporarily relocating headquarters to OH created sufficient business contacts for Philippine mining company to be "at home" there)*

SPECIFIC JURISDICTION
Court's power to adjudicate a cause of action arising out of or closely relating to the *defendant's contacts* with the forum
- Defendant *purposefully avails* themselves of the privileges and benefits of the forum state

Long-Arm Statutes
Allows state to reach outside geographical territory to exercise PJ over a defendant with *minimum contacts* with the state

- Must be consistent with Due Process Clause:
  - (1) Purposeful Availment—Purposefully establish minimum contacts with the forum state; foreseeability alone is not enough
  - (2) Substantial Nexus—Contacts must have substantial relationship to the lawsuit; fact-specific determination
  - (3) Fairness—Jurisdiction cannot offend traditional notions of fair play and substantial justice
    - Fairness factors: burden on defendant; state's interest in adjudicating suit; interstate need for efficient resolution; states' shared interest in obtaining compliance with law

❖ Int'l Shoe Co. v. Washington, 326 U.S. 310 (1945) *(Presence of salespeople in WA was continuous and systematic enough for the company to have minimum contacts under Due Process)*

❖ World-Wide Volkswagen Corp. v. Woodson, 444 U.S. 286 (1980) *(Unilateral action of plaintiff driving to OK was not sufficient contact to subject VW to PJ in OK)*

❖ _Burger King Corp. v. Rudzewicz,_ 471 U.S. 462 (1985) _(Franchisee's ongoing contractual relationship with FL was sufficient to establish minimum contacts in FL)_

Stream of Commerce
Intentionally placing products in the stream of commerce does not necessarily mean intent to go everywhere the stream carries it; additional purposeful availment must be shown

❖ _J. McIntyre Mach., Ltd. v. Nicastro,_ 564 U.S. 873 (2011) _(PJ over foreign defendant was not proper under a stream of commerce analysis absent additional purposeful availment)_

❖ _Asahi Metal Indust. Co. v. Superior Court of Cal.,_ 480 U.S. 102 (1987) _(Placing a product in the stream of commerce, without more, is not an act purposefully directed toward the forum state)_

IN REM AND QUASI IN REM JURISDICTION
The court's authority over real or personal property

Pure In Rem
- Court declares true owner of a particular piece of property located in forum state
- Suit can be filed "against" the property

Quasi In Rem Type I
- Court determines whose interest is superior among multiple parties
- Permitted over any property in the forum state

Quasi In Rem Type II
- Party does not have an interest in the property, but asks the court for an interest in the property
- Often used to enforce a separate judgment

❖ _Shaffer v. Heitner,_ 433 U.S. 186 (1977) _(In rem proceedings must satisfy due process; presence of stocks in DE was insufficient when suit was unrelated to ownership of the stock)_

SUBJECT MATTER JURISDICTION (SMJ)
The court system in which you can sue—state or federal
- Federal courts are courts of limited jurisdiction
- Must comply with the Constitution and applicable statutes

SMJ—FEDERAL QUESTION
Federal courts can hear claims "arising under federal law."
- Includes violation of a federal statute that creates a cause of action

- Includes state-law claim that implicates a federal issue if the federal issue is:
  - (1) Necessarily raised;
  - (2) Actually disputed;
  - (3) Substantial; and
  - (4) Resolvable without disrupting federal-state balance

Well-Pleaded Complaint Rule
Fed Q jurisdiction exists _only_ when federal issue is presented in P's complaint
- Ignore defendant's claims; defenses do not grant Fed Q JX
- Look at true nature of plaintiff's claims—Fed Q must be plain on the _face_ of the complaint

❖ _Louisville & Nashville R.R. v. Mottley,_ 211 U.S. 149 (1908) _(In breach of contract case, railroad's defense that it was complying with federal law when it stopped honoring lifetime passes was not sufficient to create Fed Q jurisdiction; Fed Q must be on the face of the complaint)_

❖ _Grable & Sons Metal Prods. v. Darue Eng'g & Mfg.,_ 545 U.S. 308 (2005) _(Although quiet title action is state-law claim, Grable's property was seized/sold without proper notice as required by federal statute; met all four factors for Fed Q jurisdiction)_

SMJ—DIVERSITY
Federal courts can hear disputes between parties with complete diversity, as long as the amount in controversy exceeds $75,000

Complete Diversity of Citizenship
- SMJ over disputes between citizens of different states or a U.S. citizen and a foreign citizen
- No plaintiff can have the same citizenship as any defendant
- Citizenship is determined _at the time of filing_ the suit

❖ _Strawbridge v. Curtiss,_ 7 U.S. (3 Cranch) 267 (1806) _(Complete diversity is not satisfied if any plaintiff is a citizen of the same state as any defendant)_

Exclusions from Diversity Jurisdiction
- Probate Matters (will or estate administration)
- Domestic-Relations Actions (divorce, alimony, custody, etc.)

Class Action Fairness Act (requires only _minimal_ diversity; any plaintiff must be diverse from any defendant)

Individual Citizenship

Human beings are citizens of the state in which they reside and intend to remain indefinitely

- Human being = natural person, individual
- Look for outward manifestation of intent to remain
- Can only have one state of citizenship

❖ Perry v. Mas, 489 F.2d 1396 (5th Cir. 1974) *(Married couple sued landlord (LA citizen) in federal court; couple resided in LA, but never intended to remain indefinitely; wife remained a MS citizen for diversity purposes)*

Corporate Citizenship

Corporations are citizens of the state in which they have their principal place of business AND the state in which they are incorporated.

- Can have more than one state of citizenship
- Principal place of business = "nerve center" (where officers direct, control, and coordinate corporate activities)

❖ Hertz Corp. v. Friend, 559 U.S. 77 (2010) *(A corporation's principal place of business is where officers direct, control, and coordinate corporate activities)*

Unincorporated Entities

LLCs, Partnerships, Unions, etc. are citizens of each state in which its members are domiciled

Amount in Controversy (AIC)—must *exceed* $75,000

- Includes compensatory and punitive damages; not costs, fees, interest, etc.
- Based on plaintiff's good faith assertions

- **Aggregation:** A single plaintiff can aggregate multiple claims against a single defendant to meet the AIC requirement
  - Single P cannot aggregate against multiple Ds
  - Multiple plaintiffs (typically) cannot aggregate against single defendant

SMJ—Supplemental

Allows additional state law claims to attach to the original federal question or diversity claim when the additional claims would not otherwise fall under the court's SMJ

- State law claim must be so connected to the original claim that it forms part of the **same case or controversy** (arises out of a common nucleus of operative fact/same transaction or occurrence)

❖ United Mine Workers v. Gibbs, 383 U.S. 715 (1966) *(Miner sued union under state and federal law; court did not have Fed Q or diversity SMJ over state law claim; court could exercise supplemental jurisdiction because the two claims formed part of the same case or controversy)*

Exceptions:

- **§ 1367(c)**—Discretion to decline jurisdiction when:
  - Claim raises novel or complex issue of state law;
  - Claim substantially predominates over the original claim; or
  - Court has dismissed all original claims
- **§ 1367(b)**—No supplemental jurisdiction over *plaintiff's* claims against defendants made parties under Rule 14, 19, 20, or 24 if violates complete diversity
  - No such limitation on *defendant's* claims

❖ Exxon Mobil Corp. v. Allapattah Servs., Inc., 545 U.S. 546 (2005) *(Plaintiffs joined under Rule 20 can bring additional claims under supplemental jurisdiction if they satisfy complete diversity, even if the claim does not meet the AIC requirement)*

SMJ—Removal

Process for moving a case from state to federal court
Requirements:

- (1) Claim could have been filed in federal court initially;
  - Fed Q, Diversity, or Supplemental JX
- (2) If removal is based on diversity, no defendant is a citizen of the forum state;
  - Does not prevent removal for federal question cases
- (3) All defendants must agree; and
- (4) Notice of removal must be timely
  - **30-Day Rule:** Removal must be accomplished within 30 days after grounds for removal become apparent.
  - **One-Year Rule:** No removal based on diversity is permitted more than one year after action is commenced.

Venue

The federal district in which you can sue

Proper Venue:

- (1) The district where any defendant resides if all defendants reside in the same state
  - Humans reside in the district they intend to remain indefinitely
  - Entities reside in the district where they are subject to PJ

- (2) The district where a substantial part of the events or omissions on which the claim is based occurred; or
- (3) If options (1) and (2) cannot be met, the district where any defendant is subject to PJ

Transferring Venue under § 1404(a)
- Allows transfer to another proper venue for:
  - (1) The convenience of parties and witnesses, or
    - Convenience: accessibility and availability of witnesses and evidence, not convenience to the parties
  - (2) The interest of justice
- Allows transfer to any venue all parties consent to

Forum Non Conveniens
Results in dismissal; federal court has no authority to move the case to where it should be litigated (e.g., foreign court)
- Similar factors to transfer: accessibility of witnesses and evidence
- Balance needs of the parties (private interests) against the government's interest (public interests)

❖ <u>Piper Aircraft Co. v. Reyno</u>, 454 U.S. 235 (1981) *(Dismissal was proper in a suit involving a plane crash in Scotland because Scotland was the more convenient forum even though the law was less favorable to the plaintiffs there)*

PLEADINGS
How to commence a lawsuit (complaint) and respond (answer)

Complaint
- Requires enough detail to give the defendant fair notice of the claim
- Must contain:
  - (1) Short and plain statement of the claim showing that the pleader is entitled to relief
  - (2) Short and plain statement of the grounds for the court's jurisdiction
  - (3) A demand for relief sought (may include relief in the alternative or different kinds of relief)

Answer
- *Admits or denies* allegations in the complaint
  - If not denied, allegation is deemed admitted
- **Affirmative Defenses**—Asserted in the answer
  - Argument that plaintiff's allegations fail to account for evidence that prevents defendant's liability (e.g., self-defense)

SERVICE OF PROCESS
Notice
- Due process guarantees a person's right to be informed of an action against them
- Notice must be *reasonably calculated* to inform interested parties of the action and afford them an opportunity to present objections

❖ <u>Mullane v. Cent. Hanover Bank & Trust Co.</u>, 339 U.S. 306 (1950) *(Trust beneficiaries were entitled to notice under due process before the bank merged the trusts; notice in newspaper was insufficient when bank had names and addresses)*

Process:
- (1) A copy of the complaint; and
- (2) A summons issued by the court

Service Under Rule 4
- (1) Follow state law for service in the state where the district court is located or where service is made
- (2) Personal service on the defendant by a non-party
- (3) Non-party leaves process at the defendant's dwelling or usual place of abode with someone of suitable age and discretion who resides there
- (4) Non-party delivers process to an agent authorized to receive service of process

AMENDING PLEADINGS
Applies to pleadings only (answer, complaint, etc.), not motions
- All pleadings: automatic right to amend once within 21 days of service
- Complaint: automatic right to amend 21 days after an answer or motion to dismiss has been filed
- Can amend with consent of the other party or of the court
  - Courts should grant leave to amend "as justice requires"
  - Considers: hardship to opposing party, reason for delay, whether amendment would be futile

Relation Back Under Rule 15
New Claims—Amended complaint is treated as being filed on the date of the original complaint if:
- (1) The new claim arises out of the same transaction or occurrence addressed in the original complaint; and
- (2) Adding the new claim will not prejudice the existing defendant
New Party—if amendment changes or adds a party against whom a claim is asserted, only relates back if:
- (1) Amendment will not prejudice the party's ability to defend the suit on the merits;

- (2) New party had notice of the suit within the period in which service had to occur; and
- (3) The new party knew or should have known that the action would be brought against them but for mistaken identity

Discovery Rule—in some states, statute of limitations does not start running until the plaintiff discovers (or reasonably should have discovered) the facts giving rise to the claim

JOINDER
The process for joining multiple claims and parties together in a single lawsuit

JOINDER—MULTIPLE CLAIMS
Permissive Joinder of Claims—Rule 18(a)
- May join independent or alternative claims of any nature against an opposing party
- Claims must still satisfy SMJ

Counterclaims—Rule 13
- A claim for relief made against an opposing party after an original claim has been made
- Always permissible
- **Compulsory counterclaims**—arise out of the same transaction or occurrence as the opposing party's claim
  - Lost if not asserted
  - Determining same transaction or occurrence:
    - Issues of fact and law are essentially the same;
    - Same evidence would support or refute the claims;
    - Logical relationship between the claims; and
    - Res judicata would bar a subsequent suit on either claim

Cross-Claims—Rule 13
- Made against a coparty
- Arises out of the same transaction or occurrence as the original claim
- Efficiency is served by allowing the claim

JOINDER—MULTIPLE PARTIES
Permissive Joinder of Parties—Rule 20
- Parties *may* be joined in the same action if:
  - (1) The claims asserted by or against them arise out of the same transaction or occurrence; and
  - (2) There is a question of law or fact common to all parties

Compulsory Joinder of Parties—Rule 19
- Determines when additional parties must be joined and when failure to join necessary parties requires dismissal

- A **party is necessary** if:
  - (1) Complete relief cannot be provided to existing parties in the absence of that person;
  - (2) That person's ability to protect their interests might be impaired by their absence; or
  - (3) Existing parties are at risk of multiple or inconsistent obligations without the absent party's presence

- All parties joined to the action must meet the requirements of federal **subject matter jurisdiction** and **personal jurisdiction**

- If a necessary party cannot be joined, court uses factors to determine if the party is **indispensable** such that dismissal is required:
  - Prejudice to all parties if judgment is passed without the necessary party
  - Adequacy of judgment rendered in the person's absence
  - Whether prejudice can be reduced or avoided
  - Whether plaintiff would have an adequate remedy if the action were dismissed

- Tortfeasors subject to joint and several liability *are not* indispensable parties

❖ Temple v. Synthes Corp., 498 U.S. 5 (1990) *(A doctor and hospital were not indispensable parties in a suit against the manufacturer of a medical device because it is not necessary for all joint tortfeasors to be joined as defendants in a single suit)*

THIRD PARTY PRACTICE
Impleader Under Rule 14
Allows a defending party to sue a nonparty who is or may be liable for all or part of the claim against the defending party
- Typically arises in:
  - Contribution—multiple people jointly and severally liable in tort for the same injury
  - Indemnity—Allows a defending party to collect from another person in order to cover the party's obligation to the plaintiff
- Requires the impleaded party to be liable to the defending party through a legitimate cause of action (not mistaken identity)

Claims By or Against Impleaded Parties
- Third-party D can counterclaim against the third-party P
- Third-party D can file claims against the original P that arise out of the same transaction or occurrence
- In diversity cases, the original P *cannot* assert a claim against an impleaded D if they are not diverse

because supplemental jurisdiction does not apply to this claim

OTHER MULTI-PARTY SCENARIOS
Interpleader
Allows a person holding property (stakeholder) to bring all potential claimants into a lawsuit to determine who has superior rights to the property
- Two types:
  - Federal Interpleader Rule: Rule 22
  - Federal Statutory Interpleader: § 1335

Class Actions: Rule 23
Allows a person or small group to represent the interests of a larger group
- Status as a class requires certification by the court based on certain prerequisites

ATTORNEY DUTIES: RULE 11
Every document or oral statement submitted to the court MUST be supported by:
- **(1) Good Facts**
  - Facts exist or you reasonably believe they exist
  - Allows for reasonable mistake of fact
  - Attorneys should reasonably investigate the facts

- **(2) Good Law**
  - Does not require ultimate success on the merits
  - Must have:
    - (1) reasonable belief that the law supports claims or defenses; or
    - (2) Non-frivolous argument that the law can and should be changed

- **(3) Good Faith**
  - Cannot be filed for an improper purpose (harass, cause unnecessary delay, needlessly increase litigation costs)

- Does *not* apply to discovery (covered by FRCP 37)
- Generally does *not* apply to communications made outside court proceedings

Rule 11 Sanctions
No sanctions until you leave the "safe harbor"
  - Other side serves you with a motion for sanctions, but does not file it
  - You have 21 days to withdraw the improper statement

- Typical Sanction—Money Sanctions
  - Order to pay fees related to the improper pleading
  - Can be imposed on attorney and client (except bad law violations)
- Other Sanctions:

- Pleadings can be stricken
- Arguments can be voided
- Suit can be dismissed with prejudice (extreme cases)

CHOICE OF LAW
Principles and rules by which courts determine the substantive law and rules of procedure that will govern an action

ERIE ANALYSIS
Whether state or federal law applies (vertical choice of law)

❖ <u>Swift v. Tyson</u>, 41 U.S. 1 (1842) *(Laws of the several states includes only statutory and constitutional law, not state common law)*—Overturned by <u>Erie</u>

❖ <u>Erie R.R. v. Tompkins</u>, 304 U.S. 64 (1938) *(Federal courts sitting in diversity must apply the laws of the state in which they sit, including statutory and state common law)*

- In diversity cases, federal courts must apply the law of the state in which the court sits, including statutory and state common law.
  - Prevents forum-shopping between state and federal court
  - Prevents inequitable administration of federal law

Outcome Determinative Test - Modified
- Determines whether a particular law is substantive or procedural
- Issue is whether failure to apply state law will lead to different substantive outcomes

❖ <u>Guaranty Trust Co. v. York</u>, 326 U.S. 99 (1945) *(Determine whether the failure to apply state law will lead to different outcomes)*

❖ <u>Byrd v. Blue Ridge Rural Electric Coop.</u>, 356 U.S. 525 (1958) *(Courts can weigh state and federal policy interests and apply the law that is of greater importance)*

❖ <u>Hanna v. Plumer</u>, 380 U.S. 460 (1965) *(When a valid federal statute conflicts with state law, the Supremacy Clause controls, and federal law applies)*
- If a *valid* federal statutory rule *applies*, apply the federal rule
- If no federal statutory rule applies, federal courts apply state law if it would prevent forum shopping
- Federal rule displaces conflicting state law only if the federal rule is (1) Valid, and (2) Applicable

Validity—Rules Enabling Act: FRE and FRCP
- Validity Requires:
  - Constitutional validity; and
  - Compliance with the Rules Enabling Act
- Rules Enabling Act: The FRE and FRCP cannot abridge, enlarge, or modify a substantive right

Applicability ("On Point")
- When state law applies, state law should apply
- Only federal rules that speak to the *same issue* can displace that state law
- ❖ Walker v. Armco Steel Corp., 446 U.S. 740 (1980) *(FRCP 3 governing commencement of lawsuit in federal court has no relation to state statutes of limitations, so it is not applicable to this suit and does not displace state law)*

Modern Approach to Erie Analysis
- (1) Determine whether state and federal law conflict
- (2) Determine whether the federal law is:
  - Constitutional text;
  - Statutory text; or
  - Case law interpreting such text
  - (2a) If yes, federal law controls (if valid and on point)
  - (2b) If no, apply modified outcome determinative test

MOTIONS TO DISMISS: RULE 12
Improper Forum
12(b)(1): Lack of Subject Matter Jurisdiction
12(b)(2): Lack of Personal Jurisdiction
12(b)(3): Improper Venue

Improper Service of Process
12(b)(4): Process was constitutionally insufficient
12(b)(5): Service of process was not proper

Failure to Join a Necessary Party
12(b)(7): Failure to join necessary parties under Rule 19

Waiver: Rule 12(h)(1)
The following grounds for dismissal must be asserted in a pre-answer motion or the answer, or they are waived:
- Lack of personal jurisdiction
- Improper venue
- Insufficient process
- Insufficient service of process

The following grounds for dismissal may be raised at any time:
- Lack of subject matter jurisdiction—Cannot be waived

- Failure to join a necessary party

Failure to State a Claim: Rule 12(b)(6)
- **Legal Insufficiency:** Complaint must assert a legal theory of recovery that is cognizable at law
- **Factual Insufficiency**: Complaint must assert sufficient factual allegations to state a *plausible* claim for relief
  - Eliminate mere recitations of the elements or conclusory legal assertions
  - Determine plausibility based on remaining factual allegations

❖ Bell Atlantic Corp. v. Twombly, 550 U.S. 544 (2007) *(Plaintiff in Anti-Trust case did not produce enough factual detail in the complaint to make a plausible claim that phone companies had an agreement not to compete)*

❖ Ashcroft v. Iqbal, 556 U.S. 662 (2009) *(Plaintiff did not produce enough factual detail in the complaint to make a plausible claim that Defendants purposefully adopted policy based on race, religion, or national origin)*

DISCOVERY: SCOPE AND LIMITATIONS
Subject to limitations, any matter that is <u>relevant</u> to any claim or defense is discoverable.

Relevance—Likely to make a fact in dispute more or less likely to be true

Work Product—Documents or other tangible objects created by a party or a party's attorney in anticipation of litigation are protected from discovery

❖ Hickman v. Taylor, 329 U.S. 495 (1947) *(Materials taken in anticipation of litigation and containing personal recollections and thoughts of counsel are protected from discovery)*

- **Exceptions** to Work Product Protection:
  - (1) A party can always obtain their own statement.
  - (2) A party can obtain work product for which it:
    - (a) Has a substantial need; and
    - (b) Cannot otherwise obtain without substantial hardship

Privileged Evidence—protected from discovery
- Common privileges:
  - Attorney-client privilege
  - Spousal privilege
  - Clergy-penitent privilege (some states)
  - Doctor-patient privilege (most states)

o Psychotherapist-patient privilege (federal and all states)

Undue Burden—Exists in the following circumstances:
- (1) Discovery is unreasonably cumulative or can be obtained from a less burdensome source or in a less burdensome way
- (2) The party seeking discovery already had ample opportunity to obtain the information
- (3) The burden or expense outweighs the benefits, considering the nature of the evidence, amount in controversy, and the parties' resources
- The key is *efficiency*
- ❖ Zubulake v. UBS Warburg LLC, 217 F.R.D. 309 (S.D.N.Y. 2003) *(Court may order parties to share the costs of discovery to protect the producing party from undue burden or expense)*

Non-Testifying Experts—consulted in anticipation of litigation or to prepare for trial, but NOT expected to testify
- Undiscoverable unless requesting party has:
  o (1) Extraordinary need; and
  o (2) No other way to obtain such information

Testifying Experts—expected to testify as an expert witness
- Must disclose expert report
- May also request communications related to compensation, data given to the expert, any assumptions the expert was asked to accept

DISCOVERY: DEVICES

Interrogatories—Written questions for a party to answer

Request for Admission—can ask a party to admit or deny any relevant, non-privileged matters discoverable under Rule 26

Request for Production—can ask a party to produce evidence in their custody or control

Request for Physical or Mental Examination—Available when mental or physical condition of a party is in controversy
  o Only available with court approval

Subpoena—used to obtain discovery from non-parties
  o Can be for testimony (*subpoena ad testificandum*) or documents (*subpoena duces tecum*)

Deposition—Provides opportunity to question parties and witnesses about the evidence

Use of deposition transcript at trial:
- Non-party:
  o If present at trial—can be used as impeachment
  o If absent from trial—can be used as substantive or impeachment evidence
- Party: Can be used for any purpose

Mandatory Disclosures—Rule 26(a)
Prior to trial, parties must make certain disclosures, including:
- List of all witnesses
- Documents that will be relied upon at trial
- Insurance documents

DISCOVERY: COMPLIANCE

Motion to Compel—Available if a party fails to make a mandatory disclosure or fails to respond to a properly served discovery device
- Movant must try to confer with opposing party before filing
- If successful, movant can get fees and costs related to making the motion
- If unsuccessful, non-movant can get fees and costs related to opposing the motion if it was made without substantial justification

Motion for Protective Order—Protects against annoyance, embarrassment, oppression, or undue burden or expense resulting from discovery
- Can also limit the use of evidence collected in discovery

SUMMARY JUDGMENT: RULE 56

The court shall grant summary judgment if the movant shows there is no genuine dispute as to any material fact and the movant is entitled to judgment as a matter of law

Movant Must Show
- A moving party that does not bear the burden of proof can show no genuine dispute of material fact by either:
  o Introducing own evidence; or
  o Pointing out other side's lack of evidence
- A moving party that bears the burden of proof must put forth affirmative evidence

❖ Celotex Corp. v. Catrett, 477 U.S. 317 (1986) *(In an asbestos exposure case, if the moving party does not bear the burden of proof, can show no dispute of material fact by either producing own evidence or pointing out other party's lack of evidence)*

- **Burden of Proof:** Determines which party is required to put forward evidence to establish a claim or defense
- **Affirmative Defense:** Party defending against the claim has the burden of proof in asserting an affirmative defense

No Genuine Dispute as to Any Material Fact

Based on these facts, could a reasonable jury return a verdict in favor of the nonmoving party?
- Court must make <u>all reasonable inferences</u> in favor of the non-movant
- Court will not make <u>unreasonable</u> inferences
- The law determines which facts are material

Entitled to Judgment as a Matter of Law

- (1) Plaintiff entitled to SJ if the <u>undisputed</u> facts clearly establish a claim for relief
- (2) Defendant entitled to SJ if law <u>bars</u> the claim (e.g., affirmative defense proven with affirmative evidence)

JURY TRIAL: CLAIMS AT LAW V. CLAIMS AT EQUITY

Seventh Amendment guarantees the right to a jury for federal suits at common law
- Claims at Law—Jury right applies
- Claims at Equity—No jury right
- For novel claims, court considers whether claim and remedies are analogous to historical claims under law or equity

❖ <u>Chauffeurs, Teamsters & Helpers, Local No. 391 v. Terry</u>, 494 U.S. 558 (1990) *(Union members' claims analogous to contract claims for money damages, which were historically claims at law; as a claim at law, members were entitled to a jury)*

JURY SELECTION

Federal juries consist of 6–12 people
1. Court sends jury summons to large group of randomly chosen potential jurors
- Venire: Pool of potential jurors who appear
2. Determine who is qualified to serve
- Voir dire: Questioning to determine qualification to serve
- Jurors must be unbiased
3. Ask court to dismiss particular jurors
- For cause—unlimited dismissals for bias, conflict, etc.
- Peremptory strike—can challenge up to <u>three</u> jurors without cause (cannot be based on race or gender)

❖ <u>Batson v. Kentucky</u>, 476 U.S. 79 (1986) *(Equal Protection Clause prohibits peremptory strikes based solely on race)*

Stages of a Batson Challenge:
1. Moving party establishes prima facie case of discrimination; raises presumption of discriminatory intent
2. Challenged party rebuts presumption with a race-neutral reason for the strike
3. Burden shifts back to moving party to show purposeful discrimination

TRIAL AND POST-TRIAL MOTIONS

Motion for Judgment as a Matter of Law: Rule 50(a)
- Also called Directed Verdict
- Granted if there is insufficient evidence for a jury reasonably to find for a party
- Must make all reasonable inferences in favor of the non-moving party
- Filed after either party rests its case

Renewed Judgment as a Matter of Law: Rule 50(b)
- Filed after jury returns a verdict
- Formerly called Judgment Notwithstanding the Verdict (JNOV)
- Must have moved for JMOL at trial in order to <u>renew</u> the motion after trial

Motion for a New Trial: Rule 59
Asks court to grant a new trial to prevent miscarriage of justice

Possible Grounds:
- Prejudicial misconduct of counsel, parties, jurors, or the judge
- Verdict is against the clear weight of the evidence
- Verdict is excessive or inadequate
  - Remittitur: Court may offer reduction of excessive verdict instead of a new trial
  - Additur: Court cannot increase an inadequate verdict; only option is to grant motion for new trial if appropriate
- Newly discovered evidence might have changed the outcome

APPEALS: GROUNDS

Final Judgment—Decision on the merits that leaves nothing for the court to do but execute the judgment
  - Denial of a motion to dismiss it not a final judgment

Prior to a Final Judgment:
- Orders Regarding Preliminary Injunctive Relief
- Orders Regarding Class Certification
- Certified Orders—Court certifies issue to the court of appeals
  - Close questions of law that are likely to determine the outcome of the case
- Collateral Orders—Resolves an important issue that is separate from the rest of the case
  - Delay in appeal will render it effectively unreviewable

- Court has discretion to deny if it is unfair to defendant

❖ <u>Parklane Hosiery Co. v. Shore</u>, 439 U.S. 322 (1979) *(Defendant must have had sufficient incentive to fully and vigorously litigate the first suit for offensive issue preclusion to apply against that party)*

CLAIM PRECLUSION
Prohibits the re-litigation of the same claim
Requirements:
1. Sufficiently Identical Claims—arise from the same transaction or occurrence
2. Sufficiently Identical Parties—same parties and in the same roles; sufficiently identical if:
  - New party is a successor in interest of the old party; or
  - Old party was an authorized representative of new party
3. Valid final judgment on the merits
  - Valid = court had proper jurisdiction
  - Final judgment = end of case; nothing left to decide
  - On the merits = on a claim or defense; does not include technical grounds, SMJ, PJ, venue, or service of process

ISSUE PRECLUSION
Prohibits the re-litigation of specific issues
Requirements:
1. Same issue as prior lawsuit
2. Issue was actually litigated and decided
  - Admissions and stipulations are not sufficient
3. Issue must be essential to the judgment
  - Must have been outcome determinative
4. Valid final judgment on the merits
5. Only precluded against a party to the first suit who had a full and fair opportunity to litigate the issue and lost
  - Does not require strict mutuality of parties
  - Does not permit nonparty preclusion unless the nonparty had a special relationship to the suit (e.g., privity, control of suit, etc.)

Defensive Issue Preclusion: Defendant may assert issue preclusion against a first-suit loser plaintiff

Offensive Issue Preclusion: Plaintiff may assert issue preclusion against a first-suit loser defendant

Themis
Bar Review

Constitutional Law

CONSTITUTIONAL LAW

Table of Contents

CONSTITUTIONAL LAW

PART ONE: POWERS OF THE FEDERAL GOVERNMENT

I. JUDICIAL POWER

A. SOURCE AND SCOPE

1. Source—Article III

Article III, Section 1 of the United States Constitution provides that "[t]he judicial power of the United States shall be vested in one Supreme Court and in such inferior courts as the Congress may from time to time ordain and establish."

Federal courts are generally created by the United States Congress under the constitutional power described in Article III. As noted above, Article III requires the establishment of a Supreme Court and permits the Congress to create other federal courts and place limitations on their jurisdiction. Although many specialized courts are created under the authority granted in Article I, greater power is vested in Article III courts because they are independent of Congress, the President, and the political process.

2. Scope

Article III, Section 2 delineates the jurisdiction of federal courts as limited to **cases or controversies**:

i) Arising under the Constitution, laws, and treaties of the United States;

ii) Affecting foreign countries' ambassadors, public ministers, and consuls;

iii) Involving admiralty and maritime jurisdiction;

iv) When the United States is a party;

v) Between two or more states, or between a state and citizens of another state;

vi) Between citizens of different states or between citizens of the same state claiming lands under grants of different states; or

vii) Between a state, or its citizens, and foreign states, citizens, or subjects.

a. Judicial review of congressional and executive actions

The judiciary has the power—although it is not enumerated in the text of the Constitution—to review an act of another branch of the federal government and to declare that act unconstitutional, *Marbury v. Madison*, 5 U.S. 137 (1803), as well as the constitutionality of a decision by a state's highest court, *Martin v. Hunter's Lessee*, 1 Wheat. 304 (1816). The central ideas of *Marbury v. Madison* are that (i) the Constitution is paramount law, and (ii) the Supreme Court has the final say in interpreting the Constitution.

b. Judicial review of state actions

The federal judiciary has the power, under the Supremacy Clause (Article VI, Section 2), to review state actions (e.g., court decisions, state statutes, executive orders) to ensure conformity with the Constitution, laws, and treaties of the United States. *Fletcher v. Peck*, 10 U.S. 87 (1810).

3. Limitations—Eleventh Amendment

The Eleventh Amendment is a jurisdictional bar that prohibits the citizens of one state from suing another state in federal court. It immunizes the state from suits in federal court for money damages or equitable relief when the state is a defendant in an action brought by a citizen of another state or a foreign country. In addition, the Eleventh Amendment bars suits in federal court against state officials for violating *state* law. *Pennhurst State School & Hospital v. Halderman*, 465 U.S.89 (1984).

The Supreme Court has expanded the amendment's reach to also preclude citizens from suing their own state in federal court. *Hans v. Louisiana*, 134 U.S. 1 (1890).

Note that the Supreme Court has also barred federal-law actions brought against a state government without the state's consent in its own courts as a violation of **sovereign immunity.** *Alden v. Maine*, 527 U.S. 706 (1999). Similarly, states retain their sovereign immunity from private suits brought in the courts of other states. *Franchise Tax Bd. Of Cal. v. Hyatt*, 587 U.S. ___, 139 S. Ct. 1485 (2019) (overruling *Nevada v. Hall*, 440 U.S. 410 (1979)).

a. Exceptions

There are, however, a few notable exceptions to the application of the Eleventh Amendment.

1) Consent

A state may consent to suit by waiving its Eleventh Amendment protection. *Lapides v. Board of Regents of Univ. System of Ga.*, 535 U.S. 613 (2002) (state removal of case to federal court constituted a waiver).

2) Injunctive relief

When a state official, rather than the state itself, is named as the defendant in an action brought in federal court, the state official may be enjoined from enforcing a state law that violates federal law or may be compelled to act in accord with federal law despite state law to the contrary. *Ex parte Young*, 209 U.S. 123 (1908), *Edelman v. Jordan*, 415 U.S. 651 (1974).

Note: A state also cannot invoke its sovereign immunity to prevent a lawsuit by a state agency seeking to enforce a federal right against a state official. *Virginia Office for Prot. & Advocacy v. Stewart*, 563 U.S. 247 (2011).

3) Damages to be paid by an individual

An action for damages against a state officer is not prohibited, as long as the officer himself (rather than the state treasury) will have to pay. Such is the case when an officer acts outside the law; the action is against the officer as an individual and not in his representative capacity.

4) Prospective damages

As long as the effect of a lawsuit is not to impose retroactive damages on a state officer to be paid from the state treasury, a federal court may hear an action against a state officer, even if the action will force a state to pay money to comply with a court order.

5) Congressional authorization

Congress may abrogate state immunity from liability if it is clearly acting to enforce rights created by the remedial provisions of the Thirteenth, Fourteenth, and Fifteenth Amendments (i.e., the Civil War Amendments), and does so expressly. *Fitzpatrick v. Bitzer*, 427 U.S. 445 (1976). Congress generally may not abrogate state immunity by exercising its powers under Article I (e.g., Commerce Clause powers). *Seminole Tribe of Florida v. Florida*, 517 U.S. 44 (1996).

b. Not barred by the Eleventh Amendment

1) Actions against local governments

The Eleventh Amendment applies only to states and state agencies. Local governments (e.g., counties, cities) are not immune from suit.

2) Actions by the United States government or other state governments not barred

The Eleventh Amendment has no application when the plaintiff is the United States or another state.

3) Bankruptcy proceedings

The Eleventh Amendment does not bar the actions of a Bankruptcy Court that impacts state finances. *Central Cmty. Coll. v. Katz*, 546 U.S. 356 (2006).

B. JURISDICTION OF THE SUPREME COURT

1. Original

Article III, Section 2 gives the Supreme Court "original jurisdiction" (i.e., the case may be filed first in the Supreme Court) over "all cases affecting ambassadors, other public ministers and consuls and those in which a State shall be a party." Congress may not expand or limit this jurisdiction. *Marbury v. Madison*, 5 U.S. 137 (1803). It may, however, grant concurrent original jurisdiction to lower federal courts, which it has for all cases except those between states. 28. U.S.C. § 1251.

2. Appellate

Article III, Section 2 also provides that "in all other cases before mentioned, the Supreme Court shall have appellate jurisdiction...with such exceptions, and under such regulations as the Congress shall make."

a. Means

There are two means of establishing appellate jurisdiction in the Supreme Court: certiorari (discretionary review) and direct appeal.

1) Certiorari

Almost all cases now come to the Supreme Court by way of a petition for a writ of certiorari, i.e., discretionary review. The Court takes jurisdiction only if at least four Justices vote to accept the case (the "rule of four").

2) Direct appeal

The Supreme Court **must** hear by direct appeal only a small number of cases—those that come from a decision on injunctive relief issued by a special three-judge district court panel. 28 U.S.C. § 1253. Although these panels (and appeals) were once fairly common, they are now limited to cases brought under a few specific statutes (e.g., the Voting Rights Act).

b. Limitations

Congress has some power to limit the Supreme Court's appellate jurisdiction by statute. *Ex parte McCardle*, 74 U.S. 506 (1868). There are constraints on this power, because to deny all Supreme Court jurisdiction over certain types of cases would undermine the constitutional system of checks and balances. *Boumediene v. Bush*, 553 U.S. 723 (2008) (Congress and President cannot remove Supreme Court's authority to say "what the law is" (quoting *Marbury v. Madison*, 5 U.S. 137 (1803))).

> Note that most federal cases are filed in district court and appealed, if at all, to the courts of appeals. The jurisdiction of the federal courts is set, within the framework of Article III, by statute. For example, Congress requires the amount in controversy necessary for federal jurisdiction over a case between citizens of different states to exceed $75,000. 28 U.S.C. § 1332.

c. Adequate and independent state grounds

A final state-court judgment that rests on adequate and independent state grounds may not be reviewed by the U.S. Supreme Court (or it would be an advisory opinion). The state-law grounds must fully resolve the matter (i.e., be adequate) and must not incorporate a federal standard by reference (i.e., be independent). If a state court chooses to rely on federal precedents, the court can avoid federal review by making a plain statement in its judgment or opinion that the federal cases are being used only for the purpose of guidance and did not compel the court's judgment. When it is not clear whether the state court's decision rests on state or federal law, the Supreme Court may hear the case, decide the federal issue, and remand to the state court for resolution of any question of state law. *Michigan v. Long*, 463 U.S. 1032 (1983).

C. JUDICIAL REVIEW IN OPERATION

Standing, timing (mootness or ripeness), and other issues of justiciability may dictate whether a case may be heard by a federal court.

1. Standing

Article III, Section 2 restricts federal judicial power to "cases" and "controversies." A federal court cannot decide a case unless the plaintiff has standing—a concrete interest in the outcome—to bring it. Congress cannot statutorily eliminate the constitutional standing requirement simply by allowing citizen suits, *Lujan v. Defenders of Wildlife*, 504 U.S. 555 (1992), but it can create new interests, the injury to which may establish standing, *Massachusetts v. EPA*, 549 U.S. 497 (2007).

a. General rule

To have standing, a plaintiff bears the burden of establishing three elements:

   i) **Injury in fact**;

   ii) **Causation** (the injury must be caused by the defendant's violation of a constitutional or other federal right); and

   iii) **Redressability** (the relief requested must prevent or redress the injury).

See, e.g., Lujan v. Defenders of Wildlife, 504 U.S. 555 (1992); *Valley Forge Christian College v. Americans United for Separation of Church and State, Inc.*, 454 U.S. 464 (1982).

In addition to the Article III requirements, the federal judiciary has also established a "prudential standing" requirement, i.e., that a plaintiff is a proper party to invoke a judicial resolution of the dispute. *Bender v. Williamsport Area School District*, 475 U.S. 534 (1986). Meeting this requirement depends in large part on whether the plaintiff's grievance comes within the "zone of interests" protected or regulated by the constitutional guarantee or statute under consideration. *Bennett v. Spear,* 520 U.S. 154 (1997); *Thompson v. N.Am. Stainless, LP,* 562 U.S. 170 (2011).

> **EXAM NOTE:** When answering questions about standing, eliminate answer choices involving only the substance of the claim and focus on whether the plaintiff is legally qualified to press a claim, regardless of merit.

1) Injury in fact

The injury must be both **concrete** and **particularized,** as well as **actual** or **imminent.**

a) Individualized injury

When a plaintiff has been directly injured "it does not matter how many people" were also injured; when "a harm is concrete, though widely shared," there is standing. *Massachusetts v. EPA,* 549 U.S. 497 (2007). However, even though an injury may satisfy the injury-in-fact standard, the court may refuse to adjudicate a claim by the application of the principles of prudence. Under this prudential-standing principle, an injury that is shared by all or a large class of citizens (i.e., a generalized grievance) is not sufficiently individualized to give the plaintiff standing. *Warth v. Seldin,* 422 U.S. 490 (1975).

b) Type of injury

The injury need not be physical or economic. *United States v. SCRAP,* 412 U.S. 669 (1973). A grievance that amounts to nothing more than an abstract and generalized harm to a citizen's interest in the proper application of the law does not count as an "injury in fact." *Hollingsworth v. Perry,* 570 U.S. 693 (2013). While a generalized harm to the environment does not confer standing, a harm that affects recreational "or even mere esthetic interests" is sufficient. *See Summers v. Earth Island Inst.,* 555 U.S. 488 (2009).

c) Future injury

While the threat of future injury can suffice, it cannot be merely hypothetical or conjectural, but must be actual or imminent. An injury in fact requires an intent that is concrete. *Carney v. Adams,* 592 U.S. ___, 141 S. Ct. 493 (2020) (respondent's inability to demonstrate that he was "able and ready" to apply for a judicial vacancy from which he would have been barred for not belonging to a major political party vitiated standing). When a future injury is alleged, damages cannot be obtained, but an injunction can be sought.

2) Causation

The plaintiff must show that the injury was fairly traceable to the challenged action—that is, that the defendant's conduct caused the injury. *Warth v. Seldin,* 422 U.S. 490 (1975).

3) Redressability

It must be likely (as opposed to speculative) that a favorable court decision will redress a discrete injury suffered by the plaintiff.

b. Taxpayer status

Usually, a taxpayer does not have standing to file a federal lawsuit simply because the taxpayer believes that the government has allocated funds in an improper way. However, a taxpayer does have standing to litigate whether, or how much, she owes on her tax bill. See *United States v.* Windsor, 570 U.S. 744 (2013) (litigating disallowance of estate tax exemption for surviving same-sex spouse under the Defense of Marriage Act.)

> **EXAM NOTE:** The standing of taxpayers is frequently tested on the MBE. A taxpayer has standing when the taxpayer challenges governmental expenditures as violating the Establishment Clause.

1) Governmental conduct

The conduct of the federal government, or of any state government, is too far removed from individual taxpayer returns for any injury to the taxpayer to be traced to the use of tax revenues. *DaimlerChrysler Corp. v. Cuno*, 547 U.S. 332 (2006). Long-standing precedent, however, suggests that a municipal taxpayer does have standing to sue a municipal government in federal court. *Crampton v. Zabriskie*, 101 U.S. 601 (1879).

2) Exception—Establishment Clause challenge

There is an exception for a taxpayer suit challenging a **specific legislative appropriation** made under the taxing and spending powers for violation of the Establishment Clause. *Flast v. Cohen*, 392 U.S. 83 (1968) (congressional grant to religious schools). This exception does not apply to the transfer of property to a religious organization by Congress under the Property Power, *Valley Forge Christian College v. Americans United for Separation of Church and State*, 454 U.S. 464 (1982), nor to expenditures made by the President to religious organizations from monies appropriated by Congress to the President's general discretionary fund, *Hein v. Freedom From Religion Foundation*, 551 U.S. 587 (2007), nor to a tax credit for contributions to student tuition organizations that provide scholarships to students attending private schools, including religious schools. *Ariz. Christian Sch. Tuition Org. v. Winn*, 563 U.S. 125 (2011).

c. Third-party standing

A litigant generally has no standing to bring a lawsuit based on legal claims of a third party. There are a few notable exceptions to this rule, however:

    i) If the third parties would experience difficulty or are **unable to assert their own rights,** such as a Caucasian defendant raising equal protection and due process objections to discrimination against African-American people in the selection of grand juries, *Campbell v. Louisiana*, 523 U.S. 392 (1998);

    ii) If there is a **special relationship between the plaintiff and the third parties,** such as an employer asserting the rights of its employees, a doctor asserting the rights of his patients in challenging an abortion ruling, *Singleton v. Wulff*, 428 U.S. 106 (1976), or a private school asserting its students' rights to attend despite a statute requiring attendance at public schools, *Pierce v. Society of Sisters*, 268 U.S. 510 (1925); and

    iii) If a plaintiff suffers an injury, and **the injury adversely affects the plaintiff's relationship with a third party,** the plaintiff may assert the third-party's rights. *Craig v. Boren*, 429 U.S. 190 (1976).

The rule that a litigant has no standing to bring a lawsuit on behalf of a third party is based on prudential or discretionary considerations. The federal courts may refuse to hear any case on **prudential-standing** grounds. *Elk Grove Unified School Dist. v. Newdow*, 542 U.S. 1 (2004).

1) Organizational standing

An organization may bring an action when it has suffered an injury. In addition, an organization may bring an action on behalf of its members (even if the organization has not suffered an injury itself) if:

   i)   Its members would have standing to sue in their own right; and

   ii)   The interests at stake are germane to the organization's purpose.

Hunt v. Washington State Apple Adver. Comm'n., 432 U.S. 333 (1977). When damages are sought, generally neither the claim asserted nor the relief requested can require the participation of individual members in the lawsuit. But note that the damages limitation is not constitutionally mandated and can be waived by Congress. *United Food & Commer. Workers Union Local 751 v. Brown Group*, 517 U.S. 544 (1996).

2) Parental standing

Generally, a parent has standing to bring an action on behalf of the parent's minor child. However, after a divorce, the right to bring such an action may be limited to only one of the child's parents. Moreover, when the right to bring such an action is based on family-law rights that are in dispute, the federal courts should not entertain an action if prosecution of the lawsuit may have an adverse effect on the child. *Elk Grove Unified School District v. Newdow*, 542 U.S. 1 (2004) (noncustodial parent with joint legal custody could not challenge school policy on behalf of his daughter when the custodial parent opposed the action).

d. Assignee standing

An assignee of a claim has standing to enforce the rights of an assignor, even when the assignee is contractually obligated to return any litigation proceeds to the assignor (e.g., an assignee for collection), provided the assignment was made for ordinary business purposes and in good faith. *Sprint Commc'ns Co., L.P. v. APCC Servs., Inc.*, 554 U.S. 269 (2008).

e. Citizenship standing

Citizens do not have standing to assert a claim to enforce a constitutional provision merely because they are citizens, although a citizen may bring an action against the government to compel adherence to a specific federal statute. Even in such a case, the plaintiff must have directly suffered an injury in fact.

f. Standing to assert a Tenth Amendment violation

A party has standing to challenge the constitutionality of a federal statute on the grounds that it exceeds Congress's enumerated powers and intrudes upon the powers reserved to the states by the Tenth Amendment. *Bond v. United States*, 564 U.S. 211 (2011) (defendant prosecuted for violation of federal statute).

g. Legislator's standing

Generally, a legislator who voted against a bill does not have standing to challenge the resulting statute. *Coleman v. Miller*, 307 U.S. 433 (1939) (state legislators lacked standing); *Raines v. Byrd*, 521 U.S. 811, 823 (1997) (members of Congress lacked standing).

h. Section 1983 claims

42 U.S.C. 1983 ("section 1983") provides that any person acting under color of state law who deprives any citizen of the United States (or any other person within the United States) of any rights, privileges, or immunities secured by the Constitution and laws can be held personally liable for the deprivation. Section 1983 does not provide any substantive rights. Instead, it provides a method to enforce the substantive rights granted by the Constitution and other federal laws.

1) Proper defendants

Individual government employees at any level of government may be sued under section 1983 in their individual capacities for damages, declaratory or injunctive relief. *Hafer v. Melo*, 502 U.S. 25 (1991); *City of Oklahoma City v. Tuttle*, 471 U.S. 808 (1985); *Bivens v. Six Unknown Named Agents of the Federal Bureau of Narcotics*, 403 U.S. 388 (1971). This is permitted because a suit against a government employee in his individual capacity does not represent a suit against the government entity. *Kentucky v. Graham*, 473 U.S. 159 (1985). Municipalities and local governments are also considered "persons" subject to suit pursuant to section 1983 for damages and prospective relief. *Monell v. Dept. of Social Services of New York*, 436 U.S. 658 (1978).

2) Color of state law

To use section 1983 as a remedy for the deprivation of a federally secured right, a plaintiff must show that the alleged deprivation was committed by a person acting **under color of state law**. The traditional definition of acting under the color of state law requires the defendant to have exercised power "possessed by virtue of state law and made possible only because the wrongdoer is clothed with the authority of state law." *West v. Atkins*, 487 U.S. 42, 49 (1988)(quoting *United States v. Classic*, 313 U.S. 299, 326 (1941)). Purely private conduct is not within the reach of the statute, but a private actor may be found to have acted under color of state law under certain circumstances.

> **EXAM NOTE:** The "color of state law" requirement is functionally identical to the "state action" prerequisite to trigger constitutional liability. *Lugar v. Edmondson Oil Co.*, 457 U.S. 922 (1982); *see* X. "State Action," *infra*.

2. Timeliness

An action that is brought too soon ("unripe") or too late ("moot") will not be heard.

a. Ripeness

"Ripeness" refers to the readiness of a case for litigation. A federal court will not consider a claim before it has fully developed; to do so would be premature, and any potential injury would be speculative.

For a case to be "ripe" for litigation, the plaintiff must have experienced a **real injury** (or imminent threat thereof). Hence, if an ambiguous law has a long history of non-enforcement, a case challenging that law may lack ripeness. *See Poe v. Ullman*, 367 U.S. 497 (1961).

b. Mootness

A case has become moot if further legal proceedings would have no effect; that is, if there is no longer a controversy. A **live controversy** must exist **at each stage of review,** not merely when the complaint is filed, in order for a case to be viable at that stage.

> **Example:** The classic example of mootness is the case of *DeFunis v. Odegaard,* 416 U.S. 312 (1974). The plaintiff was a student who had been denied admission to law school and had then been provisionally admitted while the case was pending. Because the student was scheduled to graduate within a few months at the time the decision was rendered, and there was no action that the law school could take to prevent it, the Court determined that a decision on its part would have no effect on the student's rights. Therefore, the case was dismissed as moot.

1) Exception—capable of repetition, yet evading review

A case will not be dismissed as moot if there is a reasonable expectation that the same complaining party will be subjected to the same action again ("capable of repetition") but that the action will not last long enough to work its way through the judicial system ("yet evading review"). *Turner v. Rogers,* 564 U.S. 431 (2011).

> **Example:** The most cited example of this exception is *Roe v. Wade,* 410 U.S. 113 (1973), when the state argued that the case was moot because the plaintiff, who was challenging a Texas statute forbidding abortion, was no longer pregnant by the time the case reached the Supreme Court. Because of the relatively short human gestation period (compared to a lawsuit), abortion litigation was readily capable of being repeated, but also likely to evade review, and the case was not dismissed as moot.

2) Exception—voluntary cessation

A court will not dismiss as moot a case in which the defendant voluntarily ceases its illegal or wrongful action once litigation has commenced. The court must be assured that "there is no reasonable expectation that the wrong will be repeated." *United States v. W.T. Grant Co.,* 345 U.S. 629 (1953).

3) Exception—collateral legal consequences

A case challenging a criminal conviction is not moot, even though the direct legal consequences no longer exist (e.g., the convicted defendant has served his sentence and is now free), if collateral legal consequences can be imposed based on that conviction (e.g., revocation of the right to vote or to serve on a jury). *Sibron v. New York,* 392 U.S. 40 (1968); *But see Spencer v. Kemna,* 523 U.S. 1 (1998) (exception does not apply to a challenge to a parole revocation decision).

4) Exception—class actions

If the named plaintiff's claim in a certified class action is resolved and becomes moot, that fact does not render the entire class action moot. *United States Parole Comm'n. v. Geraghty,* 445 U.S. 388 (1980).

3. Justiciability—Further Issues

Federal courts may invoke a variety of other reasons not to decide a case.

a. **Advisory opinions**

Federal courts may not render advisory opinions on the basis of an abstract or a hypothetical dispute. An actual case or controversy must exist.

> **EXAM NOTE:** Fact patterns involving a request for declaratory judgment are likely testing advisory opinion prohibition.

b. **Declaratory judgments**

The courts are not prohibited from issuing declaratory judgments, however, that determine the legal effect of proposed conduct without awarding damages or injunctive relief. The challenged action must pose a real and immediate danger to a party's interests for there to be an actual dispute (as opposed to a hypothetical one).

c. **Political questions**

A federal court will not rule on a matter in controversy if the matter is a political question to be resolved by one or both of the other two branches of government. *Baker v. Carr*, 369 U.S. 186 (1962).

A political question not subject to judicial review arises when:

i) The Constitution has assigned decision making on this subject to a different branch of the government; or

ii) The matter is inherently not one that the judiciary can decide.

Example: Details of Congress's impeachment procedures (constitutionally assigned to a branch other than the judiciary) and the President's conduct of foreign affairs (not within judicial competence) are examples of political questions.

Compare: The political question doctrine does not bar courts from adjudicating the constitutionality of a federal statute directing that an American child born in Jerusalem is entitled to have Israel listed as her place of birth in her U.S. passport. The Court held that the Constitution did not commit the issue to another branch of government and resolving the case would involve examining "textual, structural, and historical evidence" concerning statutory and constitutional provisions, something within judicial competence. *Zivotofsky ex rel. Zivotofsky v. Clinton*, 566 U.S. 189 (2012).

4. **Abstention**

A federal court may abstain from deciding a claim when strong state interests are at stake.

a. *Pullman* **doctrine**

A court may refrain from ruling on a federal constitutional claim that depends on resolving an unsettled issue of state law best left to the state courts. *Railroad Comm'n of Texas v. Pullman*, 312 U.S. 496 (1941).

b. *Younger* **abstention**

A court will not enjoin a pending state criminal case in the absence of bad faith, harassment, or a patently invalid state statute. *Younger v. Harris*, 401 U.S. 37 (1971). Abstention also may be appropriate with regard to a civil enforcement proceeding or a civil proceeding involving an order uniquely in furtherance of the state courts' ability to perform their judicial functions, such as a civil contempt order. *Sprint Commc'ns, Inc. v. Jacobs*, 571 U.S. 69 (2013).

II.   THE POWERS OF CONGRESS

Just as the federal courts are courts of limited jurisdiction, the powers of Congress are not plenary or exclusive. As the Tenth Amendment makes clear, the federal government may exercise only those powers specifically enumerated by the Constitution; it is state governments and the people, not the national government, that retain any powers not mentioned in the federal charter. Any action by the federal government must be supported by a source of power originating in the Constitution. Article I, Section 1 vests all legislative powers of the federal government in Congress.

> **EXAM NOTE**: Congress may amend or repeal existing law and direct that the change be applied in all related *pending* actions, i.e., those in which a final judgment has not been entered. If an exam question involves application of new legislation, pay attention to the status of any case to which it is to be applied.

> **EXAM NOTE:** Congress has no general police power to legislate for the health, safety, welfare, or morals of citizens. The validity of a federal statute on an exam question may not be justified based on "federal police power."

A.   COMMERCE

Article I, Section 8, Clause 3 of the Constitution, known as the Commerce Clause, empowers Congress "[t]o regulate Commerce with foreign Nations, and among the several States, and with the Indian Tribes." The term "commerce" has been defined to include essentially all activity—including transportation, traffic, or transmission of gas, electricity, radio, TV, mail, and telegraph—involving or affecting two or more states.

1.   Interstate Commerce

a.   Power to regulate

Congress has the power to regulate (i) the **channels** (highways, waterways, airways, etc.) and (ii) the **instrumentalities** (cars, trucks, ships, airplanes, etc.) of interstate commerce, as well as (iii) any activity that **substantially affects** interstate commerce, provided that the regulation does not infringe upon any other constitutional right. *United States v. Lopez*, 514 U.S. 549 (1995).

b.   Construed broadly

The Supreme Court has upheld acts of Congress seeking to prohibit or restrict the entry of persons, products, and services into the stream of interstate commerce, as well as acts regulating the interstate movement of kidnap victims, stolen vehicles, and telephone transmissions. However, the Commerce Clause does not give Congress the power to mandate that individuals not engaged in commercial activities engage in commerce. *Nat'l Fed'n of Indep. Bus. v. Sebelius (The Patient Protection and Affordable Care Cases)*, 567 U.S. 519 (2012) (requiring individuals not engaged in commercial activities to buy unwanted health insurance could not be sustained as a regulation of interstate commerce).

2.   "Substantial Economic Effect"

Congress has the power to regulate any activity, intra- or interstate, that in and of itself or in combination with other activities has a "substantial economic effect upon" or "effect on movement in" interstate commerce.

a.   Aggregation

With respect to an intrastate activity that does not have a direct economic impact on interstate commerce, such as growing crops for personal consumption, as long as there is a **rational basis** for concluding that the "total incidence" of the activity in the aggregate substantially affects interstate commerce, Congress may regulate even a minute amount of that total. *Gonzales v. Raich*, 545 U.S. 1 (2005) (prohibition on personal cultivation and use of medical marijuana upheld due to effect on overall interstate trade). The practical effect of this rule is that with regard to economic activity, a substantial economic effect is presumed.

> **Example:** The Supreme Court upheld congressional restriction of wheat production, even when applied to a farmer growing only 23 acres of wheat, primarily for personal use. The rationale behind the decision was that if every small farmer were allowed to grow an unrestricted amount of wheat, the combined effect could have an impact on supply and demand in the interstate market. *Wickard v. Filburn*, 317 U.S. 111 (1942).

3. Non-Economic Activity

Congress's power under the Commerce Clause to regulate **intrastate** activity that is not obviously economic (so-called "non-economic" activity) is limited to some degree by principles of federalism, at least when the regulation involves an area of traditional state concern. The non-economic activity must have a substantial economic effect on interstate commerce. *Nat'l Fed'n of Indep. Bus. v. Sebelius (The Patient Protection and Affordable Care Cases)*, 567 U.S. 519 (2012) (requiring individuals not engaged in commercial activities to buy unwanted health insurance could not be sustained as a regulation of interstate commerce); *United States v. Morrison*, 529 U.S. 598 (2000) (federal civil remedy for victims of gender-motivated violence held invalid); *United States v. Lopez*, 514 U.S. 549 (1995) (federal statute regulating possession of a firearm within 1,000 feet of a public school struck down).

B. TAXATION AND SPENDING

Article I, Section 8 provides: "Congress shall have power to lay and collect taxes, duties, imposts and excises, to pay the debts and provide for the common defense and general welfare of the United States; but all duties, imposts and excises shall be uniform throughout the United States."

> **EXAM NOTE:** If you see the terms "appropriation bill" or "authorization bill" on the exam, the power to spend is likely a consideration.

1. Taxing Power

A tax by Congress will generally be upheld if it has a **reasonable relationship to revenue production**.

> **Example:** The Affordable Health Act's individual mandate, requiring individuals to buy health insurance or pay a penalty, merely imposed a tax on those who failed to buy insurance and therefore could be sustained under the taxing power. *Nat'l Fed'n of Indep. Bus. v. Sebelius (The Patient Protection and Affordable Care Cases)*, 567 U.S. 519 (2012).

a. Any purpose

Of the three branches of the federal government, Article I, Section 8 of the Constitution gives Congress the plenary (i.e., exclusive) power to raise revenue through the imposition of taxes. The government has no burden to prove that the tax is necessary to any compelling governmental interest. Instead, the General Welfare Clause has been interpreted as permitting Congress to exercise its power to tax for any public purpose. (Note: This clause has been interpreted as having the same effect on the spending power, as discussed at § II.B.2. Spending, *infra.*)

> While the General Welfare Clause gives Congress broad power in exercising its spending and taxing powers, it does not give Congress the specific power to legislate for the public welfare in general. Such "police power" is reserved for the states.

b. Indirect tax—uniformity

The requirement that indirect federal taxes (i.e., duties, sales taxes, and import & excise taxes) must be uniform throughout the United States has been interpreted to mean **geographical** uniformity only; the product or activity at issue must be identically taxed in every state in which it is found. Differences in state law do not destroy this uniformity. *Fernandez v. Wiener*, 326 U.S. 340 (1945) (federal estate tax on "community property" valid despite variation in state laws regarding marital property).

c. Direct tax—apportionment

Article I, Section 2 provides that "[r]epresentatives and direct taxes shall be apportioned among the several states," and Article I, Section 9 provides that "no...direct tax shall be laid, unless in proportion to the Census...." A direct tax (one imposed directly on property or persons, such as an ad valorem property tax) would therefore have to be apportioned evenly among the states. The difficulty of ensuring this outcome explains Congress's reluctance to enact such taxes—or perhaps the Supreme Court's reluctance to find that federal taxes are "direct." The Sixteenth Amendment gave Congress the power to lay and collect **income tax** without apportionment among the states.

d. Export tax prohibition

Goods exported to foreign countries may not be taxed by Congress. Article I, Section 9. Under this Export Taxation Clause, a tax or duty that falls on goods during the course of exportation or on services or activities closely related to the export process is prohibited. *United States v. International Business Machines Corp.*, 517 U.S. 843 (1996) (tax on insurance premiums paid to foreign insurers of goods being exported).

e. Origination Clause

Article I, Section 7, Clause 1 provides that "All Bills for raising Revenue shall originate in the House of Representatives; but the Senate may propose or concur with Amendments as on other Bills." Known as the Origination Clause, this provision is limited to "bills that levy taxes in the strict sense of the word, and are not bills for other purposes which may incidentally create revenue." *United States v. Munoz-Flores*, 495 U.S. 385, 397 (1990), citing *Twin City Bank v. Nebeker*, 167 U.S. 196, 202 (1897).

2. Spending Power

The spending power has been interpreted very broadly. Congress has the power to **spend for the "general welfare"**—i.e., any public purpose—not just to pursue its other enumerated powers. *U.S. v. Butler*, 297 U.S. 1 (1936). For example, Congress can provide for the public funding of presidential nominating conventions as well as election campaigns. *Buckley v. Valeo*, 424 U.S. 1 (1976). Although there are areas in which Congress cannot directly regulate, it can use its spending power to accomplish such regulation indirectly by conditioning federal funding. *See South Dakota v. Dole*, 483 U.S. 203 (1987) (statute upheld withholding federal highway funds from states unless they barred the sale of alcoholic beverages to individuals under the age of 21).

Congress cannot, however, impose unconstitutional conditions, such as requiring distribution of the Ten Commandments to patients as a condition of Medicaid funding. *See id.*, 210-211; *Steward Machine Co. v. Davis*, 301 U.S. 548, 590 (1937); *Nat'l Fed'n of Indep. Bus. v. Sebelius (The Patient Protection and Affordable Care Cases)*, 567 U.S. 519 (2012). Moreover, to be enforceable, conditions must be set out unambiguously. *Arlington Cent. Sch. Dist. Bd. of Educ. v. Murphy*, 548 U.S. 291 (2006) (parents who prevailed against local school board for violation of Individuals with Disabilities Education Act could not recover expert fees from local school board under a provision providing for recovery of costs).

C. WAR AND DEFENSE POWERS

Article I, Section 8 gives Congress the power to declare war, raise and support armies, provide and maintain a navy, make rules for governing and regulating the land and naval forces, and provide for the organizing of a militia.

1. Providing for the National Defense

The authority granted to Congress under the war power is very broad. Congress may take whatever action it deems necessary to provide for the national defense in both wartime and peacetime. The Court has upheld the military draft and selective service; wage, price, and rent control of the civilian economy during wartime (and even during the post-war period); and the exclusion of civilians from restricted areas.

2. Courts and Tribunals

Congress has the power to establish military courts and tribunals under Article I, Section 8, Clause 14 and the Necessary and Proper Clause. These courts may try enemy soldiers, enemy civilians, and current members of the U.S. armed forces, but they do not have jurisdiction over U.S. civilians. U.S. citizens captured and held as "enemy combatants" are entitled, as a matter of due process, to contest the factual basis of their detention before a neutral decision maker. *Hamdi v. Rumsfeld*, 542 U.S. 507 (2004). Under the Suspension Clause of Article I, Section 9, Clause 2, all persons held in a territory over which the United States has sovereign control are entitled to habeas corpus (or similar) review of the basis for their detention, unless the privilege of seeking habeas corpus has been suspended. *Boumediene v. Bush*, 553 U.S. 723, (2008).

Because military tribunals are not Article III courts, not all constitutional protections apply (such as the right to a jury trial or grand jury indictment).

3. National Guard

National Guard units are under the dual control of the federal and state governments. Under the Militia Clauses (Art. I, Sec. 8, Cl. 15, 16), Congress has the power to authorize the President to call National Guard units to execute federal laws, suppress insurrections, and repel invasions. This constitutional authority extends to use of National Guard units in domestic situations and non-emergency circumstances, and is not subject the approval or veto of the governor of a state. *Perpich v. Dep't of Def.*, 496 U.S. 334 (1990). (Note: By statute, Congress has restricted the exercise of this constitutional authority. 10 U.S.C. §§ 331-335; 18 U.S.C. § 1385.)

D. INVESTIGATORY POWER

Congress does not have an express power to investigate, but the Necessary and Proper Clause allows Congress broad authority to conduct investigations incident to its power to legislate. *McGrain v. Daugherty*, 273 U.S. 135 (1927).

1. **Scope**

   The investigatory power may extend to any matter within a "legitimate legislative sphere." According to the Speech and Debate Clause of Article I, Section 6, members of Congress cannot be questioned in regard to activities such as speech or debate taking place during a session in either House of Congress in relation to the business before it. This provides an absolute immunity from judicial interference. *Eastland v. Unites States Servicemen's Fund*, 421 U.S. 491 (1975).

2. **Enforcement and Witness's Rights**

   A subpoenaed witness who fails to appear before Congress or refuses to answer questions may be cited for contempt. The witness is entitled to certain rights, including procedural due process (e.g., presence of counsel) and the privilege against self-incrimination.

E. **PROPERTY POWER**

   The Federal Property Clause of Article IV, Section 3 gives Congress the "power to dispose of and make all needful rules and regulations respecting the territory or other property belonging to the United States." There is no express limit on Congress's power to **dispose** of property owned by the United States. Under the Fifth Amendment, however, Congress may only **take** private property for public use (eminent domain) with just compensation and in order to effectuate an enumerated power.

F. **POSTAL POWER**

   Congress has the exclusive power "to establish post offices and post roads" under Article I, Section 8, Clause 7. Congress may impose reasonable restrictions on the use of the mail (such as prohibiting obscene or fraudulent material to be mailed), but the postal power may not be used to abridge any right guaranteed by the Constitution (e.g., the First Amendment).

G. **POWER OVER ALIENS AND CITIZENSHIP**

1. **Aliens**

   Congress has plenary power over aliens. *Fiallo v. Bell*, 430 U.S. 787 (1977). Aliens have no right to enter the United States and may be refused entry for reasons such as their political beliefs. *Kleindienst v. Mandel*, 408 U.S. 753 (1972). However, this power is subject to the constraints of the Fifth Amendment Due Process Clause for an alien within the United States. *Zadvydas v. Davis*, 533 U.S. 678 (2001). An alien may generally be removed from the United States, but only after notice and a removal hearing. 8 U.S.C. §§ 1229, 1229a.

2. **Naturalization**

   Congress has exclusive authority over naturalization. Article I, Section 8, Clause 4 allows Congress to "establish a uniform rule of naturalization."

   > **Example:** Children born abroad whose parents are U.S. citizens are not automatically entitled to U.S. citizenship. Congress can grant citizenship conditioned on the child's return to the U.S. within a specified timeframe or for a specified duration. *Rogers v. Bellei*, 401 U.S. 815 (1971).

   However, while a United States citizen may voluntarily renounce her citizenship, the right of national citizenship in the Fourteenth Amendment (the Citizenship Clause) prevents Congress from taking away a person's citizenship, unless that citizenship was obtained by fraud or in bad faith. *Afroyim v. Rusk*, 387 U.S. 253 (1967) (federal statute that stripped citizenship for voting in a foreign election struck down); *Costello v. United*

States, 365 U.S. 265 (1961) (citizen's willful failure to accurately state his occupation on a naturalization application resulted in loss of citizenship).

H. OTHER ARTICLE I POWERS

Congress has power over **bankruptcies, maritime matters, coining of money,** fixing of **weights and measures,** and **patents and copyrights.**

1. Power Over the District of Columbia

Article I, Section 8, Clause 17 provides that Congress has the power to "exercise exclusive Legislation in all Cases whatsoever, over such District (not exceeding ten Miles square) as may, by Cession of particular States, and the acceptance of Congress, become the Seat of the Government of the United States." Under this provision, which is known as the "Enclave Clause," Congress has supreme authority over Washington, D.C., and may legislate freely with regard to D.C. law.

2. Elections Clause

Article I, Section 4 of the Constitution provides: "The times, places and manner of holding elections for Senators and Representatives shall be prescribed by each state legislature, but Congress may...make or alter such regulations." The Elections Clause explicitly empowers Congress to override state laws concerning federal elections.

3. Necessary and Proper Clause

Congress is given the power to enact any legislation necessary and proper to execute any authority granted to any branch of the federal government. *McCulloch v. Maryland*, 17 U.S. 316 (1819). The Necessary and Proper Clause is not an independent source of power, but it permits Congress's otherwise designated authority to be exercised fully. This clause permits Congress to enact legislation to execute a treaty. *Missouri v. Holland*, 252 U.S. 416, 432 (1920).

> **EXAM NOTE:** Because the Necessary and Proper Clause is not an independent source of power, it is not a correct answer choice by itself unless it carries into effect other enumerated powers.

I. POWER TO ENFORCE THE THIRTEENTH, FOURTEENTH, AND FIFTEENTH AMENDMENTS (CIVIL WAR AMENDMENTS)

Each of the Thirteenth, Fourteenth, and Fifteenth Amendments contains a provision that authorizes Congress to pass "appropriate legislation" to enforce the civil rights guaranteed by those amendments.

1. Thirteenth Amendment—Ban on Slavery

Congress has the power to adopt legislation rationally related to eliminating racial discrimination, as it is among the "badges or incidents" of slavery. *Jones v. Alfred H. Mayer Co.,* 392 U.S. 409 (1968). This power has been broadly interpreted to allow Congress to regulate both private and government action, including racial discrimination by private housing sellers, private schools, and private employers. (This is the only amendment that authorizes Congress to regulate purely private conduct.) This clause also gives Congress the power to eliminate involuntary servitude.

2. Fourteenth Amendment—Equal Protection and Due Process

The Fourteenth Amendment, Section 5 Enabling Clause permits Congress to pass legislation to enforce the equal protection and due process rights guaranteed by the amendment, but not to expand those rights or create new ones. Under the separation of powers doctrine, the job of defining such rights falls to the Supreme Court. In enforcing such rights, there must be a **"congruence and proportionality"** between the injury to be prevented or remedied and the means adopted to achieve that end. *City of Boerne v. Flores*, 521 U.S. 507 (1997) (Religious Freedom Restoration Act held invalid for failure to show widespread religious discrimination and for disproportion to any purported remedial goal). Congress may override state government action that infringes upon Fourteenth Amendment rights, but it may not under this amendment regulate wholly private conduct. In the exercise of Fourteenth Amendment powers, Congress can override the Eleventh Amendment immunity of states. *Fitzpatrick v. Bitzer*, 427 U.S. 445 (1976). But Congress can only override the Eleventh Amendment immunity of states if the "congruence and proportionality" test is satisfied. *Kimel v. Fla. Bd. of Regents*, 528 U.S. 62 (2000).

3. Fifteenth Amendment—Voting

The Fifteenth Amendment prohibits both the state and federal governments from denying any citizen the right to vote on the basis of race, color, or previous condition of servitude. The courts have interpreted the right to vote to include the right to have that vote meaningfully counted. In enacting provisions based on the Fifteenth Amendment, Congress cannot treat states differently and thereby impinge on their "equal sovereignty" unless the different treatment is rationally justified by current circumstances. *Shelby Cty. v. Holder*, 570 U.S. 2 (2013).

J. QUALIFICATIONS OF MEMBERS

The qualifications for members of Congress are set forth in Article I and cannot be altered by Congress or the states. *United States Term Limits, Inc. v. Thornton*, 514 U.S. 779 (1995) (state-mandated term limits for federal representatives invalid); *Powell v. McCormack*, 395 U.S. 486 (1969) (House of Representatives could not refuse to seat a scandal-plagued member who satisfied constitutional criteria for service).

III. THE POWERS OF THE PRESIDENT

Article II, Section 1 grants the "executive power" to the President. The extent the President's executive power has been interpreted broadly by the Supreme Court, and includes the power to enforce federal law and manage the executive branch. *See Nixon v. Fitzgerald*, 457 U.S. 731 (1982). Although the Supreme Court has emphasized that the President has no power to make laws, the President's enforcement power includes the exercise of prosecutorial discretion. *Davis v. U.S.*, 512 U.S. 452 (1994). Presidents may also exercise control over agencies by issuing executive orders. Generally speaking, the President's authority is broader in the area of foreign affairs than in domestic matters.

A. DOMESTIC POWER

1. Pardon Power for Federal Offenses

Article II, Section 2 provides the President with the power to "grant reprieves and pardons for offenses against the United States, except in cases of impeachment." This power applies only to federal cases; the President may not grant pardons for state crimes. The pardon or reprieve may be granted at any time after commission of the offense. *Ex parte Garland*, 71 U.S. (4 Wall.) 333, 380 (1867). The pardon or reprieve may be made subject to conditions and may take or encompass various lesser acts, such as remission of fines, penalties, and forfeitures or commutation of sentences. *Ex parte William Wells*, 59 U.S. (18 How.) 307 (1856). The power may be exercised with respect to groups of people as well as individuals. James Carter, Executive Order 11967, issued Jan. 21, 1977 (amnesty for Vietnam War draft dodgers).

2. Veto Power

Once passed by both houses of Congress, a bill must be presented to the President. Upon presentment, the President has 10 days to act on the proposed legislation. If the President signs the bill, it becomes law. Article I, Section 7 also gives the President the power to veto any bill presented to him. The President may also veto the bill by sending it back, with objections, to the house in which it originated. Congress may override the veto and enact the bill into law by a two-thirds vote in each house.

A third option is that the President does nothing at all. If Congress is still in session at the end of the 10-day period, the bill becomes law without the President's signature. If Congress has adjourned during that time, however, the bill does not become law, because the President could not have returned it to its originating house. The President's failure to act on a bill in this situation is known as the "pocket veto" and cannot be overridden.

The President may not exercise a "line item" veto, refusing part of a bill and approving the rest, because it violates the Presentment Clause. *Clinton v. City of New York*, 524 U.S. 417 (1998).

3. Appointment and Removal of Officials

a. Appointment

Article II, Section 2 authorizes the President, **with the advice and consent of the Senate,** to appoint all "officers of the United States," including ambassadors and Justices of the Supreme Court. Congress may, however, delegate the appointment of "inferior" officials to the President alone (i.e., without Senate approval), the heads of executive departments, or the courts. "Inferior" officials are those supervised by Senate-confirmed appointees. Congress may not itself appoint members of a body with administrative or enforcement powers; such persons are "officers of the United States" and must be appointed by the President. *Buckley v. Valeo*, 424 U.S. 1 (1976) (makeup of the Federal Election Commission invalidated because a majority of its members were to be appointed by the President Pro Tem of the Senate and the Speaker of the House; the FEC's tasks were executive in nature, therefore, Congress had no right to appoint such federal officers).

b. Removal

The Constitution says nothing about the President's power to remove executive officers, but it is generally accepted that the President may remove any executive appointee without cause (and without Senate approval). Congress may not shield appointees from removal by the President by imposing a multi-tiered system in which persons at each level may be removed from office only for good cause. *Free Enterprise Fund v. Public Company Accounting Oversight Bd.*, 561 U.S. 477 (2010) (holding 15 U.S.C.S. §§ 7211(e)(6) and 7217(d)(3) unconstitutional and invalid because the multilevel protection from removal of members of the Public Company Accounting Oversight Board was contrary to Article II's vesting of the executive power in the President and contravened the Constitution's separation of powers).

Federal judges, however, are protected under Article III, Section 1, which provides that they may "hold their offices during good behavior"; they may be removed only by impeachment.

4. Authority as Chief Executive

The scope of the President's power to issue executive orders and to govern domestic affairs is extensive but not clearly delineated. The best-known exposition holds that the President's authority varies with the degree of congressional authorization of the action. Thus, when the President acts:

    i)   With the express or implied authorization of Congress, presidential authority is at its highest, and the action is strongly presumed to be valid;

    ii) When Congress has not spoken, presidential authority is diminished, and the action is invalid if it interferes with the operations or power of another branch of government; and

    iii) When Congress has spoken to the contrary, presidential authority is "at its lowest ebb," and the action is likely invalid.

Youngstown Sheet & Tube Co. v. Sawyer, 343 U.S. 579, 72 S. Ct. 863 (1952).; *See Hamdan v. Rumsfeld*, 548 U.S. 557 (2006) (military commission (i.e., tribunal) had no jurisdiction to proceed because the executive order authorizing the commission exceeded congressional limitations placed on the President to convene commissions).

5. Duty to Faithfully Execute Laws

Article II, Section 3 imposes on the President the duty to "take care that the laws be faithfully executed." Known as the "Take Care Clause," this section ensures that the President will enforce laws, despite disagreeing with them.

B. FOREIGN AFFAIRS

1. Commander in Chief

Although the President is the commander in chief of the military, only Congress may formally declare war. The President may take military action without a declaration of war in the case of actual hostilities against the United States. Congress may in turn limit the President's military activities through exercise of its military appropriation (i.e., funding) power. The questions of whether and to what extent the President may deploy troops overseas without congressional approval is unsettled; presidents routinely do so, and Congress routinely asserts its authority to approve the deployment. The courts have generally left the question to the political branches.

2. Treaties

Pursuant to the Treaty Clause (Art. II, Sec. 2. Cl. 2), the President has the exclusive power to negotiate treaties, although a treaty may only be ratified with the approval of two-thirds of the Senators present.

a. Effect of a treaty

The Constitution is superior to a treaty, and any conflict is resolved in favor of the Constitution. *Reid v. Covert*, 354 U.S. 1 (1957). A treaty has the same authority as an act of Congress; should the two conflict, the one most recently adopted controls. A non-self-executing treaty (one that requires legislation in order to implement its provisions) does not have the same force of law as an act of Congress until legislation is passed effectuating the treaty. In the absence of implementing legislation by Congress, the President does not have the authority to make a non-self-executing treaty binding on the states. *Medellin v. Texas*, 552 U.S. 491 (2008); *Youngstown Sheet & Tube v. Sawyer*, 343 U.S. 579 (1952) (Jackson, J., conc.). A ratified treaty takes precedence over any inconsistent state law. *Missouri v. Holland*, 252 U.S. 416 (1920).

3. Executive Agreements

The President has the power to enter into executive agreements with foreign nations (e.g., reciprocal trade agreements) that do not require the approval of two-thirds of the Senate. Although not expressly provided for in the Constitution, executive agreements may be made, without congressional authorization, pursuant to the President's authority over foreign affairs.

Conflicting federal statutes and treaties take precedence over executive agreements, but executive agreements take precedence over conflicting state laws.

4. International Affairs

The President represents and acts for the United States in day-to-day international affairs. In addition to appointing and receiving ambassadors, the President has the exclusive power to recognize a foreign government. *Zivotofsky v. Kerry*, 576 U.S. 1 (2015).

IV. FEDERAL INTERBRANCH RELATIONSHIPS

The separation of powers doctrine, which is inherent in the structure of the Constitution, ensures that the executive, legislative, and judicial branches of government remain separate and distinct in order to provide a system of checks and balances.

A. CONGRESSIONAL LIMITS ON THE EXECUTIVE

1. Impeachment

Article II, Section 4 states: "The President, Vice President and all civil officers of the United States shall be removed from office on impeachment for, and conviction of, treason, bribery, or other high crimes and misdemeanors." The House of Representatives determines what constitutes "high crimes and misdemeanors" and **may impeach (i.e., bring charges) by a majority vote.** The Senate tries the impeached official, and **a two-thirds vote is necessary for conviction.**

2. Appropriation

If Congress explicitly mandates an allocation, distribution, or expenditure of funds, the President has no power to impound those funds (e.g., refuse to spend them or delay the spending). The President is permitted to exercise discretion if the authorizing legislation so provides. *Train v. New York*, 420 U.S. 35 (1975); *Kendall v. United States*, 37 U.S. 524 (1838).

> **EXAM NOTE:** Separation of powers questions often center on the President trying to impound funds appropriated by Congress. Remember that if Congress fails to mandate that the funds are to be allocated, distributed, or spent, then impoundment is not a separation of powers violation.

3. Legislative Veto

It is unconstitutional for Congress to attempt a "legislative veto" of an executive action—that is, to retain direct control over the actions of an executive agency, rather than going through the proper channels of passing a bill.

Example: In *INS v. Chadha*, 462 U.S. 919 (1983), a provision of law permitted either house of Congress to overturn a decision by the Attorney General granting an alien relief from deportation. The Supreme Court held such a one-house congressional "veto" of a matter delegated to the executive to be unconstitutional as violating the carefully wrought legislative procedures set forth in Article I, which require passage of legislation by both Houses of Congress (i.e., bicameralism) and sending to the

President pursuant to the Presentment Clauses for his approval or return. Thus, the Court made clear that a two-house legislative veto would be equally unconstitutional.

B. DELEGATION OF LEGISLATIVE POWER

Because Congress is vested by Article I with "all legislative powers," it may not delegate that power to any other branch of government. This principle is known as the "nondelegation doctrine." However, delegation of some of Congress's authority to the executive branch has consistently been held constitutional, so long as Congress specifies an "intelligible principle" to guide the delegate. *Whitman v. Am. Trucking Ass'ns, Inc.*, 531 U.S. 457 (2001).

Example: The IRS has been given the power to collect taxes that are assessed under the Internal Revenue Code. Although Congress has determined the amount to be taxed, it has delegated to the IRS the power to determine how such taxes are to be collected.

Almost any legislative delegation passes the "intelligible standards" requirement, so even broadly phrased standards have been upheld.

Examples: A delegation of authority to an executive agency to regulate broadcast licenses to the extent that "public interest, convenience, and necessity require" has been upheld. *Nat'l Broad. Co. v. United States*, 319 U.S. 190 (1943). Similarly, an administrative agency could set "just and reasonable" rates for natural gas sold in interstate commerce. *FPC v. Hope Natural Gas Co.*, 320 U.S. 591 (1944).

Certain powers, however, are nondelegable, such as the power of impeachment and the power to declare war.

C. JUDICIAL LIMITATION OF CONGRESSIONAL POWER

Under the doctrine of separation of powers, Congress may not reinstate the right to bring a legal action after the judgment in the action has become final.

Example: An action brought in federal court under federal question jurisdiction was dismissed with prejudice because it was not timely filed. A statute that revived the plaintiff's right to bring the action was struck down as a violation of the separation of powers doctrine. *Plaut v. Spendthrift Farm, Inc.*, 514 U.S. 211 (1995).

Similarly, Congress cannot prescribe rules of decision to the federal courts in cases pending before it. *United States v. Klein*, 80 U.S. 128 (1872). However, when Congress changes the law underlying a judgment awarding ongoing relief, that relief is no longer enforceable to the extent it is inconsistent with the new law. *Miller v. French*, 530 U.S. 327 (2000).

D. IMMUNITIES AND PRIVILEGES

1. Judicial

A judge is absolutely immune from civil liability for damages resulting from her judicial acts, including grave procedural errors and acts done maliciously or in excess of authority unless there is a clear absence of all jurisdiction. *Butz v. Economou*, 438 U.S. 478 (1987); *Stump v. Sparkman*, 435 U.S. 349 (1978). The judge is not immune, however, to lawsuits regarding nonjudicial activities, such as hiring and firing court employees. *Forrester v. White*, 484 U.S. 219 (1988).

Prosecutors are subject to similar immunity rules. *Imbler v. Pachtman*, 424 U.S. 409 (1976). Court officers who perform ministerial duties, such as court reporters, are entitled only to qualified, not absolute, immunity. *Antoine v. Byers & Anderson*, 508 U.S. 429 (1993).

2. **Legislative**

The Speech or Debate Clause of Article I, Section 6 protects members of Congress from civil and criminal liability for statements and conduct made **in the regular course of the legislative process,** including a speech given on the floor of Congress, committee hearings, and reports. The activities of congressional aides are also protected if a legislator performing the same acts would be immune. *Gravel v. United States*, 408 U.S. 606 (1972).

> **State legislators:** The Speech or Debate Clause does not apply to state legislators, but under the principles of federalism, state legislators are immune from liability for actions within the sphere of legitimate legislative activity (*see* § VI.B.1.b.2, State legislators, *infra*).

This protection does not foreclose prosecution for a crime, including the taking of bribes, when the crime does not require proof of legislative acts or inquiring into the motive behind those acts. *United States v. Brewster*, 408 U.S. 501 (1972). This protection also does not apply to speeches made outside Congress, or the "re-publication" (i.e., repeating) of a defamatory statement originally made in Congress. *Hutchinson v. Proxmire*, 443 U.S. 111 (1979).

3. **Executive**

   a. **Executive privilege**

   Executive privilege is a privilege with respect to the disclosure of confidential information by the executive branch to the judiciary or Congress. This privilege and the more narrow presidential privilege, which applies to communications made in the performance of a president's responsibilities to shape policies and make decisions, have been recognized by the Supreme Court. The presidential privilege survives an individual president's tenure, but this privilege is not absolute. *Cheney v. United States*, 542 U.S. 367 (2004); *United States v. Nixon*, 418 U.S. 683 (1974).

   1) **Criminal trial**

      Presidential communications must be made available in a criminal case if the prosecution demonstrates a need for the information. A judge may examine the communications in camera to determine whether the communications fall within the privilege. *United States v. Nixon, supra*.

   2) **Civil proceedings**

      An executive branch decision to withhold production of information in civil proceedings will be given greater deference than in a criminal trial because the need for information is "weightier" in the latter case. In a civil case, the court may be required to consider the issue of separation of powers without first requiring the executive branch to assert executive privilege. *Cheney v. United States Dist. Court, supra*.

   3) **Historical preservation**

      Congress can require the preservation of presidential papers and tape recordings. *Nixon v. Adm'r of Gen. Servs.*, 433 U.S. 425 (1977).

   4) **State secrets**

      Claims of privilege based on national security are generally accorded enhanced deference. *United States v. Reynolds*, 345 U.S. 1 (1953) (recognizing a "state secrets" privilege). *But see In re NSA Telcoms. Records Litig.*, 564 F. Supp.

2d 1109 (2008) (the "state secrets" privilege was a common-law privilege that could be limited by congressional action).

b. Executive immunity

1) Official duties

The President may not be sued for civil damages with regard to any acts performed as part of the President's **official responsibilities.** *Nixon v. Fitzgerald*, 457 U.S. 731 (1982). The President has no immunity, however, from a civil action based on conduct alleged to have occurred **before the President took office** or completely unrelated to carrying out his job. Moreover, the President may be subject to such a suit even while in office. *Clinton v. Jones*, 520 U.S. 681 (1997).

a) Presidential advisor

A senior presidential advisor (e.g., cabinet member) is not automatically entitled to enjoy derivatively the protection of absolute executive immunity. Although the Supreme Court has stated that such an advisor may be entitled to such protection when performing special functions that are vital to national security or foreign policy, the Court has also held that an Attorney General did not qualify for absolute immunity with respect to the authorization of a warrantless wiretap for national security purposes. The burden for establishing such immunity rests with the advisor. *Harlow v. Fitzgerald*, 457 U.S. 800 (1982); *Mitchell v. Forsyth*, 472 U.S. 511 (1985).

b) Federal officials

A federal official, in performing a discretionary (as opposed to ministerial) act, is entitled to qualified immunity from liability for civil damages when the official's conduct does not violate clearly established statutory and constitutional rights of which a reasonable person would have known. This is an objective standard; a plaintiff's bare allegations of malice are insufficient to overcome this immunity. *Harlow v. Fitzgerald*, 457 U.S. 800 (1982).

> **Example:** The Attorney General, in authorizing a warrantless wiretap for national security purposes, while not entitled to absolute immunity, was entitled to qualified immunity. The unconstitutionality of this authorization was not clearly established at the time of the authorization. *Mitchell v. Forsyth*, 472 U.S. 511 (1985).

PART TWO: THE FEDERAL SYSTEM

V.   FEDERAL AND STATE POWERS

The federal system, under which the federal and state governments each have exclusive authority over some areas, yet share authority over other areas, is one of the Constitution's basic checks on governmental power.

A.   EXCLUSIVE FEDERAL POWERS

The Constitution explicitly provides for some powers of the federal government to be exclusive, such as the powers to coin money or enter into treaties. Article I, Sec. 10. Other powers are by their nature exclusively federal, such as the power to declare war and the power over citizenship; a state's attempt to exercise authority in these areas would essentially subvert the power of the federal government.

B. EXCLUSIVE STATE POWERS

The Tenth Amendment provides that all powers not assigned by the Constitution to the federal government are reserved to the states, or to the people. In theory, this gives the states expansive, exclusive power. In practice, however, given the broad interpretation of the Commerce Clause and the spending power, the federal government has very broad authority, making state power rarely exclusive.

C. CONCURRENT FEDERAL AND STATE LAWS—SUPREMACY CLAUSE

It is possible (and common) for the federal and state governments to legislate in the same area. When this happens, the Supremacy Clause (Article VI, paragraph 2) provides that federal law supersedes conflicting state law (*see* § VIII. Federal Preemption of State Law, *infra*).

VI. INTERGOVERNMENTAL IMMUNITIES

A. FEDERAL IMMUNITY

1. Regulation by the States

The states have no power to regulate the federal government—for example, by imposing state wage-and-hour laws on local federal offices—unless Congress permits the state regulation or unless the state regulation is not inconsistent with existing federal policy.

2. Taxation by the States

The federal government and its instrumentalities (such as a national bank chartered by the federal government) are immune from taxation by the states. *McCulloch v. Maryland*, 17 U.S. 316 (1819). States may, however, impose generally applicable indirect taxes so long as they do not unreasonably burden the federal government (e.g., state income taxes on federal employees). Note that imposing state sales tax on purchases made by the federal government is often unreasonably burdensome and, therefore, unconstitutional. *Panhandle Oil Co. v. Mississippi*, 277 U.S. 218 (1928).

B. STATE IMMUNITY

1. Federal Regulation

The federal government has virtually unlimited power to regulate the states.

a. Congressional action

As long as Congress is exercising one of its enumerated powers, Congress generally may regulate the states. For example, a federal minimum wage and overtime statute enacted under the commerce power can be applied to state employees. *Garcia v. San Antonio Metropolitan Transit Authority*, 469 U.S. 528 (1985). Similarly, Congress can prohibit the disclosure by state officials of personal information obtained from driver's license applications because such information constitutes an article of commerce that is being sold in interstate commerce. *Reno v. Condon*, 528 U.S. 141 (2000).

If Congress determines that a state is violating a person's civil liberties, it can place limits on that state's activities by using the power of the Fourteenth and Fifteenth Amendments. *See Oregon v. Mitchell*, 400 U.S. 112 (1970).

1) "Commandeering" limitation

Congress cannot "commandeer" state legislatures by commanding them to enact specific legislation or enforce a federal regulatory program, and it may not circumvent that restriction by conscripting a state executive officer directly.

Printz v. United States, 521 U.S. 898 (1997); *New York v. United States*, 505 U.S. 144 (1992). There is no distinction between compelling a state to enact legislation and prohibiting a state from enacting new laws—in either case Congress is precluded from issuing direct orders to state legislatures. *Murphy v. National Collegiate Athletic Assn*, 584 U.S. ___ (2018) (act preventing states from legalizing sports betting violated anti-commandeering limitation). However, through the use of the taxing and spending powers, Congress may encourage state action that it cannot directly compel.

> **Example:** In *South Dakota v. Dole*, 483 U.S. 203 (1987), the Court held that Congress could condition a provision of five percent of federal highway funds on the state's raising its drinking age to 21.

2) Requirements for conditioning funding

While, as noted, Congress, through the use of its taxing and spending powers, can encourage states to act in ways in which it cannot directly compel, such Congressional encouragement is subject to five limitations. First, the exercise of spending power must be for the "general welfare," with great deference given to Congress in its judgment. Second, the condition must be unambiguous. Third, the condition must relate to "to the federal interest in particular national projects or programs." Fourth, the condition must not induce the states to act in an unconstitutional manner. Finally, the condition may not exceed the point at which "pressure turns into compulsion." *South Dakota v. Dole at 207-11*; *Nat'l Fed'n of Indep. Bus. v. Sebelius (The Patient Protection and Affordable Care Cases)*, 567 U.S. 519 (2012).

b. Judicial action

1) Remedying constitutional violations

The federal judiciary has broad equitable powers in fashioning a remedy for a constitutional violation. For example, while a court may not directly impose a tax in order to fund a racial-discrimination remedy, it may order a local government with taxing authority to levy such a tax, and it may do so despite a state statutory limitation that would otherwise prevent such action. *Missouri v. Jenkins*, 495 U.S. 33 (1990).

2) State legislators

State legislators are absolutely immune from suit for damages and for declaratory and injunctive relief for actions within the sphere of legitimate legislative activity. *Supreme Court of Virginia v. Consumers Union of U.S., Inc.*, 446 U.S. 719 (1980); *Tenney v. Brandhove*, 341 U.S. 367 (1951).

2. Federal Taxation

Pursuant to the Supremacy Clause of Article VI, the federal government may tax a state; the Tenth Amendment does not protect a state from all federal taxation. *New York v. United States*, 326 U.S. 572 (1946) (excise tax impose on sale of mineral water could be imposed on mineral water from state-owned property); *South Carolina v. United States*, 199 U.S. 437 (1905) (federal licensing tax imposed on sellers of alcohol could be imposed on sellers who were agents of the state even when the tax was paid by the state). However, states have partial immunity from direct federal taxation that would unduly interfere with the performance of the states' "sovereign functions of government." Therefore, the federal government generally may not impose significant taxes directly on states for property used for or income received from the state's performance of basic governmental functions (e.g., public schools, state parks, etc.). *See New York v. United States*, 326 U.S. 572 (1946).

A tax on a payment made by a state to private person that is not directly imposed on the state is constitutional, even though the tax may have a substantial adverse impact on the state. *Id.*, (federal income tax on interest received by holders of state bonds); *Helvering v. Gerhardt*, 304 U.S. 405 (1938) (federal income tax on salaries of state employees).

3. Litigation Involving the United States and Its Officers

In suits between a state and the United States, the United States must consent before the state can file suit against it; conversely, the United States does not need to obtain consent from a state to file suit against that state. As between states, no consent is needed for one state to file suit against another state.

Suits against federal officers are limited, and generally prohibited, because such suits are considered to be brought against the United States if payment of the award will be made from the public treasury. However, if the federal officer acted outside the scope of his professional capacity, then a suit may be instituted against the officer individually.

Under 42 U.S.C. § 1983, a damage claim can be brought against a state official personally for violation of constitutional rights. The Supreme Court has recognized that a similar claim can be brought against federal officials. *Bivens v. Six Unknown Named Agents of Fed. Bureau of Narcotics*, 403 U.S. 388 (1971).

VII. STATE REGULATION AND TAXATION OF COMMERCE

The Constitution contemplates a system of regulation of commerce and taxation that includes both the federal and state governments.

A. THE DORMANT COMMERCE CLAUSE

The Dormant Commerce Clause (sometimes referred to as the Negative Commerce Clause) is a doctrine that limits the power of states to legislate in ways that impact interstate commerce. The Commerce Clause (Article I, Section 8, Clause 3) reserves to Congress the power "[t]o regulate commerce with foreign nations, and among the several states, and with the Indian tribes"; as a corollary, individual states are limited in their ability to legislate on such matters.

1. General Rule

If Congress has not enacted legislation in a particular area of interstate commerce, then the states are free to regulate, so long as the state or local action does not:

i) **Discriminate** against out-of-state commerce;

ii) **Unduly burden** interstate commerce; or

iii) Regulate **extraterritorial** (wholly out-of-state) activity.

> **Note:** Unlike the Comity Clause of Article IV, Section 2, the Dormant Commerce Clause does not exclude corporations and aliens from its protection against state or local action. *See* XIV.A.1. "Prohibits State Discrimination Against Nonresidents," *infra*.

2. Discrimination Against Out-of-State Commerce

A state or local regulation discriminates against out-of-state commerce if it protects local economic interests at the expense of out-of-state competitors. *See Tenn. Wine & Spirits Retailers Ass'n v. Thomas*, 588 US ___, 139 S. Ct. 2449 (2019) (a durational residency requirement for alcohol retail licenses violated the Dormant Commerce Clause because its predominant effect was to protect local economic interests at the expense of out-of-state competitors); *City of Philadelphia v. New Jersey*, 437 U.S. 617 (1978) (state statute prohibiting importation of out-of-state garbage discriminated in favor of local trash collectors); *Dean Milk Co. v. City of Madison*, 340 U.S. 349 (1959) (state law discriminated against out-of-state milk suppliers by requiring all milk sold in the city to be processed and bottled locally).

a. Necessary to important state interest

If a state or local regulation, on its face or in practice, is discriminatory, then the regulation may be upheld if the state or local government can establish that:

i)   An important local interest is being served; and

ii) No other nondiscriminatory means are available to achieve that purpose.

Hunt v. Wash. State Apple Adver. Comm'n, 432 U.S. 333 (1977). Discriminatory regulation has rarely been upheld. In a few instances, a discriminatory state or local regulation that furthers an important, non-economic state interest, like health and safety, has not been struck down. *Maine v. Taylor*, 477 U.S. 131 (1986) (upheld a prohibition against importation into the state of out-of-state live baitfish that may pose contamination hazards to local waters).

1) Burden exclusively on out-of-state businesses

The mere fact that the entire burden of a state's regulation falls on out-of-state businesses is not sufficient to constitute discrimination against interstate commerce. The Dormant Commerce Clause "protects the interstate market, not particular interstate firms, from prohibitive or burdensome regulations." *Id.* pp. 127-128. *Exxon Corp. v. Governor of Maryland*, 437 U.S. 117 (1978) (ban on refiner-owned service stations by state in which no refiners were located upheld).

b. Market-participant exception

A state may behave in a discriminatory fashion if it is acting as a market participant (buyer or seller), as opposed to a market regulator. If the state is a market participant, it may favor local commerce or discriminate against nonresident commerce as could any private business. *E.g., Reeves, Inc. v. Stake*, 447 U.S. 429 (1980) (state-owned cement plant may, in times of shortage, sell only to in-state buyers).

Be aware that the market-participant exception does not apply to challenges pursuant to the Privileges and Immunities Clause of Article IV. *See United Bldg. & Constr. Trades Council v. Camden*, 465 U.S. 208 (1984). Therefore, when a state acting as a market participant has discriminated against out-of-staters with regard to the privileges and immunities it accords its own citizens, there still must be a sufficient justification for the discrimination to avoid a violation of the Privileges and Immunities Clause of Article IV.

c. Traditional government function exception

State and local regulations may favor state and local **government** entities, though not local **private** entities, when those entities are performing a traditional governmental function, such as waste disposal. For example, an ordinance may require all trash haulers to deliver to a local **public** waste-treatment facility, but **not** to a local **private** facility. *Compare United Haulers Ass'n, Inc. v. Oneida-Herkimer Solid Waste Mgmt. Auth.*, 550 U.S. 330 (2007) (public facility), *with C &*

A *Carbone, Inc. v. Town of Clarkstown*, 511 U.S. 383 (1994) (private facility). Similarly, a state may discriminate against out-of-state interests when raising money to fund state and local government projects. *Dep't of Revenue of Kentucky v. Davis*, 553 U.S. 328 (2008) (upholding state income tax exemption for income earned on state and local bonds, but not out-of-state bonds).

d. Subsidy exception

A state may favor its own citizens when providing for subsidy. For example, a state may offer in-state residents a lower tuition rate to attend a state college or university than out-of-state residents. *Vlandis v. Kline*, 412 U.S. 441 (1973).

e. Exception—congressionally permitted discrimination

Because Congress has exclusive authority over interstate commerce, it may explicitly permit states to act in ways that would otherwise violate the Dormant Commerce Clause. *Prudential Ins. Co. v. Benjamin*, 328 U.S. 408 (1946) (state tax only on out-of-state insurance companies upheld when Congress had enacted a law permitting states to regulate insurance in any manner consistent with federal statutes). It must be unmistakably clear that Congress intended to permit the otherwise impermissible state regulation; Congress must expressly allow or "affirmatively contemplate" such state legislation. The fact that the state policy appears to be consistent with federal policy or that the state policy furthers the goals that Congress had in mind is insufficient. *South–Central Timber Dev., Inc. v. Wunnicke*, 467 U.S. 82, 90 (1984).

3. Undue Burden on Interstate Commerce

A state regulation that is not discriminatory may still be struck down as unconstitutional if it imposes an undue burden on interstate commerce. The courts will balance, case by case, the objective and purpose of the state law against the burden on interstate commerce and evaluate whether there are less restrictive alternatives. If the benefits of the state law are grossly outweighed by the burdens on interstate commerce, then even nondiscriminatory regulation may be struck down. *Pike v. Bruce Church, Inc.*, 397 U.S. 137 (1970). This balancing test is not a cost-benefit analysis or a form of close scrutiny of state economic regulation. *United Haulers Ass'n v. Oneida-Herkimer Solid Waste Mgmt. Auth.*, 550 U.S. 330 (2007).

4. "Extraterritoriality"

States may not regulate conduct that occurs wholly beyond their borders. Thus, Connecticut could not require that beer sold in Connecticut not be priced higher than beer sold in any of the four neighboring states, because the Connecticut regime had the practical effect of regulating beer prices in those states. *Healy v. Beer Inst., Inc.*, 491 U.S. 324 (1989). There may be an exception for the regulation of the internal affairs of corporations. *CTS Corp. v. Dynamics Corp.*, 481 U.S. 69 (1987).

B. STATE TAXATION OF COMMERCE

1. Interstate Commerce

Much as with regulation, the states may tax interstate commerce only if Congress has not already acted in the particular area and if the tax does not discriminate against or unduly burden interstate commerce.

a. *Complete Auto* Test

The Supreme Court applies a four-part test to determine whether a state tax on interstate commerce comports with the Commerce Clause. *Complete Auto Transit, Inc. v. Brady*, 430 U.S. 274 (1977).

1) Substantial nexus

There must be a **substantial nexus** between the activity being taxed and the taxing state. A substantial nexus requires significant (i.e., more than minimum) contacts with, or substantial activity within, the taxing state. A physical presence within the state is not required. *South Dakota v. Wayfair, Inc.*, 585 U.S. ___ (2018).

2) Fair apportionment

The tax must be fairly apportioned according to a rational formula (e.g., taxing only the state's portion of the company's business), such that interstate commerce does not pay total taxes greater than local commerce by virtue of having to pay tax in more than one state. The burden is on the taxpaying business to prove unfair apportionment.

3) Nondiscrimination

The tax may not provide a direct commercial advantage to local businesses over their interstate competitors (unless Congress specifically authorizes such a tax). A tax that is neutral on its face still may be unconstitutional if its effect is to favor local commerce. *West Lynn Creamery Inc. v. Healy*, 512 U.S. 186 (1994) (tax affecting all milk dealers, the revenue from which went to a fund used to subsidize in-state dairy farmers, violated the Commerce Clause). In addition, the denial of tax exemption to a state entity unless the entity operates primarily for the benefit of state residents may be unconstitutional. *Camps Newfound/Owatonna v. Town of Harrison*, 520 U.S. 564 (1997).

4) Fair relationship to services provided

The tax must be fairly related to the services provided by the taxing state. *Evansville-Vanderburg Airport Auth. Dist. v. Delta Airlines, Inc.*, 405 U.S. 707 (1972) (tax on airline passengers was related to benefits the passengers received from the state airport facilities).

b. Violation of other constitutional provisions

A state tax may violate more than just the Commerce Clause.

i) A tax that discriminates against nonresident individuals—for example, an income tax that exempts local residents—may violate the **Comity Clause** of Article IV. *Austin v. New Hampshire*, 420 U.S. 656 (1975).

ii) A discriminatory tax on out-of-state businesses, even if authorized by Congress and therefore allowed under the Commerce Clause, may still violate the **Equal Protection Clause** of the Fourteenth Amendment, if it cannot satisfy the rational basis test. *Metropolitan Life Ins. Co. v. Ward*, 470 U.S. 869 (1985) (promotion of domestic business by discriminating against nonresident competitors is not a legitimate state purpose).

iii) An income-based tax imposed on nonresidents that taxes income earned outside the state's borders may violate the **Due Process Clause** of the Fourteenth Amendment. *ASARCO Inc.* v. *Idaho Tax Comm'n*, 458 U.S. 307 (1982).

c. Types of taxes

1) Ad valorem property tax

An ad valorem tax is based on the value of real or personal property and is often assessed at a particular time (e.g., tax day). Such taxes, which may be imposed on the full value of the property, are generally valid, but a state may **not** levy ad valorem taxes on **goods in the course of transit** (from the time the goods are delivered to an interstate carrier or begin their interstate journey until they reach their destination). *Standard Oil Co. v. Peck*, 342 U.S. 382 (1952). However, once the goods are stopped for a business purpose (i.e., obtain a "taxable situs"), they may be taxed.

A state may tax the "instrumentalities of commerce" (airplanes, railroad cars, etc.), provided that:

i) The instrumentality has a **taxable situs** within—or **sufficient contacts** with—the taxing state (i.e., it receives benefits or protection from the state); and

ii) The tax is **fairly apportioned** to the amount of time the instrumentality is in the state.

2) Sales tax

A sales tax imposed on the seller of goods is valid as long as the sale takes place within the state. Sales tax generally does not discriminate against interstate commerce as long as there is a substantial nexus between the taxpayer and the state, and the tax is properly apportioned.

It is no longer required that the seller have a physical presence in the state. State sales taxes apply to any sellers (including online retailers) who engage in a significant quantity of business within the state. *South Dakota v. Wayfair, Inc., supra.*

3) Use tax

A use tax on goods purchased out of state but used within the taxing state is valid so long as the use tax rate is not higher than the sales tax rate on the same item. Even though a use tax does, on its face, seem to discriminate against out-of-state purchases, the rationale for its validity is that such a tax equalizes the tax on in-state and out-of-state goods. *Henneford v. Silas Mason Co., Inc.*, 300 U.S. 577 (1937).

4) "Doing business" taxes

Taxes levied against companies for the privilege of doing business in a state (made up of privilege, license, franchise, or occupation taxes) are valid as long as they pass the *Complete Auto* test (see B.1.a. "*Complete Auto* Test," above). Such a tax may be measured by a flat annual fee or by a graduated rate proportional to the amount of revenue derived from the taxing state. The burden of showing that a tax is unfairly apportioned is on the taxpayer.

2. Foreign Commerce

The Import-Export Clause of Article I, Section 10 prohibits the states, without the consent of Congress, from imposing any tax on any imported or exported goods, or on any commercial activity connected with imported goods, except what is absolutely necessary for executing its inspection laws. *Brown v. Maryland*, 25 U.S. 419 (1827).

In addition, the Commerce Clause vests in Congress the power to regulate international commerce in which the United States is involved. In addition to meeting the same requirements as a tax on interstate commerce (*see* VII.B.1.a. "*Complete Auto* Test," *supra*), a state tax on foreign commerce must not (i) create a substantial risk of *international* multiple taxation or (ii) prevent the federal government from "speaking with one voice" regarding international trade or foreign affairs issues. *Barclays Bank PLC v. Franchise Tax Board*, 512 U.S. 298 (1994).

C.   ALCOHOLIC BEVERAGE REGULATION

The Twenty-First Amendment repealed prohibition and specifically gave states the authority to prohibit the transportation or importation of alcoholic beverages into the state for delivery or use within the state. This amendment has been interpreted as giving a state the authority to regulate or outright ban the distribution and sale of alcoholic beverages within the state. However, this authority is narrowly confined. State regulations concerning alcoholic beverages are subject to the restrictions of the Dormant Commerce Clause, *Tenn. Wine & Spirits Retailers Ass'n v. Thomas*, 588 US ___ (2019) (two-year residency requirement for retail alcohol license deemed unconstitutional economic protectionism of in-state licensees), as well as the protections of the First and Fourteenth Amendments. *44 Liquormart, Inc. v. Rhode Island*, 517 U.S. 484 (1996) (Free Speech Clause); *Larkin v. Grendel's Den, Inc.*, 459 U.S. 116 (1982) (Establishment Clause); *Craig v. Boren*, 429 U.S. 190 (1976) (Equal Protection Clause).

In addition, this amendment does not prevent Congress from exercising control over economic transactions that involve alcoholic beverages under the Commerce Clause or its spending power. *324 Liquor Corp. v. Duffy*, 479 U.S. 335 (1987) (Commerce Clause); *South Dakota v. Dole, supra* (spending power).

VIII.   FEDERAL PREEMPTION OF STATE LAW

The Supremacy Clause of Article VI, Section 2 provides that the "Constitution, and the laws of the United States" are the "supreme law of the land." Any state constitutional provision or law that directly or indirectly conflicts with a federal law, including federal regulations, is void under this clause. However, the Supreme Court has frequently stated that there is a presumption against preemption, especially in areas in which states have traditionally exercised police power. *Wyeth v. Levine*, 555 U.S. 555 (2009) (health and safety).

A.   EXPRESS PREEMPTION

Federal law **expressly** preempts state law in cases in which the Constitution makes the federal power exclusive (such as the powers to coin money or declare war) or when Congress has enacted legislation that explicitly prohibits state regulation in the same area (e.g., the Federal Cigarette Labeling and Advertising Act forbids state laws that regulate either cigarette labels or the "advertising or promotion" of labeled cigarettes "based on smoking and health," 15 U.S.C. § 1334).

1.   Narrow Construction

An express federal preemption must be narrowly construed. *Altria Group, Inc. v. Good*, 555 U.S. 70 (2008) (Federal Cigarette Labeling and Advertising Act did not preempt a suit based on a state's general deceptive-practices statute because such a statute was not based on smoking and health).

Example: The National Bank Act prohibited states to "exercise visitorial powers with respect to national banks, such as conducting examinations, inspecting or requiring the production of books or records," but it was not clear from the Act's language whether it completely prohibited the state from exercising enforcement powers when state law is violated. The Court concluded that the Act's structure and purpose differentiate between the sovereign's "visitorial powers" and its power to enforce the law. While the state could not issue administrative subpoenas to banks, it could file suit to punish violations of state banking laws. *Cuomo v. Clearing House Ass'n*, 557 U.S. 519 (2009).

2. **Savings Clause**

Federal law may also contain "savings clauses" that explicitly preserve or allow state laws that regulate in the same area, e.g., 33 U.S.C. § 1365 (The Clean Water Act preserves "any right which any person (or class of persons) may have under any statute or common law.").

B.   IMPLIED PREEMPTION

1.   When Applicable

Federal preemption is **implied** when any of the following circumstances exist:

i)   Congress intended for federal law to **occupy the field** (*e.g.*, *Hines v. Davidowitz*, 312 U.S. 52 (1941) (new federal law requiring registration of all aliens preempted preexisting state law requiring registration of aliens within the state));

> Intent to occupy a field can be inferred from a framework of regulation so pervasive that Congress left no room for states to supplement it or when there is a federal interest so dominant that the federal system will be assumed to preclude enforcement of state laws on the same subject. *Rice v. Santa Fe Elevator Corp.*, 331 U.S. 218, (1947). When Congress occupies an entire field, even complementary state regulation is impermissible. Field preemption reflects a congressional decision to foreclose any state regulation in the area, even if it is parallel to federal standards. *Arizona v. U.S.*, 567 U.S. 387 (2012) (even if state may make violation of federal law a crime in some instances, it cannot do so in a field, like alien registration, that has been occupied by federal law).

ii)   The state law **directly conflicts** with the federal law by, for example, requiring conduct that is forbidden by the federal law or making it impossible (or nearly so) to comply with both, *e.g., Rose v. Arkansas State Police*, 479 U.S. 1 (1986) (federal law providing that federal death benefits for state law-enforcement officers be in addition to other state benefits preempted contrary state law requiring that other benefits be reduced by the amount of death benefits); or

> **Example 1:** Under 42 U.S.C. § 1983, all persons who violate federal rights while acting under color of state law may be sued for damages. A state law shielding state corrections officers from liability under § 1983 by excluding claims brought against them from being heard in state court violated the Supremacy Clause. *Haywood v. Drown*, 556 U.S. 729 (2009).
>
> **Example 2:** Although a federal statute provides for preemption of state tort claims with regard to medical devices approved by the Federal Drug Administration, 21 U.S.C. § 360(k), there is no express preemption with regard to prescription drugs. However, a state-imposed duty on generic drug manufacturers to warn users of dangers through labeling was preempted by an FDA rule that required the label on generic drugs to match the label of the corresponding brand name drug. The court found that it was impossible for the generic drug manufacturers to comply with both federal regulations and state law. *PLIVA, Inc. v. Mensing*, 564 U.S. 604 (2011).
>
> **Compare:** The manufacturer of a brand-name drug failed to establish preemption of a state-law duty to warn when the manufacturer was permitted under FDA regulations to change the drug label and then request FDA approval for the change. *Wyeth v. Levine, supra.*

iii) The state law **indirectly conflicts** with federal law by creating an obstacle to or frustrating the accomplishment of that law's purpose, e.g., *Perez v. Campbell*, 402 U.S. 637 (1971) (state law suspending licenses of all drivers with unpaid accident judgments frustrates the purpose of federal bankruptcy laws to provide a fresh start).

The existence of a valid purpose for a state law does not prevent federal preemption. *Id.*

2. Absence of Preemption

If federal law does not preempt state law, a state is free to enact legislation regarding the same issue. *Colorado Anti-Discrimination Comm'n. v. Continental Air Lines, Inc.*, 372 U.S. 714 (1963) (state statute prohibiting racial discrimination valid despite the existence of identical federal law). If there has not been federal preemption in a given area, a state is free to set more stringent standards than those imposed by the federal government. In addition, a state may recognize individual rights that exceed those granted by the federal constitution or federal statutes. *Pruneyard Shopping Ctr. v. Robbins*, 447 U.S. 74 (1980) (California's constitutional grant of greater free speech rights than the federal constitution confers upheld).

> **EXAM NOTE:** Under the Supremacy Clause, federal law sets a **floor** below which state law generally cannot go, but it does **not** set a **ceiling** beyond which state law cannot go.

IX. RELATIONS AMONG STATES

A. INTERSTATE COMPACTS

An interstate compact is an agreement, similar to a treaty or a contract, between two or more states. Article I, Section 10, Clause 3 (the "Interstate Compact Clause") allows states to enter into such agreements only with the consent of Congress. However, the only agreements that qualify as "compacts" requiring the consent of Congress are those that either affect a power delegated to the federal government or alter the political balance within the federal system.

B. FULL FAITH AND CREDIT

The Full Faith and Credit Clause of Article IV, Section 1 provides that "[f]ull faith and credit shall be given in each state to the public acts, records, and judicial proceedings of every other state."

1. Judgments

Full faith and credit requires that out-of-state **judgments** be given in-state effect. *Baker v. General Motors Corp.*, 522 U.S. 222 (1998). However, to be given full faith and credit, a decision must meet three requirements:

i) The court that rendered the judgment must have had **jurisdiction** over the parties and the subject matter;

ii) The judgment must have been **on the merits** rather than on a procedural issue; and

iii) The judgment must be **final**.

2. Laws (Public Acts)

The Full Faith and Credit Clause is "less demanding" with respect to choice of law and the application of the laws of other states (i.e., which state's law should apply in a situation when either might). *Id.* However, the Constitution prohibits state courts of general jurisdiction from refusing to hear a case solely because the suit is brought under a federal law, and a state may not discriminate against rights arising under federal laws. *McKnett v. St. Louis & S. F. R. Co.*, 292 U.S. 230 (1934).

PART THREE: INDIVIDUAL RIGHTS

X. STATE ACTION

The Constitution generally protects against wrongful conduct by the government, not private parties (with the exception of the Thirteenth Amendment's prohibition against slavery, which applies to private and government action). In other words, state action is a necessary prerequisite to triggering constitutional protections. A private person's conduct must constitute state action in order for these protections to apply. For example, state action may exist in cases of private parties carrying out traditional governmental functions or significant state involvement in the activities.

A. TRADITIONAL GOVERNMENTAL FUNCTION

State action is found when a private person carries on activities that are **traditionally performed exclusively by the state,** such as running primary elections or governing a "company town." *Terry v. Adams*, 345 U.S. 461 (1953); *Marsh v. Alabama*, 326 U.S. 501 (1946). By contrast, a shopping center that is open to the public does not thereby assume or exercise municipal functions, and therefore is not treated as a state actor. *Hudgens v. NLRB*, 424 U.S. 507 (1976) (shopping mall not required to permit picketing on its private sidewalks). Similarly, merely providing a product or service that the government **could** offer is not sufficient to make the provider a state actor. *Flagg Brothers v. Brooks*, 436 U.S. 149 (1978) (statutorily sanctioned but not compelled sale of goods by bailee not state action). However, the use of peremptory challenges, even by private litigants, constitutes state action because the selection of jurors is a traditional state function and because the judge (i.e., the government) plays a significant role in the process. *Edmonson v. Leesville Concrete*, 500 U.S. 614 (1992).

B. SIGNIFICANT STATE INVOLVEMENT

State action may exist if there are sufficient mutual contacts between the conduct of a private party and the government to find that the government is so pervasively entwined with the private entity that constitutional standards should apply to the private actor. *Brentwood Acad. v. Tenn. Secondary Sch. Ath. Ass'n*, 531 U.S. 288 (2001) (athletic association was a federal actor because the association was pervasively entwined with government policies and was managed and controlled by government officials in their government capacity). State action also exists if the actions of a private party and the government are so intertwined that a mutual benefit results, such as if the parties are involved in a joint venture. *Lugar v. Edmondson Oil Co.*, 457 U.S. 922 (1982) (state action was present when a clerk and sheriff acted together with a private citizen to obtain attachment against a property of the debtor). Similarly, when the government creates a corporation by special law for the furtherance of governmental objectives and retains permanent authority to appoint a majority of the directors of that corporation, the corporation is part of the government for the purposes of the First Amendment even if the enabling statute explicitly states that the corporation is a private entity. *Lebron v. Nat'l R.R. Passenger Corp.*, 513 U.S. 374 (1995).

The Supreme Court has not laid out a test to determine what constitutes significant state involvement, but some general guidelines exist. Mere licensing or regulation of a private party does not constitute state action; the state must **act affirmatively** to facilitate, encourage, or authorize the activity. *Moose Lodge No. 107 v. Irvis*, 407 U.S. 163 (1972). Even when the state explicitly prohibits behavior that violates a person's civil rights, state action may exist if it appears the state has sanctioned the violative act.

States are constitutionally forbidden from facilitating or authorizing discrimination, but they are not required to make discrimination illegal.

C. INSIGNIFICANT STATE INVOLVEMENT

Businesses that the government substantially regulates or to which the government grants a monopoly, such as utility companies, do not exercise state action. Further exclusions include nursing homes that accept Medicaid, schools that receive government funds but are operated by a private corporation, and congressional grants of a corporate charter.

XI. PROCEDURAL DUE PROCESS

The Due Process Clause of the **Fifth Amendment,** which applies against the **federal government,** provides that "[n]o person shall be ... deprived of life, liberty, or property, without due process of law."

The Due Process Clause of the **Fourteenth Amendment,** which applies against the **states,** provides that "no state shall make or enforce any law which shall ... deprive any person of life, liberty, or property, without due process of the law."

A. DUE PROCESS GENERALLY

These clauses operate at a number of levels to protect the rights of individuals and other "persons"—e.g., corporations—against the government. At the most basic level, each clause ensures that the federal and state governments must follow certain procedures before depriving any person of "life, liberty, or property." These safeguards, like notice and a hearing, are the cornerstone of **procedural due process.**

At another level, the Fourteenth Amendment, through its guarantee of rights respecting life, liberty, and property, has been interpreted to make **most provisions of the Bill of Rights** (which by its terms applies to the federal government) **applicable against the states as well.** That is, the Fourteenth Amendment Due Process Clause **incorporates** the protections of the First, Second, Fourth and Eighth Amendments, as well as most of the protections of the Fifth and Sixth Amendments. (However, the Fifth Amendment right to grand jury indictment and the Sixth Amendment right to a unanimous jury verdict in a criminal trial are not incorporated.) The Seventh Amendment right to a jury in civil trials has been held not applicable to the states.

Finally, both Due Process Clauses contain a "substantive" component that guarantees certain fundamental rights to all persons. This **substantive due process** acts as something of a catchall for rights not explicitly set forth elsewhere in the Constitution.

B. PROCEDURAL DUE PROCESS APPLIED

1. General Principles

The concept of "fundamental fairness" is at the heart of the right to procedural due process. It includes an individual's right to be **notified** of charges or proceedings against him and the opportunity to be **heard** at those proceedings. When one's liberty or property interests are adversely affected by governmental action, two questions are asked:

i) Is the threatened interest a **protected** one?

ii) If so, **what process** is due?

> Note that procedural due process only applies in quasi-judicial or adjudicatory settings, and not with respect to the adoption of general legislation. *See Minnesota State Bd. for Cmty. Colls. V. Knight,* 465 US 271 (1984).

a. Neutral decision maker

Due process entitles a person to a fair decision maker. A judge must recuse herself when she has a direct, personal, substantial, pecuniary interest in a case (i.e., actual bias) or there is a serious objective risk of actual bias. In the latter instance, proof of actual bias is not required, and subjective impartiality is not sufficient to justify a refusal to recuse. *Caperton v. A. T. Massey Coal Co.*, 556 U.S. 868 (2009).

> **Example:** An attorney running for a judgeship on the state supreme court had received a $3 million contribution that had a significant and disproportionate influence on the electoral outcome. The contribution exceeded the sum total of all other contributions the attorney had received and exceeded by 50% the combined amount spent by the attorney's and his opponent's campaigns. The contribution was made by the president of a company that had received an adverse $50 million verdict in a lower court of the state prior to the election. It was foreseeable that the judgment would be appealed to the state supreme court at the time that the contribution was made. Consequently, the Due Process Clause required the judge who had received the contribution to recuse himself. *Caperton v. A. T. Massey Coal Co., supra.*

b. Intentional conduct

Due process addresses injury that results from an intentional governmental act. Mere negligent conduct by a government employee does not trigger a due process right. *Daniels v. Williams*, 474 U.S. 327 (1986) (prisoner's injury due to correction officer's negligence was not a deprivation of liberty).

2. Protected Interests

a. Liberty

An impingement on liberty is generally construed to mean **significant** governmental restraint on one's **physical freedom,** exercise of **fundamental rights** (i.e., those guaranteed by the Constitution), or **freedom of choice or action.**

Examples of loss of liberty include commitment to a mental institution, parole revocation, and loss of parental rights. Injury to reputation alone is not a deprivation of liberty, unless the injury is so great that the individual has lost **significant employment or associational rights.**

b. Property

A cognizable property interest involves more than an abstract need or desire; there must be a "legitimate claim of entitlement" by virtue of statute, employment contract, or custom. *Board of Regents v. Roth*, 408 U.S. 564, 577 (1972) (non-tenured professor with a one-year contract had no liberty or property interest in being rehired).

The rights to government-issued licenses and continued welfare and disability benefits are legitimate property interests. For example, although a patient may have a legitimate property interest in the continued receipt of medical benefits to pay for the patient's stay in a qualified nursing home, there is no legitimate property interest in the patient's continued residence in the nursing home of the patient's choice. As a result, a patient is not entitled to a hearing before the government disqualifies a nursing home from participating in a public benefits program. *O'Bannon v. Town Court Nursing Ctr.*, 447 U.S. 773 (1980).

1) Public employment

There is a legitimate property interest in continued public employment only if there is an employment contract or a clear understanding that the employee may be fired only for cause. *Arnett v. Kennedy*, 416 U.S. 134 (1974). An "at will" governmental employee has no right to continued employment. *Bishop v. Wood*, 426 U.S. 341 (1976). If, however, the government gives the "at will" public employee assurances of continual employment or dismissal for only specified reasons, then there must be a fair procedure to protect the employee's interests if the government seeks to discharge the employee from his position. Such entitlement to procedural due process can also result from statutory law, formal contract terms, or the actions of a supervisory person with authority to establish terms of employment.

Note, though, that even those employees who lack any entitlement to continued employment cannot be discharged for reasons that in and of themselves violate the Constitution. Thus, an "at-will" governmental employee cannot be fired for having engaged in speech protected by the First Amendment. *Board of Regents v. Roth*, 408 U.S. 564 (1972). Similarly, discharge of an "at-will" governmental employee because of the employee's political views or affiliations would violate the employee's right to freedom of expression and association, unless it can be demonstrated that effective performance of the employee's job requires certain political views or affiliations. *Branti v. Finkel*, 445 U.S. 507 (1980). To be entitled to a hearing, however, the employee must make a prima facie claim that she is being discharged for reasons that violate specific constitutional guarantees. Moreover, a dismissal will be upheld if the government can prove that the employee would have been discharged in any event for reasons unrelated to any constitutionally protected activities. *Mt. Healthy City School Dist. Bd. of Educ. v. Doyle*, 429 U.S. 274 (1977).

2) Public education

There is a property right to a public education. *Goss v. Lopez*, 419 U.S. 565 (1975). Although such a right is not specifically recognized by the Constitution, all states recognize the right to a public education. *See, e.g., Serrano v. Priest*, 487 P.2d 1241 (Cal. 1971); Tex. Const. art. VII. § 1. However, the Supreme Court has never determined whether a student at a public institution of higher learning has a property (or liberty) interest in her education there. *Board of Curators of University of Missouri v. Horowitz*, 435 U.S. 78 (1978) (Supreme Court assumed without deciding that a medical student had a liberty or property interest; federal appellate court had found that the student had a liberty interest); *See Regents of University of Michigan v. Ewing*, 474 U.S. 214 (1985) (Supreme Court assumed without deciding that a medical student had a liberty or property interest; federal appellate court had found that the student had a property interest).

3. Notice and Hearing

If an individual's protected interest is threatened by governmental action, the next step is to determine what type of process is due. The Court considers three factors in determining the amount of process that is due:

i)   The **private interest** affected by the governmental action;

ii) The risk of erroneous deprivation of that interest using current procedures and the probable **value of additional or substitute safeguards**; and

iii) The **government's interest**, including the function involved and the **burden (fiscal and administrative cost)** of providing the additional process.

Mathews v. Eldridge, 424 U.S. 319 (1976). The greater the importance of the threatened interest, the greater the likelihood that the Court will require extensive procedural safeguards prior to the termination of the interest.

Generally, the person whose interest is being deprived is entitled to **notice** of the government's action by an unbiased decision maker and an **opportunity to be heard,** although the hearing need not necessarily occur before the termination of the interest.

Example: While the state must give notice and hold a hearing prior to terminating **welfare benefits,** in cases of terminating **disability benefits or public employment,** the state must give prior notice, but only a post-termination evidentiary hearing is required. *Goldberg v. Kelly*, 397 U.S. 254 (1970), *Mathews v. Eldridge*, *supra*.

When determining what procedures are required, while the government can create a liberty or property interest, the Constitution as interpreted by the Court, not the legislature, determines the minimum procedures required for the deprivation of that interest. *Cleveland Bd. of Educ. v. Loudermill*, 470 U.S. 532 (1985). Regarding the adequacy of notice, the government must provide "notice reasonably calculated, under all the circumstances, to apprise interested parties of the pendency of the action and afford them an opportunity to present their objections." *Mullane v. Cent. Hanover Bank & Tr. Co.*, 339 U.S. 306, 314 (1950).

a. Enemy combatants

United States citizens held as enemy combatants are entitled to meaningful opportunity to dispute the facts of their detention by a neutral decision maker, albeit the opportunity is adapted to reduce burdens on executive authority brought on by an ongoing military conflict. *Boumediene v. Bush*, 553 U.S. 723, (2008).

b. Parental status

Different burdens of proof are applied to termination of parental rights and paternity actions. Because termination of parental rights deprives parents of a fundamental right, the state must use clear and convincing evidence to support allegations of neglect. *Santosky v. Kramer*, 455 U.S. 745 (1982).

When a mother or child is initiating a paternity suit, due process requires proof by only a preponderance of evidence. *Rivera v. Michigan*, 483 U.S. 574 (1987). In a paternity action initiated by the state, the state must pay for the necessary blood work used in determining paternity. *Little v. Streater*, 452 U.S. 1 (1981).

c. Forfeitures

Forfeiture is an involuntary relinquishment of property that the government alleges is connected to criminal activity. Generally, the government is required to provide the owner with notice and a hearing prior to seizure of real property. *United States v. James Daniel Good Real Property*, 510 U.S. 43 (1993). However, the government is not necessarily required to provide notice prior to the seizure of personal property when there is strong justification for effecting the seizure before providing notice. *Calero-Toledo v. Pearson Yacht Leasing Co.*, 416 U.S. 663 (1974) (pre-notice seizure of yacht containing marijuana justified based on ease of moving yacht); *But see Grimm v. City of Portland*, 971 F.3d 1060 (9th Cir. 2020) (government required to provide notice prior to towing a vehicle violating parking regulations absent strong justification (e.g., car blocking traffic)).

d. Public employees

A public employee who may be discharged only for cause has a property interest in his job and therefore is generally entitled to **notice** of termination and a **pre-termination opportunity to respond.** A formal hearing is not required, as long as there is pre-termination notice, an opportunity to respond to the decision maker, and a **post-termination evidentiary hearing.** *Cleveland Bd. of Educ. v. Loudermill, supra.* If there is a significant reason for immediately removing a "for-cause" employee from the job, a prompt post-suspension hearing with reinstatement and back pay if the employee prevails constitutes sufficient due process. *Gilbert v. Homar,* 520 U.S. 924 (1997).

e. Public education

1) Academic dismissal

A student is not entitled to a hearing regarding dismissal from a public institution of higher learning. *Board of Curators of University of Missouri v. Horowitz, supra* (medical school student was fully informed respondent of the faculty's dissatisfaction with her clinical progress and the danger that this posed to timely graduation and continued enrollment); *See also Regents of University of Michigan v. Ewing, supra* (challenge to dismissal of medical student on substantive due process grounds rejected; court refused to override academic decision unless it is such a substantial departure from accepted academic norms as to demonstrate that the person or committee responsible did not actually exercise professional judgment).

2) Disciplinary suspension

When a student is suspended from public school for disciplinary reasons, due process requires that the student be given oral or written notice of the charges against him and, if he denies them, an explanation of the evidence the authorities have and an opportunity to present his side of the story. *Goss v. Lopez, supra,* at 581. However, a student whose presence poses a continuing danger to persons or property or an ongoing threat of disrupting the academic process may be immediately removed from school and the necessary notice and rudimentary hearing can follow as soon as practicable. *Id., at 582-3.*

3) Corporal punishment

While state-sanctioned disciplinary corporal punishment by a public-school authority that results in the restraint of the student and the infliction of appreciable physical pain implicates the student's liberty interests, the student is not entitled to notice or a hearing. If the punishment is excessive, the student could seek damages in a civil action. *Ingraham v. Wright,* 430 U.S. 651 (1977).

f. Government benefits

The state must give notice and hold a hearing *prior to* terminating **welfare benefits**. In cases of terminating **disability benefits,** the state must give prior notice, but only a *post-termination* evidentiary hearing is required. *Goldberg v. Kelly,* 397 U.S. 254 (1970), *Mathews v. Eldridge, supra.*

4. Court Access—Indigents

a. Court fees

The government cannot deny an indigent person access to the court system because of his inability to pay the required court fees, if such imposition of fees acts to deny a fundamental right to the indigent. Due process requires such fees to be waived. Conversely, if the matter does not involve a fundamental right, no waiver is required.

b. Right to counsel

While the Sixth Amendment provides that an indigent defendant has a constitutional right to have counsel appointed in any criminal case, including a non-summary criminal contempt proceeding in which the defendant is sentenced to incarceration (*United States v. Dixon*, 509 U.S. 688 (1993)), there is no similar due process right to have counsel appointed when an indigent defendant is held in contempt in a civil proceeding and incarcerated, but procedures must be in place to ensure a fundamentally fair determination of any critical incarceration-related question (e.g., defendant's ability to comply with order for which the defendant is held in contempt). *Turner v. Rogers*, 564 U.S. 431 (2011) (defendant held in contempt for violation of child support order; the plaintiff, who was the custodial parent seeking enforcement of the child support order, was also not represented by counsel).

XII. SUBSTANTIVE DUE PROCESS

The guarantee of substantive due process is based upon the idea that laws should be reasonable and not arbitrary.

A. STANDARD OF REVIEW

The standard of review in substantive due process cases is generally twofold: a governmental action that infringes upon a **fundamental right** is generally subject to **strict scrutiny.** If the interest infringed upon is not fundamental, then there need be only a **rational basis** for the regulation.

1. Strict Scrutiny

a. Test

The law must be the **least restrictive** means to achieve a **compelling** governmental interest.

1) Least restrictive means

For the law to be the least restrictive means to achieve the government's interest, there cannot be a way to achieve the same interest that is less restrictive of the right at issue. A law will not fail simply because there are other methods of achieving the goal that are equally or more restrictive.

Under strict scrutiny, the law should be neither over-inclusive (reaching more people or conduct than is necessary) nor under-inclusive (not reaching all of the people or conduct intended).

2) Compelling interest

Although there is no precise definition of what is "compelling," it is generally understood to be something that is necessary or crucial, such as national security or preserving public health or safety.

3) Strict in theory, fatal in fact

The strict scrutiny standard is very difficult to meet. The great majority of laws reviewed under strict scrutiny are struck down.

b. Burden of proof

The burden is on the government to prove that the law is necessary to achieve a compelling governmental interest.

c. Applicability

The strict scrutiny test is generally applied if a **fundamental right** is involved.

2. Rational Basis

a. Test

A law meets the rational basis standard of review if it is **rationally related** to a **legitimate** state interest. This is a test of minimal scrutiny and generally results in the law being upheld.

b. Burden of proof

Laws are presumed valid under this standard, so the burden is on the challenger to overcome this presumption by establishing that the law is **arbitrary or irrational.**

In court, the government's stated interest in enacting the law need not be one that it offered when the law was passed. Any legitimate reason will suffice.

This factor distinguishes rational basis review from strict scrutiny, when the government must defend the interest that it stated at the outset.

c. Applicability

The rational basis standard is used in all cases to which strict scrutiny or intermediate scrutiny does not apply. *Heller v. Doe*, 509 U.S. 312 (1993). In practice, most legislation related to lifestyle, taxation, zoning, and punitive damages is reviewed under this standard.

Although punitive damages do not violate due process, excessive damages may. The court considers whether the defendant had fair notice of the possible magnitude before it will bar a punitive-damages award.

The government cannot presume facts about an individual that will deprive that individual of certain benefits or rights. By doing so, the government creates an arbitrary classification that may violate due process as well as equal protection.

1) Retroactive legislation

The retroactive application of a statute does not in and of itself violate substantive due process. Consequently, a law that is applied retroactively must merely meet the rational basis test. *United States v. Carlton*, 512 U.S. 26 (1994) (retroactive application of estate tax law that resulted in denial of a deduction upheld). Similar treatment applies to a statutory change that is remedial in nature (i.e., affects a remedy but does not create or abolish a right). *Chase Securities Corp. v. Donaldson*, 325 U.S. 304 (1945) (lengthening of statute of limitations that permitted an otherwise time-barred lawsuit to be maintained upheld). Note, however, that the extension of a criminal statute of limitations may violate the prohibition on an ex post facto law (*see* § XVI.B. Ex Post Facto Laws, *infra*).

B. FUNDAMENTAL RIGHTS

Some rights are so deeply rooted in our nation's tradition and history that they are considered fundamental. These rights include: (i) the right to travel; (ii) the right to vote; and (iii) the right to privacy (including marriage, sexual relations, abortion, child rearing, and the right of related persons to live together). Under **strict scrutiny,** a law interfering with the fundamental rights of travel and privacy will generally be upheld only if it is **necessary** to achieve a **compelling governmental interest.** With regard to the fundamental right to vote, the level of scrutiny can depend on the degree to which this right is restricted.

Government infringement upon **nonfundamental rights**—those related to social or economic interests such as business, taxation, lifestyle, or zoning—requires only a **rational relationship** between the law and a **legitimate governmental interest.**

EXAM NOTE: If, on a question, a fundamental right is being infringed upon for all persons, the issue is likely one of substantive due process. If the right is being denied to only a particular class of persons, then equal protection is in play.

---

1. **Travel**

   a. **Interstate**

      There is a fundamental right to travel from state to state. *Shapiro v. Thompson,* 394 U.S. 618 (1969). This includes the right to enter one state and leave another, to be treated as a welcome visitor, and, for those who wish to become permanent residents, the right to be treated equally to native-born citizens with respect to state benefits. *Saenz v. Roe,* 526 U.S. 489 (1999) (state statute denying full welfare benefits to people who had not resided in the state for one year struck down; state's interests in discouraging fraud and establishing an objective residency test were not compelling).

      Reasonable residency restrictions or waiting periods may be imposed on the receipt of some government benefits. *See, e.g., Vlandis v. Kline,* 412 U.S. 441 (1973) (declining to strike down a state statute requiring one year of residence before qualifying for in-state tuition). However, durational residence requirements that impinge on the right of interstate travel by denying newcomers "basic necessities of life" are only permitted if the state can establish that they are necessary to serve a compelling state interest. In order to justify such a durational residency requirement, the state must do more than show that the policy saves money. *Mem'l Hosp. v. Maricopa Cty.,* 415 U.S. 250 (1974) (holding that a residency requirement of one year as a condition to an indigent's receiving medical care at the county's expense impermissibly burdened the right of interstate travel because fiscal savings were an insufficient state interest to uphold the requirement). Once a person qualifies as a resident, she must be treated equally. *Zobel v. Williams,* 457 U.S. 55 (1982) (division of state royalties from minerals and oil based on length of state residency unconstitutional).

   b. **International**

      Although there is a right to travel internationally, it is not a fundamental right invoking strict scrutiny. Hence, the U.S. government may limit travel to certain countries as long as it has a rational basis for doing so. *Regan v. Wald,* 468 U.S. 222 (1984).

2. **Voting and Ballot Access**

   a. **Right to vote**

      Under the Twenty-Sixth Amendment, the right to vote is fundamental to all U.S. citizens who are 18 years of age or older. This right applies to all federal, state, and local elections, including primary elections. Despite being a fundamental right, strict scrutiny does not apply to all laws that restrict this right. The level of scrutiny to which a governmental restriction of this right is subject depends on the degree to which the restriction affects the exercise of this right; the more significant the impact, the greater the degree of scrutiny. *Burdick v. Takushi*, 504 U.S. 428 (1992); *Crawford v. Marion County Election Bd.*, 553 U.S. 181 (2008).

1) Residency

A restriction on the right to participate in the political process of a governmental unit imposed upon those who reside within its borders is typically upheld as justified on a rational basis; nonresidents generally may be prohibited from voting. *Holt Civic Club v. City of Tuscaloosa*, 439 U.S. 60 (1978) (citizens who lived outside city boundaries could be denied the right to vote in city elections, even though they were subject to business licensing fees imposed by the city).

A person must be given the opportunity to prove residency before being denied the right to vote because of lack of residency. *Carrington v. Rash*, 380 U.S. 89 (1965).

a) Length of residency

A person may be required to be a resident of a governmental unit (e.g., state, city) for a short period prior to an election in order to vote in that election. *Marston v. Lewis*, 410 U.S. 679 (1973) (50-day period upheld); *Dunn v. Blumstein*, 405 U.S. 330 (1972) (three-month and one-year periods struck down).

b) Presidential elections

Congress can supersede state residency requirements with respect to presidential elections. *Oregon v. Mitchell*, 400 U.S. 112 (1970). For presidential elections, a state may not impose a residency requirement, but may require that an individual register to vote, provided that an individual may register to vote as late as 30 days before the election. 52 U.S.C.S. § 10502.

2) Property ownership

Generally, property ownership is not a valid ground upon which to restrict the right to vote. *Kramer v. Union Free School District No. 15*, 395 U.S. 621 (1969) (restriction of the right to vote on school board members to property owners or parents of school-age children struck down). A limited exception exists for elections involving special-purpose entities, such as a water-storage district. *Ball v. James*, 451 U.S. 355 (1981).

3) Poll tax

Payment of a fee in order to vote (i.e., a poll tax) in an election for federal office is prohibited by the Twenty-Fourth Amendment. More broadly, the imposition of a poll tax in order to vote in any election violates the Equal Protection Clause, as a poll tax is unrelated to voter qualifications. *Harper v. Virginia Bd. of Elections*, 383 U.S. 663 (1966).

4) Voter ID

A state may require that a citizen who votes in person present a government-issued photo ID. With regard to this neutral, nondiscriminatory requirement, the Supreme Court declined to apply a strict scrutiny standard. *Crawford v. Marion County Election Bd., supra*.

5) Felon

Pursuant to Section 2 of the Fourteenth Amendment, a state may prohibit a felon from voting, even one who has unconditionally been released from prison. *Richardson v. Ramirez*, 418 U.S. 24 (1974).

6) Write-in voting

A person's right to vote does not extend to the right to vote for any possible candidate. A state may ban all write-in candidates in both primary and general elections, at least when the state provides reasonable means by which a candidate can get on the ballot. *Burdick v. Takushi*, 504 U.S. 428 (1992) (state's legitimate interests, such as preventing unrestrained factionalism, outweighed the limited burdens placed on the right to vote by the ban).

b. Public office and ballot access

There is no fundamental right to hold office through election or appointment, but all persons do have a constitutional right to be considered for office without the burden of invidious discrimination. *Turner v. Fouche*, 396 U.S. 346 (1970).

1) Property ownership

The ownership of property cannot be made a condition of holding public office. *Turner v. Fouche, supra* (appointment to local school board).

2) Filing fee

A candidate for elected public office generally may be required to pay a reasonable filing fee, but an exorbitant filing fee, such as one that imposes the entire cost of the election on the candidates, is unconstitutional. Moreover, alternative provisions must be made for a candidate who is unable to pay the fee. *Lubin v. Parish*, 415 U.S. 709 (1974); *Bullock v. Carter*, 405 U.S. 134 (1972).

3) Public support requirements

An independent candidate for elected public office can be required to obtain the signatures of voters on a petition in order to appear on the ballot, but such a requirement cannot deny independent candidates ballot access. *Jenness v. Fortson*, 403 U.S. 431 (1971) (state requirement that an independent candidate obtain five percent of the number of registered voters at the last general election for the office in question upheld). State election laws imposing undue burdens on placing new or small parties on the state ballots must serve a compelling state interest in the regulation of a subject within the state's constitutional power. *Williams v. Rhodes*, 393 U.S. 23 (1968) (state election scheme that effectively prohibited independent candidacies in such a way as to exclude virtually all but the two major parties struck down). Unless the requirement imposes such undue burdens on minority groups, a state can deny a candidate access to the general-election ballot if the candidate failed to receive a sufficient number of votes in the primary election. *Munro v. Socialist Workers Party*, 479 U.S. 189 (1986) (minor party senatorial candidate who failed to receive one percent of the votes cast in primary election not entitled to appear on the general ballot).

4) Write-in candidates

A state may ban all write-in candidates in both primary and general elections, at least when the state provides other reasonable means by which a candidate can get on the ballot. *Burdick v. Takushi, supra.*

5) Candidate for other office

A state may prohibit a state office holder from becoming a candidate for another state office; the office holder must resign his current office in order to run for another office. *Clements v. Fashing*, 457 U.S. 957 (1982).

6) Replacement of elected official

A state may permit a political party to name a replacement for an elected public official from that party who dies or resigns while in office. *Rodriguez v. Popular Democratic Party*, 457 U.S. 1 (1982). The governor must call an election to fill a vacant congressional seat. Article I, Section 2 (House member); Seventeenth Amendment (Senator). (Note: The Seventeenth Amendment permits the state legislature to authorize the governor to appoint a temporary replacement senator.)

3. Privacy

Though it has not found that a generalized right to privacy is contained in the Constitution, the Supreme Court has recognized guaranteed "zones of privacy" under the Constitution. *See Roe v. Wade*, 410 U.S. 113 (1973). Various privacy rights have been deemed fundamental.

a. Marriage

The right to marry is fundamental. *Obergefell v. Hodges*, 576 U.S. 644 (2015) (same-sex couples); *Loving v. Virginia*, 388 U.S. 1 (1967) (interracial couples); *Turner v. Safley*, 482 U. S. 78 (1987) (prisoners); *Zablocki v. Redhail*, 434 U.S. 374 (1978) (fathers delinquent in child-support payments).

b. Contraception

Married persons have the right to use contraceptives, *Griswold v. Connecticut*, 381 U.S. 479 (1965), as do unmarried persons, *Eisenstadt v. Baird*, 405 U.S. 438 (1972). A state may not limit the sale of contraceptives to dispensation only by pharmacists or only to individuals older than age 16. *Carey v. Population Services International*, 431 U.S. 678 (1977).

c. Intimate sexual behavior

There is no legitimate state interest in making it a crime for fully consenting adults to engage in private sexual conduct—including homosexual conduct—that is not commercial in nature. *Lawrence v. Texas*, 539 U.S. 558 (2003).

d. Abortion

The landmark case of *Roe v. Wade*, 410 U.S. 113 (1973), established the principle that a woman has a fundamental right to an abortion. The Court acknowledged that this privacy right must be considered along with the state's compelling interests in protecting both the health of the pregnant woman and the potential life of the fetus. The resulting rule allowed for varying degrees of state restriction based on the trimester of the pregnancy. The decades since *Roe* have resulted in numerous, often conflicting, judicial opinions on the subject. The current standard is the "undue burden" test, the meaning of which depends on whether the fetus is viable (likely to survive outside the womb).

1) Pre-viability

An undue burden exists when the purpose or effect of a state law places **substantial obstacles** in the way of a woman's right to seek an abortion before the fetus attains viability. *Whole Woman's Health* v. *Hellerstedt*, 579

U.S. ___, 136 S. Ct. 2292 (2016); *Planned Parenthood of Southeastern Pennsylvania v. Casey*, 505 U.S. 833 (1992).

The following requirements have been held **not** to impose an undue burden:

i) A requirement that only a licensed physician may perform an abortion;

ii) A requirement that the physician must provide the woman with truthful information about the nature of the abortion procedure, the associated health risks, and the probable gestational age of the fetus;

iii) A requirement that a woman must wait 24 hours after giving informed consent before the abortion is performed;

iv) A requirement that a minor obtain her parents' consent, or if consent is not required, provide the parents with notice of the abortion. However, this consent requirement has been found to be an undue burden unless, at least for mature minors, the consent requirement can be judicially bypassed. *Planned Parenthood Association of Kansas City Missouri Inc. v. Ashcroft*, 462 U.S. 476 (1983).

v) A ban on a particular uncommon abortion technique, *Gonzales v. Carhart*, 550 U.S. 124 (2007). The Court found that the State may use its regulatory power to bar certain procedures and substitute others if it has a rational basis to act and it does not impose an undue burden.

An undue burden has been found when a state requires a woman to notify her husband before having an abortion, even when the requirement provides exceptions to the rule. *Planned Parenthood v. Casey*, 505 U.S. 833, 887 (1992) (spousal notification imposed an undue burden, even when the requirement could be bypassed with the woman's signed statement certifying that a statutory exception applied).

2) Post-viability

Once the fetus reaches viability, the state may regulate, and even prohibit, abortion, as long as there is an exception to preserve the health or life of the mother. In other words, at the point of viability, the state's interest in protecting fetal life may supersede a woman's right to choose; because the state's interest in protecting fetal life cannot supersede its interest in protecting a woman's health, however, there must be an exception for the woman's health.

3) Government funding

There is no constitutional right to have the government provide indigent women with funding for an abortion or for medical care related to an abortion, even if the government does provide indigent funding for medical care at childbirth. *Maher v. Roe*, 432 U.S. 464 (1977). Furthermore, a state may prohibit all use of public facilities and public employees in performing abortions. *Webster v. Reproductive Health Services*, 492 U.S. 490 (1989).

e. Parental rights

The fundamental parental right to make decisions regarding the care, custody, and control of one's children includes the right to privately educate one's child outside the public school system subject to reasonable educational standards imposed by the state, *Pierce v. Society of Sisters*, 268 U.S. 510 (1925), *Wisconsin v. Yoder*, 406 U.S. 205 (1972), and to limit visitation of grandparents, *Troxel v. Granville*, 530 U.S. 57 (2000).

f. Family relations

Related persons, including extended family members, have a fundamental right to live together in a single household. *Moore v. City of East Cleveland*, 431 U.S. 494 (1977).

g. Obscene material

There is a fundamental right to possess obscene material in the privacy of one's home, *Stanley v. Georgia*, 394 U.S. 557 (1969), with the exception of child pornography, *Osborne v. Ohio*, 495 U.S. 103 (1990). The state, however, may severely restrict the sale, purchase, receipt, transport, and distribution of obscene material. *Paris Adult Theater v. Slaton*, 413 U.S. 49 (1973).

h. Right to refuse medical treatment

It is an established liberty interest that a person may not be forced to undergo unwanted medical procedures, including lifesaving measures, but the Court has not ruled on whether this right is "fundamental." *Cruzan v. Missouri Department of Health*, 497 U.S. 261 (1990).

There is no fundamental right to commit suicide; therefore, the state may ban the assistance of suicide. *Washington v. Glucksberg*, 521 U.S. 702 (1997). The Court distinguished this decision from *Cruzan* by stating that forced medication is a battery, and there is a long tradition of protecting the decision to refuse unwanted medical treatment.

i. Right to avoid disclosure of personal medical information

Numerous courts include personal medical information within a "zone of privacy." *See, e.g., Doe v. Attorney General of the United States*, 941 F.2d 780 (9th Cir. 1991), *United States v. Westinghouse Electric Corp.*, 638 F.2d 570 (3rd Cir. 1980). Though the right to protect personal, confidential information is not absolute, courts weigh it against competing interests, employing a balancing test that generally includes consideration of the government's need for access to the information and the adequacy of safeguards, as well as the type and substance of the requested records and the potential for harm in non-consensual disclosure. *See C.N. v. Ridgewood Board of Education*, 430 F.3d 159, 178 (3rd Cir.2005).

4. The Second Amendment

The Second Amendment guarantees **an individual's right to possess a firearm** unconnected with service in a militia and to use that firearm for traditionally lawful purposes, such as self-defense within the home. *District of Columbia v. Heller*, 554 U.S. 570 (2008) (ban on handgun possession in the home violates Second Amendment). As mentioned previously, the Second Amendment is applicable to the states through the Fourteenth Amendment. *McDonald v. Chicago*, 561 U.S. 3025 (2010).

Like most rights, the Second Amendment right to bear arms is not unlimited. Examples of lawful regulations include imposing conditions and qualifications on the commercial sale of arms, as well as prohibitions on (i) concealed weapons, (ii) possession of firearms by felons and the mentally ill, and (iii) carrying guns in schools, government buildings, and other sensitive places. *District of Columbia v. Heller, supra.*

XIII. EQUAL PROTECTION

A. GENERAL CONSIDERATIONS

1. Constitutional Basis

a. State action

The Equal Protection Clause of the Fourteenth Amendment provides that "no state shall ... deny to any person within its jurisdiction the equal protection of the laws." This clause applies only to states and localities.

b. Federal action

Although there is no federal equal protection clause, the Supreme Court has held that the Fifth Amendment Due Process Clause includes the rights guaranteed by the Equal Protection Clause, thereby making discrimination by the federal government subject to review under the same standards as discrimination by the states. *Bolling v. Sharpe*, 347 U.S. 497 (1954).

2. Standards of Review

When reviewing government action under equal-protection theories, the Court applies one of three levels of review, depending on the classification of persons or the type of right concerned.

a. Strict scrutiny

1) Test

The law must be the **least restrictive** means to achieve a **compelling** governmental interest.

2) Burden of proof

The burden is on the government to prove that the law is necessary. Because the strict scrutiny test is a very difficult one to pass, the government rarely meets its burden, and most laws subjected to this standard of review are struck down.

3) Applicability

The strict scrutiny test is applied if a **fundamental right** or a **suspect classification** is involved. The suspect classifications are race, ethnicity, national origin, and, if the classification is by state law, alienage. (*See* § XIII.B., *infra,* for a complete discussion of suspect classifications.)

b. Intermediate scrutiny

1) Test

To be constitutional, the law must be **substantially related** to an **important** governmental interest.

2) Burden of proof

Although the Court has not clearly stated the rule, the burden appears generally to be on the government to prove that the law in question passes intermediate scrutiny. As with strict scrutiny (and unlike rational basis review), the government must defend the interest(s) it stated when the law was enacted, not just some conceivable legitimate interest.

3) Applicability

Intermediate scrutiny is used when a classification is based on **gender** or status as a **nonmarital child** (legitimacy). Note that in gender cases there must be an "exceedingly persuasive justification" for the classification, which may bring the standard in such cases closer to strict scrutiny. *See United States v. Virginia*, 518 U.S. 515 (1996).

c. Rational basis

1) Test

A law passes the rational basis standard of review if it is **rationally related** to a **legitimate** governmental interest. This is a test of minimal scrutiny. It is not required that there is actually a link between the means selected and a legitimate objective. However, the legislature must *reasonably believe* there is a link.

2) Burden of proof

Laws are presumed valid under this standard, so the burden is on the challenger to overcome this presumption by establishing that the law is **arbitrary or irrational.**

3) Applicability

The rational basis standard is used in all cases in which one of the higher standards (intermediate or strict scrutiny) does not apply. Thus, rational basis review applies to laws drawing distinctions based on age, wealth, weight, or most other classifications, as well as to any distinctions drawn for business or economic reasons.

The Court generally gives extreme deference to the legislature's right to define its objectives. In order to determine the legislature's purpose, the Court will look at the statute and the preamble. If the legislative purpose is not clear from the statute, the Court may consider any conceivable purpose that may have motivated the legislature. *U.S. Railroad Retirement Bd. v. Fritz*, 449 U.S. 166 (1980).

> Some classifications, although nominally subject to rational basis review, in practice receive heightened scrutiny. *See e.g., Romer v. Evans*, 517 U.S. 620 (1996) (sexual orientation); *Cleburne v. Cleburne Living Center, Inc.*, 473 U.S. 432 (1985) (developmental disability). When the government has acted out of animus toward or fear of a particular group, that action—even if not involving a suspect or a quasi-suspect classification—will be searchingly reviewed and may be struck down even under a rational basis test. *See e.g., United States v. Windsor*, 570 U.S. 744 (2013) (Defense of Marriage Act and same-sex marriage).

3. Proving Discrimination

To trigger strict or intermediate scrutiny, there must be **discriminatory intent** on the part of the government. The fact that legislation has a disparate effect on people of different races, genders, etc., without intent, is insufficient. Discriminatory intent can be shown facially, as applied, or when there is a discriminatory motive.

a. Facial discrimination

A law that, by its very language, creates distinctions between classes of persons is discriminatory on its face.

> **Example:** An ordinance states that only males will be considered for a city's training academy for firefighters.

b. Discriminatory application

A law that appears neutral on its face may be applied in a discriminatory fashion. If the challenger can prove that a discriminatory purpose was used when applying the law, then the law will be invalidated.

> **Example:** A city's ordinance concerning the police academy says nothing about gender, but in practice only men are considered for admission.

c. Discriminatory motive

A law that is neutral on its face and in its application may still result in a disparate impact. By itself, however, a disparate impact is not sufficient to trigger strict or intermediate scrutiny; proof of discriminatory motive or intent is required to show a violation of the Equal Protection Clause. *Arlington Heights v. Metropolitan Hous. Dev. Corp.*, 429 U.S. 252 (1977).

> **Example:** A city's paramedic training school is theoretically open to both men and women, but the entrance test includes a height requirement that disproportionately excludes women for the purpose of discriminating against women.

B. SUSPECT CLASSIFICATIONS

Laws that categorize based on race, ethnicity, national origin, or (in some cases) alienage are considered suspect and therefore require closer judicial examination. Such laws are subject to strict scrutiny and are invalid unless they are **necessary** to achieve a **compelling** governmental interest.

1. Race, Ethnicity, and National Origin

Laws or regulations that intentionally disadvantage on the basis of race, ethnicity, or national origin have almost always been struck down for failing to advance a compelling state interest. One exception was *Korematsu v. United States*, 323 U.S. 214 (1944), in which the internment of Japanese-Americans during World War II was upheld in the name of national security.

a. School integration

Because discrimination must be intentional in order to violate the Constitution, only intentional (de jure) segregation in schools violates the Equal Protection Clause. *Keyes v. Sch. Dist. No. 1*, 413 U.S. 189 (1973). Moreover, a court cannot impose a remedy that involves multiple school districts unless there is evidence of intentional segregation in each district. *Milliken v. Bradley*, 418 U.S. 717 (1974); *Missouri v. Jenkins*, 515 U.S. 70 (1995) (state not compelled to create magnet schools in order to attract students from outside the district).

If a school board does not take steps to eliminate intentional racial segregation of schools, a court can order the district to implement measures, such as busing, to remedy the discrimination. Court-ordered busing is temporary, however, and must be terminated once the "vestiges of past discrimination" have been eliminated. *Bd. of Educ. v. Dowell*, 498 U.S. 237 (1991).

b. Affirmative action

Programs that favor racial or ethnic minorities are also subject to strict scrutiny. *Adarand Constructors, Inc. v. Pena*, 515 U.S. 200 (1995) (overruling application of the intermediate standard to federal discrimination).

1) Past discrimination by government

For a governmental affirmative action program based on race to survive, the relevant governmental entity must show more than a history of societal discrimination. The government—whether federal, state, or local—must itself be guilty of specific past discrimination against the group it is seeking to favor, and the remedy must be narrowly tailored to end that discrimination and eliminate its effects. In other words, the elimination of past discrimination in a particular governmental institution is a compelling state interest; attempting to remedy general societal injustice through affirmative action is not.

2) Diversity in public universities and colleges

Race may be used as a "plus factor" (i.e., one of a range of factors to consider) in determining whether a student should be admitted to a public college or university, as there is a compelling interest in obtaining the educational benefits of a diverse student body. The use of racial quotas or of race as a determinative criterion, however, violates equal protection and is unconstitutional. *Grutter v. Bollinger*, 539 U.S. 306 (2003); *Gratz v. Bollinger*, 539 U.S. 244 (2003); *Regents of University of California v. Bakke*, 438 U.S. 265 (1978). Race may not be considered unless the admissions process used to achieve a diverse student body can withstand strict scrutiny. Strict scrutiny here requires the university to clearly demonstrate that its purpose or interest is both constitutionally permissible and substantial, and that its use of the classification is **necessary** to the accomplishment of its purpose. *Fisher v. Univ. of Texas*, 570 U.S. 297 (2013). Further, a university must regularly evaluate available data and "tailor its approach in light of changing circumstances, ensuring that race plays no greater role than is necessary to meet its compelling interest." *Fisher v. Univ. of Texas*, 579 U.S. ___, 136 S. Ct. 2198 (2016).

State laws that commit policy determinations regarding racial preferences to the voters (e.g., ballot issues) do not violate equal protection. Courts may not disempower the voters from choosing whether race-based preferences should be adopted, continued, or ended. The privilege to enact laws is a basic exercise of voters' democratic power. The constitutional validity of the choices made is a separate question. *Schuette v. Coalition to Defend Affirmative Action*, 572 U.S. 291 (2014) (upholding amendment to Michigan's constitution prohibiting state universities from considering race as part of the admission process).

3) Diversity in public elementary and high schools

A school district may not assign students to schools on the basis of race unless it is necessary to accomplish a compelling interest—e.g., remedy past discrimination. However, a district may use facially race-neutral criteria that may have the same effect, such as strategic site selection for new schools or the redrawing of attendance zones. *Parents Involved in Community Schools v. Seattle School Dist. No. 1*, 551 U.S. 701 (2007).

The Equal Protection Clause applies only to governmental action, so private persons generally are not restricted by it (*see* X. State Action, *supra*).

c. Racial gerrymandering

Race may not be the predominant factor in determining the boundary lines of legislative districts (*see* § XIII.E.2.a., Racial discrimination, *infra*).

2. Alienage

Classifications based on status as a lawful resident of the United States (as opposed to a citizen) are subject to a variety of different standards, depending on the level of government and the nature of the classification.

a. Federal classification

Because Congress has plenary power over aliens under Article I, a federal alienage classification is likely valid unless it is **arbitrary** and **unreasonable.**

> **Example:** Medicare regulations may require a five-year residency period for eligibility despite thereby excluding many lawful resident aliens. *Matthews v. Diaz*, 426 U.S. 67 (1976).

b. State classifications

1) Generally struck down

The Court will generally apply the strict scrutiny test and strike down state laws that discriminate against aliens, such as laws prohibiting aliens from owning land, obtaining commercial fishing licenses, or being eligible for welfare benefits or civil service jobs.

2) Exception—participation in government functions

A growing exception exists, however, for state laws that restrict or prohibit an alien's **participation in government functions.** Such laws need only have a **rational relationship** to a legitimate state interest. Laws prohibiting aliens from voting, serving on a jury, or being hired as police officers, probation officers, or public-school teachers have been upheld as preventing aliens from having a direct effect on the functioning of the government.

> **EXAM NOTE:** When determining whether a position or license from which aliens are excluded falls under the government function or political function exception, consider whether the position or license would allow the alien to "participate directly in the formulation, execution, or review of broad public policy" or would allow the alien to exercise "broad discretion."

c. Undocumented aliens

Undocumented aliens are not a suspect class, but the states may not deny primary or secondary public education benefits to undocumented aliens. *Plyler v. Doe*, 457 U.S. 202 (1982).

C. QUASI-SUSPECT CLASSIFICATIONS

1. Gender

Discrimination based on gender is "quasi-suspect" and subject to **intermediate scrutiny,** which is less stringent than strict scrutiny but tougher than the rational basis test. Just as with suspect classifications and fundamental rights, there must be **discriminatory intent** by the government to trigger intermediate scrutiny; disparate impact is not enough. Under intermediate scrutiny, the burden is on the state to show that a statute or regulation that treats the sexes differently is **substantially related** to an **important** governmental interest. This test applies whether the classification is invidious or benign, and it is now applied rather stringently, requiring the government to show that an "exceedingly persuasive justification" exists for the distinction, and that separate facilities (such as separate sports team facilities as state universities) are "substantially equivalent." *United States v. Virginia*, 518 U.S. 515 (1996).

a. **Discrimination against women**

Intentional discrimination through gender classification will generally be struck down under the intermediate scrutiny standard. For example, a state law giving preference to men over women to be administrators of decedents' estates was invalid. *Reed v. Reed*, 404 U.S. 71 (1971) (ease in determining who should serve as administrator is not an important interest). *See also United States v. Virginia*, 518 U.S. 515 (1996) (Virginia Military Institute could not exclude women from admission to public college based on overbroad generalizations about the physical capabilities and preferred educational methods of males and females).

b. **Discrimination against men**

Intentional discrimination against males is generally struck down for violating equal protection. However, there have been some instances of discrimination against men being upheld because of the important governmental interest:

i) Draft registration of males, but not females, *Rostker v. Goldberg*, 453 U.S. 57 (1981) (interest of preparing combat troops); and

ii) A statutory rape law that held only men criminally liable for such conduct, *Michael M. v. Sonoma County Superior Court*, 450 U.S. 464 (1981) (interest in preventing teenage pregnancy).

c. **Affirmative action (benign discrimination)**

The Court has upheld affirmative action regulations granting beneficial treatment to women over men (such as tax exemptions, increased social security benefits, and increased protection from mandatory armed forces discharge) because providing a remedy for past gender-based discrimination is an important governmental interest. *See Califano v. Webster*, 430 U.S. 313 (1977); *Schlesinger v. Ballard*, 419 U.S. 498 (1975).

2. **Legitimacy**

Classifications on the basis of status as a nonmarital child (i.e., those that distinguish between "legitimate" and "illegitimate" children) are subject to **intermediate scrutiny**—they must be **substantially related** to an **important** governmental interest. The Court will closely examine the purpose behind the distinction, and it will not uphold legislation designed to punish the offspring of a nonmarital relationship. To that end, states may not prohibit children of unmarried parents from receiving welfare benefits, *New Jersey Welfare Rights Org. v. Cahill*, 411 U.S. 619 (1973), workers' compensation benefits upon the death of a parent, *Weber v. Aetna Cas. and Sur. Co.*, 406 U.S. 164 (1972), or an inheritance from an intestate father, *Trimble v. Gordon*, 430 U.S. 762 (1977). In addition, a state cannot require a paternity action brought on behalf of an illegitimate child to be commenced within a limited time after birth in order to secure child support, while not imposing a similar time limit on a legitimate child seeking child support from a parent. *Clark v. Jeter*, 486 U.S. 456 (1988).

D. NONSUSPECT CLASSIFICATIONS

1. Age

Age discrimination in violation of the Age Discrimination in Employment Act of 1967 does not provoke heightened scrutiny; laws and other governmental actions classifying on the basis of age are reviewed under the **rational basis** standard. *See, e.g., Massachusetts Bd. of Ret. v. Murgia*, 427 U.S. 307 (1976) (police officers may be forced to retire at age 50, even if they are as physically fit as younger officers).

2. Poverty

Most statutes and regulations that classify on the basis of wealth (i.e., discriminate against the poor) are subject only to **rational basis** scrutiny and will be upheld. There is an exception for cases in which governmental action prohibits the poor from exercising a fundamental right because of a government-imposed fee; strict scrutiny will usually apply in those situations. For example, the availability of appeal in a criminal case cannot hinge on ability to pay for a trial transcript. *Griffin v. Illinois*, 351 U.S. 12 (1956). Also, poll taxes are unconstitutional because wealth is unrelated to a citizen's ability to vote intelligently. *Harper v. Virginia Bd. of Elections*, 383 U.S. 663 (1966).

3. Sexual Orientation

There is currently a division among the federal courts as to the standard of scrutiny that is applicable to discrimination on the basis of sexual orientation. The Supreme Court has struck down bans on same-sex marriage as violations of a fundamental right on both Due Process and Equal Protection grounds, and has ruled that the Civil Rights Act of 1964 protects employees against discrimination because of their sexual orientation or gender identity, *Bostock v. Dayton County*, 590 U.S. ___, 140 S. Ct. 1731 (2020), but it has not resolved the issue of whether discrimination based on sexual orientation is subject to heightened scrutiny. The government, however, cannot impose a burden upon or deny a benefit to a group of persons solely based on animosity toward the class that it affects. *Romer v. Evans*, 517 U.S. 620 (1996). Among the rights, benefits, and responsibilities of marriage to which same-sex partners must have access are birth and death certificates, which give married partners a form of legal recognition that is not available to unmarried partners. *Pavan v. Smith*, 582 U.S. ___, 137 S. Ct. 2075 (2017), citing *Obergefell v. Hodges*, 576 U.S. 644 (2016).

E. FUNDAMENTAL RIGHTS UNIQUE TO EQUAL PROTECTION

The fundamental rights guaranteed by substantive due process are often protected by equal protection principles as well. Thus, impingement of the right to vote, to travel, or to marry may trigger an inquiry under either the Due Process Clause or the Equal Protection Clause. However, certain rights and principles are particular to equal protection.

> **EXAM NOTE:** The right to *travel* and the right to *vote* are the most frequently tested fundamental rights in the area of **equal protection.** (Often, both the Due Process Clause and the Equal Protection Clause will apply. Equal protection predominates if the question emphasizes denial of a right to a particular group, and it does not apply if the denial of the right is universal.)

1. One Person, One Vote

The principle of "one person, one vote" holds that one person's vote must be essentially equal to any other person's vote. To that end, when the government establishes voting districts for the election of representatives, the number of persons in each district must be approximately equal. *Reynolds v. Sims*, 377 U.S. 533 (1964). Voter approval of a redistricting plan will not justify a violation of the "one person, one vote" rule. *Lucas v. Colorado General Assembly*, 377 U.S. 713 (1964).

a. Congressional districts

When states establish districts for congressional elections, they must achieve nearly precise mathematical equality between the districts. This restriction is imposed on the states by Article I, Section 2, which requires members of the House to be chosen by "the People of the several States." An unexplained deviation of less than one percent may invalidate the statewide congressional district plan. Variations may be justified by the state on the basis of consistently applied, legitimate state objectives, such as respecting municipal political subdivision boundaries, creating geographic compact districts, and avoiding contests between incumbent representatives. In addition, variations based on anticipated population shifts may be acceptable when such shifts can be predicted with a high degree of accuracy, and population trends are thoroughly documented. *Kirkpatrick v. Preisler*, 394 U.S. 526 (1969) (variation in population of slightly less than six percent violated the "one person, one vote" rule); *Karcher v. Daggett*, 462 U.S. 725 (1983) (variation of slightly less than 0.7 percent violated the "one person, one vote" rule).

1) Congressional apportionment of House members

Congress, in apportioning members of the House among the states pursuant to Article I, Section 2, is not held to the "mathematical equality" standard. The method adopted by Congress is entitled to judicial deference and is assumed to be in good faith. *Dept. of Commerce v. Montana*, 503 U.S. 442 (1992) (Montana's loss of a congressional seat upheld, even though retention of the seat would have placed Montana closer to the ideal population size for a congressional district).

b. State and local districts

The size of electoral districts may vary much more in the case of state and local elections, as long as the variance is not unjustifiably large. A variation of less than 10% is rebuttably presumed to be a minor deviation that does not constitute a prima facie case for discrimination. *Cox v. Larios*, 300 F. Supp. 2d 1320 (N.D. Ga.), *aff'd*, 542 U.S. 947 (2004); *Brown v. Thompson*, 462 U.S. 835 (1983). When the maximum variation is 10% or greater, the state must show that the deviation from equality between the districts is reasonable and designed to promote a legitimate state interest. *Mahan v. Howell*, 410 U.S. 315 (1973) (maximum difference of 16% in size of population between state legislative districts permitted when the state respected the boundaries of political subdivisions).

1) Bodies performing governmental functions

The "one person, one vote" rule applies to local elections of entities that perform governmental functions, even when the functions are specialized rather than general in nature. *Hadley v. Junior College Dist.*, 397 U.S. 50 (1970) (election of trustees to junior college district).

2) Relevant population

In addition to requiring relative equality with respect to the weight of a person's vote, the Equal Protection Clause generally requires the application of strict scrutiny to a restriction of voting to a particular class of persons, which generally results in the invalidation of the restriction. *Kramer v. Union Free School District No. 15*, 395 U.S. 621 (1969) (state law that restricted voting in school board election to property owners and parents with school-aged children struck down). The restriction of voting to a class of persons (e.g., landowners) and the allocation of voting weight on a basis other than personhood (e.g., the amount of land owned) has been upheld only with regard to water-district elections. *Ball v. James*, 451 U.S. 355 (1981); *See Hadley v. Junior College Dist., supra* (determination of districts for junior college trustees based on school age population violated "one person, one vote" rule). (Note: A restriction on the right to participate in the political process of a governmental unit to those who reside within its borders is typically upheld as justified on a rational basis; nonresidents generally may be prohibited from voting. *Holt Civic Club v. City of Tuscaloosa*, 439 U.S. 60 (1978).)

A state may draw its legislative districts on the basis of total population rather than eligible or registered voters. *Evenwel v. Abbott*, 578 U.S. 937 (2016).

c. At-large elections

While an election in which members of a governmental unit (e.g., county council members) are elected by all voters within that unit (i.e., an at-large election) does not violate the one-person, one-vote rule, it may conflict with another constitutional provision, such as the Equal Protection Clause. *Rogers v. Lodge*, 458 U.S. 613 (1982) (use of countywide system to elect county board unconstitutionally diluted the voting power of African-American citizens).

Note: Federal law bans at-large elections for congressional representatives in states that have more than one House member (i.e., the single-member district rule). 2 U.S.C.S. § 2c.

2. Gerrymandering

a. Racial discrimination

1) Vote dilution

When a state draws election districts for the purpose of scattering a racial or ethnic minority among several districts in order to prevent the minority from exercising its voting strength, the state's action is a violation of the Equal Protection Clause. *Gomillion v. Lightfoot*, 364 U.S. 339 (1960) (redrawing city boundaries to exclude African-American voters unconstitutional); *Rogers v. Lodge, supra*.

2) Majority-minority districts

Under the Equal Protection Clause, election districts for public office may not be drawn using race as the predominant factor in determining the boundary lines, unless the district plan can survive strict scrutiny. This restriction applies even when the district is drawn to favor historically disenfranchised groups. The state can use traditional factors—such as compactness, contiguity, or honoring political subdivisions—as the bases for the district, and it may only consider race if it does not predominate over other considerations. *Miller v. Johnson*, 515 U.S. 900 (1995). To be narrowly tailored within the strict scrutiny standard, the legislature must have a "strong basis in evidence" in support of the race-based choice that it has made. Note that the legislature need not show that its action was **actually necessary** to avoid a statutory violation, only that the legislature had **good reasons to believe** its use of race was needed. *Bethune-Hill v. Virginia State Bd. Of Elections*, 580 U.S. ___, 137 S. Ct. 788 (2017), *Alabama Legislative Black Caucus, et al. v. Alabama et al.*, 575 U.S. 254 (2015).

A district's bizarre shape can be used as evidence that race was a predominating factor, but such a shape is not necessary for a finding of racial gerrymandering. *Shaw v. Reno*, 509 U.S. 630 (1993).

a) Voting Rights Act

The Voting Rights Act (42 U.S.C. § 1973 et seq.) requires racial gerrymandering to ensure minority success in elections by creating majority-minority districts (i.e., affirmative gerrymandering). Until recently, the Act required federal pre-clearance for changes in voting rules, including redistricting, for specific southern states and a few other local governmental units. However, the formula used as a basis for subjecting jurisdictions to preclearance has been declared unconstitutional because it no longer reflects current conditions; therefore, it can no longer be used. *Shelby County v. Holder*, 570 U.S. 529 (2013). Receiving federal pre-clearance for a redistricting plan does not ensure that plan will avoid conflicting with the Equal Protection Clause. *Miller v. Johnson*, 515 U.S. 900 (1995).

The Voting Rights Act does not require a jurisdiction to maintain a particular numerical minority percentage. Instead, it requires the jurisdiction to maintain a minority's ability to elect a preferred candidate of choice. *Alabama Legislative Black Caucus, et al. v. Alabama et al.*, 575 U.S. 254 (2015).

b. Political discrimination

Partisan political gerrymandering may violate the Equal Protection Clause if the challenger can show "both intentional discrimination against an identifiable political group and an actual discriminatory effect on that group." *Davis v. Bandemer*, 478 U.S. 109, 127 (1986). However, partisan gerrymandering claims are not judiciable because they present political questions beyond the reach of the federal courts. *Rucho v. Common Cause*, 588 U.S. ___, 139 S. Ct. 2484 (2019) (lack of comprehensive and neutral principles for drawing electoral boundaries as well as the absence of rules to confine judicial intervention prevents the Court from adjudicating political gerrymandering claims).

XIV. PRIVILEGES AND IMMUNITIES CLAUSES

A. ARTICLE IV

Article IV, Section 2, known as the Comity Clause, provides that "the citizens of each state shall be entitled to all privileges and immunities of citizens in the several states."

1. Prohibits State Discrimination Against Nonresidents

The Comity Clause, in essence, prohibits one state from discriminating against the citizens of another state. In this context, the term "citizen" does not include corporations or aliens.

2. Rights Protected

Nonresident citizens are protected against discrimination with respect to fundamental rights or essential activities. Examples include the pursuit of employment, transfer of property, and access to state courts.

> **Example:** Discrimination against out-of-state residents in setting the fee for a **commercial** activity, such as a commercial shrimping license, violates the Privileges and Immunities Clause of Article IV, but similar discrimination for a **recreational** activity, such as a recreational hunting license, does not, if there is a rational basis for the fee differential. *Compare Toomer v. Witsell*, 334 U.S. 385 (1948) (fee for out-of-state commercial shrimper that was 100 times greater than the fee for an in-state shrimper unconstitutional), *with Baldwin v. Fish & Game Comm'n*, 436 U.S. 371 (1978) (fee for out-of-state resident to hunt elk that was 25 times greater than the fee for an in-state hunter constitutional).

> Note that discrimination against an out-of-state resident with regard to access to a state's natural resources may violate the Dormant Commerce Clause. *New England Power Co. v. New Hampshire*, 455 U.S. 331 (1982) (prohibition on sale of hydroelectric power outside the state unconstitutional).

3. Exception—Substantial Justification

Discrimination against out-of-state citizens may be valid if the state can show a substantial reason for the difference in treatment. A substantial reason exists if:

i) The nonresidents either cause or are a part of the problem that the state is attempting to solve; and

ii) There are no less-restrictive means to solve the problem.

> **Example:** Discrimination against nonresidents with respect to the use of scarce water resources was upheld when the purpose was to preserve natural state-owned resources. *Sporhase v. Nebraska*, 458 U.S. 941 (1982).

> **EXAM NOTE:** Although the Privileges and Immunities Clause of Article IV and the Commerce Clause are not coextensive, they tend to mutually support each other; thus, consider both when analyzing an exam question.

B. FOURTEENTH AMENDMENT—NATIONAL CITIZENSHIP

The Fourteenth Amendment provides that "[n]o state shall make or enforce any law which shall abridge the privileges or immunities of citizens of the United States." This clause protects citizens (not corporations or aliens) from infringement by the states upon the privileges or immunities of **national** citizenship.

The privileges or immunities of national citizenship include the right to travel interstate, to petition Congress for redress of grievances, to vote for national offices, to enter public lands, to be protected while in the custody of U.S. marshals, and to peaceably assemble. *Twining v. New Jersey*, 211 U.S. 78 (1908). The guarantees of the Bill of Rights, however, are not privileges or immunities of national citizenship within the context of the Fourteenth Amendment. *Slaughterhouse Cases*, 83 U.S. 36 (1873). Therefore, those rights are protected from state action only by the Due Process Clause and the Equal Protection Clause.

This provision is seldom successfully invoked; under the limiting interpretation of the *Slaughterhouse Cases,* the rights that the clause provides are redundant to rights provided elsewhere in the Constitution. Although the Supreme Court has since relied on the clause to underscore the right to move freely among states, *Saenz v. Roe*, 526 U.S. 489 (1999) (invalidating a duration requirement for welfare benefits), there has been no subsequent expansion of use; the Fourteenth Amendment's Privileges or Immunities Clause applies, in practice, only to the right to travel.

XV. TAKINGS CLAUSE

The power of the government to take private property for public purposes is known as **"eminent domain."** The Takings Clause of the Fifth Amendment acts as a check on this power; it provides that private property may not "be taken for public use, without just compensation." The Fourteenth Amendment Due Process Clause makes the Takings Clause applicable to the states.

A. PROPERTY INTEREST

For a person to challenge a governmental action as an unconstitutional taking, the person must have a property interest. When a person does not have an interest in the property that the government takes, the Takings Clause does not apply.

> **Example:** An organization of homeowners challenged a beach restoration project undertaken by a state agency and local governments. The homeowners objected to the creation of land beyond the mean high water line, which represented the boundary of the homeowners' property, because this infringed upon their right as owners of property along a shore to receive accretions and because they lost the right to control public access to the shoreline. However, because, under state law, the newly created land belonged to the state, and the homeowners did not enjoy property rights with respect to this land, there was no taking of their property rights. *Stop the Beach Renourishment, Inc. v. Fla. Dep't of Envtl. Prot.*, 560 U.S. 702 (2010). (Note: A plurality of the Supreme Court justices also found that the Takings Clause applies to a judicial taking.)

1. Types of Property

Property that may be subject to the protection of the Takings Clause includes not only land and other real property, but also tangible personal property as well as intangible property, such as contract and patent rights and trade secrets. *Ruckelshaus v. Monsanto Co.*, 467 U.S. 986 (1984); *Lynch v. United States*, 292 U.S. 571 (1934); *James v. Campbell*, 104 U.S. 356 (1882).

2. Types of Interests

In addition to the transfer of a fee simple interest in property, a taking may involve an easement, leasehold interest, or a lien. *Nollan v. California Coastal Commission*, 483 U.S. 825 (1987); *Armstrong v. United States*, 364 U.S. 40 (1960); *United States v. General Motors*, 323 U.S. 373 (1945). A taking may involve the rights of a property owner, such as the right to control access to the property. *Kaiser Aetna v. United States*, 444 U.S. 164 (1980) (federal government's imposition of public-access servitude on a waterway created on private property constituted a taking).

B. TYPES OF TAKING

1. Seizure of Property

The classic application of the Takings Clause is the seizure of private property for governmental use, such as acquiring privately held land in order to construct a courthouse or other government building. In such a case, the property owner's primary challenge to the seizure is whether he has received just compensation (*see* § XV.C., Just Compensation, *infra*).

a. Public-use challenge

A government may seize private property not only for its own direct use but also to transfer the property to another private party. Although such a seizure is subject to challenge as not being made for a public use, the taking need merely be **"rationally related** to a **conceivable public purpose."** *Hawaii Hous. Auth. v. Midkiff*, 467 U.S. 229 (1984). This is a highly deferential standard, and the burden is on the person challenging the taking to prove a lack of legitimate interest or rational basis. In addition to traditional health, safety, and welfare justifications, economic redevelopment goals constitute a sufficient public purpose to justify the seizure. *Kelo v. City of New London*, 545 U.S. 469 (2005). Moreover, a government-mandated transfer of property from one private party directly to another (e.g., from lessor to lessee) may nevertheless be for a public use. *Hawaii Housing Authority v. Midkiff*, 467 U.S. 229 (1984).

2. Damage to or Destruction of Property

A destruction of property or property rights by the federal, state, or local government can also result in a taking. The destruction need not directly benefit the government. The Takings Clause is not limited to possessory interests in property; instead, it can extend to takings of non-possessory property rights, such as easements or liens. *Armstrong v. United States*, 364 U.S. 40 (1960).

Example: A federal statute that prevented the transfer by devise or descent of fractional shares of an interest in tribal land upon the death of the owner and instead provided for such interest to escheat to the tribe constituted an unconstitutional taking when there was no provision for compensation of the owner. *Hodel v. Irving*, 481 U.S. 704 (1987).

Similarly, physical damage to property or interference with a property owner's rights by governmental action can result in a taking.

Example: County ownership of an airport that resulted in an invasion of the airspace of nearby property owners by planes taking off and landing at the airport constituted a taking. *Griggs v. Allegheny County*, 369 U.S. 84 (1962).

Note: A statute that requires an owner of property rights to take action in order to preserve an unused right does not result in a taking if the owner fails to take such action. *Texaco, Inc. v. Short*, 454 U.S. 516 (1982).

a. Exception—public peril

The governmental destruction of private property in response to a public peril does not trigger the right to compensation.

Example: The owners of infected cedar trees located near apple orchards were not entitled to compensation when the cedar trees were destroyed pursuant to a state statute in order to prevent the spread of the infection to the orchards. *Miller v. Schoene*, 276 U.S. 272 (1928).

3. Re-characterization of Property

The Takings Clause prevents a government from re-characterizing private property as public property.

Example: Interest on the purchase price of an insolvent corporation placed by the buyer in an account with the court as part of an interpleader action involving the corporation's creditors was private property. A state court's interpretation of a statutory provision that the interest was public money constituted a taking. *Webb's Fabulous Pharmacies, Inc. v. Beckwith*, 449 U.S. 155 (1980).

4. Regulatory Taking

Generally, a governmental regulation that adversely affects a person's property interest is not a taking, but it is possible for a regulation to rise to the level of a taking.

In determining whether a regulation creates a taking, the following factors are considered:

i) The economic impact of the regulation on the property owner;

ii) The extent to which the regulation interferes with the owner's reasonable, investment-backed expectations regarding use of the property; and

iii) The character of the regulation, including the degree to which it will benefit society, how the regulation distributes the burdens and benefits among property owners, and whether the regulation violates any of the owner's essential attributes of property ownership, such as the right to exclude others from the property.

Penn Central Transportation Co. v. City of New York, 438 U.S. 104 (1978).

a. Public-use challenge

In the context of a regulation, a state or local government can act under its police power for the purposes of health, safety, and welfare. In addition, a public purpose can encompass aesthetic and environmental concerns. Moreover, it is generally inappropriate for a court to examine whether a regulation substantially advances a legitimate governmental interest. (Note, however, that an arbitrary or irrational regulation may constitute a due-process violation.) *Lingle v. Chevron U.S.A. Inc.*, 544 U.S. 528 (2005).

b. Per se takings

In two instances, a regulation clearly results in a taking.

1) Physical occupation

A taking has occurred when the governmental regulation results in a **permanent physical occupation** of the property by the government or a third party, regardless of the public interest that it may serve. *Loretto v. Teleprompter Manhattan CATV Corp.*, 458 U.S. 419 (1982).

> **Example:** A law requiring a landlord to permit a cable company to install equipment on the landlord's property that would remain indefinitely constituted a taking, even though the installation had only a minimal economic impact on the landlord. *Id.*

2) No economically viable use

When a regulation results in a **permanent total loss of the property's economic value,** a taking has occurred. *Lucas v. South Carolina Coastal Council*, 505 U.S. 1003 (1992) (zoning ordinance precluding owner of coastal property from erecting any permanent structure on the land was a taking); *Tahoe-Sierra Preservation Council, Inc. v. Tahoe Regional Planning Agency*, 535 U.S. 302 (2002) (32-month building moratorium was not a taking).

> **Adverse economic impact:** A regulation that results in a dramatic decline in the value of the regulated property does not necessarily constitute a taking.

c. Post-adoption acquisition

A person who acquires property rights after the adoption of a regulation that affects those rights may nevertheless challenge the regulation as an unconstitutional taking. *Palazzolo v. Rhode Island.*, 533 U.S. 606 (2001).

5. Exaction as a Taking

A local government may exact promises from a developer, such as setting aside a portion of the land being developed for a park in exchange for issuing the necessary construction permits. Such exactions do not violate the Takings Clause if there is:

i) An **essential nexus** between legitimate state interests and the conditions imposed on the property owner (i.e., the conditions substantially advance legitimate state interest); and

ii) A **rough proportionality** between the burden imposed by the conditions on property owner and the impact of the proposed development.

Nollan v. California Coastal Commission, 483 U.S. 825 (1987) (state-required grant of an easement across beachfront property as a condition on the issuance of a building permit was a taking due to lack of essential nexus); *Dolan v. City of Tigard*, 512 U.S. 374 (1994) (state-required dedication of land to the city for use as a greenway and pedestrian/bicycle pathway in exchange for permit to expand a store and parking lot was a taking due to lack of rough proportionality).

In determining whether there is rough proportionality between the burden and the impact, the government must make an individualized determination that the conditions are related both in nature and extent to the impact.

The government's conditions must satisfy the requirements of *Nollan* and *Dolan* even when the government denies the permit and even when its demand is for money rather than property rights. *Koontz v. St. Johns River Water Mgmt. Dist.*, 570 U.S. 595 (2013).

These requirements are limited to exactions; they do not apply to regulatory takings. *Lingle v. Chevron U.S.A. Inc., supra* (rent cap was not an exaction taking, but instead was a valid regulation under the Takings Clause).

C. JUST COMPENSATION

The phrase "just compensation" has been interpreted to mean **fair market value,** which is the reasonable value of the property at the time of the taking. This value is measured in terms of the loss to the owner, not the benefit to the government.

1. Worthless Property

Property that is worthless to the owner but has value to the government may be taken without compensation.

> **Example:** Clients whose funds were held by lawyers and deposited in a trust account pursuant to state law to be paid to an entity in order to provide legal services for the poor were not entitled to compensation because each client's funds would not separately have earned interest. *Brown v. Legal Foundation of Washington*, 538 U.S. 216 (2003).

2. Only A Portion Taken

When only a portion of an owner's property is taken, the owner may also receive compensation for any diminution in value of the remaining portion that is attributable to the taking but must reduce any compensation by the value of any special and direct benefits (e.g., a highway access) conferred on the remaining portion. Additionally, an owner may receive compensation when the government gives a third party the right to occupy the property (such as when a utility is permitted to place equipment on a landowner's property). *See Kelo v. City of New London, Conn.*, 545 U.S. 469 (2005).

3. Return of Property

When governmental action constitutes a taking, the government cannot escape all liability by returning the property to its owner, but instead must pay the owner compensation for the period that the government possessed the property. *First English Evangelical Church v. County of Los Angeles*, 482 U.S. 304 (1987).

D. MANNER OF TAKING

Typically, when a property owner objects to the seizure of his property by the government, the government will institute condemnation proceedings, and the property owner can raise the Takings Clause as a defense to this action. When the governmental action that allegedly constitutes a taking is a statute, regulation, or ordinance, the property owner may institute a suit seeking an injunction or a declaratory judgment; this type of legal action is sometimes referred to as an inverse condemnation. Such actions can be brought in federal court without having to first exhaust all state court remedies. *Knick v. Township of Scott, Penn.*, 588 U.S. ___, 139 S. Ct. 2162 (2019).

XVI. PROHIBITED LEGISLATION

A. BILLS OF ATTAINDER

A bill of attainder is a **legislative** act that declares a person or group of persons guilty of some crime and punishes them without a trial. Article I, Sections 9 and 10 forbid the federal government and the states, respectively, from enacting such "legislative trials." It applies only to criminal or penal measures.

Barring particular individuals from government employment qualifies as punishment under the prohibition against bills of attainder. *United States v. Lovett*, 328 U.S. 303 (1946).

B. EX POST FACTO LAWS

The constitutional prohibition on an "ex post facto" law is confined to a retroactive change to a **criminal or penal** law. A law that is civil in purpose is treated as a criminal law only if its punitive effect clearly overrides its civil purpose. *Smith v. Doe*, 538 U.S. 84 (2003).

Under Article I, Sections 9 and 10, a **federal or state** statute will be struck down as being ex post facto if it:

i) **Criminalizes** an act that was not a crime when it was originally committed;

ii) Authorizes, after an act was committed, the imposition of a **more severe penalty** on that act;

iii) **Deprives the defendant of a defense** available at the time the act was committed; or

iv) **Decreases the prosecution's burden of proof** required for a conviction to a level below that which was required when the alleged offense was committed.

Collins v. Youngblood, 497 U.S. 37 (1990).

Example: A change in the relevant statute of limitations that resulted in the revival of a prosecution for an act of sexual abuse for which the statute of limitations had expired violates the prohibition on ex post facto laws; the change retroactively withdrew a complete defense to the crime after it had vested. *Stogner v. California*, 539 U.S. 607 (2003).

Compare: The retroactive application of state law that required registration of convicted sex offenders and child kidnappers, and public notification of information about the convicts, including name, current address, and place of employment did not constitute an ex post facto law. The law was a nonpunitive regulatory scheme enacted for the protection of the public. *Smith v. Doe, supra.*

C.   OBLIGATION OF CONTRACTS

Article I, Section 10 (i.e., the "contracts clause"), prohibits the states from passing any law "impairing the obligation of contracts." This prohibition applies only to **state legislation**— not state-court decisions and not federal legislation—that **retroactively** impairs contractual rights. It does not apply to contracts not yet entered into.

1.   Private Contracts

State legislation that **substantially** impairs a contract between private parties is invalid, unless the government can demonstrate that the interference was **reasonable** and **necessary** to serve an **important** governmental interest. *Allied Structural Steel Co. v. Spannaus*, 438 U.S. 234 (1978); *Energy Reserves Group, Inc. v. Kansas Power and Light Co.,* 459 U.S. 400 (1983). Substantial impairment generally requires that the state legislation destroy most or all of a party's rights under a preexisting contract. *See Home Bldg. and Loan Ass'n v. Blaisdell,* 290 U.S. 398 (1934); *Keystone Bituminous Coal Ass'n v. DeBenedictus,* 480 U.S. 470 (1987).

2.   Public Contracts

Impairment by the state of a **public contract** (one to which the state or local government is a party) is subject to essentially the same "reasonable and necessary" test as private contracts, but with a somewhat stricter application. The state must show that its important interest cannot be served by a less-restrictive alternative and that the impairment it seeks is necessary because of unforeseeable circumstances. *U.S. Trust Co. v. New Jersey*, 413 U.S. 1 (1977).

Note that there is no substantial impairment if the state reserved—by statute, law, or in the contract itself—the right to revoke, alter, or amend.

XVII. FREEDOM OF RELIGION

The First Amendment provides that "Congress shall make no law respecting an establishment of religion, or prohibiting the free exercise thereof." Both the Establishment Clause and the Free Exercise Clause have been incorporated into the Due Process Clause of the Fourteenth Amendment and are therefore applicable to the states.

A.   ESTABLISHMENT

When a governmental program shows preference to one religion over another, or to religion over nonreligion, strict scrutiny applies. *Bd. of Educ. v. Grumet,* 512 U.S. 687 (1994) (creation of special school district to benefit members of one religion invalid); *Larkin v. Grendel's Den, Inc.*, 459 U.S. 116 (1982) (delegating or sharing ability to make discretionary decisions, like zoning decisions, to a religious institution invalid).

1.   Standard of Review

Not every governmental action that impacts religion is unconstitutional. To determine whether a particular program violates the Establishment Clause, the Court has most often applied the three-part test developed in *Lemon v. Kurtzman*, 403 U.S. 602 (1971).

A governmental action that benefits religion is valid if:

i)   It has a **secular purpose**;

ii) Its principal or primary effect **neither advances nor inhibits** religion; and

iii) It does not result in **excessive government entanglement** with religion.

Though still applied, the Lemon test has often been modified or set aside in the Supreme Court's more recent Establishment Clause cases. *See, e.g., Am. Legion v. Am. Humanist Ass'n*, 588 U.S. ___, 139 S. Ct. 2067 (2019) (presumption of constitutionality for longstanding monuments, symbols, and practices); *Good News Club v. Milford Central School*, 533 U.S. 98 (2001) (permitting Christian organization to use public school cafeteria for after-school meetings did not violate Establishment Clause); *Bd. of Educ. v. Grumet*, 512 U.S. 687 (1994) (creation of school district to serve distinctive religious population violated Establishment Clause).

2. **Financial Aid**

   a. **Aid to religious institutions**

   Governmental financial assistance to religious institutions is permitted if the aid is secular in nature, used only for secular purposes, and, when the aid is distributed among secular and religious institutions, the distribution criteria must be religiously neutral. *Mitchell v. Helms*, 530 U.S. 793 (2000) (elementary and secondary school); *Tilton v. Richardson*, 403 U.S. 672 (1971) (college); *Bradfield v. Roberts*, 175 U.S. 291 (1899) (hospital). Aid in the form of secular textbooks, computers, standardized tests, bus transportation, school lunches, and sign language interpreters for deaf students has been upheld. While parochial elementary and secondary schools were at one time considered to be so pervasively sectarian that direct aid to them was not permitted, that is no longer the case. *Mitchell v. Helms, supra*. In applying the *Lemon* test, the third element (no excessive governmental entanglement) is not a separate requirement, but instead is one factor to be considered in ascertaining whether the second element (no advancement or inhibition of religion) has been met. *Agostini v. Felton,* 521 U.S. 203, 233 (1997).

   b. **Tax exemptions for religious organizations**

   Property-tax exemptions for religious institutions have been held valid as being equivalent to exemptions given to other charitable organizations and therefore neither advancing nor inhibiting religion. *Walz v. Tax Comm'n*, 397 U.S. 664 (1970). Tax exemptions that are available only for religious activities or organizations, however, violate the Establishment Clause as an endorsement of religion. *Texas Monthly v. Bullock*, 489 U.S. 1 (1989).

   c. **Tax deductions and aid for parochial school expenses**

   Tax deductions given to reimburse tuition expenses only for parents of students in religious schools are invalid. If such a deduction is available to *all* parents for actual educational expenses of attending any public or private school (including parochial schools), it is valid. *Mueller v. Allen*, 463 U.S. 388 (1983).

   In addition, giving parents tuition vouchers to assist them in paying religious-school tuition does not violate the Establishment Clause if the choice of whether to use the vouchers for religious or non-religious private school tuition lies with the parents. *Zelman v. Simmons-Harris*, 536 U.S. 639 (2002). However, states may deny state funds to a student pursuing a religious career without violating the Free Exercise Clause of the federal constitution. *Locke v. Davey*, 540 U.S. 712 (2004) (denial of state scholarship funds to a student seeking a career in religious instruction did not violate the Free Exercise Clause because the state was free to choose not to fund a distinct category of instruction in order to avoid the establishment of religion).

3. **Public School Activities**

Generally, officially sponsored religious activities in public schools or at public school events violate the Establishment Clause. The following practices have been held invalid as clearly promoting religion:

i) **Prayer** and **Bible reading,** *Engel v. Vitale*, 370 U.S. 421 (1962);

ii) A designated period of silence during the school day for **"meditation or voluntary prayer"** lacking any secular purpose, *Wallace v. Jaffree*, 472 U.S. 38 (1985); *but see Brown v. Gilmore*, 258 F.3d 265 (4th Cir. 2001) (divided court holding that short periods of mandatory silence did not necessarily implicate the establishment of religion, and that moment-of-silence requirements with dual legitimate purposes (i.e., a secular purpose along with a purpose to accommodate free exercise of religion) satisfy the first *Lemon* prong and may still pass the *Lemon* test);

iii) **Nondenominational (i.e., nonsectarian) prayer** at school events, *Lee v. Weisman*, 505 U.S. 577 (1992) (prayer led by a cleric at a graduation ceremony); *Santa Fe Indep. Sch. Dist. v. Doe*, 530 U.S. 290 (2000) (school policy of student-led prayer at high school football games); *but see Town of Greece v. Galloway*, 572 U.S. 565 (2014) (prayer before sessions of town council did not violate Establishment Clause due to tradition of such prayers and lack of coercion with regard to participation by nonbelievers);

iv) Posting the **Ten Commandments** on public-school classroom walls, *Stone v. Graham*, 449 U.S. 39 (1980); and

v) **Prohibiting the teaching of Darwinism** (i.e., human biological evolution), or mandating that such teaching be accompanied by instruction regarding "creation science," *Edward v. Aguillard*, 482 U.S. 578 (1987); *Epperson v. Arkansas*, 393 U.S. 97 (1968).

4. **Access to Public Facilities by Religious Groups**

If a public school allows student groups or organizations to use its facilities when classes are not in session, allowing a religious organization to use those facilities does not violate the Establishment Clause. Furthermore, to prohibit such a group from using those facilities because religious topics would be discussed would violate the First Amendment guarantee of free speech. *Good News Club v. Milford Central School*, 533 U.S. 98 (2001); *Widmar v. Vincent*, 454 U.S. 263 (1981). The Court has often responded to public educational institutions' Establishment Clause concerns by focusing on the free speech rights of religious students. *E.g.*, *Rosenberger v. Univ. of Virginia*, 515 U.S. 819 (1995) (state university could not refuse to pay for printing of religious student newspaper on Establishment Clause grounds when it funded nonreligious papers).

5. **Religious Displays**

a. **Ten Commandments**

A display of the Ten Commandments on public property is an impermissible violation of the Establishment Clause if the display has a **"predominantly religious purpose."** *McCreary County v. ACLU*, 545 U.S. 844 (2005) (Ten Commandments posted in courthouse impermissible). If the display also communicates a secular moral message, or its context conveys a historical and social meaning, it may be upheld. *Van Orden v. Perry*, 545 U.S. 677 (2005) (Ten Commandments monument on the state capitol grounds displaying 17 monuments and 21 historical markers commemorating the state's "people, ideals, and events that compose its identity" was permitted because the "Ten Commandments have an undeniable historical meaning" in addition to their "religious significance." Because of the unique historical message, which is separate from any religious message, installing the Ten Commandments in a public park did not violate the Establishment Clause). This is a highly context-dependent, case-specific inquiry.

b. Holiday displays

Government holiday displays will generally be upheld unless a reasonable observer would conclude that the display is an **endorsement** of religion. The context of the display is key—a nativity scene in a courthouse under a banner reading "*Gloria in Excelsis Deo*" was struck down as endorsing religion, but a nearby outdoor display of a Christmas tree, Chanukah menorah, and other seasonal symbols was upheld as mere recognition that Christmas and Chanukah are both parts of a highly secularized winter holiday season. *County of Allegheny v. ACLU*, 492 U.S. 573 (1989).

B. FREE EXERCISE

The Free Exercise Clause of the First Amendment has been construed to include two freedoms: the freedom to believe and the freedom to act. The degree of protection that individuals are afforded from governmental interference in religion depends on whether religious belief or conduct is involved.

1. Religious Belief

The freedom to believe in any religion or none at all is absolutely protected and cannot be restricted by law. The government may not deny benefits or impose burdens based on religious belief, *Cantwell v. Connecticut*, 310 U.S. 296 (1940); it may not require affirmation of a belief, *West Virginia State Bd. of Educ. v. Barnette*, 319 U.S. 624 (1943); and it may not determine the reasonableness of a belief, although it may determine the sincerity of the person asserting that belief, *United States v. Ballard*, 322 U.S. 78 (1944). When there is a property dispute between two religious groups, a court may not decide questions of religious doctrine, but may apply religiously neutral principles of law to resolve the dispute. *Jones v. Wolf*, 443 U.S. 595 (1979).

2. Religious Conduct

Religious conduct, on the other hand, is not absolutely protected. Generally, only state laws that **intentionally target** religious conduct are subject to strict scrutiny. Neutral laws of general applicability that have an impact on religious conduct are subject only to the rational basis test.

a. Targeting religious conduct

Strict scrutiny applies when the government purposely targets conduct because it is religious or displays religious beliefs. *Church of the Lukumi Babalu Aye, Inc. v. City of Hialeah*, 508 U.S. 520 (1993) (city ordinance banning all ritual sacrifice of animals not for the purpose of food consumption struck down as targeting the Santeria religion). A state law that is designed to suppress activity because it is religiously motivated is valid only if it is necessary to achieve a compelling governmental interest.

Other laws that have been struck down as violating the Free Exercise Clause include compulsory school attendance for the Amish, *Wisconsin v. Yoder*, 406 U.S. 205 (1972), and denial of unemployment benefits to one whose faith prevented her from taking a job that required her to work on the Sabbath, *Sherbert v. Verner*, 374 U.S. 398 (1963).

b. Generally applicable laws

Neutral state laws of general applicability that have the incidental effect of interfering with one's ability to engage in religious practices are subject only to the rational basis test. A law is not generally applicable if it invites the government to consider the particular reasons for a person's conduct by creating a mechanism for individualized exceptions. *Fulton v. Philadelphia*, 593 U.S. ___, 141 S. Ct. 1868 (2021) (refusal of city to contract with Catholic foster-child placement agency unless agency agreed to certify same-sex couples as foster parents violated Free Exercise Clause); *Employment Div. v. Smith*, 494 U.S. 872 (1990) (criminalization of peyote that did not contain an exception for use in Native American religious rituals upheld, as the ban was not motivated by any desire to burden religious conduct).

> **Example:** A parent's right to pray over a child who has contracted meningitis, rather than seeking medical assistance, may be limited by state child-neglect and manslaughter laws. Parents do not have the right to endanger the lives of their children on the grounds of freedom of religion. *See Prince v. Massachusetts*, 321 U.S. 158 (1944).

c. Access to benefits

Strict scrutiny applies when the government purposely denies a religious entity access to an otherwise available public benefit purely on account of its religious status. The avoidance of entanglement of church and state is not a sufficient governmental interest to justify this denial. *Trinity Lutheran Church of Columbia, Inc. v. Comer*, 582 U.S. ___, 137 S. Ct. 2012 (2017) (church-run preschool could not be denied, solely on the basis of its religious status, a state grant to resurface playground); *but see Locke v. Davey*, *supra* (state not required to fund degree in devotional theology as part of a state scholarship program).

d. Religious Freedom Restoration Act (RFRA)

Under the federal Religious Freedom Restoration Act, and similar acts adopted by over 20 states, even neutral laws of general applicability are subject to strict scrutiny if they substantially burden the free exercise of religion. Federal RFRA's express remedies provision permits litigants to obtain money damages against federal officials in their individual capacities. *Tanzin v. Tanvir*, 592 U.S. ___, 141 S. Ct. 486 (2020).

C. MINISTERIAL EXCEPTION TO DISCRIMINATION LAWS

Religious institutions can rely on a "ministerial exception" to federal and state employment discrimination laws in their decision to hire or fire a minister. The purpose of the ministerial exception, which is based on both the Establishment and Free Exercise Clauses of the First Amendment, is not merely to safeguard a church's decision to discharge a minister when it is made for a religious reason but also to ensure that the authority to select and control who will serve as a minister to the church's faithful, a strictly ecclesiastical matter, is solely the church's decision. The exception operates as an affirmative defense to an otherwise cognizable claim, but not as a jurisdictional bar. *Hosanna-Tabor Evangelical Lutheran Church and School v. E.E.O.C.*, 565 U.S. 171 (2012) (employee whose responsibilities included religious instruction was "minister" within scope of ministerial exception, and as such, church and school could not be held liable in E.E.O.C.'s discrimination enforcement action on her behalf).

XVIII. FREEDOM OF EXPRESSION AND ASSOCIATION

In addition to its religion clauses, the First Amendment provides that "Congress shall make no laws...abridging the freedom of speech, or of the press; or the right of the people to peaceably assemble, and to petition the Government for a redress of grievances." These aspects of the First Amendment are applicable to the states via the Fourteenth Amendment.

Freedom of expression is not absolute. While governmental regulation of the content of speech is severely constrained, governmental regulation of the time, place, and manner of speech is subject to less restriction.

A.   REGULATION OF SPEECH

1.   Expressive Conduct

Protected speech can include not only written, oral, and visual communication, but also activities such as picketing and leafleting. Expressive conduct (or symbolic speech) may also be protected as speech, but it is subject to a lesser degree of protection. Governmental regulation of expressive conduct is upheld if:

i) The regulation is **within the government's power** to enact (e.g., through a local government's police power);

ii) The regulation furthers an **important governmental interest**;

iii) The governmental interest is **unrelated to the suppression of ideas**; and

iv) The burden on speech is **no greater than necessary.**

United States v. O'Brien, 391 U.S. 367 (1968) (prohibition against burning draft cards upheld as furthering the important governmental interest in a smoothly functioning draft system).

An example of permissible regulation of expressive conduct includes upholding a ban on public nudity, such as nude dancing in adult entertainment venues, pursuant to the important governmental interest in preventing the "harmful secondary effects" of adult entertainment on neighborhoods, which is unrelated to the suppression of expression. *City of Erie v. Pap's A.M.*, 529 U.S. 277 (2000).

Examples of impermissible regulation of expressive conduct include:

i) A ban against students wearing black armbands to protest the war in Vietnam, because the government's only interest in banning the conduct was prohibiting communication, *Tinker v. Des Moines Indep. Cmty. Sch. Dist.*, 393 U.S. 503 (1969);

ii) A federal prohibition against burning the American flag because the law was intended to suppress messages of disapproval of governmental policy, rather than any conduct-related consequences of the burning of a flag, *United States v. Eichman*, 496 U.S. 310 (1990); and

iii) An ordinance prohibiting leafleting that results in littering on public streets, because the governmental interest in clean streets is insufficient justification, and such a ban on distribution is not narrowly tailored to protect the communication of information and opinion. *Schneider v. State of New Jersey Town of Irvington,* 308 U.S. 147 (1939).

The act of signing a petition constitutes expressive conduct. Public disclosure of the petition, and, thereby, the names of the individuals who signed the petition does not violate the First Amendment because such disclosure is substantially related to the important interest of preserving the integrity of the electoral process. *Doe v. Reed*, 561 U.S. 186 (2010).

2. Overbreadth

A law that burdens a substantial amount of speech or other conduct constitutionally protected by the First Amendment is **"overbroad"** and therefore void. A statute's overbreadth must be substantial both in an absolute sense and relative to the statute's plainly legitimate reach. The mere fact that some impermissible applications of a statute can be conceived of is not sufficient to render a statute overbroad. *United States v. Williams*, 553 U.S. 285 (2008). This doctrine does not apply to commercial speech. *Hoffman Estates v. The Flipside, Hoffman Estates, Inc.*, 455 U.S. 489 (1982).

In order to prevent a **"chilling effect"** on protected speech (i.e., frightening people into not speaking for fear of prosecution), overbroad statutes may be challenged as **"facially invalid"** even by those who are validly regulated on behalf of those who are not. *Broadrick v. Okla.*, 413 U.S. 601 (1973). The challenger of a law bears the burden of establishing that substantial overbreadth exists. *N.Y. State Club Ass'n v. City of N.Y.*, 487 U.S. 1 (1988).

3. Vagueness

A statute is **"void for vagueness"** if it fails to provide a person of ordinary intelligence with fair notice of what is prohibited. *United States v. Williams, supra.*

As with overbreadth, vagueness is impermissible for fear that constitutionally protected speech will be "chilled." In addition, the "void for vagueness" doctrine is grounded in the due process requirement of notice. Under due process principles, laws that regulate persons or entities must give fair notice of conduct that is forbidden or required. *FCC v. Fox Television Stations, Inc.*, 567 U.S. 239 (2012), Statutes that tie criminal culpability to conduct that involves subjective judgments without providing statutory definitions, narrow context, or settled legal meanings have been struck down for vagueness. *Reno v. ACLU*, 521 U.S. 844 (1997) (indecent speech); *Coates v. Cincinnati*, 402 U.S. 611 (1971) (annoying conduct).

4. Prior Restraints

A prior restraint is a regulation of speech that occurs in advance of its expression (e.g., publication or utterance). Prior restraints are generally presumed to be unconstitutional, with limited exceptions. *Bantam Books, Inc. v. Sullivan*, 372 U.S. 58 (1963). These rare exceptions require at a minimum that:

i) There is a **particular harm** to be avoided (like publication of troop movements); and

ii) Certain **procedural safeguards** are provided to the speaker. Examples of such safeguards include:

a) The standards must be narrowly drawn, reasonable, and definite, *Butterworth v. Smith*, 494 U.S. 624 (1990);

b) The censoring body must promptly seek an injunction, *Teitel Films v. Cusack*, 390 U.S. 139 (1968); and

c) There must be a prompt and final judicial determination of the validity of the restraint, *National Socialist Party v. Village of Skokie*, 432 U.S. 43 (1977).

The **burden is on the government** to prove that the material to be censored is not protected speech. *Freedman v. Maryland*, 380 U.S. 51 (1965).

Prior restraints have been rejected even when national security was at issue, *New York Times v. United States*, 403 U.S. 713 (1971) (Pentagon Papers), and even when press coverage threatened the fairness of a trial, *Nebraska Press Ass'n v. Stewart*, 427 U.S. 539 (1976) (prior restraint must be the only way to accomplish a goal).

5. **Unfettered Discretion**

A law or regulation that permits a governmental official to restrict speech (e.g., requires an official to issue a permit before a rally can be held) must provide definite standards as to how to apply the law in order to prevent governmental officials from having unfettered discretion over its application. Such a law or regulation must be related to an important governmental interest and contain the procedural safeguards mentioned above. A statute that gives officials unfettered discretion is void on its face; speakers need not apply for a permit and may not be punished for violating the licensing statute. *Lovell v. City of Griffin*, 303 U.S. 444 (1938).

6. **Freedom Not to Speak**

The First Amendment protects not only freedom of speech, but also the freedom not to speak. One such example is a child's right not to recite the Pledge of Allegiance. *West Virginia State Board of Education v. Barnette*, 319 U.S. 624 (1943). Similarly, the private organizers of a parade cannot be compelled by the government to include in the parade a group that espouses a message with which the organizers disagree. *Hurley v. Irish-American Gay, Lesbian & Bisexual Group of Boston*, 515 U.S. 557 (1995). Nor can the government mandate as a condition of federal funding that recipients explicitly agree with the government's policy to oppose prostitution and sex trafficking. *Agency for International Development v. Alliance for Open Society*, 570 U.S. 205 (2013). However, a state can compel a private entity (e.g., a shopping mall) to permit individuals to exercise their own free-speech rights when the private entity is open to the public and the message is not likely to be attributable to the private entity. *Pruneyard Shopping Center v. Robins*, 447 U.S. 74 (1980). A state may also require professional fundraisers to file certain public financial disclosures about fundraising activities in order to allow donors to make informed charitable contributions and to prevent fraud. *Schaumberg v. Citizens for a Better Env't*, 444 U.S. 620 (1980); *Sec'y of Md. v. Joseph H. Munson Co.*, 467 U.S. 947 (1984).

a. **Compelled financial support**

Although one can be compelled to join or financially support a group with respect to one's employment, one cannot be forced to fund political speech by that group. *Abood v. Detroit Bd. of Educ.*, 431 U.S. 209 (1977) (teacher required to pay union dues); *Keller v. State Bar of California*, 496 U.S. 1 (1990) (lawyer required to join a bar association). A student, however, can be required to pay a university activity fee even though the fee may support groups that espouse messages with which the student disagrees, at least when the fee is allocated in accord with a viewpoint-neutral scheme. *Board of Regents v. Southworth*, 529 U.S. 217 (2000).

7. **Government Speech**

When the government itself speaks, it is not constrained by the Free Speech Clause of the First Amendment. Therefore, government speech (public service announcements, agricultural marketing campaigns, etc.) need not be viewpoint-neutral. *Johanns v. Livestock Mkt'ing Ass'n*, 544 U.S. 550 (2005). This Government Speech Doctrine, however, is subject to the requirements of the Establishment Clause (*See* § XVII.A., *supra*).

a. Monuments on public property

The display of a monument on public property, even if the monument has been donated by a private person, constitutes government speech. *Pleasant Grove City v. Summum*, 555 U.S. 460 (2009) (government installed a Ten Commandments monument donated by a private person in a public park; the Court held that governmental entities may exercise "selectivity" in choosing a monument being offered by a private donor).

b. Specialty license plates

Specialty license plates, even if designed by private individuals, are government speech and, as such, the state may refuse proposed designs based on the content of those designs. *Walker v. Tex. Div., Sons of Confederate Veterans*, 576 U.S. 200 (2015) (rejection of proposed Texas license plate featuring Confederate battle flag).

c. Funding of private messages

The government may fund private messages. However, it must generally do so on a viewpoint-neutral basis. *Rosenberger v. Rector and Visitors of the University of Virginia*, 515 U.S. 819 (1995). The exception to this is when the government decides to fund artists; the decision of which artist to fund is necessarily based on the content of the artist's work. *National Endowment for the Arts v. Finley*, 524 U.S. 569 (1998).

d. Speech by government employees

When a government employee contends that her rights under the Free Speech Clause of the First Amendment have been violated by her employer, the employee must show that she was speaking as a citizen on a matter of public concern. *Borough of Duryea v. Guarnieri*, 564 U.S. 379 (2011). When a government employee is speaking pursuant to her official duties, the employee is generally not speaking as a citizen and the Free Speech Clause does not protect the employee from employer discipline. *Garcetti v. Ceballos*, 547 U.S. 410 (2006). In determining whether a government employee is speaking pursuant to her official duties, the critical question is whether the speech at issue is itself ordinarily within the scope of an employee's duties, not whether it merely concerns those duties. *Lane v. Franks*, 573 U.S. 228 (2014).

When an employee is speaking as a citizen on a matter of public concern, the First Amendment interest of the employee must be balanced against the interest of the state, as an employer, in effective and efficient management of its internal affairs. *Pickering v. Bd. of Educ.*, 391 U.S. 563 (1968); *Connick v. Myers*, 461 U.S. 138 (1983); *Borough of Duryea v. Guarnieri, supra*. This approach also applies to a government employee who petitions the government for redress of a wrong pursuant to the Petition Clause of the First Amendment. *Id.*

8. Campaign Related Speech

a. Political campaign contributions

Statutes limiting campaign contributions are subject to intermediate scrutiny: they must be "closely drawn" to correspond with a sufficiently important interest. *McConnell v. Federal Election Commission*, 540 U.S. 93 (2003); *Randall v. Sorrell*, 548 U.S. 230 (2006). The government's failure to assist a party in exercising a fundamental right does not infringe upon that right and therefore is not subject to strict scrutiny. *Ysursa v. Pocatello Education Association*, 555 U.S. 353 (2009) (state's decision to limit public employer payroll deductions for a union's political purposes did not abridge the union's right to speech).

1) Contributions to candidates

The government may limit contributions to individual candidates because excessive contributions to candidates create a danger of corruption and the appearance of corruption. *Buckley v. Valeo*, 424 U.S. 1 (1976). However, because aggregate limits on the amount a donor may contribute to candidates for federal office, political parties, and political action committees restrict participation in the political process and do little to further the prevention of "quid pro quo" corruption or the appearance of such corruption in campaign financing, they are invalid under the First Amendment. *McCutcheon v. Federal Election Commission*, 572 U.S. 185 (2014). Limits on campaign contributions to candidates for state office ranging from $275 to $1,000 have been upheld. *Nixon v. Shrink Missouri Gov't PAC*, 528 U.S. 377 (2000). However, the government cannot set differential contribution limits that penalize a candidate who finances his own campaign. *Davis v. Federal Election Commission*, 554 U.S. 724 (2008).

2) Contributions to political parties

The government may limit contributions to a political party that are used to expressly advocate for the election or defeat of a particular candidate (also known as "hard money") as well as contributions that are used for other purposes, such as promoting the party itself (also known as "soft money"). *McConnell v. Federal Election Commission, supra*. In addition, the government may require a political party to disclose contributors and recipients unless the party can show that such disclosure would cause harm to the party. *Brown v. Socialist Workers '74 Campaign Committee*, 454 U.S. 112 (1982).

3) Contributions to political action committees (PACs)

The government may limit contributions to a political action committee (PAC). *California Medical Assn. v. FEC*, 453 U.S. 182 (1981).

b. Political campaign expenditures

In contrast to campaign contributions, restrictions on expenditures by individuals and entities (including corporations and unions) on communications during an election campaign regarding a candidate are subject to strict scrutiny. So long as the source of the funding is disclosed, there is no legal limit to the amount that corporations and unions may spend on "electioneering communications." *Citizens United v. Federal Election Comm'n*, 558 U.S. 310 (2010). In addition, expenditures by a candidate on her own behalf cannot be limited. *Buckley v. Valeo, supra; Davis v. Federal Election Commission, supra.*

c. Political speakers

In addition to individuals, corporations (both nonprofit and for-profit) enjoy First Amendment protection with regard to political speech. *Citizens United, supra.* Similarly, a candidate for a judgeship has a First Amendment right to express his views on disputed legal or political issues. *Republican Party of Minnesota v. White*, 536 U.S. 765 (2002). A state law banning judicial candidates from personally soliciting campaign funds, however, does not necessarily violate the First Amendment. *Williams-Yulee v. The Florida Bar*, 575 U.S. 433 (2015).

B. REGULATION OF TIME, PLACE, AND MANNER OF EXPRESSION

The government's ability to regulate speech varies with the forum in which the speech takes place.

1. Three Categories of Forums

The Supreme Court has sorted government property that is open for speech into three categories: traditional public forums, designated public forums, and nonpublic (or limited public) forums. Speech restrictions in traditional and designated public forums are subject to the same strict scrutiny analysis, while there is a lower standard when analyzing restrictions in nonpublic forums. *Christian Legal Society v. Martinez*, 561 US 661 (2010).

2. Public Forums

A **"public forum"** may be **traditional** or **designated.** Traditional public forums are those that are historically associated with expression, such as sidewalks, streets, and parks. A designated public forum is one that has not historically been used for speech-related activities, but which the government has opened for such use, such as civic auditoriums, publicly owned theaters, or school classrooms that the public is allowed to use afterhours. The practical difference between the two is that the government can change a designated forum to a nonpublic forum, but it cannot do the same with a traditional forum.

Generally, in either type of public forum, the government may impose reasonable restrictions on the time, place, or manner of protected speech, provided the restrictions:

i) Are **content-neutral** as to both subject matter and viewpoint (i.e., it is not necessary to hear what is said in order to apply the regulation);

ii) Are **narrowly tailored** to serve a **significant governmental interest**; and

iii) Leave open ample **alternative channels for communication** of the information.

When dealing with time, place, or manner regulations, the requirement that the regulation be "narrowly tailored" does not mean that the regulation must employ the "least restrictive means" (or "least intrusive means" or "least drastic means") that will vindicate the significant governmental interest. The regulation need only promote a substantial government interest that would be achieved less effectively absent the regulation. *Ward v. Rock Against Racism*, 491 U.S. 781 (1989).

Additional restrictions, such as an absolute prohibition of a particular type of expression, will be upheld only if narrowly drawn to accomplish a compelling governmental interest, i.e., only if they satisfy strict scrutiny. *United States v. Grace*, 461 U.S. 171 (1983); *see, e.g., City of Ladue v. Gilleo*, 512 U.S. 43 (1994); *United States v. Kokinda*, 497 U.S. 720 (1990) (considering a ban on all solicitation in a public forum). Restrictions that are not content-neutral are also subject to **strict scrutiny** (*see* § XVIII.C., Regulation of Content, *infra*).

a. Residential areas

There is no right to focus picketing on a particular single residence. However, a person may solicit charitable funds in a residential area. Door-to-door solicitation does not require a permit, as long as the solicitation is for noncommercial or nonfundraising purposes. *Cantwell v. Conn.*, 310 U.S. 296, 306 (1940).

b. Injunctions

The test for the constitutionality of injunctions in public forums depends on whether the injunction is content-neutral or content-based. If an injunction is **content-neutral**, then the test is whether it burdens **no more speech than is necessary** to achieve an **important** governmental interest. On the other hand, if the injunction is **content-based,** it must be **necessary** for the government to achieve a **compelling** governmental interest.

c. Public schools

When a public school, as a designated (or limited, see below) public forum, permits the public to use its facilities, it cannot discriminate against organizations based on their beliefs. *Lamb's Chapel v. Center Moriches Union Free School District*, 508 U.S. 384 (1993) (religious organizations); *Widmar v. Vincent*, 454 U.S. 263 (1981); *Healy v. James*, 408 U.S. 169 (1972) (political organization). Similarly, a public school may provide funding and other benefits (e.g., free use of facilities) to student groups, but it must do so on a viewpoint-neutral basis.

> **Example 1:** A university that provided funds to various student publications could not withhold funds from a student religious publication on the grounds that the publication espoused religion. *Rosenberger v. Rector and Visitors of the University of Virginia*, 515 U.S. 819 (1995).
>
> **Example 2:** A public university law school could adopt an "all comers policy" with which student organizations must comply in order to receive school funding and other benefits. Under the policy, a student organization had to admit any student as a member and permit any student to hold office in the organization. Because the policy was viewpoint-neutral, its application to a religious organization was constitutional. *Christian Legal Soc'y Chapter of Univ. of California, Hastings Coll. of Law v. Martinez*, 561 U.S. 661 (2010).

3. Nonpublic Forum

A nonpublic forum (also known as a "limited public forum") is essentially all public property that is not a traditional or designated public forum. The state need not allow persons to engage in every type of speech, and may reserve the forum for certain groups or for the discussion of certain topics. Examples include government offices, jails, military bases, airport terminals, and polling places. The government may regulate speech-related activities in nonpublic forums as long as the regulation is (i) **viewpoint-neutral** and (ii) **reasonably related to a legitimate governmental interest.**

> Note that a governmental fundraising campaign is a nonpublic forum for the expression of speech. The decision to exclude some charities (but not others) cannot be made because the government disagrees with a particular organization's political views; such a decision must be ideologically neutral. *Cornelius v. NAACP Legal Def. and Educ. Fund, Inc.*, 473 U.S. 788 (1985).

a. Viewpoint-neutral

The regulation need not be content-neutral, but it must be viewpoint-neutral. In other words, the government may prohibit speech on certain issues altogether, but it may not allow only one side of an issue to be presented. For example, while a restriction on all public speeches in airports related to firearms regulation would likely be upheld, a restriction only on pro-NRA speeches would not.

> **Contrast this** with restrictions on speech in a public forum, which must be both content- and viewpoint-neutral.

b. Reasonable

The restriction on speech-related activities in nonpublic forums must only be rationally related to a legitimate governmental interest. A restriction need not be the least-restrictive means or even the most reasonable restriction to pass muster as "reasonable." For example, a city may sell commercial advertising space inside city buses but refuse to sell such space for political advertising in order to avoid the appearance of favoritism and imposition on a captive audience. *Lehman v. City of Shaker Heights*, 418 U.S. 298 (1974).

4. Personal Property

Governmental regulation of speech on a person's own private property will rarely be upheld, particularly content-based regulations. While the government has some limited powers to regulate speech on private property, outright bans on certain types of speech, such as signs in a person's yard or window, are impermissible. *City of Ladue v. Gilleo*, 512 U.S. 43 (1994) (statute banning all residential signs in order to fight "visual clutter" was found unconstitutional). Further, there is no First Amendment right to express oneself on someone else's private property (though a state's own constitution may protect such expression). *Hudgens v. NLRB*, 424 U.S. 507 (1976); *Pruneyard Shopping Center v. Robins*, 447 U.S. 74 (1980).

C. REGULATION OF CONTENT

Any governmental regulation of speech that is **content-based on its face** will only be upheld if the regulation is necessary to achieve a compelling governmental interest and is narrowly tailored to meet that interest (i.e., the **strict scrutiny** test). *Reed v. Town of Gilbert*, 576 U.S. 155 (2015) (ordinance that singled out signs bearing a particular message, the time and place of a specific event, were content based). However, even regulations that are not content-based on their face may still be content-based in application or in intent, and these laws, too, will generally be subject to strict scrutiny. *Brown v. Entm't Merchs. Ass'n*, 564 U.S 786 (2011) (state law that prohibited the sale of violent video games to minors is an unconstitutional content restriction on speech); *Simon & Schuster, Inc. v. Members of the New York State Crime Victims Board*, 502 U.S. 105 (1991). The government must identify an actual problem, and the regulation of speech must be necessary to solve that problem. This standard is incredibly stringent and is not often met. *U.S. v. Playboy Entm't Group, Inc.*, 529 U.S. 803 (2000).

However, the government may restrict speech on the basis of content if the speech falls into one of the following historic and traditional categories: obscenity, subversive speech, fighting words, defamation, or commercial speech. *U.S. v. Alvarez*, 567 U.S. 709 (2012). States are not free to create new categories of content-based restrictions without persuasive evidence that such restrictions have a long-standing history of proscription. *Brown v. Entm't Merchs. Ass'n, supra.*

1. Obscenity and Child Pornography

Neither obscene speech nor child pornography is protected by the First Amendment Free Speech Clause. *Roth v. United States*, 354 U.S. 476 (1957).

a. Obscenity test

To be considered obscene, speech must meet each part of a three-prong test developed in *Miller v. California*, 413 U.S. 15 (1973). Under the *Miller* test, the

average person, applying **contemporary community standards,** must find that the material, **taken as a whole**:

i)   Appeals to the **"prurient interest"**;

ii) Depicts sexual conduct in a **patently offensive** way; and

iii) **Lacks serious literary, artistic, political, or scientific value.**

> **EXAM NOTE:** *Standards Distinguished* – The first two prongs of this test use a contemporary **community** standard, which may be national but is generally considered to be local or statewide. A **national** standard must be applied, however, to the third prong of the test—determining the value of the work—because the work may merit constitutional protection despite local views to the contrary. *Pope v. Illinois*, 481 U.S. 497 (1987). With regard to the third prong, the judge, not the jury, determines whether this standard has been met.

Courts have recently begun to distinguish legally obscene speech from pornography. Merely establishing that speech constitutes pornography is generally insufficient to establish that the speech is obscene. Therefore, content-based restrictions on pornography are generally subject to strict scrutiny. *United States v. Playboy Entm't Grp. Inc.*, 529 U.S. 803 (2000).

Either an appellate court or a jury can assess whether the material is obscene. Evidence of similar material on newsstands is not automatically admissible, nor is expert testimony required to make such a determination.

b.   Prohibited activities

The sale, distribution, and exhibition of obscene material may be prohibited. *Stanley v. Georgia*, 394 U.S. 557 (1969). However, the right to privacy generally precludes criminalization of possession of obscenity in one's own home. *Stanley v. Georgia, supra.*

c.   Land-use restrictions

Narrowly drawn zoning ordinances may be used to restrict the location of certain adult entertainment businesses (e.g., adult theaters, adult bookstores, strip clubs) if the purpose of the regulation is to reduce the impact on the neighborhood of such establishments, but they may not be used to ban such establishments entirely. It does not matter that such establishments may be found in adjoining jurisdictions. *Los Angeles v. Alameda Books*, 535 U.S. 425 (2002); *City of Renton v. Playtime Theatres, Inc.*, 475 U.S. 41 (1986).

d.   Minors

Material that appeals to the prurient interests of minors may be regulated as to minors, even if it would not be considered obscene to an adult audience. *Ginsberg v. New York*, 390 U.S. 629 (1968). The government may not, however, block adults' access to indecent materials in order to prevent them from reaching children. *Reno v. ACLU*, 521 U.S. 844 (1997).

e.   "Scandalous" trademarks

The United States Patent and Trademark Office cannot deny registration of trademarks on the basis that they are "immoral" or "scandalous" (as previously allowed by the Lanham Act of 1946). Such provisions are unconstitutional, as they permit the USPTO to engage in viewpoint discrimination, violating the freedom of speech clause in the First Amendment. *Iancu v. Brunetti*, 588 U.S. ___, 139 S. Ct. 2294 (2019).

f. Child pornography

The First Amendment also does not protect child pornography, which is material depicting children engaged in sexually explicit conduct. Because of the state's compelling interest in protecting minor children from exploitation, the sale, distribution, and even private possession of child pornography may be prohibited, even if the material would not be obscene if it involved adults. *Osborne v. Ohio*, 495 U.S. 103 (1990); *New York v. Ferber*, 458 U.S. 747 (1982).

Simulated child pornography (i.e., pornography using young-looking adults or computer-generated images) may not be banned as child pornography. *Ashcroft v. Free Speech Coalition*, 535 U.S. 234 (2002). However, pandering (e.g., offers to sell or buy) simulated child pornography, including actual depictions of children even though the sexually explicit features are simulated, may be criminalized when the material is presented as actual child pornography. *United States v. Williams*, 553 U.S. 285 (2008).

g. Violence

Violence is not included in the definition of obscenity that may be constitutionally regulated. *Brown v. Entm't Merchs. Ass'n*, *supra*; *Winters v. New York*, 333 U.S. 507 (1948).

2. Incitement to Violence

A state may forbid speech that advocates the use of force or unlawful action if:

i)   The speech is **directed to inciting or producing imminent lawless action**; and

ii) It is **likely to incite or produce such action** (i.e., creates a clear and present danger).

Brandenburg v. Ohio, 395 U.S. 444 (1969).

Advocacy requires the use of language reasonably and ordinarily calculated to incite persons to such action. *Yates v. United States*, 354 U.S. 298 (1957). The abstract expression of ideas, including the teaching of the moral propriety or even moral necessity for a resort to force and violence, is not the same as the actual incitement of violence. There must be substantial evidence of a strong and pervasive call to violence. *Noto v. United States*, 367 U.S. 290 (1960).

3. Fighting Words

A speaker may be criminally punished for using "fighting words," which are words that **by their very nature** are likely to incite an immediate breach of the peace. *Chaplinsky v. New Hampshire*, 315 U.S. 568 (1942). Words that are simply annoying or offensive are not fighting words; there must be a genuine likelihood of imminent violence by a hostile audience. *Cohen v. California*, 403 U.S. 15 (1971).

> **EXAM NOTE:** Attempts to forbid fighting words almost always fail as vague, overbroad, or otherwise constitutionally infirm.

Statutes designed to punish only fighting words that express certain viewpoints are unconstitutional. *R.A.V. v. City of St. Paul*, 505 U.S. 377 (1992) (the Court struck down an ordinance that applied only to fighting words that insulted or provoked on the basis of race, religion, or gender).

However, actual threats of violence are outside the protection of the First Amendment, given the need to protect individuals from (i) the fear of violence, (ii) the disruption that fear engenders, and (iii) the possibility that the threatened violence will occur. *R.A.V. v. City of St. Paul*, 505 at 388.

4. Defamation

Limits on punishment for defamatory speech may apply in cases in which the plaintiff is a public official or public figure, or when a defamatory statement involves a matter of public concern. In addition to the elements of a prima facie case of defamation, the plaintiff must in these cases prove both **fault** and the **falsity** of the statement.

a. Public figure or official

A public figure is someone who is known to the general public and includes any person who has voluntarily injected herself into the public eye. The plaintiff must prove that the defendant acted with **actual malice,** i.e., knowledge of the statement's falsity or reckless disregard for whether it was true or false. *New York Times v. Sullivan*, 376 U.S. 254 (1964). Scientists who publish in scientific journals, criminals, and spouses of wealthy persons are not considered public figures.

b. Public concern

If the plaintiff is a private figure but the defamatory statement involves a matter of public concern, then the standard is lower, but the plaintiff still must establish negligence with respect to the falsity of the statement. *Gertz v. Robert Welch, Inc.*, 418 U.S. 323 (1974).

[See the Themis Torts outline for a full discussion of defamation actions.]

5. Commercial Speech

Commercial speech—advertising and similarly economically oriented expression—is entitled to an intermediate level of First Amendment protection. Restrictions on commercial speech are reviewed under a **four-part test**:

i) The commercial speech must **concern lawful activity** and be **neither false nor misleading** (fraudulent speech or speech which proposes an illegal transaction may be prohibited);

ii) The asserted governmental interest must be **substantial**;

iii) The regulation must **directly advance** the asserted interest; and

iv) The regulation must be **narrowly tailored** to serve that interest. In this context, narrowly tailored does not mean the least restrictive means available; rather, there must be a **"reasonable fit"** between the government's ends and the means chosen to accomplish those ends. *Board of Trustees of State University of New York v. Fox*, 492 U.S. 469 (1989).

Central Hudson Gas & Elec. v. Pub. Svc. Comm'n, 447 U.S. 557 (1980). Under this test, the Court has struck down laws prohibiting truthful advertising of legal abortions, contraceptives, drug prices, alcohol prices, and attorneys' fees and regulation of billboards on the basis of aesthetic value and safety.

> **Example:** A Massachusetts regulation that prohibited tobacco billboards within 1,000 feet of a school was struck down because the means—effectively barring most outdoor tobacco advertising in urban areas—were not narrowly tailored to the ends of protecting children. *Lorillard Tobacco Co. v. Reilly*, 533 U.S. 525 (2001).

Note that solicitation of funds for charitable purposes, however, is recognized as a form of protected speech. *See Village of Schaumburg v. Citizens for a Better Env't*, 444 U.S. 620 (1980). However, fraudulent charitable solicitations, such as false or misleading representations designed to deceive donor as to how donations will be used, are not protected. *Ill. ex rel. Madigan v. Telemarketing Assocs.*, 538 U.S. 600, (2003). Additionally, because there is a strong government interest in preventing fraud and allowing donors to make informed choices about their charitable contributions, the government may require professional fundraisers to file certain public financial disclosures about fundraising activities. *Village of Schaumberg v. Citizens for a Better Env't, supra*; *Sec'y of Md. v. Joseph H. Munson Co.*, 467 U.S. 947 (1984).

D. REGULATION OF THE MEDIA

Although the First Amendment specifically mentions freedom of the press, the media has no greater First Amendment rights than the general public.

1. General Considerations

The press has the right to publish information about matters of public concern, and the viewers have a right to receive it. This right may be restricted only by a regulation that is narrowly tailored to further a compelling governmental interest (i.e., strict scrutiny applies).

a. Gag orders

A gag order is a judicial order prohibiting the press from publishing information about court proceedings. Such orders are subject to prior-restraint analysis. Gag orders are almost always struck down because they are rarely the least restrictive means of protecting the defendant's right to a fair trial. The trial judge has other alternatives available, such as change of venue, postponement of the trial, careful voir dire, or restricting the statements of lawyers and witnesses. *Nebraska Press Ass'n v. Stuart*, 427 U.S. 539 (1972).

b. Attending trials

The public and the press both have the right to attend criminal trials, but this right is not absolute. It may be outweighed if the trial judge finds an **overriding** interest that cannot be accommodated by less restrictive means. The Supreme Court has not determined whether this right also applies to civil trials. However, the Supreme Court has held that the defendant's right to a public trial extended to voir dire, and the trial court must consider reasonable alternatives to closing the voir dire to the public in addressing the trial court's concerns. *Presley v. Georgia*, 558 U.S. 209 (2010).

c. No constitutional privilege to protect sources

A journalist has no First Amendment right to refuse to testify before a grand jury regarding the content and source of information relevant to the criminal inquiry. *Branzburg v. Hayes*, 408 U.S. 665 (1972).

d. Illegally obtained and private information

The First Amendment shields the media from liability for publishing information that was obtained illegally by a third party as long as the information involves a matter of public concern and the publisher neither obtained it unlawfully nor knows who did. *Bartnicki v. Vopper*, 532 U.S. 514 (2001).

Similarly, the First Amendment shields the media from liability for publication of a lawfully obtained private fact, e.g., the identity of a rape victim, so long as the news story involves a matter of public concern. *See Florida Star v. BJF*, 491 U.S. 524 (1989); *Cox Broadcasting v. Cohn*, 420 U.S. 469 (1975).

e. First Amendment conflict with state right of publicity

Some states recognize a right of publicity—the right of a person to control the commercial use of his or her identity. The right is an intellectual property right derived under state law, the infringement of which creates a cause of action for the tort of unfair competition. In *Zacchini v. Scripps-Howard Broad. Co.*, 433 U.S. 562 (1977), the Supreme Court considered a conflict between the First Amendment and a person's state-law right of publicity. A news program had televised a videotape of a daredevil's entire 15-second performance at a local fair when he was shot out of a cannon. The lower court held that the First Amendment protected the telecast from a tort suit regarding the right of publicity. The Supreme Court reversed, holding that the First and Fourteenth Amendments do not immunize the news media from civil liability when they broadcast a performer's entire act without his consent, and the Constitution does not prevent a state from requiring broadcasters to compensate performers. Note that a state government may pass a law shielding the press from liability for broadcasting performers' acts.

f. No immunity from laws of general applicability

As mentioned previously, the press has no greater First Amendment rights than does the general public, i.e., there is no special privilege allowing the press to invade the rights of others. As such, members of the press are not immune from the application of generally applicable laws, even if the application of such laws has a negative incidental effect on the ability to gather and report the news. *Cohen v. Cowles Media Co.*, 501 U.S. 663 (1991).

Example: A reporter who trespasses on another's property while investigating a story is not shielded from liability by the First Amendment.

2. Broadcast

Because the broadcast spectrum is a limited resource, radio and television broadcasters are said to have a greater responsibility to the public, and they therefore can be more closely regulated than print and other media. Broadcasters may be sanctioned, therefore, for airing "patently offensive sexual and excretory speech," even if such speech does not qualify as obscene under the *Miller* test, in the interest of protecting children likely to be listening. *FCC v. Pacifica Found.*, 438 U.S. 726 (1978).

However, public access stations are not considered to be state actors, and are thus not expected to protect free speech in the way that the government would be. *Manhattan Community Access Group v. Halleck*, 587 U.S. ___, 139 S. Ct. 1921 (2019).

3. Cable Television

The First Amendment protection provided to cable television falls somewhere between the extensive protection given to print media and the more limited protection for broadcasting. As such, a law requiring cable operators to carry local television stations is subject to intermediate scrutiny. *Turner Broad. Sys., Inc. v. FCC*, 512 U.S. 622 (1994).

Content-based regulations of cable broadcasts are subject to **strict scrutiny,** however. *United States v. Playboy Entm't. Group, Inc.*, 529 U.S. 803 (2000).

4. **Internet**

Because the Internet is not composed of scarce frequencies as are the broadcast media, and because of the reduced risk of an unexpected invasion of privacy over the Internet, any regulation of Internet content is subject to strict scrutiny. *Reno v. ACLU*, 521 U.S. 844 (1997).

E. **REGULATION OF ASSOCIATION**

Freedom of association generally protects the right to form or participate in any group, gathering, club, or organization. An infringement upon this right, however, may be justified by a compelling state interest. *See, e.g., Board of Dirs. of Rotary Int'l v. Rotary Club of Duarte*, 481 U.S. 537 (1987) (discrimination against women was not in furtherance of or necessary for any of the expressive activity undertaken by the organization); *but see Boy Scouts of America v. Dale*, 530 U.S. 640 (2000) (requiring the Boy Scouts to accept leaders who acted in a manner contrary to Boy Scout principles would unduly intrude upon the Boy Scouts' expressive associational rights).

1. **Public Employment**

An individual generally cannot be denied public employment based simply upon membership in a political organization. *Keyishian v. Board of Regents*, 385 U.S. 589 (1967).

a. **Test**

A person may only be punished or deprived of public employment based on political association if that individual:

i) Is an active member of a **subversive organization**;

ii) Has **knowledge** of the organization's illegal activity; and

iii) Has a **specific intent** to further those illegal objectives.

Scales v. United States, 367 U.S. 203 (1961) (conviction based on active, knowing, and purposive membership in an organization advocating the violent overthrow of the government upheld).

b. **Loyalty oaths**

Public employees may be required to take loyalty oaths promising that they will support the Constitution and oppose the forceful, violent, or otherwise illegal or unconstitutional overthrow of the government. *Connell v. Higgenbotham*, 403 U.S. 207 (1971). However, oaths that forbid or require action in terms so vague that a person of common intelligence must guess at the oath's meaning and differ as to its application are often found to be so vague or overbroad as to deprive an individual of liberty or property without due process. *E.g., Cramp v. Board of Public Instruction*, 368 U.S. 278 (1961) (striking down as vague a statute requiring public employees to swear that they have not and will not lend "aid, support, advice, counsel, or influence to the Communist Party"); *Shelton v. Tucker*, 364 U.S. 479 (1960) (striking down as overbroad a statute requiring teachers to file an affidavit listing every organization to which they have belonged or regularly contributed during the past five years).

2. **Bar Membership**

Although the state can inquire into the character of a candidate for bar admission, such admission cannot be denied on the basis of political association unless the candidate knowingly belongs to a subversive organization with specific intent to further its illegal ends. *Schware v. Board of Bar Exam'rs*, 353 U.S. 232 (1957). The state may, however, deny bar membership to a candidate who refuses to answer questions about political affiliations if that refusal obstructs the investigation of the candidate's qualifications. *Konigsberg v. State Bar of California*, 366 U.S. 36 (1961).

3. **Elections and Political Parties**

a. **Voters in primary elections**

A state cannot require a local political party to select presidential electors in an open primary (i.e., a primary in which any voter, including members of another party, may vote) when the national party prohibits nonparty members from voting. *Democratic Party v. LaFolette*, 450 U.S. 107 (1981). A state can require a semi-closed primary system, in which only registered party members and independents can vote in the party's primary, even if the party wants to permit anyone to vote. *Clingman v. Beaver*, 544 U.S. 581 (2005). On the other hand, a state may not prohibit a political party from allowing independents to vote in its primary. *Tashjian v. Republican Party of Connecticut*, 479 U.S. 208 (1986).

1) **Blanket primary**

A state may adopt a blanket primary system (i.e., a primary in which all voters regardless of party affiliation or lack thereof vote) that is nonpartisan. Under a nonpartisan primary system, the voters choose candidates for the general election without regard for their party affiliation. A nonpartisan blanket primary system in which a candidate identifies his own party preference or his status as an independent and that identification appears on the ballot has withstood a facial challenge, despite assertions that this self-designation violates the party's First Amendment rights as compelled speech and forced association. *Washington State Grange v. Washington State Republican Party*, 552 U.S. 442 (2008). By contrast, a partisan blanket primary system in which a party's nominees are chosen violates the party's First Amendment rights of free speech and association. *Cal. Democratic Party v. Jones*, 530 U.S. 567 (2000).

b. **Ballot access to general election**

A state may refuse to grant a political party's candidate access to the general-election ballot unless the party demonstrates public support through voter signatures on a petition, voter registrations, or previous electoral success. *Timmons v. Twin Cities Area New Party*, 520 U.S. 351 (1997); *Munro v. Socialist Workers Party*, 479 U.S. 189 (1986).

c. **Fusion candidate**

A state may prohibit a fusion candidate (i.e., a candidate who is nominated by more than one political party) from appearing on the general-election ballot as a candidate of multiple parties. This limitation on the associational rights of political parties is justified by the state's interests in ballot integrity and political stability. *Timmons v. Twin Cities Area New Party*, 520 U.S. 351 (1997).

d. Replacement candidate

When a state gives a political party the right to select an interim replacement for an elected state official who was a member of that party, the party may select the replacement through an election at which only party members may vote. *Rodriguez v. Popular Democratic Party*, 457 U.S. 1 (1982).

4. Criminal Penalty

A statute that purports to criminally punish mere membership in an association violates the First and Fourteenth Amendments. *Brandenburg v. Ohio*, 395 U.S. 444 (1969). Instead, such membership may only be criminalized if (i) the group is actively engaged in unlawful activity, or is engaging in advocacy that passes the *Brandenburg* "clear and present" danger test (i.e., speech directed to inciting or producing imminent lawless action that is likely to incite or produce such action); and (ii) the defendant knows of and specifically intends to further the group's illegal activity. *See, e.g., Whitney v. California*, 274 U.S. 357 (1927).

Themis
BarReview

LSE Key Concepts: CONSTITUTIONAL LAW
To be used with online lecture

CONSTITUTIONAL INTERPRETIVE APPROACHES

Traditional/Interpretive Approach: Interpret plain text of Constitution as a statute; may consider historical meaning, precedent, and structure of govt.

Process Theory: Focuses on representative self-government; believes Constitutional decision-making is best when it reinforces the democratic process

Rights Theory: Judiciary is committed to defend fundamental rights (from Constitution and/or natural law, etc.), regardless of majority opinion

ORIGINALISM

Text-based interpretive approach that asserts the meaning of Constitutional text was fixed at the time of drafting

- Original intent: Focused on what the framers intended their language to mean (largely abandoned in favor of original meaning)
- Original meaning: What the words used meant to a reasonable person at the time of ratification (i.e., semantic meaning); objective and public standard
- Problems: Difficult to implement; does not address textual ambiguities; precedents add complexity; principals (e.g., social power dynamics in drafting process); no results for modern developments (e.g., abortion, technology, etc.)
- ❖ District of Colombia v. Heller *(Asked whether the 2nd Amendment's right to bear arms is limited to maintaining a "well-regulated militia;" no clear originalist reading)*

JUDICIAL REVIEW

Separation of Powers (Concerns allocation of powers among branches of federal govt.)

❖ *Marbury v. Madison (Because the Constitution is law and the court has the power to decide cases in accordance with law, the judiciary can practice judicial review)*

- Judicial Review: A court with proper jurisdiction over the case before it has the power to refuse to give effect to a statute that is inconsistent with the Constitution
- Judicial Supremacy: Federal judiciary has absolute and sole authority to interpret Constitutional law (*Cooper v. Aaron; Powell v. McCormack*)

- Standing is required; taxpayer standing not usually available, except to raise an Establishment of Religion challenge to a spending program.

EXECUTIVE POWERS

- Congress cannot hire/fire executive officers without impeachment, except for special prosecutors.
- **Legislative Veto:** Reservation of power in a law delegating power to another party to veto a future exercise of that power by simple resolution
- **These are unconstitutional.
- **Unitary Executive Thesis**: Suggests that executive has unlimited powers to execute federal law, direct federal officers, and manage foreign affairs (but courts disagree and hold that some limits may apply).

CASE OR CONTROVERSY

Courts can only hear cases and controversies:

- **Ripeness:** Must be a live dispute involving actual harm or immediate threat of harm
- **Mootness:** Live controversy must exist at each stage of review, or will be dismissed as moot
- **Exception: Cases capable of repetition yet evading review are not dismissed for mootness
- **Standing:** Requires actual past or future **injury**, **causation** by defendant's conduct, and **redressability** by the court
  o Actual injury does not include ideological objection
  o No standing for injuries to someone else unless an exception applies (e.g., special relationship)
  o Taxpayers can challenge their tax liability before collection, but cannot challenge how the money is then spent (except pursuant to the Establishment Clause)

POLITICAL QUESTION DOCTRINE

Political questions (e.g., foreign affairs, military issues, and political gerrymandering in federal courts) are **always** non-justiciable.

❖ *Baker v. Carr (Held that reapportionment claims were justiciable and outlined six factors to help identify non-justiciable political questions, one of which was a "textually demonstrable constitutional commitment" to another branch)*

- **Political gerrymandering:** Non-justiciable in federal courts
- **Foreign affairs:** Usually non-justiciable

❖ Zivotofsky ex rel. Zivotofsky v. Clinton *(Political question doctrine does not bar adjudication of the constitutionality of a statute directing states to recognize Israel, because the courts are competent to review and interpret laws, even those that refer to foreign affairs)*

IMPEACHMENT

Can a sitting president be **indicted**?

❖ Morrison v. Olson *(A special prosecutor not subject to executive control can be appointed to investigate/prosecute govt. officials for certain crimes; Scalia's dissent argued that this violated the separation of powers)*

Conduct	Immunity?
Civil liability for acts in course of official duties	Sitting presidents have absolute immunity for acts in course of official duties (*Nixon v. Fitzgerald*)
Civil liability for acts before taking office	No immunity (*Clinton v. Jones*)
Criminal acts	Unclear, but Justice Dept. says no

Impeachment (accusation passed by majority vote of House of Representatives; if followed by a conviction passed by Senate by 2/3 majority vote, results in removal from office)

• Impeachment available for "treason, bribery, or other high crimes and misdemeanors" (unclear whether this includes modern crimes, crimes in/out of office, or exercises of an Article II power)

Judicial Oversight

❖ Nixon v. United States *(An impeached federal judge tried to appeal his conviction by arguing the Senate improperly delegated its power to try impeachments to a committee; Court's holdings suggested both that Senate acted properly and that the issue was a nonjusticiable political question)*

INTRO TO FEDERAL LEGISLATIVE POWERS

Necessary and Proper Clause: Power to enact any legislation necessary and proper to execute an enumerated power; not an independent source of power

No general "police power" (i.e., to promote public health, safety, welfare, or morals); these are reserved to states

THE COMMERCE POWER

Power to regulate **channels** of, **instrumentalities** of, and any activity that **substantially affects** interstate commerce

• "Substantial effects" are effectively presumed for economic and commercial activities, even for solely intrastate conduct

❖ Wickard v. Filburn *(Congress could regulate a farmer's ability to grow wheat on his own land for his own use because the aggregate effects of that intrastate activity substantially affected interstate commerce)*

• Unclear whether power applies to noneconomic activities that substantially affect interstate commerce in the aggregate; modern courts appear to have limited this power

❖ US v. Lopez *(Possession of a gun near a school was noneconomic activity; no aggregate effect on interstate commerce)*

❖ US v. Morrison *(Physical violence was noneconomic; no aggregate effect on interstate commerce)*

❖ Gonzalez v. Raich *(Growing marijuana for personal use could be regulated under the Commerce Clause; rational basis for concluding it affected national marijuana market)*

• Regulation of govt. actors engaged in same activities as private sector is permitted (e.g., minimum wage rules apply to public employers as well as private employers)

• Cannot be used to compel states to enact or enforce legislation (i.e., "**commandeering**" limitation)

❖ New York v. United States *(Cannot force enactment or enforcement of nuclear waste disposal rules)*

❖ Printz v. United States *(Cannot force state to conduct background checks required under federal law)*

OTHER FEDERAL LEGISLATIVE POWERS

Spending Power ("Tax and Spend")

• Congress can encourage states to act via taxing/spending powers (e.g., conditional funding, taxes as disincentives), but may not coerce the states.

• Any tax capable of raising revenue is within taxing power.

Civil War Amendments

• Can enact legislation to enforce 13th, 14th, and 15th Amendments

• 13th Amendment: Can legislate to prohibit private racial discrimination

• 14th Amendment: Can remedy/prevent violations of individual rights as defined by courts; must be "congruence and proportionality" between injury and the means adopted to remedy or prevent that injury

❖ Katzenbach v. Morgan *(Law preventing literacy tests as a condition of voting was proper under the enabling clause of the 14th Amendment)*

❖ City of Boerne v. Flores *(Religious Freedom Restoration Act invalidated as applied to states;*

Congress may still accommodate religious beliefs in its exercise of enumerated powers)

STATE INTERFERENCE WITH THE FEDERAL SYSTEM

Preemption (Valid federal law preempts incompatible state law)

- Incompatible laws (i.e., requiring violation of fed. law or making it impossible to comply with both) are preempted.
- Law in the same subject area is not automatically preempted, unless fed. law preempts the field.

Interstate Conflicts

- States can only tax property in the state or a proportionate share of interstate businesses.

Dormant Commerce Clause (Can only discriminate against out-of-state commerce if necessary to protect important state interest)

- "Important interest" generally means health and safety
- In-state subsidies generally allowed (in-state tuition)
- **Market Participant Exception:** State acting as market participant (buyer/seller) can discriminate against nonresident commerce
- Nondiscriminatory regulation may also be struck down if unduly burdensome on interstate commerce
- No violation if Congress consents

STATE ACTION AND INDIVIDUAL RIGHTS

State action is necessary to trigger constitutional protections (except for 13th Amendment, which also applies to private acts)

- **State action:** Action by government; may also exist when (i) private actors perform public functions, or (ii) there is significant state involvement in private activities
  - Public functions: Acts traditionally performed exclusively by the state (e.g., company towns)
  - Significant state involvement: Govt. cannot encourage or facilitate private discrimination
- Note that **anti-discrimination statutes** may apply to private conduct, even when Constitution does not.

PROCEDURAL DUE PROCESS

- When govt. takes life, liberty, or property, procedural due process requires notice and hearing.
  - Property interest: Only apples when party has legitimate claim of entitlement, not a mere expectation
  - **Includes right to continued welfare and disability benefits
  - **Includes public "for-cause" employees (requiring a pre-termination hearing)
  - **Does not include at-will employees
- Determine **what process is due** by balancing:

  - Private interest (i.e., life, liberty, property) affected;
  - Value of additional procedures in avoiding the risk of an unjust outcome; and
  - Government's interests in efficiency

THE TAKINGS CLAUSE

"Private property shall not be taken for public use without just compensation."

- **Public use** = government use (including selling to 3rd party)
- **Taking** includes (i) taking title, (ii) physical occupation by govt. or 3rd party
- Regulations restricting use or impairing value of property are not a taking UNLESS it leaves **no economically viable** use
- Just compensation = fair market value at time of taking

EQUAL PROTECTION

Level of Scrutiny	Defined	Applies if:
Strict Scrutiny*	*Must be necessary to achieve a compelling governmental interest*	*Involves fundamental right or suspect class*
Intermediate Scrutiny*	*Must be substantially related to an important governmental interest*	*Based on gender or status as non-marital child*
Rational Basis Review	*Must be rationally related to a legitimate governmental interest*	*All other cases*

To trigger strict or intermediate scrutiny, there must be **discriminatory intent; mere disparate impact can only trigger anti-discrimination statute protections*

- **Suspect classes:** Race, ethnicity, national origin, or (in some cases) alienage
- **Affirmative action:** Survives strict scrutiny (i) if specifically correct past discrimination, or (ii) as one factor to consider in college admissions decisions
- **Alienage**: Strict scrutiny applies, with two exceptions:
  - Laws by federal government based on alienage (i.e., immigration and naturalization laws) are valid unless arbitrary and unreasonable
  - Citizenship can be a prerequisite for participation in government functions (e.g., voting, jury duty, law enforcement, public school teachers), but not for private employment or govt. benefits

FUNDAMENTAL RIGHTS
- Fundamental rights trigger strict scrutiny in both Equal Protection and Substantive Due Process claims
- **Voting:** One person, one vote; requires districts of approx. equal size, but permits racial gerrymandering to increase minority representation
- Privacy includes:
  - Right to contraceptives (Griswold)
  - Engage in private sexual conduct (Lawrence)
  - Cohabitate with family (Moore v. City of E. Cleveland)
  - Parental rights (Pierce v. Society of Sisters)
- No undue burden on pre-viability **abortions** (Roe, Casey)
  - Can require informed consent, 24-hours waiting periods, and parental notification for minors
  - No spousal or parental consent requirements
  - Cannot force government financing
  ❖ Whole Woman's Health v. Hellerstedt (Courts should balance the burdens placed on abortion access against how well they actually serve govt. interests in health and safety)
  ❖ Obergefell v. Hodges (Did not call sexual orientation a suspect class, but supports marriage as fundamental right)
- **Marriage** cannot be cost-prohibitive to indigents; can be limited by age, consanguinity, or existing marriage

FREEDOM OF SPEECH
Restrictions on **time, place, or manner** upheld if:
- 1. Content-neutral (as written and applied);
- 2. Leaves alternative channels for communication; and
- 3. Narrowly tailored to serve significant governmental interest

Content-based restrictions only upheld if necessary to achieve a compelling governmental interest (i.e., strict scrutiny)
- Can be struck for vagueness (insufficient notice of restriction) or overbreadth (burdens more than needed to achieve governmental interest; not narrowly tailored)
- **Fighting Words** (i.e., words likely to incite an immediate breach of the peace) are not protected, but are hard to legislate without unconstitutional vagueness
- **Compelling govt. interests** include preventing incitement to violence, obscenity, fraud, and defamation; does not include prevention of animal cruelty

Commercial Speech (limited 1st Amendment protection)
- Generally must permit truthful and informative advertising
- May be restricted if (i) misleading, (ii) advertises illegal product or service, or (iii) restriction reasonably serves a substantial state interest

Govt. Employees (Generally cannot base employment decisions on protected acts of expression unless it interferes with official duties; exception: policy makers and their advisers)

Corporations have 1st Amendment protection with regard to political speech (*Citizens United*)
❖ United States v. Alvarez (Struck down Stolen Valor Act; lying about receiving Medal of Honor is protected speech)

THE ESTABLISHMENT CLAUSE
Lemon Test (*Lemon v. Kurztman*): Govt. action that benefits religion is valid if:
- It has a secular purpose;
- Its main effect neither advances nor inhibits religion; and
- It avoids excessive government entanglement with religion
- Lemon Test still applies, but is often modified or set aside

Modern trends focus on **endorsement** (Govt. cannot endorse one religion over another religion, or religion over non-religion)
- No **coercive** endorsement allowed

Conduct	Constitutional?
Govt. aid to religious schools/institutions	**Yes**, with secular purpose and if distributed on religiously neutral criteria
School-sanctioned prayer	**No**; coercive endorsement of religion
Voluntary student-led prayer	**Yes**
Bible readings in public school	**Yes,** as long as it is not inspirational
Ten Commandments	**Yes** as teaching tool **No** in courthouses or to inspire belief
Prohibition on teaching evolution	**No**
Legislative prayer	**Yes**
Nativity scenes on public property	**Yes**, if accompanied by something that dilutes religious message

THE FREE EXERCISE CLAUSE

- Religious belief: Absolute protection
- Religious conduct: Qualified protection

Traditional rule: Neutral laws of general applicability need not accommodate religious belief

❖ <u>Employment Div. v. Smith</u> *(criminalization of peyote with no exception for religious use was upheld).*

Religious Freedom Restoration Act: Applies strict scrutiny to neutral laws of general applicability if they substantially burden free exercise of religion; only applies to fed. govt., but many states have their own versions

❖ <u>Hosanna Tabor Evangelical Lutheran Church v. EEOC</u> *(Religious institutions can rely on a "ministerial exception" to federal and state employment discrimination laws when hiring or firing a minister)*

❖ <u>Masterpiece Cakeshop v. Colorado Civil Rights Commission</u> *(State anti-discrimination law did not apply to a baker who refused to bake a wedding cake for a same-sex couple based on the baker's religious beliefs)*

Themis
Bar Review

Contracts

CONTRACTS

Table of Contents

CONTRACTS

I. FORMATION OF CONTRACTS

A binding contract is typically created through the process of offer and acceptance, when consideration is present and when no valid defenses to contract exist.

A. DEFINITIONS AND OVERARCHING CONCERNS

1. Classification

Contracts can be classified as bilateral or unilateral.

a. Bilateral contracts

A bilateral contract is one in which a promise by one party is exchanged for a promise by the other party. The exchange of promises is enough to render them both enforceable.

b. Unilateral contracts

A unilateral contract is one in which one party promises to do something in return for an act of the other party (such as a monetary reward for finding a lost dog). Unlike in a bilateral contract, in a unilateral contract the offeree's promise to perform is insufficient to constitute an acceptance; the offeree must perform the act (find the lost dog) to accept the offer (of a monetary reward).

2. Enforceability

The absence of an essential element (such as capacity, consent, legality, form, etc.) may render the contract void, voidable, or unenforceable.

a. Void contracts

A void contract results in the entire transaction being regarded as a nullity, as if no contract existed between the parties.

b. Voidable contracts

A voidable contract operates as a valid contract, unless and until one of the parties takes steps to avoid it.

c. Unenforceable contracts

An unenforceable contract is a valid contract that cannot be enforced if one of the parties refuses to carry out its terms.

> **EXAM NOTE:** Remember that a **void** contract *cannot* be enforced, but a party may *opt* to avoid a **voidable** contract.

3. Applicable Law

The Uniform Commercial Code ("UCC") Article 2 governs transactions in goods. Although UCC Article 2 adopts much of the common law of contracts, it also codifies modifications relating to transactions in goods. Where the common law of contracts and UCC Article 2 differ, Article 2 prevails. For other types of contracts, such as those involving the sale of land or the provision of services, the common law as set forth in the Restatement (Second) of Contracts governs.

For a contract that involves both the sale of goods and a service, ask which of the two predominates.

> **Example:** Bob hires Emeril to cater his party. The contract provides that Emeril will shop for the food and cook it. The contract involves both goods (the food) and a service (Emeril cooking the food). Because the service provided here (Emeril cooking your food) is the more important aspect of the contract, common law governs.

4. Freedom of Contract

Parties are generally free to structure a contract in any manner that they see fit. Where parties do not provide for a circumstance, contract law may impose a default.

B. MUTUAL ASSENT

For a contract to be formed, there must be a manifestation of mutual assent to the exchange, which occurs upon acceptance of a valid offer to contract.

1. Offer and Acceptance

a. Offer

An offer is an objective manifestation of a willingness by the offeror to enter into an agreement that creates the power of acceptance in the offeree. In other words, it is a communication that gives power to the recipient to conclude a contract by acceptance.

1) Intent

A statement is an offer only if the person to whom it is communicated could *reasonably interpret* it as an offer. It must express the **present intent** to be legally bound to a contract. The primary test of whether a communication is an offer is whether a reasonable person receiving the communication would believe that she could enter into an enforceable deal by accepting the offer. This test is an objective test, not a subjective one. (Note: A similar objective test applies to determine whether a statement is an acceptance.)

> **Example:** Carol tells Andy, "I might be interested in buying your house." That would not be an offer because "I might" does not express a present intent to be bound.

2) Knowledge by the offeree

To have the power to accept the offer, the offeree must have knowledge of the offer.

3) Terms

The terms of the offer must be certain and definite. Under common law, all essential terms must be covered (subject matter, price, and quantity).

The UCC allows for a more liberal contract formation (i.e., a contract is formed if parties intend to contract and there is a reasonably certain basis for giving a remedy). As long as the parties intend to create a contract, the UCC "fills the gap" when a contract is silent as to terms other than quantity or subject matter, such as setting the place for delivery to be the seller's place of business, or even setting the price for the goods. Note that requirements (or output) contracts satisfy UCC formation requirements even without naming specific quantities. The UCC also implies good faith as a term.

4) Language

The offer must contain words of promise, undertaking, or commitment (as distinguished from words that merely indicate intention to sell or interest in buying). The offer must also be targeted to a number of people who could actually accept.

If a return promise is requested, then the contract is a bilateral contract. If an act is requested, then the contract is a unilateral contract.

5) What is not an offer

Offers must be distinguished from statements of opinion, or invitations to bargain.

> Compare, for example, the question, "what is your lowest price?" with the response to that question "we can quote you $5 per gross for immediate acceptance." The first question is merely an inquiry, whereas the second statement is an offer.

Advertisements normally are considered invitations to receive offers from the public unless associated with a stated reward. An advertisement may constitute an offer when the advertisement clearly specifies who may accept and how acceptance is to be made, and it leaves nothing further for negotiation.

> **EXAM NOTE:** Be careful not to mistake a true offer for language that sounds like an offer but is actually just an invitation to receive offers. The more definite the statement (e.g., "I will sell you X for…"), the more likely it is to be an offer.

b. Termination of offers

An offer can be accepted only when it is still outstanding (i.e., before the offer is terminated). Offers can be terminated in the following ways.

1) Lapse of time in offer

If the offer specifies a date on which the offer terminates, then the time fixed by the offer controls. If the offer states that it will terminate after a specified number of days, the time generally starts to run from the time the offer is received, not sent, unless the offer indicates otherwise. If the offeree is aware (or should have been aware) that there is a delay in the transmittal of the offer, the offer expires when it would have expired had there been no delay.

If the offer does not set a time limit for acceptance, the power of acceptance terminates at the end of a reasonable period of time. What is reasonable is a question of fact and depends on a variety of factors, including the nature of the contract, the purpose and course of dealing between the parties, and trade usage. For an offer received by mail, an acceptance that is sent by midnight of the day of receipt generally has been made within a reasonable period of time. Unless otherwise agreed upon, if the parties bargain in person or via telephone, the time for acceptance does not ordinarily extend beyond the end of the conversation. Restatement (Second) of Contracts § 41.

2) Death or mental incapacity

An offer terminates upon the death or mental incapacity of the offeror, even when the offeree does not know of the death or mental incapacity. An exception exists for an offer that is an option, which does not terminate upon death or mental incapacity because consideration was paid to keep the offer open during the option period, and the offer is therefore made irrevocable during that period.

Note that if an offer has been accepted, the death of the offeror will not necessarily terminate the contract.

3) Destruction or illegality

An offer involving subject matter that becomes destroyed or illegal is terminated on the happening of such an event.

4) Revocation

In general, an offer can be revoked by the offeror at any time prior to acceptance. An offer is revoked when the offeror makes a manifestation of an intention not to enter into the proposed contract. Restatement (Second) of Contracts § 42. A revocation may be made in any reasonable manner and by any reasonable means, and it is not effective until communicated. A revocation sent by mail is not effective until received.

Example: On day 1, A mails an offer to B. On day 2, A mails a revocation to B. If B receives the offer and accepts before receiving the revocation, a contract is formed.

At common law, a written revocation (as well as a written rejection or acceptance) is received when it comes into the possession of the person addressed or the person authorized to receive it on his behalf, or when it is deposited in some place he has authorized for deposit for this or similar communications. Restatement (Second) of Contracts § 68. Under the UCC, a person receives notice when: (i) it comes to that person's attention or (ii) it is duly delivered in a reasonable form at the place of business or where held out as the place for receipt of such communications. Receipt by an organization occurs at the time it is brought to the attention of the individual conducting the transaction or at the time it would have been brought to that individual's attention were due diligence exercised by the organization. UCC § 1-202.

If the offeree acquires reliable information that the offeror has taken definite action inconsistent with the offer, the offer is automatically revoked (i.e., a constructive revocation occurs). The offeror's power to revoke an offer is limited by the following items.

a) Option (promise not to revoke)

An option is an independent promise to keep an offer open for a specified period of time. Such promise limits the offeror's power to revoke the offer until after the period has expired, while also preserving the offeree's power to accept.

If the option is a promise not to revoke an offer to enter a new contract, the offeree must generally give separate consideration for the option to be enforceable. If the option is within an existing contract, no separate consideration is required. Note that in sale of goods contracts, however, a merchant's promise to keep an offer open need not be supported by consideration if it is in writing and signed.

b) Promissory estoppel

When the offeree detrimentally relies on the offeror's promise, the doctrine of promissory estoppel (*see* § I.C.3.b., *infra*) may make the offer irrevocable. It must have been reasonably foreseeable that such detrimental reliance would occur in order to hold the offeror to the offer.

c) Partial performance

If the offer is for a unilateral contract, the offeror cannot revoke the offer once the offeree has begun performance. Note, though, that the offeree must have had knowledge of the offer when she began the performance.

Once performance has begun, the offeree will have a reasonable time to complete performance. The offeree cannot be required to complete the performance, however.

d) UCC firm offer rule

Under the UCC, an offer to buy or sell goods is irrevocable if:

i) The offeror is a merchant;

ii) There are assurances that the offer is to remain open; and

iii) The assurance is contained in an authenticated writing (such as a signature, initials, or other inscription) from the offeror.

No consideration by the offeree is needed to keep the offer open under the UCC firm offer rule. UCC § 2-205.

i) Time period

If the time period during which the option is to be held open is not stated, a reasonable term is implied. However, irrevocability cannot exceed 90 days, regardless of whether a time period is stated or implied, unless the offeree gives consideration to validate it beyond the 90-day period.

ii) "Merchant" defined

For purposes of this rule, a merchant includes not only a person who regularly deals in the type of goods involved in the transaction or otherwise by his occupation holds himself out as having knowledge or skill peculiar to the practices or goods involved in the transaction, but also any businessperson when the transaction is of a commercial nature. UCC § 2-104(1) cmt. 2.

5) Rejection by counteroffer

An offer is terminated by rejection. In other words, the offeree clearly conveys to the offeror that the offeree no longer intends to accept the offer. A rejection is usually **effective upon receipt**. An offeree cannot accept an offer once it has been terminated.

A counteroffer acts as a rejection of the original offer and creates a new offer. An exception exists for an option holder, who has the right to make counteroffers during the option period without terminating the original offer.

> **EXAM NOTE:** Remember that a **counteroffer** is both a **rejection and a new offer**. Examine the offeree's statement closely. It may be a rejection, but it may also be only an inquiry (e.g., "Is that a 2005 model car?") or merely indecision (e.g., "I'll keep your offer under advisement."); in either case the offer remains open.

6) Revival of offer

A terminated offer may be revived by the offeror. As with any open offer, the revived offer can be accepted by the offeree.

> **Example:** A offers to paint B's house for $500. B rejects the offer. A states that the offer remains open. B can change her mind and accept the revived offer.

c. Acceptance

Only a party to whom an offer is extended may accept, and the acceptance forms a contract between the parties.

Generally, an offeree must know of the offer upon acceptance for it to be valid, and the terms of the acceptance must mirror the terms of the offer. For acceptance to be effective, the offeree must communicate the acceptance to the offeror.

1) Method of acceptance

The offeror, as master of the offer, can detail the manner of proper acceptance.

a) Bilateral versus unilateral offer

A **bilateral contract** is one in which a promise by one party is exchanged for a promise by the other. The exchange of promises is enough to render them both enforceable. An offer requiring a promise to accept can be accepted either with a return promise or by starting performance. Commencement of performance of a bilateral contract operates as a promise to render complete performance. Restatement (Second) of Contracts § 62.

A **unilateral contract** is one in which one party promises to do something in return for an act of the other party (e.g., a monetary reward for finding a lost dog). Unlike in a bilateral contract, in a unilateral contract, the offeree's promise to perform is insufficient to constitute acceptance. Acceptance of an offer for a unilateral contract **requires complete performance**. Once performance has begun, the offer is irrevocable for a reasonable period of time to allow for complete performance unless there is a manifestation of a contrary intent. However, the offeree is not bound to complete performance. In addition, while the offeror may terminate the offer before the offeree begins to perform, expenses incurred by the offeree in preparing to perform may be recoverable as reliance damages. Restatement (Second) of Contracts § 45.

> **EXAM NOTE:** The offeree of a unilateral contract can accept only an offer that he is aware of. In other words, if the offeree does not become aware of the offer until after acting, then his acts do not constitute acceptance.

When there is doubt as to whether an offer may be accepted by a promise to perform or by performance, the offeree may accept the offer by either. Restatement (Second) of Contracts § 32.

b) Mailbox rule

An acceptance that is mailed within the allotted response time is effective **upon posting** (not upon receipt), unless the offer provides otherwise (e.g., where an offer requires acceptance by personal delivery on or before a specified date). The mailing must be properly addressed and include correct postage.

An acceptance is effective at dispatch; a rejection is effective upon receipt.

> **EXAM NOTE:** Keep in mind that the mailbox rule applies only to **acceptance,** and therefore it almost exclusively applies to bilateral contracts (where there is one promise in exchange for another promise), because unilateral contracts request action as acceptance.

i) Rejection following acceptance

If the offeree sends an acceptance and later sends a communication rejecting the offer, the acceptance will generally control even if the offeror receives the rejection first. If, however, the offeror receives the rejection first and detrimentally relies on the rejection, the offeree will be estopped from enforcing the contract.

ii) Acceptance following rejection

If a communication is sent rejecting the offer, and a later communication is sent accepting the contract, the mailbox rule will **not** apply, and the first one to be received by the offeror will prevail.

iii) Revocations effective upon receipt

Offers revoked by the offeror are effective upon receipt.

iv) Irrevocable offer

The mailbox rule does not apply if the offer is irrevocable, as is the case with an option contract, which requires that the acceptance be received by the offeror before the offer expires. Restatement (Second) of Contracts § 63(b), cmt. f.

v) Medium

If the acceptance is by "instantaneous two-way communication," such as telephone or traceable fax, it is treated as if the parties were in each other's presence. Restatement (Second) of Contracts § 64. There is little case law with regard to email and other forms of modern communication. However, the Restatement focuses on whether the medium of acceptance is reasonable (e.g., whether it is reliable, used by the offeror, used customarily in the industry, or used between the parties in prior transactions). Restatement (Second) of Contracts § 65.

c) Means of acceptance

The traditional view required acceptance to be delivered in the same manner as the offer (e.g., if the offer is sent by telegram, acceptance must also be sent by telegram).

The modern trend allows any reasonable method of acceptance. If the offeror specifically requires acceptance by a particular method, that method will generally control.

UCC § 2-206 provides that acceptance can be by any medium reasonable under the circumstances, unless a specific medium is unambiguously required by the offer.

2) Silence

Generally, silence does not operate as an acceptance of an offer, even if the offer states that silence qualifies as acceptance (or, more likely, implied acceptance), unless:

i) The offeree has reason to believe the offer could be accepted by silence, was silent, and intended to accept the offer by silence; or

ii) Due to previous dealings or pattern of behavior, it is reasonable to believe the offeree must notify the offeror if the offeree intends not to accept.

3) Notice

An offeree of a bilateral contract must give notice of acceptance (return promise). Because acceptance becomes valid when posted, a properly addressed letter sent by the offeree operates as an acceptance when mailed, even though the offeror has not yet received the notice.

Notice of acceptance of a unilateral contract is required only when the offeror is not likely to become aware that the act is being performed or if the offeror requests such notice in the offer. Notice would be required under the same circumstances when a bilateral contract was being accepted by performance.

d. Counteroffers and mirror-image rule

1) Common-law rule

Acceptance must mirror the terms of the offer. Any modifications of the terms of the offer act as a rejection of the offer and a making of a new offer. Mere suggestions or inquiries (including requests for clarification) in a response by the offeree do not amount to a counteroffer. A conditional acceptance will terminate the offer and act as a new offer from the original offeree.

2) UCC rule—battle of the forms

The UCC does not follow the mirror-image rule. Additional or different terms included in the acceptance of an offer generally do not constitute a rejection unless the offer expressly limits acceptance to the terms of the offer.

a) Between non-merchants or if only one party is a merchant

When the contract is for the sale of goods between non-merchants or between a merchant and a non-merchant, a definite and seasonable expression of acceptance or written confirmation that is sent within a reasonable time will operate as an acceptance of the original offer even if it states terms that are additional to or different from the offer unless the acceptance is made expressly conditional on the offeror's consent to the additional or different terms. The additional or different terms are treated as a proposal for addition to the contract that is to be separately accepted or rejected in order to become a part of the contract.

b) Both parties are merchants

When both parties are merchants, not only does an acceptance that contains additional terms create a contract, but such terms are also treated as part of the contract unless the additional terms materially alter the agreement or unless the offeror objects within a reasonable time. When terms in the acceptance are different from similar terms in the offer (e.g., a different delivery date), some jurisdictions cancel out differing terms and use the provisions of the UCC as gap-fillers (called the "knockout rule"). Other jurisdictions use the terms of the acceptance to determine the scope of the agreement.

2. Excuse

a. Mistake

A legal mistake for which a court may grant a remedy is a belief that is not in accord with the facts as to a basic assumption on which the contract is based that materially affects performance of the contract. A wrong prediction about a future event is not a legal mistake.

1) Unilateral mistake

When only one of the parties is mistaken as to an essential element of the contract existing when the contract was made, and the mistaken party did not bear the risk of the mistake, either party can enforce the contract on its terms, **unless** the mistake relates to a basic assumption of the contract and has a material impact on the deal, and **either:**

    i) The non-mistaken party knew or had reason to know that the other party was mistaken, or caused the mistake; or

    ii) The mistake would make the contract unconscionable.

2) Mutual mistake

Mutual mistake occurs when both parties are mistaken as to an essential element of the contract. In such a situation, there must be a substantial difference between the deal as it was contemplated and the actual deal, with *no intent by the parties to take a risk on that element* of the transaction.

> **EXAM NOTE:** Look for words such as "as is" that show that the buyer is assuming the risk.

3) Remedies

The contract is generally *voidable* by the party that was adversely affected by the mistake.

> **Example:** Rescission of a contract to sell a cow was granted on grounds of mutual mistake when both parties completed the exchange of the cow on the mistaken understanding that the cow was barren. *Sherwood v. Walker*, 66 Mich. 568, 33 N.W. 919 (1887).

a) Reformation

When a writing that evidences or embodies an agreement in whole or in part fails to express the agreement because of a mistake of both parties as to the contents or effect of the writing, the court may at the request of a party reform the writing to express the agreement, except to the extent that rights of third parties such as good-faith purchasers for value will be unfairly affected. When reformation of the contract is available to cure a mistake, neither party can avoid the contract. Restatement (Second) of Contracts § 155.

b. Misunderstanding

Because a contract is a **meeting of the minds,** no contract exists when both parties do not intend the same meaning. If the parties think they are agreeing to the same terms, but in fact assent to different terms, and neither party knows or should know that there is a misunderstanding, there is no contract.

c. Misrepresentation, nondisclosure, and fraud

A misrepresentation made in connection with an agreement may prevent the formation of the contract or make the contract voidable by the adversely affected party. The use of an "as is" provision can shift the risk to a buyer, in the absence of unconscionability.

1) Elements

A misrepresentation is an assertion about a material element of a contract that is contrary to the facts and that induces assent by the other party who justifiably relies on the assertion.

2) Nondisclosure

Nondisclosure of a known fact is tantamount to an assertion that the fact does not exist only if the party not disclosing the fact knows that:

  i)   Disclosure is necessary to prevent a previous assertion from being fraudulent;

  ii) Disclosure would correct a mistake of the other party as to a basic assumption and the failure to disclose would constitute lack of good faith and fair dealing;

  iii) Disclosure would correct a mistake of the other party as to the contents or effect of a writing evidencing their agreement; or

  iv) The other party is entitled to know the fact because of a confidential or fiduciary relationship.

3) Types

A misrepresentation may be innocent, negligent, or fraudulent. Fraud exists if the misrepresentation is made:

  i)   Knowingly;

  ii) Without confidence in the assertion (i.e., reckless disregard for its truth); or

  iii) When the person making the assertion knows that no basis exists for the assertion.

a) Fraud in the factum

Fraud in the factum (or fraud in the execution) occurs when the fraudulent misrepresentation prevents a party from knowing the character or essential terms of the transaction. In such a case, no contract is formed, and the apparent contract is *void* (i.e., not enforceable against either party), unless reasonable diligence would have revealed the true terms of the contract.

b) Fraud in the inducement

Fraud in the inducement occurs when a fraudulent misrepresentation is used to induce another to enter into a contract. Such a contract is *voidable* by the adversely affected party if she justifiably relied on the misrepresentation in entering into the agreement.

c) Non-fraudulent misrepresentation

Even if non-fraudulent, a misrepresentation can still render a contract *voidable* by the adversely affected party. The misrepresentation must be *material* (i.e., information that would cause a reasonable person to agree or that the person making the misrepresentation knows would cause this particular person to agree) and the adversely affected party must have justifiably relied on the misrepresentation.

d. Undue influence and breach of confidential relationship

A higher standard of conduct is expected of a party to a contract who has the trust or confidence of the other party as a result of a special relationship.

1) Undue influence

Undue influence can occur in a relationship when one party is dominant and the other dependent, either due to lack of expertise or experience, or because the dependent person has diminished mental capacity. In general, the dominant party to the contract will be held to a higher standard of fairness and disclosure than he will in a contract between arms-length parties.

2) Confidential relationship

When one party to a contract has a fiduciary relationship to the other (such as trustee to beneficiary, lawyer to client, doctor to patient, financial advisor to client, and in some cases parent to child), the burden of proving that the contract is fair is usually placed upon the fiduciary.

e. Duress

Any wrongful act or threat that deprives a party of meaningful choice constitutes duress. When a party's agreement is the result of physical duress, the contract is void. When the duress is in the nature of a threat, the contract is voidable.

C. CONSIDERATION AND SUBSTITUTES

In addition to offer and acceptance, most courts require valuable consideration for an agreement to be enforceable. If either party has not given consideration, the agreement is not enforceable upon formation.

1. Bargain and Exchange

Valuable consideration is evidenced by a bargained-for change in the legal position between the parties. Most courts conclude consideration exists if there is a detriment to the promisee, irrespective of the benefit to the promissor. A minority of courts look to either a detriment or a benefit, not requiring both. The Second Restatement asks only whether there was a bargained-for exchange. Restatement (Second) of Contracts § 71.

a. Legal detriment and bargained-for exchange

For the legal detriment to constitute sufficient consideration, it must be bargained for in exchange for the promise. The promise must induce the detriment, and the detriment must induce the promise ("mutuality of consideration").

Consideration can take the form of:

i)   A return promise to do something;

ii) A return promise to refrain from doing something legally permitted;

iii) The actual performance of some act; or

iv) Refraining from doing some act.

b. Gift distinguished

The test to distinguish a gift from valid consideration is whether the offeree could have **reasonably believed that the intent of the offeror was to induce the action.** If yes, then there is consideration, and the promise is enforceable.

A party's promise to make a gift is enforceable under the doctrine of promissory estoppel if the promisor/donor knows that the promise will induce substantial reliance by the promisee and the failure to enforce the promise will cause substantial injustice.

> **Example 1:** A promises to give B $1,000 when B turns 21. The act of B attaining the age of 21 is not a bargained-for event and is thus not sufficient consideration. Note: There can be no reliance on the promise because B will turn 21 regardless of A's promise, so promissory estoppel does not apply.
>
> **Example 2:** A offers B $1,000 if B quits smoking. A is bargaining for B to quit and thus B's act is sufficient consideration. Note: If B relied on A's promise of the payment, promissory estoppel also may apply.

2. Adequacy of Consideration

The basic concept of legal detriment is that there must be something of **substance,** either an act or a promise, which is given in exchange for the promise that is to be enforced.

a. Subjective value

The benefit to the promisor does not need to have an economic value. Regardless of the objective value of an item, as long as the promisor wants it, the giving of it will constitute adequate consideration (e.g., "a mere peppercorn is enough").

b. Preexisting duty rule

1) Common law

At common law, a promise to perform a preexisting legal duty does not qualify as consideration because the promisor is already bound to perform (i.e., there is no legal detriment). Note that if the promisor gives something in addition to what is already owed (however small) or varies the preexisting duty in some way (however slight), most courts find that consideration exists. Restatement (Second) of Contracts § 73.

> **Example 1:** A borrower knows that he owes a lender $1,000 today. The borrower promises to repay the loan if the lender promises to lend the borrower an addition $100. The borrower has not provided consideration for the lender's promise.
>
> **Example 2:** A borrower knows that he owes a lender $1,000 tomorrow. The borrower offers to pay the lender $900 today if the lender agrees to forego the additional $100. The lender accepts the offer. The borrower has provided the lender with consideration for the lender's promise.

2) Exception for a third party

There is an exception to the preexisting-duty rule when a third party offers a promise contingent upon performance of a contractual obligation by a party. Under the exception, the party's promise to the third party is sufficient consideration. Restatement (Second) of Contracts § 73.

> **Example:** C contracts with P for P to install plumbing in a house being built by C for H. C subsequently becomes insolvent and walks away from the project. H contracts with P and promises to pay P the same amount P would have received from C if P installs the plumbing. P's completion of the job constitutes consideration for the promise by H, even though P was already contractually obligated to C to do the work.

c. Modification

1) Common law

At common law, modification of an existing contract must be supported by consideration. Agreements to modify a contract may still be enforced if:

i) There is a rescission of the existing contract by tearing it up or by some other outward sign, and then the entering into a new contract, whereby one of the parties must perform more than he was to perform under the original contract;

ii) There are unforeseen difficulties, and one of the parties agrees to compensate the other when the difficulties are discovered; or

iii) There are new obligations on both sides.

2) UCC and consideration

A merchant's promise to keep an offer open need not be supported by consideration if it is in an authenticated writing.

No consideration is necessary to modify a contract for the sale of goods, although there is a requirement of good faith by both parties. Thus, if one party is attempting to extort a modification, it will be ineffective under the UCC. Good faith requires honesty in fact in the conduct or transaction concerned.

> **EXAM NOTE:** Be aware of the difference between common-law and UCC rules regarding contract modification. At common law, modifications require consideration; under the UCC, they require only good faith.

d. Accord and satisfaction

Under an accord agreement, one party to a contract agrees to accept different performance from the other party than what was promised in the existing contract. Generally, consideration is required for an accord to be valid.

When a creditor agrees to accept a lesser amount in full satisfaction of the debt, the original debt is discharged **only when there is some dispute** either as to the validity of the debt or the amount of the debt, **or where the payment is of a different type than called for under the original contract.**

A "satisfaction" is the performance of the accord agreement. It will discharge both the original contract and the accord contract.

> **EXAM NOTE:** Accord and satisfaction are usually indicated on an exam when a debtor notes on a check conspicuously that a lesser payment is "**payment in full**." Remember that if the creditor endorses the check without seeing the debtor's notation, or without making another notation reserving the creditor's rights, the accord and satisfaction defense will generally prevail. The issue more commonly rests on whether the fact pattern indicates that a good-faith dispute exists.

If an accord is breached by the debtor, the creditor can sue on either the original contract **or** under the accord agreement.

e. Illusory promises

An illusory promise is one that essentially pledges nothing, because it is vague or because the promisor can choose whether or not to honor it. Such a promise is not legally binding.

> **Example:** A promises "I will give B $100, at my option." B's promise is an illusory promise.

f. Requirements and output contracts

A requirements contract is a contract under which a buyer agrees to buy all it will require of a product from the other party. An output contract is a contract under which a seller agrees to sell all it manufactures of a product to the buyer. There is consideration in these agreements, as the promisor suffers a legal detriment. The fact that the party may go out of business does not render the promise illusory.

Under the UCC, any quantities under such a contract may not be unreasonably disproportionate to any stated estimates, or if no estimate is stated, to any normal or otherwise comparable prior requirements or output.

Good faith is required under the UCC with regard to requirements and output contracts. Thus, for example, if a buyer, in good faith, legitimately no longer needs the goods, it may cancel the contract.

g. Uncertain as to law or fact

Failing to assert a claim or defense that proves to be invalid does not constitute consideration, unless the claim or defense is in fact doubtful due to uncertainty of facts or law, or if the party failing to assert the claim or defense believes in good faith that it may be fairly determined to be valid. Restatement (Second) of Contracts § 74.

3. Modern Substitutes for Bargain

a. Past or "moral" consideration

Something given in the past is typically not good consideration because it could not have been bargained for, nor could it have been done in reliance upon the promise. There is a modern trend, however, toward enforcing such promises when necessary to "prevent injustice."

> **Example:** P sees D's horse running free and knows that D is out of town. P feeds and houses the horse for two weeks awaiting D's return. When D returns, D thanks P and promises to pay P $50 at the end of the month. This promise is usually unenforceable as un-bargained-for "past consideration."

In the above example, however, P may be able to recover in quasi contract under a theory of unjust enrichment if P expected to be compensated and D received a benefit from P's actions.

b. Promissory estoppel

Promissory estoppel (or "equitable estoppel") acts as consideration when a party makes a promise that reasonably could be foreseen to induce reliance by the other party, the other party relies on that promise, and injustice can be avoided only by enforcing the promise. The remedy may be limited or adjusted as justice requires.

Thus, a court might only partially enforce a contract, depending on the circumstances.

> **EXAM NOTE:** Always consider whether there is a valid contract before considering promissory estoppel as the correct answer.

1) Charitable subscriptions

Although courts often claim to apply the doctrine of promissory estoppel to enforce promises to charitable institutions, they normally do not require evidence of reliance.

> **Example:** If A promises to give a university $1,000,000, and the university purchases land in reliance upon the promise, then the promise is enforceable under the doctrine of promissory estoppel.

c. Debts barred by the statute of limitations

A new promise to pay a debt after the statute of limitations has run is enforceable without any new consideration.

D. DEFENSES TO FORMATION

1. Capacity to Contract

Parties to a contract must be competent (i.e., have the legal capacity to be held to contractual duties). Incompetency arises because of infancy, mental illness or defect, guardianship, intoxication, and corporate incapacity.

a. Infancy

1) Disaffirmance

Infants (in most states, individuals who are under the age of 18) do not have the capacity to contract. When a contract is made by an infant with a person who does not lack capacity, it is **voidable** by the infant but not by the other party. This means that the infant may either disaffirm (void) the contract and avoid any liability under it or choose to hold the other party to the contract. The disaffirmance must be effectuated either before the individual reaches the age of majority or within a reasonable time thereafter. If the contract is not disaffirmed within a reasonable time after the individual reaches the age of majority, then the individual is deemed to have ratified the contract. If the contract is disaffirmed, the individual must restore any benefits received under the contract, if possible. Restatement (Second) of Contracts § 14.

2) Liability for necessities

When necessities are furnished to the infant, the infant must pay for them, but the recovery by the person furnishing the necessities is limited to the **reasonable value** of the services or goods (not the agreed-upon price). Recovery is under a theory of quasi contract.

Food, shelter, and clothing are clearly necessities. Statutory exceptions may also encompass insurance contracts and student loans.

b. Mental illness

If a party is adjudicated mentally incompetent and is under guardianship, contracts made by the individual are *void*. On the other hand, if there has been no adjudication or guardianship, the contracts are *voidable* and may be disaffirmed if the person is unable to understand the nature and consequences of the transaction or unable to act in a reasonable manner with regard to the transaction, and the other party has reason to know of this fact. If a contract is made during a lucid period, the contract is fully enforceable, unless the person has been adjudicated incompetent. A mentally incompetent person would be liable for the reasonable value of necessities furnished by another party, as in the case of infants (*see* § I.D.1.a., *supra*).

c. Guardianship

If a party's property is under guardianship by reason of an adjudication (such as for mental illness or defect, habitual intoxication, narcotics addiction, etc.), that party has no capacity to contract.

d. Intoxication

Intoxication of a party to a contract resulting from alcohol or drugs renders a contract *voidable* if the person entering into the contract was unable to understand the nature of the transaction and the other party had reason to know of the intoxication. Generally, the intoxicated party would be liable in quasi contract for the fair value of the goods or services furnished.

e. Corporate incapacity

When a corporation acts *ultra vires* (outside its powers), the contract is voidable. Most states allow recovery in *quantum meruit* if one party performs on the contract.

2. Illegality

If the consideration or performance that is to occur under a contract is illegal, then the contract itself is illegal and is unenforceable. If a contract contemplates illegal conduct, it is void. If a contract becomes illegal after it is formed, the duty to perform under the contract is discharged. Note that a contract is "illegal" for contract purposes when it contravenes a statute or a rule of common law; it need not involve activity that results in criminal penalties.

Examples of illegal contracts include contracts that are usurious, against public policy (e.g., contracts in restraint of marriage), for the commission of a tort or crime, or in restraint of trade.

a. Effect of illegality

Illegal transactions are not recognized or enforceable, restitution is not awarded for consideration, and no remedy is available for partial performance.

b. Exceptions

1) Ignorance

Where one party is justifiably ignorant of the facts making the contract illegal, that party may recover if the other party to the contract acted with knowledge of the illegality.

2) Party lacks illegal purpose

If only one party has an illegal purpose, the other party can recover if he did not know of the illegal purpose or knew of the illegal purpose but did not facilitate that purpose and the purpose does not involve serious moral turpitude.

> **Example:** A seller of gambling equipment can recover the price, as long as he did not become involved in illegal gambling using the equipment. *This is true even if the seller knows of the illegal purpose.*

3) Divisible contracts

Some contracts can be easily separated into legal and illegal parts so that recovery is available on the legal part(s) only.

> **Example:** The reasonable portion of a non-compete covenant can be enforced.

4) *Pari delicto* (equally at fault)

When the parties are at equal fault, neither party can claim breach of the contract by the other. If the parties are not *in pari delicto,* the "less guilty" party may be able to recover consideration from the other.

3. Unconscionability

A court may modify or refuse to enforce a contract or part of a contract on the grounds that it is "unconscionable." UCC § 2-302.

An entire contract or a contract provision is substantively unconscionable when it is so unfair to one party that no reasonable person in the position of the parties would have agreed to it. The contract or a contract provision must have been offensive at the time it was made. Unconscionability may also be applied to prevent unfair surprise. Boilerplate contract provisions that are inconspicuous, hidden, or difficult for a party to understand have been held unconscionable. Courts have also applied the doctrine of unconscionability where the process of bargaining was so unfair that the weaker party had no meaningful choice (i.e., procedural unconscionability), such as a contract of adhesion (i.e., a take-it-or-leave-it contract). Under either type of unconscionability, there usually is greatly unequal bargaining power between the parties.

The question of whether a contract is unconscionable is a question of law for the court to decide; the issue does not go to the jury.

4. Public Policy

Even if a contract is neither illegal nor unconscionable, it may be unenforceable if it violates a significant public policy (e.g., contracts in restraint of marriage).

E. IMPLIED-IN-FACT CONTRACTS AND QUASI CONTRACTS

1. Implied-In-Fact Contracts

When a person verbally expresses assent to an offer, the resulting agreement is characterized as an express contract. When a person's assent to an offer is inferred solely from the person's conduct, the resulting agreement is typically labeled an "implied-in-fact" contract. To be contractual bound, a person must not only intend the conduct but also know or have reason to know that his conduct may cause the offeror to understand that conduct as assent to the offer.

> **Example:** B joins a tour group that is walking through a downtown area learning about landmark buildings. Although B knows that members of the group have each paid the guide $15, he believes that his presence does not add to the guide's existing duties to the group. The tour guide can charge B the same fee paid by other members of the tour group because B's assent to the payment of the fee can be inferred from his conduct in joining the group.

2. Implied-In-Law ("Quasi") Contracts

When a person confers a **measurable benefit** on another, the person has **acted without gratuitous intent** (e.g., reasonably expected compensation), and allowing the other to **keep the benefit without cost is unfair,** the court can imply a "quasi contract" (or implied-in-law contract) as a method of recovery. The unfairness may arise when the recipient had the opportunity to decline the benefit but instead knowingly accepted it, or the actor had an excuse for not giving the recipient such an opportunity, such as in an emergency. This type of contract prevents unjust enrichment in cases not only in which there is no contract, but also in which there is a failed contract or a divisible contract.

When a quasi contract is implied, a promise is implied that requires the defendant to make restitution to the plaintiff, such as damages equal to the fair value of the benefit.

Example: Gardner arrives to install a sprinkler in Bill's neighbor's yard, but he accidentally starts to work in Bill's yard. Bill looks out the window and sees Gardner installing a sprinkler in his own yard and does nothing. If Gardner sued Bill, the court would find a contract implied-in-law, and the court would have the discretion to set the amount of compensation, usually the fair market value of the benefit that was conferred.

F. PRE-CONTRACT OBLIGATIONS

1. Option Contract

Generally, an offer is revocable at any time, even if the offeror has agreed to keep the offer open for a specified time. An offer can be made irrevocable, however, if the offeror promises to keep the offer open for a specific period of time *and* that promise is supported by consideration. An option contract is then formed, and the offeree usually pays an agreed amount to the offeror in order to make the offer irrevocable.

2. Construction Contracts and Promissory Estoppel

In the construction industry, an agreement not to revoke a sub-bid offer is enforceable under the theory of promissory estoppel. It would be unjust to permit the subcontractor to revoke a bid after inducing justifiable and detrimental reliance in the general contractor.

Because the sub-bid is only an outstanding offer, the **general contractor is not bound** to accept it upon becoming the successful bidder for the general contract. A general contractor can enter into a subcontract with another for a lower price.

G. WARRANTIES IN SALE-OF-GOODS CONTRACTS

UCC Article 2 allows not only for express warranties, but also for the implied warranties of merchantability and fitness for a particular purpose.

1. Express Warranty

Any promise, affirmation, description, or sample that is part of the basis of the bargain is an express warranty, unless it is merely the seller's opinion or commendation of the value of the goods. The use of a sample or model will create a warranty that the goods the buyer is to receive will be like the proffered sample or model.

Note that an express warranty can be made subsequent to the contract for sale. Technically, this would modify the original agreement, and under the UCC, no consideration is needed to make a modification enforceable.

Disclaimer clauses that conflict with express warranties are **ignored.**

> **EXAM NOTE:** A seller's opinion will not create an express warranty.

2. Implied Warranty of Merchantability

A warranty of merchantability is implied whenever the seller is a merchant. To be merchantable, goods must be fit for their ordinary purpose and pass without objection in the trade under the contract description. A breach of this warranty must have been present at the time of the sale.

Unless the circumstances indicate otherwise, the warranty can be disclaimed by use of "as is," "with all faults," or similar language that makes plain that there is no implied warranty. The disclaimer may be oral, but it must use the term "merchantability" and must be conspicuous if in writing.

If the buyer, before entering into the contract, has examined the goods or a sample or model as fully as the buyer desires, or has refused to examine the goods, there is no implied warranty with respect to defects that an examination ought to have revealed to the buyer.

3. Implied Warranty of Fitness for a Particular Purpose

A warranty that the goods are fit for a particular purpose is implied whenever the seller has reason to know (from any source, not just the buyer) that the buyer has a particular use for the goods and the buyer is relying upon the seller's skill to select the goods.

Note that this warranty will apply to any seller (i.e., the seller need not be a merchant for it to apply).

An implied warranty of fitness for a particular purpose can be disclaimed by general language (including by the use of "as is"), but the **disclaimer must be in writing and be conspicuous.**

II. THIRD-PARTY BENEFICIARY CONTRACTS

A third-party beneficiary contract results when the parties to a contract intend that the performance by one of the parties is to benefit a third person who is not a party to the contract.

A. CREDITOR AND DONEE BENEFICIARIES

The Restatement (First) of Contracts classifies third-party beneficiaries as creditor or donee beneficiaries. If performance of a promise would satisfy an actual or supposed or asserted duty of the promisee to a third party, and the promisee did not intend to make a gift to the third party, then the third party is called a **creditor beneficiary.** A creditor beneficiary has the right to sue either the promisor or promisee to enforce the contract.

> **Example:** A agrees to paint B's house in return for B's promise to pay $500 to C, because A owes C $500. C is an intended beneficiary and can recover the $500 from B.

If the promisee entered the contract for the purpose of conferring a gift on a third party, the third-party **"donee beneficiary"** is given the right to sue the promisor.

> **Example:** A pays B to build a house for C. C is a donee beneficiary of the contract between A and B.

The Restatement (Second) of Contracts abandons the "donee beneficiary" and "creditor beneficiary" categories. Instead, a third party can recover if she is an "intended beneficiary." Otherwise, she is said to be an "incidental beneficiary," with no rights to enforce the contract.

B. INTENDED BENEFICIARIES

An intended beneficiary is one to whom the promisee wishes to make a gift of the promised performance or to satisfy an obligation to pay money owed by the promisee to the beneficiary. The promisee must have an intention (explicit or implicit) to benefit the third party, otherwise the beneficiary is incidental.

Example: If A agrees to paint B's house in return for B's promise to pay $500 to C, C is an intended beneficiary and can recover the $500 from B.

C. INCIDENTAL BENEFICIARIES

An incidental beneficiary is one who benefits from a contract even though there is no contractual intent to benefit that person. An incidental beneficiary has no rights to enforce the contract.

Example: A promises to buy B a car from dealership C. The dealership is an incidental beneficiary with no grounds upon which to recover if A reneged on the promise.

D. VESTING OF BENEFICIARY'S RIGHTS

Only an intended beneficiary has a right to bring an action on the contract. An intended beneficiary of a "gift promise" (a donee beneficiary) may sue only the promisor. If the promisee tells the donee beneficiary of the contract and should reasonably foresee reliance, and the beneficiary does so rely to her detriment, promissory estoppel would apply. An intended beneficiary to whom the promisee owed money (a creditor beneficiary) may sue either the promisor or the promisee, or both, on the underlying obligation, but only one recovery is allowed.

1. When Rights Vest

The rights of an intended beneficiary vest when the beneficiary:

  i) **Materially changes position in justifiable reliance** on the rights created;

  ii) **Expressly assents** to the contract at one of the parties' request; or

  iii) **Files a lawsuit** to enforce the contract.

2. Effect of Vesting on Original Parties

Once the beneficiary's rights have vested, the original parties to the contract are both bound to perform the contract. Any efforts by the promisor or the promisee to rescind or modify the contract after vesting are void, **unless the third party agrees** to the rescission or modification.

E. DEFENSES

The promisor can raise any defense against the third-party beneficiary that the promisor had against the original promisee. Therefore, the beneficiary also becomes liable for counterclaims on the contract that the promisor could establish against the promisee. This liability can never exceed the amount that the promisor owes under the contract.

Example: A agrees to paint B's house in return for B's promise to pay $500 to C, to whom A owes $500. If the statute of limitations (or any other contractual defense) precludes A (the promisee) from recovering against B (the promisor), it will also preclude C (the intended creditor beneficiary) from recovering against B on the contract.

The promisor may not assert any defenses that the promisee would have had against the intended beneficiary.

> **Example:** In the example above, if the statute of limitations precluded C from recovering against A on the debt A owed to C, that would not affect B's obligation to C.

III. ASSIGNMENT OF RIGHTS AND DELEGATION OF DUTIES

A. DEFINITIONS

"**Assignment**" is the **transfer of rights** under a contract, and "**delegation**" is the **transfer of duties and obligations** under a contract.

B. ASSIGNMENT OF RIGHTS

Almost all contract rights can be assigned. Partial assignments are permissible, as is the assignment of future or unearned rights.

1. Limitations on Assignment

An assignment is not allowed, however, if it materially increases the duty or risk of the obligor or materially reduces the obligor's chance of obtaining performance. In addition, a contract provision can render an otherwise allowable assignment void (e.g., "any assignment of rights under this contract is void") and unenforceable by the assignee against the obligor. By contrast, a contract provision that merely prohibits an assignment (e.g., "An assignment of rights under this contract is prohibited"), while giving rise to an action for breach against the assignor, does not operate to prevent the assignor from assigning those rights (the assignor retains the power to make an assignment) nor the assignee from suing the obligor. Unless circumstances indicate the contrary, the prohibition on the assignment of a contract (e.g., "this contract may not be assigned"), does not affect the assignment of contract rights, but only bars the delegation of duties.

> **NOTE:** Courts often narrowly interpret a prohibition provision, such as by finding that such a provision only applies to a specific contractual right, and that the assignment in question thus did not violate the provision.

2. Requirements

No formalities are needed for an assignment, but there must be a present intent to transfer the right immediately. No consideration is needed, but the lack of consideration would affect revocability of the assignment.

> **Distinguish promise of a future payment:** A promise by a party to a contract to pay to monies received pursuant to the contract to third party is not an assignment of the party's contractual rights, but a promise of a future payment. As a consequence, the third party is not an assignee of the contract.

3. Rights of the Assignee

An assignee **takes all of the rights of the assignor as the contract stands at the time of the assignment** but takes **subject to any defenses that could be raised against the assignor.** The rights of the assignee are subject to set-off if the transaction giving rise to the set-off occurred prior to the time the obligor was given notice of the assignment. The assignee is also subject to any modification of the contract made prior to the time the obligor obtained notice of the assignment. Thus, payment by the obligor to the assignor can be raised as a defense, provided the payment was made before the obligor had notice of the assignment.

A subsequent assignment of the same right(s) revokes any prior *revocable* assignment. If the first assignment was an *irrevocable* assignment, the first assignee will have priority over the second assignee, unless the second assignee is a bona fide purchaser for value without notice of the first assignment, in which case, the assignee who obtains payment from the obligor or judgment first will have priority. If the second assignee knows about a prior assignment, he is estopped from asserting claim over the first assignee even if he would have otherwise prevailed.

C. DELEGATION OF DUTIES

1. In General

Generally, obligations under a contract can be delegated, unless the other party to the contract has a substantial interest in having the delegating individual perform (for example, in a personal services contract involving taste or a special skill) or when delegation is prohibited in the contract.

When obligations are delegated, the **delegator is not released from liability,** and recovery can be had against the delegator if the delegatee does not perform.

2. Novation

A novation is the substitution of a new contract for an old one, where the original obligor is released from his promises under the original agreement. A novation may be express or implied after delegation if (i) the original obligor repudiates liability to the original promise, **and** (ii) the obligee subsequently accepts performance of the original agreement from the delegatee, without reserving rights against the obligor.

3. Effect of Delegation of Performance under the UCC

Under UCC § 2-210(5), any delegation of performance under a contract for the sale of goods may be treated by the other party as creating reasonable grounds for insecurity. The other party may, without prejudice to her rights against the delegator, demand assurances from the delegatee (pursuant to UCC § 2-609, discussed at § VII.B.2.-3., *infra*).

IV. STATUTE OF FRAUDS

A. WRITING REQUIRED

Generally, oral contracts are enforceable. However, contracts that fall within the Statute of Frauds are *unenforceable* unless they are *in writing.* The writing must:

i) Be signed by the party to be charged (i.e., the person against whom enforcement is sought); and

ii) Contain the essential elements of the deal.

The writing need not be formal (i.e., receipts or correspondence can serve as memoranda). The essential elements may be in more than one writing only if one of the writings references the other(s). The writing need not be delivered. Even if it is lost or destroyed, it still operates to satisfy the Statute of Frauds, and its prior existence can be proved by oral evidence.

> **EXAM NOTE:** Note that a memorandum sufficient to satisfy the Statute of Frauds does not need to be written at the time a promise is made. The memorandum also does not have to be addressed to the promisee to be enforceable by the promisee.

B. TYPES OF CONTRACTS WITHIN THE STATUTE OF FRAUDS

Most states require that these five categories of contracts be in writing:

Marriage - A contract made upon consideration of marriage;

Suretyship - A contract to answer for the debt or duty of another;

Land - A contract for the sale of an interest in land;

One year - A contract that cannot be performed within one year from its making; and

UCC - Under the UCC, a contract for the sale of goods for a price of $500 or more.

> **EXAM NOTE:** You can remember which types of contracts are governed by the Statute of Frauds by using the mnemonic **MS. LOU** (Marriage, Suretyship, Land, One year, UCC).

1. Marriage Provision

Any agreement in consideration of marriage is within the Statute of Frauds, except mutual promises by the two to marry each other.

2. Suretyship Provision

a. Rule

Suretyship is a three-party contract, wherein one party (surety) promises a second party (obligee) that the surety will be responsible for any debt of a third party (principal) resulting from the principal's failure to pay as agreed. A suretyship induces the second party to extend credit to the third party. A promise to answer for the debt of another must generally be in writing to be enforceable.

> **EXAM NOTE:** Remember that the surety must promise the **creditor or obligee,** not just the principal, that she will pay the debt of the principal.

b. Exceptions

1) Indemnity contracts

Indemnity contracts (i.e., a promise to reimburse for monetary loss) do not fall within the Statute of Frauds.

2) Main purpose exception

In addition, if the main purpose of the surety in agreeing to pay the debt of the principal is for the surety's own economic advantage, rather than for the principal's benefit, the contract will not fall within the Statute of Frauds, and an oral promise by the surety will be enforceable.

3. Land Contracts

a. Types

A promise to transfer or buy *any interest in land* is within the Statute of Frauds. The Statute of Frauds does not apply to the conveyance itself (which is governed by separate statutes everywhere) but rather to a *contract providing for* the subsequent conveyance of land.

The following transfers are excluded from the rule: licenses, leases, and assignments of mortgages. However, the one-year rule does apply to such transfers. Consequently, a lease, license, or easement for **more than one year** must be in writing.

b. Part performance

Even if an oral contract for the transfer of an interest in real property is not enforceable at the time it is made, **subsequent acts** by either party that show the existence of the contract may make it enforceable, even without a memorandum. Such acts include:

i) Payment of all or part of the purchase price;

ii) Possession by the purchaser; or

iii) Substantial improvement of the property by the purchaser.

c. Full performance

When a party to an oral contract who has promised to convey real property performs, that party can enforce the other party's oral promise unless the promise is itself the transfer of a real property interest.

> **Example:** During a face-to-face conversation, a seller agrees to transfer land to the buyer in exchange for the buyer's promise to pay $50,000 to the seller. The seller tenders the deed to the buyer and the buyer accepts the deed. The seller can enforce the buyer's oral promise to pay $50,000 to the seller.

4. One-Year Provision

Contracts that **cannot** be performed within one year due to the constraints of the terms of the agreement must be in writing. The year starts **the day after** the contract is made. It is the time that the contract is made that is important, not the length of performance.

Note that the fact that a contract is not completed within one year does not mean that it is voidable under the Statute of Frauds. For the Statute of Frauds to apply, the *actual terms* of the contract must make it impossible for performance to be completed within one year.

Full performance will generally take the contract out of the Statute of Frauds. While part performance would not take the contract out of the Statute of Frauds, restitution would be available to the party who performed.

> **EXAM NOTE:** The test is whether the contract can be performed within one year, not whether it is likely to be performed within one year.

5. Sale of Goods for $500 or More

a. Sufficiency of the writing

When the price of goods is at least $500, the UCC requires a memorandum of the sale that must:

i) Indicate that a contract has been made;

ii) Identify the parties;

iii) Contain a quantity term; and

iv) Be signed by the party to be charged.

The memorandum needs to be signed only by the party being sued; it does not need to be signed by both parties.

A mistake in the memorandum or the omission of other terms does not destroy its validity. An omitted term can be proved by parol evidence.

Enforcement is limited to the quantity term actually stated in the memorandum.

> **EXAM NOTE:** To satisfy the Statute of Frauds, the above terms must be in writing, but that writing need not be an actual contract. It doesn't even need to be contained on one piece of paper—a series of correspondence between the parties may suffice.

b. Exceptions

1) Specially manufactured goods

No writing is required if the goods are to be specially manufactured for the buyer, are not suitable for sale to others, and the seller has made "either a substantial beginning of their manufacture or commitments for their procurement." UCC § 2-201.

2) Payment and acceptance by seller

A contract is outside the UCC Statute of Frauds to the extent that payment has been made and accepted. UCC § 2-201(3)(c). When a portion of the purchase price for a single item has been paid, most courts treat the contract as enforceable.

3) Receipt and acceptance by buyer

A contract is outside the UCC Statute of Frauds to the extent that goods are received and accepted. UCC § 2-201(3)(c). Acceptance of a part of a commercial unit is acceptance of the entire unit. UCC § 2-606(2).

4) Failure to respond to memorandum (where both parties are merchants)

If both parties are merchants and a memorandum sufficient against one party is sent to the other party, who has reason to know its contents, and that receiving party does not object in writing **within 10 days,** the contract is enforceable against the receiving party even though he has not signed it.

c. Modifications

Under UCC § 2-209(3), the requirements of the UCC Statute of Frauds must be satisfied if the contract as modified is within its provisions. Any of the above exceptions would apply, though, to take a modification out of the Statute of Frauds.

The UCC would also enforce a provision in a contract for the sale of goods that required a modification to be in writing. Thus, even if the contract was for a sale of goods valued at less than $500 or involved one of the exceptions discussed above, if the contract specifically provided that any modification be in writing, the UCC would enforce that requirement. (*See* UCC § 2-902(2).) Note that under a common-law contract, a provision requiring a modification to be in writing even though the modification would not otherwise fall within the Statute of Frauds would not be enforceable.

V. PAROL EVIDENCE

As a general rule, evidence of prior or contemporaneous agreements is not admissible to contradict the terms of a written agreement when all of the terms are completely integrated into the four corners of the agreement. In order to invoke the parol evidence rule, it must be shown that the parties intended to adopt the writing as their entire agreement.

A. INTENT OF THE PARTIES

The intent of the parties determines whether there is total, partial, or no integration. Parol evidence cannot be used to contradict any term of a writing that is the final and complete expression of the agreement between the parties, and no evidence can be introduced as to any additional promises or representations made prior to the time of the writing. A merger clause (a clause in the agreement that states that the agreement contains all the terms) is evidence of the intent to integrate.

A partially integrated agreement can be supplemented, but a completely integrated agreement cannot. The rule does not prevent a party from proving that the agreement was not final, any defects in formation, or anything that helps interpret ambiguous terms.

B. OPERATION OF THE PAROL EVIDENCE RULE

1. Contradictory Evidence

Evidence that contradicts the writing is inadmissible unless it is determined that there was no intent to integrate the agreement of the parties into the writing.

2. Supplemental Evidence

Evidence that supplements a contract that is partially integrated is admissible if it is consistent with the writing and does not contradict the terms.

Patterns of previous conduct between the parties may be admissible to show a typical course of dealing.

3. Separate Deal

Even when there is full integration, evidence may be offered if it represents a distinct and separate contract.

4. Ambiguity

Evidence may be admitted for the purpose of interpreting or clarifying an ambiguity in the agreement. This can include evidence of trade usage or even local custom to show that a particular word or phrase had a particular meaning.

5. Proving a Defense

Evidence may be admitted to prove a defense such as fraud in the inducement, mistake, failure of consideration, or failure of a condition, or to prove that the contract is void or voidable.

6. Condition Precedent

Parol evidence may also be admitted to prove a condition precedent to the existence of the contract.

7. Subsequent Agreements

The parol evidence rule does not apply to evidence of agreements between the parties subsequent to execution of the writing.

Example: Handyman has a contract with Eric to refinish Eric's deck for $300. While there, Eric asks him if he could also fix the gutter for $60. If Eric does not pay Handyman for fixing the gutter, Handyman can introduce extrinsic evidence.

8. Where Parties Attach Different Meanings

Under the Restatement (Second) of Contracts, when the parties have attached different meanings to a term in a contract, the meaning that controls will be the meaning attached by one of them, if at the time the agreement was made that party did not know of any different meaning attached by the other, and the other party knew the meaning attached by the first party.

C. UCC PAROL EVIDENCE RULE

Under UCC § 2-202, with regard to sales contracts, no evidence is admissible to show prior written or oral agreements, or contemporaneous oral agreements contradicting the contract. However, a contract can be explained or supplemented by evidence of trade usage, or course of dealings or performance. Unless the contract is found to be a complete and exclusive statement of terms, evidence of consistent additional terms may be admitted.

> **EXAM NOTE:** Remember, evidence that would be naturally omitted from a contract and does not contradict the terms of the contract usually is admissible. Any evidence that contradicts the contract will not be admissible.

VI. CONDITIONS

A condition is a future and uncertain event that must take place before a party's rights or obligations are created, destroyed, or enlarged.

Conditions must be distinguished from promises, which may be the difference between a minor breach and a complete prevention of the other party's duty to perform. If the contractual provision purports to be a statement by the party required to perform, the provision is a promise; if it is a statement by the non-performing party, it is a condition. Ambiguity is usually resolved in favor of a promise over a condition.

> **EXAM NOTE:** Remember, the failure of a **condition** relieves a party of the **obligation** to perform; the failure of a **promise** constitutes **breach**.

A condition may be express (clearly stated in the agreement), or implied (presumed based on the nature of a transaction).

A. TYPES OF CONDITIONS

1. Express Conditions

Express conditions are expressed in the contract. Words in the contract such as "on condition that" or "provided that" are typical example of express conditions. Express conditions must be complied with literally; substantial performance will not suffice. Arbitration clauses are enforceable, except when a consumer might be waiving important substantive rights.

> **EXAM NOTE:** Express conditions must be explicit. A court will not enforce a condition if the language creating the condition is ambiguous. However, where the condition is explicit, it will be strictly enforced.

2. Implied Conditions

Implied conditions that are deemed to be part of the contract because the nature of the agreement suggests that the parties truly intended the condition but failed to expressly include it, are "implied in fact" conditions. These are distinguished from "constructive" or "implied in law" conditions, which are supplied by a court if reasonable under the circumstances. Restatement (Second) of Contracts § 226 cmt. c.

> **Example:** If a banquet hall is leased for a wedding on a certain date, and the building burns before that date, the law would imply the hall's existence as a condition to the payment of the lease price and would excuse the lessor from liability.

The most common types of court-supplied implied conditions are called "constructive conditions of exchange" and arise most frequently in construction and employment contracts. A court will imply that the builder or employee must perform first (at least "substantially") before the other side's performance (the payment of money) becomes due. In addition to good faith, the UCC implies a duty of cooperation on the parties when performance of one party is dependent upon the cooperation of the other party. If a party fails to cooperate, the other party may suspend her own performance without being in breach. UCC § 2-311(3).

Substantial performance is all that is required to satisfy an implied condition.

B. TIMING OF CONDITIONS

Performance by one or both of the parties may be made expressly conditional in the contract, and the conditions may precede the obligation to perform (**condition precedent**) or may discharge the duty to perform after a particular event occurs (**condition subsequent**).

Example: A agrees to hire B if B passes the bar exam. B agrees to work as a clerk for C until B passes the bar exam. B's passing the bar exam is a condition precedent to being hired by A, and a condition subsequent to B's employment with C.

If the condition is precedent, the plaintiff has the burden of proving that the condition occurred in order to recover; if the condition is subsequent, the defendant must prove the happening of the condition to avoid liability.

A condition is only a condition subsequent if it discharges a duty that is already absolute.

C. SATISFACTION OF CONDITIONS

The approach to determine whether a condition is satisfied is usually an objective standard based upon whether a reasonable person would be satisfied. In most contracts, it is easy to conclude that all conditions have been satisfied. In contracts based upon aesthetic taste, however, the occurrence of the condition may be more difficult to determine.

1. Satisfaction Clause

When the aesthetic taste of a party determines whether the other party's performance is satisfactory (e.g., painting a family portrait), satisfaction is determined under a subjective standard. Under this standard, if the party is honestly dissatisfied, even if the dissatisfaction is unreasonable, the condition has not been met. However, the party's dissatisfaction must be in good faith, or a claim of dissatisfaction can be a breach, such as when a party is asserting dissatisfaction merely to avoid its own contractual obligation. There is a preference for the objective standard when the matter subject to a party's satisfaction involves the quality of non-unique goods or workmanship, rather than aesthetic taste. Restatement (Second) of Contracts § 228.

2. Time-of-Payment Clause

A clause in a contract making payment conditioned on the occurrence of an event is usually construed as a mere guide as to time for payment rather than as an absolute condition that must occur before payment is due.

D. DISPUTES ABOUT PERFORMANCE

1. Bilateral Contract

A party to a bilateral contract cannot recover until performance is tendered to the other party.

2. Partial Performance

a. Meaning

The doctrine of substantial performance provides that a party who substantially performs can recover on the contract even though full performance has not been tendered. If a breach of a constructive condition is minor, it will not negate substantial performance. If a breach is material, however, it will negate substantial performance.

b. Applicability

No recovery is allowed for a willful breach, which implies some attempt to cheat the other party or to provide less than was called for by the contract. The doctrine of substantial performance does *not* apply either to express conditions or to contracts for the sale of goods.

c. Damages

In general, the party who substantially performed the contract can recover the contract price minus any amount that it will cost the other party to obtain complete performance as had been promised.

3. Strict Performance Under the UCC

Under the UCC, the basic obligations of a seller are to **transfer ownership** of the goods to the buyer and to **tender goods** conforming to the warranty obligations. In general, the UCC requires "perfect tender," and substantial performance will not suffice. Substantial performance does apply under the UCC to installment contracts (*see* § VI.D.5.b., *infra*) and when the parties agree that it applies. In addition, the UCC provides that if a buyer rejects goods as nonconforming and time still remains to perform under a contract, the seller has a right to cure and to tender conforming goods (*see* § VII.F.1.b., *infra*).

a. Transferring ownership

The UCC implies a warranty of title in all sales contracts, providing that the seller automatically warrants that (i) he is conveying good title, (ii) the transfer is rightful, and (iii) the goods are delivered free from any security interest of which the buyer has no knowledge at the time of the contract. Actual knowledge by the buyer of a security interest on the goods will nullify the warranty of title.

The UCC permits disclaimer of the warranty of title, but such disclaimer must be by specific language or circumstances that give the buyer reason to know that the seller does not claim rightful title or that the seller is only purporting to sell such right as the seller or a third person possesses.

b. Tendering goods

The seller must tender the goods in accordance with the contract provisions or in accordance with the code provisions if the contract is silent on tender.

1) Time of tender

In the absence of a specific contract provision otherwise, the goods must be tendered within a reasonable time after the contract is made. UCC § 2-309.

2) Manner of tender

Unless otherwise provided in the contract, the goods are to be delivered in one delivery, unless the circumstances give either party a right to make or demand delivery in lots (as where a party would clearly have no room to store the goods if delivered all at once). UCC § 2-307.

3) Place of tender

Unless otherwise provided in the contract, the place of tender will be the seller's place of business (or residence, if the seller has no place of business), unless the goods are identified and the parties know that they are at some other location, in which case that location will be the place of tender. UCC § 2-308.

4) Method of tender

The four methods of tender are:

a) Seller's place of business

If the goods are tendered at the seller's place of business, the seller must place the goods at the disposition of the buyer and give the buyer notice, if notice is necessary to enable the buyer to take delivery.

b) Shipment contract

If the contract is a shipment contract, the seller must deliver the goods to the carrier, make a proper contract for their shipment, obtain and deliver any document necessary for the buyer to obtain possession of the goods, and give the buyer notice that the goods have been shipped.

c) Destination contract

If the contract is a destination contract, the seller must deliver the goods to a particular place (specified in the contract) and tender them there by holding the goods at the buyer's disposition and giving the buyer notice.

d) Goods in the hands of a bailee

The seller must bargain for a negotiable document of title or obtain acknowledgment from the bailee of the buyer's rights in the goods.

4. Buyer's Obligations

When a conforming tender is made, the buyer is obligated to accept and pay the price under the contract. Rejection amounts to breach of contract. A buyer has the right to inspect the goods to determine if the seller's obligations have been met.

5. Divisible or Installment Contracts

a. Common law

A divisible or installment contract is one in which the obligations imposed on the contracting parties can be separated into corresponding pairs of part performances such that each pair constitutes **agreed equivalents**. Recovery is limited to the performance promised for the corresponding portion of the contract that has been performed. Damages may be recoverable for breach of other obligations under other portions of the contract.

b. UCC

Special rules apply to installment contracts for the sale of goods. The most important difference between installment contracts and other contracts is that the perfect-tender rule does not apply; instead, the right to reject is determined by a "substantial conformity" standard. UCC § 2-612.

1) Multiple shipments

Under the UCC, an installment contract is defined as one in which the goods are to be delivered in a number of shipments, and each shipment is to be separately accepted by the buyer. Parties cannot vary or contract out of this definition under the code. Payment by the buyer is due upon each delivery, unless the price cannot be apportioned.

2) Nonconforming segment

If the seller makes a nonconforming tender or tenders nonconforming goods under one segment of an installment contract, the buyer can reject only if the nonconformity:

    i)   Substantially impairs the value of that shipment to the buyer; and

    ii)   Cannot be cured.

3) Remaining segments

Where there is a nonconforming tender or a tender of nonconforming goods under one segment of an installment contract, the buyer may cancel the contract only if the nonconformity **substantially impairs** the value of the entire contract to the buyer.

E.   SUSPENSION OR EXCUSE OF CONDITIONS

If a condition is suspended, the condition is restored upon expiration of the suspension. If the condition is excused, then the party having the benefit of the condition can never raise it as a defense.

1.   Waiver

A party whose duty is subject to the condition can waive the condition, either by words or by conduct. Courts will find waiver of a condition only if the condition is not a material part of the agreement.

The condition may be reinstated if:

    i)   The waiving party communicates a retraction of the waiver before the condition is due to occur; and

    ii)   The other party has not already suffered detrimental reliance.

2.   Wrongful Interference

A duty of good faith and fair dealing is implied into **all** (both common-law and UCC) contracts. Included in this duty is a duty not to hinder the other party's performance and a duty to cooperate, where necessary. Accordingly, if the party whose duty is subject to the condition wrongfully interferes with the occurrence of that condition, the condition is excused, and the party wrongfully interfering has an absolute duty to perform.

3.   Election

A party who chooses to continue with a contract after a condition is broken effectively elects to waive that condition.

4.   Estoppel

A party who indicates that a condition will not be enforced may be estopped from using that condition as a defense if the other party reasonably relied on the impression that the condition had been waived.

VII.   BREACH OF CONTRACT AND REMEDIES

A.   BREACH OF CONTRACT

Once a duty to perform exists, nonperformance is a breach of contract unless the duty is discharged (e.g., by agreement, statute, inability to perform, etc.).

1. **Common Law**

   Under common law, a material breach of contract (i.e., when the non-breaching party does not receive the substantial benefit of her bargain) allows the non-breaching party to withhold any promised performance and to pursue remedies for the breach, including damages. If the breach is minor (i.e., the breaching party has substantially performed), the non-breaching party is entitled to any remedies that would apply to the non-material breach. If a minor breach is accompanied by an anticipatory repudiation (*see* § VII.B, *infra*), the non-breaching party may treat the breach as a material breach.

   The party who commits a material breach of his contract obligations cannot sue for contract damages, but he would ordinarily be entitled to the fair value of any benefit conferred on the non-breaching party.

   > **EXAM NOTE:** Keep in mind that under a minor breach, the non-breaching party may be able to recover damages, but also still must perform under the contract. If the breach is material, the non-breaching party does not need to perform.

2. **UCC**

   In general, under the UCC, the seller must strictly perform all obligations under the contract, or be in breach. The doctrine of substantial performance applies only in the context of installment contracts or where the parties so provide in their contract.

B. **ANTICIPATORY BREACH**

   The doctrine of anticipatory breach is applicable when a promisor repudiates a promise before the time for performance arises or elapses. The repudiation must be **clear and unequivocal** (as opposed to mere insecurity, which results in a demand for assurances), and it may be by conduct or words.

   1. **Non-Breaching Party's Options**

      Repudiation excuses the occurrence of any condition that would otherwise prevent the repudiating party's duty from being absolute. Upon repudiation, the promisee can treat the repudiation as a breach or ignore it and demand performance. If the repudiation is ignored, continued performance by the promisee must be suspended if the performance would increase the damages of the promisor.

      a. **Limitation on options—only payment due**

         Where the only performance left is the payment of money, the aggrieved party must wait until performance is due before filing suit. In this limited situation, repudiation is not treated as an anticipatory breach.

   2. **Retraction of Repudiation**

      At common law, repudiation may be retracted until such time as the promisee (i) acts in reliance on the repudiation, (ii) signifies acceptance of the repudiation, or (iii) commences an action for breach of contract. Notice of the retraction must be sufficient enough to allow for the performance of the promisee's obligations. Under the UCC, repudiation can be retracted if the other party has not canceled the contract or materially changed position.

   3. **Inapplicability to Unilateral Contracts**

      The doctrine of anticipatory repudiation **does not apply to a unilateral contract** when the offeror withdraws the offer once the offeree has begun to perform since offeree is not required to complete her performance.

4. **Prospective Inability to Perform—Right to Demand Assurances**

A party's expectations of performance by the other party may be diminished by an event that occurs after the contract was made. A party may request **adequate assurances of performance,** which, under the UCC, must be made in writing. Until such assurances are given, the requesting party may suspend performance. If those assurances are not provided within a reasonable time (30 days is the maximum time period under the UCC), the party can treat the failure to provide assurances as a breach by anticipatory repudiation. Even then, the repudiating party can still retract his repudiation until his next performance is due, unless the other party has already materially changed his position or otherwise indicated that he considers the repudiation final.

> **EXAM NOTE:** Do not excuse a party from performing solely on the ground that the party does not expect the other party to perform.

a. **UCC—merchants**

Under the UCC, between merchants, the reasonableness of grounds for insecurity and the adequacy of any assurance offered is determined according to commercial standards. Thus, for example, if a supplier writes to a manufacturer demanding assurances of financial solvency, and the manufacturer provides its latest audited financial statements as well as a satisfactory credit report from its banker, that would likely constitute adequate assurances of its financial status.

b. **Acceptance of improper delivery or payment**

The acceptance of any improper delivery or payment does not preclude an aggrieved party from demanding adequate assurance of future performance.

c. **UCC—insolvency**

1) **Remedies when the buyer is insolvent**

If the buyer becomes insolvent before the delivery of the goods, the seller can stop goods in transit and refuse delivery except for cash.

2) **Remedies when the seller is insolvent**

A buyer who has paid for identified goods may recover the goods if the seller became insolvent within 10 days after receipt of the first installment of the contract price. Any rights of the buyer, though, may be subordinate to rights of the seller's secured creditors.

C. **DAMAGES FOR BREACH OF CONTRACT**

The primary objective of contract damages is to put the non-breaching party in the same position as if no breach had occurred. It awards both the gains prevented by the breach and the losses sustained as a direct result of the breach.

1. **Expectancy Damages**

a. **In general**

Expectancy damages are those that arise naturally and obviously from the breach and are normally measured by the **market value of the promised performance less the consideration promised** by the non-breaching party.

> **Example:** B breaches a contract with A to fix A's car for $500. A finds another mechanic, C, to fix A's car for $700, which is the market value. A can recover $200 from B.

1) Construction contracts

In construction contracts, the general measure of damages for failing to perform a construction contract is the difference between the contract price and the cost of construction by another builder.

2) Sale of goods contracts

Damages for failing to deliver goods are measured by the difference between the contract price and the market value of the goods (or the cost of cover) (*see* § VII.F.1, *infra,* for a more detailed discussion of a buyer's damages under the UCC).

3) Real estate contracts

Damages for failing to perform a real estate sale contract also are measured by the difference between the contract price and the market value.

b. Partial performance

A partially performing party can generally recover for work performed, plus expectancy damages for the work not yet performed.

> **Example:** B agrees to paint A's house for $500, which covers $400 in supplies and labor and $100 in profit. After B paints half of the house and incurs $200 in costs, A breaches. B can recover the $200 of costs already incurred, and the $100 of profit, but not the remaining $200 of costs not yet incurred.

If at the time of a breach the only remaining duties of performance are (i) those of the party in breach and (ii) for the payment of money in installments not related to one another, then breach by non-performance as to less than the whole, whether or not accompanied or followed by a repudiation, does not give rise to a claim for damages for total breach and is a partial breach of contract only. Restatement (Second) of Contracts § 243.

1) Construction contracts

In construction contracts, damages for defective or incomplete construction are measured by the cost of repair or completion. The general measure of damages for failing to perform a construction contract is the difference between the contract price and the cost of construction by another builder.

2) Sale of goods contracts

By contrast, in contracts for the sale of goods, damages for nonconformity with the contract generally are measured by the difference between the value of the goods as warranted and the actual value of the tendered nonconforming goods (*see* § VII.F.1, *infra*).

The purpose of both measures is to place the plaintiff in as good a position as if the defendant had performed the contract according to its specifications.

c. Quantum meruit

The term "quantum meruit" describes the measure of damages for recovery on a contract that is "implied in fact" (*see* § I.E, *supra*). To recover under quantum meruit, one must show that the recipient:

i) **Acquiesced** in the provision of services;

ii) **Knew** that the provider expected to be compensated; and

iii) Was **unjustly enriched.**

2. **Consequential Damages and Foreseeability**

   a. **Consequential damages**

   Consequential damages are **reasonably foreseeable losses** to a non-breaching party that go beyond expectancy damages, such as loss of profits.

   b. **Foreseeability**

   Under *Hadley v. Baxendale*, 156 Eng. Rep. 145 (Ex. Ch. 1854), damages are recoverable if they were the natural and probable consequences of breach, or if they were "in the contemplation of the parties at the time the contract was made," or were otherwise foreseeable.

   c. **Causation**

   A defendant can defend on the ground that the losses that the plaintiff seeks to recover would have occurred whether or not the defendant breached the contract.

   d. **Certainty**

   In order to recover damages, a plaintiff must prove the dollar amount of the damages with reasonable certainty. Courts are hesitant to award damages for lost profits, as they are difficult to prove. When lost profits are considered too speculative, courts often limit a party's recovery to reliance damages.

3. **Liquidated Damages and Penalties**

   A provision for liquidated damages will be enforced, and not construed as a penalty, if the amount of damages is difficult to estimate at the time that the contract is entered into and the amount stipulated in the contract is reasonable in relation to either the actual damages suffered or the damages that might be anticipated at the time the contract was made.

   Although a contract may fix the amount of damages that are recoverable in the event of a breach, because a party may not be penalized for breach, penalty clauses are unenforceable.

4. **Punitive Damages**

   Punitive damages are very rarely available in contract actions. Some statutes apply them for the purpose of punishing fraud, violation of fiduciary duty, acts of bad faith, and for deterrence.

5. **Nominal Damages**

   Damages do not need to be alleged in a cause of action for breach. If no damages are alleged or none are proved, the plaintiff is still entitled to a judgment for "nominal" damages (e.g., one dollar).

6. **Mitigating Damages**

   A party to a contract has the obligation of avoiding or mitigating damages to the extent possible by taking such steps as to not involve undue risk, expense, or inconvenience. The non-breaching party is held to a standard of reasonable conduct in preventing loss.

   A failure to take reasonable steps to mitigate damages will defeat only a claim for consequential damages. It will not deprive a non-breaching party of the opportunity to claim damages measured by the difference between the contract and market prices.

Note: The failure to mitigate does not bar recovery; it only reduces the amount that may be recovered. Note that reasonable expenses as a result of efforts to mitigate damages can be recovered, even if not connected to a successful mitigation attempt.

D.   RESTITUTION AND RELIANCE RECOVERIES

1.   Restitutionary Damages

Restitutionary damages restore to the plaintiff whatever benefit was conferred upon the defendant prior to the breach and when it would be unjust for the defendant to retain that benefit. Under some circumstances, restitutionary damages may be recovered even though the plaintiff would have suffered a loss had the defendant not breached.

Thus, if A contracts with B to paint B's house for $500, and B repudiates the contract after A has done some, but not all, of the painting, and A shows that the fair value of the work that has been done is actually $1,000, most courts allow recovery of restitutionary damages ($1,000) on the theory that otherwise the defendant would be profiting from the breach.

If, however, at the time of the defendant's breach the plaintiff has **fully performed the contract** and the defendant owes only money and not some other kind of performance, the plaintiff is not permitted to recover restitutionary damages and is limited to expectancy damages (generally the contract price minus the cost of completion).

Restitutionary damages are also available in quasi contract (*see* § I.E.2., *supra*) when there is no contract between the parties or when a contract is unenforceable, and a lack of any recovery would be unjust given that a benefit was conferred on the other party. Recovery would be limited to the fair value of the benefit conferred.

2.   Reliance Damages

Reliance damages may be recovered when the non-breaching party incurs expenses in reasonable reliance upon the promise that the other would perform. Unlike with restitutionary damages, with reliance damages, there is no requirement that the defendant benefit from the plaintiff's expenditures. These types of damages are often awarded when the consideration for a contract is based on promissory estoppel. The court can also limit the remedy as justice requires.

E.   SPECIFIC PERFORMANCE, DECLARATORY JUDGMENT

1.   Specific Performance

When damages are an inadequate remedy, the non-breaching party may pursue the equitable remedy of specific performance.

a.   Factors considered

In determining whether damages are adequate, consider the:

i)   Difficulty of proving damages with reasonable certainty;

ii)   Difficulty of procuring a suitable substitute performance by means of money awarded as damages; and

iii)   Likelihood that an award of damages will be collected.

b. Real property

Contracts involving the transfer of an interest in real property may be enforced by an order of specific performance because every parcel of **real property is considered unique.**

c. UCC

Specific performance may be granted when the goods are rare or unique or in other circumstances, such as for breach of a requirements contract in which there is not another convenient supplier.

d. Limitations

Even if the remedy of damages is inadequate, specific performance will not be granted when the court cannot supervise enforcement. Thus, courts do not grant specific enforcement of contracts for personal services, although they may restrain the breaching party from working for another.

In addition, equitable defenses such as laches (prejudicial delay in bringing the action) or unclean hands (where the non-breaching party is guilty of some wrongdoing in the transaction at issue) would be available to the breaching party.

2. Declaratory Judgment

If the rights and obligations of the parties under a contract are unclear, and an actual dispute exists between the parties concerning those rights and obligations, either party may bring a declaratory judgment action to obtain an adjudication of those rights and duties. Declaratory judgment is not available, however, to resolve moot issues or theoretical problems that have not risen to an actual dispute.

F. REMEDIES UNDER THE UCC

The following sections more specifically address the remedies that are available to buyers and sellers under the UCC.

1. Buyer's Remedies

When the seller's time for performance arises, the seller may:

i) Do **nothing** (breach by the seller);

ii) Make a **nonconforming tender** (breach by the seller);

iii) Make a **conforming tender** (performance by the seller).

a. Failure to tender

Under the UCC, the buyer has several alternative remedies if the seller fails to tender the goods:

1) Damages

Recover the market price minus the contract price. The market price is the price that existed at the time of the breach at the place where tender was to occur under the contract.

The UCC also permits recovery for incidental and consequential damages resulting from the seller's breach. Consequential damages may be limited or excluded under the UCC unless such limitation or exclusion would be unconscionable. UCC § 2-719(3).

2) Cover

Purchase similar goods elsewhere and recover the replacement price minus the contract price.

3) Specific performance

Demand specific performance for **unique** goods.

4) Replevin

The buyer can obtain identified, undelivered goods from the seller if similar goods are unavailable in the marketplace, but only if:

    i)   The seller becomes insolvent within 10 days of receiving full or partial payment from the buyer; or

    ii)   The goods were at least partially paid for by the buyer and only for family, personal, or household purposes.

b. Nonconforming tender

Under the UCC, if either the tender or the goods are nonconforming, the buyer has the **right to accept or reject** all or part of the goods. (Note that a buyer has more restrictive options in installment contracts, as discussed in § VI.D.5., *supra*.)

The buyer has the **right to inspect** the goods before deciding whether to accept or reject. Payment does not constitute "acceptance" if there is no right of inspection before payment (e.g., C.O.D., C.I.F., or C & F contracts).

1) Rejection

a) Valid rejection

A valid rejection requires that the buyer:

    i)   Give notice to the seller;

    ii)   Within a reasonable time;

    iii)   Before acceptance.

b) Retain possession

The buyer must retain possession of rejected goods for a reasonable time to allow the seller to reclaim them.

c) Perishable and non-perishable goods

In the absence of other instructions from the seller, the buyer may store non-perishable goods at the seller's expense, reship them to the seller, or sell them for the seller's account. If the goods are perishable and the seller has no local agent to whom the goods can be returned, in the absence of other instructions from the seller, the buyer is required to sell the goods on the seller's behalf.

d) Remedies

The same remedies are available to the buyer after rejection as if no tender was made by the seller (i.e., damages (including incidental and consequential damages, unless properly limited or excluded), cover, specific performance, or replevin).

Note that a failure to give notice of the breach to the seller within a reasonable time after the buyer discovers or should have discovered the breach will preclude the buyer from any remedies.

2) Acceptance

Under the UCC, the buyer accepts goods by:

i)   Expressly stating acceptance;

ii) Using the goods; or

iii) Failing to reject the goods.

The buyer can revoke acceptance (which amounts to rejection), if acceptance was with a reasonable expectation that the seller would cure and the seller did not cure, or if the defect was hidden. The revocation must occur within a reasonable time after the nonconformity or defect was or should have been discovered, and notice must be given to the seller.

3) Right to cure

The seller has a right to cure a defective tender if:

i)   The time for performance under the contract has not yet elapsed; or

ii) The seller had reasonable grounds to believe the buyer would accept despite the nonconformity.

The seller must give notice of the intent to cure and make a new tender of conforming goods. If the seller had reasonable grounds to believe that the buyer would accept despite the nonconformity, the tender must be made within a reasonable time. Once cured, the tender is considered proper and valid.

2. Seller's Remedies

a. Right to price upon acceptance

Under the UCC, the price is due after the goods are physically delivered to the buyer and the buyer has an opportunity to inspect, unless the contract provides otherwise. If the buyer refuses to pay the price, the seller may sue for the price set forth in the contract. If the contract omits a price term, the UCC supplies a reasonable price at the time for delivery. If the contract provides that the parties will agree to a price in the future and they do not so agree, the UCC would impose a reasonable price.

b. Right to reclaim goods

If the buyer was insolvent when the goods were delivered and the price is not paid, the seller can recover the goods if demand is made in 10 days, as long as no good-faith sub-purchaser has bought the goods from the buyer. In a C.O.D. (cash on delivery) sale, the seller can reclaim the goods if the buyer's check bounces.

c. Wrongful rejection

If the buyer wrongfully rejects, the seller has three alternative remedies and would also be entitled to incidental damages.

1) Collect damages

The seller would ordinarily be entitled to the contract price minus the market price at the time and place for tender, together with any incidental damages, less any expenses saved as a result of the buyer's breach.

If that measure does not put the seller in as good a position as performance would have done, then the measure of damages will be the profit (including reasonable overhead) that the seller would have made from full performance by the buyer, together with any incidental damages, less any payments received or the proceeds of a resale of the goods.

2) Resell the goods

If the seller elects to resell and sue for the contract price minus the resale price, the resale must be (i) only of goods identified in the contract, and (ii) commercially reasonable.

3) Recover the price

The seller can recover the price after rejection only if the goods are not saleable in the seller's ordinary course of business.

The price is the price as defined in the contract or, if no price is defined in the contract, a reasonable price. The seller can retain deposits paid by the buyer up to the amount stated in a liquidated-damages clause, or, in the absence of such a provision, 20% of the value of performance or $500, whichever is less.

4) Incidental damages

Note that in **addition to** any of the three remedies listed above, the seller is entitled to recover incidental damages (including storage and shipping costs).

d. Lost volume seller

The seller can recover for lost profits if the seller has a large capacity to sell goods, the seller would have made a sale if the buyer hadn't breached, and the seller sold the goods to someone else. Because of the high capacity the seller has to sell the goods, the seller can recover for lost profits, which are calculated as the contract price minus the seller's costs.

3. Risk of Loss

a. General rules

The UCC assumes that the risk of loss is on the seller until some event occurs (i.e., the delivery obligations under the contract) that shifts the risk to the buyer.

If the goods are identified and the contract authorizes the seller to ship the goods by carrier, the event necessary to shift the risk of loss is dependent upon whether the contract is a "shipment" or "destination" contract (*see* § VI.D.3.b, *supra,* regarding shipment and destination contracts). If the contract is a "shipment" contract, risk of loss passes to the buyer when the seller gives possession of the goods to the carrier and makes a proper contract for their shipment. If the contract is a "destination" contract, risk of loss passes to the buyer when the seller tenders at the place specified in the contract.

If the contract does not require the transfer of the goods by carrier, risk of loss passes to the buyer upon the taking of physical possession if the seller is a merchant; otherwise, risk passes on tender of delivery, unless otherwise agreed.

b. Special rules

Remember these three special rules regarding risk of loss:

i) If the seller delivers nonconforming goods, the risk of loss remains on the seller until the buyer accepts or there is a cure;

ii) If the buyer rightfully revokes acceptance, the risk of loss shifts back to the seller to the extent of any lack of insurance coverage by the buyer;

iii) If the buyer repudiates or breaches after the goods have been identified but before the risk of loss shifts, the risk of loss is immediately shifted to the buyer to the extent of any lack of insurance coverage on the part of the seller.

c. Effect of placement of risk of loss

When risk of loss is on the buyer and the goods are lost or destroyed, the buyer will be liable for the contract price of the goods. If risk of loss is on the seller and the goods are lost or destroyed, the seller is liable for damages for non-delivery or must tender replacement goods.

4. Stoppage in Transit

A seller can stop the goods in transit due to the buyer's insolvency, but if due to the buyer's breach, goods can be stopped in transit only if shipped in carload lots.

The seller cannot stop goods in transit once the:

i) Buyer has received the goods;

ii) Carrier or warehouseman has acknowledged the buyer's rights;

iii) Goods have been reshipped by carrier; or

iv) Title has been given or negotiated to the buyer.

5. Insurable Interest

a. Seller's insurable interest

Under UCC Article 2, the seller retains an insurable interest as long as the seller retains title to the goods or has a security interest in them. Unless the contract specifies otherwise, the title passes from the seller to the buyer when the seller completes his or her delivery obligations. At that point, the seller's insurable interest ceases unless the seller retains a security interest in the goods.

b. Buyer's insurable interest

The UCC provides that the buyer obtains an insurable interest in the goods as soon as the goods are "identified to the contract."

6. Title and Good-Faith Purchasers

a. Entrusting provisions

The UCC provides that delivery of goods by the owner to one who sells goods of that kind gives to the transferee the power to convey good title to a buyer in ordinary course. A "buyer in ordinary course" is one who in good faith and without knowledge of a third party's ownership rights or security interest buys from someone selling goods of that kind.

b. Voidable title

When the true owner of goods sells them to another, but the sale is voidable because of fraud, because of lack of capacity, or because it was a cash sale and the buyer failed to pay or paid with a dishonored check, the buyer may transfer good title to a good-faith purchaser.

VIII. DISCHARGE

The promisor may not be liable for nonperformance if some supervening event or change in circumstances arises after formation of the contract that discharges the promisor's duty to perform.

A. IMPOSSIBILITY

The defense of impossibility is permitted only when performance is impracticable because of extreme and unreasonable difficulty or expense. The impossibility must be in the nature of the thing to be done (objective impossibility) and not in the inability of the promisor to do it (subjective impossibility).

The defense of impossibility usually is valid if:

    i)   Performance becomes illegal after the contract is made;

    ii)   The specific subject matter of the contract is destroyed;

    iii) The performing party in a personal-services contract dies or becomes incapacitated.

Note that a party may recover in quasi contract for any benefit that was conferred prior to impossibility.

> **EXAM NOTE:** If the contract is to perform services that can be delegated, it is not discharged by the death or incapacity of the party who was to perform the services.

The defense of impracticability is permitted when the subject matter of the contract is not destroyed but it is impracticable to perform.

The defense is valid if:

    i)   An unforeseeable event has occurred;

    ii)   Non-occurrence of the event is a basic assumption on which the contract was made;

    iii) The event made performance impracticable;

    iv) The party who is seeking discharge is not at fault; and

    v)   The party seeking discharge did not bear the risk.

B. FRUSTRATION OF PURPOSE

The doctrine of frustration of purpose applies when unforeseen events arise that make a contract impossible to perform, entitling the frustrated party to rescind the contract without paying damages.

Example: A contracts with B to buy a commercial building to rent, and while the sale is pending, the building is condemned by the city as unsafe for any use. A can back out of the purchase without obligation.

C. IMPRACTICABILITY OF PERFORMANCE UNDER THE UCC

The UCC implies three conditions into contracts for the sale of goods, which must be satisfied before performance is excused: (i) a contingency has occurred; (ii) the contingency has made performance impracticable; and (iii) the nonoccurrence of that contingency was a basic assumption upon which the contract was made.

1. **Total Impracticability**

   Impracticability of performance provides an excuse (defense) for nonperformance of the contract similar to impossibility at common law. This excuse exists when:

   i) Goods identified at the time of contracting are **destroyed**;

   ii) Performance becomes **illegal**; or

   iii) Performance has been made **"impracticable."**

   The excuse applies only when the event was not foreseeable and when nonoccurrence of the event was a basic assumption of the contract.

2. **Partial Impracticability**

   When impracticability affects only part of the seller's ability to perform, the goods actually produced must be apportioned among all the buyers with whom the seller has contracted. The buyer, however, may refuse to accept and may cancel the contract.

   When the agreed method of transportation or payment becomes impracticable, (i) the performing party must use a commercially reasonable substitute if available, and (ii) substitute performance must be accepted.

D. RESCISSION

The non-defaulting party to a contract can cancel or rescind the contract, which requires a return of any deposits or other benefit conferred on the other party.

Rescission can also occur by the mutual agreement of the parties. The surrender of rights under the original contract by each party is consideration for the rescission by mutual agreement.

In cases of third-party beneficiaries, a contract is **not** discharged by mutual rescission if the rights of the third-party beneficiary have already vested.

E. RELEASE

A release is a writing that manifests an intent to discharge another party from an existing duty. For common-law contracts, the release must generally be supported by consideration to discharge the duty.

Under the UCC, however, a claim or right can be discharged in whole or in part without consideration by a written waiver or renunciation signed and delivered by the aggrieved party. No consideration is needed to support the release.

Themis
Bar Review

Law School Essentials: CONTRACTS
To be used with online lecture

OVERVIEW OF CONTRACTS
Three BIG questions:
1. Has an enforceable contract been **formed**?
2. Has the contract been **performed/excused**?
3. What are the **remedies** for breach?

COMMON LAW OR THE U.C.C.
- Common Law = Services
- U.C.C. 2 = Goods
  - Applies to merchants and nonmerchants
- Mixed Contracts
  - Rule #1: All or nothing rule (exception: divisible contracts)
  - Rules #2: Predominant purpose test
- ❖ Conwell v. Gray Loon Outdoor Marketing Group *(Website creation and maintenance is a services contract)*

THE OFFER
Manifestation of willingness to enter agreement that creates power of acceptance
- Objective test
  - Ask: Would a reasonable person think outward words/actions manifested an intent to be bound?
  - Look for situations with humor or anger
- ❖ Embry v. Hargadine, McKittrick *(Employer's statement "don't let it worry you" was sufficient under the objective test; a reasonable person would interpret that as agreement to renew employment contract)*
- ❖ Lucy v. Zehmer *(Agreement on back of bar bill while intoxicated was still a serious intent to be bound.)*

DEFECTIVE FORMULATION OF AGREEMENT
Defective formulation (Two reasonable interpretations of material term on both sides)
- ❖ Raffles v. Wichelhaus *(Peerless Problem, no contract was formed)*

IS IT REALLY AN OFFER?
- Specific
- Genuine intent to be bound
- Directed at specific offeree (exception: contest/reward offers)
- Offer must give power to accept
- ❖ Lonergan v. Scolnick *(Seller told buyer via letter to act fast, but acceptance came after seller sold to another; court held no power of acceptance created because final round of approval remained with the seller)*

ADVERTISEMENTS
General Rule: Ads are not offers, but invitations to deal (except when specific w/ no room for negotiation)
- ❖ Leonard v. PepsiCo *(Court says the ad was a joke and it was an ad, thus not an offer to get a jet with Pepsi points)*
- ❖ Lefkowitz v. Great Minneapolis Store *(First come, first served for specific fur coat; court held because it was specific, it is an offer)*

ACCEPTANCE
Manifestation of willingness to enter the agreement
- Offeror is master of the offer
- Unilateral contract (acceptance by action)
- Bilateral contract (acceptance by return promise)
- ❖ Carlill v. Carbolic Smoke Ball Co *(Woman accepted offer in ad to pay anyone who used their smoke ball and still became sick; court held it was unilateral offer with acceptance by performance)*

COMMUNICATING ACCEPTANCE
Acceptance must be communicated to the offeror.
- ❖ Hendricks v. Behee *(Buyer's offer accepted/signed by seller, but not communicated to buyer, so buyer's revocation was effective)*

ACCEPTANCE BY PERFORMANCE
Unilateral offer (accepted only by performance)
  - Part performance: must allow performance to be completed once started
- ❖ Ever-Tite Roofing Corp. v. Green *(Offer indicated performance would be acceptance*
- ❖ Glover v. Jewish War Veterans *($500 reward for information leading to arrest; court ruled lack of knowledge of reward prior to performance is not a contract)*

ACCEPTANCE BY SILENCE
- **Implied in fact-contracts** (communicating with gestures/actions)
- ❖ Wrench v. Taco Bell *(Use of Chihuahua acts as acceptance to marketing plan even without formally accepting)*
- **Unintentional acceptance** (must intend to accept)
- **History of dealing** (silence in the past may imply silence is acceptable)
- ❖ Amons v. Wilson *(Wilson rejected order for shortening after 12 days of silence; court held past experience informed the silence as acceptance)*

THE MAILBOX RULE AND TIMING OF ACCEPTANCE
Acceptance is effective when sent

- DOESN'T APPLY (1) if something else sent first, (2) to other communications, (3) to options
- ❖ Adams v. Lindsell *(establishes Mailbox Rule)*

REJECTION, COUNTEROFFER, AND THE MIRROR IMAGE RULE
Rejection, common law counteroffer and **conditional acceptance** squashes the offer

- **Mirror Image Rule** (terms of CL acceptance must match offer or it's a counteroffer)
- "If," "but only," "on condition" squash CL offer
- ❖ Minneapolis & St. Louis Railway v. Columbus Rolling Mill *(acceptance following earlier counteroffer/rejection does not revive initial offer)*

UCC 2-207 AND THE BATTLE OF THE FORMS
- **UCC 2-207(1)** (acceptance can be valid, even if it contains additional or different terms)
  - ○ Must be timely, reasonable, and not conditional upon new or different terms
- **UCC 2-207(2)** (new term only controls IF (1) both parties are merchants, (2) new term doesn't materially alter deal, (3) offer didn't limit acceptance to its terms, (4) offeror doesn't object.

Knockout Rule (different terms in offer and acceptance knock each other out)
- Difficult for new terms to govern

LEONARD PEVAR V. EVANS PRODUCTS CO.
An illustration of 2-207 and Battle of the Forms at work

❖ *(Dispute as to whether there was an oral contract followed by confirming memo, whether forms constituted offer and acceptance, or whether purported acceptance was really a counteroffer due to "unless" provisio; case remanded)*

TERMINATING OFFERS
SIX ways to terminate:
1. Express revocation by offeror to offeree
2. Constructive revocation – offeree learns offeror has acted in a way inconsistent with ability to contract
3. Rejection by offeree
4. Counteroffer by offeree (counter-inquiry or indecision are ok)
5. Death of offeror

6. A reasonable amount of time has passed
Remember: offeror can choose to **revive** offer.

IRREVOCABLE OFFERS
General rule is that offers revocable any time prior to acceptance.

❖ Dickinson v. Dodds *(Seller's statement that buyer had until 9am Friday to accept his offer was not binding; seller free to revoke.)*
Four types of irrevocable offers:

1. Offeree buys an **option**
❖ Humble Oil v. Westside Investment *(Buyer's purchase of an option kept the offer open, even when Buyer proposed different terms that may have otherwise been a counteroffer)*

2. **UCC Merchant's firm offer** (merchant; written; explicit promise not to revoke; lasts for as long as stated in the offer or a "reasonable time" not to exceed three months)

3. **Unilateral**, if offeree has started performance (offeree is entitled to finish, but doesn't have to)

4. Reasonable, detrimental, foreseeable **reliance** by offeree (often contractor/subcontractor)

❖ James Baird v. Gimbel Bros. *(Subcontractor's initial bid was too low and revoked before acceptance; no contract)*
❖ Drennen v. Star Paving *(Subcontractor's bid was too low and revoked before acceptance; here, in contrast with the court in James Baird, the court said the contract was irrevocable for a time because the contractor detrimentally relied on that offer.)*

OVERVIEW OF CONSIDERATION

Quid pro quo (some legal detriment or benefit)
1. Who is making the promise? (promisor to promisee)
2. Is there a benefit OR a detriment?
3. Was this bargained for?

❖ Hamer v. Sidway *(Uncle promised nephew $5000 to refrain from drinking, smoking, swearing, and gambling until age 21; this detriment to promisee was consideration.)*
❖ Pennsy Supply v. American Ash *(American Ash offered free AggRite, and Pennsy Supply took it; in a breach of warranty action, court ruled that there was a contract because American Ash wanted the stuff removed—that was a benefit.)*

ADEQUACY OF CONSIDERATION
Nominal Consideration is not ok.

❖ <u>In re Green</u> *(when plaintiff sought damages of $375,000, court determined that original $1 consideration must have been insufficient)*

PRE-EXISTING DUTY RULE AND MODIFICATION
Pre-existing Duty Rule (promise to do something you are already legally obligated to do is not consideration)

Modification now valid without consideration if:
1. Modification occurred before performance;
2. Prompted by unexpected change in circumstances;
3. Fair and equitable.

Mutuality of Obligation – meaningful obligation on each side
- Can't be illusory
- Requirements and output contracts are ok
- Court will read obligations into exclusive dealing contracts, satisfaction conditions

CONSIDERATION SUBSTITUTES
Reliance (Promissory Estoppel): (1) reasonable (2) detrimental reliance on promise, and (3) injustice avoided only by enforcement.

❖ <u>Ricketts v. Scothorn</u> *(detrimental reliance creates enforceable K)*
❖ <u>Kirksey v. Kirksey</u> *(decided before detrimental reliance; no K despite changed circumstances)*

Quasi-K (Implied-in-fact K or Restitution): (1) P confers benefit on D (2) with expectation of payment and (3) it's unfair for D not to pay (i.e., did D have a chance to decline or good reason otherwise?).

Past Consideration: insufficient unless moral obligation + subsequent promise

DEFENSES TO CONTRACT FORMATION
1. Indefiniteness: K missing important term
2. Incapacity: lack of mental acuity
3. Mistake
4. Fraud, misrepresentation, or nondisclosure
5. Duress: forcing another into K
6. Unconscionability: unfair deal
7. Illegality or against public policy

Void: a nullity; no K ever existed (illegal K)
Voidable: valid K unless/until party takes steps to avoid

- o Unenforceable: valid K, but can't be enforced if one party refuses to perform

- **Indefiniteness**
  - o Court may step in to interpret ambiguities and enforce the K; if they can't, void
  ❖ <u>Varney v. Ditmars</u> (*"some projects" and "a fair share" is too indefinite to enforce*)
  ❖ <u>Baer v. Chase</u> (*Sopranos case; "remuneration commensurate with value of services" too indefinite*)

- **Incapacity**
  - o **Minors** (minor can void K unless for necessities; can ratify after turning 18)
  - o **Mental illness** – (1) no understanding of consequences of actions (doesn't matter what other party knows); (2) can't act in a reasonable manner w/r/t transaction (only voidable if other party knows of incapacity).
  ❖ <u>Heights Realty v. Phillips</u> (*mentally ill seller not liable to listing agent for commission*)
  - o **Intoxication** (only if extreme and other side knows)

- **Mistake**
  - o **Mutual** – both parties are mistaken (mistake of fact, relates to basic assumption, material, impacted party did not assume risk)
  ❖ <u>Sherwood v. Walker</u> (*both parties think cow is barren and price cow accordingly; K avoided*)
  ❖ <u>Beachcomber Coins v. Boskett</u> (*both parties think dime was rare; it wasn't, and K avoided*)
  - o **Unilateral** – only one party is mistaken (to avoid K, all of the above + mistake would make K unconscionable or other side knew, had reason to know, or caused mistake.)

- **Fraud** (misrepresentation of (1) present (2) material fact that (3) the other party justifiably relies on)
  - o **In the inducement:** lie to get someone to sign K
  - o **In the execution:** trick into signing something other party doesn't know is a K
- **Nondisclosure** (one party stays silent as to a material fact that the other party doesn't know)
  ❖ <u>Hill v. Jones</u> (*nondisclosure of termite infestation, when asked, voided K*)

- **Duress** (improper threat that deprives party of meaningful choice to contract)
  ❖ <u>Rubenstein v. Rubenstein</u> (*subjective standard applied to void contract on grounds of duress*)
  - o **Economic duress** – threat related to economic prospects

❖ Austin Instrument v. Loral Corp *(threatening to cancel existing K unless company agreed to an additional K constituted economic duress)*
- **Undue Influence** (intense pressure on a party who seems weak minded or highly susceptible)
- **Unconscionability** (terms or bargaining process so one-sided as to be unenforceable)
  - Procedural unconscionability: defect in bargaining process (look for surprise or absence of meaningful choice)
  - Substantive unconscionability: problematic terms
❖ Williams v. Walker-Thomas Furniture *(enforcement of cross-collateralization clause was unconscionable, substantively and procedurally)*
❖ Ferguson v. Countrywide Credit *(one-sided arbitration clause substantively unconscionable)*

- **Illegality** (K is void if its subject matter is illegal, though K ancillary to illegal activity may be enforced)
❖ Sinnar v. Le Roy *(no recovery of funds given to illegally procure liquor license)*
- **Against Public Policy** (not illegal but law won't encourage; e.g., broad exculpatory clauses; incentivizing divorce)

STATUTE OF FRAUDS
Applies to: K made in consideration of marriage, suretyship, one year, UCC, real property

Satisfied by:

- **Performance** (at CL, full performance of a services K was enough)
- **Writing** signed by party against whom K is being enforced (must indicate K has been made, ID the parties, and contain essential elements of K)
❖ Crabtree v. Elizabeth Arden *(two different documents combined to satisfy the SOF)*
- **Under UCC:**
  - Signed writing containing quantity
  - Part performance, as to quantity delivered/accepted
  - "Substantial beginning" of custom-made goods
  - Judicial admission
  - Failure to object to merchant's confirming memo

PERFORMANCE OBLIGATIONS
PAROL EVIDENCE RULE (PER)
If there is a comprehensive writing, earlier statements not in this agreement are not part of the deal

- Does not apply to later statements/modifications
- **Integration** (comprehensive agreement; can be full or partial)

❖ Mitchill v. Lath *(promise to destroy icehouse prior to written K was barred by PER)*
❖ Masterson v. Sine *(exclusivity of option not necessarily barred by PER; simple K wasn't a full integration)*
  - Merger clause ("full & complete agreement b/w parties")
  - Extrinsic term, naturally omitted – not barred by PER
  - UCC presumes partial integration unless term would have "certainly" been included
- PER does not apply to: defenses; evidence of second, separate deal; evidence to interpret ambiguity.

INTERPRETATION
Clearing up ambiguity instead of canceling K

❖ PG&E v GW Thomas Drayage *(dispute as to meaning of "indemnify" was cleared up by earlier conversations b/w the parties)*
❖ Frigaliment Importing v. BNS *(to determine definition of "chicken," court looked to multiple sources including (1) contract itself, (2) preliminary negotiations, (3) trade usage, etc. – did not violate PER)*
❖ Panera v. Qdoba *(is a burrito a sandwich?)*

DUTY OF GOOD FAITH
Can't prevent or hinder the other side's performance

❖ Patterson v. Meyerhofer *(D-buyer's bidding on land against P-seller at auction violated good faith)*
- Must exercise discretion with good faith
❖ Neumiller Farms v. Cornett *(P's use of "chipping to satisfaction" condition to take advantage of market drop was a violation of good faith)*
- **Modification of K** (valid under UCC if made in good faith)

WARRANTIES AND CONDITIONS
- **Warranty** (promise re: a term that explicitly shifts risk to party making the promise)
- **UCC warranties:**
  - Express warranties – promise re: the goods that is part of the basis of the bargain (e.g., use of sample or model)
  - Implied warranty of merchantability – goods the merchant normally sells are fit for their ordinary purpose – can be disclaimed by very conspicuous language (either using "merchantability" or "as is")
  - Implied warranty of fitness for a particular purpose – buyer relies on seller's expertise to

select proper goods; can be extended by non-merchant – can be disclaimed.

- **Conditions** (shift risk by stating that one party's K obligations only kick in if a future event takes place)
  - **Express** – "only if," "provided that," "on condition that"; must be strictly satisfied
- ❖ Dove v. Rose Acre Farms (*working 9.5 out of a required 10 weeks would not satisfy an express condition*)
  - **Satisfaction condition**: usually objective (reasonable person standard), but sometimes subjective (aesthetic) and must only exhibit good faith.
- Conditions may be waived by party being protected or excused
  - **Implied** – CL Constructive Condition of Exchange

- **Constructive Condition of Exchange** (one party's performance is conditioned on the other party's performance)
  - Strict performance isn't req.
  - Substantial performance is enough if it's not a material breach and is not willful.
- ❖ Jacob and Youngs v. Kent (*use of identical, but not specified, pipe was substantial performance; K satisfied; no damages because no decrease in market value*)
  - Even if substantial compliance, may still be damages for cost to complete performance (and limited by decrease in market value)
  - Breaching party can't recover in K (maybe quasi-K)
- **Divisibility** (K can be "chunked up" to determine substantial performance)

UCC Perfect Tender Rule
Perfect Goods (buyer can refuse if not perfect)
- Can revoke acceptance of goods if defect discovered within reasonable time
- If seller fails to deliver perfect goods and (1) there is still time left for performance of K or (2) seller had reasonable grounds to think goods would be acceptable, buyer has to give seller chance to **cure.**

Perfect Delivery (default is one delivery of goods)
- Installment Ks: agreement authorizes or requires delivery in separate lots
  - Buyer can't reject a specific delivery that isn't perfect unless there is a substantial impairment that can't be cured.

Excuse of Conditions
Waiver (party who enjoys protection of the condition waives it by words or conduct)
- ❖ Clark v. West (*law prof who drank while writing casebook claimed that publisher waived condition by estoppel*)
- Waiver by estoppel
- Waiver by election
- Waiver by interference (protected party wrongfully interferes or hinders occurrence of condition)
- Waiver as a matter of law

CHANGED CIRCUMSTANCES
Impossibility (can no longer be performed)
Impracticability (can perform with great difficulty)
- Examples: K becomes illegal, subject of K is destroyed, "special person" in a services K dies or becomes incapacitated
- Hinders **ability** to perform, **not cost** of performance
- ❖ US v. Wegematic Corp. (*no excuse of impracticability when computer manufacturer overestimated its ability to deliver new technology*)
- **Unforeseen Event**, nonoccurrence of which was a basic assumption of the K; no fault
- **Death after a K** does not usually excuse performance; estate is liable
  - Exception if there is something special about the party to perform K

Frustration of Purpose (can be performed, but entire reason for K has been undermined)
- ❖ Krell v. Henry (*tenant who rented apt for its view of coronation parade was excused when parade was postponed*)

REMEDIES FOR BREACH OF CONTRACT
- CCE (withhold your own performance)
- Anticipatory Repudiation (stop own performance when it appears other side is going to breach)
- Money Damages (expectation damages, reliance damages, restitution)
- Liquidated Damages (specified in K)
- Emotional Distress and Punitive
- Equitable relief (court order, not money)

Anticipatory Breach (one party repudiates before performance is due)
Nonbreaching party has two options:
1. Treat as breach and sue immediately for damages
2. Ignore repudiation, demand performance, and see what happens
Repudiating party can retract repudiation as long as other side hasn't (1) sued, or (2) acted in reliance on breach.

❖ Wholesale Sand & Gravel v. Decker (*P's repeated failure to show up to complete driveway constituted anticipatory repudiation; D excused from performance*)
UCC allows for demanding adequate assurance of performance if reasonable grounds for insecurity

Expectation Damages (put the party in the same economic position they'd been in if the K had been performed – forward looking)
- Compare value of **performance w/o breach** to **performance w/** breach
- Same methodology in **UCC**
- ❖ Hawkins v. McGee (*hairy hand*)
- ❖ Sullivan v. O'Connor (*botched nose job*)

Type of Damage	Expectations
Doctor's fee	No
Hospital expenses	Only for third operation
Pain/suffering (1 & 2)	No
Pain/suffering (3)	Yes
Lost earnings	Yes

Limitations on Expectation Damages
- Have to be proven with *reasonable certainty*
- The **Hadley Rule** – unforeseeable consequential damages are not recoverable unless breaching party had some reason to know about the possibility
  - General damages (anyone would suffer from breach)
  - Consequential damages (unique to this plaintiff)
- ❖ Hadley v. Baxendale (*failure to deliver mill shaft caused mill to shut down for 5 days; D not responsible for lost profits, which were unforeseeable*)
- **Mitigation** – breached-against party must take reasonable steps to reduce damage from breach
  - If refusal to mitigate, law calculates damages as if there had been mitigation
  - D has to prove mitigation failure
  - Mitigation efforts must be reasonably similar to original K
- ❖ Parker v. Twentieth Century Fox (*Shirley MacLaine case – offer of new movie role was not reasonably similar to original K role; no failure to mitigate*)

When Paying Party Breaches
Incomplete Performance – non-breaching party can't continue to perform if paying party breaches; will adjust the recovery price if the performing party finishes

Expectation Damages = contract price – amount already paid – amount that would be needed to finish the job

Lost Volume Profits (LVP) – if seller is a retailer who sells this type of product all the time, mitigation could result in under-compensation for breach
- ❖ Locks v. Wade (*jukebox owner had many jukeboxes to let, so finding another renter wasn't mitigation; LVP*)
  - Look for lots of supply and limited buyers

When Performing Party Breaches
Normally, hire someone else—if it costs the same, no problem; if it costs less, you've benefited; if it costs more, you can sue for the extra
Market value v. cost to complete (CTC):
Remember Jacob & Youngs v. Kent (*wrong brand of wrought-iron pipe in house*). CTC would be cost to tear down house + build a new house + cost of pipes = overcompensating for breach. **Alt method: decrease in market value** (DMV) – how much lower is the market value of what you got vs. what you K'ed for.
- ❖ Peevyhouse v. Garland Coal & Mining Co (*after mining, D didn't complete land restoration agreed to; CTC was $25k, DMV was $300; in highly criticized case, court awarded DMV*)

Emotional Distress and Punitive Damages
Almost never awarded in K
Emotional distress damages: breaching party should expect that failure to deliver will lead to major distress (e.g., funeral services).
- ❖ Lane v. Kindercare (*emotional distress was recoverable when day care center forgot about a child*)
Punitive damages: maybe when it looks as if the breach might also be a fraud.
- ❖ Boise Dodge Inc. v. Clark (*dealer described car as "new," but had set back the odometer on the used car*)

ALTERNATIVE CALCULATION OF MONEY DAMAGES
Reliance Damages: attempt to put party in same economic position as if the K had never been formed
- What loss has P incurred that would not have taken place but for the breached K?
- Usually, party must elect **either** expectation or reliance, but not both
Restitution Damages: attempt to give P amount equal to **economic benefit** P has incurred on D
- ❖ Sullivan v. O'Connor (*botched nose job*)

Type of Damage	Reliance	Restitution
Doctor's fee	Yes	Yes
Hospital expenses	Yes	No

Pain/suffering (1 & 2)	Yes	No
Pain/suffering (3)	Yes	No
Lost earnings	Yes	No

LIQUIDATED DAMAGES

Damages negotiated in the K that are due upon breach.

To be enforceable:

- Amount of liquidated damages must be **reasonable at the time of K** and
- Actual damages for breach would be **uncertain in amount** and **difficult to prove**

Otherwise, **unenforceable penalty**

❖ Southwest Engineering v. US (*liquidated damages upheld; reasonable/proportionate and difficult to calculate*)

SPECIFIC PERFORMANCE AND EQUITABLE REMEDIES

The exception, not the norm; awarded **when money damages are considered inadequate** – e.g., unique goods like the *Saturday Night Fever* dance floor

- Specific performance is presumptively allowed in **real estate transactions**; real estate is unique
- Presumptively not available in **personal services Ks**
  - o Might get an injunction prohibiting breaching party from working for a competitor

❖ Lumley v. Wagner (*court would not force opera singer to perform, but prohibited her from performing at a competing London theatre for an amount of time*)

❖ Walgreen v. Sara Creek Property (*K not to lease space in mall to another pharmacy; P sought an injunction; D wants to pay damages; ct awarded injunction because damages would be too speculative; left determining that amount to the parties themselves*)

Themis
Bar Review

Criminal Law

CRIMINAL LAW

Table of Contents

CRIMINAL LAW

I. **GENERAL PRINCIPLES**

The elements of a criminal offense include the *mens rea*, or guilty mind; the *actus reus*, the bad or unlawful act; and causation. With the exception of strict liability crimes, which have no *mens rea*, every statute defining a substantive criminal offense proscribes a particular *mens rea* and *actus reus* that must be proved by the prosecution beyond a reasonable doubt in order for criminal liability to result.

> **EXAM NOTE:** Remember that your professor may prefer to focus on the Model Penal Code, the common law, or the law of a particular state. Keep this in mind when preparing for your exam and when you analyze each element of a crime. If possible, look at prior exams to get a sense of what your professor tends to test.

A. *ACTUS REUS* — **ACTS AND OMISSIONS**

Before there can be a crime, there must be a criminal act (*actus reus*). The criminal act must be a voluntary, affirmative act causing a criminally proscribed result. The act requirement may also be satisfied by an "omission" or failure to act under circumstances imposing a legal duty to act. A bad thought standing alone cannot result in criminal liability.

1. **Physical Act**

   In general, a criminal act must be a physical act. A bad thought standing alone cannot result in criminal liability.

   a. **Speech**

      Speech can constitute a physical act. For example, in the crime of extortion, the verbal threat is the act. A mere statement of intent generally would not be enough to constitute an *actus reus*, but speech that encourages someone to commit a crime could be an *actus reus*.

   b. **Possession**

      Possession of an object can constitute a physical act. Generally, there must be conscious knowledge of the possession of the object, but the possessor need not know that such possession is illegal. Under the Model Penal Code, possession can be a criminal act only if the defendant knew she had possession of the object and was aware of such possession for a sufficient period to have been able to terminate such possession. MPC § 2.01(4).

2. **Voluntary Act**

   The criminal act must be physical and voluntary. Actions during unconsciousness, sleep, or hypnosis are not voluntary. Other acts that are not considered voluntary are reflexive or convulsive acts, and conduct that is not the product of the actor's determination.

   > **Example:** Person A pushes Person B into a bystander, injuring the bystander. Person B cannot be held criminally liable.

   If an epileptic knows of the possibility of a seizure and engages in the voluntary act of driving a car, has a seizure while driving, and causes a fatal accident, the epileptic is criminally responsible.

> **Example:** An epileptic may still be criminally responsible if (i) he knows of the possibility of seizure; and (ii) the last act was voluntary.

The best example where liability is not generally imposed is for acts committed while sleep-walking.

2. Failure to Act When Duty Exists

A legal duty to act and the failure to do so results in criminal liability in these five instances:

i) Imposed by statute (e.g., obligation to file tax return; obligation to register for selective service);

ii) Contract (e.g., lifeguard saving drowning person; nanny who neglects a baby's care);

iii) Special relationship (e.g., parent's duty to her child, or duty to one's spouse);

iv) Detrimental undertaking (e.g., when defendant, with no duty otherwise, undertakes to assist a victim, leaving the victim in worse condition after such assistance); and

v) Causation (e.g., failing to aid after causing victim's peril).

The defendant must have knowledge of the facts giving rise to the duty to act and fail to act. Additionally, it must be reasonably possible for the defendant to perform the duty.

> **Contrast absence of a duty:** When there is not a duty to act, a defendant is not criminally liable by failing to help others in trouble. A mere bystander has no duty to act. Note that no matter how unsympathetic your professor may make the bystander seem for not acting, there is generally no legal duty to act if the bystander had no involvement with the peril.

> **EXAM NOTE:** If your exam contains more than one actor, ask yourself what is different about the actions of each actor, and ask what makes one actor liable for something that the other may not be liable for. It is unlikely the professor is asking you to answer the same thing for each actor. Figure out what facts are different and how they may change the result as to each one.

B. *MENS REA*—STATE OF MIND

Mens rea is the requirement of a guilty mind or legally proscribed mental state a defendant must possess in order to commit a crime. Except for strict liability crimes, a crime is committed when a criminal act (*actus reus*) is coupled with a guilty mind—both the mental and physical elements exist at the same time. Strict liability crimes have no *mens rea* requirement and only require an *actus reus*.

1. Specific Intent Crimes

Specific intent crimes require that the defendant possess **a subjective desire, specific objective, or knowledge to accomplish a prohibited result**. When dealing with specific intent crimes, it is necessary to identify specific intent for two reasons. First, the prosecution must prove the specific intent in order to prosecute the defendant; and second, certain defenses (e.g., voluntary intoxication and unreasonable mistake of fact) are applicable only to specific intent crimes.

At common law, the specific intent crimes include:

i) **F**irst-degree murder;

ii) **I**nchoate offenses (attempt, solicitation, conspiracy);

iii) **A**ssault with intent to commit a battery; and

iv) **T**heft offenses (larceny, larceny by trick, false pretenses, embezzlement, forgery, burglary, robbery).

> **EXAM NOTE:** A simple way to remember the common-law specific intent crimes is by using the mnemonic "FIAT." Whenever a fact pattern defines the crime as requiring "the intent to…," the crime is a specific intent crime.

2. **Malice Crimes**

The crimes of common law murder and arson require **malice, a reckless disregard of a high risk of harm**. Although these two crimes appear to have an "intent" requirement (e.g., intent to kill), malice only requires a criminal act without excuse, justification, or mitigation. Intent can be inferred from the accomplishment of the act.

3. **General Intent Crimes**

General intent crimes require only the **intent to perform an act** that is unlawful. Examples include battery, rape, kidnapping, and false imprisonment.

Motive is not the same as intent. The motive is the reason or explanation for the crime and is immaterial to the substantive criminal offense.

a. **Transferred intent**

When a defendant acts with an intent to cause harm to one person or object and that act directly results in harm to another person or object, the defendant can be liable for the harm caused under the doctrine of transferred intent.

Example: D points a gun at A, intending to shoot and kill A, but accidentally shoots and kills B instead. D is guilty of two crimes: the murder of B under the doctrine of transferred intent and the attempted murder of A.

Note that the doctrine of transferred intent applies only to "bad aim" cases and not to cases of mistaken identity.

Example: If D shoots at A and hits A, although mistakenly believing that A is B, the doctrine of transferred intent is unnecessary because D hit the very body he intended to hit; the intent, therefore, does not need to be transferred—D is guilty of shooting A.

Transferred intent, also known as the unintended victim rule, is usually confined to homicide, battery, and arson. Any defenses that the defendant could assert against the intended victim (e.g., self-defense) may also transfer to the unintended victim.

Note that transferred intent does not apply to attempted crimes, only completed crimes.

Example: D shoots at A with the intent to kill him, but D instead shoots B. The shot does not kill B, but merely injures her. D can be convicted of the attempted murder of A and of battery against B, but cannot be convicted of the attempted murder of B.

The Model Penal Code, while not specifically recognizing the doctrine of transferred intent, does recognize liability when purposely, knowingly, recklessly, or negligently causing a particular result is an element of an offense. This element can be established even if the actual result is not within the purpose or contemplation of the defendant, or is not within the risk of which the defendant is aware, so long as the result differs from the intended, contemplated, or probable result only insofar as (i) a different person or different property is harmed or (ii) the contemplated injury or harm would have been more serious or more extensive than the harm actually caused. MPC § 2.03.2(2, 3).

4. **Model Penal Code**

A crime defined by statute generally states the requisite *mens rea*. The following levels of culpability are based on the Model Penal Code ("MPC").

a. **Purposely**

When a defendant acts "purposely" his conscious objective is to engage in the conduct or to cause a certain result. MPC 2.02(2)(a).

b. **Knowingly or willfully**

"Knowingly" or "willfully" requires that the defendant be **aware that his conduct is of the nature required by the crime** or that circumstances required by the crime exist. In other words, the defendant must be aware or know that **the result is practically certain to occur** based on his conduct. MPC 2.02(2)(b).

c. **Recklessly**

"Recklessly" requires the defendant **to act with a conscious disregard of a substantial and unjustifiable risk** that a material element of a crime exists or will result from his conduct. The risk must constitute a gross deviation from the standard of conduct of a law-abiding person. MPC 2.02(2)(c). Mere realization of the risk is not enough.

d. **Negligently**

A defendant acts "negligently" when that defendant **should be aware of a substantial and unjustifiable risk** that a material element of a crime exists or will result from his conduct. The risk must constitute a gross deviation from the standard of care of a reasonable person in the same situation. MPC 2.02(2)(d). Furthermore, similarly to tort law, violation of a statute or ordinance may be evidence of liability.

e. **Hierarchy of mental states**

The MPC mental states are ordered from negligence as the lowest degree of fault to purposefully as the highest level of fault. Consequently, if a statute specifies a mental state, proof of a more culpable mental state satisfies the mens rea requirement. For example, if a statutory crime required that an act be undertaken knowingly, establishing that the act was committed purposefully satisfies the mens rea requirement with respect to that act. MPC § 2.02(5).

f. *Mens rea* **not stated**

If the requisite *mens rea* is not stated in a criminal statute, it is established if the defendant acted at least recklessly. If the *mens rea* does not state the culpable mind applicable to all material elements of the crime, then the *mens rea* applicable to one material element is applicable to all material elements, unless a contrary purpose plainly appears. MPC § 2.02(3),(4).

5. **Strict Liability Crimes**

A strict liability crime does not require a *mens rea*. Examples of strict liability crimes include statutory rape, bigamy, regulatory offenses for public welfare, regulation of food, drugs, and firearms, and selling liquor to minors.

a. **Public welfare offense**

A public welfare offense is a strict liability crime for which no *mens rea* is required. Conduct that is subject to stringent public regulation includes that which could seriously threaten the public's health or safety or is inherently dangerous.

Examples: Typical examples include adulteration of food or drugs, regulation of waste disposal, and selling liquor to minors.

b. **Degree of penalty**

In general, when courts look to determine whether a crime is a public welfare offense, the degree of the penalty imposed by the statute can often be determinative if the statute is unclear. Thus, if the penalty imposed is severe (e.g., the crime is classified as a felony), a court looking at the issue may find an intent requirement in the statute and treat the offense as not a strict liability crime.

c. **Statutory interpretation**

Statutes rarely specifically state that strict liability is imposed. Rather, they generally just omit any *mens rea* requirement at all. Courts are then faced with a statutory interpretation requirement to decide if the legislature really meant to impose strict liability. If the statute is complex, but easy to innocently violate, or imposes a severe penalty, a court may be likely to find a *mens rea* requirement and therefore avoid finding strict liability.

> **EXAM NOTE:** When given a statute on an exam, read that statute carefully for hints about the *mens rea* requirement. Look for words like "with intent" (specific intent crime), "knowingly" or "recklessly" (general intent crime), or no mention of *mens rea*, which may be a strict liability crime.

6. **Vicarious Liability**

Vicarious liability differs from strict liability in that strict-liability crimes require only a personal act on the part of the defendant (*actus reus*); vicarious liability crimes do not require an *actus reus* by the defendant. Instead, vicarious liability imposes criminal liability on the defendant for the *actus reus* of a third party.

a. **Application to strict-liability crimes**

Courts often impose vicarious liability for strict-liability crimes, most commonly when an employer or principal is vicariously liable for the crimes of an employee or agent. However, sometimes it is unclear whether the legislature intended for vicarious liability to apply to a strict-liability offense. When the punishment for a strict-liability crime is light, courts are more likely to find that vicarious liability applies. The modern trend is to limit vicarious liability to regulatory crimes.

Vicarious liability may present due process issues because it can involve criminal liability without a personal act on the part of the defendant. Although imprisonment for a faultless crime may have constitutional due process implications, when the punishment for a crime is merely a fine, the application of vicarious liability is unlikely to constitute a denial of due process.

b. Application to corporations

When dealing with corporations, common law held that corporations had no criminal liability because a corporation could not form the necessary *mens rea*. Modern statutes, on the other hand, impose vicarious liability on corporations when the offensive act is performed by an agent of the corporation acting within the scope of his employment or when the act is performed by a high-ranking corporate agent who likely represents corporate policy. Under the MPC, a corporation may be held criminally liable if (i) the corporation fails to discharge a specific duty imposed by law, (ii) the board of directors or a high-ranking agent of the corporation acting within the scope of his employment authorizes or recklessly tolerates the offensive act, or (iii) the legislative purpose statutorily imposes liability on a corporation for a specific act. The individual agent of the corporation who violated the statute may also be held criminally liable, and the corporation's conviction does not preclude conviction of the individual. MPC § 2.07.

7. Causation

When mens rea is a requirement of a crime, that mens rea must generally cause the actus res. In addition, the defendant's act must cause the particular result made unlawful by statute.

8. Mistake as a Defense

a. Mistake of fact

1) Negation of intent

Mistake of fact may negate criminal intent but it must be an "honest mistake." The defense applies differently between specific and general intent crimes. Mistake of fact is never a defense to a strict liability crime because strict liability offenses do not have a *mens rea.*

2) Reasonableness of mistake

a) Specific intent crimes

A mistake of fact is a defense to a specific intent crime, even if the mistake is unreasonable.

> **Example:** An athlete takes an expensive gold watch from a table mistakenly thinking that it was her inexpensive black plastic sports watch. Even though the athlete's mistake of fact is unreasonable, the athlete lacks the intent to steal necessary to commit larceny, a specific intent crime.

b) General intent and malice crimes

A mistake of fact must be reasonable in order to be a defense to a general intent or malice crime.

3) MPC approach

Under the MPC, a mistake or ignorance of fact that negates the required state of mind for a material element of a crime is a defense.

> **EXAM NOTE:** When considering a mistake of fact defense, consider whether the crime the defendant is charged with is one of specific intent, general intent, or strict liability.

b. Mistake of law

Mistake or ignorance of the law generally is not a valid defense, except when:

i) There is reliance on the decision of a court, administrative order, or official interpretation of the law determined to be erroneous after the conduct;

ii) A statute defining a *malum prohibitum* crime (i.e., a crime for engaging in conduct not obviously wrong, such as a failure to obtain a license) was not reasonably made available prior to the conduct; or

iii) An honestly held mistake of law negates the required intent.

> **Example:** A forcibly takes money from B to settle a debt that B owed to A. A has the mistaken belief that the law allows for self-help in such situations. A's belief negates the specific intent required for the crime of robbery (i.e., the specific intent to gain control over the property of another person).

Incorrect or bad legal advice from an attorney is not itself a valid mistake-of-law defense, but it may negate the required intent or mental state for a material element of the crime.

> Similarly, a mistake of law as to the existence of a defense does not permit a defendant to raise the defense unless one of the exceptions enumerated above applies.

> **EXAM NOTE:** There are some modern statutory crimes that expressly require a defendant to know of a legal prohibition. Read any statute that your professor gives you carefully to determine if it contains such a requirement.

C. JURISDICTION

Criminal jurisdiction addresses the authority of the federal and state governments to create criminal laws and the courts to enforce those laws.

1. Constitutional Limits on Authority

a. State authority

State authority to create crimes is based on the states' broad, inherent police power that is implicitly recognized by the Tenth Amendment.

b. Federal authority

Federal authority to create crimes is limited. There is no federal common law of crimes; all are statutory. Under the U.S. Constitution, Congress is granted power over only a handful of crimes, including treason and currency counterfeiting.

c. State and federal authority

Under the Constitution, neither federal nor state governments may criminalize conduct that has already occurred (i.e., an ex post facto law) or impose punishment without a trial (i.e., a bill of attainder). The Due Process Clauses of the Fifth and Fourteenth Amendments prevent both federal and state governments from imposing criminal liability without giving clear warnings as to the conduct prohibited. *Papachristou v. City of Jacksonville*, 405 U.S. 156, 162-63 (1972) (vagrancy ordinance struck down as "void for vagueness").

Additionally, many jurisdictions are in the process of eliminating multiple convictions against a defendant with more than one offense if those multiple offenses were all part of the same criminal transaction. Some states have statutorily prohibited such convictions, while other states apply the doctrine of merger or double jeopardy to eliminate the multiple convictions.

2. Territorial Considerations

a. Federal

Congress has the power to criminalize conduct occurring over federally owned or controlled territory (national parks or the District of Columbia), United States nationals abroad, and conduct on ships or airplanes.

b. State authority

A state has the authority to prosecute a person for a crime committed within the state and for a crime that is only partly committed within the state if an element of the crime is committed within the state. In addition, the following actions may also be prosecuted by the state:

i) Conduct outside the state that constitutes an attempt to commit a crime within the state;

ii) Conduct outside the state that constitutes a conspiracy to commit an offense within the state when an overt act in furtherance of the conspiracy occurs within the state;

iii) Conduct within the state to commit attempt, solicitation, or conspiracy of a crime in another jurisdiction when the state and the other jurisdiction recognize the crime; and

iv) The failure to perform outside the state a duty imposed by the state.

D. PARTIES TO A CRIME

Under the modern rule, in most jurisdictions, the parties to a crime can be a principal, an accomplice, and an accessory after the fact.

At common law, the principal was called the principal in the first degree, and an accessory who was actually or constructively present at the scene of the crime was called the principal in the second degree. An accomplice who was not present at the crime scene was called an accessory before the fact or after the fact, depending on when he provided assistance.

1. Principal

A principal is the person whose **acts or omissions are the *actus reus*** of the crime, or, in other words, the perpetrator of the crime. The principal must be actually or constructively present at the scene of the crime. A principal is constructively present when some instrumentality he left or controlled resulted in the commission of the crime.

If two or more people are directly responsible for the *actus reus*, they are joint principals (i.e., co-principals).

2. Accomplice Liability

An accomplice (i.e., an accessory before the fact or a principal in the second degree) is a person who, with the requisite mens rea, aids or abets a principal prior to or during the commission of the crime.

Note: In general, the mental state required for accomplice liability is the intent to assist the principal in committing the underlying crime. If, however, the underlying crime requires only recklessness or negligence as a *mens rea*, most jurisdictions require only this lesser *mens rea* for accomplice liability with regard to that crime.

a. Accomplice's status

Some states draw a distinction between an accessory before the fact and a principal in the second degree based upon presence at the scene of the crime. An accomplice who is physically or constructively present during the commission of the crime is a principal in the second degree. For example, a getaway driver some distance from the scene is deemed constructively present and will be considered a principal in the second degree.

An accomplice who is neither physically nor constructively present during the commission of the crime, but who possesses the requisite intent, for example someone who helped plan the crime or acquired tools or weapons necessary to commit the crime, is an accessory before the fact.

b. Accomplice's mental state

1) Majority rule

Under the majority and MPC rule, a person is an accomplice in the commission of an offense if he acts with the purpose of **promoting or facilitating** the commission of the offense. The accomplice must solicit, aid, agree, or attempt to aid in the planning or commission of the crime, with the intent that the crime actually be committed. Model Penal Code § 2.06(3). Mere knowledge that another person intends to commit a crime is not enough to make a person an accomplice.

2) Minority rule

A minority of states hold a person liable as an accomplice if he **intentionally or knowingly** aids, induces, or causes another person to commit an offense. *See, e.g.*, Ind. Code Ann. § 35-41-2-4. Under the minority rule, any voluntary act that actually assists or encourages the principal in a known criminal aim is sufficient for accomplice liability even if the person does not act with the intent of aiding the commission of the crime.

3) Criminal facilitation

In jurisdictions that have adopted the majority rule, a person encouraging or assisting a criminal who is not guilty of the crime itself as an accomplice may be guilty of a lesser crime, such as criminal facilitation.

4) Reckless or negligence mental state crimes

When the crime committed by the principal only requires the principal to act recklessly or negligently (e.g., involuntary manslaughter), a person may be an accomplice to that crime under the majority rule if the person merely acts recklessly or negligently with regard the principal's commission of the crime, rather than purposefully or intentionally. *See* Model Penal Code § 2.06(4).

c. Accomplice's criminal liability

An accomplice is responsible for the crime to the same extent as the principal. If the principal commits crimes other than the crimes for which the accomplice has provided encouragement or assistance, an accomplice is liable for the other crimes if the crimes are the natural and probable consequences of the accomplice's conduct.

Example: D encourages E to burn V's house and E does so. The fire spreads to W's house and it was foreseeable that it would do so. D is an accomplice to the burning of W's house.

An accomplice may be criminally liable even though the accomplice cannot be a principal.

> **Example:** A woman who could not commit rape at common law as a principal could be liable for rape if she aided the male principal (e.g., restraining the victim) in his rape of the victim.

d. Withdrawal

To legally withdraw (and therefore avoid liability for the substantive crime), the accomplice must (i) repudiate prior aid, (ii) do all that is possible to countermand prior assistance, and (iii) do so before the chain of events is in motion and unstoppable.

A mere change of heart, flight from the crime scene, arrest by law enforcement, or an uncommunicated decision to withdraw is ineffective to constitute withdrawal. Notification to the legal authorities must be timely and directed toward preventing others from committing the crime.

> **EXAM NOTE:** Be careful not to confuse these rules with the rules regarding withdrawal for inchoate offenses such as solicitation, attempt, and conspiracy. The rules are different.

e. Persons not accomplices

1) Class protected by a statute

A person who is a member of the class protected by a statute cannot be an accomplice. For example, a girl who is below the age of consent is not liable as an accomplice to her own statutory rape, even if she gave encouragement to the male defendant.

2) Crime requiring a second person

If the crime requires another party, the other party is not, simply by engaging in the criminal act, guilty of the crime as an accomplice. For example, the buyer of drugs is not guilty of the crime of distributing drugs simply by purchasing the drugs (but he may be guilty of a different crime).

3) Innocent agent

An "innocent agent" would not be an accomplice.

> **Example:** A is duped by D into taking her friend's laptop and delivering it to D, who had told A that the laptop was really his and that the friend had meant to return it to him. While D may be liable as a principal for larceny of the laptop, A, an innocent agent, would not be guilty of any crime either as a principal or an accomplice.

f. Effect of principal's status

At common law, the accomplice could be convicted of a crime only if the principal was also previously convicted of the crime. However, a principal in the second degree could be convicted even if the principal in the first degree was not convicted. A small minority of jurisdictions still subscribes to this approach. By statute, however, in most jurisdictions, an accomplice may be convicted of a crime even if the principal is not tried, is not convicted, has been given immunity from prosecution, or is acquitted.

3. **Accessory After the Fact**

An accessory after the fact is a person who aids or assists a felon in avoiding apprehension or conviction after commission of the felony. An accessory after the fact must know that a felony was committed, act specifically to aid or assist the felon, and give the aid or assistance for the purpose of helping the felon avoid apprehension or conviction. An accessory after the fact is not subject to punishment for the crime committed by the felon, but instead has committed a *separate crime*, frequently labeled "obstruction of justice" or "harboring a fugitive."

a. **Failure to report a crime**

The mere failure to report a crime does not by itself make a person an accessory after the fact (though it may be a separate crime if a statute specifically makes it a crime to fail to report a crime). However, a person who gives false information to the police in order to prevent the apprehension of a felon can be an accessory after the fact.

b. **Misprision of felony**

Misprision is a common-law misdemeanor that punishes a failure to report or the hiding of a known felon.

The defendant must have (i) had full knowledge that the principal committed and completed the felony alleged, (ii) failed to notify the authorities, and (iii) taken an affirmative step to conceal the crime. *U.S. v. Ciambrone*, 750 F.2d 1416, 1417 (1986).

c. **Compounding a crime**

A person who receives valuable consideration for agreeing not to prosecute a crime may be guilty of compounding a crime.

E. **RESPONSIBILITY**

1. **Insanity**

Insanity encompasses mental abnormalities that may affect legal responsibility. It is a legal term rather than a psychiatric term. The four tests for insanity are the *M'Naghten* test, the irresistible-impulse test, the *Durham* rule, and the Model Penal Code test. These tests expressly exclude the "sociopathic" or "psychopathic" criminals who have a tendency to commit antisocial and sometimes violent acts and are incapable of experiencing guilt; the fact that a defendant has such tendencies does not mean that he has the requisite mental disease or defect. A defendant who puts his sanity at issue can be compelled to submit to psychiatric testing after being informed of his Fifth Amendment rights.

> **EXAM NOTE:** Remember that the elements for insanity under any of these standards must have been present at the time of the crime that is at issue for insanity to be a defense to that crime.

a. **M'Naghten test**

Under the M'Naghten test, the defendant is not guilty if, because of a defect of reason due to a mental disease, the defendant did not know either (i) the nature and quality of the act or (ii) the wrongfulness of the act.

Without knowing that the act is wrong, a defendant could not have formed the requisite criminal intent. Therefore, it is important to assess whether the defendant's actions would have been criminal if the facts, as he believed them to be, supported his delusions. However, a defendant is not necessarily exculpated simply because he believes his acts to be morally right, although a few states do allow for such a defense. Loss of control because of mental illness is not a defense under this test. This is the "right from wrong" test.

b. Irresistible impulse test

Under the "irresistible impulse" test, the defendant is not guilty if he lacked the capacity for self-control and free choice because mental disease or defect prevented him from being able to conform his conduct to the law. The loss of control need not be sudden. This is an impulse the defendant cannot resist.

c. Durham rule

Under the Durham rule, a defendant is not guilty if the unlawful act was the product of the defendant's mental disease or defect, and would not have been committed but for the disease or defect. This is the "but for" test.

d. Model Penal Code test

The Model Penal Code combines the M'Naghten and irresistible impulse tests. The defendant is not guilty if, at the time of the conduct, he, as a result of a mental disease or defect, did not have substantial capacity to appreciate the wrongfulness of the act, or to conform the conduct to the law.

> **EXAM NOTE:** Again, when preparing for your exam, remember to consider which insanity rule your professor focused on in class. If it is unclear from a fact pattern which insanity rule applies, be prepared to discuss what would happen to the defendant under each of the different standards.

e. Burden of proof

In the majority of jurisdictions, the defendant has the burden of proving insanity. The level of proof required in these jurisdictions can be either a preponderance of the evidence or clear and convincing evidence. Other jurisdictions require the defendant to overcome the presumption of sanity by introducing evidence of the defendant's insanity, and then shift the burden of persuasion to the prosecution, which has to prove beyond a reasonable doubt that the defendant is sane.

f. Incompetence to stand trial

There is a distinction between the assertion of the insanity defense as a defense to a crime and the assertion of insanity as a basis for not having a defendant stand trial on the grounds of incompetence. Generally, a defendant will be held incompetent to stand trial if she is unable to understand the proceedings against her and assist counsel in her defense. In many jurisdictions, the burden of proof with regard to incompetence to stand trial is statutorily placed on the defendant.

2. Intoxication

Intoxication can be caused by any substance (e.g., alcohol, drugs, or prescription medicine). There are two types of intoxication defenses, voluntary and involuntary.

a. Voluntary intoxication

Voluntary intoxication is the intentional taking of a substance known to be intoxicating; actual intoxication need not be intended.

1) Specific intent crimes

Voluntary intoxication is a defense to specific intent crimes if it prevents the formation of the required intent. Without the required intent, not all of the elements of the crime can be established. For example, intoxication may prevent the formation of the premeditation required for first-degree murder, but not second-degree murder.

Under the MPC, voluntary intoxication is a defense to crimes for which a material element requires a mental state that is purposely or knowingly and the intoxication prevents the formation of that mental state. MPC § 2.08(1),(2).

2) When inapplicable

Voluntary intoxication is not a defense when the intent was formed before intoxication, or the defendant becomes intoxicated for the purpose of establishing the defense of voluntary intoxication. Voluntary intoxication is not a defense to crimes involving malice, recklessness, or negligence, or for strict liability crimes.

Note: Although common law murder and arson sound like specific intent crimes as they require the "intent to kill" or the "intent to burn," they are malice crimes and the specific intent defenses (e.g., voluntary intoxication) do not apply.

b. Involuntary intoxication

Involuntary intoxication is a defense when the intoxication serves to negate an element of the crime, including general as well as specific intent and malice crimes. To be considered involuntary, the intoxicating substance must have been taken:

i) Without knowledge of the intoxicating nature of the substance, including substances taken pursuant to medical advice; or

ii) Under duress.

Although intoxication and insanity are two separate defenses, excessive drinking and drug use may bring on actual insanity. Thus, intoxication can give rise to an insanity defense if the requirements for that defense are met.

3. Immaturity/Infancy

At common law, a child under the age of seven could not be convicted of a crime. A child at least seven years old but less than 14 years old was rebuttably presumed to be incapable of committing a crime. A child at least 14 years old could be charged with a crime as an adult.

Modern statutes have modified this and provide that no child can be convicted of a crime until a certain age is reached, usually between the ages of 11 and 14.

F. TYPES OF CRIMES

There are two basic types of crimes—felonies and misdemeanors. A felony is a crime that is punishable by death or imprisonment for more than one year; a misdemeanor is a crime punishable by imprisonment for one year or less or by a fine or by both.

II. HOMICIDE

A. DEFINITION

Homicide is the killing of a living human being by another, and includes the offenses of murder and manslaughter. At common law, homicide was divided into three categories: (i) homicide justified by law, (ii) criminal homicide, and (iii) excusable homicide. Criminal homicides were divided into three offenses: murder, voluntary manslaughter, and involuntary manslaughter.

Common-law murder is the unlawful killing of another living human being with malice aforethought. Malice can be shown by any one of the following states of mind: (i) intent to kill, (ii) intent to do serious bodily injury, (iii) reckless indifference to human life (depraved-heart murder), and (iv) intent to commit a felony (felony murder). (*See* § II.B., Types of Homicide, *infra*.) Manslaughter includes two types: voluntary and involuntary. Voluntary manslaughter involves an intentional killing, and involuntary manslaughter is an unintentional killing.

1. Killing a Person

In order for a homicide to occur, a living human being must die. A body need not be found; death can be established by circumstantial evidence.

A person cannot be killed twice. Shooting a corpse is not homicide, but can be a crime (e.g., abuse of a corpse).

At common law, a fetus is not a living person.

2. Causation

To prove a homicide, the prosecution must show that the defendant caused the victim's death. The prosecution must prove both actual and proximate causation.

a. Actual cause

If the victim would not have died **but for** the defendant's act, then the defendant's act is the actual cause (i.e., cause-in-fact) of the killing. When the defendant sets in motion forces that led to the death of the victim, the defendant is the actual cause of the victim's death.

Example: A mechanical device set up by the defendant kills an individual. The defendant is considered to have caused that individual's death.

1) Substantial factor

Actual causation can be found when there are multiple causes, (i.e., other persons are also responsible for the victim's death) and the defendant's act was a substantial factor in causing the death.

Simultaneous acts by different individuals who are acting independently may each be considered the actual cause of a victim's death, even though the victim would have died in the absence of one of the acts.

Example: Two individuals simultaneously shoot a third individual. Either of the shots would have killed the victim. Each shot is considered the actual cause of the victim's death.

2) Independent cause

A defendant's act will not be deemed the cause when a victim is killed by an independent cause before the defendant's act can kill the victim.

> **Example:** A plans to kill B by stabbing him. A approaches B, finding him lying on the bed in a nonresponsive state. A assumes that B is asleep and stabs him multiple times. In reality, however, B had died one hour previously due to a massive heart attack. A's actions did not cause B's death; therefore, there is no homicide (A may be guilty of attempted murder).

3) Victim's preexisting condition

A victim's preexisting condition that contributes to the victim's death does not supplant the defendant's conduct as an actual cause of the victim's death.

> **Example:** A victim has heart condition. The defendant hits the victim with a club intending to kill the victim, but the blow would not have killed the victim if the victim had not had the heart condition. The defendant's actions are nevertheless the actual cause of the victim's death.

4) Mercy killing

Providing a person with the **means** by which that person can commit suicide generally does not make the provider guilty of murder as an accomplice (because suicide is not homicide) but instead guilty of a lesser crime, such as assisting a suicide. Note, however, that consent is not a defense to homicide, so a "mercy killing" (i.e., euthanasia) can be a criminal homicide even if the person was willing to die because of a painful terminal illness.

b. Proximate cause

Proximate cause (i.e., legal cause) exists only when the defendant is deemed legally responsible for a homicide. For the defendant to be legally responsible for a homicide, the death must be foreseeable. A death caused by the defendant's conduct is deemed foreseeable if death is the natural and probable result of the conduct. Even if there is some intervening act, the defendant will still be held responsible unless the intervening act was so out-of-the-ordinary that it would be unjust to hold the defendant criminally responsible for the outcome. Or, as the MPC explains it, when the injury suffered is generally of the type intended by the defendant, proximate causation exists if the injury is "not too remote or accidental in its occurrence to have a [just] bearing on the actor's liability or on the gravity of his offense." MPC § 203(2)(b). Actions by a third party (e.g., negligence by the doctor treating the victim), as well as actions by the victim (e.g., suicide to escape the pain that resulted from the injuries inflicted by the defendant), are generally foreseeable. However, actions by third parties will relieve the defendant of liability if they are independent of the defendant's conduct and unforeseeable, or dependent on the defendant's conduct and "abnormal" (i.e., not just unforeseeable, but unusual or extraordinary in hindsight). 2 Wayne R. LaFave, Substantive Criminal Law § 14.5(d), at 453 (2d ed. 2003). Actions by a force of nature that are not within the defendant's control are generally not foreseeable (e.g., a lightning strike that kills a victim the defendant tied to a tree).

An act that accelerates death is a legal cause of that death.

> **EXAM NOTE:** A common situation in which the issue of proximate cause arises is when the felony murder rule applies. A frequently applied standard is that the homicide must be a natural and probable consequence of the defendant's actions.

c. Year and one day rule

At common law, the defendant's act was conclusively presumed not to be the proximate cause of the killing if the victim died more than one year and one day after the act was performed. Most states have either abolished this rule or have extended the time period of responsibility.

B. TYPES OF HOMICIDE

1. Murder

Common-law murder is the:

i)   Unlawful (i.e., without a legal excuse);

ii) Killing;

iii) Of another human being;

iv) Committed with **malice aforethought**.

"Malice aforethought" includes the following mental states: intent to kill, intent to inflict serious bodily injury, reckless indifference to an unjustifiably high risk to human life (depraved heart), or the intent to commit certain felonies (felony murder).

a. Intent to kill

Conduct, accompanied by the intent to kill, which is the legal cause of the death of a living person, constitutes intent-to-kill murder unless the legal circumstances surrounding the homicide are such that the crime is reduced to voluntary manslaughter. An inference of intent to kill may be made if an intentional use of a deadly weapon was used in the commission of the crime.

Example: A intends to kill B, and by his conduct of shooting B, kills him.

b. Intent to inflict serious bodily harm

A person who intends to do serious bodily injury or "grievous bodily harm," but actually succeeds in killing, is guilty of murder despite the lack of intention to kill.

Example: A intentionally hits B over the head with a baseball bat, intending to hurt B but not kill him, and B later dies from a skull fracture.

Intent to inflict serious bodily harm is an unintentional killing that results in death.

Intent to inflict serious bodily harm can be inferred from the use of a deadly weapon to inflict the bodily injury.

c. Depraved heart

A killing that results from reckless indifference to an unjustifiably high risk to human life is a depraved-heart murder.

Example: A stands on top of a highway overpass and for a joke drops a bowling ball into on-coming traffic, resulting in the death of B, a passing motorist.

Depraved-heart murder is an unintentional killing that results in death. There is a split among jurisdictions as to whether the requisite depravity exists when a defendant is actually unaware of the risk involved in the conduct, but the majority of states and the MPC impose liability only when the defendant actually realizes the danger. (The minority objective standard imposes guilt if a reasonable person would have recognized the danger.) Note that even those states that ordinarily follow a subjective standard allow a conviction if the reason the defendant failed to appreciate the risk was due to voluntary intoxication.

Generally, reckless driving alone will not lead to a charge of depraved-heart murder. Such a charge would be appropriate only if the reckless driving was extreme, such as if it were combined with intoxication or other aggravating factors. *See, e.g., Cook v. Commonwealth,* 129 S.W.3d 351 (Ky. 2004) (an intoxicated defendant driving at an excessive speed); *State v. Woodall,* 744 P.2d 732 (Ariz. Ct. App. 1987) (intoxicated defendant drove almost 70 mph on a 40-mph double curve).

d. Felony murder

Felony murder is an unintended killing proximately caused by and during the commission or attempted commission of an inherently dangerous felony. The felonies traditionally considered inherently dangerous are: **B**urglary, **A**rson, **R**ape, **R**obbery, and **K**idnapping. [Mnemonic: **BARRK**]. (Common-law felonies also include murder, manslaughter, mayhem, and sodomy, but the BARRK crimes are most commonly tested in the context of felony murder; neither murder nor manslaughter can be the basis for a felony-murder charge.) To convict a defendant of felony murder, the prosecution must establish the underlying felony and that the defendant committed that felony. In addition, in most states, any aggravated felony committed with the use of a dangerous weapon is subject to the felony-murder rule. However, such an aggravated felony must be independent of the killing itself to qualify as an underlying felony for felony murder (e.g., aggravated battery cannot be the basis for a felony-murder charge).

Example: X accidentally shoots the owner of a home while committing a burglary. X can be charged with felony murder.

There is no charge of attempted felony murder if the unintended victim does not die. Generally, co-felons (including accessories) are vicariously liable for the death if the death is a foreseeable consequence of the underlying inherently dangerous felony.

If one of two co-felons kills the other during the commission or attempted commission of a dangerous felony, this will also constitute felony murder. If the co-felon is killed by a victim or a police officer, though, the defendant is generally not guilty of felony murder.

Note: The underlying felony will generally "merge" into the crime of felony murder for the purposes of Double Jeopardy. That is, the predicate felony is generally deemed a lesser-included offense of the felony murder. For example, in the majority of jurisdictions, a defendant who kills the proprietor of a store while committing a robbery can be punished only for felony murder; the robbery conviction would "merge" into the felony-murder conviction. A minority of jurisdictions have enacted statutes explicitly allowing cumulative punishment for both the felony murder and the underlying felony.

1) Defenses to felony murder

One of the following circumstances can constitute a defense to a felony-murder charge:

i) A valid defense to the underlying felony;

ii) The felony was not distinct from or independent of killing itself (e.g., aggravated battery);

iii) Death was not a foreseeable result or a natural and probable consequence of the felony (i.e., there was no proximate causation); or

iv) Death occurred after the commission of the felony and the ensuing flight from the scene of the crime.

2) Killing by felony victim or police

a) Death of bystander

When **someone other than a co-felon** is killed by a police officer or dies as a result of resistance by the victim of the felony, the felon's liability for that death will depend on whether an agency theory or proximate-cause theory is applied. Under an agency theory, the felon will not be liable for the death of a bystander caused by a felony victim or police officer because neither person is the felon's agent. Under the proximate-cause theory, liability for the bystander's death may attach to the felon because the death is a direct consequence of the felony.

The same analysis is applicable when a victim of the underlying felony or a police officer is killed by someone who is not one of the felons.

b) Death of co-felon

When a co-felon is killed by a victim or a police officer either in self-defense or to prevent escape, under the *Redline* doctrine (*Commonwealth v. Redline*, 391 Pa. 486 (1958)), the defendant is generally not guilty of felony murder. The killing by the victim or the police officer is considered justifiable homicide. Some jurisdictions even extend this to the situation in which a co-felon kills herself. If one co-felon kills another co-felon while committing the underlying felony, jurisdictions are split on allowing a felony murder charge.

2. Statutory Crimes of Murder

At common law, there were no degrees of murder. Under modern statutory rules, murder is generally divided into two degrees: first-degree and second-degree murder.

a. First-degree murder

First-degree murder is generally defined as a deliberate and premeditated murder. First-degree murder, defined in this manner, is a specific-intent crime, which means that specific-intent defenses are available for a defendant (*see* I.B.1. Specific Intent Crimes, *supra*). In addition, felony murder is frequently classified as first-degree murder.

1) Created by statute

Because the specific criteria for first-degree murder are established only by statute, a homicide cannot be first-degree murder without a corresponding statute.

2) Premeditation

The distinguishing element of first-degree murder is premeditation, meaning the defendant reflected on the idea of killing or planned the killing. The amount of time needed for premeditation may be brief. It must be long enough after forming the intent to kill for the defendant to have been fully conscious of the intent and to have considered the killing (i.e., a time for reflection). This requirement does not apply to felony murder.

3) During the commission of an inherently dangerous felony

If a murder is committed during the perpetration of an enumerated felony, it may be first-degree murder. The most commonly enumerated felonies are **B**urglary, **A**rson, **R**ape, **R**obbery, and **K**idnapping. [Mnemonic: **BARRK**].

4) Heinous murder

A murder resulting from an egregious act, such as ambush (i.e., lying in wait), torture, bombing, terrorism, or poisoning, may be classified as first-degree murder.

b. Second-degree murder

Second-degree murder is a homicide committed with the necessary malicious intent: the intent to kill, the intent to do great bodily injury, or a depraved-heart murder. In addition, a murder that occurs during the commission of a felony other than the felonies that trigger first-degree murder may statutorily be treated as second-degree murder.

> **EXAM NOTE:** Be sure to differentiate between second-degree murder and first-degree murder when answering exam questions. First-degree murder is a specific intent crime, whereas second-degree murder, like common law murder, is a malice crime.

3. Voluntary Manslaughter

Voluntary manslaughter is homicide committed with malice aforethought, but also with mitigating circumstances.

a. "Heat of passion"

Murder committed in response to adequate provocation (i.e., in the "heat of passion") is voluntary manslaughter. The "heat of passion" means that the defendant was provoked by a situation that could inflame the passion of a reasonable person to the extent that it could cause that person to momentarily act out of passion rather than reason. The defendant cannot have been set off by something that would not bother most people.

> **EXAM NOTE:** Remember that "heat of passion" is NOT a defense; it merely reduces murder to voluntary manslaughter.

1) Adequate provocation

A serious battery, a threat of deadly force, or discovery of adultery by a spouse constitutes adequate provocation. Usually mere words, such as taunts, do not.

While an intentional killing committed when resisting arrest is generally murder, the intentional killing can be manslaughter if the arrest is unlawful and the defendant acts in the "heat of passion."

2) "Cooling off"

If there was sufficient time between the provocation and the killing for a reasonable person to cool off, then murder is not mitigated to manslaughter. If there was sufficient time to cool off for a reasonable person even though the defendant himself did not regain self-control, the murder is not mitigated to manslaughter.

> **EXAM NOTE:** If the fact pattern shows that there was sufficient time to cool off and the defendant did not calm down, the murder is not mitigated to manslaughter.

Second provocation: Even when the defendant has "cooled off," a second encounter with the victim may give rise to another situation in which the defendant acts in the "heat of passion."

3) Causation

There must be a causal connection between provocation, passion, and the fatal act. There will.

4) Transferred provocation

When, because of a reasonable mistake of fact, the defendant is in error in identifying her provoker or accidentally kills the wrong person, she will be guilty of voluntary manslaughter if that would have been her crime had she killed the provoker. If, however, the defendant, in her passion, intentionally kills another person known to her to be an innocent bystander, then there will be no mitigation, and murder, rather than voluntary manslaughter, will apply.

b. Imperfect defense

In many states, murder may be reduced to voluntary manslaughter when the defendant contends that his use of deadly force was necessary in defense of himself or others, but (i) the defendant started the altercation or (ii) the defendant unreasonably (if truly) believed in the necessity of using deadly force.

For a more detailed discussion of imperfect self-defense and self-defense for an initial aggressor, *see* § V.B.1, Self-Defense, *infra*.

4. Involuntary Manslaughter

Involuntary manslaughter is an unintentional homicide committed with criminal negligence (recklessness under the MPC) or during an unlawful act.

a. Criminal negligence

Criminal negligence is grossly negligent action (or inaction when there is a duty to act) that puts another person at a significant risk of serious bodily injury or death. It requires more than ordinary negligence for tort liability and something less than the extremely reckless conduct required for depraved-heart murder. For example, the failure of a parent, under a duty of care, to provide medical care to a sick minor child constitutes criminal negligence.

Under the Model Penal Code rule, the defendant must have acted recklessly, which is a "gross deviation from the standard of conduct that a law-abiding person would observe in the actor's situation." MPC § 2.02(2)(c). The defendant must have been actually aware of the risk his conduct posed.

b. Unlawful act

The unlawful act may occur in one of two ways:

i)   Under the misdemeanor-manslaughter rule, which is a killing committed in the commission of a *malum in se* (wrong in itself) misdemeanor; or

ii) A killing committed in the commission of a felony that is not statutorily treated as first-degree felony murder or second-degree murder.

The term "*malum in se*" means "wrong in itself," or "inherently evil," and includes crimes such as assault and battery. "*Malum prohibitum*" refers to wrongs that are merely prohibited, (i.e., not inherently immoral or hurtful, but wrong due to a statute), such as a parking violation, smuggling, or failure to obtain a license. A homicide resulting from a wrong that is *malum prohibitum* will constitute involuntary manslaughter only if the unlawful act was willful or constituted criminal negligence.

c. Causation

There must be a causal connection between the unlawful act and the death for involuntary manslaughter to apply.

III. OTHER CRIMES

A. CRIMES AGAINST PROPERTY

1. Larceny

Larceny is the:

i) Trespassory;

ii) Taking and;

iii) Carrying away;

iv) Of the personal property;

v) Of another;

vi) With the intent to permanently deprive that person of the property (i.e., intent to steal).

a. Trespass

The property must be taken without the owner's consent. If the original taking was without consent, yet was not unlawful because there was no intent to steal at the time of the taking, larceny may be committed at a later time if the intent to steal is later formed. Under the "continuing trespass" rule, the original trespass is deemed to be "continuing" in order for the criminal act to coincide with the criminal intent. The defendant's original taking must have been wrongful (e.g., a taking based on knowledge that the property belonged to another, such as a taking with the intent to borrow and return the property).

b. Taking

The taking (also known as caption) requirement is satisfied by any trespassory removal of the property from the owner's possession into another's control.

1) Destruction of property in owner's possession

The destruction of property while it is in the owner's possession (e.g., breaking an object held by the owner) is not a taking.

2) Use of agent

If the defendant uses an agent, even one unaware of the defendant's criminal intent, a taking occurs.

c. Carrying away (asportation)

The carrying away requirement (also known as asportation) is satisfied by even a slight movement of the property (e.g., inches).

d. Personal property

The property taken must be personal, not real property. Electricity or gas supplied by a utility constitutes personal property.

1) Intangibles

At common law, only tangible property could be the subject of a larceny. Today, larceny has generally been expanded to include intangibles. Documents that represent the rights to intangible property (e.g., stocks, bonds) are treated as personal property.

2) Services

Modern theft statutes usually criminalize obtaining services without paying for them (i.e., the theft of services).

3) Real property items

The taking of fixtures (i.e., items affixed to real property) or real property items (e.g., trees, unharvested crops) is not larceny when the defendant's act of severance occurs immediately before the carrying away of the fixture or other real property items. However, when the real property items have previously been severed from the land by the owner, they become personal property (e.g., picked apples), and the carrying away of such items can be larceny.

e. Another's property

The property must be in the possession of someone other than the defendant.

Contrast with embezzlement: For embezzlement, the defendant is legally entrusted with the property by the owner and then the defendant later fraudulently converts the property to his own use. With larceny, the initial taking must be trespassory; there cannot be lawful entrustment by the owner. This is the main difference between the two crimes.

1) Owner of property

The owner of property (i.e., a person who has title to it) can commit larceny when someone other than the owner (e.g., lessee) is entitled to current possession of the property.

2) Thief

Larceny may even be committed against a thief. The taking of stolen property taken from a thief can constitute larceny unless the taker has a superior possessory interest in the property (e.g., an owner or a lessee of the property).

3) Joint owners

A joint owner of property who takes possession of the property from a co-owner is not guilty of larceny because the taker has an equal right to possess the property.

4) Constructive possession

"Constructive possession" means legal possession if factual possession does not exist.

An owner has constructive possession of property when actual possession, but not title, is taken from her by fraud. The crime is called "larceny by trick." *See* § III.A.3, Larcen by Trick, *infra*.

a) Employee's control over employer's property

Low-level employees can only be guilty of larceny whereas high-level employees are typically guilty of embezzlement. An employer generally has constructive possession of property in the hands of a lower-level employee. Such an employee has custody, not possession, of the employer's property. A higher-level employee (e.g., company president) who has greater authority with respect to the employer's property may have possession of, rather than custody of, such property and may be guilty of embezzlement, rather than larceny, for taking the property.

b) Bailee possession

A bailee is guilty of larceny if, with intent to steal, the bailee opens and takes property from closed containers belonging to the bailor. Otherwise, the bailee simply has possession.

5) Abandoned vs. lost property

Property that has been abandoned by its owner (i.e., the owner has surrendered all rights to the property) is not subject to larceny. Property that has been lost by its owner can be the subject of larceny if, at the time of the finding, the finder knows the owner or believes that he can locate the owner and the finder possesses the necessary intent to permanently deprive the owner of the property.

6) Mistakenly delivered property

Property that has been mistakenly delivered may be the subject of larceny if the recipient of the property realizes that a mistake has been made at the time of the receipt of the property and the recipient possesses the necessary intent to permanently deprive.

a) Special problems

When a defendant takes legitimate possession of an item, but he discovers another item enclosed in the larger item (the container), the issue arises as to whether the defendant had possession of the enclosed item at the time the defendant legitimately possessed the larger item. If so, there is no larceny because the defendant has not taken the property from another's possession. However, determining whether or not there is possession is a difficult task. Larceny may depend on whether or not the parties intended to transfer the container. If the intent is to transfer, then no larceny is committed because the defendant effectively takes immediate possession of both items. A few states hold that the defendant does not take possession of the enclosed property until he discovers it. At which point, if he forms the intent to keep the property, then he is guilty of larceny.

f. Intent to permanently deprive

Larceny is a **specific intent** crime. At the time of the taking, the intent to permanently deprive the owner of the property must be present at the time of the taking. There is no defense of restoration if the defendant later has a change of heart and restores the property to the rightful owner. The crime is complete at the time of the taking.

> **Examples:** The intent to permanently deprive the owner of the property can occur when the defendant takes property with the intent to claim a reward, the defendant intends to throw away or abandon the property, the defendant intends to sell the property back to the owner, or the defendant intends to pledge or pawn the property without being able to redeem it.

1) Insufficient intent

The necessary specific intent does not exist when the defendant's intent is to:

i) Borrow property with the ability to return it;

ii) Pay for merchandise that she has the means to buy; or

iii) Take money as repayment of a debt.

a) Intent to borrow

If the defendant intends only to borrow the property with the ability to do so, then larceny does not occur because there is no intent to permanently deprive the owner of the property, (e.g., borrowing a car to run an errand).

> **EXAM NOTE:** If property is taken with the intent to return the property and is accidently damaged or destroyed, larceny has not occurred.

> **Example:** D takes A's car to run an errand. On the way back to A's house, D is in a car accident and A's car is totaled. D is not guilty of larceny.

b) Intent to pay

A defendant's intent to pay for property is not sufficient to prevent larceny when the property is not offered for sale.

c) Repayment of debt

If a defendant takes property with the honest belief that she is entitled to the property as repayment of a debt (i.e., a claim of right), then the taking does not constitute larceny. (Note, however, that a claim of right cannot serve as a justification for robbery in most states.)

d) Rewards

A defendant intending to return property in expectation of claiming a reward has not committed larceny, unless his intent is to return the property only upon receiving the reward.

2) Sufficient intent

There is sufficient intent if the defendant intends to create a substantial risk of loss or if the defendant intends to sell the goods back to the owner.

3) Time for measuring intent

The intent to permanently deprive is generally measured at the time of the taking. The continuing trespass rule may apply to stretch the time at which intent is measured. *See* § III.A.3.a.1, *supra.*

2. Larceny by Trick

Larceny by trick is

i) Larceny

ii) Accomplished by fraud or deceit

iii) That results in the conversion of the property of another.

Larceny by trick requires that the defendant fraudulently induce the victim to deliver possession of, but not title to, the property to the defendant.

a. False representation of material present or past fact

The representation (whether oral, written, or by actions) must be false in fact and be of a material past or present fact. A prediction about a future event, a false promise, or an opinion such as sales talk or puffing is not sufficient.

b. Reliance by the victim

The victim must rely upon the false representation, and that reliance must cause the victim to give possession to the defendant. This standard is subjective, not objective.

c. Conversion of property

Unlike larceny, larceny by trick requires that the property be converted. Property is converted when the defendant, in a manner so serious as to deprive the victim of the use of the property, deprives the victim of possession of the property or interferes with the property. The deprivation must be substantial enough to justify a court to order the defendant to pay the full fair market value of the property.

Contrast with false pretenses: Under larceny by trick, the defendant obtains possession. Under false pretenses, the defendant obtains title. *See* § III.A.5, False Pretenses *infra.*

3. Forgery

Forgery is the:

i) Making;

ii) Of a false writing;

iii) With apparent legal significance; and

iv) With the intent to defraud (i.e., make wrongful use of the forged document).

a. Making

Making includes creating, altering, or fraudulently inducing another to sign a document when that person is unaware of the significance of the document. The defendant need not use the document; the crime is complete upon the "making" of the document. When property is acquired by use of the forged document, the defendant may also be guilty of another crime, such as false pretenses (*see* § III.A.5, False Pretenses, *infra*).

b. False writing

The writing itself must be false, instead of merely including false information in an otherwise genuine document. (Note: Signing another person's name on a check or other commercial paper makes the check itself false.) When there is an alteration, the alteration must be material.

c. Apparent legal significance

A document has legal significance if it has value beyond its own existence. A contract, deed, will, or check has value beyond the document itself; a painting does not.

d. Intent to defraud

The defendant must intend to make wrongful use of the writing, (e.g., cashing a check with a forged drawer's signature). There must be intent to defraud, even if no one actually is defrauded.

4. Embezzlement

Embezzlement is the:

i) Fraudulent;

ii) Conversion;

iii) Of the property;

iv) Of another;

v) By a person who is in lawful possession of the property.

a. Conversion

Conversion is a serious interference with the owner's rights to the property by inappropriately using property held pursuant to a trust agreement either by selling it, damaging it, or unreasonably withholding possession. The defendant need not personally benefit from the conversion. No movement or carrying away of the property is required. If it is unclear whether there was a conversion of the property, the victim must demand a return of the property and the embezzler must refuse to return the property before a claim for embezzlement can be made.

b. Intent to defraud

The defendant must intend to defraud the owner of the property. If the defendant intends to return the exact property that is converted and has the ability to do so at the time that the intent is formed, the defendant lacks the intent to defraud the property owner. If the defendant intends to return similar property or the cash equivalent of the value of the property, the defendant has the intent necessary to commit embezzlement. A conversion pursuant to a claim of right also is not embezzlement.

c. Type of property

Property that is subject to larceny is also subject to embezzlement. In some states, real property, as well as personal property, may be embezzled.

d. Another's property

The property embezzled must belong to another. The inability to fulfill a contractual obligation (e.g., pay back a loan) is not embezzlement.

e. Lawful possession

The embezzler must be in lawful possession of the property at the time that the intent to defraud occurs, although some states limit embezzlement to property entrusted to the embezzler.

> **Example:** O's car breaks down and he entrusts it to M, a mechanic, for repair. M fixes the car and then sells it to T. M has committed embezzlement. He was a bailee of the car, in lawful possession, when he sold it to the T.

5. False Pretenses

False pretenses (also called "obtaining property by false pretenses" or "larceny by false pretenses") is:

i)   Obtaining title to the property;

ii) Of another person;

iii) Through the reliance of that person;

iv) On a known false representation of a material past or present fact; and

v)   The representation is made with the intent to defraud.

a. Title must pass

Title to the property must pass from the victim to the defendant. Title can be obtained without possession of the property, but mere possession does not constitute false pretenses. If the defendant subjectively believes that he owns the property in question, he will not be guilty of false pretenses.

> **Contrast larceny by trick:** Mere possession of the property without legal title by a defendant can be sufficient for larceny by trick.

b. Type of property

Generally, property that may be subject to larceny is also subject to false pretenses.

c. False factual representation

The representation must be false and must be of a material past or present fact. A prediction about a future event, a false promise, or an opinion, such as sales talk or puffing, is not sufficient. The representation may be made orally, in writing, or by actions (e.g., resetting a car's odometer). Silence does not constitute a representation, even when the defendant is aware of the owner's misunderstanding, unless the defendant caused the misunderstanding or the defendant has a fiduciary obligation to the victim.

d. Reliance by the victim

The victim must rely upon the false representation, and that reliance must cause the victim to pass title to the defendant. This standard is subjective, not objective.

e. Intent to defraud

The defendant must know that the representation is false and specifically intend to defraud. Most courts find that a defendant acts knowingly and has knowledge of a particular fact when he is aware of a high probability of the fact's existence and deliberately avoids learning the truth. A few states require actual knowledge of a particular fact.

A defendant has the intent to defraud required to establish false pretenses when she intends that the person to whom the false representation is made will rely upon it.

6. Robbery

Robbery is:

i) Larceny;

ii) From the person or presence of the victim;

iii) By force or intimidation.

a. Elements of larceny

All of the elements of larceny are necessary for robbery. Larceny is the (i) trespassory, (ii) taking and carrying away, (iii) of the personal property of another, (iv) with the intent to steal (*see* III.A.1. Larceny, *supra*).

b. From the person or presence

The property taken must be on the victim's person or within the victim's reach or control (from the presence of the victim). For example, if a victim is restrained by the defendant within the victim's home prior to the seizure of the property, items taken from the entire house can be treated as "from the victim's presence."

c. By force or intimidation

The taking of the property must be accomplished by force or intimidation. The force or imitation must occur before the taking, simultaneously with the taking, or immediately following the taking to retain the stolen property or to effect an escape.

1) Force

The force used by the defendant must be more than the amount necessary to effectuate taking and carrying away the property.

When a pickpocket takes the victim's property without the victim's knowledge, the taking does not constitute robbery unless the victim notices the taking and resists. Similarly, most state courts that have considered the issue have said that purse-snatching is not robbery unless additional circumstances transform the larceny into a robbery. Such circumstances are present when the victim notices the taking and resists, or when the victim is intimidated, knocked down, struck, or injured by greater force than is required to carry away the property.

> **EXAM NOTE:** Regarding the degree of force necessary for robbery, remember that slight force is sufficient. Common law required that the force must be manifested immediately before or at the same time as the taking, while the modern trend in many jurisdictions is that the force may be immediately following the taking (e.g., during escape).

2) Intimidation

The threat must be of immediate serious physical injury to the victim, a close family member, or other person present. A threat to damage or destroy property, other than the victim's home, probably is not sufficient.

d. Merger

Larceny, assault, and battery all merge into robbery or attempted robbery.

7. Extortion

a. Common law

At common law, extortion was the unlawful taking of money by a government officer.

b. Modern approach

Most jurisdictions have enacted statutes that more broadly define extortion as the taking of money or property from another by threat. In most jurisdictions, it is the making of threats (rather than obtaining the property) that is the essence of the crime. In a minority of jurisdictions, however, the accused must actually obtain the property to be guilty.

Extortion differs from robbery in two respects:

i) The threats need not be of immediate harm, nor need they be of a physical nature (e.g., threatening future exposure of the victim's marital infidelity); and

ii) The property intended to be taken need not be on the victim or in his presence.

8. Burglary

Common law burglary is the:

i) Breaking and;

ii) Entering;

iii) Of the dwelling;

iv) Of another;

v) At nighttime;

vi) With the specific intent to commit a felony therein.

a. Breaking

Breaking is accomplished by using force to create an opening into a dwelling, such as by shattering a window or kicking in a door. The force used may be slight, such as opening an unlocked door or window.

Note: It is not a breaking to enter a dwelling through an open door or window, unless the opening must be enlarged in order to allow the entry.

1) Breaking without use of force

If entry is obtained by fraud or threat, there is a breaking. If the defendant had consent by the owner to enter, no breaking occurs unless the consent was obtained by fraud or the defendant exceeded the scope of such consent.

2) Breaking within dwelling

If entry is gained with consent, a breaking can still occur if the defendant breaks into a part of the dwelling structure, such as by opening a closet door or wall safe. The mere opening of an object within the dwelling, such as a desk drawer, trunk, or box, does not constitute a breaking.

3) Use of force to exit—No breaking

The use of force to exit a dwelling does not constitute a breaking.

Most states now require only that the defendant enter the premises; a breaking is not required. The common law requires a breaking.

b. Entering

Entering occurs when any portion of the defendant's body (e.g., a hand through a broken windowpane) or an instrument used by the defendant to gain entry (e.g., rock thrown through a window), crosses into the dwelling without permission through the opening created by the breaking.

> **EXAM NOTE:** Breaking and entering need not happen at the same time, but the entering must follow the breaking.

c. Dwelling of another

A dwelling is a structure regularly occupied for habitation. It need not be occupied at the time of the breaking, but must not be abandoned.

All states have statutes that expand the type of structure to include non-dwellings, such as businesses, buildings, or cars, and surrounding areas, such as the yard.

The dwelling must be that of another person. A person cannot burglarize his own dwelling, but the owner of a dwelling who has transferred the possessory interest to another (e.g., a tenant) can be guilty of burglary.

d. Nighttime

Nighttime occurs during the period of darkness between sunset and sunrise. It is not considered nighttime if there is sufficient natural daylight to see the burglar's face.

The common law required that the breaking and entering occur during nighttime. Only a very few states require that all forms of burglary be committed at night, although many states impose more severe penalties on nighttime burglaries.

e. Specific intent to commit a felony

At the time of the breaking and entering, the defendant must have the intent to commit a felony (e.g., larceny, robbery, rape, murder, etc.) inside the dwelling.

A defendant who fails to commit the underlying felony may nevertheless be guilty of burglary as well as attempt with regard to the underlying felony. If the underlying felony is completed, it does **not** merge with the burglary.

Many states have broadened the scope of the crimes intended to be committed to include misdemeanor thefts.

9. Arson

Arson is the:

i)   Malicious;

ii) Burning;

iii) Of the dwelling;

iv) Of another.

a. Malice

Malice does not require ill will. The defendant is not required to intend to burn the dwelling of another; it is sufficient that the defendant performs an act with reckless disregard that creates a substantial risk of such burning.

b. Burning

The damage to the dwelling must be caused by fire. Smoke damage alone is insufficient. In addition, the damage must affect the structure of the building; mere scorching (i.e., discoloration due to heat) of the walls and burning of the contents of the dwelling are insufficient. When the dwelling is constructed of wood, there must be at least a charring of the wood (i.e., damage to the wood itself).

c. Another's dwelling

Ownership is not required. The test is whether a person has the right to possession or occupancy of the dwelling. Many states have expanded arson to include the burning of one's own dwelling. At common law, however, the burning of one's dwelling (house burning) that was located near other houses or in a city was only a misdemeanor, and burning one's own building for insurance fraud was not considered arson.

> Most states have expanded arson to include the burning of buildings other than dwellings, but burning the contents of a building alone does not constitute arson.

10. Possession Offenses

Possession of a prohibited object (e.g., drug paraphernalia, burglar's tools) or a substance (e.g., illegal narcotics) is unlawful if the defendant exercises control over such object or substance. The defendant is not required to be aware that possession of the object is illegal. Dominion and control must exist for a period long enough to have provided the defendant with an opportunity to cease such dominion and control.

11. Receiving Stolen Goods

Receiving stolen property is a statutory crime that requires:

i) Receiving control of stolen property;

ii) Knowledge that the property is stolen; and

iii) Intent to permanently deprive the owner of the property.

Knowledge that the property is stolen must coincide with the act of receiving the property. Only control, not possession, is necessary. The goods must have actually been stolen at the time they are received and the defendant must believe that they have been stolen.

12. Legislative Changes to Theft Crimes

There are several changes made to the common law property offenses under the MPC and through states' criminal codes. Larceny, false pretenses, embezzlement and receipt of stolen goods are treated as a single statutory crime of theft. The definition of property has been expanded to cover intangibles, services, and documents. In addition, the defendant need only have unauthorized control over the property.

B. **CRIMES AGAINST THE PERSION**

1. **Battery**

Battery is the:

i)   Unlawful;

ii) Application of force;

iii) To another person;

iv) That causes bodily harm to that person or constitutes an offensive touching.

a. **Unlawful**

"Unlawful" means that the force is applied without legal excuse. Excessive use of force by a police officer during an arrest is unlawful.

b. **Application of force**

The touching, however slight, must result in bodily harm (e.g., a bruise) or an offensive touching (e.g., an unwanted kiss). The force can be applied by a third party acting under the defendant's direction or by an object controlled by the defendant (e.g., a brick thrown by the defendant).

Example: D hits H in front of H's wife, W. W is so upset at D's action that she suffers a seizure. D cannot be charged with battery against W, as there was no physical touching. D can, of course, be charged with battery for hitting H.

c. **To the person of another**

The application of force to an object near, carried by, or attached to the victim constitutes a battery if the victim suffers bodily harm or an offensive touching.

Example: A battery occurs if a defendant kicks a cane used by a victim for support causing the victim to fall and injure herself.

d. **Requisite intent**

Battery is a general intent crime that includes not only intentional conduct but also criminal negligence (i.e., conduct that carries a high degree of risk to others).

e. **Consent defense**

Although consent is generally not a defense to a crime, consent may be a defense to a battery. Consent may be explicit (e.g., a signed authorization for surgery) or implicit (e.g., participation in an athletic event).

f. **Aggravated battery**

Battery may carry a greater penalty, by statute, when serious bodily injury is inflicted or bodily injury is caused by the use of a deadly weapon.

2. **Assault**

Assault is:

i)   An attempt to commit a battery; or

ii) Intentionally placing another in apprehension of imminent bodily harm.

Battery Distinguished: The defendant **must** cause bodily injury or actually touch the victim (or something attached to his person) for a battery to occur. An assault can occur if the defendant does not touch the victim.

a. Attempted battery

The defendant must take a substantial step toward the commission of a battery. Like all attempt crimes, the defendant must have the specific intent to commit a battery.

b. Fear of harm

The "fear of harm" type of assault (also called "apprehension assault") is a general intent crime—the defendant must intend to cause bodily harm or apprehension of such harm. The victim's apprehension must be reasonable. Unlike attempted battery, because actual apprehension is necessary, the victim's lack of awareness of the threat of harm is a defense to this type of assault.

c. Consent defense

As is the case with battery, consent may be a defense to assault.

d. Aggravated assault

Assault may carry a greater penalty, by statute, when a deadly weapon is used.

3. Mayhem

Mayhem is a common-law felony battery that causes the dismemberment or permanent disfigurement of a person. It is the equivalent of modern statutory aggravated battery.

4. Kidnapping

Kidnapping is the:

i) Unlawful;

ii) Confinement of a person;

iii) Against that person's will;

iv) Coupled with either:

    a) The movement; or

    b) The hiding of that person.

Note: There is no requirement for a ransom demand in order to establish kidnapping.

a. Unlawful

The unlawful requirement excludes legally sanctioned actions, such as the imprisonment of a felon by the state after his conviction.

b. Confinement

The victim's freedom of movement must be significantly restricted. It is not enough that the victim is prevented from taking a path or entering an area; the victim must be prevented from leaving an area or compelled to go to a place the victim does not want to go.

c. Against the victim's will

The confinement must be accomplished by force, threats, or fraud.

Consent of the victim to the confinement is a defense if given by a person with the capacity to consent. A child cannot consent to be taken out of the control of a parent or guardian.

d. Movement

The victim need only be moved a short distance (e.g., forced from driver's seat into the trunk of car). If the kidnapping occurs incident to another crime (e.g., robbery), the movement must be more than is necessary for the commission of that crime in order for a defendant to be liable for both kidnapping and the separate offense.

e. Hidden location

Instead of movement, the victim may be concealed for a substantial period of time at a hidden location.

f. Enhanced punishment

A kidnapping that results in bodily injury, interferes with a governmental function, or is done for the purpose of collecting a ransom may be subject to enhanced punishment, by statute.

5. False Imprisonment

False imprisonment is the:

i) Unlawful;

ii) Confinement of a person;

iii) Without consent.

a. Unlawful

The confinement is unlawful unless is it consented to or specifically authorized by law.

b. Confinement

Confinement may be effected by forcing a person to go where he does not want to, or preventing him from going where he does want so long as no alternative routes are available to him. This may be done by actual force, threat of force, or a show of force.

3. Consent

To be effective, consent must be given freely, and the one consenting must have the capacity to do so.

C. RAPE AND STATUTORY RAPE

1. Rape

Rape is:

i) Unlawful;

ii) Sexual intercourse;

iii) With a female;

iv) Against her will by force or threat of immediate force.

Most modern statutes are gender-neutral and have replaced the force requirement with lack of consent.

a. Unlawful—exclusion of husband

At common law, a husband could not rape his wife. Most states have either abolished this restriction or removed the immunity if the husband and wife have separated or filed for divorce.

b. Sexual intercourse

Actual penetration, however slight, is required; emission is not.

c. With a female

Traditionally, the victim of rape could only be a woman. Most states recognize homosexual rape as a crime labeled "sexual assault" rather than rape. Most states also have defined rape in a gender neutral manner; under such statutes, a woman could be the perpetrator of a rape.

d. Without consent

When a woman consents to sexual intercourse, rape has not occurred. Consent does not exist if intercourse is procured by force or threat of harm, or when the female is unable to consent due to a drug-induced stupor or unconsciousness.

1) Threat of harm

Consent is ineffective if a woman consents to sexual intercourse due to threat of harm, although the harm threatened must be imminent and must involve bodily harm. Economic duress is not sufficient.

2) Fraud

Fraud rarely negates consent. Consent obtained by fraud regarding the nature of the act itself—fraud in factum (e.g., the defendant convinces victim the act is not intercourse but part of a medical exam)—is not a valid defense. Consent obtained by fraud in inducement (e.g., a promise of marriage in exchange for sex) is a valid defense.

3) Resistance of victim

Resistance of the victim is not required, but can be evidence of the victim's lack of consent.

e. Intent

Rape is a general intent crime requiring only the intent to commit intercourse without consent of the female. Intent is negated if a defendant reasonably believes the victim's lack of resistance indicates consent.

2. Statutory Rape

Statutory rape is sexual intercourse with a person under the age of consent. It is a strict-liability crime with respect to the age of the victim. Consent by the underage victim is not a defense. A defendant's reasonable mistake of fact concerning the victim's age is not a defense.

IV. INCHOATE CRIMES

The term "inchoate" literally means "unripened." With an inchoate offense, the intended crime need not be committed to be guilty. The inchoate offenses are solicitation, conspiracy, and attempt. Inchoate offenses are specific intent crimes.

A.   MERGER

Traditionally, under the doctrine of merger, if a person's conduct constitutes both a felony and a misdemeanor, then the misdemeanor merges into the felony, and the person can be convicted of the felony but not the misdemeanor. However, if the crimes are of the same degree, i.e., all felonies or all misdemeanors, then there is no merger of the crimes.

Modern law does not subscribe to the doctrine of merger based on the felony-misdemeanor distinction, but does apply this doctrine with respect to solicitation and attempt and the solicited or completed crime. A defendant may be tried, but not punished, for solicitation and the completed crime or for attempt and the completed crime. Solicitation and attempt are said to "merge" into the completed crime.

Contrast conspiracy: Unlike a solicitation and attempt conviction, a conviction for conspiracy does *not* merge into a conviction for the completed crime.

In addition, a defendant may be tried, but not punished, for more than one inchoate offense (i.e., solicitation, conspiracy, and attempt) based on conduct designed to culminate in the commission of the same crime. MPC 5.05(3).

Note: The Double Jeopardy Clause generally prohibits a defendant from being convicted of both a crime and a lesser-included offense (i.e., an offense all the elements of which are also elements of the more-significant crime), such as robbery and larceny. Many jurisdictions characterize this prohibition as a "merger" of the lesser-included offense into the greater.

B.   SOLICITATION

Solicitation is the:

i)   Enticing, encouraging, requesting, or commanding of another person;

ii) To commit a crime;

iii) With the intent that the other person commits the crime.

1.   Encouragement

The encouragement may take the form of enticement, incitement, request, or command. The crime is completed upon the encouragement. The other person need not agree to commit the crime.

2.   Relationship to Other Crimes

If the other person does agree, the solicitor and the person being solicited may also become co-conspirators.

3.   Defenses to Solicitation

a.   Renunciation

At common law, renunciation was no defense to solicitation. Under the Model Penal Code, voluntary renunciation may be a defense, provided the defendant thwarts the commission of the solicited crime.

b.   Factual impossibility

Factual impossibility is not a defense to solicitation. If a solicitor is part of group that was meant to be exempted by the statute, the solicitor cannot be guilty of solicitation (e.g., minor female soliciting sex cannot be guilty of statutory rape).

Example: D goes into a bar and asks X to kill D's husband. If X says no, D can be charged with the crime of solicitation. If X says yes, D can be charged with conspiracy to commit murder. If X actually kills D's husband, the solicitation charge would merge into the underlying murder charge. D could then be charged with both conspiracy to commit murder (which does not merge—see the discussion below) and murder, but not solicitation (which does merge).

C. CONSPIRACY

Conspiracy is:

i) An agreement;

ii) Between two or more persons;

iii) To accomplish an unlawful purpose;

iv) With the intent to accomplish that purpose.

The majority rule and federal law, as well as the MPC, now require the commission of an overt act, which can be legal or illegal, in furtherance of the conspiracy to complete the formation of the conspiracy. At common law, no overt act was required for the conspiracy to be complete.

1. Agreement

The agreement need not be a formal document, or even in writing; an oral agreement is sufficient. An agreement need not be specifically articulated, but can be inferred from a concerted action by the defendants. Thus, depending on the circumstances, silence could even indicate agreement.

> **EXAM NOTE:** Watch out for a situation in which a defendant shares an objective of the conspiracy, but helps the conspirators secretly, without their knowledge. There is no agreement with the defendant, so there cannot be a conspiracy. Note that the defendant could still be charged with aiding and abetting the conspirators' crime.

2. Number of Conspirators

At common law, there is no such thing as a unilateral conspiracy because two or more persons are required to form a conspiracy. This is often referred to as a "bilateral" approach to or theory of conspiracy.

However, the modern trend and the MPC is to allow a "unilateral" conspiracy. Under this approach, the focus of liability is on the individual defendant and his agreement to the object of the conspiracy. A unilateral conspiracy may be formed when *only one party* actually agrees, such as when another party merely feigns agreement, or if the alleged co-conspirators are ultimately acquitted.

a. Feigned agreement

When only one conspirator has the intent to agree, such as when the other conspirator is a governmental agent or pretends to go along with the crime to warn police, there is a conspiracy under the "unilateral" approach but there is no conspiracy at common law unless another participant is involved.

b. Protected by statute

When the purpose of a criminal statute is to protect a type of person (e.g., a statutory rape statute protects the underage participant), there is no conspiracy between the protected party and the targeted defendant.

c. Wharton Rule

Under the Wharton Rule, if a crime requires two or more participants (e.g., adultery) there is no conspiracy unless more parties than are necessary to complete the crime agree to commit the crime. Although there is no conspiracy, the participants may be found guilty of the underlying crime itself. Because the MPC does not require the participation of at least two conspirators, this rule does not apply to conspiracies under the MPC.

d. Corporation and its agents

A corporation can conspire with its own agents with some limitations. In some jurisdictions, there can be no conspiracy between a corporation and a single agent of that corporation. A conspiracy between the corporation and multiple agents of the same corporation may in most jurisdictions satisfy the plurality requirement. A corporation or its agents can enter into a conspiracy with another corporation or agents of that corporation.

e. Prosecution of other conspirators

A conspirator cannot be convicted of conspiracy if all other conspirators are acquitted at the same trial. In other circumstances, such as when co-conspirators are never tried or apprehended, a conspirator may be convicted of conspiracy if the prosecution proves the existence of a conspiracy.

f. Spouses as co-conspirators

Common law did not consider husband and wife as co-conspirators because the law viewed them as a single entity. However, they could, as an entity, conspire with a third person. Nearly every jurisdiction has abolished this common law concept.

3. Unlawful Purpose

Under federal law and the modern trend, "unlawful purpose" is limited to criminal conduct. In some states, even the achievement of a lawful purpose through illegal means can be the subject of a conspiracy. If, however, the conspirators simply conspire to do something that is not illegal, they cannot be found guilty of conspiracy, even if they believed that what they were planning to do was illegal.

4. Specific Intent

Conspiracy is a specific intent crime. A conspirator must have the intent to agree, and the intent to commit the criminal objective. The intent to agree may be inferred from conduct of the parties.

> **Example:** Conspiracy to commit arson requires specific intent, even though the substantive offense of arson only requires malice. Similarly, a conspiracy to commit a strict-liability crime requires intent.

Because the intent to agree and commit the crime are elements of conspiracy, criminal liability for a conspiracy cannot be based solely on knowledge of the existence of the conspiracy. For example, a merchant who supplies goods to a conspirator knowing that the conspirator intends to use the goods in furtherance of the objective of the conspiracy is not a member of the conspiracy simply because the merchant possessed such knowledge. Instead, the merchant must take an additional step to show such intent, such as selling the goods at an exorbitant price, basing the price of the goods on a percentage of the conspiracy's "take," or ordering specially manufactured goods that the merchant does not normally sell.

5. Overt Act Requirement

An overt act was not required at common law, but it is now a required element of a conspiracy under federal law, the MPC, and in a majority of states. When an overt act is required, the conspiracy crime is not complete until the overt act is performed in furtherance of the conspiracy. The overt act can be performed by any co-conspirator, with or without the knowledge of all co-conspirators. The overt act can be lawful or unlawful. However, the MPC does not require an overt act if the conspiratorial crime is a felony in the first or second degree.

Contrast attempt: To constitute attempt, the defendant must have taken a substantial step toward commission of the crime. A mere preparatory act is insufficient for attempt.

6. Scope of Conspiracy

a. Crimes committed by co-conspirators

Under the Pinkerton rule, a conspirator can be convicted of both the offense of conspiracy and all substantive crimes committed by any other co-conspirators acting in furtherance of the conspiracy. Under the Model Penal Code, the minority view, a member of the conspiracy is not criminally liable for such crimes unless that member aids and abets in commission of the crimes.

b. Multiple crimes, single conspiracy

A single conspiracy may have numerous criminal objectives. Not all of the co-conspirators even need to know the identities of all of the other co-conspirators or all of the details of the criminal organization. It is only necessary that all co-conspirators agree to further the common scheme or plan. Multiple conspiracies arise when the objectives and/or crimes are not committed in furtherance of the same agreement, common scheme, and plan.

c. Unknown conspirators, single conspiracy

1) Chain relationship

Persons who do not know each other can be members of the same conspiracy if there is a **community of interest** in the achievement of the object of the conspiracy. A community of interest is usually found when the activities of each person resemble links of a chain, such as a scheme to acquire and distribute drugs. In such a conspiracy, all of the members of the community of interest are liable for the acts of the others in furtherance of the conspiracy.

2) Hub-spoke relationship

A scheme that resembles a hub with spokes, such as the processing of fraudulent loans by one person that were submitted by numerous other individuals, is less likely to have a community of interest. In such a case, the "hub" and each "spoke" are usually treated as having formed a separate conspiracy from all of the other hub-spoke combinations. Thus, the common hub will be liable for all of the conspiracies, but the spoke members are not liable for the acts of the other conspirators.

7. Impossibility

Factual impossibility (that it was factually impossible to complete the intended crime) is not a defense to conspiracy. Legal impossibility (that the intended act is not criminal in nature) may be a defense if the object of the agreement is not a crime.

Example: A and B agree to steal a painting from a house at night when the owners are out of town. The painting turns out to be missing from the house on the night that they break and enter to steal it. A and B will still be liable for conspiracy to commit burglary, despite the factual impossibility.

8. Withdrawal

a. Effect on liability for conspiracy

At common law, withdrawal was not a defense to conspiracy because the conspiracy is complete as soon as the parties enter into the agreement. Under the federal rule, which is also the majority rule, withdrawal is possible between the date of the agreement and the commission of the overt act. In order to withdraw, notice must be communicated to the other co-conspirators, or the police must be advised of the existence of a conspiracy in a timely manner. Upon completion of the overt act, the conspiracy is formed and withdrawal is no longer possible. Under the MPC and the minority view, subsequent withdrawal is possible only if the defendant acts voluntarily to "thwart the success" of the conspiracy.

b. Effect on liability for substantive crimes

A defendant may limit his liability as a co-conspirator for the substantive crimes that are the subject of the conspiracy by withdrawing from the conspiracy at any time after it is formed. For this purpose, he may withdraw by giving notice to his co-conspirators or timely advising legal authorities of the existence of the conspiracy even though such an action does not thwart the conspiracy.

> While a defendant is not liable as a co-conspirator for crimes committed in furtherance of the conspiracy after an effective withdrawal from the conspiracy, the defendant may nevertheless be liable as an accomplice for subsequent crimes committed by his former co-conspirators for which he has given aid. (*See* I.D.2.c. "Withdrawal," *supra*.)

9. Termination

It is important to determine when a conspiracy ends for purposes of determining the statute of limitations and the admissibility of acts or declarations made by the conspirators in furtherance of the crime. Generally, the act of concealing the conspiracy is not treated as a part of the conspiracy.

10. Punishment

Jurisdictions vary widely with regards to penalty provisions for conspiracies. Some jurisdictions make conspiracy a misdemeanor regardless of the objective, while other jurisdictions provide maximum sentencing depending on the objective. Still others allow for a permissible maximum, regardless of the objective. Nevertheless, sometimes the sentencing for conspiracy is more severe than the punishment for the crime itself.

D. ATTEMPT

An attempt requires a specific intent to commit a criminal act coupled with a substantial step taken toward the commission of the intended crime, which fails to be completed. An attempt is:

i) A **substantial step** towards the commission of a crime; coupled with

ii) Intent to commit the crime.

If the crime is successfully completed, the attempt is merged into the completed crime.

1. Substantial Step Test

A subjective test, called the "substantial step" test, is applied to determine whether an attempt has occurred. Under this test, conduct does not constitute a substantial step if it is in mere preparation; the act must be conduct that tends to effect the commission of a crime.

a. Acts

Any of the following acts may constitute a substantial step if they corroborate the defendant's criminal purpose (From the MPC):

i) Lying in wait, searching for, or following the intended victim;

ii) Unlawful entry into the place contemplated for the commission of the crime;

iii) Enticing the intended victim to go to such place;

iv) Possession of materials specially designed for committing the crime;

v) Possession of materials to be used in the commission of the crime at or near the place of commission; and

vi) Soliciting an innocent agent to engage in criminal conduct.

b. "Dangerous proximity" test

Some states continue to apply the traditional common-law "dangerous proximity" test. Under this test, an attempt does not occur until the defendant's acts result in a dangerous proximity to completion of the crime.

> **EXAM NOTE:** Remember, a substantial step for purposes of attempt is not equivalent to the overt act required for a conspiracy. It is a much more significant act.

2. Specific Intent

The defendant must possess the specific intent to perform an act or attain a result, which, if completed, would constitute the target crime, even if the target crime is not a specific intent crime.

> **Example:** Arson is not a specific intent crime, but attempted arson is. An attempt to commit a strict liability crime is also a specific intent crime.

There is no attempt to commit negligent crimes like involuntary manslaughter because a defendant's act cannot be both intentional and negligent.

3. Impossibility

Impossibility is not a defense to attempt if the crime attempted is factually impossible to commit due to circumstances unknown to the defendant. If, however, the act intended is not a crime (i.e., a legal impossibility), the defendant is not guilty of attempt. In such a case, even when statutes purport to have done away with the impossibility defense, there is always a provision that allows for legal impossibility.

> **Example:** D shoots V, believing that V is sleeping. V actually was already dead. D is guilty of attempted murder, but not murder.

4. Abandonment

At common law, once the defendant has taken a substantial step toward the commission of the offense, the defendant may not legally abandon the attempt to commit the crime because of a change of heart. Upon the completion of a substantial step, the crime of attempt is completed; there can be no abandonment or withdrawal.

Some states do recognize voluntary abandonment as a defense to attempt. Even then, abandonment is not voluntary if it is motivated by a desire to avoid detection, a decision to delay commission of the crime until a more favorable time, or the selection of another similar objective or victim. Abandonment by the defendant does not constitute a defense for an accomplice who did not join in the abandonment or withdrawal.

V. DEFENSES

A. GENERALLY

1. Justification and Excuse

Defenses may be divided into the categories of justification and excuse. When the defendant's actions, despite being criminal, are socially acceptable, the defendant has acted justifiably. Self-defense and defense of others are examples of justification defenses. When the defendant has a disability that makes the defendant not responsible for her actions, the defendant's criminal behavior is excused. Insanity, intoxication, and duress are examples of excuse defenses. This distinction does not affect the applicability or operation of these defenses.

2. Mistake of Fact

When a defendant is factually mistaken (e.g., the defendant thinks that the victim is holding a pistol that instead is a toy gun), the defendant may generally rely on a defense if the mistake is a reasonable one. In determining the reasonableness of the mistake, the defendant's physical characteristics, experiences, and knowledge are taken into account. An unreasonable factual mistake is a defense only to a specific intent crime.

B. SPECIFIC DEFENSES

1. Self-Defense

One who is not the aggressor is justified in using reasonable force against another person to prevent immediate unlawful harm to himself. The harm to the defendant must be imminent, not a threat of future harm. The defendant can use only as much force as is required to repel the attack.

a. Deadly force

Deadly force is force that is intended or likely to cause death or serious bodily injury. Deadly force may be justified in self-defense only when it is reasonably necessary to prevent death or serious injury or to prevent the commission of a serious felony involving a risk to human life.

b. Nondeadly force

Nondeadly force is force that is not intended or likely to cause death or serious bodily injury and may be used to repel nondeadly force.

c. Retreat

There is never an obligation to retreat before employing nondeadly force. Under the majority view, retreat is not required even when deadly force is used in self-defense. Under the minority view (states that follow the so-called "retreat doctrine"), retreat is required if it can be safely accomplished. Even under the minority view, however, retreat is never required when the person employing deadly force is in his own home (i.e., the "castle doctrine").

d. Imperfect right of self-defense

Imperfect self-defense occurs when the person claiming self-defense unjustifiably kills the attacker. The purpose of the rule is to reduce the charge from murder to voluntary manslaughter. The rule, adopted in most states, is applied when the defendant cannot claim perfect self-defense for some reason. For example, a defendant honestly but unreasonably believes that deadly force is required to prevent death or serious bodily injury.

e. Aggressor's right to use self-defense

It is possible for an initial aggressor to gain the right to act in self-defense in two circumstances: (i) an aggressor using nondeadly force is met with deadly force, or (ii) the aggressor must, in good faith, completely withdraw from the altercation, and must have communicated that fact to the victim.

2. Defense of Others

A person has the right to defend others under the same circumstances that self-defense would be acceptable. Defense of others is not limited to defending family members, but extends to anyone the defendant reasonably believes has the right of self-defense.

3. Defense of Property

A person in lawful possession of property that is threatened by the conduct of another, and who has no time to seek assistance from law enforcement, may take reasonable steps, including the use of nondeadly force to protect the property. To use force, the defender must reasonably believe that the real property is in immediate danger of unlawful trespass or that personal property is in immediate danger of being carried away and that the use of force is necessary to prevent either. The force cannot be unreasonably disproportionate to the perceived harm.

There is no right to use deadly force in defending property, with one exception. Generally, a person may use deadly force to prevent or terminate forcible entry into a dwelling if the occupant reasonably believes that the intruder intends to commit a felony inside. The use of deadly force against an intruder exiting the dwelling is generally not permissible. A deadly mechanical device cannot be used to protect property, although non-deadly mechanical devices or objects (such as barbed wire) may be used.

Note: Any right to use deadly force in the protection of a dwelling is limited to the dwelling (i.e., one's occupied residence). Thus, a gardening shed on the edge of the property would likely not be covered by this right. Any room in the residence, however, would be covered.

EXAM NOTE: When analyzing a question in which it appears someone harmed or killed another to protect property, consider whether that person could argue that they were really attempting to protect their own life or the life of another (e.g., using deadly force to prevent someone from stealing a car if there is a baby in the car).

4. Arrest

A police officer or a person acting under police direction is justified in using reasonable force to make a lawful arrest or to prevent the escape from one already in lawful custody.

a. Right to arrest

The right of a police officer to arrest a suspect is often specified by statute. A police officer can lawfully arrest a suspect, with or without a warrant, if the suspect has committed a crime in the officer's presence or if the officer has probable cause to believe that the defendant committed a felony offense outside of his presence. A civilian acting without police direction in making an arrest (e.g., a "citizen's arrest") who makes a mistake, even a reasonable mistake, as to the commission of the crime is not entitled to rely on this defense, but may do so if the civilian makes a reasonable mistake as to the identity of the perpetrator of the crime.

b. Use of force to arrest

A police officer can use nondeadly force to arrest a suspect. A police officer can use deadly force to arrest a suspect if the suspect represents a threat to either the officer or third parties.

c. Resisting unlawful arrest

A defendant may use nondeadly force to resist an unlawful arrest, but never deadly force. Some jurisdictions do not permit the use of force at all and require defendants to seek legal redress for an unlawful arrest.

5. Prevention of Crimes

Anyone can use deadly force to prevent the commission of a serious felony involving a risk to human life, and may use nondeadly force to prevent the commission of a felony or a breach-of-the-peace misdemeanor. A private citizen who makes a mistake, even a reasonable mistake, as to the commission of a serious felony by the victim is not entitled to rely on this defense.

6. Public Authority

Actions taken by public officials pursuant to legal authority (e.g., court ordered seizure of property, state-sanctioned executions) are justified.

7. Parental Authority

The use of reasonable force in the exercise of parental authority (i.e., discipline) by a parent or by a person in charge of a child (e.g., a teacher), is justified if exercised for the benefit of the minor child.

8. Duress

A third party's unlawful threat which causes a defendant to reasonably believe that the only way to avoid death or serious bodily injury to himself or another is to violate the law and causes the defendant to do so, allows the defendant to claim the duress defense. The defendant's fear of harm must have been both an actual fear and objectively reasonable.

Duress is not a defense to intentional murder. A defendant charged with felony murder may claim duress as a defense to the underlying felony and avoid conviction for felony murder.

9. Necessity

If the forces of nature (e.g., storm, fire) cause the defendant to commit what would otherwise be a crime, the defendant may be justified in doing so based upon necessity. The law prefers that the defendant, when faced with two evils, avoids the greater evil by choosing the lesser evil, e.g., the destruction of property to prevent the spread of a fire.

The defendant is not entitled to assert necessity if he set the natural forces in motion (e.g., set the fire) or if there is a reasonably apparent noncriminal alternative. In addition, economic necessity does not justify theft. For example, an unemployed worker may not steal food from the grocery store.

Necessity is a result of natural forces; duress results from human actions.

Note, though, that the MPC does not explicitly limit the defense of necessity to natural forces.

> **EXAM NOTE:** While the defendant may escape criminal liability, the defendant may be compelled by tort law to reimburse the victim for any losses.

10. Consent

Consent of the victim is not a defense to a crime unless the consent negates a required element of the crime or precludes the harm sought to be avoided by the crime. Such consent must be voluntarily and freely given, involve no fraud, and given by one competent to consent.

Consent is a defense to rape (unless the woman is a minor), since rape is defined as sexual intercourse without consent. Consent is also a defense to kidnapping if an adult (but not a minor) consents to traveling with the defendant.

a. Bodily injury

Consent to bodily injury or to conduct that may cause bodily injury may constitute a defense when the injury is not serious or, with regard to a sporting event or similar activity, the conduct and injury are reasonably foreseeable (i.e., boxing).

b. Ineffective consent

Consent may be ineffective when given by a legally incompetent person; by a victim who is unable to make a reasonable judgment due to age, mental disease or defect, or intoxication; or by a victim whom the law seeks to protect. Consent obtained by fraud, duress, or deception may also be ineffective.

11. Entrapment

Entrapment is the conception and planning of an offense by a law enforcement officer, and his procurement of its commission by a defendant who would not have committed that offense except for the trickery, persuasion, or fraud of the officer. If an officer merely offers an already-predisposed person the opportunity to commit a crime, it is not entrapment. In other words, the defendant must lack any pre-disposition to commit the crime. Entrapment can occur through the use of an undercover agent, but not by a private citizen. The modern trend allows a defendant to deny participation in an event, yet still raise the defense of entrapment. Traditionally, the defendant was precluded from using the entrapment defense if he denied his participation in the event.

a. Subjective approach

The subjective approach to defining entrapment is the majority position among the states and has also been adopted by the U.S. Supreme Court. Under this approach, the focus is on the defendant. Entrapment occurs when (i) the crime is induced by a government official or agent, and (ii) the **defendant was not predisposed** (i.e., ready and willing) to commit the crime.

b. Objective approach

Under the objective approach, which has been advanced by the MPC and adopted by a few states, the **focus is on the government's action** and the effect those actions would have on a hypothetical innocent person. This approach requires the government official or agent to have induced or encouraged the defendant to commit a crime by employing methods of persuasion or inducement that **create a substantial risk** that the crime will be committed by an otherwise law-abiding citizen.

12. Alibi

An alibi is a defense whereby a defendant denies his participation in a crime because he asserts that he was elsewhere when the alleged crime was committed. An alibi is not an affirmative defense; the defendant is not required to prove that he was elsewhere when the crime was committed. Instead, the burden remains on the prosecution to prove that the defendant was the person who committed the crime.

Themis
Bar Review

LSE Key Concepts: Criminal Law
To be used with onine lecture

WHAT IS CRIMINAL BEHAVIOR?
1. *Conduct* (not just thoughts)
2. With a specific *mental state* (mens rea)
3. That *inflicts or threatens* (causation)
4. *Harm* to individual or public interests
5. *Without justification or excuse*

ACTUS REUS – CONDUCT
1. *Conduct*
2. *Causation*
3. *Social Harm*
- **Conduct itself**
  - Must involve an **act** (brain moving the body; outside force, thoughts, status – not acts)
  - Act must be **voluntary** (involves the mind, not just the brain; involuntary acts are unauthorized by the mind; habit acts are voluntary)

❖ Martin v. State *(drunk at home and then taken into public place by police; not responsible because he was not voluntarily in public)*

Martin v. State variations	Act?	Voluntary?
Sober person who walks outside and drinks heavily; acts disorderly	Yes	Yes
Drunk person who walks outside and then acts disorderly	Yes	Yes
Drunk person who has a seizure, falling outside	Yes	No
Drunk person carried outside at his request	Yes	Yes
Drunk person carries outside against his will	No	No
Walks outside; remains quiet; hypnotized by police and becomes disorderly	Yes	No

  - **Timing**: act and mental state must occur together (concurrence of the elements)
  - **Omissions**: Common law (CL) imposes no duty to help
    - Exceptions (very similar under MPC):
      1. Statute
      2. Status- or relationship-based duty
      3. Contract
      4. Voluntary assumption of care and seclusion
      5. Creation of risk or danger

- **Attendant circumstances** (conditions that must be present in conjunction with conduct that constitute the crime)

  - **Objective facts** only (e.g., whether a building is a residence; whether it's nighttime, etc.)

MENS REA – INTENT
Types of Intent:

- *Purposely* (it is the purpose or goal to achieve a result)
- *Knowingly* (consciously aware that the result is likely; subjective and objective; result substantially certain to occur)
- *Recklessly* (aware of substantial and unjustifiable risk)
- *Negligence* (should have been aware of substantial and unjustifiable risk; gross deviation from reasonable person)
- *Intentionally* (purposely or knowingly)
- *Maliciously* (purposely or recklessly; probably also knowingly)
- *Willfully* (intentionally, knowingly, "evil purpose," and sometimes intent to violate law)
- *Corruptly, feloniously, fraudulently, designedly, wantonly*
- *Strict liability* (liability without regard to fault)

Proving Intent:
- **Scope**
  - Must be proven as to **behavior** and **result**
  - Attendant circumstance elements are often **strict liability**
  - Intent does not equal **motive**
- **Evidence:**
  - Confession or admission
  - Circumstantial evidence (inferring intent from conduct and attitude)
  - Motive

❖ Regina v. Cunningham *(removal of gas meter caused gas leak and near asphyxiation of neighbor)*

Specific v. General Intent:

- **General intent:** intent as to the basic conduct in the statute
- **Specific intent:** extra layer of intent, express or implied
  - Acting to do a specific wrong in the future
  - Acting with a specific motive or purpose
  - Acting with knowledge of certain attendant circumstances

Transferred Intent:
Defendant's acts cause harm to a different **victim**, of a different **type**, or to a different **degree**.
- Intent **does** transfer to different **victims**
- Intent **does not** transfer to different **types** of harm (harm to people, property, or security)
- Liability attaches to the **lesser degree** crime

MODEL PENAL CODE CULPABILITY LEVELS
Hierarchy of culpability levels:
1. Purpose
2. Knowledge
3. Recklessness
4. Negligence
*Strict Liability (implied)

- Evidence proving higher levels also proves lower
- Each material element has its own culpability level
- Strict liability can only result in fines, not jail time

Culpability	Conduct	Attendant Circ.	Result
Purpose	Conscious purpose or object	N/A	Conscious purpose or object
Knowledge	Aware conduct is of a specified nature	Aware they exist	Practically certain
Recklessness	N/A	Conscious disregard of sub. & unjust. risk	Conscious disregard of sub. & unjust. risk
Negligence	N/A	Unreas. lack of awareness of sub. & unjust. risk	Unreas. lack of awareness of sub. & unjust. risk
Strict Liability	N/A	N/A	N/A

Ambiguities:
- No culpability level – at CL, check history; in MPC, **recklessness is the default**
- Multiple actus reus elements but one culpability level – **single culpability level modifies all** absent clear contrary purpose

Intent Issues:
- No general v. specific issues; every element needs own level
- Transferred intent: intent usually is not transferred with 2 exceptions:
  o **Different victim** (NOT *additional* victim)
  o Different **degree** (liability attaches to lesser harm)
    ▪ NOT different **type**

CRIMINAL INTENT – STRICT LIABILITY
Punishment imposed **without regard** to D's **mental state**

- MPC: **not incarceration** crimes
- CL: look to **congressional intent** (express or implied)
  o **Public welfare** offenses
❖ US v. Staples (*owning an automatic weapon is not inherently dangerous + severe punishment = no strict liability; holding* **does not** *go so far to say that absence of mens rea requirement, default standard is knowledge*)
❖ Morissette v. US (*"knowing conversion" of property requires knowledge of ownership; collector who thought bomb casings were abandoned is not guilty*)

CRIMINAL INTENT – MISTAKE OF FACT
Honest mistake as to **attendant circ.** that the government must prove as an **element** of the crime
- NOT an affirmative defense; goes to prima facie case
  o **Specific Intent** – negated by honest mistake of fact, even unreasonable
  o **General Intent** – mistake must be honest and reasonable
  o **Strict Liability** – mistake has no effect
❖ People v. Navarro (*D took wooden beams from construction site that he thought were abandoned; negated specific intent*)
- **MPC**: mistake of fact is a defense when it negatives degree of culpability
  o No general vs. specific intent
  o No reasonable vs. unreasonable mistake

CRIMINAL INTENT – MISTAKE OF LAW
Usually, ignorance of law is no excuse. Here are the exceptions.

Traditional/Reasonable Reliance (mistake as to the definition or coverage of the law)
- Reasonable reliance on **official statement of the law** that authorized behavior at the time but was later declared wrong
- "Official statement" sources:
  o **Statute** later declared invalid
  o **Judicial decision** of higher court later overturned
  o **Official interpretation** from person or public body charged with interpreting or enforcing the law
❖ NY v. Marrero (*C.O. believed he was covered by peace officer exception, but based only on his own interpretation; guilty*)

Elemental Claim (no knowledge of law whose statute specifically requires knowledge)
- Only works with **specific intent** crimes
- Reasonable mistake does not excuse **general intent** crime
- ❖ Cheek v. US (*not guilty of "willful" tax evasion because D didn't think he owed taxes on certain money*)

Due Process Claim (no fair notice of the law's existence)
- Affirmative defense
- ❖ Lambert v. California (*no notice that D had to register as a felon w/in 5 days of moving, so no violation*)
- *Factors:* 1. *omission, not action*
  2. *based on status, not activity*
  3. *offense regulatory, not dangerous*

MPC: Mistake of Law defense if:
- If it negates culpability required (elemental)
- If statute has not been made public (due process)
- If reliance on official statement (reasonable reliance)

CAUSATION – ACTUAL CAUSE

But-for Causation (the result would not have occurred when it did but for the D's conduct)
- Temporal element is key

Concurrent Sufficient Causes (CSC) (two Ds, acting independently, commit two separate acts, each of which is sufficient to cause the result in question)
- Not accomplices; both can be but-for causes

Acceleration Causation (non-fatal blow accelerates death; still a but-for cause)
- Only one D inflicts mortal bow

MPC: temporal and CSC but-for causation

CAUSATION – PROXIMATE CAUSE

Once but-for cause has been found, is it fair to hold D guilty?

Intervening Events:
- Act of God
- Act of independent third party that aggravates or accelerates harm, or unexpected manner of harm
- Act or omission of victim

Factors in Assessing Liability:
- De minimis contribution (*D's conduct insubstantial compared to intervening event*)
- Omissions (*rarely to negative acts cut off responsibility for affirmative act*)
- Intended consequences (*if result wrongdoer intends comes about, even in a roundabout way, D is guilty; actual manner must match*)

- Apparent safety (*if victim reaches position of apparent safety, D should no longer be liable*)
- Free, deliberate, and informed human intervention (*after D's attach on victim, chain of causation won't go back to D*)
- Reasonable foreseeability (*D can't escape liability if intervening act was reasonably foreseeable*)

MPC: asks whether result is "too remote or accidental"

PARTICIPANTS IN CRIME
Traditionally
- Principal in the first degree ("*triggerman*")
- Principal in the second degree (*present and participates, e.g., lookout*)
- Accessory before or after (*not present, but gives assistance*)

Modern
- Principal (*person who commits the crime*)
- Accomplices (*principals in the second degree, accessories before the fact*)
  - Principals and accomplices subject to **full liability**
- Accessories after the fact (*lower liability*)

ACCOMPLICE
Conduct: assistance, aid, encouragement
- Physical conduct (*providing equipment, casing scene, signaling/lookout, getaway driver, blocking victim's escape*)
- Psychological influence (*counseling, soliciting, encouraging*)
  - Mere presence, uncommunicated intent, acquiescence – not enough
  - Presence + support – enough (low bar)
- Omission (*duty to act but fails w/ desire for crime to occur*)
  - Unsuccessful attempt to aid is not enough
- **MPC Conduct:**
  - Soliciting principal
  - Aiding, agreeing to aid, or attempting to aid principal
  - Having a legal duty but failing to take action
  - Unsuccessful aid IS enough (CL minority, too)

Intent: Two levels of intent:
  1. Intent to **assist principal**
  2. Intent for **underlying offense** to occur:

  - Intent for principal to commit **actus reus**
  - Intent for principal's acts to produce **results**
  - Intent as to **attendant circumstances**
- Intent re: **actus reus**
  - Purpose, not just knowledge
  - CL and MPC

❖ *People v. Lauria (phone service used by prostitutes; owner knew of but had no real interest in prostitution)*
- Intent re: **results**
  - If reckless or negligence required for underlying crime, MPC and majority require only recklessness or negligence from accomplice
    - Minority requires purpose or knowledge
  - If purpose or knowledge for principal, then purpose or knowledge for accomplice
- Intent re: attendant circumstances
  - Little caselaw and MPC is silent

Extent of Accomplice Liability
Liability extends to any crime that is the **natural & probable consequence** of the crime the accomplice wanted to result
- MPC rejects that rule; only **accomplice's own mental state**

HOMICIDE
Homicide: Killing of a person without justification or excuse.
Murder: Killing of a person with malice aforethought.
Manslaughter: Killing of a person w/o malice aforethought.

Four main types of murder:
1. Intent to kill (*purposely or knowingly causing death*)
2. Intent to cause great bodily injury ("GBI") (*wanting or knowing actions will cause GBI, and death results*)
3. Depraved heart (*acting with extremely reckless disregard for human life, and death results*)
4. Felony murder (*acting with intent to commit a felony, and death results*)

Two types of manslaughter:
1. Voluntary (intentional) (*intent to kill developed in the heat of passion, during that heat, result of reasonable provocation*)
2. Involuntary (unintentional) (*death results from act done w/o due caution; negligent homicide; misdemeanor manslaughter*)

	Murder (Malice)	Manslaughter (No Malice)
Intent to Kill	Intent-to-kill murder	Voluntary manslaughter
No Intent to Kill	Intent-to-cause-GBI murder, depraved-heart murder, felony murder	Involuntary manslaughter, negligent homicide, misdemeanor manslaughter

MPC Homicide:
No degrees of murder
No "malice aforethought"
Criminal homicide is the **purposely, knowingly, recklessly, or negligently** causing the death of another.
Three types of MPC Homicide:
1. Murder
2. Manslaughter
3. Negligent homicide

INTENTIONAL MURDER
First-Degree Murder – premeditated and deliberate OR statutory criteria (e.g., lying in wait, police officer)
Second-Degree Murder – intentional, but not premeditated
Premeditation & Deliberation – heightened intent; planned

Premeditation	Deliberation
Forethought	Reflection
Does not require deliberation	Requires premeditation
Takes time	Takes time

Evidence: planning, motive, manner of killing, provocation, conduct/statements, ill will, additional blows, nature of wounds
MPC murder: homicide committed purposely or knowingly
❖ *Midgett v. State (father who killed son in drunken rage showed no premeditation)*
❖ *State v. Forrest (mercy killing of father constituted premeditation)*

VOLUNTARY MANSLAUGHTER
Intentional killing done in the heat of passion, produced by adequate provocation, before D has had time to cool off; need causal connection between provocation, passion, and fatal act.

Traditionally limited categories (e.g., finding spouse in bed with another); now anything that could cause **reasonable person** to act in an **uncontrolled emotional state**.
- Issue for the jury
- Words are not enough
- Reasonable person is average, sober, and "normal" mental capacity; psychological issues not considered
MPC: murder under extreme mental or emotional disturbance

	Heat of Passion (CL)	Extreme Emotional Disturbance (MPC)
Must victim be provoker?	Yes. If another killed, must be accidental.	No link between source of EED and victim.
Cooling-off time	Can't claim provocation after cooling off.	EED can build over time
Proportionality	Response intensity :: provocation intensity	Not relevant

UNINTENTIONAL KILLINGS FROM RISKY BEHAVIOR

E.g., firing gun into crowd, driving drunk, Russian roulette, not feeding child, unsecure dangerous animals, dropping heavy items off a tall building

Second-Degree Murder (Depraved-Heart Murder) (death resulting from acting with extreme recklessness and manifesting extreme indifference to the value of human life)

- Wanton, arrogant, conscious disregard for life
- Objective components (e.g., risk of death); subjective components (e.g., knew behavior put human life at risk)

Involuntary Manslaughter (consciously disregards risk to human life (but not extreme disregard) or gross negligence – gross deviation from standard of care)

MPC:

- **Extreme Reckless Murder** (almost purpose or knowledge)
- **Manslaughter** (ordinary recklessness)
- **Negligent Homicide** (gross deviation)

FELONY MURDER

Homicide caused during **the commission or attempted commission of a felony**

- No mens rea as to homicide; only felony needs to be intended
- **MPC:** commission of listed felonies creates a presumption supporting **"extreme recklessness"** murder charge
- Even without felony-murder statute, almost any felony-murder charge could also be filed as intent-to-cause-GBI murder or depraved-heart murder

Limitations

1. **Inherently dangerous felony** (IDF) (*only IDF give rise to felony murder*)

- Abstract approach: precedent or statutory elements (i.e., can the crime be performed without substantial risk to life?)
- Facts of the case approach: was the manner in which D committed the felony inherently dangerous?
- MPC: a list of felonies (like abstract approach) but both D and Prosecutor can argue, based on the facts of the case, that felony-murder charge is not/is appropriate

2. **Independent felony** (no merger) (*felony must be independent of the homicide; is the felony assaultive?*)

- Abstract approach: low-level homicides are always assaultive, non-assaultive crimes can be used, assaultive crimes cannot be used
- Purpose approach: facts of the case; what was the defendant's purpose? If only to cause harm, not a predicate felony; if another purpose, can be used

3. **In furtherance...**(*killing must be part of the felony itself*)

- Temporal connection: during commission, attempt, or escape
- Causal connection: but-for and proximate causation
  - Agency rule (majority) – responsible for deaths caused by felon and accomplices; not by police officers
  - Proximate cause rule (minority) – responsible for any killing by felon, accomplice, or anyone else if the act was set in motion by behavior of felon or accomplices

ATTEMPT LIABILITY

With intent to commit a substantive offense, D intentionally performs act that brings D close to committing target offense

- Complete attempt (*D does everything necessary to commit target offense, but harm doesn't result*)
- Incomplete attempt (*D has taken some, but not all, steps necessary for target offense*)

Conduct (Actus Reus)

- Complete attempt – same as for target offense
- Incomplete attempt – more than just "mere preparation"
  - Temporal proximity b/w act and threatened harm
  - Seriousness of threat (more serious = earlier attempt)
  - Strength of evidence of intent

Jurisdictional Actus Reus Tests

1. Last Act (D performed all acts believed necessary for target?)
2. Indispensable Element (last indispensable req. element?)
3. Physical Proximity (w/in actor's power to complete crime almost immediately?)

4. Dangerous Proximity (is D dangerously close to success?)
5. Unequivocality (D's conduct unambiguously manifests criminal intent)
6. Probable Desistance (what's the point of no return?)
7. Abnormal Step (any step toward target beyond where ordinary person would go?)
8. MPC Substantial Step (purposely takes act that is a substantial step in course of conduct culminating in crime?)

Intent (Mens Rea)
Two intents required:
1. D must **intentionally commit** the acts = substantial step
2. D must act with **specific intent** to commit the target crime
What did D intent as to result?
❖ People v. Gentry (*husband pours gas on wife, who ignites by stove; attempted murder only if specific intent to kill her*)
MPC attempt: purpose or knowledge of target crime; broad
- No attempted felony murder at CL (need specific intent)
- No attempted depraved-heart murder (unintentional by def.)
- Yes attempted voluntary manslaughter
- No attempted involuntary manslaughter

Target Offense	Attempt Liability Possible?
Intentional Crime	Yes
Non-intentional Crime	No

Attendant Circumstances
CL: knowledge as to attendant circumstances required
Modern Rule 1: knowledge not required; recklessness
Modern Rule 2: knowledge not required; proof of mens rea for underlying/target offense (MPC rules)

Affirmative Defenses
Factual impossibility (not a defense at CL or MPC)
Abandonment (can D abandon after crossing attempt line? Depends on how close to committing target offense)

PROPERTY OFFENSES
Basic Theft Crimes
Larceny (*taking an carrying away the property of another w/o consent and w/ intent to permanently deprive*)
- Virtually any movement = carrying away
- Any personal property

- Specific intent to permanently deprive owner (borrowing doesn't count, but destruction or conversion is not req.)
Embezzlement (*theft of property given to hold temporarily*)
- Often seen in cases with cashiers or auto mechanics
Larceny by Trick (*theft of property given because D lies to get owner's consent*)
Theft by False Pretenses (*obtaining title to property—not just possession—by fraudulent representation*)
Burglary (*breaking and entering a property with the intent to commit a theft or felony inside that property*)
- Actus reus is not the theft or the felony, but the breaking and entering with intent; crime is against the property
- Nighttime might be an attendant circumstance
Robbery (not a property crime) (*theft by force or threat of force from the body of another*)
- Crime is against the person
- Rightful owner can still be a robber if taking property by force or threat of force

CONSPIRACY
An **agreement**, express or implied, between two or more people to commit a criminal act or series of acts.
- **Traditional CL:** Nothing else required
- **Modern Law**: Requires at least one overt act in furtherance
- **MPC**: Conspiracy if D agrees with others to (1) commit an offense, (2) attempt to commit an offense, (3) solicit another to commit an offense, or (4) aid another person in planning or committing an offense

Consequences of Conspiracy
- **Pinkerton Doctrine** (any member of conspiracy is responsible for any reasonably foreseeable crime committed by any other member in furtherance of that conspiracy)
- D can be tried **alone or jointly** in venue of **any overt act**
- **Hearsay** from conspirators can prove co-conspirators' guilt

Proving Conspiracy
- Testimony of co-conspirators
- Circumstantial evidence

Overt Act
- Any act; does not need to be illegal
- Liability for conspiracy is earlier on the timeline than attempt
- Overt act can be done by any conspirator and all are liable

- MPC has dropped overt act requirement for serious offenses

Intent – two specific intents required
1. Intent to agree
2. Intent to successfully commit the crime
- Purpose is required; can be inferred from circumstances

Conspiracy with Undercover Officer?
- At CL – no two-person conspiracy with undercover officer
- MPC – yes two-person conspiracy with undercover officer

No Merger with Target Offense
- Can be convicted of conspiracy and target offense
- Can be convicted of conspiracy even if acquitted of target
- MPC: merger; can't be convicted of both

Shapes of Conspiracy (Wheel v. Chain)
Is there one big conspiracy or several small ones?
❖ Kotteakos v. US (*one broker and 31 seekers of fraudulent loans; whether there was one conspiracy with 32 participants or 31 conspiracies depends on awareness of other conspirators*)
❖ Blumenthal v. US (*distillery owner, distributors, retailer or illegal whiskey; D knows of other conspirator's involvement, also responsible for their crimes.*)

Defenses
- **Impossibility** is not a defense at CL or MPC
- **Abandonment or withdrawal**:
  - CL – must communicate w/d to each co-conspirator; no liability for subsequent crimes (but not retroactive)
  - MPC – must renounce criminal purpose and thwart success of enterprise to have a full defense

---

RAPE AND STATUTORY RAPE
Knowingly having sexual intercourse with another person without that person's consent.
- Modern laws are gender neutral
- Some form of marital immunity in minority of jurisdictions

Actus Reus – Nonconsent
- Proof of force or threat of force AND/OR proof of resistance by victim
- "No"
- Absence of affirmatively expressed consent
- Other forms (e.g., drugged, unconscious, mentally disabled)
- Rape by fraud?

  - Fraud in the inducement: convincing someone to have sex by telling lies (e.g., about willingness to marry) – NO RAPE
  - Fraud in the facts: telling someone penetration is with a medical instrument – RAPE

Mens Rea – D's knowledge of Nonconsent
- Recklessness (*honest mistake about consent, reasonable or unreasonable*)
- Negligence (*honest and reasonable mistake*)
- Strict liability (*no mistake is permissible*)
- D's will argue proof of nonconsent (actus reus) first, before claiming mistake

Statutory Rape (sexual intercourse with a person who is not old enough to provide consent; negligence or strict liability)

DEFENSES
Strategies
Procedural Bars (public policy limitations) (*no ruling on the merits; case is dismissed or not filed*)
- Statute of limitations, immunity, defect in the pleading
Failures of Prosecution's Proof (*poking holes in the theory of proof on any element*)
- Mistake of fact, mistake of law, proximate cause
Defenses Specific to the Crime Charged (*after prosecution has closed its case-in-chief*)
- Abandonment of an attempt crime
Justification (*D's acts were morally right*)
- Self-defense, necessity
Excuses (*acknowledges crime, but D shouldn't be blamed*)
- Infancy, insanity, duress, due process mistake of law, reasonable reliance mistake of law

---

SELF-DEFENSE AND DEFENSE OF OTHERS
- **Reasonable amount of force**
  - Can use deadly force to meet threat of deadly force, non-deadly force with non-deadly force
  - Deadly force is intended or likely to cause death or GBI
  - Must be **proportionate**
  - **MPC:** deadly force may be used to prevent rape or kidnapping
- **Reasonable and sincere belief necessary**
  - Danger must be **imminent** (pressing or urgent)
  - Non-aggressor (first aggressor—the one who "ratchets up" to deadly force—cannot later claim self-defense)
  - Words are not enough
  - **MPC:** first person who purposely provokes deadly force cannot use self-defense

- **Withdrawal** (retreat and communicate intent to withdraw)
❖ US v. Peterson (*D who went after thief of wipers with a pistol was not entitled to use deadly self-defense, even when victim had responded to pistol with lug wrench*)
  - **Retreat** – traditionally, retreat was necessary if possible
    - **Slight majority:** no duty to retreat ("Stand Your Ground" laws)
    - **Minority and MPC:** still a duty to retreat if safe; even in these jurisdictions "Castle Doctrine" says no duty to retreat if attacked in own home.
  - **Reasonableness is an objective standard**
    - Unreasonable belief gives rise to voluntary manslaughter in minority of jurisdictions ("imperfect self-defense")
- **Defense of Others** (right of intervenor is co-extensive with victim's right to use force in self-defense)
  - Force must appear reasonably necessary (need not be correct)
  - **MPC:** no more force than third party would use; actually believe force is necessary; unreasonable use can give rise to reckless/negligent homicide

NECESSITY

a.k.a. Choice of Evils Doctrine (D's acts, though illegal, were necessary to prevent an even greater harm from occurring; no lawful alternatives)
- **Clear and imminent danger**
- **Action will abate the danger** (direct causal claim between action and harm)
- **No reasonable lawful alternatives**
- **Harm is less serious than the harm trying to prevent**
  - Reasonably foreseeable harms
  - Facts as they reasonably appear
  - Harm avoided > harm caused (NOT equal to)
- **Choice does not contradict legislative history**
- **Clean hands** (D is not responsible for the situation)
- **MPC:** notable changes – no clean hands requirement (though D could be prosecuted for recklessness or negligence); imminence is not required (but is considered); no distinction between natural and man-made forces
- **Not generally a defense to homicide**
❖ Regina v. Dudley and Stephens (*lifeboat inhabitants drew straws to kill and eat one to avoid starvation; court said no necessity defense; can't impose comparative value to lives*)
  - **MPC:** does not rule out choice of evils in homicide context

EXCUSES

D acknowledges crime, but should not be blamed or punished because of circumstances
Infancy (*D not old enough to understand actions*)
Duress (*D acting under threat of GBI*)
- Threat must involve threat of serious violence (not economic or embarrassment) by another person
- Use of force must be imminent (not future)
- Threat must be directed at D or someone close to D
- Clean hands
- Severity (threatened force need not exceed crime committed)
  - Not available as a defense to intentional homicide
- Coerced party is acquitted; coercing party should be convicted of the offense committed
- **MPC:** "person of reasonable firmness" replaced CL elements; can raise in a homicide prosecution
Insanity
Affirmative defense; D must produce evidence regarding mental condition (preponderance or clear and convincing evidence)
- D must prove **mental disease or defect** and that **because** of that defect:
  - **M'Naughten:** D did not know the **nature and quality** of the act AND/OR did not know it was **wrong**
  - **Irresistible Impulse:** Lost power to choose b/w right and wrong OR actions were not subject to **free will**
  - **MPC:** lacked substantial capacity to **appreciate criminality** of the conduct or conform conduct to the law

FUNCTIONS OF PUNISHMENT

The state's deliberate infliction of suffering an stigma on an individual who has done something wrong.
Forms: fine, probation, community service, imprisonment, execution, ancillary penalties
Moral Justification (supported by **good reason** and **proportional** to its purpose)

Utilitarianism	Retributivism
Justification lies in the useful purposes that punishment serves.	Punishment is justified because the offender deserves it.

Utilitarianism (useful consequences of punishment)
- Deterrence (individual and general)
- Rehabilitation
- Incapacitation (prevention)
- Legitimization of the legal system
- Norm reinforcement and expression
- Restitution and healing for victims

Retributivism (punitive)
- Symbol of hate that D should feel
- Treats wrongdoer with dignity as a full human being responsible for choices
- Repaying debt to society

Quantity and Type of Punishment

Utilitarianism	Retributivism
Depends on how much punishment is necessary to deter/rehabilitate/incapacitate, etc.	Depends on how bad act was, how much harm was cause, and how bad we think the actor is; can be mitigated by circumstances

Unpleasantness: assumption is that prison time will be experienced as a form of pain (not always the case)

Reasons Not to Punish
- Cost
- Criminal education in prison
- Loss of industry or parenting time
- Brutalizes offenders and society
- Fear of punishment can affect integrity of legal system

Themis
Bar Review

Property

PROPERTY

Table of Contents

PROPERTY

I. GAINING OR LOSING TITLE TO PERSONAL PROPERTY

A. TYPES OF PROPERTY

There are different types of property, which include real and personal property.

1. Real Property

Real property is property that cannot be moved. Real property usually consists of land, items attached to the land, and items that are associated with the land. Real property can be converted to personal property by severance, while personal property can be converted to real property by annexation.

2. Personal Property

Personal property is property that is movable. Personal property usually consists of personal possessions and items that are not real property.

a. Fixtures

Under the fixture concept, chattel is converted from personal to real property by attaching it to the land or immobile structures affixed to the land. The chattel is then considered a part of the land and passes with the ownership of the land.

Trade fixtures are items attached to real property for the purpose of carrying on a business. Trade fixtures may be removed by a tenant at the conclusion of the tenant's lease.

> **EXAM NOTE:** When evaluating a question for fixture issues, be sure to determine if there was intent on the part of the owner to make the questioned item a part of the land. If that appears to be the case, then the item will likely be considered a fixture on the land and move with the real property.

b. Leaseholds

Leases of land for any period of time are technically classified as personal property and are, for historical reasons, classified as chattels-real. This technical classification has little modern significance or effect, and leases should be analyzed as estates in land. The issue might arise, however, if a decedent were to devise, for example, "all of my real property..." to an assignee.

c. Crop conveyance and mortgage

Crops such as trees, bushes, grass, and other vegetation that grow spontaneously, without having been planned for, are defined as *fructus naturales* and considered to be real property. Crops such as fruits, vegetables, and grains that farmers and others plan for and plant are defined as *fructus industriales* and are personal property.

When conveying land, any crops that grow on the land, including those produced on an annual basis, are conveyed with the land, unless a reservation to the contrary is made in the deed or will. Older mortgages on the land prevail over newer mortgages on the crops.

1) Doctrine of emblements

Former tenants have the right to enter land to cultivate and remove crops that were planted before they terminated their interest in the land. Two requirements must be met for this to occur: (i) the tenancy must have been for an undetermined period of time or have been a life estate, and (ii) the tenancy must have been terminated under conditions other than the tenant's fault.

B. GAINING OR LOSING OWNERSHIP

There are several ways ownership of personal property can be acquired. Personal property can be acquired by capture, creation, conversion, discovery, adverse possession, accession, confusion, and gift. Ownership can be lost through abandonment, fraud, or one of the methods of acquiring ownership. It can be effectively, though not technically, lost by an owner who loses or misplaces it. In most instances, owners of personal property must give consent to transfer the property. When evaluating which goods pass in a sale and title transfer, the *intent of the parties* prevails.

1. Capture of Unowned Property

The classic example of unowned property is wild animals. Wild animals that are not domesticated and are in their own natural state are considered unowned. Only when they are captured and converted to possessions are they considered personal property. *Pierson v. Post*, 3 Cai. 175 (N.Y. 1805). If an animal escapes from its owners, is not properly marked, and returns to its natural habitat, the animal becomes unowned again.

a. Discovery rule

The discovery rule provides a framework for the concept that a person who discovers real or personal property has the best title to the property. This rule is most often associated with the European claims to the title of land inhabited and possessed by sovereign indigenous nations. The discovery doctrine was established by a number of U.S. Supreme Court decisions, including *Johnson v. M'Intosh*, 21 U.S. 543 (1823).

b. Possession

Animals become possessions when an individual manifests the intent to own by exercising actual or constructive **dominion and control.** For example, an animal that is hunted, trapped, and caught is considered to be in the constructive possession of the person who caught it. The act of hunting the animal without actually obtaining it does not constitute constructive possession unless a vested property right has been created by mortally wounding the animal such that capture is inevitable.

In cases of animals that escape from their owner's property and periodically return to the owner's land or when the owner makes an effort to recapture an animal that is attempting to escape, the owner does not lose title. Additionally, owners do not lose title in marked animals that escape when the owner makes all efforts to recapture the animals.

c. Trespass

If an individual enters onto the land of another without permission and traps and catches an animal, he forfeits his property right in favor of the landowner.

d. Violating a statute

If a person traps and captures an animal in violation of a statute, he loses ownership of the animal. For example, if a hunter does not have a valid hunting license in the state where he is hunting and traps and captures an animal, then he would lose the right to title in that animal.

2. Creation of New Property

The most obvious example of the creation of new property is the authorship of written or otherwise recorded works. An author's written works are protected by copyright laws under federal statute. 17 U.S.C. § 301(a). In order for an author to seek protection, she must meet several requirements, including that:

i) The work must be in an actual form and not be a mere thought or idea for future work;

ii) The work must be original and new and not a reworked version of something old; and

iii) The work must be "fixed" in a tangible medium of expression for a significant period of time.

a. Protections

Protection under the copyright laws usually includes the owner's lifetime plus 70 years. If the owner was anonymous, the period could be for 95 years from publication or 120 years from the creation of the work. Authors must properly register their copyrights. Until a work is registered, authors cannot bring a suit for copyright infringement.

b. Limitations

Authors do not have protection against individuals who independently create works that are similar to their work. *Cheney Bros. v. Doris Silk Corp.*, 35 F.2d 279 (2d Cir. 1930), *Smith v. Chanel, Inc.*, 402 F.2d 562 (9th Cir. 1968).

C. BAILMENTS

1. Definition

A bailment is defined as a person's (the bailor's) delivery of her goods or chattel to another person (the bailee) to hold for a period of time. The bailor *does not* transfer title to the bailee. Instead, the bailee has a right of possession arising from the terms of the bailment and must return the property according to those same terms.

These transfers are made without transfer of title, and no express contract is required.

2. Bailment Elements

There are four elements to a bailment. The bailee must:

i) Physically possess the property;

ii) Knowingly possess the property;

iii) Know exactly what is possessed; and

iv) Consent to the possession.

If the bailee is responsible for an article and there is a component of it that is hidden, he cannot be held responsible for the concealed portion.

Example: If a person leaves her car with a valet, the valet is responsible for the bailment (the car). If the person left a laptop on the floor in the back and did not tell the valet it was there, then the valet cannot be responsible for the loss of the laptop. This is because the valet did not know it was there at the time the car was given to him.

Note that most bailments are conditional bailments, in which the bailor gives the bailee possession for a specific purpose. For instance, Sally bails her car to Bob so that he can watch it while she is gone. Can he drive it? Probably, unless they have agreed otherwise. Can he drag race with it? Most likely not, unless they have otherwise specifically agreed. Can he sell it to an interested stranger? Definitely not, as that would completely defeat his ability to give the car back to Sally when she returns.

One common type of conditional bailment is a **consignment,** whereby the bailor gives the goods to a bailee who is authorized to sell the goods for the consignor. Another is a **pledge,** whereby a bailor gives a bailee goods as security for the performance of an obligation that the bailor owes to the bailee. Bailees who violate the conditions of the bailment are strictly liable for any damages that arise as a result of their violations of the terms of a bailment.

3. Bailments Distinguished from Other Transactions

a. Employer relationships

An employee's use of goods that are owned by an employer is not a bailment because the employer never loses control over the goods.

b. Consignment

As mentioned above, consignees are authorized to sell goods on behalf of the owner of the goods (the consignor). These are considered special bailments solely for the purpose of a sale. A consignor's rights are superior to those of all the consignee's creditors, as well as to the trustee in a bankruptcy proceeding.

c. Sale

A sale is different from a bailment because a sale requires transfer of ownership whereas a bailment requires only transfer of possession. The test for whether a transaction involving an item was bailed or sold is whether there is **an obligation to restore the item.** A transaction is considered to be a bailment *if the item must be returned* in the same or in an altered form (as with a clothing alteration). The transaction is a sale if the receiver has the discretion to return another item of equal value or money equaling the value of the item.

4. Bailee's Standards of Care

The duties of the bailee vary widely on the basis of the reasons for the bailment. There are three general categories of bailments and a different default duty of care that applies to each. Parties can agree to different duties of care, but professional bailees—those who act as a bailee as a business—cannot waive duty altogether and must limit their liability expressly.

a. Slight diligence

The bailee owes a duty only of slight diligence when the bailment is solely for the benefit of the bailor.

b. Ordinary care

Ordinary care is due when there is a mutual benefit for both the bailor and bailee in the situation. This includes most commercial bailment situations, including bailments to common carriers.

c. Great diligence

The bailee owes a duty of great diligence when the bailment is solely for the benefit of the bailee.

D. FINDING LOST, MISPLACED, OR ABANDONED PROPERTY

Owners who lose or misplace their property are not denied their right to title. However, someone who abandons his property loses title to that property.

1. Lost and Misplaced Property

Owners who unintentionally lose their property do not lose title to it. The question of who claims possession against all the world *except* the true owner, however, may depend on where it is found, by whom, and whether a reasonable person would believe that the property was truly lost or merely mislaid.

a. Finder of lost property

Someone who finds lost property is entitled to keep it, unless the finder was trespassing or the true owner is identified. *Favorite v. Miller*, 176 Conn. 310 (1978).

When items are found in a highly private location where the public is not invited, the owner of that location will retain possessory rights over the finder.

Employees who find property while engaged in an act that their employer directs them to perform are not entitled to the property. The employer gains ownership.

b. Finder of misplaced property

Misplaced property is property that reasonably seems to have been intentionally placed in a particular location, but then appears to have been forgotten.

A finder of misplaced property does not obtain possession of the property. The finder's right to the misplaced property falls after that of the original owner and the owner of the property on which the misplaced item was found. *McAvoy v. Medina*, 93 Mass. 548 (1866).

2. Abandoned Property

Personal property is abandoned when the owner has the full intention to leave the property and give up title and possession to it.

> **EXAM NOTE:** It is essential in the case of abandoned property to show there was intent on the part of the owner to give up the property. The mere passage of time is not enough to constitute abandonment. *Columbus-America Discovery Grp. v. Atlantic Mut. Ins. Co.*, 974 F.2d 450 (4th Cir. 1992).

If an intermediary that has no interest in the property holds abandoned property, the property escheats to the state in which the property is located.

3. Treasure Trove

Treasure troves include property that is concealed and is anticipated to be recovered at a later time. A treasure trove is usually gold or silver that is found hidden and the owner is not known. Treasure troves can also include paper instruments that provide information regarding ownership of gold or silver.

Under common law, treasure troves differed from other lost property. Someone who found a treasure trove, even if that person was a trespasser, could retain ownership against anyone but the true owner. However, today most states apply the rules that are associated with lost property to treasure troves and do not recognize this common-law category.

4. Rights and Duties of Possessors

A quasi-bailee is someone who has obtained possession of property against everyone but the true owner. The quasi-bailee even has the right to sue someone who may have wrongfully taken the property from him, as long as it is not the true owner. A quasi-bailee has a duty to locate the true owner if he might know or have a reasonable means of finding out the identity of the true owner. If the quasi-bailee neglects to find the true owner, then he may be brought up on criminal or civil charges.

E. ACCESSION OF GOODS AND MATERIALS TO PERSONAL PROPERTY

Accession is the process of adding value to property by the expenditure of labor or adding new materials. Generally, the accession of materials to an owner's goods, whether in the course of repairs or otherwise, transfers ownership of the materials accessed to the owner of the original goods on which the work was done. In a non-gratuitous setting, of course, the tradesman will be owed payment for his labor and his materials and will have a lien against the goods on which the accession occurs. If there has been confusion by one party about who owned either the base goods or the goods used for repair, and if the newly added chattel cannot be detached from the property, then there is a question as to who owns the improved chattel. The result is determined by whether the trespasser (i.e., the party who was wrong about original ownership) was acting in good faith (i.e., whether he was a willful trespasser).

> **EXAM NOTE:** For questions that ask about title to property that has significantly increased in value after being taken from the original owner, you will have to scrutinize closely to determine if the trespasser was willful or innocent.

1. Innocent Trespasser

In cases of an innocent trespasser, the original owner retains title, and while the trespasser cannot bring an action for compensation against the owner, the owner can seek damages for conversion or replevin. In cases where the property has been completely changed or greatly increased in value by the innocent trespasser, the trespasser may claim title to the goods. The original owner thus may not recoup the chattel but can sue for damages.

When an innocent trespasser mistakenly improves the real property of another, the owner of the real property has the option to sell the land to the improver or pay the improver the fair value of the improvement.

2. Willful Trespasser

A willful trespasser cannot gain rights to title by accession. The original owner is entitled to keep the property in its enhanced state, regardless of how much added value the accession may have created. Additionally, the original owner can sue the trespasser for damages for conversion or replevin if the value of the goods to the owner is impaired by the accession.

F. GIFTS

A gift is a voluntary transfer of property without payment or consideration. It is important to note that promises to make gifts in the future are not binding; the gift occurs only when the actual transaction takes place.

1. Gifts *Inter Vivos*

These include gifts that require delivery, acceptance, and the donor's intent.

a. Intent of donor

In order for intent of the donor to exist, the person must have the *intent and mental capacity* to make the gift.

Intent can be *conditional.* Thus, for instance, because engagement gifts are given in anticipation of an impending marriage, there is a presumption that they are given on the condition that the marriage will take place. If the marriage does not take place, then gifts should be returned. However, it has been concluded that an engagement ring is not given with the same conditional intent, and courts have thus not required that the ring be returned. When the courts determine conditional intent, they look at factors including the donor's expressed intent and background behavior, the type of property being given, whether fraud has occurred, and whether (of course) conditions that were attached to the gift were met.

b. Delivery

The delivery requirement exists so as to provide a clear manifestation of the donor's intention to divest herself of title and possession. The decisive factor in determining whether a gift has been adequately delivered is whether the putative donor has the power to reclaim the property. Delivery can be accomplished in the following manners:

i) Actual physical delivery;

ii) Constructive delivery;

iii) Delivery in writing; and

iv) Symbolic delivery.

Proper agents of the donor or the grantee may, as ever, stand in the shoes of their principals. Control of the gift—and the opportunity to take it back—does not pass from the donor until it passes also from the donor's agent.

1) Actual physical delivery

For actual physical delivery to take place, the donee must take dominion and possession over the property.

2) Constructive delivery

If it is not feasible to deliver an item because its location or size would make physical delivery impossible, then the donor can instead surrender control of the item. A mere declaration of intent to give a gift is insufficient to constitute constructive delivery.

3) Delivery in writing

If a donor clearly expresses written intent to give a gift, clearly describes the subject being gifted, signs the document, and passes the writing out of his control with the intention that it reach the donee, then that is a sufficient method of delivery.

4) Symbolic delivery

When actual physical delivery is impossible or impractical, delivery may be symbolic, as by the donor giving some object that is not the actual gift, but is symbolic of it. This is most often accomplished by delivery of a written instrument. *See, e.g., In re Cohn*, 187 App. Div. 392 (N.Y. 1919).

c. Examples of delivery-related issues

The following circumstances illustrate the requirement that delivery must demonstrate the intent to make a gift as well as transfer control of the gift.

1) Checks

A donor's delivery of a check to a donee is not enough to make the gift a success. The full transfer is not complete until the donee takes the check to the bank and cashes it or the bank deposits the funds into the donee's account. This is because the donor retains the ability to make the gift valueless until it has been drawn upon.

2) Stocks

When stocks are transferred with donative intent, a valid gift has been completed, even if the donor continues to receive dividends until the time of his death.

3) Promissory notes

Because a promissory note is merely a promise to deliver money in the future, the manual delivery of such a note does not constitute a valid gift. If, however, a promissory note is drawn in favor of the donor, who subsequently transfers it to the donee, then the gift is valid.

4) Bank savings deposits

Delivering a bank book with the intent to make a gift provides the donee with sufficient dominion to qualify as delivery, assuming that the bank book is the only means of accessing the funds in the account.

d. Acceptance of gifts

Acceptance of a gift is presumed. Refusal of a gift must be by an express affirmative act.

2. Gifts *Causa Mortis*

Gifts *causa mortis* are gifts given in contemplation of death. The elements are identical to those for *inter vivos* gifts (mental capacity, personal property, delivery and acceptance), with the additional requirement that the donor act in contemplation of imminent death.

a. Imminence

In order for a gift *causa mortis* to be valid, it must be given in anticipation of impending death, such as an actual life-threatening illness. An abstract fear of death, such as someday drowning or dying in a plane crash, is not enough to be considered impending death.

b. Anticipation of death versus recovery

Although older cases required that the donor actually die from the anticipated cause, the modern trend is to find a valid gift so long as the donor did not **recover** from the illness. That is, if the donor recovers from the illness that placed him in contemplation of death, then the gift is revoked. If, however, the donor merely died from a different cause, but never actually recovered from the impending illness, the gift is valid.

Example: A woman with terminal cancer makes an otherwise valid gift *causa mortis* to her niece. One month later, she is killed in a car accident. Although she did not die from the illness that placed her in contemplation of death, there was no "recovery" from her illness, and the gift is valid.

c. Revocation

A gift *causa mortis* is not valid if it is revoked. Such a gift may be revoked by an affirmative act on the part of the donor indicating the intent to revoke the gift, or if the donee predeceases the donor.

G. REMEDIES

If a person is wrongfully deprived of her property, there may be remedies to recover her rights. Such remedies include conversion, replevin, trespass, and trover.

i) Conversion is an action that forces breachers or tortfeasors to purchase at full price goods that they have damaged or misdelivered;

ii) Replevin is an action taken to recover the actual property or chattel;

iii) Trespass is an action that seeks to recover monetary damages incurred by reason of the lack of possession; and

iv) Trover is an action to recover the value of the property or chattel in addition to damages for lack of possession.

II. ADVERSE POSSESSION

A. REAL PROPERTY

The doctrine of adverse possession allows ownership to be granted to a person who exercises exclusive physical possession of a piece of property for a certain amount of time. Title acquired by adverse possession is as good as title traceable to a prior record owner. For possession to ripen into title, possession must be continuous, actual, open and notorious, hostile, and exclusive. In some jurisdictions, the possessor must pay the property taxes during the possession. Government-owned land cannot be adversely possessed.

1. Continuous

Possession must be continuous and uninterrupted for a period of time as defined by statute (or, 20 years at common law). Seasonal or infrequent use may be sufficiently continuous if it is consistent with the type of property that is being possessed (e.g., land at a summer camp).

a. Tacking

An adverse possessor may tack on his predecessor's time in order to satisfy the statutory period, as long as there is privity satisfied by any non-hostile nexus (such as blood, contract, deed, or will). The periods of possession must pass directly from one possessor to the next, without any gaps.

Tacking is not allowed when there is an actual, wrongful exclusion of a party entitled to possession from the property (ouster).

b. Disability of owner

The statute of limitations will not run against a true owner who is afflicted with a disability (e.g., insanity, infancy, imprisonment) at the inception of the adverse possession.

2. **Actual, Open, and Notorious**

Possession must be open and notorious, such that a reasonable true owner would become aware of the claim. Uses that are hidden (such as underground wiring or piping) are insufficient to satisfy this requirement.

3. **Hostile**

The adverse possessor must possess the land without the owner's permission and with the intent to claim the land as his own against the claims of others for it to be considered "hostile." The majority of jurisdictions do not require that the possession be hostile in the sense that the possessor purposefully seeks to defeat the owner's title. The intent of the possessor is irrelevant in many jurisdictions. Most jurisdictions that consider intent will grant title to a possessor who, in good faith, thought he had the legal right to possess (i.e., believed the property was not owned or thought that he owned the property). A minority of jurisdictions instead require the possessor to know that the land belongs to another.

4. **Exclusive**

Possession cannot be shared with the true owner, although two or more people can join together to create a tenancy in common by adverse possession.

5. **Scope of Possession**

    a. **Constructive adverse possession**

    If a person enters property under color of title (a facially valid will or deed) and only actually possesses a portion of the property, constructive adverse possession can give title to the whole. The amount possessed must be a reasonable portion of the whole.

    b. **Below surface area**

    The adverse possessor acquires the rights to the subsurface (e.g., mineral rights), unless those rights belong to a third party. In order to acquire title to the mineral rights by adverse possession, the possessor would have to mine the minerals and meet the other requirements for adverse possession.

    c. **Future interests**

    The adverse possessor acquires the estate held by the person who has legal possession at the time that the adverse possession began. In other words, the adverse possession period does not run against future interests that exist at the time that the adverse possession begins, but it does apply to future interests created from a fee simple absolute estate after the adverse possession has begun.

B. **PERSONAL PROPERTY**

A trespasser takes possession of someone else's property, either intentionally or innocently, but without permission. If the trespass meets the elements listed below and lasts throughout the whole period in which the title owner could bring an action to regain possession, then at the end of the statute of limitations period, the trespasser becomes the rightful owner of the property. If the former owner wishes to recover the property, he must bring a cause of action *before* the relevant statute of limitations runs.

1. **Elements**

In order for the statute of limitations to take hold and start running, possession of personal property (as with real property) must be:

    i) Actual;

ii) Open and notorious;

iii) Hostile and adverse (without consent); and

iv) Exclusive and continuous throughout the entire statutory period.

The open-and-notorious element proves particularly difficult to satisfy in the context of adverse possession of personal property. Courts may require a showing that the owner has demanded return of the property and that the possessor has refused, before finding that the elements of open-and-notorious and hostility are satisfied. In the absence of such a showing, the court may presume that the trespassory possession was in fact either concealed or permissive.

2. Passage of Title

Title to the property passes when the statute of limitations expires.

3. Tacking

Possessors of the property may merge their respective periods of possession when there is privity (the property was sold, given, or bequeathed to the next owner).

4. Tolling the Statute of Limitations

Under certain conditions, the statute of limitations is "tolled" and does not run. Tolling occurs, for example, when a plaintiff suffers from a physical or mental disability that does not allow her to maintain an action.

III. REAL PROPERTY OWNERSHIP

Ownership of real property may be transferred from one person to another by sale, gift, or devise. The seller or donor is called the "grantor," and the buyer or recipient is called the "grantee." This section will discuss both present and future possessory interests in land (which are subject only to the rights of others), and other sections will discuss non-possessory interests in land (which are subject to specific restrictions as to the use of the land).

A. PRESENT ESTATES

In order to be categorized as a freehold, an estate must be (i) immobile (either land or some interest derived from or affixed to land), and (ii) for an indeterminate duration (as opposed to leasehold, which is for a limited duration). The owner of a present estate has the right to currently possess the property.

1. Fee Simple Absolute

Fee simple absolute is the most common form of property ownership and the broadest ownership interest recognized by law. It is absolute ownership of potentially infinite duration, is freely alienable (i.e., easily bought or sold), and has no accompanying future interest. Although common law required words of limitation (e.g., "and heirs"), conveyances that are ambiguous are now considered fee simple by default (e.g., "to B").

Example: A conveys Blackacre "to B and his heirs." C conveys Whiteacre to "B." Both conveyances give B a fee simple absolute estate in the property.

Note that using the limitation "and heirs" does not restrict the ability of the transferee of a fee simple absolute interest or other real property interest to transfer that interest during the transferee's life, nor limit the people to whom the interest may be transferred to the transferee's heirs.

The fee simple absolute is a present estate that does not terminate unless the owner dies intestate without heirs, in which case the property escheats to the state.

2. Defeasible Fees

As with a fee simple absolute estate, a defeasible fee is ownership of potentially infinite duration. But, unlike a fee simple absolute estate, a defeasible fee **may be terminated by the occurrence of an event**. Three defeasible fee simples that you will encounter are (i) fee simple determinable, (ii) fee simple subject to a condition subsequent, and (iii) fee simple subject to an executory interest.

> **EXAM NOTE:** If a statement in a conveyance of real property merely indicates a grantor's desire, intent, or purpose for which the property is to be used rather than imposing a condition on the ownership of the property itself, the property interest is treated as a fee simple absolute, rather than a defeasible fee.

a. Fee simple determinable

A fee simple determinable is a present fee simple estate that is **limited by specific durational language** (e.g., "so long as," "while," "during," "until"), such that it terminates automatically upon the happening of a stated condition, and full ownership of the property is returned to the grantor. The fee simple determinable is freely alienable, devisable, and descendible, but always subject to the stated condition.

> **EXAM NOTE:** A fee simple determinable looks just like a fee simple absolute except that it has a provision that makes it automatically end upon the happening of an event.

1) Future interest in grantor—possibility of reverter

When, upon the occurrence of the stated condition, the estate automatically reverts back to the grantor, the future interest is known as a **"possibility of reverter."** The estate reverts back to the grantor whether or not the language of the grant specifically mentions the owner of this future interest. A possibility of reverter is freely alienable by the grantor, both during his life and upon his death.

> **Example:** A conveys Blackacre "to B and his heirs, until B gets married." The estate reverts back to A if B gets married. Therefore, B has a fee simple determinable in Blackacre, and A has a possibility of reverter.

> **EXAM NOTE:** Absent language to the contrary, a fee simple determinable is a present possessory estate followed by a possibility of reverter in the grantor.

2) Future interest in third party—executory interest

When, upon the occurrence of the stated condition, the estate automatically reverts to a third party (i.e., a person other than the grantor or the holder of the present interest), the future interest is known as an **"executory interest."** The estate reverts back to a third person only when the language of the grant specifies this person. An executory interest is freely alienable by the third party, both during his life and upon his death. In this circumstance, the present interest is most often referred to a "fee simple subject to an executory interest," although some refer to it as a "fee simple determinable subject to an executory interest."

> **Example:** A conveys Blackacre "to B and his heirs, until B gets married, then to C." B has a fee simple subject to an executory interest in Blackacre, and C has an executory interest. A does not have an interest in Blackacre.

b. Fee simple subject to condition subsequent

A fee simple subject to a condition subsequent is a present fee simple that is **limited in duration by specific conditional language.** Upon the occurrence of the condition, the **grantor** (or his successor interest) **has the right to terminate this estate**.

> **EXAM NOTE:** Typical language that indicates a fee simple subject to a condition subsequent: "provided that," "on condition that," "but if."

1) Compare to fee simple determinable

As with a fee simple determinable, the fee simple subject to a condition subsequent is freely alienable by the owner during his life, and upon his death it is devisable and descendible.

Unlike a fee simple determinable, termination of a fee simple subject to a condition subsequent is not automatic. Upon occurrence of the stated condition, the present fee simple **will terminate only if the grantor affirmatively demonstrates intent to terminate** (e.g., by bringing an action to recover possession).

If the language in the conveyance is ambiguous, courts typically adopt a preference for the fee simple on condition subsequent.

2) Right to terminate

In the conveyance, the grantor must explicitly retain the right to terminate the fee simple subject to a condition subsequent (known as the **"right of entry," "right of reentry,"** or the **"power of termination"**). This right is devisable and descendible, but it cannot be transferred during the owner's lifetime. The owner may waive this right, but the mere failure to assert it does not constitute a waiver.

> **Example:** A conveys Blackacre "to B and his heirs, but if B gets married, then A can reenter Blackacre." B will retain ownership until A exercises his right to reenter. B has a fee simple subject to a condition subsequent in Blackacre, and A has a right of reentry. (Even if B gets married, B will retain his current possessory estate in Blackacre until A exercises his right to terminate B's estate.)

c. Fee simple subject to executory interest

A fee simple subject to an executory interest (sometimes referred to as a "fee simple subject to an executory limitation") is a present fee simple estate that is limited in duration by specific conditional language (e.g., "provided that," "on condition that," "but if"), such that, upon the occurrence of the specified condition, title will automatically pass to a **third party** (i.e., someone other than the grantor or the holder of the present fee).

1) Future interest in third party

The future interest held by the third party is an executory interest. An executory interest is freely alienable by the third party, both during his life and upon his death. Unlike the corresponding future interest in the grantor (right of entry), the executory interest automatically comes into existence; there is no need for the third party to take any action (e.g., an eviction action).

> **Example:** A conveys Blackacre "to B and his heirs; but if B gets married, then to C." In Blackacre, B has a fee simple subject to an executory interest, C has an executory interest *(technically a shifting executory interest as discussed in I.B.5.a., below),* and A does not have an interest. (Note: C's interest is subject to the Rule Against Perpetuities.)

3. Fee Tail

A fee tail is a freehold estate that limits the estate to the grantee's lineal blood descendants by specific words of limitation (e.g., "heirs of the body"). The fee tail estate has been eliminated in most states because it is treated as a fee simple absolute.

4. Life Estate

A life estate is a present possessory estate that is limited in duration by a life. The language must be clear, and the duration must be measured in terms of a life, not a number of years (e.g., "to A for life"). Upon the end of the measuring life, title reverts to the grantor or specified remainderman. This future interest is known as a "reversion."

> **Example 1:** A conveys Blackacre "to B for the life of B." B has a life estate in Blackacre, which terminates upon B's death. A has a reversion; upon B's death, ownership of Blackacre reverts to A.
>
> **Example 2:** A conveys Blackacre "to B for B's life, and then to C." B has a life estate in Blackacre, which terminates upon B's death. C has a remainder; upon B's death, ownership of Blackacre vests in C.

The life estate is not subject to the Rule Against Perpetuities.

a. Measuring life is grantee

To be a life estate, the interest granted must be measured by the life of a human being and be qualified only by non-time limitations. Unless otherwise specified, the measuring life is the grantee.

> **Example:** A conveys Blackacre to "B for life." B has a life estate that is measured by his own life.

A life estate is fully transferable during the life of the person by whom the life estate is measured. Because the interest terminates at the death of the person by whom the life estate is measured, a life estate measured by the grantee's life is generally neither devisable nor descendible. If the life estate is received by will or intestacy, the life tenant may renounce the estate if he so chooses. In the states that have done away with the common-law curtesy and dower custom, a surviving spouse has a statutory right to take a portion of the estate.

In states that continue curtesy and dower, a conveyance from the husband to a bona fide purchaser without the wife's joining in the conveyance does not defeat dower. Similarly, a wife's dower rights are not defeated by the husband's creditors.

b. Measuring life is a third party

A life estate measured by the life of a third party is also called a life estate *pur autre vie.*

> **Example:** A conveys Blackacre to "B for the life of C." A granted a life estate to B for the life of C.

c. Rights and obligations

A life tenant has the right of possession, the right to all rents and profits during possession, and the right to lease, sell, or mortgage the property (right of alienation). To the extent the property can produce income, life tenants have the obligation to pay all ordinary taxes on the land and interest on the mortgage. If the property is not producing an income, the life tenant is responsible for taxes and mortgage interest to the extent of the reasonable rental value of the land. The life tenant also has the duty not to commit waste.

The life tenant is under no obligation to insure the land for the benefit of the remainderman and is not responsible for damage caused by third-party tortfeasors.

d. Waste

The rights of a holder of a life estate are limited by the doctrine of waste. Under this doctrine, a life tenant must deliver the property in essentially the same condition that it was in when she took possession. The holder of a future interest in the property (e.g., remainder, executory interest, reversion) may enter the land to inspect for waste, and she may seek damages and an injunction to prevent waste.

Other estates: Although the doctrine of waste typically arises in the context of a life estate, it comes into play with abuse or alteration of real property by any person who is holds a property interest that is not a fee simple interest.

1) Affirmative waste

Affirmative (or voluntary) waste is the result of overt conduct that causes a decrease in the value of the property. The holder of a vested future interest may bring suit for damages, and the holder of any future interest may bring suit for an injunction. Limited exceptions exist for the exploitation of natural resources (e.g., minerals, timber) if such use was authorized by the grantor, was in effect at the time the tenancy began, or is necessary to maintain the property.

2) Permissive waste

Permissive waste occurs when the life tenant "permits" the premises to deteriorate through neglect, a failure to preserve the property, or a failure to reasonably protect the property. To maintain the property and avoid permissive waste, the life tenant is required to make reasonable repairs but need not spend more than the amount of income generated by the property, or, if the life tenant is in actual possession of the property, its fair rental value. The life tenant's duties include paying any property taxes and mortgage interest associated with the property and, in some jurisdictions, the duty to pay insurance premiums.

3) Ameliorative waste

At common law, a life tenant was prohibited from engaging in acts that changed the property's value (even those that enhanced the value), unless all future interest holders were known and consented. The current majority rule allows life tenants to physically alter structures on the property when necessary to make reasonable use of the property.

B. FUTURE INTERESTS

A future interest is an interest in presently existing property, or in a gift or trust, which may commence in use, possession, or enjoyment sometime in the future.

1. Reversion

A reversion (or "reverter") is the future interest held by the grantor who grants a life estate or estate for years but does not convey the remaining future interest to a third party. Reversions are not subject to the Rule Against Perpetuities.

2. Possibility of Reverter

A possibility of reverter is a future interest retained by a grantor when a fee simple determinable is conveyed.

3. Right of Reentry

A right of reentry (also called "right of entry" or "power of termination") is a future interest retained by the grantor after a fee simple subject to a condition subsequent is granted.

4. Remainder

Generally, a remainder is a future interest created in a grantee that is capable of becoming an estate that is presently possessory upon the natural expiration of a prior possessory estate (e.g., a life estate, estate for years) that is created in the same conveyance in which the remainder is created. However, by definition, a remainder interest cannot follow a defeasible fee interest. A remainder can be either vested or contingent.

a. Class interests

A class interest consists of a group of unspecified persons whose number and identity and share of the interest are determined in the future (e.g., at the death of the donor). Usually, the group is of children.

Example: A conveys a gift "to my children." Here, A conveys a class gift to an unspecified group because the recipients (i.e., those who will qualify as A's children upon A's death) are not known until A dies.

1) Vested remainder

A vested remainder is an interest that is not subject to any conditions precedent and is created in an ascertainable grantee.

Example: A conveys Blackacre "to B for life, and then to C and his heirs." Here, the grantee, C, is ascertainable.

a) Vested subject to open

If a conveyance grants a remainder to a class of grantees and at least one of the grantees receives a vested remainder at the time of the conveyance, that vested remainder is subject to open (i.e., the property interest is uncertain because other grantees may become vested and able to share in the grant).

Example: A conveys "to B for life, and then to B's children as they turn 18." B has three children upon death, X (10 years old), Y (15 years old), and Z (20 years old). Z has a vested remainder subject to open because the property interest may be shared if Y and/or X become vested (i.e., reach age 18).

Once a class closes, any person who might otherwise have become a class member (e.g., later-born siblings) cannot claim an interest in the property as a class member.

Although those born after the class closes are generally not part of the class, *those already in gestation upon closing are* included in the class.

Absent a closing date, the rule of convenience closes the class when any member of the class becomes entitled to immediate possession of the property.

Example: A conveys "to B for life, and then to C's children." If the conveyance does not specify when the class closes, the class closes when B dies, regardless of any of C's children born after B's death.

b) Vested subject to complete divestment

A vested remainder subject to complete divestment indicates that the occurrence of a condition subsequent will completely divest the remainder interest.

Example: A conveys "to B for life, and then to C; but if C has no children, then to D's children." C has a vested remainder interest, but if he is not survived by his children at the time of B's death, then C's interest will be divested.

b. Contingent remainder

A remainder is contingent if it is created in a grantee that is unascertainable, or if it is subject to an express condition precedent to a grantee's taking. This normally occurs in one of two circumstances: (i) when the property cannot vest because the beneficiary is unknown, or (ii) when the property cannot vest because the known beneficiary is subject to a condition precedent that has not yet occurred.

Example: A conveys "to B for life, remainder to C's heirs." If C is alive at the conveyance, C's heirs are not yet ascertainable, and the remainder is contingent.

Contingent remainders were destroyed at common law if they had not vested by the time the preceding estate terminated. In such a situation in most states today, the grantor's reversion becomes possessory, and the person holding the contingent remainder takes a springing executory interest, which becomes possessory if and when the condition precedent is met.

c. Rule in *Shelley's Case*

At common law, the rule in *Shelley's Case* prevented contingent remainders in the grantee's heirs by defeating the grantor's intent and changing the interest that the grantor purported to give to the grantee and his heirs to a vested remainder in the grantee. The rule in *Shelley's Case* changes the state of the title to two successive freehold estates in the grantee. Under the doctrine of merger, both the present and future interests are merged so that the grantee takes in fee simple absolute. Most jurisdictions have abolished the rule in *Shelley's Case,* and the parties now take the present and future interests according to the language in the deed.

Example: A conveys "to B for life, remainder to B's heirs." If the rule in *Shelley's Case* applies, after the merger, B will receive the property in fee simple absolute.

If the rule in *Shelley's Case* has been abolished, B has a life estate, and B's heirs have a contingent remainder in the subject property.

d. Doctrine of Worthier Title

The Doctrine of Worthier Title is a rule of construction similar to the rule in *Shelley's Case* (except that it prevents against remainders in the grantor's heirs) and still applies in some states. The presumption is in a reversion to the grantor.

5. Executory Interests

An executory interest is a future interest in a third party that is not a remainder and that generally cuts the prior estate short upon the occurrence of a specified condition. In addition, a future interest that follows a fee simple determinable and is held by a third party (rather than the grantor) is an executory interest, even though it arises naturally out of the termination of the fee simple determinable, because a remainder never follows a defeasible fee and an executory interest is the only other future interest held by a third party.

There are two types of executory interests: shifting executory interests and springing executory interests.

a. Shifting executory interest

A shifting executory interest divests the interest of the grantee by cutting short a prior estate created in the same conveyance. The estate "shifts" from one grantee to another on the happening of the condition.

Example: A conveys "to B and his heirs, but if C returns from Paris, then to C." This conveyance creates a fee simple subject to an executory limitation in B, and a shifting executory interest in C.

b. Springing executory interest

A springing executory interest divests the interest of the grantor or fills a gap in possession in which the estate reverts to the grantor.

Example: A conveys "to B for life, and one year after B's death to C and his heirs." This conveyance creates a life estate in B, a one-year reversion in A (in fee simple subject to an executory limitation), and a springing executory interest in C.

6. Transferability of Remainders and Executory Interests

Vested remainders are fully transferable inter vivos, devisable by will, and descendible by inheritance. Today, executory interests and contingent remainders are transferable inter vivos in most jurisdictions, although under common law they were not transferable; both are devisable and descendible. It is important to note that most states permit any transferable future interest to be reached by creditors, except for those interests held by unascertainable or unborn persons.

7. Classification of Interests

It is important to classify the various interests in a disposition clause in order (i.e., from left to right) because the characterization of the first interest usually determines the characterizations of the following interests. For example, a contingent remainder can follow a contingent remainder but cannot follow a fee simple.

Example 1: A conveys Blackacre "to B for life, then to C if C survives B; but if C does not survive B, on B's death to D."

B has a present life estate. C has a future interest, which is a remainder because it can become possessory upon the termination of the preceding possessory interest (i.e., B's life estate), and is a contingent remainder because C's taking is conditioned on C surviving B. D also has a future interest, which is a remainder because it can become possessory upon the termination of B's life estate; it is a contingent remainder because D's taking is contingent on C not surviving B.

Now consider the following language that results in the same outcome (i.e., C owns Blackacre if C survives B, and D owns Blackacre if C does not) but different property interests for C and D immediately after the conveyance.

Example 2: A conveys Blackacre "to B for life, and on B's death to C. But if C predeceases B, on B's death to D."

B has a present life estate. C has a future interest, which is a remainder because it can become possessory upon the termination of B's life estate. C's remainder is vested because C is ascertainable **and** there is no condition precedent that C must satisfy to take Blackacre. However, C's vested remainder is subject to complete if a condition subsequent (C predeceasing B) occurs. D has a future interest, but it is not a remainder because C's interest is not an estate of a fixed duration, but is instead a fee simple estate, which has an unlimited duration. However, if the condition subsequent occurs, D would be entitled to take possession of Blackacre, thereby cutting short C's interest. Consequently, D has a shifting executory interest.

The above two examples demonstrate the importance of examining each clause independently and classifying each interest in the proper order.

C. RULE AGAINST PERPETUITIES

Under the Rule Against Perpetuities ("Rule"), specific future interests are valid only if they must vest or fail by the end of a life in being, plus 21 years.

Example 1: A conveys Blackacre "to B for life, and then to the first male descendant of B, then to C." This provision violates the Rule because it may be many generations before there is a male descendant of B, if at all.

Example 2: A conveys Blackacre "to B for life, and then to B's first son who reaches the age of 18, then to C." This provision is valid because any son of B will attain age 18 within 21 years after B's death.

Note the difference in the examples above. In Example 1, the opportunity for B to have a male descendant does not end after he dies. Because there is a possibility that the devise will neither vest nor fail within a life in being plus 21 years, the Rule is violated.

On the other hand, in Example 2, once B dies, his opportunity to have children ends, and so the clock starts. If, when he dies, B has at least one son under the age of 18, then it is certain to be less than a life in being plus 21 years before the condition either vests (son reaches 18) or fails (son dies).

1. Affected Future Interests

The Rule applies only to the following interests: contingent remainders, vested remainders subject to open, executory interests, powers of appointment, rights of first refusal, and options. It does *not* apply to future interests that revert to the grantor (i.e., reversion, possibility of reverter, right of reentry).

a. Trust interests

Even though a beneficiary of a trust holds only an equitable interest in the trust property, such an interest may be subject to the Rule.

2. Measuring Lives

The application of the Rule is determined by one or more measuring (or, validating) lives. A measuring life must be human, but there can be more than one measuring life, provided the number of such lives is reasonable. If a measuring life is not specified, the measuring life is the life directly related to the future interest that is subject to the Rule.

> **Example 1:** A devises Blackacre "to B for life, and then to B's children who reach the age of 25." B's life is the measuring life.

If there is not a measuring life, the applicable testing period is 21 years from the time that the future interest is created.

> **Example 2:** A devises Blackacre "to a charity for so long as the property is used as an animal shelter, and then to C." Because there is not a measuring life, C's interest must vest or fail within 21 years of the creation of C's interest in order to satisfy the Rule. Because there is not a guarantee regarding the future use to which Blackacre is put, C's interest violates the Rule.

3. Creation Events

The Rule tests the future interest as of the time that it is created. For example, a future interest created by a will is tested as of the testator's death.

4. "Vest or Fail" Requirement

The Rule requires that the future interest either vest or fail to vest within the applicable time period. If there is *any possibility* that it will not be known whether the interest will vest or fail within that period, the Rule has not been satisfied.

5. Effect of Violation

If a future interest fails to satisfy the Rule, **only the offending interest fails.** In the rare case when the voiding of the future interest undermines the grantor's intent, the entire transfer is voided.

6. Special Rule for Transfer to a Class

If the transfer of a future interest is made to a class and the Rule voids a transfer to any member of a class, the transfer is void as to all class members, even those whose interests are already vested (i.e., "bad as to one, bad as to all").

> **Example:** A devises Blackacre "to B for life, and then to B's children who have graduated from college." At the time of A's death, B had two children: X, who had graduated from college, and Y, who had not. X has a vested remainder subject to open; Y, as well as any after-born children of B, has a contingent remainder. At the time of B's death, Y has also graduated from college and B has had a third child, Z, who is in elementary school. Because it may take Z more than 21 years to graduate college and thereby vest his interest, not only is Z's interest void under the Rule, but X and Y's interests are also void.

a. Rule of convenience as a savior

The rule of convenience, which is a rule of interpretation, can operate to prevent the application of the Rule to a class transfer. Under this rule, membership in a class closes whenever any member of the class is entitled to immediate possession of a share of the class gift.

Example 1: A conveys Blackacre "to B for life, and then to B's grandchildren." At the time of the conveyance, B has one grandchild, X. X has a vested remainder subject to open. Although B may have grandchildren born more than 21 years after B's or X's death, the class will close upon B's death because B has a grandchild, X. Consequently, X and any other grandchildren born prior to B's death will take Blackacre. The Rule will not apply to void their interests in Blackacre.

Since the rule of convenience is a rule of interpretation, it does not apply when the grantor specifies that the class should remain open even though a member of the class is entitled to immediate possession of a share of the class gift. In addition, the application of the rule of convenience to a class transfer does not automatically forestall the application of the Rule.

Example 2: In the example at § I.B.8.f. Special rule for transfer to a class (class gifts), *supra*, (A devises Blackacre "to B for life, and then to B's children who have graduated from college"), although the class closes upon B's death because both X and Y have vested remainder interests, Z, as a child of B, is also a member of the class. Because Z's interest may not vest within 21 years of B's death, the remainder interests of all of B's children are void because of the Rule.

EXAM NOTE: Beware of fact patterns with class gifts to grandchildren of an *inter vivos* grantor instead of a testator. An *inter vivos* transfer is more likely to violate the Rule because the donor may have more children, while a deceased testator most likely will not.

b. Exceptions

There are two main exceptions to the "bad as to one, bad as to all" rule for class transfers. Both transfers of a specific dollar amount to each class member (e.g., "$50,000 to each grandchild who survives his parent") and transfers to a subclass that vests at a specific time (e.g., "to the children of B, and upon the death of each, to that child's issue") are tested separately. Any person who is entitled to the transferred interest is not prohibited from taking that interest simply because there are other members of the class who are prohibited from taking the interest.

7. Exceptions

a. Charity-to-charity exception

If property passes from one charity to another charity, the interest of the receiving charity is not subject to the Rule.

Example: Blackacre is conveyed "to charity B, as long as the premises are used for a school, and then to charity C." The executory interest of charity C may not vest within the time allotted by the Rule, but, because the Rule does not apply to charity-to-charity transfers, C's executory interest is valid.

2) Option and right of first refusal exception

The Rule does not apply to an option to purchase the property that is held by a current leasehold tenant. If the current tenant can transfer such an option, then this exception does not apply to a subsequent holder of the purchase option. In addition, the Rule does not apply to an option contract or a right of first refusal when the property right is created in a commercial transaction.

8. Common Rule Violations

a. Class transfers—"survival beyond age 21" condition

If a transfer to a class is conditioned on the class members surviving to an age beyond 21 and the class is open, the transfer to the class violates the Rule.

Example: A conveys Blackacre "to B for life, and then to B's children who reach the age of 30." At the time of the conveyance, B has one child, X, who is 35 years old. X has a vested remainder subject to open; B's potential children have a contingent remainder. The contingent remainder violates the Rule because it is possible that B could have another child who would not attain the age of 30 until more than 21 years after B's death. Because the contingent remainder is invalid, X's vested remainder subject to open is also invalid as a consequence of the "bad as to one, bad as to all" rule for class transfers.

b. Fertile octogenarian

Anyone, regardless of age or physical condition, including an 80-year-old woman (i.e., the fertile octogenarian) is deemed capable of having children for the purposes of the Rule. Some states have set an age limit (e.g., 55 years old) beyond which it is rebuttably presumed that a woman cannot have a child.

Example: A conveys Blackacre "to B for life, then to B's children who reach the age of 30." At the time of the conveyance, B is 90 years old, with one child, X, who is 35 years old. X has a vested remainder subject to open, since B, despite her age, is assumed to be capable of having another child. Because the contingent remainder in that child would violate the Rule, X's interest is also void under the "bad as to one, bad as to all" rule.

c. Unborn spouse

If an interest following a widow's life estate cannot vest until the widow dies, it violates the Rule.

Example: A conveys Blackacre "to B for life, then to B's widow for life, then to B's children who are then living." The contingent remainder in B's children violates the Rule because B's widow may be someone who is not yet alive at the time of the conveyance. The contingent remainder would not violate the rule if the life estate was conveyed to a particular person (e.g., B's current spouse) instead of "B's widow."

d. Defeasible fee followed by an executory interest

An executory interest that follows a defeasible fee violates the Rule, unless there is a time limit on the vesting of the executory interest that satisfies the Rule.

If the limit on the defeasible fee is durational (e.g., "so long as," "while"), the striking of the executory interest leaves the grantor with the possibility of reverter. If the limit on the defeasible fee is a condition subsequent (e.g., "but if," "upon the condition that"), the striking of the executory interest leaves the holder of the defeasible fee with a fee simple absolute interest in the property.

Example 1: A conveys Blackacre "to B for so long as the property is used for residential purposes; if it is not, then to C." B has a fee simple subject to an executory interest; C has an executory interest. Since C's executory interest could become possessory after the expiration of the testing period for the Rule, C's interest is stricken and A has a possibility of reverter in Blackacre.

> **Example 2:** A conveys Blackacre "to B; but if the property is used for residential purposes, then to C." B has a fee simple subject to an executory interest; C has an executory interest. Since C's executory interest could become possessory after the expiration of the testing period for the Rule, C's interest is stricken and B owns Blackacre in fee simple absolute.

e. Conditional passage of interest

If there is a condition imposed on the passing of a future interest subject to the Rule that is not confined to a specified time limit that meets the Rule's testing period, such as probating the will, or termination of a current military conflict, the future interest runs afoul of the Rule.

9. Statutory Changes

A majority of the states have adopted the Uniform Statutory Rule Against Perpetuities which adopts a "wait and see" stance with respect to the applicability of the Rule. Under this stance, an otherwise invalid interest is valid if it does in fact vest within 90 years of its creation. A few states have simply repealed the Rule altogether.

D. CONCURRENT ESTATES

A concurrent estate (or co-tenancy) is ownership or possession of real property by two or more persons simultaneously. The most common concurrent estates are tenancy in common, joint tenancy, and tenancy by the entirety.

1. Tenancy in Common

Any tenancy with two or more grantees creates a tenancy in common (and is thus considered the "default" or "catch-all" co-tenancy when neither joint tenancy nor tenancy in the entirety exists). In most states, there is a presumption that a conveyance to two or more persons creates a tenancy in common rather than a joint tenancy. Equal right to possess or use the property (unity of possession) is required, and **no right of survivorship** exists. Each co-tenant holds an undivided interest with unrestricted rights to possess the whole property, regardless of the size of the interest. Without the right of survivorship, each tenant can unilaterally devise, encumber, or freely transfer his interest to anyone, and the interest of the other tenants in common will not be affected. A tenant in common may also transfer his interest to another by a lease. The other tenants in common are entitled to share possession with the lessee and to receive a share of the rental profits from the lessor-tenant in common.

2. Joint Tenancy

A joint tenancy exists when two or more persons own property **with the right of survivorship** (i.e., upon the death of a joint tenant, the interest terminates and automatically goes to the surviving joint tenants). Modern law calls for a clear expression of intent along with survivorship language.

> **EXAM NOTE:** To determine if a joint tenancy was created, look for survivorship language.

a. Four unities

The joint tenancy must be created with each joint tenant having the equal right to possess or use the property (unity of **p**ossession), with each interest equal to the others (unity of **i**nterest), at the same time (unity of **t**ime), and in the same instrument (unity of **t**itle).

> MNEMONIC: **PITT**
>
> Unlike a joint tenancy, a tenancy in common requires only the unity of possession.

b. Severance

Although an interest in a joint tenancy cannot be devised, joint tenants can convey all or part of their individual interests during their lifetimes (inter vivos) to a third party, thereby severing the joint tenancy.

1) Effect of severance on remaining joint tenants

Once the joint tenancy interest is transferred inter vivos, the right of survivorship to that interest is destroyed and converted to a tenancy in common. A conveyance by only one of more than two joint tenants does not destroy the joint tenancy of the remaining joint tenants.

Note that any lien against one joint tenant's interest also terminates upon that tenant's death, such that the lien does not encumber the surviving tenants' interests.

2) Mortgages

A joint tenant may grant a mortgage interest in the joint tenancy property to a creditor. In **lien theory** states (the majority), the mortgage is only a lien on the property and does not sever the joint tenancy absent a default and foreclosure sale. In **title theory** states (the minority), the mortgage severs title and the tenancy between the joint tenants and creditor is converted into a tenancy in common.

3) Leases

There is a split among jurisdictions with respect to how to handle joint tenancies when one joint tenant leases his interest. Some jurisdictions hold that the lease destroys the unity of interest and thus severs the joint tenancy, while other jurisdictions believe that the lease merely temporarily suspends the joint tenancy, which would resume upon expiration of the lease.

4) Intentional killings

When one co-tenant intentionally kills the other co-tenant, some states allow the felonious joint tenant to hold the property in constructive trust for the deceased joint tenant's estate. This means that the surviving joint tenant does not profit from the felony but is able to keep his interest in the property. Other jurisdictions have statutes that sever the joint tenancy upon a felonious killing of one joint tenant by another joint tenant.

3. Tenancy by the Entirety

Tenancy by the entirety is a joint tenancy between married persons with a right of survivorship. The same rules for joint tenancy apply to tenancy by the entirety, plus the joint tenants must be married when a deed is executed or the conveyance occurs (the fifth **unity of person**). Neither party can alienate or encumber the property without the consent of the other. Tenancy by the entirety is used in many states and is analogous to community property in the states that recognize that type of property ownership.

4. Rights and Obligations

a. Possession

Unless there is an agreement to the contrary, each co-tenant has the right to possess all of the property. A co-tenant is generally not required to pay rent to the other co-tenants for the value of her own use of the property, even when the other co-tenants do not make use of the property. Similarly, a co-tenant is generally not required to share profits earned from the use of the property, such as from a business conducted on the property.

As a consequence of each tenant's right to possess the entire property, a co-tenant's exclusive use of the property does not, by itself, give rise to adverse possession of the interest of another cotenant.

1) Ouster

When a co-tenant refuses to allow another co-tenant access to the property, the ousted co-tenant may bring a court action for ouster to gain access to the property and to recover the value of the use of the property for the time during which the co-tenant was denied access to the property.

2) Natural resources

A co-tenant is entitled to the land's natural resources (e.g., timber, minerals, oil, gas) in proportion to her share.

b. Third-party rents

A co-tenant must account to other co-tenants for rent received from third parties, but he can deduct operating expenses when calculating net proceeds. Third-party rents are divided based on the ownership interest of each tenant.

c. Operating expenses

A co-tenant can collect contribution from the other co-tenants for paying more than his portion of necessary or beneficially spent operating expenses (e.g., taxes or mortgage interest), unless he is the only one in physical possession of the property and his use of it is equal to or outweighs the overpayment. Note that an owner in sole possession can collect only for the amount that exceeds the rental value of the property.

d. Repairs and improvements

A co-tenant does not have a right to be reimbursed by other co-tenants for repairs made to the property, even when those repairs are necessary. However, the majority view is that contribution for necessary repairs can be compelled in actions for accounting or partition. A co-tenant may, in some jurisdictions, maintain a separate action for contribution, as long as the other co-tenants have been notified of the need for the repair.

Similarly, except in actions for accounting or partition, a co-tenant does not have a right to reimbursement for improvements made to the property. As noted, when a third party is occupying the property, the co-tenant who collects rent from the third party can subtract expenses for necessary repairs from the rent received before sharing the rent with the other co-tenants.

5. Partition

a. Who may partition

A tenant in common or a joint tenant generally has the right to unilaterally partition the property, but a tenant by the entirety *does not* have this right. Property can be partitioned either voluntarily (if the co-tenants agree in writing on the division of land) or involuntarily (by court action).

The holder of a future interest who shares that interest with another (e.g., jointly held remainder interest) does not have the right to immediate possession and therefore cannot maintain an action for involuntary partition.

b. Effect of partition

In a partition action, the court divides the jointly owned property into distinct portions, or, if division of the property is not practicable or fair, the court may sell the property at a public auction and distribute the proceeds among the co-tenants in accordance with their ownership interests.

c. Restriction on partition

An agreement by co-tenants not to seek partition is enforceable. However, the agreement must be clear and the time limitation must be reasonable.

E. TRANSFER OF REAL PROPERTY

In order to transfer a real property interest, the grantor must demonstrate the intent to make a present transfer of the interest (e.g., delivery of the deed) and the grantee must accept the interest. In addition, pursuant to the Statute of Frauds, the transfer of a real property interest must be evidenced by a writing (e.g., a valid deed). Finally, the grantee may be able to protect his property interest against others' claims by recording the deed.

1. Intent to Transfer (Delivery)

The grantor must, at the time of transfer, intend to make a present transfer of a property interest to the grantee. Note that the interest itself may be a future interest, such as when a parent retains a life estate in a residence and transfers a remainder interest to an adult child.

Typically, this intent is manifested by delivery of the deed. Delivery may be completed by physically handing or mailing the deed to the grantee or the grantee's agent. However, intent can be implied from the words and conduct of the grantor, such as when the grantor drafts and records a deed.

Although it is often stated that a deed must be delivered in order for a real property interest to pass (i.e., a delivery requirement), the term "delivery" is used as shorthand for the existence of the necessary grantor intent. Physical transfer of a deed is not required and is not conclusive evidence of the grantor's intent.

a. Retention of deed by grantor

When the grantor keeps the deed, intent to transfer is not presumed. Instead, parol evidence is admissible to establish whether the grantor had the intent to make a present transfer of the property interest.

b. Transfer of deed to grantee

Transfer of a deed to the grantee creates a presumption that the grantor intended to make a present transfer of the property interest. Parol evidence is admissible to show that the grantor lacks such intent (e.g., the grantor only intended to create a mortgage not to effect an outright transfer). However, when the grantor transferred the deed to the grantee subject to an oral condition (i.e., a condition that does not appear in the deed), parol evidence is not admissible and the condition is not enforceable.

c. Transfer of deed to third party

1) Grantor's agent

When the grantor transfers the deed to her own agent (e.g., an attorney), the transfer is treated as if the grantor had retained the deed, even where the grantor has instructed the agent to deliver the deed to the grantee at some future time or upon the happening of an event. Until the grantor's agent delivers the deed to the grantee, the grantor can demand that the agent ignore the prior instruction and return the deed to the grantor.

2) Grantee's agent

When the grantor transfers the deed to the grantee's agent, the transfer is treated as if it had been made to the grantee herself.

3) Independent agent—gift

If the grantor purportedly gives property to a grantee through a third party and places a condition on the transfer of the deed by the third party to the grantee, whether delivery has taken place depends on the grantor's language. If the grantor retains an absolute right to recover the deed, no valid delivery exists because transfer of title was not clearly intended.

If the grantor does not retain a right to retrieve the deed, the key is whether the grantor intends to make a present gift of a property interest. If so, the grantor cannot later void the gift. Instead, the conditional transfer is treated as creating a future property interest in the grantee.

When the third party's transfer of the deed to the grantee is conditioned on the death of the grantor, the grantor's transfer of the deed to the third party must evidence the intent to make a present gift. When the grantor's intent is that the gift itself be effective only upon the grantor's death, the transfer can be ineffective due to a failure to comply with the requirements for a testamentary transfer (i.e., the Statute of Wills).

4) Independent agent—contract

When a contract for the sale of real property calls for the seller to give the deed to an independent third party (i.e., an escrow agent) and conditions the release of the deed to the buyer on the happening of an event, typically payment of the purchase price, the escrow agent is obligated to transfer the deed to the buyer if and when the condition occurs.

a) Retrieval by grantor

When there is a written contract, the grantor cannot require the escrow agent to return the deed prior to the failure of the condition to occur. When the contract is oral, the grantor can reclaim the deed from the escrow agent because the Statute of Frauds requires a writing for a land sale contract to be enforceable.

b) Escrow agent

When the escrow agent delivers the deed to the buyer prior to the performance of the condition, title to the property remains with the seller. This is true even when the buyer then transfers the property to a third party, even a person who purchases the property in good faith (i.e., a bona fide purchaser). An exception exists when the seller permits the buyer to possess the property.

c) Time of transfer

In general, title to the property remains in the seller until the condition is satisfied. Once the condition is satisfied, title automatically vests in the buyer. The date of transfer can relate back to the date that the grantor deposited the deed in escrow when, before the condition is satisfied, the grantor dies, becomes incapacitated or marries, or the grantee dies.

d. Acceptance

Acceptance is required for a transfer to be complete, and the grantee is generally presumed to have accepted any beneficial conveyance. Acceptance relates back to the time the deed was transferred, unless a bona fide purchaser or creditor of the grantor would be negatively affected by doing so.

If the grantee rejects the deed, no title passes and the grantor holds the title. If, howeer, the grantee accepts the deed and then changes his mind even a moment later, an entirely new deed must be created in order for the grantee to convey the title back to the original grantor.

2. Valid Deed

Valid deeds abide by the Statute of Frauds and include all necessary terms, such as the grantor's signature, named grantee, words of transfer, and a description of the property. Unlike a contract, **consideration is not required**.

a. Parties

The **grantor** and **grantee** must be identified. In addition, the grantor's signature is required, but in most states it need not be witnessed nor acknowledged (notarized). The grantee need not sign the deed. A deed that does not identify the grantee is ineffective until the grantee's name is added or determined.

b. Words of transfer

The portion of a deed that contains the words that transfer an interest from the grantor to the grantee is called a granting clause ("do grant and convey"). Any language evidencing a present intent to transfer will suffice.

c. Description of property

The description of the property must be reasonably definite, but extrinsic evidence is admissible to clarify. A habendum clause (e.g., "to have and to hold") in a deed defines the interest conveyed. When there is an irreconcilable difference between the granting clause and the habendum clause, the granting clause prevails. Descriptions by metes and bounds or by street address are acceptable but not required to sufficiently describe the property. When there is a conflict between descriptions of the property in the deed, descriptions based on monuments (e.g., from oak tree east to tool shed) are given priority over area descriptions (e.g., "100 acres").

Fraudulent documents are ineffective to convey title, even if they are relied upon by bona fide purchasers. Deeds executed through duress, mistake, or undue influence, or by minors or persons who are otherwise incapacitated, are deemed voidable.

3. Recording Act

While a deed need not be recorded to be valid and convey good title, all states have enacted recording acts, which establish priorities among conflicting claims to real property interests and promote certainty of title. Nearly all instruments affecting real property interests may be recorded, including easements, covenants, leases, contracts to convey, and mortgages. Some states also require the grantor to acknowledge the deed before a notary public before accepting it for recording, in an attempt to prevent fraudulent transfers. Unless the recording act governs, the common law rule of "first in time, first in right" generally applies to determine priorities.

a. Types of statutes

The three types of recording statutes are notice, race, and race-notice.

1) Notice statute

A purchaser need only purchase without notice of the prior interest to prevail under a notice statute. Notice statutes tend to protect subsequent purchasers against interest holders who could have, but failed to record documents describing their interests.

> **Example of notice statute:** "No conveyance or mortgage of real property shall be good against subsequent purchasers for value and *without notice* unless the same be recorded according to law."

> **EXAM NOTE:** Remember that a bona fide purchaser need not record in order to prevail over a prior interest in a notice jurisdiction, but must record to prevail against a subsequent purchaser.

2) Race statute

A minority of states have race statutes, under which a purchaser who records first prevails, regardless of his knowledge of any prior conflicting interests.

> **Example of race statute:** "No conveyance or mortgage of real property shall be good against subsequent purchasers for value unless the same be *first recorded* according to law."

3) Race-notice statute

A race-notice statute requires a subsequent purchaser to take the interest without notice of a prior conflicting interest, **and** be the first to record.

> **EXAM NOTE:** Look for words in the statute like "in good faith" in conjunction with phrases like "first duly recorded," which are present in a race-notice statute.

> **Example of race-notice statute:** "No conveyance or mortgage of real property shall be good against subsequent purchasers for value and *without notice* unless the same be *first recorded* according to law."

b. Paid value

Only a grantee who pays value for an interest in real property is entitled to protection under the recording statutes.

1) Mortgages

Mortgagees are considered to have "paid value" and are protected by the recording acts, unless the mortgage is not given simultaneously with a loan (such as when the mortgage is given after the loan is created).

2) Judgment liens

Creditors are protected only against claims that arise after a judgment lien against the debtor is recorded, unless otherwise indicated by statute. But, the majority of jurisdictions protect purchasers of property at a judicial sale against all unrecorded interests subject to the recording act.

3) Donees, heirs, and devisees

Grantees who acquire title of property by gift, intestacy, or devise are not protected by the recording act against prior claims to the same property, even when those claims are not recorded.

4) Shelter rule

Grantors who are protected by the recording act protect (or, "shelter") their grantees who would otherwise be unprotected. The **exception** to the shelter rule is that a purchaser who is not a bona fide purchaser cannot convey to a bona fide purchaser and then buy the property back to obtain the status of a bona fide purchaser.

c. Notice

As discussed *supra*, only purchasers who give value in good faith and without notice of a prior claim will prevail in notice or race-notice jurisdictions. "Notice" can be actual, by inquiry, or constructive. Whether a purchaser has notice is tested as of the time of the conveyance of the property to the purchaser. Notice obtained by the purchaser after the conveyance does not prevent the purchaser from enjoying the benefit of the recording act.

1) Actual notice

A grantee possessing actual, personal knowledge of a prior interest cannot prevail under a notice or race-notice recording statute.

2) Inquiry notice

If a reasonable investigation would have disclosed the existence of prior claims, the grantee is considered to possess inquiry notice, and cannot prevail against those prior claims. The purchaser is charged with whatever knowledge a reasonable inspection of the property would have disclosed. In most states, taking a quitclaim deed does not in itself create inquiry notice of prior claims.

Example: A's deed to B references a restrictive covenant entered into by A and B at the time of the deed. The deed is recorded, but the covenant is not contained in the deed. Any purchaser in A's chain of title will be charged with knowledge of the covenant and its contents.

3) Constructive notice

Grantees are held to have constructive notice of all prior conveyances that were properly recorded.

a) Tract index

All properties in a tract index system are listed by location on a separate page that includes all conveyances and encumbrances.

b) Grantor-grantee indexes

Each yearly index is usually alphabetized by the last names of grantors and grantees.

When searching the chain of title, the potential purchaser must first search for the grantor's name as a grantee (to ensure good title) in the grantee index, then the name of the grantor's grantor must be searched as a grantee, and so on, until the title has been searched back to its inception (common law rule) or as far back as the recording statute provides. Some states have search cut-off dates. Then, the grantors are searched as grantors to verify the chain of title.

c) Related searches

Title searches also should include a search of tax assessment and judgment lien records, as well as the marriage, divorce, and probate records for every named grantor and grantee.

d. Priorities

Interests are placed in order of priority based on the relevant statute (notice, race, and race-notice). The protected interest that is first in time is satisfied first, followed by the junior interests in order of time.

e. Rule application

Example 1: First, O conveys Blackacre to A, but A does not record. Second, O then conveys Blackacre to B, who has no notice of the earlier conveyance to A. Next, A records. Then, B records. B sues A to quiet title in Blackacre. What is the result?

i) Under a race statute, the first in time to record prevails. In the situation above, A wins because A was the first to record.

ii) Under a notice statute, regardless of who records first, those who in good faith purchase without notice prevail. So, in the above scenario, B wins because B took without notice.

iii) In a race-notice jurisdiction, B is unable to prove that he had both no notice *and* recorded first. Because A recorded first, A wins.

Example 2: First, O conveys an easement in Blackacre to A, but A does not record. Second, O then conveys Blackacre in fee simple absolute to B, who knows of the earlier conveyance to A. Next, B records. Then, A records. B sues A for title to Blackacre. What is the result?

i) Under a race statute, B wins and the easement is extinguished because B recorded first.

ii) Under a notice statute, A wins because B had notice of A's rights at the time of purchase.

iii) In a race-notice jurisdiction, A prevails and can enforce the easement against B because B is unable to show that he both recorded first *and* purchased without notice of A's prior claim.

Example 3: First, O promises A in writing that O will use Blackacre only for residential purposes, and the parties intend that this burden will run with the land. A does not record the promise. O then conveys Blackacre in fee simple absolute to B, who has no notice of O's earlier promise to A. Next, B records. Then, A records the promise. B then conveys a fee simple absolute estate in Blackacre to C, who has actual knowledge of O's promise to A. C uses Blackacre for non-residential purposes. A sues C to enforce O's promise to A, seeking damages and an injunction. What is the result?

    i) Under a race statute, C wins, even though C records after A. In this situations, A's recording is outside C's chain of title, so it does not constitute "winning the race" for the purposes of a race statute. Also, because B's interest in Blackacre "wins" over A's, and C relies on B's title, C wins.

    ii) Under a notice statute, C wins even though C had notice. The shelter doctrine shelters C by making B's title marketable, because B was a good faith purchaser. Therefore, B passes his title to C, and C takes B's status as a good faith purchaser.

    iii) In a race-notice jurisdiction, C wins because the shelter doctrine applies.

f. Chain of title problems

1) Wild deed

Although an instrument is recorded and indexed in the recording office, it may not be recorded in such a way as to give notice to subsequent purchasers (i.e., the deed may not be in the "chain of title"). A recorded deed that is not within the chain of title is a "wild deed."

Example 1: First, O conveys Blackacre to A, but A does not record. Second, A conveys Blackacre to B, and B records. O then conveys Blackacre to C, who has no notice of the earlier conveyances to A or B. Next, C records. Then, A records the deed from O to A. B sues A for title to Blackacre. What is the result?

    i) Under a race statute, C prevails even though B recorded the deed from A to B before C recorded the deed from O to C, because the deed from A to B was a "wild deed," outside C's chain of title. In performing a standard title search, C would have searched in the grantor index for deeds listing O as the grantor from the date the deed granting Blackacre to O was executed to the date C recorded the deed from O to C. No deed from O to A would have been discovered in such a search, and without finding a deed from O to A, B would not be expected to look for a deed from A to B.

    ii) Under a notice statute, C prevails because he had no actual notice of the conveyances from O to A and from A to B, and the deed from A to B did not give him constructive notice because it was a wild deed.

    iii) In a race-notice jurisdiction, C prevails for a combination of the two reasons above: C had no actual or constructive notice of O's deed to A, and B's prior recording of the deed from A to B does not count because it is a wild deed.

2) Deed recorded late

Example 2: O conveys Blackacre to A, but A does not record. Next, O conveys Blackacre to B, who has actual notice of the conveyance from O to A, and B records. Then, A records. Next, B conveys to C, who has no actual notice of the O-to-A conveyance. C sues A for title to Blackacre. What is the result?

    i) Under a race statute, C prevails even though A recorded the deed, because A's deed was recorded outside C's chain of title. Remember that under the standard title search, C would only research the grantor index under O's name until the date that B recorded the deed from O to B. Because O's deed to A was filed after that date, it is not considered "duly recorded" for the purposes of a race statute.

 ii) Under a notice statute, C wins because C had no notice and because A's deed was recorded outside C's chain of title.

 iii) In a race-notice jurisdiction, C wins because both race and notice requirements are met.

3) Deed recorded early (estoppel by deed)

Under the estoppel by deed doctrine, a grantor who conveys an interest to land by warranty deed before actually owning it is estopped from later denying the effectiveness of her deed. Consequently, when the grantor does acquire ownership of the land, the after-acquired title is transferred automatically to the prior grantee. However, under the majority rule, a subsequent purchaser from the same grantor who takes without notice can obtain good title, despite the doctrine of estoppel by deed, in a notice or race-notice jurisdiction. The purchaser is generally required to search the grantee index for a grantor's name only as far back as the date on which the grantor's name appears as a grantee (i.e., the date on which the grantor acquired the property). That date is the earliest date that a grantor's name must be searched on the grantor index for a conveyance by the grantor. The recording of a transfer made by the grantor before that date is not treated as giving the purchaser constructive notice of the transfer.

4) Title insurance

Title insurance protects owners or lenders against the actual monetary loss due to such matters as title defects and lien problems. Title defects are most often created as the result of errors in the title examining process, as well as title recording errors. Forged instruments and undelivered deeds also create title defects because they do not transfer title and are void.

Lien problems result from the invalidity or unenforceability of mortgage liens. Additionally, tax liens and judgments create defects that do not allow for the proper transference of title.

4. Types of Deeds

a. General warranty deed

The grantor of a general warranty deed guarantees that he holds six covenants of title, which are discussed below.

1) Present covenants

Present covenants embodied in the general warranty deed are the covenant of seisin, the covenant of the right to convey, and the covenant against encumbrances.

The covenant of seisin warrants that the grantor owns the land as it is described in the deed. The covenant of the right to convey guarantees that the grantor has the right to transfer title. The covenant against encumbrances guarantees that the deed contains no undisclosed encumbrances.

2) Future covenants

Future covenants run with the land, and the statute of limitations does not begin to run until the grantee's rights are encroached. The grantor of a general warranty deed promises to protect the grantee against subsequent lawful claims of title or encroachment (the covenant of quiet enjoyment and the covenant of warranty).

In some jurisdictions, the grantor also promises to do whatever is necessary to pass title to the grantee if it is later determined that the grantor omitted something required to pass valid title (future covenant of further assurances).

3) Breach of covenant

a) Time of breach

Breach of the present covenants occurs at the time of conveyance. A breach of the covenant of seisin and right to convey arises when the grantor is not the owner. A property that is encumbered at the time of conveyance creates a breach of the covenant against encumbrances. In most states, these present covenants do not run with the land. Consequently, a subsequent grantee cannot sue to enforce them against the original grantor. However, some states allow a remote grantee to sue the original grantor for breach of the covenant against encumbrances. *See* Uniform Land Transactions Act § 2-312.

Conversely, a breach of future covenants occurs only upon interference with possession and runs to successive grantees. The party seeking liability must provide the covenantor with notice of the claim.

b) Recovery

A buyer can recover for breach of the covenant against encumbrances the lesser of the difference in value between title with and without the defect, or the cost of removing the encumbrance.

Recovery for the covenants of enjoyment or warranty is the lesser of the purchase price or the cost of defending title.

Recovery for the covenants of seisin, right to convey, or further assurances is the lesser of the purchase price or the cost of perfecting title.

c) After-acquired title

When a person who purports to transfer real property that he does not own subsequently becomes the owner of that property, the after-acquired title doctrine provides that title to the property automatically vests in the transferee. Most often, this doctrine is applied to the grantor of a warranty deed. A related doctrine, estoppel by deed, prevents the grantor from asserting ownership of the after-acquired property.

b. Special warranty deed

A special warranty deed contains the same covenants of title as a general warranty deed, but only warrants against defects arising during the time the grantor has title.

c. Quitclaim deed

Unlike a warranty deed, a quitclaim deed promises **no covenants of title.**

A common form of quitclaim deed is the tax deed, which is used by government authorities when selling properties seized for nonpayment of taxes.

The grantee in a quitclaim deed (or a grant deed or warranty deed) receives no better title than what the grantor possessed.

F. SECURITY INTERESTS IN REAL PROPERTY

The owner of an interest in real property may convey or retain that interest as security for the payment of an obligation, usually a loan. The obligation typically takes the form of a promissory note, which sets out the terms of the transaction. This document reflects only the personal obligation of the debtor and need not be filed in order to enforce the mortgage. If the obligation is not repaid when due, the holder of the security interest will choose either to take title to the real estate or sell it and use the proceeds to repay the debt along with legal fees.

The two main forms that a security interest may take are a mortgage and a deed of trust.

1. Mortgage

A mortgage is an interest in real property that serves as security for an obligation. The obligation may be owed by the person who conveys the interest (i.e., the **mortgagor)** or a third party. The **mortgagee** is the person with the security interest in the real property, typically a bank.

As a conveyance of an interest in real property, the mortgage must satisfy the Statute of Frauds.

a. Lien theory versus title theory states

In a **majority** of the states, the mortgagor is treated as the owner of the real property interest and the mortgagee is treated as the holder of lien on that interest. These states are referred to as lien states. By contrast, in a **minority** of states, the mortgagee is treated as the owner of the real property interest and the mortgagor possesses the right to regain ownership of the real property upon satisfaction of the obligation. These states are referred to as title states.

1) Effect on joint tenancy

In a lien state, a mortgage interest is treated as a lien that does not affect a joint tenancy until foreclosure. In a title state, the joint tenancy is severed upon the granting of a mortgage, and the interest is converted into a tenancy in common. In either case, upon foreclosure, the mortgagee may only foreclose on the undivided tenancy in common interest of the mortgagor, and the interests of other co-tenants to the property are not affected.

2. Mortgage Alternatives

a. Deed of trust

In some states, a deed of trust (or trust deed) is used in place of a mortgage. The borrower (landowner) delivers a note to a third-party trustee as collateral security for the payment of the note to the beneficiary (lender), with the condition that the trustee re-conveys the title to the borrower upon payment of the note. Upon default, the beneficiary instructs the trustee to sell the land to repay the note. In a defective transfer of a deed-of-trust transaction, an equitable lien can be argued when a property is transferred without proper payment of the mortgage. For most purposes, a deed of trust is treated the same as a mortgage.

b. Installment land contract

An installment land contract (i.e., contract for deed) is a contract whereby the seller retains title until the buyer makes the final payment under an installment payment plan. Traditionally, an installment land contract allowed the seller to keep all installment payments and retake possession if the buyer failed to make a single payment, even if the buyer had made almost all of the installment payments.

States vary in their methods to assist a buyer in default. Some states treat an installment land contract as a mortgage, requiring the seller to foreclose on the property to gain clear title. Other states offer the buyer the equitable right of redemption. Still others allow the seller to retain ownership of the property but require some form of restitution to the buyer.

c. Absolute deed

An absolute deed (also known as a "Deed of Absolute Sale") is free of all liens and encumbrances and is used to transfer unrestricted title to property. When there is an obligation created prior to or contemporaneously with this transfer, the grantor may prove that the transfer was not actually a sale but instead a disguised mortgage. If proven, a court will treat the transfer as an equitable mortgage.

1) Evidentiary issues

The grantor must prove existence of such an agreement by clear and convincing evidence. Parol evidence is admissible to establish the existence of such an agreement because the deed was not intended to be a complete integration of the parties' agreement. In addition, the Statute of Frauds does not prevent the introduction of oral evidence to explain or interpret the written deed (i.e., to show that the deed was subject to an agreement that the property serve as security for an obligation).

2) Grantee's sale to bona fide purchaser

If the grantee sells the property to a bona fide purchaser, the grantor cannot recover the property from the bona fide purchaser. However, the grantor can seek to recover the difference between the value of the property and the amount of the outstanding obligation.

d. Conditional sale and repurchase

When real property is sold and then leased back to the seller, usually for a long period of time with the option to repurchase the property, the transaction may constitute the creation of security interest in the property, a disguised mortgage, rather than a sale-leaseback arrangement. Among the factors the court will take into account when determining the true character of the transaction are the equivalency of the lease payments to the fair market rental value of the property and the likelihood that the seller-lessee will exercise his right to repurchase the property at the end of the lease period.

3. Effect of Transfer by Mortgagor

The transfer by the mortgagor of mortgaged property can have significant ramifications for both the mortgagor and transferee. Restatement (Third) of Property §§ 5.1-5.5.

a. Mortgagor's liability

Unless the mortgagee-lender agrees to release the mortgagor-borrower from liability for the loan, the mortgagor-borrower remains personally liable on the loan obligation after the transfer of the mortgaged property. If the transferee assumes the mortgage obligation, then the mortgagor-borrower becomes secondarily liable as a surety, and the transferee becomes primarily liable on the mortgage loan. In the event the mortgagor-borrower makes mortgage payments, she can immediately seek reimbursement from the transferee.

1) Lender's modification or release of transferee's obligation

As transferor, the original mortgagor-borrower is relieved of personal liability when the mortgagee-lender impairs the original mortgagor-borrower's right of recourse against the transferee by modifying the terms of the loan or releasing the transferee from personal liability on the obligation. For example, a complete release from liability granted by the mortgagee-lender to the transferee usually results in the discharge of the mortgagor-borrower's personal liability on the mortgage obligation. The traditional rule is that the original mortgagor-borrower is completely relieved of personal liability by a modification in the terms of the loan. Some states and the Restatement limit the relief to the amount that original mortgagor-borrower's right of recourse is impaired. Restatement (Third) of Property: Mortgages, § 5.3, cmt. b.

2) Lender's release or impairment of security interest

The original mortgagor-borrower is also relieved of personal liability if the mortgagee-lender releases or impairs the property subject to the mortgage. Some states provide that a release completely discharges the mortgagor-borrower's personal liability. Other states and the Restatement provide that the mortgagor's personal liability is discharged only to the extent of the value of the property released. Restatement (Third) of Property: Mortgages, § 5.3, cmt. c.

Note: The reason that the mortgagor-borrower is "let off the hook" (i.e., released from personal liability to the mortgagee-lender) is that the mortgagee-lender's release of the mortgage eliminates the mortgagor-borrower's ability to be subrogated to the mortgagee-lender's mortgage interest. If the mortgagor-borrower were not released from personal liability, the mortgagor-borrower would remain liable to the mortgagee-lender, but would not have the protection of the mortgage in seeking to recoup from the transferee the amount paid to the mortgagee-lender.

3) Due-on-sale clause

Most mortgages contain a due-on-sale clause. This clause provides that, upon the transfer of mortgaged property, the lender has the option to demand immediate payment of the full amount of the outstanding obligation, including interest, unless the lender has given its written permission for the transfer. In exchange for this permission, the lender may increase the interest rate on the loan or demand an "assumption fee." Due-on-sale clauses are federally enforceable. 12 USC § 1701j–3.

Other transfers: Although labeled a "due on sale" clause, the clause typically covers any type of transfer.

a) Residential property exception

Residential real property, which includes property containing fewer than five dwelling units, is not subject to federal enforcement of a due-on-sale clause with respect to a variety of transfers including the automatic "transfer" of a joint tenancy interest upon the death of the borrower, a transfer by will or intestacy to a relative upon the death of the borrower, a transfer to the spouse or child of the borrower, a transfer to an ex-spouse due to a divorce, and a transfer to the borrower's living trust. 12 USC § 1701j–3(d).

4) Due-on-encumbrance clause

Similar to a due-on-sale clause, a due-on-encumbrance clause gives the lender the right to accelerate a mortgage obligation upon the mortgagor's obtaining a second mortgage or otherwise encumbering the property. A due-on-encumbrance clause is generally enforceable to the same extent as a due-on-sale clause. Restatement (Third) Property: Mortgages, § 8.1, cmt. b.

b. Transferee's liability

1) Assuming mortgage obligation—personal liability

If the transferee-buyer assumes the mortgage obligation, then, upon default, the transferee-buyer, as well as the mortgagor-borrower, is personally liable to the lender. Most jurisdictions do not require that the assumption agreement be in writing; if proven, an oral agreement is enforceable.

2) "Subject to" mortgage obligation—no personal liability

If the transferee-buyer takes title "subject to" an existing mortgage obligation, then the transferee-buyer is not personally liable upon default. The mortgaged property is the principal and the transferor-seller is the only party liable for a deficiency. The transferee-buyer takes title, which allows him to possess the land, but that possession has no effect on any deficiency. If a deed is silent or ambiguous as to the transferee-buyer's liability, then the transferee-buyer is considered to have taken the property subject to the mortgage obligation.

4. Effect of Transfer by Mortgagee

a. Proper party to pay

If the promissory note given by the mortgagor-borrower is a negotiable instrument, then the mortgagor-borrower is generally obligated to pay the holder of the note. This is true even when the mortgagor-borrower does not have notice that the original mortgagee has transferred to the note to a third party. However, a promissory note given in connection with a mortgage may not be a negotiable instrument because the note does not contain the words of negotiability (i.e., "pay to the order of" or "pay to bearer") or payment is subject to the conditions that prevent negotiability. In such cases, the modern trend is that the mortgagor may pay the original mortgagee until the mortgagor receives notice of the transfer. Restatement (Third) of Property: Mortgages § 5.5.

b. Method of transfer

If the promissory note is non-negotiable, ownership of the note may be transferred by a separate document that assigns the mortgagor's right to the transferee. If the promissory note is a negotiable instrument, it may be transferred only by negotiation, which may require not only delivery of the note but also its indorsement.

c. Transfer of mortgage and note

The promissory note and the mortgage that serves as security for the note are typically transferred together.

1) Transfer of mortgage without note

Jurisdictions are split with regard to the effect of transferring a mortgage without the note. Because the note is the principal evidence of the debt, many states treat a transfer of the mortgage alone as void. Other jurisdictions, however, treat the note as having automatically been transferred along with the mortgage, unless the parties to the transfer agree otherwise.

2) Transfer of note without mortgage

When the note is transferred without the mortgage, the mortgage is treated as having been automatically transferred along with the note, unless the parties to the transfer agree otherwise. Although it is customary for the transferee to obtain and record a mortgage assignment, no separate written assignment of the mortgage is necessary for the transferee to be entitled to enforce the mortgage. Restatement (Third) of Property: Mortgages § 5.4.

5. Pre-foreclosure Rights and Duties

a. Mortgagee's right to possession

Whether the mortgagee may take possession of the real property depends on the theory of title that the jurisdiction follows.

In a **lien theory state**, the mortgagee cannot take possession prior to foreclosure because the mortgagor is considered to be the owner of the real property until foreclosure.

In a **title theory state**, legal title is in the mortgagee until the mortgage has been fully satisfied. Thus, the mortgagee is theoretically entitled to take possession at any time, although the mortgagee is typically prohibited by the terms of the mortgage from taking possession of the property before default occurs. The mortgagee-in-possession can make repairs, take rent, prevent waste, and lease out vacant space. While in practice this may seem advantageous, few mortgagees take advantage of this right because of the liability risks involved. A mortgagee-in-possession assumes a duty to take reasonable care of the property, and she incurs liability as if she were the owner. Some mortgagees instead opt to have the court appoint a receiver to manage the property and intercept the rents prior to foreclosure.

A minority of jurisdictions follow the **intermediate title theory**, which in practice operates similar to the title theory. Under this theory, the mortgagor retains legal title until default, and, upon the mortgagor's default, it vests legal title in the mortgagee.

Regardless of the theory adhered to by a jurisdiction, the mortgagee may take possession of the real property if the mortgagor abandons the property.

b. Waste

The mortgagor has a duty not to commit waste at least to the extent that the waste impairs the mortgagee's security. This duty exists even if the mortgagor is not otherwise in default.

c. Equity of redemption

After default on the obligation, but **prior to** a foreclosure sale, the mortgagor may regain clear title to the property under the doctrine of equity of redemption by paying the amount of the loan obligation currently owed, which, if there is an acceleration clause (*see* E.1.a. Acceleration clause, *below*), can be the full amount of the unpaid loan obligation, plus any accrued interest. Many states recognize a statutory right of redemption that permits the mortgagor to reclaim the property after a foreclosure sale (*see* § V.E.3.a.1. Statutory right of redemption, *below*).

1) Deed in lieu of foreclosure

In lieu of foreclosure, a mortgagor may convey all interest in the property to the mortgagee ("deed in lieu of foreclosure"). This permits the mortgagee to take immediate possession of the property without any further legal formalities, but it requires the consent of both the mortgagor and the mortgagee. The mortgagee generally may reserve the right to pursue a deficiency as measured by the difference between the outstanding mortgage obligation and the fair market value of the property against the mortgagor, but the mortgagor may bring an equitable action to set aside the conveyance if it is not reasonable and fair.

2) Clogging the equity of redemption

A mortgagor may waive his right to redeem after the mortgage is executed in exchange for good and valuable consideration. However, courts routinely reject attempts by the mortgagee to deny the mortgagor this right (i.e., to "clog" the equity of redemption) prior to default, such as by the inclusion of a waiver clause in the mortgage.

6. Foreclosure Methods

A mortgagee may generally foreclose on a mortgage when the obligation to which the mortgage relates is in default. Typically, this occurs when the mortgagor fails to make timely loan payments.

a. Notice to mortgagor

In order for a mortgagee to foreclose on a mortgage, the mortgagee must give the mortgagor prior notice.

b. Sale

1) Judicially supervised

All states permit a mortgagee to foreclose on a mortgage through a judicially-supervised public sale of the mortgaged property.

2) Privately supervised

More than half of the states also permit a mortgagee to foreclose on a mortgage through a privately-conducted public sale of the mortgaged property when the mortgage contains a "power of sale" clause. This method is more common in states that recognize a deed of trust as the security instrument and in such states is typically conducted by the trustee pursuant to the "power of sale" clause in the deed of trust. Typically this method is faster and cheaper than a judicially supervised sale.

c. Strict foreclosure

A few jurisdictions recognize the strict foreclosure method in which a court orders the mortgagor to pay the mortgage within a certain time period. If the mortgagor does not pay within the time period, then the mortgagee takes title free and clear.

d. Timing of enforcement of note and mortgage

Most states permit the mortgagee to elect whether to bring an action to enforce the mortgage obligation (e.g., note) against the mortgagor-borrower personally or to initiate an action to foreclose on the mortgage. To the extent that the obligation is not satisfied by pursuing one type of action, the mortgagee may be able to then pursue the other enforcement action.

7. Foreclosure—Priority of Interests

If there is more than one interest (e.g., two or more mortgages) in the property being foreclosed, a valid foreclosure terminates any interest in the foreclosed property that is junior to the interest being foreclosed, but has no effect on any senior interest.

In determining the priority of interests (i.e., whether an interest is junior or senior to another interest), the basic "first in time, first in right" rule is applied. However, this rule is subject to various exceptions.

a. Purchase-money mortgage exception

A purchase-money mortgage is a mortgage granted to (i) the seller of real property or (ii) a third-party lender, to the extent that the loan proceeds are used to acquire title to the real property or construct improvements on the real property if the mortgage is given as part of the same transaction in which title is acquired. A purchase-money mortgage has priority over mortgages and liens created by or that arose against the purchaser-mortgagor prior to the purchaser-mortgagor's acquisition of the property, whether or not recorded. This priority of a purchase-money mortgage generally exists with respect to a judgment lien against the purchaser-mortgagor that pre-dates the purchaser-mortgagor's acquisition of the property and an after-acquired property clause in a mortgage of other property granted by the purchaser-mortgagor prior to the purchaser-mortgagor's acquisition of the property in question. (*see* § V.E.2.f. After-acquired property, *below*). In addition, a purchase-money mortgage has priority over a vendor's lien, such as an equitable vendor's lien that arises when the seller of real property takes a promissory note for part of the purchase price but does not take a mortgage.

A seller's purchase-money mortgage generally has priority over a purchase-money mortgage given to a third-party lender by a buyer to aid the buyer in acquiring the property from the seller. The priority of third-party purchase-money mortgages is determined chronologically, subject to any other applicable exception. Restatement (Third) of Property: Mortgages §§ 7.2, 7.5.

b. Unrecorded mortgage exception

A mortgage, as an interest in property, is subject to the state recording act. Consequently, a subsequent mortgage that satisfies the requirements of the applicable recording act has priority over an unrecorded prior mortgage. For example, in a notice jurisdiction, the mortgagee who receives her mortgage without knowledge of a prior unrecorded mortgage has priority over the holder of the unrecorded mortgage.

c. Subordination agreement between mortgagees

The holder of a prior mortgage can agree to subordinate his interest to the holder of a subsequent mortgage. This agreement is enforceable unless the mortgage is not sufficiently described or specified.

d. Mortgage modifications and replacements

A senior mortgagee who enters into an agreement with the mortgagor to modify the mortgage or the obligation it secures subordinates his interest to a junior mortgagee's interest to the extent that the modification is materially prejudicial to the junior mortgagee's interest. The senior mortgagee's interest otherwise remains superior to the junior mortgagee's interest. Similarly, when a senior mortgagee releases a mortgage and, as part of the same transaction, replaces it with a new mortgage, the new mortgage retains the same priority as the former mortgage, except to the extent that any change in the terms of the mortgage or the obligation it secures is materially prejudicial to the holder of a junior interest in the real estate. Restatement (Third) of Property: Mortgages § 7.3(a)(1), (b).

e. Future-advances mortgages

A **future-advance mortgage** is a mortgage given by a borrower in exchange for the right to receive money from the lender in the future. This type of mortgage is also known as a "line of credit." It is often used for home equity, construction, business, and commercial loans, and can provide for obligatory advances or optional advances. If payments are obligatory, the future advance mortgage has priority with respect to amounts loaned both before and after the mortgagee has notice of the subsequent mortgage. If, however, the payments under a future-advances mortgage are optional, the subsequent mortgage has priority over payments made after the future-advance mortgagee has notice of the subsequent mortgage. There is a split among the states as to whether actual notice is required or whether constructive notice is sufficient. In addition, the modern trend is to treat all future advances, including optional advances, as having priority over a subsequent mortgage.

8. Foreclosure—Effect on Various Parties

a. Mortgagor

A foreclosure sale eliminates the mortgagor's interest in the property.

1) Statutory right of redemption

Many states permit the mortgagor to reclaim the property after a foreclosure sale. In these jurisdictions, during a fixed period of time (typically between three months and two years), the mortgagor has the right to compensate the party who purchased the property at the foreclosure sale and reclaim the property.

b. Purchaser of property

The purchaser of property at a foreclosure sale takes the property free and clear of any junior mortgage and subject to any senior mortgage. In addition, the purchaser may be subject to the mortgagor's statutory right of redemption.

c. Senior interest

The rights of the holder of a senior interest are generally not affected by a foreclosure sale.

d. Junior interests

All interests that are junior to the mortgage that is being foreclosed are generally destroyed.

1) Omitted party

The holder of a junior interest must be given notice of the foreclosure and made a party to the foreclosure action. This provides the junior interest with an opportunity to redeem the property by paying off a senior interest. If the holder of a junior interest is not made party to the action, her interest is not affected by the foreclosure action.

2) "Marshalling of assets"

Generally, a creditor whose debt is secured by a mortgage on multiple properties can elect which property to subject to a foreclosure sale. However, when a senior mortgage is foreclosed and the mortgage covers multiple properties, the holder of a junior mortgage on some but not all of these properties can petition the court to apply the equitable doctrine of **"marshalling of assets."** Under this doctrine, the holder of the senior mortgage may be compelled to first foreclose on the properties for which only that holder possess a mortgage in order to protect the security interest of the holder of the junior mortgage, so long as it does not prejudice the interest of the holder of the senior mortgage or a third party. If there are multiple junior interests, property subject to the more recently created interests is subject to foreclosure prior to property subject to the more remotely created interests (i.e., **the "inverse order rule"**).

9. Foreclosure—Distribution of Proceeds

The proceeds from a foreclosure sale are applied first to the costs associated with the sale, second to the balance and interest of the mortgage obligation being foreclosed, and third to the mortgage obligations owed to junior interest holders in the order of the priority of their interests. Any remainder is paid to the debtor-mortgagor.

10. Personal Liability of Mortgagor for Deficiency

When the mortgagor signs a note and gives a mortgage, in most states, the mortgagee is permitted to bring an action based on the note itself before bringing an action to foreclose on the mortgage. In addition, after bringing a foreclosure action, the mortgagee is permitted by many states to bring a deficiency action against the mortgagor if the foreclosure sale proceeds are insufficient to satisfy the mortgage obligation. Some states disallow this action when the mortgagee forecloses via a privately-supervised foreclosure sale or when the mortgage is a purchase-money mortgage. In addition, some states limit the amount that may be recovered in a deficiency action to the fair market value of the property when the value of the property falls below the amount of the deficiency.

11. Payment by a Third Party—Subrogation

A person who pays off another person's mortgage obligation may become the owner of the obligation and the mortgage to the extent necessary to prevent unjust enrichment. Among the circumstances in which the equitable remedy of subrogation is appropriate is when the payor (i.e., subrogee) is under a legal duty to pay the obligation, or when the payor does do so to protect his own interest or on account of misrepresentation, mistake, duress, fraud or undue influence. Restatement (Third) Property-Mortgages § 7.6.

a. Amount paid

Subrogation is not permitted where the full obligation secured by the mortgage is not discharged. (Note: An obligation may be fully discharged even though the payor pays less that the face value of the obligation if the payor does so as a result of a negotiated settlement with the obligee.) In the case of a partial discharge, a payor who is a subordinate mortgagee may be able to add the amount paid to the balance of the subordinate mortgage and recover the amount upon foreclosure.

12. Defenses

A mortgage is generally enforceable only to the extent that the underlying obligation is enforceable. A mortgage is subject to the same defenses as the underlying obligation secured by the mortgage (e.g., mistake, duress, failure of consideration, fraud, or lack of capacity). In addition, when the interest on the mortgage obligation violates state usury law, the lender will forfeit the interest, but generally not the principal due on the loan.

a. Transferee who assumes mortgage

A donee who takes property that has been mortgaged is entitled to assert the donor's defenses against the mortgagee. However, a transferee who purchases real property and agrees to assume an existing mortgage obligation generally may not raise defenses that the mortgagor-transferor could have raised against enforcement of the mortgage obligation, such as statute of limitations, forgery, lack of capacity, or failure of consideration. Restatement (Third) of Property: Mortgages § 5.1, cmt. g.

b. Transferor's right to raise transferee's defenses

In general, a mortgagor who becomes a surety with respect to a mortgage obligation upon the transfer of the property to a person who assumes that obligation is entitled to the benefit of any favorable modification of the obligation, such as a lower interest rate or an extension of time to pay. The mortgagor-transferor may raise such a modification as a defense to the mortgagee's attempt to enforce the original terms of the mortgage obligation. However, the mortgagor-transferor is not entitled to raise defenses that are personal to the transferee, such as lack of capacity or a discharge in bankruptcy. Restatement (Third) of Property: Mortgages § 5.3, cmt. i.

13. Discharge

A mortgage obligation may be discharged by payment of the debt secured by the mortgage or by acceptance by the mortgagee of a deed in lieu of foreclosure. In addition, the doctrine of merger may be applied to eliminate a mortgage.

a. Mortgagor's right of prepayment

Traditionally, in the absence of clause permitting a mortgagor to prepay a mortgage obligation, the mortgagor had no such right. Under the modern trend, the presumption is reversed and prepayment is permitted unless the mortgage contains a clause prohibiting prepayment. With regard to the imposition of a prepayment penalty by the mortgagor, about half of the states prohibit it or place restrictions of various sorts on the imposition of the penalty (e.g., limitation on rate of interest of the loan, limitation on the amount or rate of the penalty, limitation of the penalty to the first few years of the mortgage) if the mortgage is on residential property. Restatement (Third) of Property: Mortgages § 6.1.

b. Merger

Under the doctrine of merger, when a mortgagee's interest in real property and the interest in the same property retained by the mortgagor are acquired by the same person, courts treat the mortgage as having merged into a fee ownership of the property. However, the Restatement contends that this doctrine should be limited to ownership of two consecutive estates in land by the same person and should not be applied to mortgages. Restatement (Third) of Property: Mortgages § 8.5.

IV. LANDLORD AND TENANT

The relationship between a landlord and a tenant can create four different estates. The relationship is generally governed by a contract, called the "lease," which contains the covenants of the parties.

The promises of the landlord and the tenant are generally independent of each other; in other words, each party must perform his promises regardless of whether or not the other party performs his promise.

A. TYPES OF TENANCIES

There are four types of landlord-tenant estates:

i)   Tenancy for years;

ii) Periodic tenancy;

iii) Tenancy at will; and

iv) Tenancy at sufferance.

1. Tenancy for Years

A tenancy for years is an estate measured by a fixed and ascertainable amount of time.

a. Term

A tenancy for years may be any length of time (e.g., one week, six months, five years).

b. Creation

A tenancy for years is created by an agreement between the landlord and the tenant. The Statute of Frauds applies to a tenancy for years that is longer than one year; such agreements must be in writing. A lease subject to the Statute of Frauds is voidable until the tenant takes possession and the landlord accepts rent from the tenant.

c. Termination

1) At end of term

Termination occurs automatically upon the expiration of the term; no notice is required. Any right to renew the agreement must be explicitly set out in the lease.

2) Prior to end of term

Termination may also occur before the expiration of the term, such as when the tenant surrenders the leasehold (i.e., the tenant offers and the landlord accepts return of the leasehold). In addition, although at common law the doctrine of independent covenants usually prevented the breach of a covenant in the lease by a tenant or landlord from giving the other party the right to terminate the lease, most states recognize that the breach of certain specific leasehold covenants (e.g., the tenant's payment of the rent, and the landlord's covenants of quiet enjoyment and implied warranty of habitability) can give rise to a right to terminate the lease.

2. Periodic Tenancy

A periodic tenancy is a repetitive, ongoing estate measured by a set period of time (e.g., a month-to-month lease) but with no predetermined termination date.

a. Term

A periodic tenancy automatically renews at the end of each period until one party gives a valid termination notice. The Statute of Frauds does not apply to a periodic tenancy because its nature is that it is for a non-fixed term.

b. Creation

A periodic tenancy can be created by express agreement, implication (e.g., the failure of an express agreement to mention a termination date), or operation of law (e.g., a holdover tenant).

c. Termination

Because a periodic tenancy automatically renews, notice is required to terminate.

1) Notice—timing

Notice of termination must be given before the beginning of the intended last period of the periodic tenancy.

> **Example 1:** A landlord who wants to terminate a month-to-month tenancy as of March 31st must give notice of the termination to the tenant before the first day of March.

For a year-to-year periodic tenancy, notice must be given at least six months (rather than one year) in advance. Many states have further reduced the advance notice period for a periodic tenancy of more than a month (e.g., one month for a year-to-year tenancy). Notice that is given late is generally treated as effective to terminate the tenancy as of the end of the following period.

> **Example 2:** A landlord who wanted to terminate a month-to-month tenancy that began on January 1st as of March 31st gave notice of the termination to the tenant on March 5th. The notice is effective to terminate the month-to-month tenancy as of the end of April.

A notice of termination is generally effective only as of the last day of the period (e.g., the end of the month for a month-to-month tenancy that began on the first day of the month).

> **Example 3:** A landlord wanted to terminate a month-to-month tenancy that began on January 1st as of March 15th. The landlord gave notice of the termination to the tenant on February 14th. The notice is effective to terminate the month-to-month tenancy as of the end of March.

2) Other ways to terminate

The same circumstances discussed with regard to a tenancy for years may also give rise to the termination of a periodic tenancy prior to the end of a term.

3. Tenancy at Will

a. Term

A tenancy at will is a leasehold estate that does not have a specific term and continues until terminated by either the landlord or tenant.

b. Creation

A tenancy at will can be created by the express agreement of the parties or by implication if a person is allowed to occupy the premises, such as when the parties are negotiating a lease. Note that, unless this tenancy is expressly created, the payment of rent by the tenant converts a tenancy at will into a periodic tenancy.

c. Termination

At common law, a tenancy at will could be terminated by either party without advance notice, but the tenant had to be given a reasonable time in which to vacate the premises. By statute, most states now require that a party give advance notice in order to terminate a tenancy at will, and some states allow only the tenant to terminate the lease at will. A tenancy at will can also be terminated by the death of either party, waste or assignment by the tenant, and transfer or lease of the property to a third party by the landlord. Restatement Second of Property: Landlord-Tenant §1.6.

If it is not clear from the language of the lease that it is a tenancy at will, it may be construed as a determinable estate (e.g., an estate for years determinable). A tenancy that is terminable at the will of one party only may be unconscionable. Restatement Second of Property: Landlord-Tenant §1.6, cmt. g.

4. Tenancy at Sufferance

A tenancy at sufferance (holdover tenancy) is the period of time after the expiration of a lease during which the tenant remains on the premises without the landlord's permission.

> **EXAM NOTE:** Know the difference between a tenancy at will, which is created by the agreement of the landlord and the tenant, and a tenancy at sufferance, which is created by the actions of the tenant alone.

A tenancy at sufferance is terminated if the tenant vacates the premises or the landlord evicts the tenant. In such case, the tenant is obligated to pay the reasonable value of his use and occupancy of the premises, which typically is a daily rate determined by reference to the previous rent. In addition, the tenant is liable for reasonably foreseeable special damages that result from his holding over, such as the cost of evicting the tenant. Alternatively, the landlord can terminate the tenancy at sufferance by binding the tenant to a new tenancy.

a. Holdover tenant

When a tenant continues to occupy the premises without the landlord's agreement after the original lease expires, the tenant is considered to be a "holdover tenant." The landlord can continue the relationship by treating the holdover tenant as a periodic tenant or a tenant at sufferance. Alternatively, the landlord may file a lawsuit for unlawful detainer if the holdover tenant remains after serving a written notice to vacate (or "quit").

The tenant is not considered to be a holdover tenant if the tenant leaves a few articles of personal property behind or the tenant's occupation is for only a few hours. Circumstances out of the tenant's control (e.g., severe illness) and seasonal leases are also exempt from the holdover doctrine.

1) Periodic tenant

By accepting rent after the termination of a lease, the landlord creates a periodic tenancy, the terms of which mirror the previous terminated lease. Notwithstanding the foregoing, no periodic lease of a residence can be implied for greater than one month, and of a commercial structure no longer than one year, due to Statute of Frauds requirements.

2) Tenant at sufferance

If the landlord refuses to accept rent from a holdover tenant, the tenant is considered wrongfully in possession, and the landlord may evict the tenant without notice.

3) Self-help

Most states no longer allow the landlord to use self-help, but require instead that she (i) properly serve the tenant with notice of a lawsuit and (ii) obtain a court judgment of possession.

4) Rent

A landlord can impose a higher rent on a holdover tenant if the landlord informed the tenant of the new rent prior to the expiration of the old lease. Otherwise, the rent of the old lease applies.

B. ASSIGNMENT AND SUBLETTING

Absent any language to the contrary, a lease can be freely assigned or sublet. Because a lease is both a contract and a conveyance, these can be independent grounds for liability.

1. Assignment versus Sublease

An assignment is a complete transfer of the tenant's remaining lease term. Any transfer for less than the entire duration of the lease is a sublease.

2. Assignee's Rights and Liabilities

Assignee tenants are in privity of estate with the landlord and are thus liable to the landlord for the rent and any other covenants in the lease that run with the lease. However, if the assignee tenant reassigns the leasehold to a subsequent tenant, the assignee tenant's privity with the landlord ends. Thus, he is no longer liable because the subsequent tenant is now in privity with the landlord.

3. Sublessee's Rights and Liabilities

Because the sublessee is not in privity of estate or contract with the landlord, the sublessee is not liable to the landlord for the rent or any other covenants in the lease but is liable to the lessee. However, if the sublessee expressly assumes the rent covenant (or any other covenants), he becomes personally liable to the landlord. While the sublessee can enforce all covenants made by the original lessee in the sublease, the sublessee cannot enforce any covenants made by the landlord.

4. Original Tenant's Rights and Liabilities

The privity of estate held by the original tenant terminates upon a successful assignment by the tenant to the assignee. But, because the original tenant remains in privity of contract with the landlord (because both are parties to the lease agreement), the original tenant remains liable for all the covenants in the lease—even after a successful assignment. Absent an agreement by the landlord to release the original tenant from liability (i.e., a **novation**), the original tenant remains liable to the landlord for the entire duration of the lease.

5. Landlord Assignments

A landlord may assign his ownership interest, usually through a deed, to a third party without the tenant's consent. The tenant is required to continue his rent obligation and any other covenant under his lease to the new landlord, provided that the covenants touch and concern the land. Likewise, the assignee landlord, as well as the original landlord, is bound to the tenant by the covenants of the lease.

6. Limitations on Assignment and Subletting

a. Prohibition

When a lease prohibits the tenant from assignment or subletting the leasehold, the tenant may nevertheless assign or sublet the premises. However, the landlord generally can then terminate the lease for breach of one of its covenants and recover any damages.

b. Landlord's permission

When a lease prevents assignment or subletting without the permission of the landlord, and the lease is silent as to a standard for exercising that permission, the modern trend imposes a requirement that the landlord may withhold permission only on a **reasonable ground in relationship to the property being leased** and not on a whim or personal prejudice. The traditional rule is that the landlord may withhold permission at his discretion. Non-assignment and non-sublease clauses are valid but narrowly construed.

A clause that prohibits assignment does not automatically also prohibit subletting.

c. Waiver by landlord

An assignment or sublease may be waived if the landlord knows of either the assignment or sublease and does not object. When a landlord consents to an assignment or waives her right to object, she cannot then object to a subsequent assignment. This prohibition on an objection to a subsequent assignment does not apply to subsequent subleases, and a minority of jurisdictions do not impose such a prohibition even on a subsequent assignment.

C. DUTIES OF LANDLORD

1. Give Possession

In most states, a tenant is relieved of the obligation to pay rent if the landlord fails to deliver actual possession of the leasehold premises. The minority rule requires only that the landlord deliver legal possession.

2. Duty to Repair

Under the common law, there was no implied duty on the part of the landlord to repair leased premises. However, the majority of jurisdictions today enforce an implied duty upon the landlord to repair under a residential lease, even when the lease attempts to place the burden on the tenant, except for damages caused by the tenant. Failure to make these repairs may constitute a constructive eviction or violate the implied warranty of habitability.

3. Warranty of Habitability

With regard to most **residential** leases, particularly when the dwelling is multi-family, there is an implied warranty of habitability. The landlord must maintain the property such that it is reasonably suited for residential use. The landlord's failure to comply with applicable housing code requirements constitutes a breach of this warranty, particularly with regard to violations that substantially threaten the tenant's health and safety. This warranty generally cannot be waived by the tenant, either by express language in the lease or by taking possession of the property with knowledge of the conditions.

If the premises are not habitable, then the tenant may choose to (i) refuse to pay rent, (ii) remedy the defect and offset the cost against the rent, or (iii) defend against eviction. Generally, before the tenant can withhold the rent or remedy the defect, she must first notify the landlord of the problem and give him a reasonable opportunity to correct the problem.

4. **Covenant of Quiet Enjoyment**

Every lease (both commercial and residential) contains an implied covenant of quiet enjoyment, which is breached only when the landlord, someone claiming through the landlord, or someone with superior title disrupts the possession of the tenant. Off-premises actions of third parties will not suffice.

The landlord is not liable for acts of other tenants but he has a duty to take action against a tenant's nuisance-like behavior and to control the common areas. Any actions by the landlord that breach this covenant amount to an **actual or constructive eviction** of the tenant. However, not every interference with the use and enjoyment of the premises amounts to a constructive eviction. Temporary or *de minimis* acts not intended to amount to a permanent expulsion do not amount to constructive eviction.

a. **Actual eviction**

If the landlord removes the tenant from the premises, the total eviction terminates the lease and ends the tenant's obligation to pay rent.

b. **Partial eviction**

If the tenant is prevented from possessing or using a portion of the leased premises, the tenant may seek relief for a partial actual eviction. The type of relief granted depends on who prevented the possession.

1) **Landlord**

The tenant is completely excused from paying rent for the entire premises if the landlord is responsible for partial eviction.

2) **Third parties**

The tenant must pay the reasonable rental value of the premises occupied if the partial eviction is by a third party with a superior claim to the property.

The tenant is not excused from paying rent if a third-party adverse possessor/trespasser partially evicts the tenant.

c. **Constructive eviction**

If the landlord breaches a duty to the tenant, such as failing to make a repair, that substantially interferes with the tenant's use and enjoyment of the leasehold (e.g., fails to provide heat or water), then the tenant's obligation to pay rent is excused due to constructive eviction **only if the tenant gives notice and adequate time to permit the landlord to fulfill his duty and vacates** the property within a reasonable amount of time.

d. **Retaliatory eviction**

Under the doctrine of retaliatory eviction, a landlord may not evict a residential tenant as retaliation for the tenant's reporting a housing code violation to the appropriate authorities or for refusing to pay rent when the landlord breaches the warranty of habitability. This doctrine also prevents a landlord from retaliating against a residential tenant by refusing to renew a periodic tenancy.

V.   LAND USE RESTRICTIONS

Commonly tested disputes about the use of land revolve around use of another's land (by easement, profit, or license) or restriction of use of one's own land (by covenants running with the land or equitable servitude).

A.   EASEMENTS

An easement is the right held by one person to make specific, limited use of land owned by another. The land that is subject to the easement is the servient estate, whereas the land that benefits from an easement on a servient estate is the dominant estate.

> **EXAM NOTE:** When a fact pattern involves the use of another's land, consider three questions:
>
> 1. Was an easement created?
>
> 2. If so, what is the scope of the easement?
>
> 3. Was the easement terminated?

1.   Classification of Easements

a.   Easements by grant and reservation

An affirmative easement gives another the right to use the land for a specific purpose.

An easement by reservation is created when a grantor conveys land but reserves an easement right in that land for his own use and benefit (and not for a third party).

b.   Easements appurtenant and profit in gross

Easements are presumed to be appurtenant (i.e., tied to the land) unless there are clear facts to the contrary. The benefits of an easement must correspond directly to the use and enjoyment of the possessor of the dominant estate.

An easement is "in gross" if it was granted to benefit a particular person (as opposed to the land).

> **Example:** A owns lakefront property and grants B, who lives in a town across the lake, an easement to gain access to the lake at a certain point on A's property. A created an easement in gross because it benefits B, not any land owned by B.

2.   Types of Easements

a.   Express easements

An express easement arises when it is affirmatively created by the parties in a writing that is in compliance with the Statute of Frauds.

The scope of an express easement is determined by the terms of the written grant or reservation.

b.   Easements by necessity and implication

1)   Easement by necessity

An easement by necessity is generally created only when property is virtually useless (e.g., landlocked) without the benefit of an easement across neighboring property. In addition, in order for an easement by necessity to be created, both the dominant and servient estates must have been under common ownership in the past and the necessity must have arisen at the time that the property was severed and the two estates were created. However, unlike an easement by implication, a quasi easement need not have existed at the time that both estates were under common ownership (i.e., there need not be a showing of prior use).

> **Example:** B owns an undeveloped parcel of land, which B subdivides into two lots. B sells one of the lots to A and retains the other lot for himself. The only access to a public road from the lot purchased by A is through the lot retained by B. Even though the deed makes no mention of an easement across B's lot and there has not been a prior path from A's lot across B's lot to the public road, A has an easement by necessity across B's lot to the road.

The scope of an easement by necessity is limited to the nature and extent of the necessity, and is determined by the parties' conduct.

2) Easement by implication

If an easement was previously used on the servient estate by an earlier owner, the court may find that the parties intended the easement to continue if the prior use was continuous, apparent (open and obvious), and reasonably necessary to the dominant land's use and enjoyment (distinguish from an easement by necessity, which requires strict necessity).

Because an owner cannot have an easement on his own land, this is considered a "quasi" easement. The scope of a quasi easement is determined by the prior use that gave rise to the easement, but can change over time if the changes are reasonably foreseeable at the time of conveyance.

Easements may also be implied without an existing use in a conveyance of lots sold in a subdivision with reference to a recorded plat or map that details streets leading to lots. Individuals who buy lots have an implied easement to be able to get to their lots that does not expire even if a public easement held by the city or county is vacated in the future.

c. Easements by prescription

Easements can be obtained by prescription similarly to the way land can be acquired by adverse possession. There must be continuous, actual, open, and hostile use for the statutory period (or 20 years). Unlike adverse possession, the use need not be exclusive (such as a public easement to access a beach).

The scope of an easement by prescription is limited to the nature and extent of the adverse use.

d. Easements by estoppel

Good faith, reasonable detrimental reliance on permission by a servient estate holder may create an easement by estoppel to prevent unjust enrichment.

> **Example:** A allows B to use a road on A's land to gain access to B's land, and B builds his house with the road being its main access point, improving the road with pavement and foliage. Thereafter, A tells B that he can use the road only if B pays $500; A closes off the road when B refuses. B likely has an easement by estoppel because he relied on the ability to use the road when he built his house, and unjust enrichment may otherwise result.

Distinguish this example from easement by prescription, which requires that the use be hostile (i.e., no permission was given). To prove an easement by estoppel, there must be permission to use the property, plus detrimental reliance on that permission (as in the example above).

e. Negative easements

A negative easement (or "restrictive covenant") prevents the owner from using land in particular ways. To be valid, a negative easement must be expressly created by a writing signed by the grantor and it is typically recognized only in relation to restricting use of light, air, support, or stream water from an artificial flow.

Example: A conveys a lot adjacent to his own to B, with an agreement that no structure will be built that would obstruct the light and air of A's land. This is a negative easement of light and air, because it deprives B from enjoying the property to the fullest extent. Negative easements are really restrictive covenants.

3. Transfer

a. Easement appurtenant

An easement appurtenant is transferred with the land to which it relates. Consequently, the benefit is transferred automatically with the transfer of the dominant estate, and the burden likewise is transferred automatically with the transfer of the servient estate.

b. Easement in gross

Traditionally, an easement in gross could not be transferred, but most courts now look to the intent of the parties to determine whether the parties intended only the holder of the easement in gross to enjoy the right, in which case it is not transferable, or whether the parties intended the holder to be able to transfer it.

Whether a transferable easement in gross can be apportioned turns on whether the easement in gross is exclusive or non-exclusive. A non-exclusive easement may not be divided up, but an exclusive easement may be. However, the division of an exclusive easement in gross is subject to the one-stock rule. Under this rule, the use that the transferees make of the easement collectively is limited by the use that the transferor made of the easement (i.e., his "stock").

4. Termination

a. Release

An easement can terminate by a writing that expressly releases the easement right and complies with the Statute of Frauds.

b. Merger

An easement is terminated if the owner of the dominant or servient estate acquires fee title to the other estate; the easement is said to "merge" into the title. The easement is not automatically revived on the separation of the property into the previous dominant and servient estates.

Note that the easement does not merge if the owner acquires less than fee title.

c. Severance

Any attempt to convey an appurtenant easement separate from the land it benefits terminates (or "severs") the easement.

d. Abandonment

An easement can be terminated if the owner of the easement acts in an affirmative way that shows a clear intent to relinquish the easement right.

Mere statements of intent without affirmative conduct are insufficient to constitute abandonment, but they may constitute estoppel. Mere non-use of the easement is also not sufficient to extinguish the easement right.

> **Example:** B is the owner of an easement across A's land for access to a beach. B does not like the beach and builds a brick wall across his land, blocking the entranceway to the easement. B's easement is terminated by abandonment.

e. Destruction and condemnation

Destruction of a structure on the servient estate by natural forces can terminate an easement if the easement is related to the structure (e.g., access to a lighthouse). Condemnation of the servient estate also terminates an easement. Note that some courts permit the holder of the easement to receive compensation because of the condemnation.

f. Prescription

If an easement holder fails to protect his easement against a trespasser for the statutory period, his easement right may be terminated by prescription.

g. Estoppel

If the servient estate owner changes position to his detriment in reliance on statements or conduct of the easement holder that the easement is abandoned, the easement holder may be estopped from asserting the easement.

h. Sale to a bona fide purchaser

If a **written easement** is granted but not recorded, then, depending on the applicable recording act, the easement may not be enforceable against a bona fide purchaser of the servient estate. The easement itself is not terminated.

5. Scope of Easement

The scope of an easement is not defined by its physical characteristics, but by its purpose. In determining the scope of an express easement, courts will look to the reasonableness of the use and the intent of the original parties to the easement. When the language used to create the easement is too general to determine the specific purpose of the easement, ambiguities are resolved in favor of the grantee.

The scope of an easement by necessity or implication is determined by the extent of the necessity. In other words, courts examine the circumstances surrounding the easement and will consider the easement's future foreseeable use, so long as any changes in use are reasonable.

Changes in the use of an easement are also examined for reasonableness, with the understanding that the original parties most likely contemplated not only its present use but also its future use.

6. Profits

A profit is an easement that confers the right to enter another's land and remove specific natural resources (such as oil, gas, minerals, timber, or game).

Although a profit can be either exclusive or non-exclusive, most are construed as non-exclusive. If it is exclusive, the holder of the profit has an unlimited and exclusive right to take the subject matter of the profit from the land. If it is non-exclusive, the right to take the profit is either limited by quantity, time, or use, or it is shared with another. Exclusive rights may be assigned and apportioned, as long as the apportionment is not wholly inconsistent with the original agreement.

Non-exclusive rights are assignable, but apportionment is not permitted when the burden on the servient estate is increased. Under the "one stock" rule, the transferees are limited to the amount of material taken by the transferor (i.e., his "stock"), and this quantity is divided up by transferees taking the profit.

Profits are created and analyzed similarly to easements, except that profits cannot be created by necessity.

7. Licenses

As with an easement, a license is a nonpossessory right to enter another's land for some delineated purpose. Unlike an easement, a license is freely revocable unless coupled with an interest or detrimentally relied upon, in which case the license is irrevocable. An irrevocable license based on detrimental reliance is the functional equivalent of an easement by estoppel with one exception: an easement continues to bind successors to the servient estate while a license only binds the licensor. When the language of the permission is ambiguous, courts prefer to interpret the language as granting a license.

A license coupled with an interest occurs when, for example, a grantor creates a life estate for A with the remainder to B. During A's life tenancy, B has an irrevocable license to enter the land and inspect for waste, due to his future interest in the land.

A license may be created without consideration or a writing. Because no writing is required, a license is created when there is an oral attempt to create an easement or written attempt otherwise fails due to the Statute of Frauds.

In addition to a specific revocation by the licensor, a license is revoked when the licensor dies or the servient estate is transferred. Traditionally, a license could not be transferred by the licensee and the attempt to do so resulted in the loss of the license.

8. Duty to Maintain

The owner of the easement has the right and the duty to maintain the easement for its purpose unless otherwise agreed between the owner of the easement and the owner of the servient land. The duty to contribute, however, is dependent upon the reasonableness of the repair. Specifically, the repairing party must give the contributing parties adequate notification and a reasonable opportunity to participate in decisions regarding the repairs. Moreover, the repairs must be performed adequately, properly, and at a reasonable price. *See* Restatement (Third) of Property § 4.13 (2000).

B. COVENANTS RUNNING WITH THE LAND

Unlike easements, profits, and licenses (which grant affirmative rights to use land), real covenants and equitable servitudes restrict the right to use land. When damages are sought to enforce the covenant, the covenant is called a "real covenant." When an injunction is sought to enforce a covenant, it is called an "equitable servitude." The requirements discussed below are necessary for both the benefit and the burden to run with the land, unless otherwise indicated.

1. Requirements to Run

Covenants run with the land (subsequent owners may enforce or be burdened by the covenant).

a. Writing

In order for a covenant to be enforceable, it must first comply with the Statute of Frauds. The only exception is an implied reciprocal servitude, which does not require a writing.

b. Intent

The parties must intend for the rights and duties to run with the land. Look for either explicit language like "and his heirs and assigns," or implication from the totality of the document and circumstances.

c. Touch and concern

The covenant must "touch and concern the land," which generally means that the person seeking enforcement must establish that the benefit or burden affects both the promisee and the promisor as owners of land and not merely as individuals.

Most courts would find that an affirmative covenant to maintain insurance for improvements on the land touches and concerns the servient estate. However, generally, most courts are hesitant to find that affirmative covenants touch and concern the land for fear that the covenant will unnecessarily encumber the land.

The modern trend shifts the burden by superseding the touch-and-concern requirement. Instead, the covenant is presumed valid unless it is contrary to public policy, imposes an unreasonable restraint on alienation or trade, or is unconscionable. If not, the covenant is valid unless illegal or unconstitutional. Restatement (Third) of Property: Servitudes § 3.2.

d. Notice—burden only

Under the recording acts, a subsequent purchaser without notice of a burdening covenant is not bound by it. Such notice can be constructive (recorded in the chain of title), actual (awareness that the covenant exists), or inquiry (duty to find out).

e. Privity

1) Horizontal privity—burden only

For the burden to run, the original parties to the covenant must have privity of estate at the time the agreement creating the covenant is entered into. This means that there must be some shared property interest apart from the covenant itself. (Note: Horizontal privity is not required for the benefit to run.)

2) Vertical privity

The successor to property can be held to the covenant (i.e., the burden runs) only if title to the entire servient estate (as measured durationally (e.g., a fee simple interest), not geographically (e.g., 20 acres)) can be traced back to the promisor. The successor to the property can enforce the covenant (i.e., the benefit runs) as long as the property interest possessed by the successor is at least some portion of the property interest held by the promisee.

3) Modern trend: no privity required

The Restatement of Property relies less on privity to determine running of the benefit and the burden than on a distinction between affirmative and negative covenants. The benefits and burdens of an affirmative covenant run to the successor of an estate of the same duration as the estate of the original party. Negative covenants, on the other hand, are analyzed similarly to easements.

f. Specific examples

There are certain burdens that come with their own specific problems. First, **money** that is used in connection with the land, such as association fees, as a general rule will run with the land. With **covenants not to compete,** although the burden of restricting land use touches and concerns the land, some courts have refused to permit the benefit to run with the land because the covenant does not affect the land's physical use. Finally, a **racially based covenant** that disallows an owner from transferring his property to another because of the person's race is never enforceable because to enforce it would violate the Fourteenth Amendment.

2. Equitable Servitudes

Equitable servitudes are covenants about land use that are enforced at equity by injunction.

a. Requirements

For a servitude to be enforced at equity, it must be in writing and meet the following requirements.

i) There must be **intent** for the restriction to be enforceable by successors in interest for the benefit to run and enforceable against successors in interest for the burden to run;

ii) The servitude must **touch and concern** the land; and

iii) If the person against whom the servitude is to be enforced is a purchaser, he must have notice (whether **actual, record, or inquiry notice**) of the servitude.

The requirement of notice (item iii, above), which is based on the principle that the acquisition of legal title by an innocent purchaser defeats a prior equitable claim, is independent of the effect of the recording act on the enforcement of an equitable servitude.

> Unlike with a real covenant, with an equitable servitude, a party seeking to enforce it need not show privity, but the party is limited to equitable remedies.

b. Implied reciprocal servitudes

Most jurisdictions impose the following requirements to enforce an implied reciprocal servitude: (i) there must be **intent to create** a servitude on all plots (i.e., the promise must be reciprocal), (ii) the servitude must be **negative** (i.e., a promise to refrain from doing something), and (iii) the party against whom enforcement of the servitude is sought must have actual, record, or inquiry **notice**. To establish intent, a common scheme must be established. Note that no writing is required for an equitable servitude created by implication.

3. Termination of Covenants

Like easements, covenants, equitable servitudes, and implied reciprocal servitudes terminate upon written release, merger of title, abandonment, estoppel, condemnation, or sale to a bona fide purchaser.

4. Changed Circumstances

If a restriction on a property no longer makes sense to enforce because of drastic changes in the surrounding area since the restriction was first contemplated, the restriction will not be enforced. A good indication that the neighborhood has changed is a variance in zoning ordinances.

> **Example:** A small subdivision restricts lots to residential use. Forty years later, the subdivision is next to a major thoroughfare and the land in the surrounding area is largely commercial and industrial. The restriction for residential use will likely be unenforceable on the theory that its value was lost with the drastic change of the neighborhood.

C. WATER RIGHTS

1. Theories

a. Riparian rights

The riparian doctrine states that water belongs to those who own the land bordering the water course (known as riparians). Riparians share the right of reasonable use of the water. One riparian is liable to another for unreasonable interference with the other's use. Domestic use trumps commercial use and can be unlimited.

b. Prior appropriation

Most western states have adopted the doctrine of prior appropriation, which states that the water belongs initially to the state, but the right to divert and use it can be acquired by an individual, regardless of location. Rights are determined by priority of beneficial use. The norm for allocation is first in time, first in right. Any productive or beneficial use of the water, including use for agriculture, is sufficient to create appropriation rights.

2. Waterways

Rights in navigable waters are limited by the government's right to protect the use of the waterway for transportation. Rights to non-navigable waters vary in their treatment depending on the theory in which the jurisdiction subscribes. Most jurisdictions, including those that have adopted the doctrine of reasonable use, treat non-navigable water rights (including all underground water) in the same manner as surface water rights. Some jurisdictions that have adopted an appropriation system have also applied it to non-navigable waters, including underground ponds and lakes. At least one jurisdiction has adopted a correlative rights standard, which gives a landowner a proprietary right to the portion of water that correlates to his proportion of land over the underground waterway.

3. Groundwater

The majority view allows the surface owner to make "reasonable use" of the groundwater. Contrast this with the doctrine of absolute ownership followed by some eastern states, which allows the surface owner total and complete discretion over water extraction and use. The western states, on the other hand, tend to follow the prior appropriation doctrine.

4. Surface Water

In about half of the states, the landowner may make changes or improvements to his land to combat the flow of surface water ("common enemy doctrine"). Some jurisdictions limit this right to prohibit unnecessary harm to another's land. On the other hand, about half of the states prevent the landowner from altering the rate or natural flow of water ("natural flow theory"). However, most of those states have mitigated the rule to permit **reasonable** changes in water flow. This is a growing trend and requires balancing the harm against the utility.

5. Support Rights

A landowner has the right to have the land supported in its natural state.

a. Lateral support

A landowner must not alter the land by excavation so as to cause the lateral support it provides to adjoining land to be weakened or removed. When the adjoining land is in its natural state (i.e., undeveloped), a landowner who excavates on his own land is strictly liable for any damage caused to adjoining land by the excavation.

When the adjoining land has been improved, such as by a building, the landowner is strictly liable for any damage caused by to the adjoining land and its improvements by the excavation if that land would have collapsed in its natural state. When the weight of an improvement at least contributes to the collapse of the adjoining land, the landowner is not strictly liable for damage caused to the adjoining land and its improvements. Instead, the landowner's negligence with regard to the excavation must be established in order for the adjoining landowner to recover damages.

b. Subjacent support

The right to subjacent support (i.e., support from beneath the surface of the land) arises when the owner of land grants the right to mine on his land to a third party. The owner of the mineral rights is strictly liable for any failure to support the land and any buildings on the land at the time the rights were conveyed. The owner is liable only for negligence for damage to any improvements built after the conveyance of the rights.

D. GOVERNMENT REGULATION OF LAND

The following concepts should be read in conjunction with the detailed discussion of the Fifth and Fourteenth Amendments in the Themis Constitutional Law outline.

1. Zoning

State and local governments may regulate the use of land through zoning laws, subject to the limitations of the Fifth and Fourteenth Amendments of the Constitution.

Zoning laws may be used to segregate incompatible uses from developing in the same area. They are enacted for the protection and safety of the communities' citizens. Single-family residences are normally considered the highest and best use in zoning ordinances. Commercial and industrial uses are lower uses and generally incompatible with residential neighborhoods. Unusual uses, like funeral homes, require special-use permits, even if the district authorizes that type of use.

a. Exemptions and variances

In certain situations, an owner may be exempt from a zoning ordinance. If an owner can demonstrate that a particular zoning ordinance exacts a unique hardship on him, then he may request a variance as long as the variance is not contrary to the public welfare.

b. Relationship to covenants

A zoning restriction establishes a "ceiling" beyond which a private covenant cannot go, but it does not set a "floor" below which a private covenant cannot go.

> **Example**: A zoning ordinance requires that a residence be set back at least 50 feet from the edge of the property. A covenant that requires a setback of 100 feet is enforceable. A covenant that requires a setback of 25 feet does not override the zoning restriction and cannot justify the location of a residence that is set back only 35 feet.

> **EXAM NOTE:** Fact patterns about zoning ordinances that contain standard restrictions are typically not far enough outside the norm to be constitutional violations.

2. Eminent Domain

A taking occurs when the government takes title to land, physically invades land, or severely restricts the use of land. Courts look to whether an essential nexus exists between the legitimate state interest stated as the justification for the taking/restriction and any conditions imposed on the property owner.

Valid exercises of police power include regulations that have the purpose of protecting the public from harm, or ensuring a public benefit.

A landowner can recover damages equal to the reduction in value to his property resulting from a partial taking.

Themis
Bar Review

LSE Key Concepts: PROPERTY
To be used with online lecture

PROPERTY IN CONTEXT: BIG PICTURE
Property law = rights among people relating to things
- *Rights* (e.g., to use, exclude, alienate, possess, destroy)
- *Among people* (relational and limited by rights of others)
- *Things* (real and personal, tangible and intangible, etc.)

FIRST POSSESSION
Issue: How to establish ownership over something unowned
General rule: First in time, first in right
- Possession ≠ Ownership
❖ Johnson v. M'Intosh *(Doctrine of discovery; held that indigenous tribes in America only had rights of occupancy to land, and could not sell valid titles to the land)*
- "Possession" can be situational and relative
❖ Pierson v. Post *(Fox case; ownership can be established by capture)*

SUBSEQUENT POSSESSION
Coming into possession of something that is already owned by someone else
Abandoned property: True owner has relinquished all rights to it   = Finder becomes new owner
Lost property: True owner unintentionally parted with it
= Finder acquires best title against all except (i) the true owner or (ii) prior possessor
Mislaid property: True owner intentionally put it somewhere and accidentally left it there = Finder acquires no rights

ADVERSE POSSESSION (AP)
A doctrine that can allow a **wrongful possessor's** use of property to blossom into **rightful** ownership
- If owner does not eject the possessor before the SOL runs, adverse possessor receives title that relates back to the beginning of the AP
- Possession must be: (i) actual, (ii) open and notorious, (iii) hostile, and (iv) continuous for the statutory period (consistent with nature of property).
❖ Marengo Cave v. Ross *(Court ruled that underground use of a cave was not sufficiently visible to satisfy*

adverse possession's "open and notorious" requirement)

ADVERSE POSSESSION – SPECIAL ISSUES
- **Color of Title:** AP based on a faulty writing (e.g., bad deed or fraudulent contract)
  o Some states require color of title or shorten the SOL for color of title
  o **Constructive Adverse Possession** applies: Allows possessor to acquire whole property described in faulty writing, even if only actually possessed part of it

- **Tacking:** Allows a possessor to "tack on" a predecessor's time to satisfy continuity for the statutory period
  o Requires privity (i.e., voluntary transactional relationship) with predecessor
- **Tolling:** Situations where running of the SOL pauses; includes owner's disability (infancy, imprisonment, mental incapacity)

GIFTS
A voluntary transfer of property without payment or consideration
- Gifts of real property must satisfy Statute of Frauds
- Valid gifts = **irrevocable**.
Gifts inter vivos require the following (in any order!):
- Present **intent** to make an irrevocable gift;
- **Delivery** to donee (actual, constructive, or symbolic); and
- **Acceptance** (presumed if gift had value)
❖ Gruen v. Gruen *(Father wanted to gift painting to son and delivered a note instead of the painting; note was effective symbolic delivery)*
Wedding/Engagement Gifts: Courts are split between treating them as (i) conditional gifts that must be returned if marriage does not occur, or (ii) typical irrevocable gifts.

GIFTS CAUSA MORTIS
A gift made in anticipation of donor's death; considered a will substitute
- Same requirements as inter vivos gifts, PLUS:
  o Given motivated by and in contemplation of imminent death; and
  o Donor must actually die
- Courts split on whether gifts in contemplation of **suicide** are enforceable gifts causa mortis.

ESTATES IN LAND

Estates are interests in things; property law determines who holds these interests.
- **Time**: Estates in land are measured by how long they last
- Possession may be simultaneous or consecutive
- May be a present estate or future interest

A **vested** interest gives the holder an immediate right to title.

THE FEE SIMPLE ABSOLUTE & LIFE ESTATE

- **Fee Simple Absolute**: Unlimited estate including all rights; can be devised or alienated; can last indefinitely
- **Life Estate**: Lasts for duration of measuring lifetime; leaves a future interest; can be measured by holder's life or the life of another (i.e., pur autre vie)

THE FEE SIMPLE DETERMINABLE

A present fee interest that is capable of being indefinite, but may be cut short because it is limited by specific **durational language**
- **Magic words**: "So long as," "While," or "During which time"
- Followed by **Possibility of Reverter** held by grantor; vests automatically

THE FEE SUBJECT TO A CONDITION SUBSEQUENT

A present fee interest that is capable of being indefinite, but may be cut short because it is limited by specific **conditional language**
- **Magic words**: "But if," "On the condition that," or "Provided that"
- Followed by **Right of Entry** held by grantor; does not vest automatically
  - If future interest is held by third-party, present interest becomes fee simple subject to executory limitation.

THE FEE SIMPLE SUBJECT TO EXECUTORY LIMITATION

A present fee interest that is capable of being indefinite, but may be cut short **by a future interest held by a third party**
- Operates like Fee Simple Subject to Condition Subsequent, except (1) third-party holds the future interest, and (2) divests automatically
- **Executory Interests**: Future interest held by a third party and divesting a Fee Simple Subject to Executory Limitation

  - **Shifting**: Grantee divests another grantee
  - **Springing**: Grantee divests the grantor

REVERSIONS & REMAINDERS

- **Reversions**: Future interest held by the grantor; always vested; follows natural expiration of a lesser estate
- **Remainders**: Three types, but always held by a grantee after natural expiration of prior estate
  - **Vested**: Taker is ascertained and no conditions precedent apply
  - **Contingent**: Remainder in unascertained party or subject to condition precedent
  - **Vested Subject to Open**: Class gift where at least one member is vested

Present Estate	Future Interest
Fee Simple Determinable	Grantor: Possibility of Reverter
Fee Simple Subject to Condition Subsequent	Grantor: Right of Entry
Life Estate; Term Estate (e.g., leaseholds)	Grantor: Reversion 3rd Party: Remainder
Fee Simple Subject to Executory Limitation	3rd Party: Executory Interest

SPECIAL ISSUES IN ESTATES

Waste: When multiple parties have interests in the same property (concurrently or consecutively), one party's actions (or inactions) must not injure the other party's interests

❖ <u>McIntyre v. Scarbrough</u> *(Life-estate holder failed to maintain property; holder of vested remainder successfully moved to dissolve present estate to prevent further waste)*
- **Permissive**: Inaction leading to waste
- **Voluntary**: Affirmative action leading to waste
- **Ameliorative**: Improvements against the wishes of other interest holders

Cy Pres: Equitable power to fix a conveyance when it cannot be satisfied by its terms
- Often applies for gifts with charitable purpose
- Can be prevented with a clause in the conveyance

THE RULE AGAINST PERPETUITIES (RAP)

Purpose: Prevents an owner from tying up future interests for more than two generations (life +21 years) by striking future interests unless they will vest or fail within that time
- **Validating life**: Look for person who determines if future interests will vest or fail (i) in their lifetime,

(ii) at their death, or (iii) within 21 years of their death

Three steps:

- Does **RAP** apply? Only to **contingent future interests** (i.e., contingent remainders, vested remainder subject to open, and executory interests)
- Is there a **validating life**? Determine the **last** moment in time the interest could possibly vest or fail, and ask if that moment could be after everyone **alive at the time of conveyance** (i.e., lives in being) has been dead 21 years.
- **Assess.** If interest could vest or fail 21 years after all lives in being are dead, there is no validating life; strike that interest.

PESKY RAP PROBLEMS

- **RAP Assumptions:** Everyone can have kids (regardless of age and/or fertility); and everyone dies.
- **Unborn Widow:** Contingent future interests after gifts to unnamed "widows" fail for lack of a validating life in being
  - O to A for life, **then to A's widow (W)**, then to A's issue then living (Won't know who W is until A dies; W might not be alive at conveyance; if W outlives A by 21 years, A's living issue's interest will neither vest nor fail within 21 years of A's death; future interest for A's issue FAILS RAP for lack of validating life)
- **Fertile Octogenarian:** Try testing RAP problems by assuming everyone reproduces then dies
  - O to A for life, then to A's first child who reaches 25 (Because we assume A can reproduce until their death, it is possible for A to have a living child who has not died or reached 25 within 21 years of A's death)
- **Magic Gravel Pit:** Ill-defined deadlines (e.g., events that could take a year or 100 years) can extend indefinitely
  - O to A for life, but when O's gravel pit is fully exhausted, to B (Assume gravel pit is bottomless; strike B's interest)

RAP TRENDS

Savings clauses: may prevent RAP violations (e.g., "Any interest deemed to violate RAP shall terminate 21 years after the last life in being has died.")

"Wait and See" approach (Modern trend): Let events play out and only strike interests that do not vest/fail within the period (90 years for USRAP)

- Applies to Options and Rights of First Refusal
- ❖ Symphony Space v. Pergola Properties *(RAP applies to all option agreements, including rights of first refusal)*

TENANCY IN COMMON (CONCURRENT OWNERSHIP)

Concurrent ownership interests = **simultaneous**; law assumes concurrent owners occupy the **same space** at the **same time**.

- **Tenancy in Common** (Default): **Separate** but **undivided** interests; no right of survivorship; shares need not be equal
- **Partition:** Equitable action to transform concurrent ownership interests into separate ownership interests
  - In Kind (default): Physically divide the land
  - In Sale: Land is sold and profits distributed

JOINT TENANCY (CONCURRENT OWNERSHIP)

Concurrent estate where joint tenancy have equal and undivided interests with rights of survivorship

Right of Survivorship: Upon death, a joint tenancy automatically goes to the surviving joint tenants; tenancy cannot be devised

Creation language: "As joint tenants with a right of survivorship" (although some courts require less)

Four Unities for Joint Tenancies **(TTIP)**

1. Time: Must be created at same time
2. Title: Must be created by same instrument
3. Interest: Must be same interest (estate, amount)
4. Possession: Tenants must have right to possess the whole

Losing a unity severs joint tenancy as to that interest (becomes tenancy in common)

SPECIAL TOPICS IN CONCURRENT OWNERSHIP

Tenancy by the Entirety (minority rule):

- Special joint tenancy for spouses; requires TTIP unities plus marriage; right of survivorship applies
- Encumbrances: Not subject to debts and liens of one spouse

Other Issues in Concurrent Ownership

- **Possession:** Generally, each concurrent owner has right to possess the whole
- **Ouster:** Tenant in possession denies possession to another co-tenant
- **Rent** received and **necessary operating expenses** are divided according to ownership interests.
- No right to reimbursement for **improvements or necessary repairs**; only credit upon partition
- Co-tenants generally not fiduciaries

TENANCIES (LANDLORD/TENANT)

Landlord/Tenant law is governed by contract law (re: lease agreement) and property law (re: estates and future interests).

- **Term of Years:** Lease for fixed amount of time; terminated automatically at end of term
- **Periodic tenancy:** Continues for successive periods until a party terminates (usually not in middle of a period)
- **Tenancy at Will:** Lease based on affirmative agreement that can be terminated by either party at any time
- **Tenancy of Sufferance:** Leasehold in name only, resulting when tenant "holds over" after a lease ends; landlord must decide to (1) re-rent to tenant, or (2) evict

TRANSFERS (LANDLORD/TENANT)

Assignment: Tenant transfers her entire interest
Sublease: Tenant transfers less than entire interest
❖ Ernest v. Conditt *(Parties called their agreement a "sublease," but court held that it was an "assignment" because it transferred the entire leasehold interest)*
Assignment: Landlord can collect rent from tenant (privity of contract) or transferee (privity of estate)
Sublease: Landlord can only collect rent from tenant
- If lease silent, can transfer without permission; if lease requires permission, landlord can only refuse for commercially reasonable reason (under majority rule; minority allows refusal in landlord's discretion)

CONDITIONS OF LEASEHOLD (LANDLORD/TENANT)

Covenant of Quiet Enjoyment: Every lease includes a covenant that landlord will not disrupt tenant's possession; may take form of actual or constructive eviction
- o Actual: Wrongful eviction
- o Constructive: Conditions are so bad that they are akin to eviction
- o Breached if conditions substantially interfere with tenant's ability to make proper use of the premises

Constructive Eviction as Remedy: Upon breach, tenant can: (1) give notice, (2) give landlord reasonable opportunity to fix it, (3) stop paying rent, and (4) vacate the leasehold
Warranty of Habitability: (Residential only) Landlord must provide healthy and safe living conditions; similar to constructive eviction, but need not leave to recover

LAND TRANSACTIONS

Two stages to land transactions:
1. *Contract Stage*: Parties negotiate terms; liability based on contract
2. *Deed Stage*: Seller transfers property; liability based on deed
Statute of Frauds: Essential terms of transfer must be in a writing signed by the party against whom the agreement will be enforced, **unless an exception applies**:
Part Performance is evidence that the contract existed (e.g., payment of all/part of purchase price, buyer taking possession, or improvements by buyer)
Detrimental Reliance: Party reasonably relied on contract and will suffer hardship if not enforced

SELLER'S DUTIES AT CONTRACT STAGE

Implied covenant of marketable title (title free from unreasonable risk of litigation) included in all land sale contracts
- **Standard:** According to a reasonable buyer
- **Remedy:** Buyer rescinds contract
Seller of a residence has duty to disclose all material defects (substantially affect the value of the home, health and safety of occupant, or desirability)
❖ Reed v. King *(Failure to disclose that a murder had occurred in the residence breached the duty to disclose)*
❖ Johnson v. Davis *(Seller misrepresented water damage as wallpaper glue, breaching duty to disclose)*
The three basic types of remedies to "contract-stage" breaches:
- Damages
- Rescission
- Specific Performance

DEEDS

Legal instrument used to transfer property
- Deed must contain (i) identity of parties, (ii) reasonable description of property, (iii) granting clause showing intent to make a transfer, and (iv) signature of grantor
Three types of deeds:
- **Quitclaim:** Seller makes no warranties about title
- **Special Warranty:** Seller warrants that seller has not caused defects to title
- **General Warranty:** Seller warranties against all defects

LAND TRANSACTIONS IV

Present Covenants (regarding condition of land/title at time of conveyance)
- *Seisin*: Deed describes land in question
- *Right to Convey*: Seller has power to transfer the land

- *Against Encumbrances*: No undisclosed strains on title

Future Covenants (regarding future conditions or conduct)
- *Quiet Enjoyment*: Buyer's possession will not be disturbed
- *Warranty*: Seller will defend buyer against future claims of a third party
- *Further Assurances*: Grantor will fix future problems that arise

Deed must be (i) delivered, and (ii) accepted.
- *Delivery*: Requires grantor's intent to convey the land; does not require physical delivery; cannot be speculative; can be made to agent
- *Acceptance*: Presumed if transfer has value

COMMON LAW RECORDING

Recording (puts others on notice of an ownership claim to property)
- Can help assure title, but is not required by law
- Can record deeds, property interests, judgments, etc.
- Recording does not affect validity of a deed, only its enforceability against **subsequent purchasers**
- **Common Law:** First in time, first in right
- **Recording Statutes:** Protect certain subsequent purchasers from losing their interests under the common-law rule
  - When no party can claim the protection of the recording statute, common law still controls

RACE STATUTES

First to record wins; look for language like "first recorded" or "first to record"
- *"No conveyance or mortgage of real property shall be good against subsequent purchasers for value unless the same be **first recorded** according to law."*

NOTICE STATUTES

Subsequent purchaser wins if she takes **without notice** of a prior unrecorded conveyance; look for language like "in good faith" or "without notice"
- *"No conveyance or mortgage of real property shall be good against subsequent purchasers for value and **without notice** unless the same be recorded according to law."*

Three types of notice:
- **Actual:** Real, personal knowledge of prior transfer
- **Constructive:** Prior interest is property recorded (i.e. record notice)
- **Inquiry:** Should have been on notice had they look at the land or documentation (e.g., someone occupying the land or deed mentions another interest)

RACE NOTICE STATUTES

Subsequent purchaser wins if she takes **without notice** of a prior unrecorded conveyance, **and records first**; combines requirements of other statutes
- *"No conveyance or mortgage of real property shall be good against subsequent purchasers for value and **without notice** unless the same be **first** recorded according to law."*

EASEMENTS

Non-possessory right to use land
- Affirmative (right to do something on another's land)
- Negative (right to prevent someone else from doing something on their own land)
- *Dominant Estate*: Land benefited by easement
- *Servient Estate*: Land burdened by easement
- Two classifications of easements:
  - Appurtenant: Easement benefits holder in use of a particular piece of property
  - In Gross: Easement benefits the holder personally, regardless of where they live

Express Easement: Created by express grant; must satisfy SOF because it creates an interest in land
Easement by Estoppel: License (i.e., use permission) that become irrevocable because of detrimental reliance
❖ Holbrook v. Taylor *(Detrimental reliance on license to use a road made it irrevocable and created an easement by estoppel)*
Easement by Prescription: Effectively created by adverse possession for statutory period; does not require exclusive use like averse possession
Easement by Necessity: Arise after a larger parcel is subdivided to grant a landlocked parcel necessary access to public roads
- **Implied Easement (Prior Use):** Landowner uses one side of property to benefit another, severs and sells the burdened portion, and continues the prior use

SCOPE OF EASEMENTS

❖ Henley v. Continental Cablevision *(Landowner gives easement to a utility company, who gives a license to a cable company; license for additional cables was permitted because they did not increase burden on servient estate)*
❖ Davis v. Bruk *(Burdened landowner not permitted to unilaterally move a right-of-way easement)*
Termination of Easements
- **Release**: Holder executes a formal written release

- **Expiration**: Terminates naturally under the terms of the easement (e.g., end of stated term)
- **Merger**: Ends if the dominant and servient estates come under the same owner
- **Abandonment**: Holder affirmatively relinquishes the easement, and servient owner relies on it
- **Prescription**: Terminated by adverse possession

REAL COVENANTS
Real Covenant (Promise re: use of land that is enforced against successors in interest at law by an award of damages)
- Promise needs to be in **writing** (i.e. satisfy SOF)
- Original parties must **intend** for the promise to bind successors in interest (i.e., to run with land)
- Promise must **touch and concern** the land
- Successors must have **notice**
- Real covenants require **privity** (i.e. transactional agreement)
  - o **Horizontal**: Between the original parties making the promise (only required for burden to run with land)
  - o **Vertical**: Between the previous holder and the successor in interest (required for benefits and burdens)

EQUITABLE SERVITUDES
Equitable Servitude (Promise re: use of land that is enforced against successors in interest at equity by injunctions)
- **Requirements**: (i) Writing; (ii) Intent to run with the land; (iii) Touch and concern the land; and (iv) Notice

Reciprocal Negative Easement (Negative covenant implied when a seller intends to create a servitude on all plots in accordance with a common scheme; party against whom enforcement is sought must have notice)
❖ Sanborn v. McLean *(Landowner sells multiple residential lots as part of a planned subdivision; lots sold later as part of the same planned subdivision are also residential, even if sold without reference to the restriction)*

ZONING AND TAKINGS
Zoning (Local govt. power to regulate property use in its jurisdiction to segregate incompatible land uses)
- Power comes from state police powers and municipality enabling statutes
❖ *Village of Euclid v. Amber Reality (Upheld practice of zoning)*

- **Variance:** Administrative approval of a new use in violation of current zoning rules
- **Nonconforming Uses:** Use that was proper before a change to zoning rules; owner may seek approval to continue as long as they can show a **vested right**
  - o **Vested Right:** Owner must have proper building permit and have made substantial progress toward achieving the nonconforming use when the zoning law goes into effect

Takings (5th Amendment; private property cannot be taken for public use without just compensation)
- **Eminent Domain:** Government (1) takes private property for its own public use or to give to another for public use, or (2) physically occupies private property
❖ Kelo v. New London *(City took private property for economic development; interpreted as public use)*
❖ US v. Causby *(Military flights regularly flying low over landowner's property was a taking)*
- **Regulatory Taking:** Private property is regulated to the point that its value decreases
❖ Lucas v. South Carolina Coastal Council *(Zoning ordinance prohibiting any development on owner's beachfront property was a regulatory taking)*

Themis
Bar Review

Torts

Themis
BarReview

TORTS

Table of Contents

TORTS

I. INTENTIONAL TORTS INVOLVING PERSONAL INJURY

A. GENERALLY

A prima facie case for any intentional tort, including those not involving personal injury, must include proof of an **act**, **intent**, **and causation**.

1. Act

The act must be voluntary, meaning that the defendant must have the state of mind that directed the physical muscular movement. Failure to act when there is a duty to do so also fulfills this element.

2. Intent

The defendant acts **intentionally** if:

i) He acts with the **purpose** of causing the consequences of his act; or

ii) He acts knowing that the consequence is **substantially certain** to result.

Restatement (Third) of Torts: Liability for Physical and Emotional Harm § 1 (2010). (Hereinafter, "Rest. 3d § xx.")

Note: Intent is satisfied even if the actor does not intend to cause harm to the victim.

a. Children and the mentally incompetent

A majority of courts hold that both **children** and those who are **mentally incompetent** can be held **liable for intentional torts** if they either act with a purpose or know the consequences of their acts with a substantial certainty.

b. Transferred intent

Transferred intent exists when a person intends to commit an intentional tort against one person, but instead commits:

i) A **different intentional tort** against that person;

ii) The intended tort **against a different person**; or

iii) A different intentional tort against a different person.

Example 1: If the defendant throws a hardball in the direction of the plaintiff, intending only to scare her (assault), but the ball strikes the plaintiff, the defendant is liable to the plaintiff for the battery. **The intent to commit one intentional tort** (the assault) **suffices to satisfy the intent requirement for another intentional tort**, the battery. Conversely, if the defendant intends to strike the victim and cause contact but instead misses and scares the plaintiff, the intent to cause the battery suffices for the intent required for the assault.

Example 2: If the defendant throws a punch intending to strike the man standing next to him, but he misses and instead strikes a third party, then the intent to commit a battery on the man suffices to complete the intent requirement for the battery to the third party under the doctrine of **transferred intent.**

Example 3: If the defendant throws a punch intending to strike the man standing next to him, and he misses both that man and a third party who is standing nearby, but he causes that third party to experience apprehension of an imminent harmful or offensive bodily contact, then the intent to commit a battery on the man "transfers" and suffices to complete the tort of assault against the third party.

Transferred intent applies only when the intended tort and the resulting tort are among the following: **battery, assault, false imprisonment, trespass to land, and trespass to chattels.** Note, in particular, that transferred intent **does not apply** to the torts of intentional infliction of emotional distress or conversion.

3. Causation

Causation exists when the resulting harm was legally caused by the defendant's act. Causation is also established when the defendant's conduct is a substantial factor in creating the harm.

B. BATTERY

1. Elements

A defendant is liable to the plaintiff for **battery** when he:

i)   Causes a **harmful or offensive contact** with the person of another; and

ii)   Acts **with** the **intent** to cause such contact or the apprehension of such contact.

2. Lack of Consent

There is no battery if the plaintiff consented to the act, either expressly or by virtue of participating in a particular event or situation (such as being bumped on a crowded subway or playing in a football game). *See* § II.A. Consent, *infra*.

3. Harmful or Offensive Contact

Contact is harmful when it causes injury, physical impairment, pain, or illness.

Contact is **offensive when a person of ordinary sensibilities** (i.e., a reasonable person) would find the contact offensive (objective test).

Note that a **defendant may be liable if he is aware that the victim is hypersensitive but proceeds to act nonetheless**. In such a case, the fact that a reasonable person would not find the contact offensive is not a defense.

The plaintiff need not be aware of the contact when it occurs in order to recover.

Example: If an operating room attendant inappropriately touches the patient while she is under the effect of anesthesia, there may be a battery even though the patient was not aware of the touching.

4. Plaintiff's Person

Contact with anything **connected to** the plaintiff's person qualifies as contact with the plaintiff's person for the purposes of battery (e.g., a person's clothing, a pet held on a leash, or a bicycle ridden by the plaintiff).

5. Causation

The act must in fact result in contact of a harmful or offensive nature. A defendant who sets in motion a chain of events that causes contact with the plaintiff, whether the contact is direct or indirect, is liable (e.g., a tripwire set by the defendant that causes the plaintiff to fall).

6. Intent

To act intentionally, a defendant must act with either (i) the purpose of bringing about the consequences of that act or (ii) the knowledge that the consequences are substantially certain to occur.

In some cases, depending on the jurisdiction and the factual context, a defendant may be liable if he intends merely to bring about the contact. While the contact must be harmful or offensive, the defendant need not intend that result (single intent rule). In other cases, depending on the jurisdiction and the factual context, a defendant may be required not only to intend to bring about a contact, but also to intend that the contact be harmful or offensive (double intent rule).

The doctrine of transferred intent applies to battery.

7. Damages

a. No proof of actual harm is required

No proof of actual harm is required; the plaintiff may recover nominal damages even though no actual damage occurred (to vindicate her right to physical autonomy).

b. Punitive damages

Many states allow recovery of **punitive damages** if the defendant acted outrageously or with malice (i.e., a wrongful motive, or a conscious or deliberate disregard of a high probability of harm). *See* § IV.F.7. Punitive Damages, *infra*.

c. Defendant liable for unforeseen consequences

Under the **thin ("eggshell") skull rule**, the defendant is **not** required to foresee the extent of damages in order to be held liable for all damages. The defendant is liable for any damages that ensue, even if she did not intend them and even if they could not have been reasonably foreseen.

Example: If the defendant inappropriately pinches a stranger on a bus, he will be liable for battery. If it then turns out that the victim is a hemophiliac and bleeds to death, the defendant will be liable for all damages appropriately awarded for the wrongful death.

C. ASSAULT

An assault is the plaintiff's reasonable apprehension of an imminent harmful or offensive bodily contact caused by the defendant's action or threat with the intent to cause either the apprehension of such contact or the contact itself.

1. Bodily Contact

Bodily contact is not required for assault.

The prototypical assault occurs when the plaintiff sees the defendant throw a punch at him. Regardless of whether the punch connects (and therefore causes a battery), **the apprehension of the contact** is sufficient for assault.

2. Reasonable Apprehension

A plaintiff's apprehension must be **reasonable**. Unlike with battery, the plaintiff must be aware of or have knowledge of the defendant's act.

The defendant's apparent ability to cause harm (e.g., a "real-looking" toy gun) can be sufficient to place the plaintiff in apprehension of harm.

Even if the victim is confident that he can prevent the threatened harm, there may still be an assault.

> **Example:** A 100-pound man tries to hit a 300-pound professional football player. Even though the football player is not afraid of the man, is confident that he can avoid being hit, and does, in fact, avoid being hit, there is still an assault. If however, the man aims a gun at the football player, but the football player knows that the gun is not loaded, there is no assault because the football player knows that the threat is incapable of being performed at that time.

3. Imminence

The threatened bodily harm or offensive contact must be **imminent,** i.e., without significant delay. Threats of future harm are insufficient, as are threats made by a defendant too far away to inflict any harm.

> **Example:** If the defendant calls and threatens the plaintiff from across the city, then the threat is not imminent and therefore there is no assault.

4. Mere Words

It is sometimes said that "**mere words alone do not constitute an assault**." However, words coupled with conduct or other circumstances may be sufficient. If the defendant is able to carry out the threat imminently and takes action designed to put the victim in a state of apprehension, then there may be an assault.

> **Example:** If the defendant sneaks up behind the plaintiff in a dark alley and utters in a menacing voice, "Your money or your life," then an assault may be complete.

5. Intent

The defendant must intend to cause the plaintiff's apprehension of an imminent harmful or offensive contact or intend to cause harmful or offensive bodily contact with the victim.

The defendant's own words, however, can negate the intent.

> **Example:** If the defendant says, "If you were not such a good friend, I would punch you," then there is no assault.

The doctrine of transferred intent applies to assault.

6. Damages

No proof of actual damages is required. The victim can recover **nominal damages** and, in appropriate cases, **punitive damages**. If the plaintiff sustains **damages from physical harm**, such as a heart attack resulting from the assault, then he may recover these as well.

D. INTENTIONAL INFLICTION OF EMOTIONAL DISTRESS

A defendant is liable for intentionally or recklessly acting with **extreme** or **outrageous conduct** that causes the plaintiff severe emotional distress.

1. Intent

The defendant must intend to cause severe emotional distress or must act with recklessness as to the risk of causing such distress. The traditional doctrine of transferred intent does not apply to intentional infliction of emotional distress when the defendant intended to commit a **different** intentional tort (such as a battery) against a different victim. Instead, this situation is governed by the rules for third-party victims. See Section 4, below. However, transferred intent **may** apply to intentional infliction of emotional distress if, instead of harming the intended person, the defendant's extreme conduct harms another.

2. **Extreme or Outrageous Conduct**

Conduct is extreme or outrageous if it **exceeds the possible limits of human decency**, so as to be entirely intolerable in a civilized society. Liability does not extend to mere insults, threats, or indignities. A defendant's conduct must be such that ordinary people would conclude that it is **"outrageous."**

> **Example:** As a practical joke, the defendant tells the plaintiff that his wife was killed in an accident.

Courts are more likely to find a defendant's abusive language and conduct to be extreme and outrageous if either:

   i) The defendant is in a position of **authority or influence** over the plaintiff, such as a police officer, employer, or school official, or traditionally an innkeeper or an employee of a common carrier; or

   ii) The plaintiff is a member of a group with a **known heightened sensitivity** (e.g., young children, pregnant women, or elderly persons).

3. **Acts Directed Toward Third Parties**

When the defendant's conduct is directed at a third-party victim, that defendant is liable if he intentionally or recklessly causes severe emotional distress to:

   i) A member of the victim's **immediate family** who is present at the time of the defendant's conduct (and the defendant is aware of such presence), whether or not such distress results in bodily injury; or

   ii) Any other bystander who is present at the time of the conduct (and the defendant is aware of such presence), if the distress **results in bodily injury**.

Restatement (Second) of Torts § 46 (1965). (Hereinafter, "Rest. 2d § xx.")

> **Example:** If the defendant draws a pistol and threatens to shoot a woman in her husband's presence, and the husband suffers severe emotional distress, he may recover.

> **EXAM NOTE:** This section applies to bystander recovery in general. It is not limited to situations in which a third-party victim experiences physical injury.

4. **Causation**

The plaintiff may establish causation by a showing that the defendant's actions were a **factual cause** of the plaintiff's distress.

Special rules of causation apply in cases in which a bystander makes a claim of severe emotional distress. When the defendant has caused severe **physical** harm to a third party and the plaintiff suffers severe emotional distress as a result, the plaintiff can recover if:

   i) The plaintiff was **present** when the defendant inflicted the harm;

   ii) The plaintiff was a **close relative** (i.e., a member of the same immediate family) of the injured person; and

   iii) The defendant **had knowledge** of both of the above facts.

The plaintiff does not need to prove the above facts if the defendant's **design or purpose** was to cause severe distress to the plaintiff.

5.   Damages

The plaintiff must prove severe emotional distress beyond what a reasonable person could endure.

In many cases, the very extreme and outrageous character of the defendant's conduct itself provides evidence that the plaintiff experienced severe mental distress. In other words, the more extreme the defendant's conduct, the less evidence is required of the severity of the plaintiff's emotional distress.

If the plaintiff is **hypersensitive,** however, and experiences severe emotional distress unreasonably, then there is no liability **unless the defendant knew** of the plaintiff's heightened sensitivity.

Most courts do not require the plaintiff to prove physical injury except in the case of bystander recovery when the plaintiff is not a member of the immediate family of the person to whom the defendant's extreme and outrageous conduct is personally directed (*see* § 3 Acts Directed Toward Third Parties, *above*).

E.   FALSE IMPRISONMENT

False imprisonment results when a person acts:

  i)   Intending to **confine or restrain** another within boundaries fixed by the actor;

  ii)   Those actions directly or indirectly **result in such confinement;** and

  iii) The other is **conscious of the confinement** or is **harmed by it**.

1.   Confined Within Boundaries

The plaintiff must be confined within a bounded area in which the plaintiff's freedom of movement in all directions is limited. The bounded area may be large and need not be stationary. An area is not bounded if there is a **reasonable** means of safe escape.

2.   Methods of Confinement

The defendant may confine or restrain the plaintiff by the use of physical barriers, physical force, direct or indirect threats (to the plaintiff, a third party, or the plaintiff's property), or by the invalid use of legal authority, duress, or the failure to provide a reasonable means of safe escape.

Shopkeeper's Privilege: A shopkeeper's reasonable (in both duration and manner) detention of a suspected shoplifter is **not** an invalid use of authority and hence is **not** a false imprisonment.

Furthermore, a court may find that the defendant has confined the plaintiff when she has refused to perform a duty to release the plaintiff from an existing confinement or provide a means of escape.

Example: If a child accidentally locks herself in a restroom in a restaurant, the restaurant may be liable if it intentionally fails to assist her in unlocking the door to obtain her release.

The defendant's use of moral pressure or future threats does not constitute confinement or restraint. The plaintiff is not imprisoned if she submitted willingly to confinement.

3. **Time**

   The length of time of the confinement or restraint is immaterial, except as to the determination of the extent of damages.

4. **Intent**

   The defendant must act with the purpose of confining the plaintiff or act knowing that the plaintiff's confinement is substantially certain to result.

   If the confinement is due to the defendant's negligence rather than his intentional acts, then the defendant may be liable under the rules governing negligence but not under the intentional tort of false imprisonment. If the imprisonment occurs by pure accident and involves neither the defendant's intent nor his negligence, then there is no recovery.

   The doctrine of transferred intent applies to false imprisonment.

5. **Knowledge of confinement**

   Most courts hold that the plaintiff must be aware of her confinement at the time it occurs. The Second Restatement provides that the plaintiff must either be aware of her confinement at the time it occurs or must suffer some actual harm from the confinement. Rest. 2d § 42.

6. **Damages**

   It is not necessary to prove actual damages (except when the plaintiff is unaware of the confinement). Punitive damages may be imposed in appropriate cases.

II. **DEFENSES TO INTENTIONAL TORTS INVOLVING PERSONAL INJURY**

A. **CONSENT**

1. **Express Consent**

   The plaintiff expressly consents if she, by words or actions, manifests the willingness to submit to the defendant's conduct. The defendant's conduct may not exceed the scope of the consent.

   a. **Mistake**

      Consent by mistake is valid consent unless the defendant **caused** the mistake or **knew** of it and **took advantage** of it.

   b. **Fraud**

      Consent induced by fraud is invalid if it goes to an **essential** matter. If the fraud that induced the consent goes only to a collateral matter, then the consent is still valid.

   c. **Duress**

      Consent given while under duress (physical force or threats of physical force) is not valid. The threat, however, must be of **present action,** not of future action. In general, threats of economic duress will not be enough to render a plaintiff's consent invalid.

2. **Implied Consent**

   The plaintiff's consent is implied when the plaintiff is silent (or otherwise nonresponsive) in a situation in which a reasonable person would object to the defendant's actions.

a. Emergency situation

When immediate action is required to save the life or health of a patient who is incapable of consenting to treatment, such consent is ordinarily unnecessary. Courts generally say that consent is "implied in fact," but it probably is more accurate to say that the treatment is privileged.

Even in an emergency situation, however, a competent and conscious patient's right to refuse treatment cannot be overridden.

b. Injuries arising from athletic contests

Consent may also be implied by custom or usage (e.g., participation in a contact sport). The majority of jurisdictions that have considered the issue of when a participant in an athletic contest can recover have concluded that the injured player can recover only for a reckless disregard of a player's safety, such as a violation of a safety rule designed primarily to protect participants from serious injury.

c. Mutual consent to combat

In the case of boxing or prizefighting, most courts hold that the plaintiff consents to intentional torts when he engages in the fighting, and he is therefore precluded from recovering for any injuries sustained.

In the case of street-fighting and other illegal activities, the courts are divided. A **majority** holds that consent to such acts is not a defense because one cannot consent to a criminal act. **The Second Restatement and a significant minority** of courts now hold to the contrary, however. Rest. 2d § 60.

3. Lack of Capacity

A plaintiff's lack of capacity due to youth, intoxication, or incompetence may negate the validity of her consent.

B. SELF-DEFENSE

1. Use of Reasonable Force

A person may use **reasonable force** to defend against an offensive contact or bodily harm that she **reasonably believes** is about to be intentionally inflicted upon her. The force used in self-defense must be reasonably proportionate to the anticipated harm. A person's mistaken belief that she is in danger, so long as it is a **reasonable mistake,** does not invalidate the defense.

2. Use of Deadly Force

The defendant may use deadly force only if she has a reasonable belief that force sufficient to cause serious bodily injury or death is about to be intentionally inflicted upon her.

3. No Obligation to Retreat

In a majority of states, by judicial decision or a "stand your ground" statute, a person is **not required to retreat** before using force, including deadly force, in defense. In a minority of states, a person has a duty to retreat before she may use deadly force in defense, if she can do so safely, but this duty does not apply if the defendant is in (or within the curtilage of) her own home. Restatement (Second) of Torts § 65.

4. **Initial Aggressor**

The initial aggressor is not entitled to claim self-defense **unless** the other party has responded to non-deadly force with deadly force.

5. **Third-Party Injuries**

The actor is **not liable** for injuries to **bystanders** that occur while he is acting in self-defense, so long as those injuries were accidental, rather than deliberate, and the actor was not negligent with respect to the bystander.

C. DEFENSE OF OTHERS

One is justified in using **reasonable force** in defense of others upon a reasonable belief that the **defended party would be entitled to use self-defense.** It is no longer required that the force be used to defend a member of the defendant's own family or someone otherwise under the defendant's legal protection. The defender may use force that is proportionate to the anticipated harm to the other party. He is not liable for acting on a mistaken belief that the third party is in danger as long as his belief is reasonable.

D. DEFENSE OF PROPERTY

1. **Reasonable Force Allowed**

A person may use reasonable force to defend her property if she reasonably believes it is necessary to prevent tortious harm to her property.

2. **Use of Deadly Force Not Allowed**

Deadly force **may not be used** merely in defense of property. A person may **never** use a deadly mechanical device (e.g., a spring-loaded gun) to defend her property.

3. **Reasonable Force to Prevent Intrusion Upon Real Property**

A possessor of land generally may use reasonable force to prevent or terminate another's intrusion upon her land. However, the possessor may not use force to prevent or terminate the visitor's intrusion on her land if the visitor is acting under necessity (*see* § III.C.6. Necessity as a Defense to Trespass, *infra*). In addition, a landowner is generally entitled to use reasonable force only after making a request that the trespasser desist and the trespasser ignores the request. Such a request is not required if the landowner reasonably believes that a request will be useless or that substantial harm will be done before it can be made. Restatement (Second) of Torts § 77.

The land possessor is not liable for using force if she makes a reasonable mistake with respect to an intrusion occurring on her land.

4. **Recapture of Chattels**

A person may use reasonable force to reclaim her personal property that another has wrongfully taken. If the original taking was lawful (e.g., a bailment) and the current possessor of the property has merely retained possession beyond the period of time to which the owner consented, then only peaceful means may be used to reclaim the chattel.

5. **Force to Regain Possession of Land**

At common law, an owner or possessor of land was permitted to use reasonable force to regain possession of that land from one who had wrongfully taken possession of it. However, modern statutes provide procedures for recovery of realty; therefore, the use of force is no longer allowed.

E. PARENTAL DISCIPLINE

A parent may use reasonable force or impose reasonable confinement as is necessary to discipline a child, taking into consideration the age of the child and the gravity of the behavior. An educator has the same privilege, unless the parent places restrictions on that privilege.

F. PRIVILEGE OF ARREST

1. Felony

a. Arrest by private citizen

A private citizen is privileged to use force (e.g., commit a battery or false imprisonment tort) to make an arrest in the case of a felony if the felony has in fact been committed and the arresting party has reasonable grounds to suspect that the person being arrested committed it.

It is a defense to make a reasonable mistake as to the **identity of the felon** but not as to the **commission of the felony.**

b. Arrest by police officer

A police officer must reasonably believe that a felony has been committed and that the person she arrests committed it. Unlike a private citizen, a police officer who makes a mistake as to the commission of a felony is not subject to tort liability.

2. Misdemeanor

In the case of a misdemeanor, a police officer may make an arrest if the misdemeanor is being committed or reasonably appears about to be committed **in the presence** of the officer. When the person effecting the arrest is a private citizen, the misdemeanor must also be a breach of the peace.

III. HARMS TO PERSONAL PROPERTY AND LAND

A. TRESPASS TO CHATTELS

1. Definition

A defendant is liable for trespass to chattels (i.e., tangible personal property) if she **intentionally interferes with the plaintiff's right of possession** by either:

i) **Dispossessing** the plaintiff of the chattel; or

ii) **Using or intermeddling with** the plaintiff's chattel.

2. Intent

Only the intent to do the interfering act is necessary; the defendant need not have intended to interfere with another's possession of tangible property.

The doctrine of transferred intent applies to trespass to chattels.

3. Appropriate Plaintiffs

An action for trespass to chattels may be brought by **anyone with possession or the immediate right to possession** of the chattel.

4. Mistake

Mistake of law or fact by the defendant about the legality of his actions is **not** a defense.

5.   Damages

In a case of **dispossession**, a plaintiff may recover for:

i)   The **actual damages caused** by the interference; **and**

ii) The **loss of use**.

In circumstances of **use or intermeddling**, the plaintiff may recover only when there are **actual damages**.

6.   Remedy

The plaintiff may be entitled to compensation for the **diminution in value** or the **cost of repair**.

B.   CONVERSION

1.   Definition

A defendant is liable for conversion if he **intentionally** commits an act **depriving the plaintiff of possession** of her chattel or **interfering** with the plaintiff's chattel in a manner **so serious as to deprive the plaintiff of the use of the chattel.** The plaintiff's damages are the chattel's full value at the time of the conversion.

Only personal property and intangibles that have been reduced to physical form (e.g., a promissory note) can be converted.

2.   Intent

The defendant must only intend to commit the act that interferes; intent to cause damage is not necessary. Mistake of law or fact is no defense (e.g., a purchaser of stolen goods is liable to the rightful owner). Transferred intent does not apply to conversion. The defendant must have intended to exercise control over the particular piece of property.

Accidentally damaging the plaintiff's chattel is not conversion if the defendant had permission to use the property.

3.   Interference

The defendant interferes with the plaintiff's chattel by exercising **dominion or control** over it. Examples of acts of conversion include wrongful acquisition, transfer, or detention; substantially changing; severely damaging or destroying; or misusing the chattel.

Note that if the original acquisition of the chattel was not wrongful, then the plaintiff must demand the return of the chattel **before** she sues for conversion.

4.   Distinguishing Conversion From Trespass to Chattels

There is no specific rule as to what behavior constitutes conversion, as opposed to trespass to chattels; it is a matter of degree of seriousness. The following factors are considered:

i)   The **duration and extent** of the interference;

ii) The defendant's **intent to assert a right inconsistent** with the rightful possessor;

iii) The defendant's **good faith**;

iv) The **expense or inconvenience** to the plaintiff; and

v) The **extent of the harm** to the chattel.

Generally, the greater the degree of these factors, the greater the likelihood that a conversion has occurred. Conversion is an exercise of dominion or control over the plaintiff's personal property such that the court is justified in requiring the defendant to pay the plaintiff the full value of the property.

> **Example:** If an embittered defendant steals his ex-girlfriend's car and drives it into a lake, that is conversion. If he merely hits the hood of her car once with a hammer, that is trespass to chattels.

5. Damages

The plaintiff may recover **damages in the amount of the full value of the converted property** at the time of the conversion. Alternatively, the plaintiff may bring an action for replevin to recover the chattel.

C. TRESPASS TO LAND

Trespass to land occurs when the defendant's **intentional** act causes a **physical invasion** of the land of another.

1. Intent

The defendant need only have the **intent to enter the land** (or to cause a physical invasion), not the intent to commit a wrongful trespass. In other words, the defendant **need not know that the land belongs to another.** Mistake of fact is not a defense.

> **Example:** An erroneous survey of the defendant's property leads the defendant to believe that an annoying cherry tree is on her property when in fact it is on her neighbor's property. She intentionally enters her neighbor's land and cuts down the tree. Even though she reasonably believed that the tree was on her property, she is liable for trespass to land.

The doctrine of transferred intent applies to trespass to land.

2. Physical Invasion

The defendant need not personally enter onto the plaintiff's land; intentionally flooding the plaintiff's land, throwing rocks onto it, or intentionally emitting particulates into the air over the land will each suffice.

Additionally, the defendant's failure to leave the plaintiff's property after his lawful right of entry has expired constitutes a physical invasion.

A trespass may be committed on, above, or below the surface of the plaintiff's land.

3. Appropriate Plaintiffs

Because it is the right to possession that is being protected, **anyone in actual or constructive possession of land may bring an action for trespass** (e.g., owner, lessee, or even an adverse possessor).

4. Distinguished From Nuisance

Trespass always requires an invasion or intrusion of land; nuisance may or may not involve intrusion.

An action for trespass protects the possessor's interests in the land; an action for nuisance protects the use and enjoyment of land. *See also* § III.D. Nuisance, *infra*.

If no physical object enters onto the plaintiff's land (e.g., the defendant's floodlights project onto the plaintiff's land or damage results from the defendant's blasting), then the case is generally treated as a nuisance or strict liability action (discussed in §§ III.D. Nuisance and V. Strict Liability, *infra*).

5. Damages

No proof of actual damages is required. The defendant is liable for all consequences of the trespass, though, even if she had no reason to foresee them.

6. Necessity as a Defense to Trespass

The privilege of necessity is available to a person who enters or remains on the land of another (or interferes with another's personal property) to prevent serious harm, which typically is substantially more serious than the invasion or interference itself. The privilege of necessity applies only to intentional torts to property, including trespass to land, trespass to chattels, and conversion.

a. Private necessity

Private necessity is a **qualified** privilege to protect an interest of the defendant or a limited number of other persons from serious harm. The privilege applies if the interference was **reasonably necessary** to prevent a serious injury from nature or another force not connected with the property owner. A defendant is not entitled to exercise this privilege on behalf of another if the defendant knows or has reason to know that the other person is unwilling for the defendant to take such action. Despite this privilege, the property owner is entitled to recover **actual damages**, but cannot recover nominal or punitive damages nor use force to eject the defendant. Restatement (Second) of Torts § 197.

> **Example:** During a severe storm, the owner of a boat secures the boat to a dock to prevent the destruction of the boat. The storm winds knock the boat against the dock, causing damage to the dock. The defendant is not liable as a trespasser to the plaintiff for nominal damages, but is liable to the dock owner for the actual damages to the dock.

b. Public necessity

Under the doctrine of public necessity, private property may be intruded upon or destroyed when necessary to protect a large number of people from public calamities, such as the spreading of a fire, the spreading of disease, or the advance of a hostile military force.

The privilege is absolute. As long as the defendant acts reasonably, he is not liable for any damage to the property. He is not liable even if the original entry was not necessary, as long as he **reasonably believed** that the necessity existed. The privilege lasts only as long as the emergency continues.

The privilege is available to private citizens or public officials, should the plaintiff seek to hold a public official personally liable.

c. Application to torts affecting damages to chattels

Necessity and public necessity also are privileges to the torts alleging damage to personal property, i.e., trespass to chattels and conversion. *See* §§ III.A-B, *supra*.

D. NUISANCE

1. Private Nuisance

a. Definition

A private nuisance is a thing or activity that **substantially and unreasonably interferes** with another individual's **use or enjoyment** of his land.

b. Nature of the defendant's conduct

The interference must be intentional, negligent, reckless, or the result of abnormally dangerous conduct to constitute nuisance.

c. Appropriate plaintiffs

Anyone with **possessory** rights in real property may bring a nuisance claim.

d. Substantial interference

A substantial interference is one that would be **offensive, inconvenient, or annoying to a normal, reasonable person in the community**. A person with special sensitivities can recover only if the average person would be offended, inconvenienced, or annoyed. Conversely, a "thick-skinned" plaintiff who is not offended, inconvenienced, or annoyed is nevertheless entitled to recover if an average reasonable person would be, although the amount of damages may be affected.

e. Unreasonable interference

The interference is unreasonable if the injury caused by the defendant **outweighs the usefulness** of his actions.

f. Distinguished from trespass

1) Physical invasion

Trespass requires a **physical invasion** of the plaintiff's property. Nuisance does not require physical invasion, but **physical invasion may constitute a nuisance.**

> **Example:** If the defendant's factory emits particulates that settle on the plaintiff's property, then the defendant may be liable for **both** trespass and private nuisance.

2) Substantial interference

Private nuisance requires **substantial interference** with the plaintiff's use and enjoyment of her property. Trespass, however, does not require a substantial intrusion.

> **Example:** A defendant's merely walking onto the plaintiff's land, if unprivileged and not consented to, is a trespass.

3) Duration

Generally, a nuisance is continuous. A trespass may be a one-time event, episodic, or continuous.

g. Access to light

Historically, courts have refused to find the obstruction of sunlight as creating a private nuisance.

h. Defenses to private nuisance

Apart from challenging the elements of nuisance, the defenses available to a defendant turn on whether the defendant's conduct is intentional, reckless, negligent, or abnormally dangerous. For example, the plaintiff's negligence or assumption of the risk may be a defense to a nuisance (or reduce recovery in a comparative-fault jurisdiction).

1) Regulatory compliance

The fact that a defendant complies with a statute, local ordinance, or administrative regulation is not a complete defense to a nuisance action. However, such statutory or regulatory compliance may be admitted as evidence as to whether the interference with the plaintiff's use and enjoyment of her land is unreasonable. For example, zoning regulations are typically regarded as admissible evidence in actions for nuisance, but they are not determinative.

2) Coming to the nuisance

It is generally **not a defense** that the plaintiff "came to the nuisance" by purchasing property in the vicinity of the defendant's premises with knowledge of the nuisance operated by the defendant. However, the fact that the plaintiff moved to the nuisance is not irrelevant; it may be considered by the jury in determining whether the plaintiff can recover for the nuisance.

In other words, the plaintiff's coming to the nuisance **does not entitle the defendant to judgment** as a matter of law, but it is **evidence that the jury may consider.**

Conversely, ownership of land prior to the defendant's entry into the neighborhood will not, by itself, make the defendant's action a nuisance. The test is whether the defendant's action is unreasonable.

2. Public Nuisance

a. Definition

A public nuisance is an unreasonable interference with a right common to the general public. (Note: Public nuisance does not necessarily involve land, but it is included in this part of the outline because of its common historical roots with private nuisance.) Typical examples of public nuisance include air pollution, pollution of navigable waterways, interference with the use of public highways, and interference with the public's use of parks or other public property.

A private citizen has a claim for public nuisance only if she suffers harm that is different in kind from that suffered by members of the general public.

Example 1: If the defendant pollutes a river, a plaintiff who fishes in the river cannot bring a claim for public nuisance. However, a plaintiff who operates a fishing camp on the banks of the river and suffers a substantial economic loss may do so.

Example 2: A dynamiting operation causes rocks to block a public highway. All members of the community are harmed by the nuisance. Consequently, a driver who suffers economic harm, such as a loss of business, due to the blockage, cannot recover.

> **Example 3:** Same facts as in Example 2, but in this case, a rock strikes the driver's car, cracking the windshield. The driver has suffered harm different from the general community and may bring an action in public nuisance.

In most instances, state statutes or local ordinances specifically declare something to be a public nuisance, such as running a house of ill repute or a disorderly tavern, gambling on Sundays, or growing certain types of thorny bushes.

Public authorities can either (i) seek injunctive relief to abate (prevent the continuation of) the public nuisance, or (ii) criminally prosecute the defendant.

b. Applying principles derived from the law of private nuisance

The law of public nuisance is extremely vague and varies greatly from one jurisdiction to another. However, the **modern trend** is to transpose much of the law governing private nuisance onto the law of public nuisance. For example, most courts hold that a defendant's conduct must be (i) intentional and unreasonable, (ii) negligent or reckless, or (iii) actionable under the principles governing abnormally dangerous activities. Furthermore, the defenses available to defendants in private nuisance actions typically apply in public nuisance actions.

3. Remedies for Nuisance

a. Damages

The usual remedy for nuisance is damages. All resulting harm is recoverable, including damages for reduction in the value of real property, personal injury, and harm to personal property.

1) Utility of the defendant's conduct

Even if the utility of the defendant's conduct outweighs the gravity of the harm, damages (but not injunctive relief) may be available if the harm is serious and the financial burden of compensating for the harm would not make the defendant's continuing conduct unfeasible. In other words, while it may be reasonable for the defendant to engage in the conduct, it is unreasonable for the defendant to do so without paying for the harm done.

2) Continuing nuisance

If the nuisance is a continuing one and the court deems it "permanent," then it will award the plaintiff all past and future damages, which prevents plaintiffs from returning to the court to collect damages in the future.

Occasionally, courts award **temporary damages** measured by the damages that have occurred prior to trial and within the statute of limitations. In these instances, plaintiffs may return to the court in the future to collect additional temporary damages if the nuisance continues.

b. Injunctive relief

If monetary damages are inadequate and the nuisance would otherwise continue, then courts may grant injunctive relief. In determining whether an injunction is appropriate, the courts will **"balance the equities,"** that is, weigh the social utility of the defendant's conduct against the harm caused to the plaintiff and others. However, the court need not consider the relative hardships if the defendant's sole purpose was to cause harm to the plaintiff or to violate the common standards of decency (sometimes called a "spite nuisance").

4. Abatement

a. Private nuisance

A person may enter another's land in order to abate a private nuisance after giving the defendant notice of the nuisance, after which the defendant refuses to act. The amount of force used may be only that which is reasonable to abate the nuisance; the plaintiff is liable for any additional damage.

b. Public nuisance

One who is entitled to recover for a public nuisance has the right to abate that nuisance by self-help, as one would with a private nuisance. However, in the absence of unique injury, a public nuisance may be abated only by a public authority.

IV. NEGLIGENCE

EXAM NOTE: Negligence is a very commonly tested subject on law school exams. In addition to memorizing the elements, be sure to know that the defendant must:

i) Fail to exercise the care that a reasonable person in his position would exercise; and

ii) Act in a way that breaches the duty to prevent the foreseeable risk of harm to anyone in the plaintiff's position, and the breach must be the cause of the plaintiff's injuries.

A. DEFINITION

Negligence is **conduct** (the commission of an act or the failure to act), without wrongful intent, that falls below the minimum degree of ordinary care imposed by law to protect others against unreasonable risk of harm.

1. Standard of Care

There are two (sometimes competing) approaches for defining the basic standard of care in negligence.

a. Traditional approach

Most courts define the standard of care as what a **reasonably prudent person** under the circumstances would or would not do.

b. Restatement (Third) approach

The modern trend is to define negligence **as the failure to exercise reasonable care under all the circumstances,** and then use an economic or cost-benefit analysis to determine whether reasonable care has been exercised. For example, the Third Restatement calls for courts, when determining whether a person has acted without reasonable care, to weigh the following factors:

i) The **foreseeable likelihood** that the person's conduct will result in **harm,**

ii) The **foreseeable severity of** any **harm** that may result, and

iii) The **burden of precautions to eliminate or reduce the risk of harm.**

Rest. 3d: Liability for Physical and Emotional Harm § 3.

2. Elements of Negligence

A prima facie case for negligence consists of four elements:

i) **Duty**, the obligation to protect another against unreasonable risk of injury;

ii) **Breach**, the failure to meet that obligation;

iii) **Causation**, a close causal connection between the action and the injury; and

iv) **Damages**, the loss suffered.

B. DUTY

In general, a duty of care is owed to all foreseeable persons who may be injured by the defendant's failure to follow a reasonable standard of care. An actor has a duty to exercise reasonable care when the actor's conduct creates a risk of physical harm. Rest. 3d: Liability for Physical or Emotional Harm § 7.

1.   Failure to Act

Generally, there is no duty to act affirmatively, even if the failure to act appears to be unreasonable. For more on this principle, and the exceptions to it, *see* § IV.B.5. Affirmative Duty to Act, *below*.

2.   Foreseeability of Harm

Most courts today hold that if the defendant is acting affirmatively, then **the foreseeability of harm to another resulting from the defendant's failure to use reasonable care is sufficient to create a general duty to act with reasonable care.** This is a change from 19th-century negligence law under which the plaintiff was required to show an independent or autonomous source of duty, such as a contract, a statute, or a regulation.

3.   Foreseeability of Harm to the Plaintiff

a. Cardozo (majority) view

The majority rule is that a duty of care is owed to the plaintiff only if she is a member of the class of persons who might be foreseeably harmed (sometimes called "foreseeable plaintiffs") as a result of the defendant's negligent conduct. According to Judge Cardozo's majority opinion in *Palsgraf v. Long Island R. R. Co.*, 162 N.E. 99 (N.Y. 1928), the defendant is liable only to plaintiffs who are **within the zone of foreseeable harm.**

b. Andrews (minority) view

The minority view, articulated in Judge Andrews's minority opinion in *Palsgraf*, states that if the defendant can foresee harm to **anyone** as a result of his negligence, a duty is owed to **everyone (foreseeable or not) harmed** as a result of his breach. However, the plaintiff still may not be able to recover, because a particular plaintiff's injury may not be closely enough connected to the defendant's negligence for the court to conclude that it was proximately caused by the defendant's negligence. In other words, the issue is one of duty for Judge Cardozo, but one of proximate cause for Judge Andrews. *See* § IV.E.3., *infra*. Rest. 3d: Liability for Physical and Emotional Harm § 29 cmt. n.

4.   Specific Classes of Foreseeable Plaintiffs

a. Rescuers

A person who comes to the aid of another is a foreseeable plaintiff. If the defendant negligently puts either the rescued party or the rescuer in danger, then he is liable for the rescuer's injuries. To the extent that a rescuer's efforts are unreasonable, comparative responsibility should be available to reduce, rather than to bar, recovery by a rescuer. Rest. 3d: Liability for Physical and Emotional Harm § 32.

An emergency professional, such as a police officer or firefighter, is barred from recovering damages from the party whose negligence caused the professional's injury if the injury resulted from a risk inherent in the job ("firefighter's rule").

b. Intended beneficiaries

A defendant is liable to a third-party beneficiary if the legal or business transaction that the beneficiary is a part of is prepared negligently by the defendant, and the defendant could foresee the harm of completing the transaction.

c. Fetuses

Fetuses are owed a duty of care if they are viable at the time that the injury occurred. *See* § IV.G.4. "Wrongful Life" and "Wrongful Birth" Claims, *infra*.

5. Affirmative Duty to Act

In general, there is no affirmative duty to act. However, there are some notable exceptions to that rule.

a. Assumption of duty

A person who voluntarily aids or rescues another is liable for injury caused by a failure to act with reasonable ordinary care in the performance of that aid or rescue.

Note that some states have enacted **"Good Samaritan" statutes** to protect doctors and other medical personnel when they voluntarily render emergency care. These statutes exempt medical professionals from liability for ordinary negligence; however, they do not exempt them from liability for gross negligence.

b. Placing another in peril

A person who places another in peril is under a duty to exercise reasonable care to prevent further harm by rendering care or aid.

c. By contract

There is a duty to perform contractual obligations with due care.

d. By authority

One with actual ability and authority to control another, such as parent over child and employer over employee, has an affirmative duty to exercise reasonable control. Generally, this duty is imposed upon the defendant when the defendant knows or should know that the third person is apt to commit the injuring act.

Example: A parent may be liable for failing to control the conduct of a child who uses a dangerous instrumentality to injure a plaintiff.

e. By relationship

A defendant with a unique relationship to a plaintiff, such as business proprietor-patron, common carrier-passenger, employer-employee, or parent-child, may have a duty to aid or assist the plaintiff and to prevent reasonably foreseeable injury to her from third parties.

C. THE STANDARD OF CARE

1. Reasonably Prudent Person

In most cases, the standard of care imposed is that of a **reasonably prudent person under the circumstances**. This standard is an **objective** one, measured by what a reasonably prudent person would do, rather than whether a particular defendant is acting in good faith or using her best efforts. A defendant is required to exercise the care that a reasonable person under the same circumstances (i.e., in her position, with her information and competence) would recognize as necessary to avoid or prevent an unreasonable risk of harm to another person. In determining whether particular precautions were warranted, a jury should weigh the probability and gravity of the injury against the burden of taking such precautions.

a. Mental and emotional characteristics

Under this standard, the defendant is presumed to have average mental abilities and the same knowledge as an average member of the community. The defendant's own mental or emotional disability is not considered in determining whether his conduct is negligent, unless the defendant is a child. In other words, **a mentally disabled person is held to the standard of someone of ordinary intelligence and knowledge**.

Most courts hold that if a defendant possesses special skills or knowledge, she is held to a higher standard, i.e., she must exercise her superior competence with reasonable attention and care.

b. Physical characteristics

The defendant's particular physical characteristics (e.g., blindness) are taken into account in determining the reasonableness of the defendant's behavior. The reasonableness of the conduct of a defendant with a physical disability will be determined based upon a reasonably careful person with the same disability. Rest. 3d: Liability for Physical and Emotional Harm § 11. For example, a blind pedestrian must act as any other reasonable blind person would act under the circumstances.

c. Intoxication

Intoxicated individuals are held to the same standards as sober individuals unless their intoxication was involuntary.

d. Children

The standard of care imposed upon a child is that of a **reasonable child of similar age, intelligence, and experience.** Unlike the objective standard applied to adult defendants in negligence actions, the standard applicable to minors is more subjective in nature because children are unable to appreciate the same risks as an adult.

However, a child engaged in an adult activity, such as driving a car, is held to the same standard as an adult. Courts regard children of a particularly young age as incapable of negligent conduct. Under the Third Restatement, children under the age of five are generally incapable of negligent conduct. Rest. 3d: Liability for Physical and Emotional Harm § 10.

2. Cost-Benefit Analysis

In many cases, courts describe the primary factors to consider in determining whether the defendant has acted negligently to be:

i)   The foreseeable likelihood that the defendant's conduct would cause harm;

ii) The foreseeable severity of any resulting harm; and

iii) The defendant's burdens (costs or other disadvantages) in avoiding the harm.

In fact, the Third Restatement defines negligence using these terms rather than the reasonable person standard.

3. **Custom**

   a. **Within a community or industry**

   Evidence of a custom in a community or industry is admissible as evidence to establish the proper standard of care, but such evidence is not conclusive. The entire community or industry may be negligent.

   b. **Safety codes**

   Safety codes promulgated by industries, associations, and governmental bodies for the guidance of operations within their respective fields of interest are admissible to prove custom.

   c. **Professionals**

   A professional person (e.g., doctor, lawyer, or electrician) is expected to exhibit the **same skill, knowledge, and care as an ordinary practitioner in the same community.** A specialist may be held to a higher standard than a general practitioner because of his superior knowledge.

   Establishing negligence by a professional person generally requires expert testimony to establish both the applicable standard of care and the defendant's deviation from that standard. However, when the defendant's negligence is so apparent that a layperson can identify it, expert testimony will not be required. *See, e.g., Palmer v. A.H. Robins Co.*, 684 P.2d 187 (Colo. 1984) (Because the standard of care was regarded as within the common knowledge of a layman when the surgeon amputated the wrong leg, no expert testimony was required to establish the standard of care.).

   d. **Physicians**

   1) **Local vs. national standard**

   Traditionally, physicians were held to the "same or similar locale" rule of custom: did the physician's actions comport with those customarily employed by doctors in the same locale or in similar localities? While some jurisdictions have retained the traditional rule, the majority of jurisdictions now apply a national standard to physicians, including physicians who are specialists.

   2) **Informed consent**

   Physicians are under a specific obligation to explain the risks of a medical procedure to a patient in advance of a patient's decision to consent to treatment. Failure to comply with this "informed consent" doctrine constitutes a breach of the physician's duty owed to the patient and is actionable as medical malpractice (medical negligence). Doctors are **not** under an obligation to disclose when the:

   i) Risk is a **commonly known** risk;

   ii) Patient is **unconscious**;

   iii) Patient **waives or refuses** the information;

   iv) Patient is **incompetent** (although the physician must make a reasonable attempt to secure informed consent from a guardian); or

v) Disclosure would be **too harmful** to the patient (e.g., would upset the patient enough to cause extreme illness, such as a heart attack).

A **majority** of jurisdictions hold that the required level of disclosure of risks is governed by custom among medical practitioners. However, a significant **minority** holds that the physician must disclose any "material risk," that is, any risk that might make a difference to a reasonable person in deciding whether to proceed with the surgery or other medical treatment.

4. Negligence *Per Se*

The standard of care can sometimes be determined by statute. In most jurisdictions, the violation of such a statute establishes negligence as a matter of law (a conclusive presumption as to duty and breach). A minority of jurisdictions hold that violation of the statute is merely evidence of negligence (a rebuttable presumption as to duty and breach).

a. Basic rule

i) A criminal or regulatory statute (or an administrative regulation or municipal ordinance) imposes a penalty for violation of a specific duty;

ii) The defendant violates the statute by failing to perform that duty;

iii) The plaintiff is in the class of people **intended to be protected** by the statute; and

iv) The harm is of the type the statute was **intended to protect against**.

Once negligence per se is established, in order for the defendant to be liable, the plaintiff must prove that his injuries were proximately caused by the defendant's violation of the statute.

b. Proof of a defendant's compliance is not dispositive

Generally speaking, compliance with a statute, regulation, or ordinance does not prove the absence of negligence. However, sometimes, if the defendant's conduct complies with certain types of federal regulatory statutes, such as those establishing comprehensive regulatory schemes, compliance with the federal requirements may preempt common-law tort actions.

c. Defenses

1) Compliance is impossible

Even in those jurisdictions in which negligence *per se* results in negligence as a matter of law, the defendant can avoid liability by proving either that compliance was **impossible** under the circumstances or that an **emergency** justified violation of the statute.

2) Violation was reasonable under the circumstances

The defendant's violation of a statute is excused and is not negligence if the violation is reasonable in light of the defendant's **physical disability** or incapacitation, if the defendant is a **child**, or if the defendant exercises **reasonable care** in attempting to comply with the statute. Rest. 3d: Liability for Physical and Emotional Harm § 15.

In addition, if the statute imposes an obligation only under certain factual circumstances that are not usually present, and the defendant is **not aware** that these circumstances are present and further proves that his ignorance was reasonable, then the defendant's violation of the statute is excused for the purposes of negligence *per se*.

Finally, if the requirements of the statute at issue were presented to the public in a **confusing** manner (e.g., extremely vague or ambiguous), then the defendant's violation is excused. Rest. 3d: Liability for Physical and Emotional Harm § 15.

d. Violation by a plaintiff

The violation of a statute, regulation, or ordinance by a plaintiff may constitute contributory negligence per se. The same requirements apply.

5. Standards of Care for Specific Classes of Defendants

a. Common carriers and innkeepers

Under the common law, a majority of jurisdictions held common carriers (e.g., operators of planes, trains, buses) and innkeepers to the highest duty of care consistent with the practical operation of the business. Under this approach, common carriers and innkeepers could be held liable for "slight negligence."

A majority of courts continue to hold **common carriers** to this higher standard. However, most courts today hold that an **innkeeper** (hotel operator) is liable only for **ordinary negligence**.

Note, however, that the Third Restatement approach is slightly different: common carriers and innkeepers must exercise reasonable care toward their passengers and guests. Although generally there is no affirmative duty to act, common carriers and innkeepers have a duty to act based on a special relationship. They must use reasonable care under the circumstances with regard to risks that arise out of the relationship with their passengers and guests. Rest. 3d: Liability for Physical and Emotional Harm § 40.

> **EXAM NOTE:** Be certain to apply the carriers and innkeepers standards only to passengers or guests.

b. Automobile drivers

In most jurisdictions, automobile drivers owe ordinary care to their guests as well as their passengers (those who confer an economic benefit for the ride). However, a minority of jurisdictions distinguish between the two with "guest statutes," which impose only a duty to refrain from gross or wanton and willful misconduct with a guest in the car. Proof of simple negligence by the driver will not result in recovery by the plaintiff-guest.

c. Bailors and bailees

A bailment occurs when a person (the bailee) temporarily takes possession of another's (the bailor's) personal property, such as when a driver leaves his car with a valet. The duty of care that must be exercised by a bailor or bailee varies depending on the type of bailment.

1) Bailor's duty

A gratuitous bailor (e.g., the owner of a power saw who lends it without charge to a friend) has a duty to inform the bailee only of **known** dangerous defects in personal property, but a compensated bailor (e.g., a commercial entity that leases a power saw to a customer) must inform a bailee of defects that are known or **should have been known** by the bailor had he used reasonable diligence.

2) Bailee's duty

When a bailor receives the sole benefit from the bailment, the bailee has a lesser duty to care for the property and is liable only if he has been grossly negligent. In contrast, when a bailee receives the sole benefit from the bailment, he must exercise extraordinary care for the bailor's property. Slight negligence on the bailee's part will result in liability for any injuries to the property from failure to properly care for or use it. In a bailment for mutual benefit, the bailee must take reasonable care of the bailed property.

d. Modern trend

The modern trend has been to get away from distinctions in the level of care and to regard the relationship between the parties as simply one of the circumstances in the light of which conduct is to be measured by the standard of reasonable care.

e. Emergency situations

The applicable standard of care in an emergency is that of a reasonable person in the same situation. In other words, less may be expected of the reasonably prudent person who is forced to act in an emergency, but only if the defendant's conduct did not cause the emergency.

6. Possessors of Land

The term "possessors of land" as used here includes owners, tenants, those in adverse possession, and others in possession of land. The fact that a plaintiff is injured while on someone else's land does not affect the liability of a defendant other than the land possessor. Only land possessors are protected by the rules limiting liability to trespassers or licensees. Everyone else—for example, easement holders (e.g., a utility company with power lines on the land) or those licensed to use the land (e.g., hunters)—must exercise reasonable care to protect the trespasser or the licensee.

In general, possessors of land owe a duty only to those within the boundaries of their land. The duty to entrants on the land includes:

i) **Conduct** by the land possessor that creates risks;

ii) **Artificial conditions** on the land;

iii) **Natural conditions** on the land; and

iv) Risks created when any of the **affirmative duties** discussed in § IV.B.5. Affirmative Duty to Act, *supra*, are applicable.

a. Two approaches

Approximately one-half of all jurisdictions continue to follow traditional rules that provide that the standard of care owed to land entrants depends upon whether the land entrant is an invitee, a licensee, or a trespasser.

Courts in the other half of jurisdictions (as well as the Third Restatement) require that a standard of reasonable care applies to all land entrants except trespassers, abolishing the distinction between invitees and licensees. (In the case of the Third Restatement, the rule applies to all land entrants except for "flagrant" trespassers (*see* b.2) Modern and Third Restatement approach, *below.*)

a) Known or obvious dangers

A land possessor must take reasonable precautions for known or obvious dangers when the possessor should anticipate the harm despite such knowledge or obviousness. However, when the danger is open and obvious to the entrant, a warning will ordinarily not provide additional protection against harm. Consequently, if the only purpose of a warning would be to provide notice of a danger that is open and obvious, there is no liability for failing to provide such a warning. In addition, even when a warning is required, an entrant who encounters an obviously dangerous condition and fails to exercise reasonable self-protective care is contributorily negligent.

b. Trespassers

A trespasser is someone who enters or remains upon the land of another **without consent or privilege** to do so.

1) Traditional approach

A landowner is obligated **to refrain from willful, wanton, reckless, or intentional misconduct** toward trespassers.

a) Spring-guns and other traps

The use of a "spring-gun" or other trap set to expose a trespasser to a force likely to inflict death or grievous bodily injury will lead to liability for the land possessor. The land possessor cannot do indirectly what he would be forbidden to do directly (e.g., shoot the trespasser).

b) Discovered trespassers

Land possessors owe a duty toward **discovered or anticipated trespassers** to warn or protect them from **concealed, dangerous, artificial conditions.** There is no duty to warn of natural conditions or artificial conditions that do not involve risk of death or serious bodily harm. Land possessors also have a duty to use reasonable care while conducting activities on their land, as well as to control the activities of third parties on their property.

When a land possessor **should reasonably know** that trespassers are consistently entering his land (e.g., frequent trespassers using a footpath to cut across the corner of the property), the possessor owes a duty to the **anticipated trespasser**, regardless of the land possessor's actual knowledge of the trespasser's presence.

c) Undiscovered trespassers

Land possessors generally owe no duty to undiscovered trespassers, nor do they have a duty to inspect their property for evidence of trespassers.

d) Attractive nuisance

Under the "attractive nuisance" doctrine, a land possessor may be liable for **injuries to children** trespassing on the land if:

  i) An artificial condition exists in a place where the land possessor knows or has reason to know that **children are likely to trespass;**

ii) The land possessor knows or has reason to know that the condition poses an **unreasonable risk** of death or serious bodily injury to children;

iii) The children, because of their youth, do not discover or **cannot appreciate the danger** presented by the condition;

iv) The utility to the land possessor of maintaining the condition and the burden of eliminating the danger are **slight compared to the risk of harm** presented to children; and

v) The land possessor fails to exercise **reasonable care** to protect children from the harm.

Restatement (Second) of Torts § 339 (1965).

2) Modern and Third Restatement approach

A few states now take the approach that land possessors owe trespassers, like all other land entrants, a reasonable standard of care under all the circumstances. Of course, the fact that the land entrant is trespassing, particularly if he is undiscovered, is one fact that the jury may consider in deciding whether the land possessor has exercised reasonable care.

The Third Restatement § 52 provides that although a duty of reasonable care is owed to trespassers, only the duty not to act in an intentional, willful, or wanton manner to cause physical harm is owed to **flagrant trespassers** who are not imperiled and unable to protect themselves. A burglar in a home would be a flagrant trespasser but someone injured while walking in a public park at midnight, despite the presence of a posted notice that the park was closed after dusk, would not be. This distinction has not been widely adopted by the courts.

c. Invitees: traditional approach

An invitee is either:

i) A **public invitee**—Someone invited to enter or remain on the land for the purposes for which the land is held open to the public; or

ii) A **business visitor**—Someone invited to enter or remain on the land for a purpose connected to business dealings with the land possessor.

A land possessor owes an invitee the duty of reasonable care, including the duty to use reasonable care to **inspect** the property, **discover** unreasonably dangerous conditions, and **protect** the invitee from them.

However, the duty of reasonable care owed to an invitee does not extend beyond the scope of the invitation, and the invitee is **treated as a trespasser** in areas beyond that scope.

1) Non-delegable duty

The land possessor's duty to invitees is a non-delegable duty. For example, even if a store owner hires an independent contractor to maintain the escalator in her store, she will remain liable if the contractor negligently fails to properly maintain the escalator. This same principle of non-delegable duty applies under the modern approach (discussed below) under which the land possessor owes most land visitors a duty of reasonable care.

2) Recreational land use

In some jurisdictions, a land possessor who opens his land to the public for recreational purposes is not liable for injuries sustained by recreational land users so long as he does not charge a fee for the use of his land, unless the landowner acts willfully and maliciously or, in some jurisdictions, with gross negligence.

d. Licensees: traditional approach

A licensee is someone who enters the land of another with the express or implied permission of the land possessor or with a privilege. Examples of licensees include:

i) **Social guests**—Note, they may be "invited," but they are still licensees, not invitees;

ii) Those whose presence is **tolerated** by the land possessor such as children who routinely cut across the land on their way home from school; and

iii) **Emergency personnel** such as police, firefighters, and emergency medical technicians.

The land possessor has a duty to either **correct or warn** a licensee of **concealed dangers** that are either **known** to the land possessor or which **should be obvious** to her. The land possessor **does not have a duty to inspect** for dangers. In addition, the land possessor must exercise **reasonable care** in conducting activities on the land.

e. Invitees and licensees: modern and Restatement approach

Approximately one-half of all jurisdictions and the Third Restatement now require the land possessor to exercise **reasonable care under all circumstances to all land entrants except trespassers** (or in the case of the Third Restatement, all land entrants except for "flagrant trespassers." *See* § IV.C.6.b. Trespassers, *supra*). The land possessor must use **reasonable care to prevent harm posed by artificial conditions** or conduct on the land.

If the land possessor is commercial, then he also must use reasonable care to prevent harm to the visitor posed by natural conditions. A non-commercial land possessor must use reasonable care to prevent harm posed by natural conditions only if the possessor is aware of the risk, or the risk is obvious.

f. Liability of landlords and tenants

Because the obligations associated with property are owed by the possessor of the land, a lessee (tenant) assumes any duty owed by the lessor (the landlord) once the lessee takes possession.

1) Landlord's liability

The landlord, though, remains liable for injuries to the tenant and others occurring:

i) In **common areas** such as parking lots, stairwells, lobbies, and hallways;

ii) As a result of **hidden dangers** about which the landlord **fails to warn** the tenant;

iii) On premises **leased for public use**;

iv) As a result of a hazard caused by the landlord's **negligent repair**; or

v) Involving a hazard that the landlord has **agreed to repair**.

2) Tenant's liability

As an occupier of land, the tenant continues to be liable for injuries to third parties arising from dangerous conditions within the tenant's control, regardless of whether the landlord has liability.

g. Off-premises victims

A landowner generally does not owe a duty to a person not on the premises (e.g., passerby, owner of adjacent land) who is harmed by a **natural condition** on the landowner's premises. An exception exists, however, with respect to trees in urban areas.

With respect to an **artificial condition,** the landowner generally owes a duty to prevent an unreasonable risk of harm to persons who are not on the premises. Similarly, with respect to an activity conducted on the premises by the owner or by someone subject to the owner's control, the landowner generally owes a duty of reasonable care to persons who are not on the premises.

h. Sellers of real property

Sellers of real property owe a **duty to disclose** to buyers those concealed and unreasonably dangerous conditions known to the seller. These are conditions that the buyer is unlikely to discover upon reasonable inspection. The seller's liability to third parties continues until the buyer has a reasonable opportunity, through maintenance and inspection, to discover and remedy the defect.

D. BREACH OR VIOLATION OF DUTY OF CARE

1. Burden of Proof

The plaintiff must establish all four elements of negligence (duty, breach, causation, damage) by a **preponderance of the evidence**. A breach of duty occurs when the defendant departs from the conduct expected of a reasonably prudent person acting under similar circumstances. The evidence must show a greater probability than not that (i) the defendant failed to meet the required standard of care, (ii) the failure was the proximate cause of the injury, and (iii) the plaintiff suffered damages. The plaintiff can demonstrate such failure by introducing evidence of the required standard of care through custom and usage, violation of a statute, or *res ipsa loquitur*.

2. *Res Ipsa Loquitur*

Under the doctrine of *res ipsa loquitur*, the trier of fact may infer the existence of the defendant's negligent conduct in the absence of direct evidence of such negligence. *Res ipsa loquitur* is **circumstantial evidence** of negligence that does not change the standard of care.

> **EXAM NOTE:** *Res ipsa loquitur* does not apply if there is direct evidence of the cause of the injury.

a. Traditional requirements

Under the traditional standard for *res ipsa loquitur,* still used in many jurisdictions, the plaintiff must prove that:

i) The accident was of a kind that **ordinarily does not occur** in the absence of negligence;

ii) It was caused by an agent or instrumentality within the **exclusive control** of the defendant; and

iii) It was not due to any action **on the part of the plaintiff**.

In establishing that the accident was of a kind that ordinarily does not occur in the absence of negligence, the plaintiff need not conclusively exclude all other possible explanations. It is enough that the facts proved reasonably permit the conclusion that negligence is the more probable explanation. Restatement (Second) of Torts § 328D.

b. Modern trends

Even under the traditional requirements, courts often generously interpret the "exclusive control" requirement.

> **Example:** The defendant hires an independent contractor to clean and maintain his store premises. The plaintiff is injured when she slips on a floor negligently left wet by an independent contractor. Courts will find that the duty to maintain the premises open to the public is a non-delegable duty, such that the defendant continued to be in "exclusive control." Therefore, *res ipsa loquitur* can be used to find that the defendant breached a duty of reasonable care.

1) Medical malpractice

In medical malpractice cases in which several physicians, nurses, and other medical personnel have access to the plaintiff during surgery, a small number of jurisdictions apply *res ipsa loquitur,* finding that each defendant has breached a duty of care unless he can exonerate himself. In the absence of such exonerating evidence, the courts hold all defendants jointly and severally liable. *See, e.g., Ybarra v. Spangard,* 25 Cal. 2d 486 (1944).

2) Product liability

In negligence cases involving products, even if the product passes through many hands—those of the manufacturer, the distributor, the retail store, and the consumer/user—if the manufacturer wrapped the package or it is clear that any negligence took place during the production process, **many courts ignore the exclusivity requirement**.

3) Comparative fault jurisdictions

Courts in the vast majority of jurisdictions that have adopted comparative fault also are inclined to loosely apply the third requirement—that the harm must not be due to any action on the part of the plaintiff (whether such action constitutes contributory negligence or not)—because such a requirement would otherwise be in tension with the law holding that the plaintiff's contributory negligence is no longer a total bar to recovery.

c. Third Restatement

In light of the fact that the majority of jurisdictions generously apply the traditional requirements for *res ipsa loquitur,* the Third Restatement of Torts has re-articulated the requirements of the doctrine in the following manner:

The fact finder may infer that the defendant has been negligent when:

i) The accident that caused the plaintiff's harm is a type of accident that ordinarily happens as a result of negligence of a class of actors; and

ii) The defendant is a relevant member of that class of actors.

Note that a group approach to res ipsa loquitur is generally supportable only if the parties in the group have an ongoing relationship pursuant to which they share responsibility for a dangerous activity. Restatement (Third) of Torts: Liability for Physical and Emotional Harm § 17.

However, because the Third Restatement was only recently adopted, few courts have adopted this precise articulation of the doctrine.

d. Procedural effect of *res ipsa loquitur*

If the plaintiff establishes a prima facie case of *res ipsa loquitur*, then the trial court should deny the defendant's motion for a directed verdict and the issue of negligence must be decided by the trier of fact. In most jurisdictions, *res ipsa loquitur* does not require that the trier of fact find negligence on the defendant's part. It simply establishes an **inference** of negligence sufficient to avoid dismissal of the plaintiff's action.

E. CAUSATION

The plaintiff must prove that the defendant's actions were both the actual cause (also known as the factual cause or "cause-in-fact") and the proximate cause (i.e., within the scope of liability) of the plaintiff's injury.

1. Cause In Fact

a. "But-for" test

If the plaintiff's injury would not have occurred **but for** the defendant's tortious act or omission, then the defendant's conduct is a factual cause of the harm. If the injury would have occurred despite the defendant's conduct, then there is no factual cause.

b. Multiple and/or indeterminate tortfeasors

The "but-for" test of causation often will not work if:

i) There are multiple tortfeasors and it cannot be said that the defendant's tortious conduct necessarily was required to produce the harm;

ii) There are multiple possible causes of the plaintiff's harm but the plaintiff cannot prove which defendant caused the harm; or

iii) The defendant's negligent medical misdiagnosis increased the probability of the plaintiff's death, but the plaintiff probably would have died even with a proper diagnosis.

1) Substantial factor

When but-for causation does not work, most courts substitute a substantial-factor test. In cases in which the conduct of two or more defendants may have contributed to a plaintiff's indivisible injury, each of which alone would have been a factual cause of that injury, the test is whether the defendant's tortious conduct was a **substantial factor** in causing the plaintiff's harm.

The *Restatement (Second) of Torts* promoted the substantial-factor test, but the Third Restatement is highly critical of it and drops it. Under the Third Restatement, in cases in which several causes or acts may have contributed to the plaintiff's injury, each of which alone would have been a factual cause of the plaintiff's injury, each cause or act is regarded as a factual cause of the harm. Rest. 3d: Liability for Physical and Emotional Harm § 27.

2) Concurrent tortfeasors contributing to an individual injury

When the tortious acts of two or more defendants are each a factual cause of an indivisible injury to the plaintiff, the defendants are jointly and severally liable.

3) Alternative causation

If the plaintiff's harm was caused by (i) one of a small number of defendants—usually two and almost never more than four or five, (ii) each of whose conduct was tortious, and (iii) all of whom are present before the court, then the court may shift the burden of proof to each individual defendant to prove that his conduct was not the cause in fact of the plaintiff's harm.

4) Concert of action

If two or more tortfeasors were **acting pursuant to a common plan or design** and the acts of one or more of them tortiously caused the plaintiff's harm, then all defendants are jointly and severally liable.

Example: Two defendants agree to a drag race and one of them injures another driver or a passenger during the race. Both are jointly and severally liable to the plaintiff.

c. Loss of chance of recovery

When a physician negligently misdiagnoses a potentially fatal disease and thereby reduces the patient's chance of survival, but the patient's chance of recovery was less than 50% even prior to the negligent misdiagnosis, the plaintiff ordinarily cannot prove that but for the physician's negligence the plaintiff's death would not have occurred. A majority or substantial minority of courts now hold that the plaintiff can recover reduced damages based on the loss-of-chance doctrine.

Under this doctrine, the plaintiff can recover an amount equal to the total damages recoverable as a result of the decedent's death multiplied by the difference in the percentage chance of recovery before the negligent misdiagnosis and after the misdiagnosis.

Example: The plaintiff's total damages are $1,000,000, and his chances of survival were 40% without the negligent misdiagnosis and 25% after the misdiagnosis. The plaintiff will recover $150,000 ($1,000,000 × (40% − 25%)).

2. Causal Linkage

Most often, when the plaintiff proves that the defendant's tortious conduct was a **but-for cause** of his injury, he also implicitly proves that the defendant's conduct increased the probability that the plaintiff would be harmed.

However, in a few cases, it is purely coincidental that the defendant's tortious conduct was the but-for cause of the plaintiff's injury.

Example: A passenger in a car is injured because the wind blows down a tree and the car is positioned under the tree at the moment it falls only because the driver has been traveling at an unreasonably unsafe speed. While the passenger would not have been injured but for the driver's negligent speeding, most courts would find that the driver should not be found to be a cause of the accident under the doctrine of causal linkage, i.e., the driver's conduct did not increase the probability that the plaintiff would be harmed.

3. Proximate Cause (Scope of Liability)

In addition to proving actual causation, the plaintiff must prove that the defendant's tortious conduct was a proximate cause of her harm. Some courts and the Third Restatement replace the proximate causation terminology with the issue of whether the plaintiff's harm was within the **"scope of liability"** of the defendant's conduct. A defendant's liability is limited to those harms that result from the risks that made the defendant's conduct tortious. Rest. 3d: Liability for Physical and Emotional Harm § 29.

> **EXAM NOTE:** Remember that there must be factual cause for proximate cause to exist, and if factual cause exists, then proximate cause exists unless there are intervening acts.

a. Limitation on liability

The basic idea of proximate causation (or, scope of liability) is that there must be limits on liability for the tortious acts of the defendant. There are two sub-issues in proximate causation:

1) Which plaintiffs can recover?

a) Majority rule

Recall that a majority of jurisdictions hold that the defendant does not owe a duty of care to the plaintiff unless the plaintiff is among the class of victims who might **foreseeably be injured** as a result of the defendant's tortious conduct. This is the Cardozo approach in *Palsgraf v. Long Island R. R. Co.*, 162 N.E. 99 (N.Y. 1928). *See* § IV.B.3. Foreseeability of Harm to the Plaintiff, *supra*.

b) Minority/Restatement rule

In the minority of jurisdictions—and in the Third Restatement—which plaintiffs can recover is determined by whether harms to them were proximately caused by the defendant's tortious conduct or were within the scope of liability of the defendant's conduct. This is the Andrews approach in *Palsgraf*.

Under the Andrews approach, whether the plaintiff's harms are proximately caused by the defendant's conduct requires consideration of the following factors:

i) Is there a **natural and continuous sequence** between cause and effect?

ii) Was the one a **substantial factor** in producing the other?

iii) Was there a **direct connection** without the intervention of too many intervening causes?

iv) Was the cause **likely to produce** the effect?

v) Could the defendant have **foreseen** the harm to the plaintiff?

vi) Is the cause **too remote** in time and space from the effect?

2) Types of risk

The second proximate cause (scope of liability) issue is whether the plaintiff can recover for the specific type of risk that harmed her. For example, even if the court decides that a duty of care is owed to a specific plaintiff, a ship owner, because there is a foreseeable risk that a defendant stevedore's dropping of a plank into the hold of a ship might dent the ship, is the defendant still liable when the dropped plank unforeseeably causes vapors in the hull of the ship to ignite, totally destroying the ship? Again, there are two approaches.

a) Direct cause

A majority of U.S. courts hold that the plaintiff can recover when the defendant's tortious acts are the **direct cause** of the plaintiff's harm—a cause **without the intervention of independent contributing acts**. In deciding whether the plaintiff can recover for a particular type of harm, these courts look at many of the same factors that Judge Andrews considered in *Palsgraf*. These jurisdictions hold that the foreseeability of the type of harm does not necessarily preclude liability.

b) Unforeseeable type of risk

A strong minority of U.S. jurisdictions hold that whether a plaintiff can recover for a particular type of risk is determined by whether or not that particular risk is **foreseeable as a result of the defendant's tortious conduct**. If it is not, then there is no proximate cause and the plaintiff cannot recover.

b. Extent of damages

Even though a strong minority of jurisdictions hold that the type of risk that produces the plaintiff's harm must be foreseeable, under the "thin skull" or "eggshell skull" rule, the **extent of the damages need never be foreseeable**. Thus, the defendant is liable for the full extent of the plaintiff's injuries due to the plaintiff's pre-existing medical condition or vulnerability, even if the extent is unusual or unforeseeable.

c. Intervening and superseding causes

Many proximate cause questions involve intervening and superseding causes.

1) Intervening cause

An intervening cause is a factual cause of the plaintiff's harm that contributes to her harm after the defendant's tortious act has been completed.

2) Superseding cause

A superseding cause is any intervening cause that **breaks the chain of proximate causation between the defendant's tortious act and the plaintiff's harm**, thereby preventing the original defendant from being liable to the plaintiff.

a) Foreseeability

Most courts hold that an **unforeseeable** intervening cause is a superseding cause that therefore breaks the chain of causation between the defendant and the plaintiff. Examples of foreseeable intervening forces include subsequent medical malpractice, disease, or accident; negligence of rescuers; normal forces of nature; or efforts to protect a person or property. Examples of unforeseeable superseding causes include extraordinary acts of nature ("Acts of God") and criminal acts and/or intentional torts of third parties.

b) Negligent intervening causes

As a general guideline, **negligent intervening acts are usually regarded as foreseeable** and do not prevent the original defendant from being held liable to the plaintiff.

> **Example:** The defendant negligently injures the plaintiff in an auto accident. The plaintiff seeks treatment for the resulting broken leg, and the treating physician commits malpractice that results in the amputation of the leg. Because the original driver-defendant's negligence was a but-for cause of the amputated leg and because medical malpractice is foreseeable, the driver's negligence is also a proximate cause of the amputated leg, and he may be held liable for damages caused by the entire injury including the consequences of the amputation.

c) Criminal intervening causes

Criminal acts of third parties are generally regarded as **unforeseeable superseding causes,** and therefore break the chain of causation between the original defendant's negligence and the plaintiff's harm.

However, if the duty breached by the defendant is one of **failing to use reasonable care to protect the plaintiff** and the plaintiff is harmed by a **criminal act**, then the original defendant remains liable.

> **Example:** A middle-school student is assaulted during a field trip. Her teacher failed to use reasonable care to protect her. The fact that the intervening cause of her harm, the assault, was criminal will not preclude the student and her parents from holding the school liable.

d) Effect of non-superseding intervening causes

If the intervening negligent act is not a superseding cause, then the original defendant and the actor responsible for the intervening negligent act can be held jointly and severally liable to the plaintiff.

> **EXAM NOTE:** Remember that the original tortfeasors remain liable unless the results of an intervening negligent act are **unforeseeable**. In particular, keep in mind that medical malpractice is foreseeable, and therefore it is not a superseding cause that breaks the chain of causation and insulates the defendant from liability.

F. DAMAGES

1. Actual Damages

The plaintiff must prove actual harm, i.e., personal injury or property damages, in order to complete the requirements of liability for negligence. Unlike actions for intentional torts, nominal damages are not recoverable in negligence actions. In addition, a plaintiff who suffers only economic loss without any related personal injury or property damage cannot recover such loss through a negligence action. However, once a plaintiff has proven non-economic injury, he is entitled to recover both economic and non-economic damages. Attorney's fees and interest from the date of damage are not recoverable in a negligence action.

2. Compensatory Damages

The general measure of compensatory damages is compensation that would make the victim whole, as if he had never suffered the injury.

3. Mitigation of Damages, Avoidable Consequences

The plaintiff must take reasonable steps to mitigate damages. Although sometimes phrased as a "duty to mitigate," this "duty" is not an obligation that the plaintiff owes to the defendant but instead is a limitation on the plaintiff's recovery due to the failure to avoid harm that could have been avoided by the use of reasonable effort after the tort was committed. For example, if the victim fails to use reasonable care to treat a wound, resulting in infection and the loss of a limb, she ordinarily will not be able to recover for the infection or lost limb. In a contributory-negligence jurisdiction, the failure to mitigate precludes the plaintiff from recovering for any additional harm caused by aggravation of the injury. In a comparative-negligence jurisdiction, the failure to mitigate is taken into account, but it does not categorically prevent recovery.

4. Personal Injury: Categories of Damages

The typical categories of damages recoverable in a personal injury action include:

i) Medical and rehabilitative expenses, both past and future;

ii) Past and future pain and suffering (e.g., emotional distress); and

iii) Lost income and any reduction in future earnings capacity.

Under the **"eggshell-skull rule,"** the defendant is liable for the full extent of the plaintiff's injuries that may be increased because of the plaintiff's preexisting medical condition or vulnerability, even if the extent is unusual or unforeseeable.

5. Property Damage

a. General rule

When the plaintiff's real or personal property is injured or destroyed by the defendant's tortious conduct, the general rule is that the plaintiff may recover the difference between the fair market value of the property immediately before the injury and immediately after the injury.

b. Cost of repairs

In the case of tortious harm to personal property, most courts also allow the cost of repairs as an alternative measure of damages, provided that the cost of repairs does not exceed the value of the property.

c. Household items

In the case of household items, such as clothing and appliances, courts often hold that replacement value is the measure of damages.

6. Collateral-Source Rule

a. Traditional rule

Under the traditional rule, benefits or payments provided to the plaintiff from outside sources (such as medical insurance) are not credited against the liability of any tortfeasor, nor is evidence of such payments admissible at trial. Even under the traditional rule, payments made to the plaintiff by the defendant's insurer are not considered payments from a collateral source, and such payments are credited against the defendant's liability.

b. Modern trend

A majority of states have passed statutes that either eliminate the collateral source rule entirely or modify its application (e.g., not applicable in medical malpractice cases).

7. Punitive Damages

The plaintiff may be entitled to punitive damages if he can establish by clear and convincing evidence that the defendant acted willfully and wantonly, recklessly, or with malice. Torts that inherently involve a malicious state of mind or outrageous conduct (such as intentional infliction of emotional distress) may often result in punitive damages for the plaintiff. Note that in many states that availability of punitive damages as a remedy is determined by statute. There are also constitutional limitations on the amount of a punitive damages award. The Supreme Court has declined to impose a bright-line ratio which a punitive damages award cannot exceed, but has observed that very few awards exceeding a single-digit ratio between punitive and compensatory damages will satisfy due process. *State Farm v. Campbell*, 538 U.S. 408 (2003).

G. SPECIAL RULES OF LIABILITY

1. Negligent Infliction of Emotional Distress

There are three types of cases in which a defendant may breach the duty to avoid negligently inflicting emotional distress upon a plaintiff. Whether a duty exists may depend upon whether the harm and the plaintiff are reasonably foreseeable. Some states deny recovery because one or the other is too speculative and thus not foreseeable.

a. Zone of danger

A plaintiff can recover for negligent infliction of emotional distress from a defendant whose tortious conduct placed the plaintiff in harm's way if the plaintiff demonstrates that:

i)   He was within the "**zone of danger**" of the threatened physical impact—that he feared for his own safety because of the defendant's negligence; and

ii) The threat of physical impact caused emotional distress.

1) Proof of emotional distress

The majority rule is that the emotional distress must be manifested by **physical symptoms** (e.g., nightmares, shock, ulcers). The severity of symptoms required varies by jurisdiction. A few states as well as the Restatement allow recovery for serious emotional disturbance without a physical manifestation of harm. Restatement (Third) of Torts: Liability for Physical and Emotional Harm § 4, comment d.

Compare to intentional infliction of emotional distress, under which the plaintiff must prove more than negligence (intentional or reckless extreme or outrageous conduct) but need not prove any physical injury.

b. Bystander recovery

Most states allow a bystander plaintiff outside the zone of danger to recover for emotional distress if that plaintiff:

i)   Is closely related to the person injured by the defendant;

ii) Was present at the scene of the injury; and

iii) Personally observed (or otherwise perceived) the injury.

A majority of jurisdictions have not expanded liability to an unmarried cohabitant. However, some jurisdictions do allow engaged cohabitants to recover.

1) Proof of emotional distress

As with a plaintiff who is in the zone of danger, for a plaintiff who is a bystander, the majority rule is that the emotional distress must be manifested by **physical symptoms** (e.g., nightmares, shock, ulcers).

c. Special relationship

The duty to avoid negligent infliction of emotional distress exists without any threat of physical impact or physical symptoms in cases in which there is a special relationship between the plaintiff and the defendant. The most common examples are a mortician mishandling a corpse or a common carrier mistakenly reporting the death of a relative.

Example: A physician negligently misdiagnoses a patient with a terminal illness that the patient does not have, and the patient goes into shock as a result.

2. Wrongful Death and Survival Actions

a. Wrongful-death actions

A decedent's spouse, next of kin, or personal representative may bring suit to recover **losses suffered as a result of a decedent's death** under wrongful death actions created by state statutes. Under typical statutes, the recoverable damages include the **loss of support** (income) as a result of the decedent's death, as well as the **loss of companionship, society, and affection** experienced by the surviving family members, **but not pain and suffering**. Recovery, however, is limited to what the deceased would have recovered had he lived. Additionally, the decedent's creditors have no right to institute a claim against the amount awarded.

b. Survival actions

Survival statutes typically enable the personal representative of a decedent's estate to pursue **any claims the decedent herself would have had at the time of her death**, including claims for damages resulting from both personal injury and property damage. Such claims often involve damages resulting from the tort that injured the decedent and later resulted in her death.

Example: If the decedent was negligently injured by the driver of another automobile and lingered—out of work, in the hospital, and in extreme pain—for one year before passing away, his estate would be able to recover for his **medical expenses** from the time he was injured until his death, for his **loss of income** during this time, and for the **pain and suffering** he experienced.

Most states do not allow survival of tort actions involving intangible personal interests (such as defamation, malicious prosecution, or invasion of privacy) because they are considered too personal to survive the decedent's death.

Note: If a jurisdiction recognizes both wrongful death and survival actions, there is no double recovery.

3. Recovery for Loss Arising From Injury to Family Members

a. Spouses

One spouse may recover for loss of consortium and services as a result of injuries to the other spouse resulting from the defendant's tortious conduct.

b. Parent-child

A parent may recover damages for loss of services if a child is injured due to the defendant's tortious conduct. Many jurisdictions allow a parent to recover for loss of the child's companionship in a wrongful-death action if the child is killed, but only a few jurisdictions allow a parent to recover for such damages if the child is injured but lives.

Similarly, many jurisdictions allow a child to recover for loss of the parent's companionship in a wrongful-death action, but most do not allow the child to recover such damages if the parent is injured but lives. In a wrongful-death action, the child's claim for loss of support resulting from the decedent's death will be brought by the statutorily designated adult family member as part of the wrongful-death action.

c. Limitations

The amount of damages recoverable in a derivative action (an action arising solely because of tortious harm to another) for interference with family relationships is reduced in a comparative-fault jurisdiction (and eliminated in a contributory-negligence jurisdiction) by the injured family member's contributory negligence. Thus, if the damages recovered in the injured family member's own action are reduced by the plaintiff's comparative fault, then the damages recoverable by his family members in their derivative action will also be reduced.

4. "Wrongful Life" and "Wrongful Birth" Claims

a. Wrongful life

Most states do not permit actions by a child for "wrongful life" based on the failure to properly perform a contraceptive procedure or failure to diagnose a congenital defect, even if the child is born with a disability. A few states permit this action, but they limit the child's recovery to the special damages attributable to the disability.

b. Wrongful birth

Conversely, many states do permit parents to recover for "wrongful birth" (failure to diagnose a defect) or "wrongful pregnancy" (failure to perform a contraceptive procedure). Generally, the mother can recover damages for the medical expenses of labor as well as for pain and suffering. In the case of a disabled child, the parents may be able to recover damages for the additional medical expenses of caring for that child, and, in some states, may recover for emotional distress as well.

H. VICARIOUS LIABILITY

Vicarious liability is a form of strict liability in which one person is liable for the tortious actions of another. It arises when one person has the right, ability, or duty to control the activities of another, even though the first person was not directly liable for the injury. It is, of course, a defense to vicarious liability that the conduct of the person subject to the plaintiff's conduct was not tortious.

1. **Liability of an Employer for an Employee's Torts**

   a. **Employer's right of control**

   As a rule, a person is an employer if the person has the right to control the means and methods by which another performs a task or achieves a result. The person subject to this right is an employee. Absent a right to control, the person is likely an independent contractor.

   b. **Scope of employment**

   An employer is liable for the tortious conduct of an employee that is within the **scope of employment**. Conduct within the scope of employment includes acts that the employee is employed to perform or that are intended to profit or benefit the employer.

   > **Note:** Careful instructions directed to the employee do not insulate the employer from liability—even when the employee acts counter to the instructions—if the employee is acting within the scope of employment.

   1) **Intentional torts**

      An employer may be liable for the intentional tort of an employee. For example, when **force is inherent** in the employee's work (e.g., a bouncer at a bar), the employer may be responsible for injuries the employee inflicts in the course of his work. However, if an employee, acting on a long-standing personal grudge, punches a customer of the employer's store, the employer probably will not be held liable. In addition, if the **employer authorizes the employee** to act on his behalf, and the employee's position provides the opportunity to commit an intentional tort, the employer may be liable (e.g., when an employee with the power to sign contracts enters into a fraudulent contract with a third party, the employer may be liable). As with negligence, the test is whether the employee was acting within the scope of employment. Restatement (Third) of Agency § 7.07.

   2) **Detour and frolic**

      An employer may be liable for a tort committed by the employee during an employee's detour (a minor and permissible deviation from the scope of employment) but not for an employee's frolic (an unauthorized and substantial deviation).

   > **EXAM NOTE:** The employer and employee will be jointly and severally liable (*see* § IV.J.1. Joint and Several Liability, *infra*) for torts committed by the employee within the scope of employment.

   c. **Direct liability**

   In addition to vicarious liability for torts committed by an employee within the scope of employment, an employer is liable for its own negligence in the hiring, training, supervising, or entrustment of an employee. Generally, the employer's liability extends only to actions taken by the employee within the scope of the employment.

2. **Torts Committed By Independent Contractors**

   a. **Generally no vicarious liability**

   Those who engage an independent contractor are generally not vicariously liable for the torts of the independent contractor.

b. Distinguished from employee

An independent contractor is one engaged to accomplish a task or achieve a result but who is not subject to another's right to control the method and means by which the task is performed or the result reached.

    i)   Independent contractors tend to have specialized skills or knowledge, e.g., physicians and plumbers; and

    ii)   Independent contractors tend to work for many employers, while employees more often work for a single employer.

c. Non-delegable duties

A person who hires an independent contractor is vicariously liable for certain conduct, including:

    i)   **Inherently dangerous activities**;

    ii)   **Non-delegable duties** arising out of a relationship with a specific plaintiff or the public (i.e., activities that are inherently risky or that affect the public at large, such as construction work adjacent to a public highway);

    iii)   The duty of a storekeeper or other operator of premises open to the public to keep such premises in a reasonably safe condition; and

    iv)   In a minority of jurisdictions, the duty to comply with state safety statutes.

d. Apparent agency

Under the rule of apparent agency, a person who hires an independent contractor to perform services is subject to vicarious liability for physical harm if (i) the services are accepted in the reasonable belief that the person or the person's employees are rendering the services, and (ii) the independent contractor's negligence is a factual cause of harm to one who receives the services, and such harm is within the scope of liability. The reasonable belief must be traced to manifestations of the person, but the injured person need not be the person who accepts the services based on that belief.

> **Example:** On a hot summer day, a brother and sister are walking on a city sidewalk in the neighborhood in which they live. The sister passes out. The brother hails a taxi. Painted on the taxi is the name of a taxi company that owns the taxi. The driver of the taxi is an independent contractor. The brother places his sister into the taxi, enters himself, and directs the taxi to drive them home. On the way there, the taxi, as a result of the driver's carelessness, hits a car. Both the brother and sister are injured. The taxi company is vicariously liable to the sister, as well as the brother, for the negligence of the taxi driver, even though only the brother relied on the identification of the taxi company as the provider of the taxi services.

e. Negligence in selection or supervision

A party who selects or supervises an independent contractor may be liable for his own negligence in selecting or supervising the independent contractor.

3. Business Partners and Joint Enterprise Participants

Partners in a partnership are jointly and severally liable for torts committed within the scope of the partnership. Participants in a joint enterprise, in which each has a common purpose with the other participants and there is a mutual right of control, may be liable for the tortious acts of each other that are committed within the scope of the business purposes.

By contrast, a member of a limited liability company (LLC) is generally not personally liable for torts committed by another member of the LLC.

4. Automobile Owners

a. Negligent entrustment

The owner of a vehicle (or any other object that carries the potential for harm, such as a gun or lawn mower) may be liable for the negligent acts of a driver or user to whom the car or other property was entrusted if the owner knew or should have known of the user's negligent propensities.

b. Family-purpose doctrine

Many jurisdictions, through either legislative enactments or judicial decisions, have adopted the family-purpose doctrine, providing that the owner of an automobile may be liable for the tortious acts of **any family member** driving the car with permission.

c. Owner liability statutes

Many jurisdictions have enacted statutes that provide that the owner of an automobile may be liable for the tortious acts of **anyone** driving the car with permission.

5. Parents and Their Children

a. No vicarious liability

The general rule is that parents are not vicariously liable for their minor child's torts. **Exceptions** to this general rule include situations in which:

i) The child commits a tort while acting as **the parent's agent**;

ii) State statutes provide for the liability of parents when children commit specified acts such as **vandalism or school violence**; or

iii) State statutes require that a parent, when he signs for the child's driver's license application, assumes liability for any damages caused by negligent acts that the child commits while driving a car.

b. Negligence of parents

Parents, however, are liable for their *own* negligence with respect to their minor child's conduct. A parent is under a duty to exercise reasonable care to prevent a minor child from intentionally or negligently harming a third party, provided the parent:

i) Has the ability to control the child; and

ii) Knows or should know of the necessity and opportunity for exercising such control.

In such circumstances, a parent who fails to exercise control may be liable for harm caused by the child, even though the child, because of his age, is not liable. Rest. 2d § 316.

Example: A father gives a gun to his six-year-old son. Although the son lacks the necessary maturity and judgment to operate the gun independently in a safe manner, the father allows the son to use the gun when the father is not present.

The son, while aiming the gun at a toy in his yard, misses and accidentally shoots a neighbor. The father, because of his failure to properly supervise his son, can be liable for the injury suffered by the neighbor that is directly attributable to the son's conduct, even though the son himself will not be liable because of his age.

6. "Dram Shop" Liability

Many states recognize, either by statute (a "dram shop act") or by judicial decision, a cause of action against the seller of intoxicating beverages when a third party is subsequently injured due to the buyer's intoxication. Most states limit liability to situations in which the buyer was a minor or was intoxicated at the time of the sale. Some states extend liability to a social host who serves intoxicating beverages to a minor. The states are divided as to whether the cause of action is grounded in negligence or strict liability.

7. Bailment Liability

A bailor may be liable for his own negligent actions but generally is not vicariously liable for the tortious acts of his bailee, except for those limited situations described above, such as bailments involving automobiles or parents and children.

I. LIMITATION OF LIABILITY RESULTING FROM DEFENDANT'S IDENTITY OR RELATIONSHIPS ("IMMUNITIES")

Traditionally, governmental entities, charities, and family members were immune from liability. Today, these immunities have been largely eliminated, but the rules governing the liability of these defendants continue to differ from those governing other tortfeasors.

1. Liability of the Government and Its Officers

a. Federal government

Under the Federal Tort Claims Act ("FTCA"), the U.S. government waives immunity in tort actions, with the following exceptions:

i) Certain enumerated torts (assault, battery, false imprisonment, false arrest, malicious prosecution, abuse of process, libel and slander, misrepresentation and deceit, and interference with contract rights);

ii) Discretionary functions (i.e., planning or decision making, as opposed to operational acts);

iii) Assertion of the government's immunity by a government contractor in a products liability case if the contractor conformed to government specifications and warned the government of any known dangers in the product; and

iv) Certain traditional governmental activities (i.e., postal, tax collection or property seizure, admiralty, quarantine, money supply, and military activity).

When the U.S. government waives its sovereign immunity under the FTCA, it is liable in the same manner and to the same extent that a private person under the same circumstances would be liable, but it is not liable for punitive damages.

b. State governments

Most states have waived sovereign immunity, at least partially, through legislation. Simultaneously, however, they have imposed limits on the amount of recovery and the circumstances under which the state can be held liable. They also have created procedural barriers to recover that do not exist in claims against private defendants. **State tort claims acts vary greatly** and therefore each act must be read carefully.

Unless otherwise provided in the legislation, the same terms and conditions apply to the liability of state agencies—including prisons, hospitals, and educational institutions—as to the state itself.

c. **Municipalities**

1) **Usually governed by state tort claims act**

Today, the liability of municipalities, other local governments, and their agencies usually is governed by the provisions of state tort claims acts.

2) **Governmental vs. proprietary functions**

Traditionally, immunity attached to the performance of traditional government functions (such as police and court systems) but did not attach when a municipality was performing a "proprietary" function that often is performed by a private company (such as utilities and parking lots).

3) **Public-duty rule**

The public-duty rule provides that there is no liability to any one citizen for the municipality's failure to fulfill a duty that is owed to the public at large, unless that citizen has a special relationship with the municipality that creates a special duty. A special relationship can be shown by:

   i) Promises or actions on the part of the municipality demonstrating an affirmative duty to act on behalf of the injured party;

   ii) Knowledge by the municipality's agents that failure to act could lead to harm;

   iii) Direct contact between the municipality's agents and the injured party; and

   iv) The injured party's justifiable reliance on the municipality's affirmative duty.

d. **Government officials**

1) **Discretionary functions**

When a government official is personally sued, immunity applies if she is performing **discretionary functions** entrusted to her by law so long as the acts are done without malice or improper purpose.

2) **Ministerial functions**

There is no tort immunity for carrying out ministerial acts, such as driving while on government business.

3) **Highly ranked officials**

Many highly ranked government officials, such as legislators performing their legislative functions, judges performing their judicial functions, prosecutors, and some upper-echelon officials of the executive branches, are usually absolutely immune from personal liability.

4) **Federal immunity**

Under the so-called "Westfall Act," 28 U.S.C. § 2679(b)(1), the remedy against the United States under the FTCA for torts committed by federal employees precludes any personal liability on the part of a federal employee under state tort law.

2. Intra-Family Immunity

Intra-family immunity applies only to personal injuries, not to property damage.

a. Interspousal immunity

Traditionally, interspousal immunity prevented one spouse from suing the other in a personal-injury action. In most jurisdictions today, however, interspousal immunity has been extinguished, and either spouse can now institute a cause of action for personal injury against the other spouse.

b. Parent-child immunity

Traditionally, parents were immune from tort claims brought by their children. In recent decades, however, there has been a clear trend toward abolishing or greatly restricting parental immunity, but abrogation has proceeded more slowly than in the case of interspousal immunity.

Courts generally allow parents to be held liable in areas other than **core parenting activities.** For example, most states allow children to sue parents:

i) For injuries arising from **automobile accidents**;

ii) In extreme cases, such as those involving **sexual abuse and intentional tortious conduct;** and

iii) When the parent is acting in a **dual capacity,** such as when the parent is a physician treating the child for an injury (medical malpractice claim allowed).

3. Charitable Immunity

Most states have either totally or partially eliminated the common-law rule of charitable immunity. Some states cap the amount of damages recoverable from a charitable institution.

J. SHARING LIABILITY AMONG MULTIPLE DEFENDANTS

1. Joint and Several Liability

a. Definition

Under the doctrine of joint and several liability, each of two or more defendants who is found liable for a single and indivisible harm to the plaintiff is subject to liability to the plaintiff **for the entire harm**. The plaintiff has the choice of collecting the entire judgment from one defendant, the entire judgment from another defendant, or portions of the judgment from various defendants, as long as the plaintiff's entire recovery does not exceed the amount of the judgment.

b. Application

Examples of when joint and several liability applies include, among other instances, when:

i) The tortious acts of two or more tortfeasors combine to produce an indivisible harm (*see* § IV.E.1.b.2. Concurrent tortfeasors contributing to an individual injury, *supra*);

ii) The harm results from the acts of one or more tortfeasors acting in concert (*see* § IV.E.1.b.4. Concert of action, *supra*);

iii) Alternative liability applies (*see* § IV.E.1.b.3. Alternative causation, *supra*);

iv) Res ipsa loquitur is used against multiple defendants (such as in a surgical setting), and the plaintiff is unable to identify the tortfeasor whose acts were negligent (*see* § IV.D.2. Res Ipsa Loquitur, *supra*); and

v) The employer and the employee are both held liable (*see* § IV.H.1. Liability of an Employer for an Employee's Torts, *supra*).

2. Contribution

If two or more tortfeasors are subject to liability to the same plaintiff, and one of the tortfeasors has paid the plaintiff more than his fair share of the common liability, then he may sue any of the other joint tortfeasors for contribution, and recover anything paid in excess of his fair share. Additionally, a person seeking contribution must prove that the person against whom contribution is sought would have been liable to the plaintiff in an amount and share equal to or greater than the amount sought as contribution. *See* Rest. 3d (Apport.) § 23.

a. Determining fair shares

In most jurisdictions, each party's fair share is determined by comparing how far each tortfeasor departed from the standard of reasonable care.

b. Intentional tortfeasor

Generally, a party who has committed an intentional tort may not seek contribution from another tortfeasor.

3. Several (Proportionate) Liability

A majority of states now restrict or reject joint and several liability. Many instead recognize **pure several liability**, under which **each tortfeasor is liable only for his proportionate share** of the plaintiff's damages. In most of these jurisdictions, each defendant's share of liability is determined in accordance with how far each deviated from the standard of reasonable care. In other words, the more culpable defendant pays the higher proportion of the damages.

4. Satisfaction and Release

Once a plaintiff has recovered fully from one or a combination of defendants, she is barred from pursuing further action against other tortfeasors. The plaintiff generally may not receive double recovery.

If the plaintiff has not been wholly compensated, it is now the usual rule that a release of one tortfeasor does not release the others but instead diminishes the claim against the others, ordinarily by the amount of compensation received from the released tortfeasor. However, a release may bar claims against other tortfeasors if either (i) the release agreement so provides or (ii) the plaintiff has been entirely compensated for his losses.

5. Indemnification

Indemnification is the shifting of the entire loss from person to another.

a. Vicarious liability

Indemnification generally applies when a person is vicariously liable for the other's wrongdoing. The person who has discharged the liability is entitled to indemnity from the actual wrongdoer who was primarily responsible for the harm (e.g., an employer who pays a judgment for the tort of an employee because of the employer's vicarious liability).

b. Complete reimbursement

A tortfeasor can seek complete reimbursement (indemnity) from another tortfeasor when:

i) There is a **prior indemnification agreement** between the parties (e.g., in the construction industry, a contractor may agree to indemnify a subcontractor for the latter's negligence that may occur in the future);

ii) There is a significant difference between the blameworthiness of two defendants such that **equity requires a shifting of the loss** to the more blameworthy defendant;

iii) Significant **additional harm is subsequently caused by another tortfeasor** (i.e., one defendant pays the full judgment, including for additional harm caused by the malpractice of the treating physician); or

iv) Under **strict products liability**, each supplier has a right of indemnification against all previous suppliers in a distribution chain.

Note: Indemnity in degree of blameworthiness is rejected in jurisdictions with comparative negligence systems. These states apportion damages based on relative fault, although indemnification is allowed in other instances when it is not based on degree of fault.

K. DEFENSES TO NEGLIGENCE

1. Contributory Negligence

Contributory negligence occurs when a plaintiff **fails to exercise reasonable care** for her own safety and thereby **contributes to her own injury**. Note that when a plaintiff is suing a defendant for the negligent rendering of services, such as medical services, the plaintiff's negligent conduct in creating the condition that the defendant has been employed to remedy is not taken into account.

a. Contributory negligence: traditional rule

At common law, and in a handful of states, the plaintiff's contributory negligence (i.e., failure to exercise reasonable care for her own safety) is a **complete bar to recovery**, regardless of the percentage that the plaintiff's own negligence contributed to the harm.

Examples of contributory negligence include:

i) A plaintiff's violation of a statute that is designed to protect against the type of injury suffered by the plaintiff; the plaintiff's violation of a statute cannot be used as a defense, however, when a safety statute is interpreted to place the entire responsibility for the harm suffered by the plaintiff on the defendant (e.g., workplace safety statutes when an injury occurs to someone not covered by workers' compensation);

ii) A plaintiff-pedestrian's crossing the street against the light; and

iii) A plaintiff driving at an unreasonable speed that deprived him of the opportunity to avoid a traffic accident.

A rescuer who takes significant risks when attempting a rescue may also be permitted to recover, despite the rescuer's negligence.

Note: Contributory negligence is **not** a defense to an intentional tort, gross negligence, or recklessness.

Traditional reasons for the rule denying recovery have included punishing a plaintiff who has herself been negligent and deterrence, in that people are more likely to be careful about their own safety if they know they cannot recover for their injuries if they are not themselves careful.

b. Last clear chance

In contributory-negligence jurisdictions, the plaintiff may mitigate the legal consequences of her own contributory negligence if she proves that the defendant had the last clear chance to avoid injuring the plaintiff but failed to do so. This doctrine has been abolished in most comparative-fault jurisdictions.

1) Helpless plaintiff

A plaintiff who, due to his own contributory negligence, is in peril from which he cannot escape is in helpless peril. In such cases, the defendant is liable if she **knew or should have known** of the plaintiff's perilous situation and could have avoided harming the plaintiff but for her (the defendant's) own negligence.

2) Inattentive plaintiff

A plaintiff who, due to his own contributory negligence, is in peril from which he could escape if he were paying attention is an inattentive or oblivious plaintiff. The defendant is liable only if she has **actual knowledge** of the plaintiff's inattention.

c. Comparative fault

Rejecting the "all-or-nothing" approach of contributory negligence, almost all jurisdictions have adopted some form of comparative fault (comparative negligence), which attempts to apportion damages between a defendant and a plaintiff based on their relative degrees of fault. There are two basic forms of comparative fault.

1) Pure comparative negligence

In jurisdictions that have adopted the doctrine of pure comparative negligence, a plaintiff's contributory negligence is not a complete bar to recovery. Instead, the plaintiff's full damages are calculated by the trier of fact and then reduced by the proportion that the plaintiff's fault bears to the total harm (e.g., if the plaintiff's full damages are $100,000, the plaintiff is 80% at fault, and the defendant is 20% at fault, then the plaintiff will recover $20,000). Only a minority of jurisdictions have adopted the pure comparative negligence approach.

2) Modified or partial comparative fault

A majority of comparative-fault jurisdictions apply modified comparative fault. In these jurisdictions:

 i) If the plaintiff is **less at fault than the defendant**, then the plaintiff's recovery is **reduced by his percentage of fault**, just as in a pure comparative-fault jurisdiction;

 ii) If the plaintiff is **more at fault than the defendant**, then the plaintiff's **recovery is barred**, just as in a contributory-negligence jurisdiction;

 iii) In the vast majority of modified comparative-fault jurisdictions, if the plaintiff and the defendant are found to **be equally at fault**, then the

plaintiff recovers 50% of his total damages. In a few modified comparative-fault jurisdictions, the plaintiff recovers nothing when the jury finds that the plaintiff and the defendant are equally at fault.

3) Multiple defendants

In either a pure comparative-fault or a modified comparative-fault jurisdiction, the plaintiff's degree of negligence is compared to the total negligence of all defendants combined.

4) Relationships to other defenses

    i) Last clear chance no longer applies as a separate doctrine in comparative-fault jurisdictions.

    ii) Comparative fault will reduce the plaintiff's recovery even if the defendant's conduct is willful, wanton, or reckless, but it will not reduce the plaintiff's recovery for intentional torts.

    iii) The impact of comparative fault on assumption of risk is considered in § IV.K.2.c. Unreasonably proceeding in face of known, specific risk, *below*.

5) Illustrations

    i) Single defendant, pure comparative—The defendant is 55% negligent and the plaintiff is 45% negligent in causing the accident. They each have $100,000 in damages. The plaintiff will recover $55,000 from the defendant ($100,000 minus $45,000, which represents the plaintiff's proportionate fault of 45%), and the defendant will recover $45,000 from the plaintiff. The plaintiff will have a net recovery of $10,000 because the defendant's damages will be offset against the plaintiff's damages.

    ii) Single defendant, modified or partial comparative—Same facts as above, except that the defendant will not recover anything because he was more than 50% at fault.

    iii) Multiple defendants, modified or partial comparative—Two defendants are negligent: Defendant 1 is 20% negligent; Defendant 2 is 45% negligent. Combined, their negligence is 65%. The plaintiff is 35% negligent. The plaintiff can recover $65,000 from either Defendant 1 or Defendant 2 under the theory of joint and several liability. The paying defendant can then seek contribution from the nonpaying defendant. If either defendant suffered damages, he also has a right of recovery against either of the other two negligent parties because each one's negligence is less than the total negligence of the other two.

d. Imputed contributory negligence

Imputed contributory negligence occurs when another person's fault is "imputed" to the plaintiff to prevent or limit his recovery due to the other person's fault. For example, an employee's negligent driving may prevent or reduce an employer's recovery from a third party if the employer's car is damaged by the third party's negligence. The fault of one business partner can be imputed to another business partner as contributory negligence when the second party is suing a third party.

Imputed contributory negligence is disfavored. Imputed contributory negligence does not apply to:

i) A married plaintiff whose spouse was contributorily negligent in causing the harm, in a suit against a third party;

ii) A child plaintiff whose parent's negligence was a contributing cause of her harm, in a suit against a third party;

iii) An automobile passenger suing a third-party driver if the negligence of the driver of the car in which the passenger was riding also contributed to the accident; or

iv) An automobile owner in an action against a defendant driver for negligence when the driver of the owner's car also was negligent.

> **EXAM NOTE:** Common fact patterns of imputed fault to look for on examinations are ones involving the employers and their employees and business partners.

e. Distinguishing comparative fault, contribution, and several liability

Comparative fault, contribution, and several liability all involve comparing the level of egregiousness of fault of parties in tort litigation. However, each of these concepts operates in a different context:

i) Comparative fault always involves comparing the fault of a plaintiff with the fault of one or more defendants;

ii) Contribution involves comparing the degrees of fault of co-defendants in an action or as the result of a motion by one co-defendant against another co-defendant; it does not affect the liability of any of the defendants to the plaintiff;

iii) Several liability, in the minority of jurisdictions where it operates, involves comparing the levels of fault of the co-defendants; however, unlike with contribution, the issue is how much the plaintiff will receive from each defendant.

2. Assumption of the Risk

a. Exculpatory clauses in contracts

In general, parties can contract to disclaim liability for negligence. But, courts **will not** enforce exculpatory provisions:

i) Disclaiming liability for reckless or wanton misconduct or gross negligence;

ii) When there is a gross disparity of bargaining power between the parties;

iii) When the party seeking to apply the exculpatory provision offers services of great importance to the public that are a practical necessity for some members of the public such as medical services;

iv) If the exculpatory clause is subject to typical contractual defenses such as fraud or duress; or

v) When it is against public policy to enforce agreements that insulate people from the consequences of their own negligence.

Some jurisdictions require that the contract explicitly state that claims "based on negligence" are disclaimed.

Generally, **common carriers, innkeepers, and employers cannot disclaim liability for negligence**. State statutes often provide that certain additional businesses cannot disclaim liability for negligence.

Many courts now hold that **disclaimer of liability by contract negates** the fact that the defendant owes a **duty of care** to the plaintiff in the first place. This causes the plaintiff's prima facie case for negligence to fail, rather than acting as an affirmative defense of assumption of the risk.

b. Participants and spectators in athletic events

In a negligence claim brought by a spectator of or a participant in an athletic event or similar activity, the spectator or participant necessarily subjects himself to certain risks that are usually incident to and inherent in the game or activity. Some courts hold that the other players or facility owners therefore do not owe the spectators a duty of care; others allow the defendant to defend against the claim using the affirmative defense of assumption of the risk.

c. Unreasonably proceeding in the face of known, specific risk

Traditionally, and in many jurisdictions today, a plaintiff's **voluntarily encountering a known, specific risk** is an affirmative defense to negligence that affects recovery. Most courts hold that the voluntary encountering must also be **unreasonable**.

In **contributory-negligence** jurisdictions and in a minority of comparative-fault jurisdictions, this form of assumption of the risk remains a **total bar** to recovery.

In most **comparative-fault** jurisdictions, this form of assumption of the risk has been merged into the comparative-fault analysis and merely **reduces recovery**. The plaintiff's awareness of the risk is taken into account in determining the degree to which the plaintiff is at fault, but it also can be considered in determining the reasonableness of the plaintiff's or the defendant's actions.

> ***Consent distinguished:*** Consent is a defense to intentional torts, whereas assumption of the risk applies to negligence actions and actions alleging strict liability.

V. STRICT LIABILITY

A prima facie case for strict liability requires (i) an absolute duty to make the plaintiff's person or property safe, (ii) breach, (iii) actual and proximate causation, and (iv) damages.

The three general situations in which strict liability is imposed are:

    i)   **D**angerous activities;

    ii)   **A**nimals; and

    iii)   **D**efective or dangerous products.

MNEMONIC: DAD

> **EXAM NOTE:** The "DAD" situations are the **only** situations in which a defendant can be liable without fault.

A. ABNORMALLY DANGEROUS ACTIVITIES

1. Basic Rule

A defendant engaged in an abnormally dangerous activity may be held strictly liable—without any proof of negligence—for personal injuries and property damage caused by the activity, regardless of precautions taken to prevent the harm. Rest. 3d: Liability for Physical and Emotional Harm § 20.

2. **Definition of "Abnormally Dangerous"**

Abnormally dangerous means that an activity:

i) Creates a **foreseeable and highly significant risk** of physical harm even when reasonable care is exercised; and

ii) The activity is **not commonly engaged in**.

In addition to these requirements, in evaluating whether an activity is abnormally dangerous, courts often consider the **gravity of the harm** resulting from the activity, the **inappropriateness of the place** where the activity is being conducted, and the **limited value** of the activity to the community.

EXAM NOTE: The focus is on the inherent nature of the activity, not on how careful the defendant may or may not have been in conducting the activity.

Common abnormally dangerous activities include mining, blasting, using explosives, fumigating, crop dusting, excavating, disposing of hazardous waste, storing gasoline in residential areas, storing toxic chemicals and gases, and storing large quantities of water and other liquids.

Jurisdictions are split as to whether fireworks displays constitute an abnormally dangerous activity. Some compare the activity to blasting, finding that fireworks displays are not commonly engaged in and present substantial risks that cannot be eliminated with the exercise of reasonable care. Other jurisdictions, relying on the Second Restatement of Torts, have found that their value to the community outweighs the risks, and do not find the activity abnormally dangerous.

Damage or injury caused by flying aircraft is no longer subject to strict liability, though a few states still apply the doctrine to ground damage from an airplane crash.

3. **Scope of Risk**

Strict liability for an abnormally dangerous activity exists **only if harm that actually occurs results from the risk that made the activity abnormally dangerous in the first place**.

Example: A defendant drops a heavy package of explosives on the plaintiff's foot, severely injuring it. The injury did not result from the risk of an explosion, which is the risk that makes the use of explosives an abnormally dangerous activity.

As in the case with superseding causes in negligence (*see* § IV.E.3.c. Intervening and superseding causes, *supra*), the defendant's liability can be cut off by unforeseeable intervening causes.

B. **THE RULE OF *RYLANDS V. FLETCHER***

A defendant is strictly liable for the consequences that occur when he "...for his own purposes brings on his lands and collects and keeps there anything likely to do mischief if it escapes, must keep it at his peril, and, if he does not do so, is prima facie answerable for all the damage which is the natural consequence of its escape." *Rylands v. Fletcher*, LR 3 HL 330 (1868) (involving the release of water from the defendant's reservoir onto the plaintiff's property). The narrow holding of *Rylands*—that an owner of property with a dam on it is strictly liable for the harm caused by the release of water due to the bursting of the dam— is still followed. However, the broader principle of strict liability for harm caused by any dangerous object brought onto property by the landowner is no longer always followed. Instead, courts usually hold that only abnormally dangerous activities are subject to strict liability.

C. ANIMALS

1. Wild Animals

The Second Restatement of Torts defined wild animals as animals in a category that is "not by custom devoted to the service of mankind at the time and in the place in which it is kept." Restatement Second of Torts § 506(1). The Third Restatement narrows this definition by excluding animals that pose no obvious risk of causing substantial personal injury. Under the Third Restatement, a wild animal is an animal that belongs to a category of animals (e.g., species) that:

    i)   Have not been generally domesticated in the United States; and

    ii)   Are likely, unless restrained, to cause personal injury.

Restatement (Third) of Torts: Liability for Physical and Emotional Harm § 22.

Example 1: An elephant in the United States that has been tamed and exhibited as part of a circus strikes a circus acrobat with its trunk. The elephant is categorized as a wild animal even though, in other countries, it has been domesticated. Because an unrestrained elephant is likely to cause personal injury due to its strength and temperament, an elephant would be a wild animal under both the Second and Third Restatements.

Example 2: A pet snake escapes its enclosure and bites its owner's roommate. Snakes are not generally domesticated in the United States, and would be considered wild animals under the Second Restatement. However, under the Third Restatement, whether the snake is considered "wild" depends on the particular species of snake; a garter snake would not be considered "wild" because its species is not likely to cause personal injury, but a rattlesnake, even if defanged, would be considered "wild" because it belongs to a species of animals that are likely to cause personal injury.

Under both rules, a wild animal remains a wild animal despite being tamed for a number of years and even though its departure from that tameness is sudden and unexpected.

Example 3: A veterinarian raised a young chimpanzee as a pet. She kept the chimpanzee in her home and diligently trained and socialized it for many years. The chimpanzee has always adapted easily to meeting new people and has never injured anyone. One day, without warning, the chimpanzee bites a visitor to the veterinarian's house. Because the chimpanzee is a wild animal, strict liability will apply.

a. Dangerous propensity

The owner or possessor of a wild animal is strictly liable for harm caused by the animal, in spite of any precautions the possessor has taken to confine the animal or prevent the harm, if the harm arises from a **dangerous propensity** that is **characteristic of such a wild animal** or of which the owner **has reason to know**.

b. Plaintiff's fearful reaction

Strict liability applies to an injury caused by a **plaintiff's fearful reaction to the sight of an unrestrained wild animal**, in addition to injuries caused directly by the wild animal's dangerous propensity.

2. Abnormally Dangerous Animals

a. Known to be abnormally dangerous

The owner or possessor of an animal is strictly liable for injuries caused by that animal if he **knows or has reason to know** that the animal has **dangerous propensities abnormal for the animal's category or species**, and the harm results from those dangerous propensities. Otherwise, at common law, the owner of a domestic animal is generally liable only for negligence. Restatement (Third) of Torts: Liability for Physical and Emotional Harm § 23.

> **Example:** A defendant suffered injuries when he was thrown from his neighbor's young horse. Even if the neighbor knew that the young horse was "high strung" and "skittish," these traits are unlikely to establish that the neighbor knew or had reason to know that the horse had **abnormal dangerous propensities** because of how common it is for horses to have these traits. However, if the neighbor knew that the horse had an unusual habit of throwing all of its riders, strict liability may apply.

b. "Dog-bite" statutes

Many states have enacted "dog-bite" statutes that hold owners of dogs or other domestic animals designated in the statute strictly liable for damages resulting from personal injuries.

3. Trespassing Animals

The owner or possessor of any animal, wild or domestic (other than household pets), is strictly liable for any reasonably foreseeable damage caused by the animal while trespassing on the land of another. The exception for household pets (the Third Restatement specifically mentions dogs and cats) does not apply if the owner knows or has reason to know that the dog or cat is intruding on another's property in a way that has a tendency to cause substantial harm. The general negligence standard applies if an animal strays onto a public road and contributes to an accident there. Restatement (Third) of Torts: Liability for Physical and Emotional Harm § 21.

4. Landlord's Liability

In most jurisdictions, the landlord is not liable for harms caused by animals owned by his tenants because the landlord lacks the required element of control over the animal. Some jurisdictions impose liability on the landlord based on negligence if the landlord is aware of the dangerous propensities of the dog or other animal and has control under the terms of the lease of the tenant's possession of animals.

D. DEFENSES TO STRICT LIABILITY

1. Contributory Negligence

In contributory-negligence jurisdictions, the plaintiff's contributory negligence is not a defense to strict liability, i.e., it does not bar recovery.

2. Comparative Fault

Courts are divided, and in some comparative-fault jurisdictions, the plaintiff's negligence does not reduce the plaintiff's recovery under a strict-liability claim. Other jurisdictions would allow recovery to be reduced by the comparative fault of the plaintiff. Restatement (Third) of Torts: Liability for Physical and Emotional Harm § 25.

3. Assumption of the Risk

The plaintiff's assumption of the risk bars his recovery in a strict-liability action. This defense is also referred to as "knowing contributory negligence."

4. Statutory Privilege

Performance of an essential public service (e.g., construction of utility or sewer lines) exempts one from strict liability; however, liability may still exist under a negligence theory.

VI. PRODUCTS LIABILITY

A product may be defective because of a defect in its **design** or **manufacture** or because of a **failure to adequately warn** the consumer of a hazard related to the foreseeable use of the product.

When a plaintiff files a products liability case, he generally has at least three possible claims on which to base an action: **negligence, strict products liability**, and **breach of warranty**. Each type of claim requires different elements. (The Third Restatement provides for only a single cause of action in the absence of additional facts, and some courts have begun to adopt this approach.)

If, however, the defendant intended or knew with substantial certainty the consequences of the defect, then the cause of action could be based on an intentional tort. As with any intentional tort claim, punitive as well as compensatory damages are recoverable. The same defenses germane to each type of tort are applicable.

A. NEGLIGENCE

As with any negligence action, the plaintiff must prove duty, breach, causation, and damages to prevail.

1. Duty

The commercial manufacturer, distributor, retailer, or seller of a product owes a duty of reasonable care to **any foreseeable plaintiff** (i.e., a purchaser, user, or bystander).

2. Breach

Failure to exercise **reasonable care** in the inspection or sale of a product constitutes breach of that duty. The plaintiff must establish not only that the defect exists, but that the defendant's negligent conduct (lack of reasonable care) led to the plaintiff's harm. In other words, had the defendant exercised reasonable care in the inspection or sale of the product, the defect **would have been discovered,** and the plaintiff would not have been harmed. The plaintiff also has the option of invoking *res ipsa loquitur* if the defect could not have occurred without the manufacturer's negligence.

Note: The individual defendant must have breached his duty to reasonably inspect or sell. Unlike in strict products liability, the negligence of others in the supply chain cannot be imputed. Rather, the plaintiff has the burden of proving fault on the part of any particular defendant.

3. Causation

The plaintiff must prove factual and proximate causation.

Note: When a retailer sells a product with a known defect and without giving adequate warnings about the defect, the failure to warn may be a superseding cause, breaking the chain of causation between the manufacturer and the injury.

4. Damages

The plaintiff is entitled to recover damages resulting from any personal injury or property damage. A claim for purely economic loss is generally not allowed under either a negligence theory or a strict-liability theory, but it must be brought as a breach-of-warranty action.

5. Defenses

The standard negligence defenses of contributory/comparative negligence and assumption of the risk apply.

B. STRICT PRODUCTS LIABILITY

Under strict liability, the manufacturer, retailer, or other distributor of a defective product may be liable for any harm to persons or property caused by such product.

> **EXAM NOTE:** Strict products liability is only one way that a manufacturer or supplier of a product can be held liable for a plaintiff's injuries. Remember also to consider breach of warranty and negligence.

1. Elements of Claim

In order to recover, the plaintiff must plead and prove that:

i) The product was **defective** (in manufacture, design, or failure to warn);

ii) The defect existed at the time the product left the defendant's control; and

iii) The defect **caused the plaintiff's injuries** when the product was used in an **intended or reasonably foreseeable way**.

2. Defective Product

A product is defective when, at the time of the sale or distribution, it contains a manufacturing defect, a design defect, or inadequate instructions or warnings (i.e., failure to warn).

a. Manufacturing defect

A manufacturing defect is a **deviation from what the manufacturer intended** the product to be that causes harm to the plaintiff. The test for the existence of such a defect is whether the product **conforms to the defendant's own specifications**.

b. Design defect

Depending on the jurisdiction, courts apply either the **consumer-expectation test** or the **risk-utility test** to determine whether a design defect exists. Many jurisdictions use various hybrids of the two tests, and some states allow the plaintiff to prove a design defect under either test.

i) *Consumer expectation test:* Does the product include a condition not contemplated by the ordinary consumer that is **unreasonably dangerous** to him?

ii) *Risk-utility test:* Do the risks posed by the product **outweigh its benefits**?

Under the risk-utility test, in a majority of jurisdictions and under the Third Restatement, the plaintiff must prove that a **reasonable alternative design** was available to the defendant and the failure to use that design has rendered the product not reasonably safe. The alternative design must be economically feasible.

> **Note:** Merely providing a warning does not necessarily prevent a product from being unreasonably dangerous.

c. Failure to warn

An action brought under a failure-to-warn theory is essentially the same as a design defect claim, but the defect in question is the manufacturer's failure to provide an adequate warning related to the risks of using the product. A failure to warn defect exists if there were **foreseeable risks of harm, not obvious to an ordinary user** of the product, which risks could have been reduced or avoided by providing reasonable instructions or warnings. The failure to include the instructions or warnings renders the product not reasonably safe.

1) Prescription drugs and medical devices

Under the "learned-intermediary" rule, the manufacturer of a prescription drug or medical device typically satisfies its duty to warn the consumer by informing the prescribing physician, rather than the patient, of problems with the drug or device. Restatement (Third) of Torts: Products Liability § 6 (1998). There are several exceptions, including, most importantly:

i) If the manufacturer is aware that the drug or device will be dispensed or administered without the personal intervention or evaluation of a healthcare provider, such as when a vaccine is administered through a mass inoculation; and

ii) As a result of a federal statute, in the case of birth control pills.

d. Inference of defect

A plaintiff is entitled to a res ipsa loquitur–like inference that a product defect existed if the harm suffered by the plaintiff:

i) Was of a kind that ordinarily occurs as a result of a product defect; and

ii) Was not solely the result of causes other than a product defect existing at the time of sale or distribution.

Rest. 3d: Products Liability § 3.

This inference is frequently applied in cases involving a manufacturing defect when the product is lost or destroyed as a consequence of the incident that caused the plaintiff's harm.

3. Plaintiffs

To bring a strict-liability action, a plaintiff is **not** required to be in privity of contract with the defendant. **Anyone foreseeably injured** by a defective product or whose property is harmed by the product may bring a strict-liability action. Appropriate plaintiffs include **not only purchasers**, but also **other users** of the product and even **bystanders** who suffer personal injury or property damage.

4. Defendants

a. Business of seller

To be subject to strict liability for a defective product, the defendant must be in the **business of selling** or otherwise distributing products of the type that harmed the plaintiff.

b. Chain of distribution

Included as a seller are the **manufacturer** of the product, its **distributor**, and its **retail seller**.

c. Even if not responsible for the defect

If the seller is a commercial supplier of the product, the seller is subject to strict liability for a defective product, even if the revenue from sales of the product is not a significant portion of its business. The seller is generally strictly liable even if the seller was not responsible for the defect in any way and even when the product is not purchased directly from the seller. However, a retail seller or other distributor of a prescription drug or medical device is subject to liability for harm caused by the drug or device only if:

(i) At the time of sale or other distribution the drug or medical device contains a manufacturing defect; or

(ii) At or before the time of sale or other distribution of the drug or medical device the retail seller or other distributor fails to exercise reasonable care and such failure causes harm to persons.

d. Seller of a component part

The commercial supplier of a component, such as sand used in manufacturing cement or a switch used in an electrical device, is subject to liability if the component itself is defective, but not when the component is incorporated into a product that is defective for another reason. However, the commercial supplier of a component may be liable if that supplier substantially participates in the process of integrating the component into the design of the assembled product and that product is defective due to the integration.

e. Indemnification

Ordinarily, if the plaintiff recovers from the retailer solely for a product defect that existed at the time the product left the manufacturer's control, the retailer can recover from the manufacturer in an indemnification action.

f. Lessor

Generally, a lessor of a commercial product (e.g., car, boat, tools) is subject to strict liability for a defective product.

g. Products and services

A product is tangible personal property distributed commercially for use or consumption. A service is not a product. A seller that provides both products and services generally is **liable if the defective product is consumed**, such as food at a restaurant, but not if the product is only used, such as the vendor of a balloon ride when the balloon itself is defective. Hospitals and doctors generally are treated as providing a service, rather than a product, in cases in which the defective product is used as a tool, loaned to the patient, or even implanted in the patient.

h. Exclusions

1) Casual seller

Because the seller must be in the business of selling similar products, a casual seller, such as an individual car owner who sells a car to his neighbor or an accountant who sells her office furniture to another businessperson, is **not subject to strict liability**.

2) Auctioneer

Similarly, an auctioneer of a product generally is not subject to strict liability with respect to the products auctioned.

5.   Damages

As with negligence claims, the plaintiff is entitled to recover damages for any personal injury or property damage. A claim for **purely economic loss generally is not allowed under a strict-liability theory** but must be brought as a breach-of-warranty action, as must a claim for harm to the product itself and any consequential damages arising therefrom.

6.   Defenses

a.   Comparative fault

In a comparative-fault jurisdiction, the plaintiff's own negligence reduces his recovery in a strict-products-liability action in the same manner as it is in a negligence action. For example, in a pure comparative-fault jurisdiction, the plaintiff's recovery is reduced by the percentage that the plaintiff's fault contributed to causing her injury.

b.   Contributory negligence

In a contributory-negligence jurisdiction, the plaintiff's negligence generally is not a defense to a strict-products-liability action when the plaintiff negligently failed to discover the defect or misused the product in a reasonably foreseeable way, but it generally is when the plaintiff's fault consisted of unreasonably proceeding in the face of a known product defect.

Note: Suppliers are required to anticipate reasonably foreseeable misuses of their products.

c.   Assumption of risk

Voluntary and knowing assumption of the risk is a complete bar to recovery in contributory-negligence jurisdictions and in a small number of the comparative-fault jurisdictions. In most comparative-fault jurisdictions, a plaintiff's assumption of a risk will reduce his recovery in proportion to degree of fault, but it will not be a complete bar to recovery. Assumption of the risk is a subjective standard. The plaintiff must be aware of the danger and knowingly expose himself to it.

d.   Product misuse, modification, or alteration by the user

The misuse, alteration, or modification of a product by the user in a manner that is neither intended by nor reasonably foreseeable to the manufacturer typically negates liability. On the other hand, foreseeable misuse, alteration, or modification usually does not preclude recovery.

A majority of comparative-fault jurisdictions treat product misuse as a form of fault that reduces, but does not eliminate, the plaintiff's recovery. A significant minority of comparative-fault jurisdictions, and most contributory-negligence jurisdictions, hold that product misuse totally bars recovery.

e. Substantial change in product

If the product substantially changes between the time it is distributed by the manufacturer and the time it reaches the consumer (e.g., a part is reconditioned), then this change may constitute a superseding cause that cuts off the liability of the original manufacturer.

f. Compliance with governmental standards

Most often, compliance with governmental safety standards is not conclusive evidence that the product is not defective. On the other hand, the jury can consider evidence introduced by the defendant that the product complied with governmental standards and also evidence offered by the plaintiff on the product's failure to comply with these standards in deciding whether the product is defective.

However, if a product complies with federal safety statutes or regulations, a state tort claim act may be "pre-empted" if (i) Congress has explicitly so indicated, (ii) Congress has comprehensively regulated the field (i.e., "field preemption"), or (iii) it would be impossible for the manufacturer to comply with both the federal regulation and the requirements of state tort law.

g. "State of the art"

In failure-to-warn and design-defect cases, the manufacturer may introduce as evidence the level of relevant scientific, technological, and safety knowledge existing and reasonably feasible at the time of the product's distribution. In most jurisdictions, compliance with this "state of the art" standard does not bar recovery against the manufacturer as a matter of law. However, many states have enacted statutes providing that compliance with the state-of-the-art standard is a total bar to recovery.

h. Statute of limitations issues

The statute of limitations begins to run against the plaintiff with a personal injury whenever he discovers, or in the exercise of reasonable care should discover, his injury and its connection to the product. As a result, the statute of limitations may not preclude an action against a manufacturer or other seller until many decades after the manufacture and distribution of the product. For example, asbestos-related diseases may not manifest themselves until decades after the distribution of the asbestos insulation and the plaintiff's exposure to it.

i. Contract disclaimers, limitations, and waivers

A **disclaimer** or limitation of remedies or other contractual exculpation (i.e., waiver) by a product seller or other distributor **does not generally bar** or reduce an otherwise valid products-liability claim for personal injury.

> **EXAM NOTE:** The immunity created by workers' compensation statutes protects only the plaintiff's employer from most tort claims brought by the victim. It does not provide any immunity for other defendants. Frequently, the plaintiff-employee is injured while working with a defective machine tool or with a toxic substance, such as asbestos insulation. Workers' compensation does not bar his claim against the manufacturer of these products.

C. WARRANTIES

Products-liability actions brought under warranty theories generally may be brought not only against a retailer of a product, but also against a manufacturer or distributor of goods, at least when damages are sought for personal injury or property damage.

1. **Implied Warranties**

   a. **Two types**

      1) **Merchantability**

         The implied warranty of merchantability warrants that the product being sold is **generally acceptable and reasonably fit for the ordinary purposes for which it is being sold**. The seller must be a merchant with respect to the kind of goods at issue.

      2) **Fitness for a particular purpose**

         The implied warranty of fitness warrants that a product is fit for a particular purpose, but only if the **seller knows the particular purpose** for which the product is being purchased and the buyer **relies on the seller's skill or judgment in supplying the product**.

   b. **Claims**

      Any product that fails to live up to either of the above warranties constitutes a breach of the defendant's warranty; the **plaintiff need not prove any fault** on the defendant's part.

      The plaintiff may recover damages for personal injury and property damage, as well as for **purely economic loss**.

      Alternative versions of the Uniform Commercial Code (UCC) provisions governing warranties provide differing versions of who can recover. For example, the most restrictive UCC provisions allow only the purchaser or a member of her family or household to recover, while a more inclusive variation essentially allows any foreseeable victim to recover.

2. **Express Warranties**

   An express warranty is a guarantee—an **affirmation of fact or a promise**—made by the seller regarding the product that is part of the **basis of a bargain**. A seller is liable for any breach of that warranty, regardless of fault. Damages for personal injury or property damage are recoverable.

3. **Defenses to Warranty Claims**

   a. **Disclaimers**

      Although the seller generally can disclaim warranties, in the case of **consumer goods, any limitation of consequential damages for personal injury is prima facie unconscionable**.

      In the case of express warranties, a disclaimer is valid only if it is consistent with the warranty, which it usually is not.

   b. **Tort defenses**

      1) **Assumption of the risk**

         Most jurisdictions hold that the plaintiff's unreasonable, voluntary encountering of a known product risk bars recovery.

      2) **Comparative fault**

         Most comparative-fault jurisdictions reduce recovery based on warranty claims in the same way they would strict-products-liability claims.

3) Contributory negligence

In contributory-negligence jurisdictions, most courts hold that contributory negligence does not bar a plaintiff's warranty claim, except when the contributory negligence consists of the unreasonable encountering of a known risk (i.e., the overlap between contributory negligence and assumption of the risk).

4) Product misuse in implied warranty claims

With or without using the language of "product misuse," most courts find that product misuse prevents recovery under the implied warranty of merchantability when the product is warranted to be fit for "ordinary purposes."

5) Failure to provide notice of breach

A warranty claim generally fails if the plaintiff fails to provide the seller with notice of the breach of warranty within the statutorily required time period (when applicable) or a reasonable period of time.

VII. DEFAMATION, INVASION OF PRIVACY, AND BUSINESS TORTS

A. DEFAMATION

A plaintiff may bring an action for defamation:

i) If the defendant's **defamatory language**;

ii) Is **of or concerning** the plaintiff;

iii) Is **published** to a third party who **understands** its defamatory nature; and

iv) **Damages** the plaintiff's reputation.

For **matters of public concern**, the plaintiff is constitutionally required to prove fault on the part of the defendant. If the plaintiff is either **a public official or a public figure**, then the plaintiff must prove actual malice**.**

1. Defamatory Language

Language that diminishes respect, esteem, or goodwill toward the plaintiff, or that deters others from associating with the plaintiff, is defamatory. The plaintiff may introduce extrinsic facts to establish defamation by innuendo.

An opinion is actionable if the defendant implies that there is a factual basis for that opinion. *See Milkovich v. Lorian Journal Co.*, 497 U.S. 1 (1990); *Gertz v. Welch, Inc.*, 418 U.S. 323 (1974).

2. "Of or Concerning" the Plaintiff

A reasonable person must believe that the defamatory communication refers to this particular plaintiff and holds him up to scorn or ridicule in the eyes of a substantial number of respectable members of the community.

If the defamatory language applies to a group, then a member of the group can maintain a defamation action only if the group is so small that the matter can reasonably be understood to refer to that member, unless there is other evidence that the language refers to that particular member.

Note: A deceased individual cannot be defamed. A corporation, partnership, or unincorporated association may be defamed if the language prejudices it in conducting its activities or deters others from dealing with it.

3. **Publication**

   a. **To a third party**

   Publication of defamatory matter is its intentional or negligent communication to a third party, i.e., to someone other than the person being defamed.

   > **Example:** If an employer confronts her employee in a face-to-face conversation during which no one else is present and no one can overhear the conversation and tells him that he is being fired because he embezzled company funds, then there is no publication and no defamation.

   > **EXAM NOTE:** Questions on defamation often center on the publication requirement. Remember that the statement must be **intentionally or negligently made to a third party**. Beware of fact patterns in which the publication requirement is not met, such as those involving a third party learning about the statement through no fault of the defendant's, or when no third party hears the statement at all.

   b. **Republication**

   A person who **repeats** a defamatory statement may be liable for defamation even though that person identifies the originator of the statement and expresses a lack of knowledge as to the truthfulness of the statement.

   c. **Internet service providers**

   A federal statute provides that internet service providers are not publishers for the purpose of defamation law.

4. **Constitutional Requirements**

   Since the Supreme Court's opinion in *New York Times v. Sullivan,* 376 U.S. 254 (1964), which held that the First Amendment affects the plaintiff's right to recover under the common-law tort of defamation, constitutional requirements now underlie many aspects of defamation law. These constitutional requirements affect fundamental aspects of defamation law in various ways depending on (i) the category into which the plaintiff fits and (ii) the nature of the defamatory communication.

   a. **Public official**

   A public official is someone in the hierarchy of government employees who has, or appears to have, **substantial responsibility for or control over the conduct of government affairs**. **Candidates for public office** are also treated as public officials.

   b. **Public figure**

   The constitutional requirements are the same when the plaintiff is a public figure as when she is a public official. There are two ways in which a plaintiff may be categorized as a public figure:

   - i) *General purpose public figures*—Plaintiffs who occupy positions of such **persuasive power and influence in society** that they are deemed public figures for all purposes; and

   - ii) *Limited purpose or special purpose public figures*—Plaintiffs **who thrust themselves to the forefront of particular public controversies** in order to influence the resolution of the issues involved. These plaintiffs are treated as public figures **if the defamatory statement relates to their**

participation in the controversy, but they are treated as private figures if the defamation relates to any other matter.

c. **Private individual**

1) **Matter of public concern**

If the plaintiff is a **private individual** (neither a public figure nor a public official) and the statement involves a matter of **public concern**, then the defendant is entitled to **limited constitutional protections**, though not as significant as those available when the person being defamed is either a public official or a public figure.

2) **Not a matter of public concern**

If the plaintiff is a **private individual** and the statement is **not a matter of public concern**, then there are **no constitutional restrictions** on the law of defamation. However, many states now apply the same principles of defamation law to all cases involving private individuals as plaintiffs.

5. **Falsity**

a. **Matters of public concern**

If either (i) the defamatory statement relates to a matter of public concern or (ii) the plaintiff is a public official or a public figure, then the plaintiff must prove that the **defamatory statement is false** as part of her prima facie case.

b. **Private individual plaintiff/not a matter of public concern**

At common law and in some states today, a private individual plaintiff suing for defamation regarding a statement that does not involve a matter of public concern is **not required to prove falsity** as part of her prima facie case. However, the defendant may prove the truth of the statement as an affirmative defense.

6. **Fault**

a. **Public official or public figure**

If the plaintiff in a defamation action is either a public official or a public figure, then the plaintiff is required to prove that the defendant acted with **actual malice;** that is, he either had **knowledge that the statement was false or acted with reckless disregard as to the truth or falsity of the statement.** To establish a reckless disregard for the truthfulness of a statement, the plaintiff must prove that the defendant entertained **serious doubts** about its truthfulness; mere failure to check facts is not sufficient. *New York Times Co. v. Sullivan*, 376 U.S. 254 (1964); *St. Amant v. Thompson*, 390 U.S. 727 (1968).

b. **Private individual/matter of public concern**

If the plaintiff in a defamation action is a private individual and the defendant's statement involves a matter of public concern, then the plaintiff is constitutionally required to prove that the **defendant acted with fault—either negligence or actual malice**. *Gertz v. Robert Welch, Inc.*, 418 U.S. 323 (1974). The level of fault will determine what damages may be recovered.

c. **Private individual/not a matter of public concern**

If the plaintiff in a defamation action is a private individual and the defendant's statement does not involve a matter of public concern, then the constitutional requirements do not apply. At common law, the defendant was strictly liable.

Most states today require **at least negligence** by the defendant for all defamation actions, and some now require actual malice in all defamation actions.

7. Libel and Slander Distinguished

a. Libel

Defamation by words **written, printed, or otherwise recorded** in permanent form is libel.

1) Television and radio

Today it is generally—though not universally—accepted that defamatory **radio and television broadcasts are libel,** regardless of whether they are spoken from a script.

2) Email and other electronic communication

Most courts addressing the issue have held that e-mail messages can be categorized as **libel**. It is not yet clear whether courts will hold that tweets and text messages are libel or slander.

3) General and presumed damages

Subject to the constitutionally imposed limits on damages recoverable in a defamation action, the libel plaintiff need only prove **general damages** in order to complete the prima facie tort of libel. General damages are any damages that **compensate the plaintiff for harm to her reputation**. Under the common law, the plaintiff was entitled to recover "presumed damages" as part of general damages. The plaintiff did not need to prove that she actually incurred any damages; her lawyer only needed to invite the jury to award the damages that they believed flowed from the defendant's defamatory communication.

4) Libel *per quod*

In some jurisdictions, under the doctrine of libel *per quod*, if the nature of the defamatory statement requires proof of extrinsic facts to show that the statement is defamatory, then the plaintiff must prove either special damages or that the statement fits into one of the four categories of statements that satisfy the requirements of slander per se.

b. Slander

Defamation by **spoken word, gesture, or any form other than libel** is slander. To recover for slander, the plaintiff must plead and prove one of the following.

1) Special damages

Special damages require the plaintiff to prove that a third party **heard** the defendant's defamatory comments and **acted adversely** to her. Most often, special damages involve an economic loss to the plaintiff, e.g., loss of employment or loss of business, but they also would include such things as the plaintiff's fiancé breaking off the engagement or a friend refusing to host the plaintiff in her home after hearing the defamatory comments.

2) Slander per se

Under the doctrine of slander per se, a plaintiff alleging slander need not plead and prove special damages if the statement defaming her fits into one of four categories.

To qualify as slander per se, the defamatory statement must accuse the plaintiff of one of the following.

i) *Committing a crime.* In many jurisdictions, the crime must be one involving moral turpitude or one that subjects the criminal to imprisonment.

ii) *Conduct reflecting poorly on the plaintiff's trade or profession.* Traditionally, accusing a navigator, teacher, or holy person of being a drunk satisfied this requirement, but the same accusation against a salesperson did not.

iii) *Having a loathsome disease.* Traditionally, loathsome diseases included illnesses such as leprosy or a sexually transmitted disease.

iv) *Sexual misconduct.* In modern times, examples of cases falling within this sub-category, as well as the previous one, are very rare. A few courts have held that trading sex for drugs constitutes sexual misconduct. Traditionally, this category applied when a person imputed unchaste behavior to a woman. This typically meant adultery. Under the equal protection requirements of the Fourteenth Amendment, a state would likely be required to give such protection to men, as well.

3) Parasitic damages

Once the plaintiff satisfies the requirements of the slander per se prima facie tort by proving either special damages or slander per se, at common law she could recover general damages as parasitic damages.

4) Constitutional constraints

Damages recoverable in a slander action, as well as damages recoverable in a libel action, are subject to the constitutional limitations discussed below.

8. Constitutional Limitations on Damages

If the plaintiff is a private figure and the matter is one of public concern, presumed and punitive damages may not be awarded if the plaintiff establishes the defendant's fault without proving actual malice. *Gertz v. Robert Welch Inc., supra.* However, if the plaintiff is a private figure and the matter is not one of public concern, presumed and punitive damages may be awarded even if the plaintiff establishes the defendant's fault without proving actual malice. *Dun & Bradstreet, Inc. v. Greenmoss Builders, Inc.*, 472 U.S. 749 (1985).

9. Defenses

a. Truth

Truth is an absolute defense to a claim of defamation.

> **Falsity as an element of a cause of action:** For a defamation action brought by a public official or figure, by a limited public figure, or by a private figure regarding a statement about a matter of public concern, the falsity of the statement is an element that the plaintiff must prove.
>
> **Common-law distinction:** The plaintiff need not prove fault or falsity for common-law defamation. Defamatory statements are presumed to be false, and the defendant must assert truth as a defense.

A truthful statement is not defamatory. A statement that contains slight inaccuracies may nevertheless be considered to be true and therefore not defamatory. A statement that a person has engaged in conduct that is substantially different from the conduct in which the person did in fact engage is not considered to be true, even if the person's actual conduct was equally or more morally reprehensible.

> **EXAM NOTE:** If a statement is true but seems like defamation, consider whether it constitutes intentional infliction of emotional distress or invasion of privacy.

b. Consent

Consent by the plaintiff is a defense, but as with other torts, a defendant cannot exceed the scope of the plaintiff's consent.

c. Absolute privileges

Statements made under the following circumstances are shielded by absolute privilege:

i) In the course of **judicial proceedings** by the participants to the proceeding (e.g., witnesses, parties, lawyers, judges);

ii) In the course of **legislative proceedings**;

iii) Between **spouses** concerning a third person; and

iv) **Required publications** by radio, television, or newspaper (e.g., statements by a political candidate that a station must carry and may not censor).

Statements made by participants in the course of judicial proceedings must be related to the proceedings in order to be privileged. A similar limitation applies to statements made by witnesses in a legislative proceeding. However, no such limitation exists for statements made by a legislator in a legislative proceeding.

d. Qualified (conditional) privilege

Statements made under the following circumstances are subject to a conditional privilege:

i) In the **interest of the publisher** (defendant), such as defending his reputation;

ii) In the **interest of the recipient of the statement** or a third party; or

iii) Affecting an important **public interest**.

Qualified privileges most often occur in the contexts of employment references, credit reports, and charges and accusations within professional societies and among members of religious and charitable organizations.

1) Abuse of privilege

A qualified privilege may be lost if it is abused. Generally, a privilege is abused by making statements outside the scope of the privilege or by acting **with malice**. Traditionally, the malice required was **express** malice—hatred, ill will, or spite. Today, most jurisdictions hold that **actual malice**, i.e., knowledge that a statement is false or acting with a reckless disregard as to the truth or falsity of the statement, will defeat a qualified privilege.

2) Burden of proof

The burden is on the defendant to prove that a privilege, whether absolute or qualified, exists. It is, therefore, an **affirmative defense**. The burden is then on the plaintiff to prove that the privilege has been abused and therefore lost.

B.   INVASION OF PRIVACY

The right of privacy **does not extend to corporations**, only to individuals. Additionally, because the right of privacy is a personal right, in most instances, this right terminates upon the death of the plaintiff and does not extend to family members.

Invasion of privacy is not a single tort but includes four separate causes of action.

MNEMONIC: I FLAP (Intrusion, **F**alse **L**ight, **A**ppropriation, **P**rivate facts**)**

1.   Misappropriation of the Right to Publicity

A majority of states recognize an action for the misappropriation of the right to publicity, which is based on the right of an individual to control the commercial use of his identity. The plaintiff must prove:

   i) *The defendant's unauthorized appropriation of the plaintiff's name, likeness, or identity* (Most often commercial appropriation cases involve the use of the plaintiff's name or picture, but this is not required. A television or radio production might mimic the plaintiff's distinctive vocal patterns. Also, an action may be maintained when the defendant uses other items closely associated with the plaintiff, such as a specially designed car with unique markings associated with a racecar driver.)

   ii) For the **defendant's advantage**, commercial or otherwise;

   iii) **Lack of consent**; and

   iv) Resulting **injury**.

The states are split as to whether this right survives the death of the individual, with some states treating it as a property right that can be devised and inherited.

2.   Intrusion Upon Seclusion

Many states recognize an action for unreasonable intrusion upon the plaintiff's private affairs (also referred to as intrusion upon seclusion). The defendant's act of **intruding,** physically or otherwise, into the plaintiff's private affairs, solitude, or seclusion, if the intrusion is **highly offensive to a reasonable person** establishes liability. Eavesdropping on private conversations by electronic devices is considered an unreasonable intrusion. Photographing a person in a public place generally is not, unless the photograph is taken in a manner that reveals information about the person that the person expects to keep private even in a public place.

Note: Unlike the other forms of invasion of privacy, no publication is required to establish liability.

3.   Placing the Plaintiff in a False Light

A minority of jurisdictions recognize a separate tort of false light. The plaintiff must prove that the defendant (i) **made public** facts about the plaintiff that (ii) placed the plaintiff in a **false light,** (iii) which false light would be **highly offensive to a reasonable person**.

Attributing to the plaintiff **views** that he does not hold or **actions** that he did not take may constitute placing him in a false light. Similarly, falsely asserting that the plaintiff was a victim of a crime or once lived in poverty may be sufficient for the false light tort.

Most jurisdictions require that the plaintiff prove **actual malice** by the defendant. As considered in the discussion of defamation, this may be constitutionally required in many instances.

4. **Public Disclosure of Private Facts About a Plaintiff**

   a. **Elements**

   In order to recover, the plaintiff must show that:

   i) The defendant **gave publicity to a matter concerning the private life** of another; and

   ii) The matter publicized is of a kind that:

   a) Would be **highly offensive** to a reasonable person; and

   b) Is not of **legitimate concern** to the public.

   b. **Publicity**

   The requirement of publicity in the public disclosure tort requires far broader dissemination of the information than is required under the "publication" requirement of defamation. The information must be communicated at large or to so many people that it is substantially certain to become one of public knowledge.

   c. **Disfavored tort**

   Because the public disclosure tort involves the dissemination of true facts, it clearly is in tension with the First Amendment's freedoms of speech and press. Accordingly, the tort is disfavored in the modern era.

   d. **Disclosure of dated material**

   Today, most courts hold that the public disclosure of even dated material—for example, a criminal conviction from decades ago—is a matter of public interest and therefore does not create liability.

5. **Damages**

   The plaintiff need not prove special damages for any of the invasion of privacy torts. Emotional distress and mental distress are sufficient.

6. **Defenses**

   a. **Defamation defenses**

   The defenses of absolute and qualified privileges applicable in defamation actions also apply to privacy actions brought on "false light" or "public disclosure of private facts" grounds. These defenses are not applicable if the defendant was intrusive.

   b. **Consent**

   Consent is a defense to invasion of privacy actions. A defendant's mistake as to consent negates this defense, no matter how reasonable the mistake.

   > **EXAM NOTE:** Remember that truth is not a defense to invasion of privacy, whereas it is a complete defense to defamation.

C. INTENTIONAL MISREPRESENTATION

A prima facie case of intentional misrepresentation is established by proof of the following six elements.

1. Defendant's False Representation

The misrepresentation must be of **a material fact**. Usually the defendant actively misrepresents the facts, such as through deceptive or misleading statements or pictures. Sometimes the misrepresentation occurs through the active concealment of a material fact, such as when the seller of a house places paneling over the basement walls in order to conceal that the foundation is in terrible condition.

There generally is no duty to disclose a material fact or opinion to the other party. However, there may be an affirmative duty to disclose a fact when the other party is:

   i)   In a fiduciary relationship with the defendant;

   ii) Likely to be misled by statements previously made by the defendant ("partial disclosure"); or

   iii) (In a minority of jurisdictions) About to enter into a transaction under a mistake as to what the basic facts of the transaction are, the defendant is aware of this, and the customs of the trade or other objective circumstances suggest that the other party would expect the defendant to disclose these facts.

2. Scienter

The defendant must have **known** the representation to be false or must have acted with reckless disregard as to its truthfulness.

3. Intent

The defendant must have intended to induce the plaintiff to act (or refrain from acting) in reliance on the misrepresentation.

4. Causation

The misrepresentation must have caused the plaintiff to act or to refrain from acting. That is, the plaintiff must have actually relied on the misrepresentation.

5. Justifiable Reliance

The **plaintiff's reliance must have been justifiable**. Reliance is not justifiable if the facts are obviously false or if the defendant is stating a lay opinion. However, the plaintiff is under no duty to investigate the truth or falsity of the statement.

6. Damages

The plaintiff **must prove actual damages** to recover; nominal damages are not awarded. Consequential damages may also be awarded.

In a majority of jurisdictions, the measure of recovery in misrepresentation cases is the "benefit of the bargain" rule (the difference between the actual value received in the transaction and the value that would have been received if the misrepresentation were true).

The Second Restatement and a handful of states allow the plaintiff to choose between the benefit of the bargain and the out-of-pocket losses measures of damages.

A small minority of states limit the plaintiff's recovery to his out-of-pocket losses (similar to the typical tort law measure of recovery).

In all jurisdictions, the plaintiff is not permitted to recover damages for emotional distress.

D. NEGLIGENT MISREPRESENTATION

1. Elements and Scope

Under the law of a majority of jurisdictions, as well as that outlined in the Second Restatement:

i) The defendant, usually an accounting firm or another supplier of commercial information, who

ii) Provides false information (the "misrepresentation") to the plaintiff as a result of the defendant's negligence in preparation of the information,

iii) Is liable to the plaintiff for pecuniary damages caused by the plaintiff's justifiable reliance on the information, provided that

iv) The plaintiff is either in a contractual relationship with the defendant or is a third party known by the defendant to be a member of the limited group for whose benefit the information is supplied, and

v) The information must be relied upon in a transaction that the supplier of the information intends to influence or knows that the recipient of the information intends to influence.

Under this rule, the accountant who regularly conducts audits and furnishes financial statements and opinions routinely required by lenders, investors, purchasers, or others is not liable unless she is informed that an identified third party or third parties will be using the statement for a particular purpose.

Note: This tort generally is confined to commercial transactions; the defendant is not liable to the public in general, but only to the particular plaintiffs to whom the representation was made or to those the defendant knew would rely on it. In addition, the defendant is liable only if the plaintiff uses the information for its intended purpose or a substantially similar one.

2. Defenses

Unlike in intentional misrepresentation, in negligent misrepresentation, negligence defenses (e.g., contributory negligence or comparative fault) can be raised.

3. Damages

The plaintiff can recover reliance (out-of-pocket) damages, as well as consequential damages, if negligent misrepresentation is proven with sufficient certainty.

4. Distinguished From Ordinary Negligence

The ordinary rules of negligence apply when physical harm is a foreseeable result of a negligent misrepresentation.

Example: A defendant air traffic controller is liable for ordinary negligence when he negligently gives the pilot of an airplane incorrect information about the plane's location and speed and, as a result, the passenger-parachutist jumps to his death in Lake Erie instead of at the target airfield.

E. INTENTIONAL INTERFERENCE WITH BUSINESS RELATIONS

1. Intentional Interference With a Contract

a. Elements

To establish a prima facie case for intentional interference with a contract, the plaintiff must prove that the defendant:

i) **Knew** of a **contractual relationship** between the plaintiff and a third party;

ii) **Intentionally interfered** with the contract, **resulting in a breach**; and

iii) The breach caused **damages** to the plaintiff.

b. Nature of contractual relationship

In the majority of states, the contract in question **must be valid and not terminable at will**. However, a minority of states will allow the cause of action to be brought for interference with a contract that is terminable at will.

A contract that is voidable by one of the parties to the contract, such as due to a violation of the Statute of Frauds, may be the subject of tortious interference unless the party elects to void the contract.

c. Interference with performance other than inducing breach

The defendant may be liable whenever he prevents a party from fulfilling its contractual obligations or adds to the burden of a party's performance, even if the defendant does not induce the party to breach its contractual obligation. To be considered tortious, a defendant's actions must **substantially exceed** fair competition and free expression, such as persuading a bank not to lend money to a competitor.

d. Justification

A defendant's interference usually will be found to be justified if it is not motivated by an improper purpose. Some courts require the plaintiff to prove that the breach was induced by an improper purpose. Considerations of health, safety, morals, or ending poor labor conditions are proper purposes. For example, a defendant who tries to convince a U.S. clothing store to stop buying fabrics from a foreign textile manufacturer known for its inhumane labor conditions will not be liable for interference with a contract.

A defendant might claim that the interference is within the privilege of fair competition. If the contract is terminable at will, the defendant's attempt to induce a third party to breach its contract with the plaintiff can be justified if the defendant is a business competitor of the plaintiff who is in an existing contractual relationship with the third party.

2. Interference With Prospective Economic Advantage

A defendant may be liable for interfering with a plaintiff's expectation of economic benefit from third parties even in the absence of an existing contract.

When there is no valid contract in place between the plaintiff and the third party, courts require more egregious conduct on the part of the defendant in order to hold him liable. A defendant who is the business competitor of the plaintiff will not be held liable for encouraging the third party to switch his business to the defendant.

Some jurisdictions require that the defendant's conduct, in order to be actionable, must be either "independently tortious" (e.g., consist of fraud or assault) or violate provisions of federal or state law. Other jurisdictions and the Second Restatement engage in a more open-ended balancing process to decide whether the defendant's conduct is improper.

3. Theft of Trade Secrets

The plaintiff must own a valid trade secret (i.e., information that provides a business advantage) that is not generally known. The owner of the secret must take reasonable precautions to protect the secret, and the defendant must have taken the secret by improper means.

F. INJURIOUS FALSEHOODS

1. Trade Libel

Trade libel imposes tort liability for **statements injurious to a plaintiff's business or products**. Unlike defamation, it is not intended to compensate for harm to the personal reputation of the owner/manager of the business. Proof of special damages is required. Damages for mental suffering are not available. The plaintiff must prove:

i) Publication;

ii) Of a derogatory statement;

iii) Relating to the plaintiff's title to his business property, the quality of his business, or the quality of its products; and

iv) Interference or damage to business relationships.

2. Slander of Title

Similar to trade libel, slander of title protects against false statements that harm or call into question the plaintiff's ownership of real property. The plaintiff must prove:

i) Publication;

ii) Of a false statement;

iii) Derogatory to the plaintiff's title;

iv) With malice;

v) Causing special damages;

vi) As a result of diminished value in the eyes of third parties.

G. WRONGFUL USE OF THE LEGAL SYSTEM

1. Malicious Prosecution

A person is liable for malicious prosecution when:

i) She **intentionally and maliciously** institutes or pursues, or causes to be instituted or pursued;

ii) For an **improper purpose**;

iii) A legal action that is brought **without probable cause**; and

iv) That **action is dismissed** in favor of the person against whom it was brought.

Most jurisdictions have extended malicious prosecution to include civil cases as well as criminal actions. The civil action is sometimes known as wrongful institution of civil proceedings.

The plaintiff may recover for any damage proximately caused by the malicious prosecution, including legal expenses, lost work time, loss of reputation, and emotional distress.

Note that judges and prosecutors enjoy **absolute immunity** from liability for malicious prosecution.

2. **Abuse of Process**

Abuse of process is the misuse of the power of the court. To recover for abuse of process, the plaintiff must prove:

i)   A legal procedure set in motion in proper form;

ii) That is "perverted" to accomplish an ulterior motive;

iii) A willful act perpetrated in the use of process that is not proper in the regular conduct of the proceeding;

iv) Causing the plaintiff to sustain damages.

For abuse of process, unlike malicious prosecution, the existence of probable cause—and even whether the defendant ultimately prevails on the merits—is **not** determinative in precluding liability. Rather, **the essence of the tort is using the legal process for an ulterior motive, such as extorting payment or recovering property**.

Example: A local school board of education sued a teacher's union and subpoenaed 87 teachers for a hearing in order to prevent the teachers from walking a picket line during a labor dispute between the union and the board of education.

Note that abuse of process, like malicious prosecution, does not require ill will or spite, but it does require proof of damages.

Themis
BarReview

LSE Key Concepts: TORTS

WHAT IS A TORT?
Non-contractual civil wrong; typical remedy damages

INTENTIONAL TORTS GENERALLY
1. *Voluntary Act*: Defendant's state of mind directed physical movement
2. *Intent*: Act w/ purpose or knowing consequence substantially certain to result
3. *Causation*: Conduct was substantial factor in creating harm
❖ Vosburg v. Putney *(Child kicked another child; voluntary act intending to make contact resulting in serious harm; children or mentally incompetent can be liable w/requisite intent)*

BATTERY
Harmful/offensive contact w/ another

- *Harmful*: Contact that causes injury, pain
- *Offensive*: Person of ordinary sensibilities would find objectively offensive (exception: known sensitivity)
- *Contact*: Anything connected to person; awareness not required (e.g., unconscious patient)
❖ Garret v. Dailey *(Child pulled chair out; contact w/ the ground suffices)*
- *Intent* to cause contact (or substantial certainty of contact)
  o Intent relates to the CONTACT
Damages: Whatever the victim suffers, even if Eggshell Plaintiff (*Vosburg*)

ASSAULT
Voluntary act causing reasonable apprehension of imminent harmful or offensive contact

- *Intent*: Act w/ intent to cause apprehension or the contact itself
- *Harm*: Concern of contact must be objectively reasonable; awareness required; need not involve fear
- *Imminent*: Future harm not enough; words and circumstances may suffice

TRANSFERRED INTENT
Intent to commit intentional tort transfers across people and across torts

- Types: Person to person; Tort to tort; Tort and person
- Does NOT apply to IIED (tort to tort)
- Purpose: morality, deterrence

FALSE IMPRISONMENT
Act w/ intent to confine/restrain another within fixed boundaries, resulting in confinement such that plaintiff is conscious of or harmed by the confinement

- *Confined/restrained*
  o Freedom of movement limited in all directions
  o Does not need to be small or stationary
  o No reasonable means of escape
  o Examples: physical barriers, force, threat of force, invalid invocation of authority, duress, coercion, refusal to set free (failure to provide safe means of escape)
- *Intent*
  o Purpose of confining
  o Knowing confinement substantially certain to result
  o Negligence does not suffice for intentional tort
- *Knowledge of Confinement*
  o Plaintiff must be aware OR suffer actual harm
  o Do not need to be conscious if harmed by confinement
Shopkeeper's privilege in some jurisdictions (detain shoplifter for reasonable time/manner)
❖ Coblyn v. Kennedy's *(reasonableness measured against an objective standards)*

INTENTIONAL INFLICTION OF EMOTIONAL DISTRESS
Defendant is liable for **IIED** when (1) acting intentionally or recklessly, (2) w/ extreme or outrageous conduct, and (3) causing severe emotional pain.

Extreme/outrageous conduct (Must exceed limits of human decency so as to be intolerable to society)
❖ Wilkinson v. Downton *(Joking/lying about husband dying in car wreck was extreme/outrageous)*
❖ Trentadue v. US *(Prison mistreated prisoner corpse to extreme/outrageous degree)*
- Look for power differential, plaintiff as member of group w/ special sensitivity
- Emotional pain (objective standard: beyond what reasonable person would endure)
- Hyper-sensitive plaintiff (beyond reasonable person standard, unless defendant knew about sensitivity)

TRESPASS TO LAND
Intentionally causing the physical invasion of another's land

- *Physical invasion*
  - Entering land without permission
  - Refusing to leave after entering w/ permission
  - Causing something else to invade (flood, rocks)
- *Intent*
  - Intent is only to enter the land; need not intend the trespass to be wrongful
  - Awareness not required; mistake of fact is no defense
- ❖ Public Service Co. of Colorado v. Van Wyk *(Above-ground power lines causing noise/radiation on land was intangible and not physical invasion)*
- **Damages** (Proof of damages not required)

PRIVATE NUISANCE

Substantial and unreasonable interference w/ enjoyment of one's land

- *Substantial:* Objectively offensive, inconvenient, annoying to normal, reasonable person.
- *Unreasonable:* When the injury outweighs usefulness of the conduct (cost-benefit analysis)
- ❖ Pestey v. Cushman *(Smelly dairy farm; court held unpleasant odors from sewage is unreasonable)*
- Defenses
  - Regulation compliance not a defense
  - Coming to the nuisance is only a factor

	Trespass	Nuisance
What's protected?	Right to exclude	Use & enjoyment
If no physical intrusion?	Likely not trespass	May be nuisance

---

PUBLIC NUISANCE

Unreasonable interference w/ a right common to the general public

- Private Citizen Claim: Only private citizens that have suffered an injury different in kind from the general public has standing
- State Claim: Govt. brings suit on behalf of public, acting as guardian of public rights under parens patriae

Remedies:
- Typical remedy: Injunction (abate the nuisance)
- Damages (continue, but pay damages)
- Continuing nuisance: Permanent damages (past and future)

TRESPASS TO CHATTELS AND CONVERSION

Trespass to Chattels: Intentional interference w/ plaintiff's right to tangible personal property by dispossessing OR using/intermeddling w/ plaintiff's use of the chattel

- *Intent*
  - Need only intend the interfering act
  - Mistake of law not a defense
- *Damages*
  - Dispossession: Actual damages and loss of use
  - Use or intermeddling: Actual damages only (diminution in value/cost of repair)

Conversion: Intentional act that deprives plaintiff of use, or interferes enough to effectively deprive plaintiff of the use

- Intent
  - Only requires intent to commit the act
  - Mistake of law or fact no defense
  - Accidentally depriving after permissive use NOT conversion
- **Damages** (Full value of chattel at time of conversion)

	Trespass to Chattels	Conversion
Severity	less serious	more serious
Duration	shorter	longer
Intent	Just messing	Claiming right
Other factors	good faith, more convenient, less harm	greater harm, more expense, less convenient

---

SELF DEFENSE AND DEFENSE OF PROPERTY

Self-Defense (Force must be reasonably proportionate to threatened harm; reasonable mistake does not invalidate; no duty to retreat in majority of states, but depends on state law)

❖ Courvoisier v. Raymond *(Cop w/ reasonable belief victim had a gun could act w/ reasonably proportionate force)*

- Deadly Force: Only w/ reasonable belief defendant is threatened w/ deadly force or serious bodily injury
- Initial aggressor: Generally cannot claim self-defense
- Liable for deliberately/negligently injured bystanders

Defense of Others (Same requirements, and must reasonably believe the defended party could legally use self-defense)

Defense of Property (Must reasonably believe necessary to prevent tortious harm; must be reasonable

- No deadly force, including traps (*Bird* and *Katko*)
- Permitted to prevent/end intrusion on land unless visitor claims necessity; or recapture wrongfully taken chattels
- Not permitted to regain possession of land (modern rule)

Consent And Other Defenses

Express consent: Words or actions show willingness to submit to conduct

	Is consent invalidated?
Mistake?	No, unless defendant caused or took advantage of mistake
Fraud?	Yes, if induced by material fraud
Duress?	Yes (but not if duress is just economic)

Implied consent: Silence where reasonable person would object, or contact is expected and ordinary; includes emergencies and sports (except for reckless disregard)

Parental Discipline (permits reasonable force or confinement)

Privilege of Arrest

- **Private Citizen:** Only for felonies actually committed; reasonable mistake of identity of felon permitted
- **Officer:** Reasonable mistakes of identity and/or whether felony was actually committed are allowed
- **Misdemeanors:** For private citizens, must breach the peace

Necessity

Defense to trespass to land/chattels committed to prevent substantially more serious injury

- **Public:** To protect many from **public calamity**; no damages owed
- **Private:** To safe own life/property; actual damages owed for harm caused by trespass
- ❖ Ploof v. Putnam *(Dock owner releases trespassing boat into a storm; crew and boat injured; boat owner claims private necessity as defense to trespass)*
- ❖ Vincent v. Lake Erie Transportation Co. *(Trespassing boat damages dock while tied in a storm; boat owner owed damages to dock owner for the damaged dock, even though necessity allowed the boat to trespass)*

Negligence

Negligence (Failure to exercise reasonable care, in **breach** of a **duty, causing damages**)
- ❖ Donoghue v. Stevenson *(Dead snail in bottle)*

Negligence — Duty

General rule (3rd Restatement): Defendant owes foreseeable plaintiffs a duty to exercise reasonable care in conduct that risks physical harm; generally no duty to act

- ❖ Palsgraf v. Long Island Railroad *(Fireworks dropped on a railroad indirectly leads to a bystander's injuries)*
- **Cardozo/Majority:** Duty only to plaintiffs in zone of foreseeable harm
- **Andrews/Minority:** Duty owed to everyone harmed
- Defendant owes duty to rescuers
- ❖ Wagner v. International Ry *("Danger invites rescue")*
- **Firefighter's Rule:** Emergency personal cannot recover damages for injuries from risks inherent to the job
- ❖ Strauss v. Belle Realty *(Tenant falls in common area of building during power outage; could not sue utility company due to lack of privity w/ the company in the area where injured)*

Failure To Act And Affirmative Duty To Act

No affirmative duty to help others (*Yania v. Bigan*) unless:

- **Risk Creation:** Placing others in peril creates a duty to prevent further harm
- ❖ Montgomery v. National Convoy *(Drivers on snowy road)*
- **Special Undertaking:** Rescuers must act w/ reasonable care
- ❖ Farwell v. Keaton *(Incomplete/unreasonable first aid)*
- **By Authority:** Parties w/ control over another (e.g., parent-child, employer-employee)
- **Special Relationships** (e.g., common carrier–passenger, innkeeper-guest)
- ❖ Farwell v. Keaton *(Friendship might create duty)*
- ❖ Tarasoff v. Regents of Univ. of Cal. *(Therapist may have duty to prevent harm to third parties)*

Duty — Standard Of Care: Part 1

Reasonably prudent person standard (By default, defendant must act as a reasonably prudent person under the circumstances; objective standard)
- ❖ Vaughn v. Menlove *(burning haystack damages neighbor's property; objective standard of care not met)*

	Trait modifies the standard of care?
Physical?	YES (same/similar condition)
Mental/Emotional?	NO
Special Knowledge/Skill?	YES (higher standard)
Children?	Below certain age: N/A Usually YES ("Similar age, intelligence, and experience") NO for adult activities
Intoxication?	NO (unless involuntary)
Emergencies?	YES (same situation)

Duty – Standard Of Care: Part 2

Common Carriers and Innkeepers
- *Common Law:* Utmost care
- *Modern Rule:* Common carriers = utmost care; no higher standard for innkeepers
- *3rd Restatement* (e.g., *Bethel v. NYC Transit Authority*): Being an innkeeper or common carrier is just another circumstance to consider in determining "reasonable care"

Owners and Occupiers of Land
- Traditional (Tripartite) Approach:
  - *Invitees:* Inspect for and remedy dangers
  - *Licensees:* Correct or warn of dangers
  - *Trespassers:* No misconduct; warn if discovered
- Modern Approach: Status of land entrant just another circumstance to consider
  - CA dropped all categories, but most states just abolished invitee/licensee distinction
  - 3rd Restatement (minority): No duty to flagrant trespassers

Attractive Nuisance: Duty owed to trespassing children who are attracted to a dangerous artificial condition

Negligence – Breach

Breach (Defendant fails to exercise standard of care owed to plaintiff)
- **Traditional:** Reasonably Prudent Person
- **Economists:** Hand Formula (*Carroll Towing*)
  - Weigh the burden of precaution (B) against probability (P) and cost of loss (L); $B vs. P x $L
- ❖ Adams v. Bullock (*Child electrocuted by streetcar live wire in unforeseeable accident*)

Shortcuts For Defining Breach

Custom (Majority practice within an industry)
- Usually relevant but not dispositive
- ❖ The TJ Hooper (*Boat in a storm had no radios; whether boats customarily have radios was relevant, but not dispositive, to whether there was a breach*)
- **Professionals:** Custom defines negligence
Statutes (Unexcused statutory violation is
Negligence Per Se (*Martin v. Herzog*))
- **Excuse:** Compelling reason not to follow statute
- ❖ Tedla v. Ellman (*Pedestrians on wrong side of road*)
- Statutory purpose must be relevant to breach
- ❖ Gorris v. Scott (*Unrestrained sheep on ship fall overboard; statute requiring sheep to be kept in pens to prevent diseases is not grounds for negligence per se*)

Circumstantial Evidence And Res Ipsa Loquitur

- **Circumstantial Evidence:** Indirectly relates to establishing breach
- **Res Ipsa Loquitur:** "The thing speaks for itself"
  - **Elements:** (1) Accident ordinarily does not occur without negligence; (2) cause was within exclusive control of defendant; and (3) not plaintiff's fault
  - **3rd Restatement:** "Does this type of accident usually happen due to the negligence of someone in Defendant's position?"
- ❖ Byrne v. Boadle (*Barrel of flour falls from flour shop window and hits plaintiff*)
- ❖ Ybarra v. Spangard (*Surgical team sued for plaintiff's unexplained pain post-surgery*)

Causation – Cause In Fact: Part 1

Cause in Fact (actual causation)
- **But-For Test:** Injury would not have occurred "but for" defendant's negligence (shown by preponderance of the evidence)
- **Substantial Factor:** Defendant's negligence was a substantial factor in causing plaintiff's harm

Causation – Cause In Fact: Part 2

Multiple Tortfeasors, Indivisible Injury (Each tortfeasor's conduct was sufficient to cause a single, indivisible harm)
- All are jointly and severally liable
Alternative Causation (Multiple parties acted negligently, but only one actually caused the harm)
- All are liable unless they show that they did not cause the injury (i.e., burden shifts to defendants)
- ❖ Summers v. Tice (*Two hunters negligently fire in plaintiff's direction; hunters each must prove that their own shot did not injure plaintiff*)
Market Share Liability
- ❖ Sindell v. Abbott Labs (*Liability allotted based on manufacturer's market share of the defective product*)
Loss of Chance (Negligent misdiagnosis of plaintiff who had <50% chance of survival further reduces the chance of survival)
- Applies where but-for causation cannot be shows due to pre-existing low chance of survival

Causation – Proximate Cause: Part 1

- **Proximate Cause** (legal cause): Does the harm caused fall within the scope of liability for defendant's negligent conduct?
- ❖ Ryan v. NY Central RR (*Fire caused by train engine in a shed that spread to neighboring buildings was too*

remote to be the proximate cause of damage to plaintiff's property)
- **Eggshell Plaintiff Rule**: Defendant is liable for full extent of damages, even if the extent is not foreseeable
- ❖ Vosburg v.Putney (Child suffers unforeseeably severe injuries from minor kick to the leg)

CAUSATION – PROXIMATE CAUSE: PART 2
- **Foreseeability:** Type of harm must be within the scope of liability
- ❖ Berry v. Sugar Notch (Tree branch falls on speeding trolley; speeding was a cause-in-fact of the damage, but not the proximate cause)
- ❖ In Re Polemis (Knocking over a board creates a spark that ignites an explosive substance, triggering the total destruction of the ship; proximate cause exists)
- ❖ Wagon Mound (Ship pours oil into a harbor; the oil unforeseeably ignites and burns a dock; no proximate cause because fire damage was unforeseeable)

	Intervening Cause	Superseding Cause
Is D still liable?	Yes	No
Chain of causation?	Not broken	Broken
Type of harm?	Foreseeable	Unforeseeable

- ❖ Atherton v. Devine (Second accident in the ambulance on the way to the hospital was within the scope of defendant's liability because it is an intervening cause)
- ❖ Bigbee v. Pacific Telephone (Car crashing into a phone booth was not within the scope of the phone company's liability for the placement of the booth)

DAMAGES – COMPENSATORY DAMAGES
- **Compensatory damages:** For actual harm and expenses; must prove actual damage
- Failure to **mitigate** damages may reduce recovery
- **Personal injury damages** include medical expenses, lost income, and pain and suffering (single-recovery rule applies)
- **Property damages** can be calculated as difference in FMV, cost of repairs, or replacement value.
- Collateral Source Rule:
  - **Traditional:** Payments from outside sources (e.g., insurance) do not reduce liability
  - **Modern trend:** Rule eliminated or altered
- **Tax Consequences**: Compensatory damages not taxed

- Percentage may go to a contingency fee; courts generally prohibited from instructing juries to account for these fees

DAMAGES – PUNITIVE DAMAGES
- **Punitive damages:** To punish and deter conduct when defendant acts willfully, wantonly, recklessly, or w/ malice
  - At common law, must "shock the conscience"
- Three Due Process limitations (14th Amendment):
  - Must be in line w/ **reprehensibility** of conduct
  - Comparable to **criminal fines** for same conduct
  - **Single-digit ratio** (punitive vs. compensatory damages)

DAMAGES – LIMITATIONS
- Nominal damages not permitted for negligence
- **Pure economic harm:** Negligently inflicted economic harm absent either physical injury or property damage
- ❖ 532 Madison (Store lost income while road was closed due to defendant's negligence; defendant not liable)
- ❖ Deepwater Horizon Disaster (Victim compensation fund for victims of oil spill allowed for pure economic harm)
- **Plaintiff** can recover for **NIED** by showing:
  - Risk of physical injury
  - Within zone of danger
  - Emotional distress resulting in bodily harm
- **Bystander** recovery for **NIED** under **Dillon Rule** if:
  - Closely related to victim
  - **Present** at scene
  - Personally observed the accident

NEGLIGENCE – CLAIMS

	Survival Action	Wrongful Death
Brought by decedent's:	Personal representative	Spouse, next of kin, or personal representative
On behalf of:	Decedent/Plaintiff	Themselves
Possible damages include:	Medical costs Pain and suffering Lost income	Lost economic support Companionship and society

Loss of Consortium: Recovery after wrongful death/injury of a spouse for loss of companionship, services, and/or emotional support, etc.
- Loss of child: Parent might recover; more likely for wrongful death than injury
- Loss of parent: Child can recover for lost companionship in wrongful death

Negligent Failure To Perform Contraceptive Procedure (or to diagnose congenital defect):
- If brought by **child**, called **wrongful life**; <u>not recognized</u> in most states
- If brought by **parent**, called **wrongful birth**; <u>permitted</u> in many states to recover medical expenses and/or pain and suffering

VICARIOUS LIABILITY

Defendant liable for another's negligence
- **Respondeat Superior:** Employers are vicariously liable for employees' torts occurring w/in scope of employment; plaintiff can recover from employee or employer
  - **Scope of Employment:** (1) Acts employed to perform, (2) Activities that profit/benefit employer, or (3) Acts intrinsic to the employment relationship

	Detour	Frolic
Scope of Employment?	Yes	No
Employer liable?	Yes	No

  - Employer can also be independently negligent (negligent hiring)
  - **Apparent Agency doctrine:** Independent contractors (IC) will be treated as an employee (EE) when:
    - Victim reasonably believed IC was an EE;
    - Based on manifestations from employer; and
    - IC's negligence caused harm to victim
- Vicarious liability may also apply to other situations (business partners, car owners, and parents/children).

ALLOCATION OF LIABILITY

- **Joint and Several Liability:** Each tortfeasor liable for a single indivisible harm is liable for the whole harm
  - Plaintiff can collect from any defendant
  - No double recovery
  - **Contribution:** Tortfeasor who paid more than their fair share can collect from the others
- **Pure Several Liability:** Each tortfeasor is liable only for his independent proportionate share of plaintiff's damages
- **Modified Joint and Several Liability:** Joint liability only applies when tortfeasor's share of fault is above some proportion (determined by statute)
- Fault allocated evenly at common law; now juries decide.
- **Indemnification:** Shift loss from one party to another

IMMUNITIES

No duty owed; no recovery for damages

- **Sovereign Immunity:** Generally applies to actions against state and federal govt. agencies
- **Federal Tort Claims Act:** Waives sovereign immunity, but not for (1) some intentional torts, (2) discretionary functions, (3) contractors conforming to govt. specifications, and (4) traditional govt. activities.
- **States:** Tort Claims Acts are common, but vary greatly
- **Municipalities:** Immunity for traditional govt. functions; not for proprietary/private functions
- **Govt. Officials:** Immunity for discretionary functions (policy); not for ministerial acts (job)

	Common Law	Today
Charities	Immunity	No immunity
Interspousal	Immunity	No immunity
Parent-child	Parental immunity	Generally no immunity, except core parenting activities

DEFENSES – CONTRIBUTORY NEGLIGENCE AND COMPARATIVE FAULT

Contributory Negligence: At common law, plaintiff's contributory negligence bars plaintiff's recovery
❖ Leroy Fibre Co. v. Chicago, Milwaukee & St. Paul Ry. *(Keeping straw near a railroad where sparks might ignite it was not contributory negligence)*
  - **Last Clear Chance:** Plaintiff can recover if defendant had last clear chance to avoid harm and did not take it
❖ Fuller v. Illinois RR *(Train had last chance to stop)*
❖ Davies v. Mann *(Wagon had last chance to stop)*
Pure Comparative Fault: Recovery reduced by plaintiff's share of fault
- Modified Comparative Fault:
  - P%<D% = Recovery reduced by plaintiff's fault
  - P%>D% = No recovery
  - P%=D% = 50% or no recovery
- For comparative fault, compare plaintiff's fault to combined fault of all defendants.

DEFENSES – ASSUMPTION OF RISK

Assumption of Risk (Plaintiff knowingly and willingly accepted risk of harm and cannot recover)
- **Express:** Plaintiff assumes risk by a **contractual waiver** that is (1) **clear** and **unequivocal**, and (2) acceptable on **public policy** grounds
❖ Dalury v. SKI, Ltd. *(Skier injured at ski park; court finds the waiver unenforceable on public policy grounds)*
- **Implied:** Plaintiff willingly accepted the risk by her actions (some states divide into primary and secondary)

❖ Murphy v. Steeplechase Amusement Co. ("Flopper" case; plaintiff implied assumption of risk by getting on ride)
  o Primary: Defendant owes no further duty to plaintiff
  o Secondary: Defendant argues plaintiff was negligent

STRICT LIABILITY – INTRODUCTION AND ANIMALS
If defendant caused harm, defendant is liable
- Owner of **wild animals** strictly liable for harm caused by:
  o **Dangerous propensity** that is characteristic of the animal or that the owner should know of; and
  o Plaintiff's **fearful reaction** to seeing the animal **unrestrained**
- No strict liability for animals harming **trespassers**, except for injuries inflicted by a **vicious watchdog**.
- Owner of **domestic animals** strictly liable if owner knows or has reason to know animal's **dangerous propensities**
  o Local "Dog Bite" statutes may also apply to certain types of injuries.
- Owners of **trespassing animals** are strictly liable for any reasonably foreseeable damage caused by animal while trespassing; for **household pets**, owner must know or have reason to know of the trespass

ABNORMALLY DANGEROUS ACTIVITIES AND DEFENSES
Abnormally Dangerous Activity (Creates foreseeable and highly significant risk of physical harm even when reasonable care is exercised, and is not a matter of common usage (e.g., explosives, mining, fumigation, hazardous waste disposal))
- Harm must result from abnormally dangerous risk to trigger strict liability.
- **Airplanes:** Owners and operators traditionally strictly liable for falling objects
❖ Rylands v. Fletcher (Old English case; reservoir burst and flooded neighbor's mine)
  o Broad Rule: Landowner strictly liable for an artificial condition of the land that escapes (no longer followed)
  o Narrow Rule: Landowner strictly liable for dangerous accumulations of water (better reflects American law)
Defenses to Strict Liability Actions

	Effect of Plaintiff's Conduct
Contributory Negligence State	Negligence not a bar to recovery
Comparative Fault State	Courts divided Negligence usually reduces recovery
Assumption of Risk	**Bars recovery**

PRODUCTS LIABILITY – INTRODUCTION
Three Types of Actionable Defects: Manufacturing, Design, and Inadequate Warning
Three Types of Product Liability Lawsuits
Negligence (duty, breach, causation, and damages)
Breach of Warranty
- Implied: Merchantability or Fitness
- Express: Affirmations or promises about fitness or safety of products
- Seller can disclaim some, but not all, warranties.
Strict Products Liability elements:
- Defect (unreasonably dangerous defective condition);
- Existed when product left defendant's control; and
- Caused plaintiff's injury

PRODUCTS LIABILITY – STRICT LIABILITY ACTIONS
2nd Restatement: Strictly liable for harm if: (1) seller is in the business of selling the product, (2) product was defective when it left seller's control, and (3) defect causes plaintiff's harm
- **Proper Defendants:** Anyone in manufacturing or distribution chain (no privity required)
❖ MacPherson v. Buick (Plaintiff could sue manufacturer for defect without a contract)
❖ Takata Airbags (Can sue anyone in manufacturing or distribution chain for damage caused by airbags)
  o **Indemnification** within the chain is possible
  o **Casual sellers** not strictly liable
- **Proper Plaintiff:** Anyone foreseeably injured by a defect

PRODUCTS LIABILITY –DEFECTS AND DAMAGES
- **Manufacturing Defect:** Any deviation from what manufacturer intended product to be that harms plaintiff (compare to manufacturers specifications)
❖ Escola v. Coco-Cola Bottling Co. (Shattering bottle was not how the product was intended to function)
- **Design Defect:** Product's intended specifications are themselves defective (e.g., Ford Pinto engine placement)
  o **Consumer Expectation Test:** Less safe than ordinary consumer expects (tends to apply to simpler designs)
❖ Campo v. Scofield (Met consumer expectation by functioning properly w/ no latent or hidden risks of injury)

- o **Risk-Utility Test:** Risks posed by product outweigh its benefits
  - ▪ Majority: Plaintiff also must show a **reasonable alternative design (RAD)**
- ❖ Barker v. Lull Engineering *(Use risk-utility test to compare actual product with a RAD)*
- **Failure to Warn:** Foreseeable risk of harm, not obvious to user, which could have been reduced or avoided by reasonable warnings
- ❖ Borel v. Fibreboard Paper Products Corp *(Asbestos case determined by the reasonableness of warnings)*
- **Damages:** Can recover for personal injury or property damage, but not pure economic loss

PRODUCTS LIABILITY – DEFENSES
- Defendants have duty to anticipate and warn users about foreseeable misuse.

	Defense if:	Not a defense:
Contributory Negligence States	Barred if P unreasonably proceeds in face of known danger (i.e., assumed risk)	If P failed to discover defect; OR P foreseeably misused product
Comparative Fault States	Recovery reduced in the same manner as in a negligence action (see *Daly v. General Motors Corp.*)	No reduction of recovery in minority of comparative fault states
Misuse Alteration	Unforeseeable (i.e., assumed risk)	Foreseeable

- ❖ Daly v. General Motors Corp *(Defense can present evidence of plaintiff's fault, and jury can allocate fault for plaintiff's injuries between defect and plaintiff's negligence)*
- ❖ LeBoeuf v. Goodyear Tires *(DUI is foreseeable misuse)*
- **Compliance w/ govt. standards:** Usually relevant, not dispositive (unless **preemption** applied)
- ❖ Wyeth v. Levine *(Preemption applies to generic prescription drugs)*
"State of the Art" defense: Varies state-to-state; generally allows defendant to introduce evidence that the product was as safe as possible given the "state of the art" when it was distributed

DEFAMATION – COMMON-LAW ELEMENTS
False information injurious to someone's reputation
Libel: Written, printed, or recorded in permanent form (e.g., radio/TV broadcasts, e-mail)

Slander: Spoken word, gesture, or forms other than libel
- Common-Law (CL)Elements:
  - o Defamatory language
    - ▪ Must be false.
    - ▪ Opinions are actionable if declarant implies knowledge of facts to support the opinion.
  - o **Of and concerning** plaintiff (i.e., reasonable person must believe language refers to plaintiff, or to a small group of which Plaintiff is a member)
  - o Published/distributed to third party
    - ▪ Includes repeating /reprinting another's statements
    - ▪ Does NOT include internet service providers
  - o Damages plaintiff's reputation

CL Absolute Privileges: Judicial and legislative proceedings; spouses; required radio/TV publications
CL Conditional Privileges: Defending defendant's reputation; public interest; response to charge for third party

DEFAMATION – CONSTITUTIONAL REQUIREMENTS
❖ New York Times v. Sullivan *(Defamation actions are limited by the 1st Amendment)*
Plaintiff must prove falsity (by clear and convincing evidence if plaintiff is a **public figure**)
Standard of Liability:

	Private Concern	Public Concern
Public Figure or Official	No constitutional limits; common law usually requires **negligence**	Plaintiff must show **actual malice*** by clear and convincing evidence
Private Figure		**(i) Fault** for compensatory damages **(ii) Actual malice*** for punitive or presumed damages

*Actual malice: Defendant knew statement was false or acted with reckless disregard as to its truthfulness (i.e., scienter)
Public Official: Anyone in govt. with authority, while acting in that role
Public Figure: Can be unlimited (public for all purposes), limited (public for a particular issue), or involuntary

INVASION OF PRIVACY (I-FLAP)
Intrusion upon Seclusion (Defendant intrudes on plaintiff's private affairs, solitude, or seclusion in a manner objectionable to a reasonable person)
❖ Nader v. GM *(Court found no invasion of privacy where GM sought information in public knowledge and did not unreasonably intrude on Nader's privacy)*

❖ Galella v. Onassis (Court found intrusion where paparazzi regularly harassed plaintiff and her children; no 1st Amendment protection for torts committed gathering news)

False Light (Defendant presents facts that place plaintiff in an offensive false light)

Appropriation of Likeness (Unauthorized appropriation of plaintiff's name of likeness for defendant's commercial advantage)

❖ Midler v. Ford Motor Co. (Bette Midler impersonator used in commercial without her consent to sell cars)

Public Disclosure of Private Facts (Defendant gives publicity to the private life of another that (1) would be highly offensive to a reasonable person, and (2) is not a legitimate public concern)

- Disfavored because it involves **true** information

INTENTIONAL AND NEGLIGENT MISREPRESENTATION

Intentional Misrepresentation

- *Deceptive/misleading statement* (or failure to disclose material fact if defendant has duty to disclose)
- *Defendant's knowledge or reckless disregard of falsity*
- *Intent to induce plaintiff's action or inaction*
- *Actual reliance by plaintiff*
  - "Puffing" is not actionable.

Duty to disclose if (1) defendant is fiduciary, (2) plaintiff was likely misled by prior statements, or (3) defendant knows plaintiff is mistaken about basic facts

Damages: Actual pecuniary loss; recovery generally "benefit of bargain"

Negligent Misrepresentation (Defendant provides false information due to negligent preparation)

- Plaintiff must **justifiably rely** on information defendant **intended** to influence plaintiff, and plaintiff must be (1) in contractual relationship w/ defendant OR (2) part of small group defendant knows have this information
- **Damages:** Out-of-pocket and consequential